Topographic Map Symbols		Geologic Map Symbols

Topographic Map Symbols

Elevation markers

Contour lines

Index contour lines —100—

Depression contour lines

Water elevation 9600

Spot elevation x 9136

Boundaries

National

State

County, parish, municipal

Township, precinct, town

Incorporated city, village, or town

National or state reservation

Small park, cemetery, airport, etc.

Land grant

Buildings and Structures

Buildings

School

Church

Cemetery † cem

Barn and warehouse

Wells (non-water) ○ oil ○ gas

Open-pit mine, quarry, or prospect

Tunnel → – – – ←

Benchmark ⊗BM △8025

National Park

Campsite

Bridge

Roads and Railroads

Divided highway

Road

Trail

Railroad

Geologic Map Symbols

Sedimentary Rocks

Breccia

Conglomerate

Dolomite

Limestone

Mudstone

Sandstone

Siltstone

Shale

Igneous and Metamorphic Rocks

Extrusive

Intrusive

Metamorphic

Features

River

Water well ○ ● ● ● ◍ water

Spring ○∨

Lake

Glacier

HOLT
CALIFORNIA

Earth Science

Mead A. Allison

Arthur T. DeGaetano

Jay M. Pasachoff

HOLT, RINEHART AND WINSTON
A Harcourt Education Company

Orlando • **Austin** • New York • San Diego • London

About the Authors

Mead A. Allison, Ph.D.

Tulane University, New Orleans, Louisiana

Mead Allison received his Ph.D. in oceanography from State University of New York. He is an associate professor of Earth and environmental sciences at Tulane University in Louisiana, where he teaches introductory geology and upper-level courses in sedimentology and marine geology.

Arthur T. DeGaetano, Ph.D.

Cornell University, Ithaca, New York

Arthur DeGaetano received his Ph.D. in meteorology from Rutgers University. He is an associate professor of Earth and atmospheric sciences at Cornell University in New York, where he teaches introductory climatology and upper-level courses in atmospheric thermodynamics and physical meteorology. Dr. DeGaetano is also the director of the Northeast Regional Climate Center.

Jay M. Pasachoff, Ph.D.

Williams College, Williamstown, Massachusetts

Jay Pasachoff received his Ph.D. in astronomy from Harvard University. He is the Field Memorial Professor of Astronomy and the director of the Hopkins Observatory at Williams College in Massachusetts, where he teaches introductory and upper-level courses in astronomy. In addition, Dr. Pasachoff has written several popular college-level astronomy textbooks.

ISBN 0-03-092207-0

4 5 6 048 09 08 07

California

As you read the following pages and work through the unpacking of the California Earth Sciences Standards, you will discover the big ideas and key concepts that your teacher expects you to learn and understand.

You will see three things:

1 **>**
what the standard actually says

2 **What's it mean?**
an explanation to help you understand the big ideas within the standard

3 **Review Question**
a typical standards review question

California
The Golden State

State capitol, Sacramento

Cliffs on the coastline of the Pacific Ocean, Big Sur

Mountains in the High Sierra

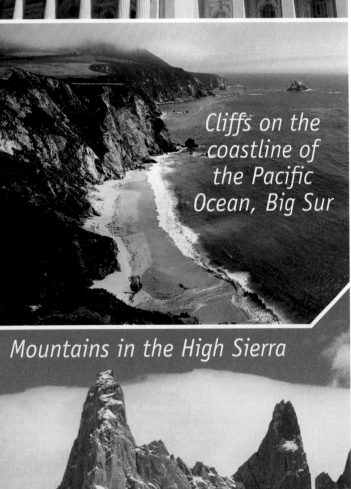

Earth's Place in the Universe

>1. Astronomy and planetary exploration reveal the solar system's structure, scale, and change over time. As a basis for understanding this concept:

What's it mean? Astronomy, the study of the universe, and planetary exploration show us the size, shape and history of the solar system.

>a. Students know how the differences and similarities among the sun, the terrestrial planets, and the gas planets may have been established during the formation of the solar system.

What's it mean? ...the sun, the terrestrial planets and the gas planets are very different from one another yet share some similarities. These differences and similarities may have been established when the solar system formed... Go to Chapter 27, Planets of the Solar System, for help.

Review Question All of the outer planets in the solar system are large except
   A. Saturn.
   B. Uranus.
   C. Neptune.
   D. Pluto.

Not Tested* Standards that all students should have the opportunity to learn, identified with an asterisk (*), are not tested.

>b. Students know the evidence from Earth and moon rocks indicates that the solar system was formed from a nebular cloud of dust and gas approximately 4.6 billion years ago.

What's it mean? ...the ages and the chemical compositions of Earth and moon rocks provide evidence that the solar system formed from a nebular cloud of dust and gas approximately 4.6 billion years ago... Go to Chapter 27, Planets of the Solar System, for help.

Review Question The hypothesis that states that the sun and the planets developed out of the same cloud of gas and dust is called the
  A. Copernicus hypothesis.
  B. solar hypothesis.
  C. nebular hypothesis.
  D. Galileo hypothesis.

>c. Students know the evidence from geological studies of Earth and other planets suggest that the early Earth was very different from Earth today.

What's it mean? ...the evidence, such as the chemical composition of Precambrian rocks and the intense cratering on terrestrial planets, shows that the conditions on the early Earth were different from today... Go to Chapter 27, Planets of the Solar System, for help.

Review Question The first atmosphere of Earth was made mostly of
  A. helium.
  B. oxygen.
  C. carbon dioxide.
  D. methane.

>d. Students know the evidence indicating that the planets are much closer to Earth than the stars are.

What's it mean? ...the evidence, such as the parallax measurements of stars and the planets, shows that the planets are much closer to the Earth than to the stars... Go to Chapter 30, Stars, Galaxies, and the Universe, for help.

Review Question The change in position of a nearby star as seen from different points on Earth's orbit compared with the position of a faraway star is called
  A. parallax.
  B. blue shift.
  C. red shift.
  D. a Cepheid variable.

>e. Students know the Sun is a typical star and is powered by nuclear reactions, primarily the fusion of hydrogen to form helium.

What's it mean? ...the primary source of power for typical stars such as our sun comes from nuclear fusion reactions. In a nuclear fusion reaction hydrogen atoms are fused together forming helium atoms and releasing enormous amounts of energy... Go to Chapter 29, The Sun, for help.

Review Question The number of hydrogen atoms that fuse to form a helium atom is
  A. two.
  B. four.
  C. six.
  D. eight.

Yosemite National Park

>f. Students know the evidence for the dramatic effects that asteroid impacts have had in shaping the surface of planets and their moons and in mass extinctions of life on Earth.

What's it mean? ...the evidence that asteroids shaped the surface of planets and moons and caused mass extinctions on Earth include large impact craters surrounded by concentric ridges of displaced material and the presence of iridium in rock layers formed during periods of extinction... Go to Chapter 9, A View of Earth's Past, for help.

Review Question What evidence supports the hypothesis that a meteorite impact led to the Cretaceous-Tertiary mass extinction?
  A. rock layers rich in iridium formed at the end of the Cretaceous Period
  B. the position of the Earth's continents at the end of the Cretaceous Period
  C. rock layers rich in volcanic ash formed at the end of the Cretaceous Period
  D. an increase in the abundance of mammals at the end of the Cretaceous Period

>g.* Students know the evidence for the existence of planets orbiting other stars.

What's it mean? ...the evidence that planets exist in orbits around other stars includes observations of slight periodic changes in the wavelengths of light reaching us from these stars... Go to Chapter 27, Planets of the Solar System, for help.

>2. Earth-based and space-based astronomy reveal the structure, scale, and changes in stars, galaxies, and the universe over time. As a basis for understanding this concept:

What's it mean? From astronomical observations made both on the ground and in space, we have learned about the shape, size, and history of the universe.

>a. Students know the solar system is located in an outer edge of the disc-shaped Milky Way galaxy, which spans 100,000 light years.

What's it mean? ...the solar system is at the outer edge of the 100,000-light-year diameter, disc-shaped Milky Way galaxy... Go to Chapter 30, Stars, Galaxies, and the Universe, for help.

Review Question What type of galaxy is the Milky Way galaxy?
   A. barred spiral
   B. irregular
   C. spiral
   D. elliptical

>b. Students know galaxies are made of billions of stars and comprise most of the visible mass of the universe.

What's it mean? ...galaxies are large groups of stars. Most of what we can see in the universe is galaxies... Go to Chapter 30, Stars, Galaxies, and the Universe, for help.

Review Question Large-scale groups of stars bound together by gravitational attraction are known as
   A. galaxies.
   B. multiple star systems.
   C. Cepheids.
   D. clusters.

Death Valley National Park

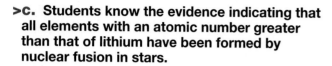

>c. Students know the evidence indicating that all elements with an atomic number greater than that of lithium have been formed by nuclear fusion in stars.

What's it mean? ...the evidence, such as the observation that elements with atomic numbers greater than lithium form in supernovas, indicates that all elements with atomic numbers greater then lithium formed by nuclear fusion inside stars... Go to Chapter 30, Stars, Galaxies, and the Universe, for help.

Review Question The heaviest element formed in the core of a star is
   A. iron.
   B. carbon.
   C. helium.
   D. nitrogen.

>d. Students know that stars differ in their life cycles and that visual, radio, and X-ray telescopes may be used to collect data that reveal those differences.

What's it mean? ...people can use a variety of telescopes to learn that different stars do not have the same life cycles... Go to Chapter 30, Stars, Galaxies, and the Universe, for help.

Review Question Which of the following choices lists the colors of stars from hottest to coolest?
   A. red, yellow, orange, white, blue
   B. orange, red, white, blue, yellow
   C. yellow, orange, red, blue, white
   D. blue, white, yellow, orange, red

Joshua trees

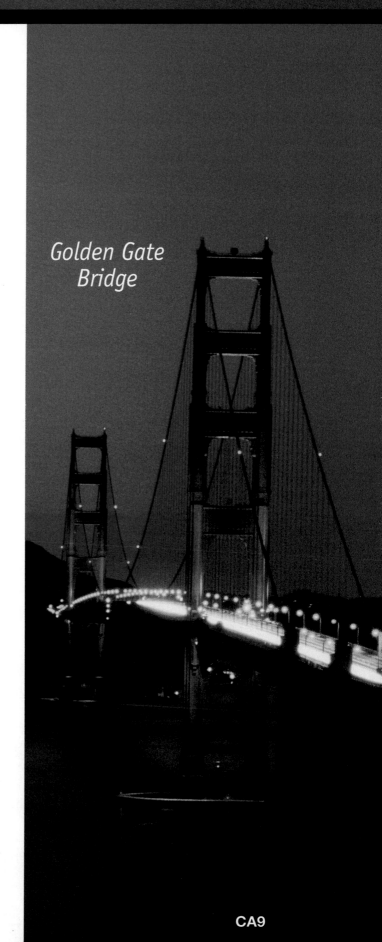

>e.* **Students know accelerators boost sub-atomic particles to energy levels that simulate conditions in the stars and in the early history of the universe before stars formed.**

What's it mean? ...accelerators are machines that create high-energy conditions by smashing subatomic particles together. Accelerators can simulate conditions that existed in the early universe and inside stars... Go to Chapter 4, Earth Chemistry, for help.

>f.* **Students know the evidence indicating that the color, brightness, and evolution of a star are determined by a balance between gravitational collapse and nuclear fusion.**

What's it mean? ...the color, brightness, and evolution of stars are determined by a balance between gravitational collapse and nuclear fusion. This evidence comes from such things as observing the temperatures and compositions of many stars at different points in their life cycles... Go to Chapter 30, Stars, Galaxies, and the Universe, for help.

>g.* **Students know how the red-shift from distant galaxies and the cosmic background radiation provide evidence for the "big bang" model that suggests that the universe has been expanding for 10 to 20 billion years.**

What's it mean? ...the stretching out of light waves from distant galaxies and the cosmic background radiation provide evidence that the universe began to expand 10 to 20 billion years ago... Go to Chapter 30, Stars, Galaxies, and the Universe, for help.

Golden Gate Bridge

Answers: 2c) A, 2d) D

Dynamic Earth Processes

>3. Plate tectonics operating over geologic time has changed the patterns of land, sea, and mountains on Earth's surface. As the basis for understanding this concept:

What's it mean? The Earth's crust is divided into large plates that pull apart, push together, and slide past each other. The movements of these big pieces of the crust are responsible for the shape of the Earth's surface.

>a. Students know features of the ocean floor (magnetic patterns, age, and sea-floor topography) provide evidence of plate tectonics.

What's it mean? ...many features on the ocean floor, such as magnetic patterns, age and sea-floor spreading, provide evidence to support plate tectonics—the idea that the Earth's crust is divided into large plates that pull apart, push together, and slide past each other... Go to Chapter 10, Plate Tectonics, for help.

Review Question An underwater mountain chain that formed by sea-floor spreading is called a
   A. divergent boundary.
   B. subduction zone.
   C. mid-ocean ridge.
   D. convergent boundary.

>b. Students know the principal structures that form at the three different kinds of plate boundaries.

What's it mean? ...at the three kinds of plate boundaries mountains, rift valleys and earthquakes form or occur... Go to Chapter 10, Plate Tectonics, for help.

Review Question New ocean floor is constantly being produced through the process known as
   A. subduction.
   B. continental drift.
   C. sea-floor spreading.
   D. terranes.

Lassen Volcanic National Park

>**c.** Students know how to explain the properties of rocks based on the physical and chemical conditions in which they formed, including plate tectonic processes.

What's it mean? ...the properties of rocks, such as texture and mineral composition, are based on the physical and chemical conditions in which they formed. Plate tectonic processes also affect the properties of rocks... Go to Chapter 6, Rocks, for help.

Review Question The large, well-developed crystals found in some samples of granite are a sign that
 A. the lava from which it formed cooled rapidly.
 B. the magma contained a lot of dissolved gases.
 C. the lava from which it formed cooled slowly.
 D. water deposited minerals in the rock cavities.

>**d.** Students know why and how earthquakes occur and the scales used to measure their intensity and magnitude.

What's it mean? ...why and how an earthquake occurs depends on factors such as the location of the earthquake. The size of an earthquake can be measured on a variety of scales... Go to Chapter 12, Earthquakes, for help.

Review Question Earthquakes that cause severe damage are likely to have what characteristic?
 A. a deep focus
 B. an intermediate focus
 C. a shallow focus
 D. a deep epicenter

>**e.** Students know there are two kinds of volcanoes: one kind with violent eruptions producing steep slopes and the other kind with voluminous lava flows producing gentle slopes.

What's it mean? ...volcanoes have different characteristics, based on the type of eruptions they produce, and are classified into different types... Go to Chapter 13, Volcanoes, for help.

Review Question Explosive volcanic eruptions commonly result from
 A. mafic magma.
 B. felsic magma.
 C. aa lava.
 D. pahoehoe lava.

Answers: 3a) C, 3b) C, 3c) C, 3d) C, 3e) B

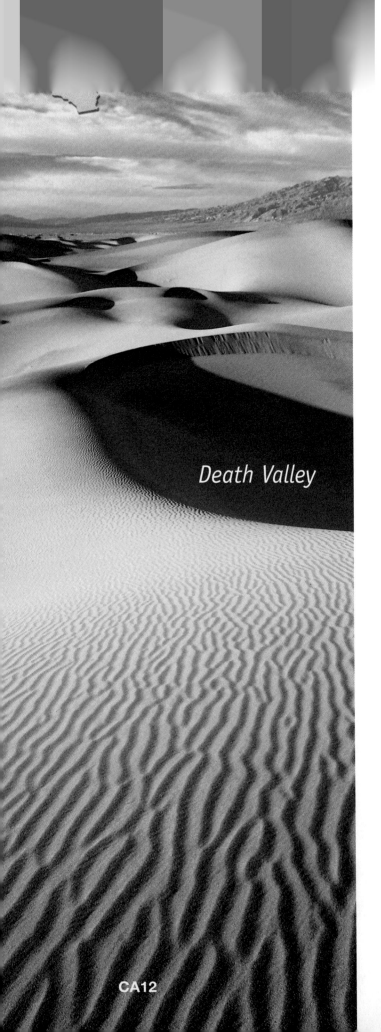

Death Valley

>**f.*** Students know the explanation for the location and properties of volcanoes that are due to hot spots and the explanation for those that are due to subduction.

What's it mean? ...isolated volcanoes are related to hot spots in the Earth's crust. These volcanoes have specific properties that differ from the properties of the volcanoes associated with subduction... Go to Chapter 13, Volcanoes, for help.

Energy in the Earth System

>**4.** Energy enters the Earth system primarily as solar radiation and eventually escapes as heat. As a basis for understanding this concept:

What's it mean? Radiation from the sun is the ultimate source of most of the energy on Earth. The Earth releases this energy as heat.

>**a.** Students know the relative amount of incoming solar energy compared with Earth's internal energy and the energy used by society.

What's it mean? ...how much energy comes from the sun in the form of solar radiation can be compared to the energy produced inside the planet, and the energy people use... Go to Chapter 2, Earth as a System, for help.

Review Question Energy can enter the Earth system from internal sources through convection and from external sources through
   A. radioactive energy.
   B. wave energy.
   C. wind energy.
   D. solar energy.

>**b.** **Students know the fate of incoming solar radiation in terms of reflection, absorption, and photosynthesis.**

What's it mean? ...some solar radiation is reflected back into space, some is absorbed by the atmosphere and surface, and some is used by plants to make food... Go to Chapter 2, Earth as a System, for help.

Review Question What happens to most of the solar radiation that reaches Earth and is *not* reflected back into space?
  A. It is absorbed by the ozone layer.
  B. It is reradiated as shortwave radiation.
  C. It is used in chemical reactions by plants.
  D. It is reradiated as longwave radiation.

>**c.** **Students know the different atmospheric gases that absorb the Earth's thermal radiation and the mechanism and significance of the greenhouse effect.**

What's it mean? ...there are certain gases in the atmosphere that absorb radiation reflected off the Earth's surface. This mechanism, known as the greenhouse effect, plays an important role in many processes that take place on Earth... Go to Chapter 22, The Atmosphere, for help.

Review Question The process by which the atmosphere slows Earth's loss of heat to space is called the
  A. greenhouse effect.
  B. Coriolis effect.
  C. doldrums.
  D. convection cell.

Answers: 4a) D, 4b) B, 4c) A

Los Angeles skyline

>d.* Students know the differing greenhouse conditions on Earth, Mars, and Venus; the origins of those conditions; and the climatic consequences of each.

What's it mean? ...the nature of the greenhouse condition, the origins of this condition, and the consequences on the condition in climate differ on Earth, Mars, and Venus... Go to Chapter 27, Planets of the Solar System, for help.

>5. Heating of Earth's surface and atmosphere by the sun drives convection within the atmosphere and oceans, producing winds and ocean currents. As a basis for understanding this concept:

What's it mean? Heat energy from the sun is transferred through the Earth's surface and atmosphere by the movement of winds and ocean currents.

>a. Students know how differential heating of Earth results in circulation patterns in the atmosphere and oceans that globally distribute the heat.

What's it mean? ...the Earth heats up unevenly, but this heat energy is distributed through global circulation patterns in the atmosphere and the oceans... Go to Chapter 21, Movements of the Ocean, for help.

Review Question What role do convection currents in the ocean and atmosphere have in regulating climate?
A. They set up atmospheric circulation.
B. They prevent deep-water currents.
C. They restrict energy to local use.
D. They ensure a balance of precipitation.

Mono Lake

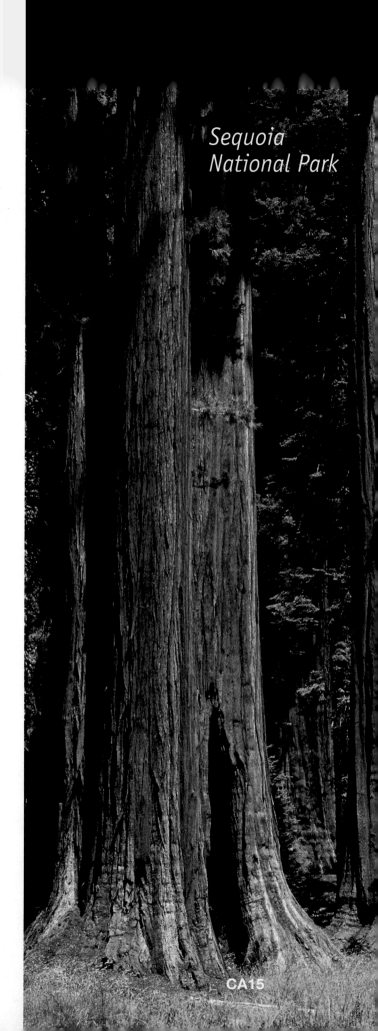

Sequoia National Park

>b. Students know the relationship between the rotation of Earth and the circular motions of ocean currents and air in pressure centers.

What's it mean? ...the everyday turning of the Earth on its axis affects currents in both the ocean and the atmosphere. These currents move in circular patterns... Go to Chapter 22, The Atmosphere, for help.

Review Question In the Northern Hemisphere, the Coriolis effect causes winds moving toward the North Pole to be deflected in which of the following ways?

    A. Winds are deflected to the right.
    B. Winds are deflected to the left.
    C. Winds are deflected in unpredictable patterns.
    D. Winds are not deflected by the Coriolis effect.

>c. Students know the origin and effects of temperature inversions.

What's it mean? ...temperature inversions, a layer of warm air trapping cooler air near the surface, are caused by factors such as the shape of the land. An example of an effect of temperature inversions is a layer of trapped air pollution... Go to Chapter 22, The Atmosphere, for help.

Review Question Why might a city located on the Great Plains have fewer air-pollution incidents related to temperature inversions than a city near the Rocky Mountains?

    A. The Great Plains are at lower elevations where the cool air necessary for temperature inversions is rarely found.
    B. The topography of the Great Plains is flatter allowing air to circulate without being trapped.
    C. Cities on the Great Plains have strict laws that regulate levels of air pollution in order to prevent temperature inversions.
    D. Cities located on the Great Plains are smaller, produce less air pollution, and so have fewer temperature inversions.

>**d.** Students know properties of ocean water, such as temperature and salinity, can be used to explain the layered structure of the oceans, the generation of horizontal and vertical ocean currents, and the geographic distribution of marine organisms.

What's it mean? ...differing temperatures and levels of dissolved salts can explain the layering of ocean water, the horizontal and vertical movement of ocean currents, and the distribution of marine life... Go to Chapter 20, Ocean Water, for help.

Review Question The temperature of ocean water is dependent on all of the following except
 A. depth
 B. the amount of solar energy it receives
 C. water movement
 D. the number of organisms living in it

>**e.** Students know rain forests and deserts on Earth are distributed in bands at specific latitudes.

What's it mean? ...the locations of rain forests, areas with annual rainfall patterns of over 200 cm per year, and deserts, areas with annual rainfall patterns of less than 25 cm per year, are found at specific distances north and south of the equator... Go to Chapter 25, Climate, for help.

Review Question Which climate is characterized by high temperatures and is located in a band along the equator?
 A. middle-latitude
 B. mediterranean
 C. tropical
 D. steppe

>**f.*** Students know the interaction of wind patterns, ocean currents, and mountain ranges results in the global pattern of latitudinal bands of rain forests and deserts.

What's it mean? ...the location of rain forests and deserts at certain distances north and south of the equator is the result of interactions between wind patterns, ocean currents and mountain ranges... Go to Chapter 25, Climate, for help.

>**g.*** Students know features of the ENSO (El Niño southern oscillation) cycle in terms of sea-surface and air temperature variations across the Pacific and some climatic results of this cycle.

What's it mean? ...the ENSO (El Niño southern oscillation) affects sea surface and air temperatures across the Pacific. Some climatic features, such as flooding and drought, result from this cycle... Go to Chapter 25, Climate, for help.

San Francisco and the Golden Gate Bridge

>6. **Climate is the long-term average of a region's weather and depends on many factors. As a basis for understanding this concept:**

What's it mean? Weather, which is determined by a number of factors, is what occurs day to day. The climate of an area represents the average weather conditions over a long period of time.

>a. **Students know weather (in the short run) and climate (in the long run) involve the transfer of energy into and out of the atmosphere.**

What's it mean? ...both short-term weather and long-term climate involve energy transfers in and out of the atmosphere... Go to Chapter 25, Climate, for help.

Review Question Which statement best compares how land and water are heated by solar energy?
   A. Water heats up faster and to a higher temperature than land does.
   B. Land heats up faster and to a higher temperature than water does.
   C. Water heats up more slowly but reaches a higher temperature than land does.
   D. Land heats up more slowly and reaches a lower temperature than water does.

>b. **Students know the effects on climate of latitude, elevation, topography, and proximity to large bodies of water and cold or warm ocean currents.**

What's it mean? ...the climate of a region is determined by a number of things: distance from the equator, height above sea level, surface features, and closeness to large bodies of water and ocean currents... Go to Chapter 25, Climate, for help.

Review Question When a moving air mass encounters a mountain range, the air mass
   A. stops moving.
   B. slows and sinks.
   C. rises and cools.
   D. reverses its direction.

Answers: 5d) D, 5e) C, 6a) B, 6b) C

Tidepool, Monterey

>c. Students know how Earth's climate has changed over time, corresponding to changes in Earth's geography, atmospheric composition, and other factors, such as solar radiation and plate movement.

What's it mean? ...Earth's climactic changes correspond to changes in landforms, gases in the atmosphere, levels of energy coming from the sun, and the movement of crustal plates... Go to Chapter 25, Climate, for help.

Review Question In samples of atmospheric gases taken from ice cores, high levels of carbon dioxide indicate that the sample is from a time period that had
  A. a warm climate.
  B. a cool climate.
  C. high amounts of precipitation.
  D. low amounts of precipitation.

>d.* Students know how computer models are used to predict the effects of the increase in greenhouse gases on climate for the planet as a whole and for specific regions.

What's it mean? ...computer models can be used to predict the effects of greenhouse gases on global climate as well as for specific regions... Go to Chapter 24, Weather, for help.

Biogeochemical Cycles

>7. Each element on Earth moves among reservoirs, which exist in the solid earth, in oceans, in the atmosphere, and within and among organisms as part of biogeochemical cycles. As a basis for understanding this concept:

What's it mean? The Earth is made up of a limited number of elements, and these elements cycle through various Earth systems as well as living systems over time.

>a. **Students know the carbon cycle of photosynthesis and respiration and the nitrogen cycle.**

What's it mean? ...the carbon cycle is the exchange of carbon between organisms and the nonliving parts of the environment. This occurs when plants produce their own food, use the food as a source of energy, and exchange oxygen and carbon dioxide with the environment. The nitrogen needed by plants also cycles through the environment... Go to Chapter 22, The Atmosphere, for help.

Review Question Before plants can take up nitrogen, it must first be fixed. This means that
  A. Bacteria in the soil excrete atmospheric nitrogen.
  B. Nitrogen compounds change into carbon dioxide.
  C. Bacteria decay into nitrogen compounds.
  D. Nitrogen is changed into nitrogen compounds.

>b. **Students know the global carbon cycle: the different physical and chemical forms of carbon in the atmosphere, oceans, biomass, fossil fuels, and the movement of carbon among these reservoirs.**

What's it mean? ...the cycling of carbon in different chemical and physical forms, such as solid limestone and carbon dioxide gas, through temporary storage in the atmosphere, oceans, living things, and in fossil fuel, takes place on a global scale... Go to Chapter 2, Earth as a System, for help.

Review Question As part of the global carbon cycle, which of the following represents a possible sequence of reservoirs and processes for an atom of carbon?
  A. respiration → limestone → erosion → natural gas
  B. coal → photosynthesis → atmosphere → decomposition
  C. ocean water → limestone → respiration → natural gas
  D. atmosphere → photosynthesis → plant remains → combustion

Answers: 6c) A, 7a) D, 7b) D

Los Angeles

>c. Students know the movement of matter among reservoirs is driven by Earth's internal and external sources of energy.

What's it mean? ...the movement of matter, such as carbon and nitrogen, among temporary storage locations is driven by the Earth's internal and external sources of energy... Go to Chapter 2, Earth as a System, for help.

Review Question Which of the following methods of internal energy transfer drives volcanic activity on Earth's surface?
 A. radioactive decay
 B. convection
 C. kinetic transfer
 D. conduction

>d.* Students know the relative residence times and flow characteristics of carbon in and out of its different reservoirs.

What's it mean? ...it takes different lengths of time for carbon atoms to move through the various stages of the carbon cycle... Go to Chapter 2, Earth as a System, for help.

Structure and Composition of the Atmosphere

>8. Life has changed Earth's atmosphere, and changes in the atmosphere affect conditions for life. As a basis for understanding this concept:

What's it mean? The Earth's atmosphere responds to changes in living things. At the same time, living things are affected by changes in the atmosphere.

>a. Students know the thermal structure and chemical composition of the atmosphere.

What's it mean? ...the atmosphere is made up of layers that vary in temperature and in the mixture of gases in each layer... Go to Chapter 22, The Atmosphere, for help.

California sea lion

Yosemite National Park

Review Question Which of the following statements best describes the relationship of atmospheric pressure to altitude?

   A. The atmospheric pressure increases as the altitude increases.

   B. The atmospheric pressure increases as the altitude decreases.

   C. The atmospheric pressure varies unpredictably at different altitudes.

   D. The atmospheric pressure is constant at all altitudes.

>b. **Students know how the composition of Earth's atmosphere has evolved over geologic time and know the effect of outgassing, the variations of carbon dioxide concentration, and the origin of atmospheric oxygen.**

What's it mean? …the balance of chemicals that make up the Earth's atmosphere has changed during geologic time. Volcanic eruptions filled the early atmosphere with gases from inside the Earth, carbon dioxide levels have fluctuated, and organisms have released atmospheric oxygen… Go to Chapter 27, Planets of the Solar System, for help.

Review Question In the process of photosynthesis, green plants give off

   A. hydrogen.

   B. oxygen.

   C. carbon dioxide.

   D. helium.

Anza-Borrego

>c. Students know the location of the ozone layer in the upper atmosphere, its role in absorbing ultraviolet radiation, and the way in which this layer varies both naturally and in response to human activities.

What's it mean? ...the ozone layer is located in the upper atmosphere and absorbs harmful ultraviolet radiation that would otherwise reach the Earth's surface. The ozone layer varies in response to both natural and human activity... Go to Chapter 22, The Atmosphere, for help.

Review Question How does the ozone layer benefit living things on Earth?
- A. It prevents chlorofluorocarbons from entering the atmosphere.
- B. It allows ultraviolet rays to enter the atmosphere.
- C. It prevents ultraviolet rays from entering the atmosphere.
- D. It allows chlorofluorocarbons to enter the atmosphere.

California Geology

>9. The geology of California underlies the state's wealth of natural resources as well as its natural hazards. As a basis for understanding this concept:

What's it mean? The state of California has a wealth of both natural resources and natural hazards that result from geology.

>a. Students know the resources of major economic importance in California and their relation to California's geology.

What's it mean? ...geologic resources, such as minerals, play a role in the economy of California... Go to Chapter 7, Resources and Energy, for help.

Review Question Which of the following is an example of a nonrenewable resource?
A. natural gas
B. sunlight
C. falling water
D. wind

>b. Students know the principal natural hazards in different California regions and the geologic basis of those hazards.

What's it mean? ...different regions of California have different natural hazards associated with them. Geologic processes are the basis for these hazards... Go to Chapter 12, Earthquakes, for help.

Review Question Energy waves that produce an earthquake begin at what location on or within Earth?
A. the epicenter
B. the seismic gap
C. the focus
D. the shadow zone

>c. Students know the importance of water to society, the origins of California's fresh water, and the relationship between supply and need.

What's it mean? ...water is a vital resource for humans. It is important to know where California's fresh water comes from and what must be done to insure that water needs can be met with the state's supply... Go to Chapter 16, Groundwater, for help.

Review Question Any body of rock or sediment in which water can flow and be stored is called a(n)
A. well.
B. aquifer.
C. sinkhole.
D. artesian formation.

Answers: 8c) C, 9a) A, 9b) C, 9c) B

>d.* Students know how to analyze published geologic hazard maps of California and know how to use the map's information to identify evidence of geologic events of the past and predict geologic changes in the future.

What's it mean? ...geologic hazard maps of California are published that can be used to identify evidence of past geologic events such as earthquakes as well as to predict future geologic changes such as mudslides... Go to Chapter 3, Models of the Earth, for help.

Investigation and Experimentation

>1. Scientific progress is made by asking meaningful questions and conducting careful investigations. As a basis for understanding this concept and addressing the content in the other four strands, students should develop their own questions and perform investigations. Students will:

What's it mean? Scientists learn more about the world by asking questions. They find answers to these questions through investigations and experiments. To understand this and understand the other four strands, students should ask their own questions and carry out their own investigations. Students will:

>a. Select and use appropriate tools and technology (such as computer-linked probes, spreadsheets, and graphing calculators) to perform tests, collect data, analyze relationships, and display data.

What's it mean? Choose and use the right tools and equipment (such as probes connected to computers, spreadsheet software that makes data tables, and calculators that plot graphs) to make observations, and to collect information, interpret information, and display information... Go to Chapter 5, Minerals of Earth's Crust, for help.

Golden Gate Bridge

Yosemite National Park

>j. **Recognize the issues of statistical variability and the need for controlled tests.**

What's it mean? Identify and understand the variability of results and that controlled tests can limit the variation... Go to Chapter 1, Introduction to Earth Science, for help.

Review Question Why do scientists use control groups in experiments?
  A. A control helps identify the response of a subject to a variable.
  B. A control helps identify the variables in an experiment.
  C. Control groups eliminate the need for peer review.
  D. Control groups reduce the need for precise measurements.

>k. **Recognize the cumulative nature of scientific evidence.**

What's it mean? Understand that new scientific knowledge is built on and extends knowledge that was obtained previously by scientists... Go to Chapter 27, Planets of the Solar System, for help.

Review Question How did Newton's ideas about the orbits of the planets differ from Kepler's ideas?
  A. Newton claimed that the planets revolved around the Earth in elliptical orbits.
  B. Newton described the movement of planets as having circular orbits, while Kepler described them as having elliptical orbits.
  C. Kepler described the movement of planets as having elliptical orbits, but Newton provided causes for these elliptical orbits.
  D. Kepler claimed that the planet revolved around the Earth in elliptical orbits.

>l. Analyze situations and solve problems that require combining and applying concepts from more than one area of science.

What's it mean? The branches of science are not isolated fields of knowledge. Concepts from investigations in one field of science can be applied to other fields... Go to Chapter 10, Plate Tectonics, for help.

Review Question Support for Wegener's hypothesis of continental drift includes evidence of changes in
   A. climatic patterns.
   B. Panthalassa.
   C. terranes.
   D. subduction.

>m. Investigate a science-based societal issue by researching the literature, analyzing data, and communicating the findings. Examples of issues include irradiation of food, cloning of animals by somatic cell nuclear transfer, choice of energy sources, and land and water use decisions in California.

What's it mean? Look into a current science topic that affects society by studying written information, examining data, and reporting what has been learned. Examples of topics include treating food with radiation, cloning animals by exchanging cell parts, choosing ways to get energy, and making decisions about how to use water and land in California... Go to Chapter 12, Earthquakes, for help.

Review Question Which of the following changes in rock may one day be used to help forecast earthquakes?
   A. small changes in crystal size
   B. the radioactive decay of isotopes trapped in the rock
   C. changes in the levels of greenhouse gases
   D. changes in the tilt of the ground

California palm trees

>n. **Know that when an observation does not agree with an accepted scientific theory, the observation is sometimes mistaken or fraudulent (e.g., the Piltdown Man fossil or unidentified flying objects) and that the theory is sometimes wrong (e.g., Ptolemaic model of the movement of the Sun, Moon, and planets).**

What's it mean? Understand that when information gathered does not match an idea agreed on by scientists, the information is sometimes wrong (for example, seeing flying saucers) and sometimes, the scientific idea is wrong (for example, the idea that the Sun revolves around Earth)... Go to Chapter 1, Introduction to Earth Science, for help.

Review Question If experimental results do not match their predictions, scientists generally will

    A. repeat the experiment until they do match.
    B. make the measurements more precise.
    C. revise their working hypothesis.
    D. change their experimental results.

Steiner Street, San Francisco

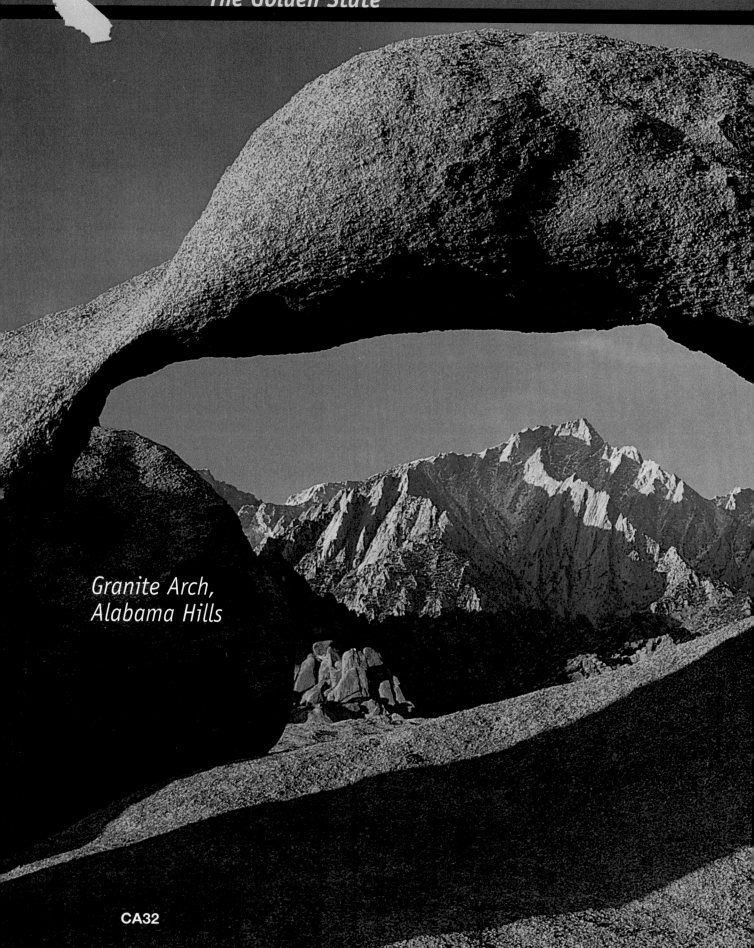

California
The Golden State

Granite Arch,
Alabama Hills

CA32

HOLT
Earth Science

Mead A. Allison

Arthur T. DeGaetano

Jay M. Pasachoff

HOLT, RINEHART AND WINSTON

A Harcourt Education Company

Orlando • **Austin** • New York • San Diego • London

About the Authors

Mead A. Allison, Ph.D.

Tulane University, New Orleans, Louisiana

Mead Allison received his Ph.D. in oceanography from State University of New York. He is an associate professor of Earth and environmental sciences at Tulane University in Louisiana, where he teaches introductory geology and upper-level courses in sedimentology and marine geology.

Arthur T. DeGaetano, Ph.D.

Cornell University, Ithaca, New York

Arthur DeGaetano received his Ph.D. in meteorology from Rutgers University. He is an associate professor of Earth and atmospheric sciences at Cornell University in New York, where he teaches introductory climatology and upper-level courses in atmospheric thermodynamics and physical meteorology. Dr. DeGaetano is also the director of the Northeast Regional Climate Center.

Jay M. Pasachoff, Ph.D.

Williams College, Williamstown, Massachusetts

Jay Pasachoff received his Ph.D. in astronomy from Harvard University. He is the Field Memorial Professor of Astronomy and the director of the Hopkins Observatory at Williams College in Massachusetts, where he teaches introductory and upper-level courses in astronomy. In addition, Dr. Pasachoff has written several popular college-level astronomy textbooks.

ISBN 0-03-092207-0

4 5 6   048 09 08 07

Acknowledgments

Authors

Mead A. Allison, Ph.D.
Associate Professor
Department of Earth
and Environmental
Sciences
Tulane University
New Orleans, Louisiana

Arthur T. DeGaetano, Ph.D.
*Director, Northeast
Regional Climate
Center*
Associate Professor
Department of Earth and
Atmospheric Science
Cornell University
Ithaca, New York

Jay M. Pasachoff, Ph.D.
*Director, Hopkins
Observatory*
*Field Memorial Professor
of Astronomy*
Williams College
Williamstown,
Massachusetts

Feature Development

Susan Feldkamp
Science Writer
Manchaca, Texas

Inclusion Specialist

Ellen McPeek Glisan
Special Needs Consultant
San Antonio, Texas

California Close-Up

A. Eugene Fritsche, Ph.D.
*Professor Emeritus
of Geology*
Department of
Geological Sciences
California State
University, Northridge
Northridge, California

Academic Reviewers

Paul Asimow, Ph.D.
*Assistant Professor
of Geology and
Geochemistry*
Geological and Planetary
Sciences
California Institute of
Technology
Pasadena, California

John A. Brockhaus, Ph.D.
*Professor of Geospatial
Information Science*
Geospatial Information
Science Program
United States Military
Academy
West Point, New York

Wesley N. Colley, Ph.D.
Professor of Astronomy
Department of
Astronomy
University of Virginia
Portsmouth, Virginia

Roger J. Cuffey, Ph.D.
Professor of Paleontology
Department of
Geosciences
Penn State University
University Park,
Pennsylvania

Scott A. Darveau, Ph.D.
*Associate Professor of
Chemistry*
Department of
Chemistry
University of Nebraska
at Kearney
Kearney, Nebraska

Turgay Ertekin, Ph.D.
*Professor and Chair of
Petroleum and Natural
Gas Engineering*
Petroleum and Natural
Gas Engineering
Program
Penn State University
University Park,
Pennsylvania

Deborah Hanley, Ph.D.
Meteorologist
Florida Division of
Forestry
Department of
Agriculture and
Consumer Services
Tallahassee, Florida

Steven Jennings, Ph.D.
*Associate Professor of
Geography*
Geography and
Environmental Studies
University of Colorado at
Colorado Springs
Colorado Springs,
Colorado

Joel S. Leventhal, Ph.D.
*Emeritus Scientist,
Geochemistry*
U.S. Geological Survey
Denver, Colorado

Mark Moldwin, Ph.D.
*Associate Professor of
Space Physics*
Earth and Space
Sciences
University of California,
Los Angeles
Los Angeles, California

Sten Odenwald, Ph.D.
Astronomer
Astronomy and Space
Physics
NASA-Goddard Space
Flight Center
Greenbelt, Maryland

Henry W. Robinson, Ph.D.
Meteorologist
Office of Services
National Weather
Service
Silver Spring, Maryland

Kenneth H. Rubin, Ph.D.
Associate Professor
Geology and Geophysics
University of Hawaii
Manoa, Hawaii

Daniel Z. Sui, Ph.D.
*Professor of Geography
and Holder of the
Reta A. Haynes
Endowed Chair in
Geosciences*
Department of
Geography
Texas A&M University
College Station, Texas

Vatche P. Tchakerian, Ph.D.
Professor
Geosciences
Texas A&M University
College Station, Texas

Dale E. Wheeler, Ph.D.
*Associate Professor of
Chemistry*
A. R. Smith Department
of Chemistry
Appalachian State
University
Boone, North Carolina

Acknowledgments, continued

Teacher Reviewers

Lowell S. Bailey
Earth Science Educator
Bedford-North Lawrence
High School
Bedford, Indiana

**Shawn Beightol,
M.S. Ed.**
Chemistry Teacher
Michael Krop Senior
High School
Miami, Florida

David Blinn
Science Teacher
Wrenshall High School
Wrenshall, Minnesota

**Daniel Brownstein,
MAT/MA**
*Science Department
Chair*
Hastings High School
Hastings, New York

Glenn Dolphin
Earth Science Teacher
Union-Endicott High
School
Endicott, New York

Alexander Dvorak
Science Teacher
Heritage School
New York, New York

Jeanne Endrikat
Science Chair
Lake Braddock
Secondary School
Burke, Virginia

Anthony P. LaSalvia
*Curriculum Coordinator
and Science Teacher*
New Lebanon Central
Schools
New Lebanon, New York

Keith A. McKain
Earth Science Teacher
Colonel Richardson High
School
Federalsburg, Maryland

Marie E. McKay
*Earth and Environmental
Science Teacher*
Ashbrook High School
Gastonia, North Carolina

Mike McKee
*Science Department
Chair*
Cypress Creek High
School
Orlando, Florida

Christine V. McLelland
*Distinguished Earth
Science Educator in
Residence*
Education and Outreach
Geological Society of
America
Boulder, Colorado

Tammie Niffenegger
*Science Chair and
Teacher*
Port Washington High
School
Port Washington,
Wisconsin

Scott Robertson
*Earth Science and
Physics Teacher*
North Warren Central
School District
Chestertown, New York

Teresa Tucker
Science Teacher
Northwest Community
Schools
Jackson, Michigan

Lab Testing

**Shawn Beightol,
M.S. Ed.**
Chemistry Teacher
Michael Krop Senior
High School
Miami, Florida

**Daniel Brownstein,
MAT/MA**
*Science Department
Chair*
Hastings High School
Hastings, New York

Eric Cohen
Science Educator
Westhampton Beach
High School
Westhampton Beach,
New York

Alonda Droege
Science Teacher
Highline High School
Burien, Washington

Alexander Dvorak
Science Teacher
Heritage School
New York, New York

Randa Flinn, M.S.
*Teacher and Science
Curriculum Facilitator*
Northeast High School
Broward County, Florida

Erich Landstrom
*NASA SEU Educator
Ambassador*
Boynton Beach
Community High
School
Boynton Beach, Florida

Tammie Niffenegger
*Science Chair and
Teacher*
Port Washington High
School
Port Washington,
Wisconsin

Scott Robertson
*Earth Science and
Physics Teacher*
North Warren Central
School District
Chestertown, New York

Teresa Tucker
Science Teacher
Northwest Community
Schools
Jackson, Michigan

Standardized Test Prep Reviewers

Russell Agostaro
*Program Development
Specialist*
Office of Funded
Programs, Newburgh
Enlarged City School
District
Newburgh, New York

Lou Goldstein
*Staff Development
Specialist for Middle
Level Science* (retired)
New York City
Department of
Education
New York, New York

Sheila Lightbourne
Curriculum Specialist
Okaloosa School District
Fort Walton Beach,
Florida

Craig Seibert, M. Ed.
*Science Coordinator of
Collier County Public
Schools*
Collier County Public
Schools
Naples, Florida

continued on page 951

CONTENTS IN BRIEF

CONTENTS

STUDYING THE EARTH — Unit 1

Environmental
Connection

COMPOSITION OF THE EARTH

Unit **2**

HISTORY OF THE EARTH

Unit 3

Environmental Connection

THE DYNAMIC EARTH

RESHAPING THE CRUST

Environmental
Connection

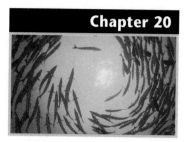
ATMOSPHERIC FORCES

Unit 7

Environmental Connection

- **Be alert, and walk with care in the lab.** Be aware of others near you and your equipment.

- **Do not take food, drinks, chewing gum, or tobacco products into the lab.** Do not store or eat food in the lab.

- **NEVER taste chemicals or allow them to contact your skin.** Keep your hands away from your face and mouth, even if you are wearing gloves.

- **Exercise caution when working with electrical equipment.** Do not use electrical equipment with frayed or twisted wires. Be sure that your hands are dry before using electrical equipment. Do not let electrical cords dangle from work stations. Dangling cords can cause you to trip and can cause an electrical shock.

- **Use extreme caution when working with hot plates and other heating devices.** Keep your head, hands, hair, and clothing away from the flame or heating area. Remember that metal surfaces connected to the heated area will become hot by conduction. Gas burners should be lit only with a spark lighter, not with matches. Make sure that all heating devices and gas valves are turned off before you leave the lab. Never leave a heating device unattended when it is in use. Metal, ceramic, and glass items do not necessarily look hot when they are hot. Allow all items to cool before storing them.

- **Do not fool around in the lab.** Take your lab work seriously, and behave appropriately in the lab. Lab equipment and apparatus are not toys; never use lab time or equipment for anything other than the intended purpose. Be aware of the safety of your classmates as well as your safety at all times.

Emergency Procedures

- **Follow standard fire-safety procedures.** If your clothing catches on fire, do not run; WALK to the safety shower, stand under it, and turn it on. While doing so, call to your teacher. In case of fire, alert your teacher and leave the lab.

- **Report any accident, incident, or hazard—no matter how trivial—to your teacher immediately.** Any incident involving bleeding, burns, fainting, nausea, dizziness, chemical exposure, or ingestion should also be reported immediately to the school nurse or to a physician. If you have a

close call, tell your teacher so that you and your teacher can find a way to prevent it from happening again.

- **Report all spills to your teacher immediately.** Call your teacher rather than trying to clean a spill yourself. Your teacher will tell you whether it is safe for you to clean up the spill; if it is not safe, your teacher will know how to clean up the spill.

- **If you spill a chemical on your skin, wash the chemical off in the sink and call your teacher.** If you spill a solid chemical onto your clothing, brush it off carefully without scattering it onto somebody else and call your teacher. If you get liquid on your clothing, wash it off right away by using the faucet at the sink and call your teacher.

When You Are Finished

- **Clean your work area at the conclusion of each lab period as directed by your teacher.** Broken glass, chemicals, and other waste products should be disposed of in separate, special containers. Dispose of waste materials as directed by your teacher. Put away all material and equipment according to your teacher's instructions. Report any damaged or missing equipment or materials to your teacher.

- **Wash your hands with soap and hot water after each lab period.** To avoid contamination, wash your hands at the conclusion of each lab period, and before you leaving the lab.

Safety Symbols

Before you begin working in the lab, familiarize yourself with the following safety symbols, which are used throughout your textbook, and the guidelines that you should follow when you see these symbols.

 Eye Protection

- **Wear approved safety goggles as directed.** Safety goggles should be worn in the lab at all times, especially when you are working with a chemical or solution, a heat source, or a mechanical device.

- **If chemicals get into your eyes, flush your eyes immediately.** Go to an eyewash station immediately, and flush your eyes (including under the eyelids) with running water for at least 15 minutes. Use your thumb and fingers to hold your eyelids open and roll your eyeball around. While doing so, ask another student to notify your teacher.

- **Do not wear contact lenses in the lab.** Chemicals can be drawn up under a contact lens and into the eye. If you must wear contacts prescribed by a physician, tell your teacher. In this case, you must also wear approved eye-cup safety goggles to help protect your eyes.

- **Do not look directly at the sun or any light source through any optical device or lens system, and do not reflect direct sunlight to illuminate a microscope.** Such actions concentrate light rays to an intensity that can severely burn your retinas, which may cause blindness.

 Clothing Protection

- **Wear an apron or lab coat at all times in the lab to prevent chemicals or chemical solutions from contacting skin or clothes.**

- **Tie back long hair, secure loose clothing, and remove loose jewelry so that they do not knock over equipment, get caught in moving parts, or come into contact with hazardous materials.**

 Hand Safety

- **Do not cut an object while holding the object in your hand.** Dissect specimens in a dissecting tray.

- **Wear protective gloves when working with an open flame, chemicals, solutions, or wild or unknown plants.**

- **Use a hot mitt to handle resistors, light sources, and other equipment that may be hot.** Allow all equipment to cool before storing it.

 Hygienic Care

- **Keep your hands away from your face and mouth while you are working in the lab.**

- **Wash your hands thoroughly before you leave the lab.**

- **Remove contaminated clothing immediately.** If you spill caustic substances on your skin or clothing, use the safety shower or a faucet to rinse. Remove affected clothing while you are under the shower, and call to your teacher. (It may be temporarily embarrassing to remove clothing in front of your classmates, but failure to rinse a chemical off your skin could result in permanent damage.)

- **Launder contaminated clothing separately.**

Sharp-Object Safety

- **Use extreme care when handling all sharp and pointed instruments, such as scalpels, sharp probes, and knives.**

- **Do not cut an object while holding the object in your hand.** Cut objects on a suitable work surface. Always cut in a direction away from your body.

- **Do not use double-edged razor blades in the lab.**

Glassware Safety

- **Inspect glassware before use; do not use chipped or cracked glassware.** Use heat-resistant glassware for heating materials or storing hot liquids, and use tongs or a hot mitt to handle this equipment.

- **Do not attempt to insert glass tubing into a rubber stopper without specific instructions from your teacher.**

- **Notify immediately your teacher if a piece of glassware or a light bulb breaks.** Do not attempt to clean up broken glass unless your teacher directs you to do so.

Electrical Safety

- **Do not use equipment with frayed electrical cords or loose plugs.**

- **Fasten electrical cords to work surfaces by using tape.** Doing so will prevent tripping and will ensure that equipment will not fall off the table.

- **Do not use electrical equipment near water or when your clothing or hands are wet.**

- **Hold the rubber cord when you plug in or unplug equipment.** Do not touch the metal prongs of the plug, and do not unplug equipment by pulling on the cord.

- **Wire coils on hot plates may heat up rapidly.** If heating occurs, open the switch immediately and use a hot mitt to handle the equipment.

Heating Safety

- **Be aware of any source of flames, sparks, or heat (such as open flames, electric heating coils, or hot plates) before working with flammable liquids or gases.**

- **Avoid using open flames.** If possible, work only with hot plates that have an on/off switch and an indicator light. Do not leave hot plates unattended. Do not use alcohol lamps. Turn off hot plates and open flames when they are not in use.

- **Never leave a hot plate unattended while it is turned on or while it is cooling off.**

- **Know the location of lab fire extinguishers and fire-safety blankets.**

- **Use tongs or appropriate insulated holders when handling heated objects.** Heated objects often do not appear to be hot. Do not pick up an object with your hand if it could be warm.

- **Keep flammable substances away from heat, flames, and other ignition sources.**

- **Allow all equipment to cool before storing it.**

Fire Safety

- **Know the location of lab fire extinguishers and fire-safety blankets.**

- **Know your school's fire-evacuation routes.**

- **If your clothing catches on fire, walk (do not run) to the emergency lab shower to put out the fire. If the shower is not working, STOP, DROP, and ROLL!** Smother the fire by stopping immediately, dropping to the floor, and rolling until the fire is out.

Safety with Gases

- **Do not inhale any gas or vapor unless directed to do so by your teacher.** Never inhale pure gases.

- **Handle materials that emit vapors or gases in a well-ventilated area.** This work should be done in an approved chemical fume hood.

Caustic Substances

- **If a chemical gets on your skin, on your clothing, or in your eyes, rinse it immediately and alert your teacher.**

- **If a chemical is spilled on the floor or lab bench, alert your teacher, but do not clean it up yourself unless your teacher directs you to do so.**

How to Use Your Textbook

Your Roadmap for Success with *Holt Earth Science*

Get Organized

Do the **Pre-Reading Activity** at the beginning of each chapter to create a **FoldNote,** which is a helpful note-taking and study aid. Use the **Graphic Organizer** activity within the chapter to organize the chapter content in a way that you understand.

STUDY TIP Go to the Skills Handbook section of the Appendix for guidance on making FoldNotes and Graphic Organizers.

Read for Meaning

Read the **Objectives** at the beginning of each section, because they will tell you what you'll need to learn. **Key Terms** are also listed for each section. Each key term is highlighted in the text and is defined in the margin. After reading each chapter, turn to the **Chapter Highlights** page and review the **Key Concepts,** which are brief summaries of the chapter's main ideas. You may want to do this even before you read the chapter.

STUDY TIP If you don't understand a definition, reread the page on which the term is introduced. The surrounding text should help make the definition easier to understand.

⬈ Be Resourceful—Use the Web

SciLinks boxes in your textbook take you to resources that you can use for science projects, reports, and research papers. Go to **scilinks.org** and type in the **SciLinks code** to find information on a topic.

Visit go.hrw.com
Find resources and reference materials that go with your textbook at **go.hrw.com.** Enter the keyword **HQ6 Home** to access the home page for your textbook.

Consider Environmental Issues

As you read each section, look for passages marked with oak leaves—one at the beginning of the passage and one at the end. These passages contain information that is directly related to important environmental issues.

Prepare for Tests

Section Reviews and **Chapter Reviews** test your knowledge of the main points of the chapter. Critical Thinking items challenge you to think about the material in different ways and in greater depth. The **Standards Assessment** that is located after each Chapter Review helps you sharpen your test-taking abilities.

STUDY TIP Reread the Objectives and Chapter Highlights when studying for a test to be sure you know the material.

Use the Appendix

Your **Appendix** contains a variety of resources designed to enhance your learning experience. These resources include the **Skills Handbook,** which provides helpful study aids, **Mapping Expeditions** and **Long-Term Projects** activities, and **Reference Tables** and **Reference Maps.**

Figure 6 ▶ This stone lion sits outside Leeds Town Hall in England. It was damaged by acid precipitation.

acid precipitation precipitation, such as rain, sleet, or snow, that contains a high concentration of acids, often because of the pollution of the atmosphere

Acid Precipitation

Natural rainwater is slightly acidic because it combines with small amounts of carbon dioxide. But when fossil fuels, especially coal, are burned, nitrogen oxides and sulfur dioxides are released into the air. These compounds combine with water in the atmosphere to produce nitric acid, nitrous acid, or sulfuric acid. When these acids fall to Earth, they are called **acid precipitation.**

Acid precipitation weathers some rock faster than ordinary precipitation does. In fact, many historical monuments and sculptures have been damaged by acid precipitation, as shown in **Figure 6.** Between 1940 and 1990, acid precipitation fell regularly in some cities in the United States. In 1990, the Acid Rain Control Program was added to the Clean Air Act of 1970. These regulations gave power plants 10 years to decrease sulfur dioxide emissions. The occurrence of acid precipitation has been greatly reduced since power plants have installed scrubbers that remove much of the sulfur dioxide before it can be released.

Section 1 Review

1. **Identify** three agents of mechanical weathering. 🖥7c

2. **Describe** how ice wedging weathers rock. 🖥7c

3. **Explain** how two activities of plants or animals help weather rocks or soil. 🖥7c

4. **Compare** mechanical and chemical weathering processes. 🖥7c

5. **Identify** and describe three chemical processes that weather rock. 🖥7c

6. **Compare** hydrolysis, carbonation, and oxidation. 🖥7c

7. **Summarize** how acid precipitation forms.

CRITICAL THINKING

8. **Making Connections** What two agents of weathering would be rare in a desert? Explain your reasoning. 🖥7c, IE.1d

9. **Understanding Relationships** Automobile exhaust contains nitrogen oxides. How might these pollutants affect chemical weathering processes? 🖥7c, IE.1d

CONCEPT MAPPING

10. Use the following terms to create a concept map: *weathering, oxidation, mechanical weathering, ice wedging, hydrolysis, abrasion, chemical weathering, carbonation,* and *acid precipitation.* 🖥7c

348 Chapter 14 **Weathering and Erosion**

Visit Holt Online Learning

If your teacher gives you a special password to log onto the **Holt Online Learning** site, you'll find your complete textbook on the Web. In addition, you'll find some great learning tools and practice quizzes. You'll be able to see how well you know the material from your textbook.

Unit 1 STUDYING THE EARTH

► Earth scientists can be found everywhere on Earth, braving conditions from the extreme heat of an active volcano to the frozen depth of a glacier. The Muir Glacier at Alaska's Glacier Bay National Park can be explored and studied through this ice cave.

Chapter 1

Introduction to Earth Science

Sections

1 What Is Earth Science?

2 Science as a Process

What You'll Learn

- What areas of study make up Earth science
- How Earth scientists study the planet
- Why the work of Earth scientists is important to society

Why It's Relevant

An understanding of Earth science is vital in determining how the environment affects human society and how human society affects the air, water, and soil of Earth.

PRE-READING ACTIVITY

Four-Corner Fold

Before you read this chapter, create the **FoldNote** entitled "Four-Corner Fold" described in the Skills Handbook section of the Appendix. Label each flap of the four-corner fold with a topic from the chapter. Write what you know about each topic under the appropriate flap. As you read the chapter, add other information that you learn.

▶ The movement of rocks like this one in an area called *Racetrack Playa*, in Death Valley, California, has intrigued Earth scientists for years. Scientists have many hypotheses as to how rocks that weigh over 320 kg can move more than 880 m. However, no one knows for sure how these rocks move.

California Content Standards

IE.1a Students will select and use appropriate tools and technology (such as computer-linked probes, spreadsheets, and graphing calculators) to perform tests, collect data, analyze relationships and display data.

IE.1b Students will identify and communicate sources of unavoidable experimental error.

IE.1c Students will identify possible reasons for inconsistent results, such as sources of error or uncontrolled conditions.

IE.1d Students will formulate explanations using logic and evidence.

IE.1f Students will distinguish between hypothesis and theory as science terms.

IE.1g Students will recognize the usefulness and limitations of models and theories as scientific representations of reality.

IE.1j Students will recognize the issues of statistical variability and the need for controlled tests.

IE.1k Students will recognize the cumulative nature of scientific evidence.

IE.1l Students will analyze situations and solve problems that require combining and applying concepts from more than one area of science.

IE.1m Students will investigate a science-based societal issue by researching the literature, analyzing data, and communicating the findings. Examples of issues include irradiation of food, cloning of animals by somatic cell nuclear transfer, choice of energy sources, and land and water use decisions in California.

IE.1n Students will know that when an observation does not agree with an accepted scientific theory, the observation is sometimes mistaken or fraudulent (e.g., the Piltdown Man fossil or unidentified flying objects) and that the theory is sometimes wrong (e.g., the Ptolemaic model of the movement of the Sun, Moon and planets).

What Is Earth Science?

California
Content
Standards

IE.1d Students will formulate explanations
using logic and evidence.
IE.1k Students will recognize the cumulative

nature of scientific evidence.
IE.1l Students will analyze situations and solve
problems that require combining and applying

concepts from more than one area of science.

For thousands of years, people have looked at the world around them and wondered what forces shaped it. Throughout history, many cultures have been terrified and fascinated by seeing volcanoes erupt, feeling the ground shake during an earthquake, or watching the sky darken during an eclipse.

Some cultures developed myths or stories to explain these events. In some of these myths, angry goddesses hurled fire from volcanoes, and giants shook the ground by wrestling underneath Earth's surface. Modern science searches for natural causes and uses careful observations to explain these same events and to understand Earth and its changing landscape.

The Scientific Study of Earth

Scientific study of Earth began with careful observations. Scientists in China began keeping records of earthquakes as early as 780 BCE. The ancient Greeks compiled a catalog of rocks and minerals around 200 BCE. Other ancient peoples, including the Maya, tracked the movements of the sun, the moon, and the planets at observatories like the one shown in **Figure 1.** The Maya used these observations to create accurate calendars.

For many centuries, scientific discoveries were limited to observations of phenomena that could be seen with the unaided eye. Then, in the 16th and 17th centuries, the inventions of the microscope and the telescope made seeing previously hidden worlds possible. Eventually, the body of knowledge about Earth became known as Earth science. **Earth science** is the study of Earth and of the universe around it. Earth science, like other sciences, assumes that the causes of natural events, or phenomena, can be discovered through careful observation and experimentation.

OBJECTIVES

▶ **Describe** two cultures that contributed to modern scientific study. IE.1k

▶ **Name** the four main branches of Earth science. IE.1l

▶ **Discuss** how Earth scientists help us understand the world around us. IE.1k

KEY TERMS

Earth science
geology
oceanography
meteorology
astronomy

Earth science the scientific study of Earth and the universe around it

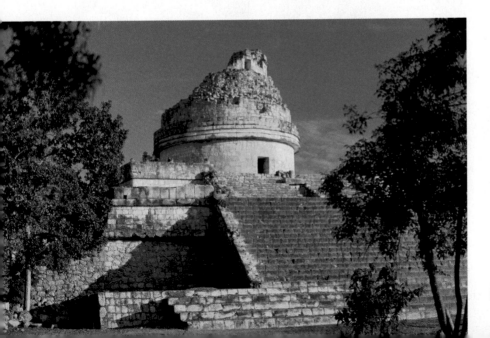

Figure 1 ▶ El Caracol, an observatory built by the ancient Maya of Mexico, is the oldest known observatory in the Americas. Mayan calendars show the celestial movements that the Maya tracked by using observatories.

Branches of Earth Science

The ability to make observations improves when technology, such as new processes or equipment, is developed. Technology has allowed scientists to explore the ocean depths, Earth's unseen interior, and the vastness of space. Earth scientists have used technology and hard work to build an immense body of knowledge about Earth.

Most Earth scientists specialize in one of four major areas of study: the solid Earth, the oceans, the atmosphere, and the universe beyond Earth. Examples of Earth scientists working in these areas are shown in **Figure 2.**

Geology

The study of the origin, history, processes, and structure of the solid Earth is called **geology.** Geology includes many specialized areas of study. Some geologists explore Earth's crust for deposits of coal, oil, gas, and other resources. Other geologists study the forces within Earth to predict earthquakes and volcanic eruptions. Some geologists study fossils to learn more about Earth's past. Often, new knowledge forms new areas of study.

Oceanography

Oceans cover nearly three-fourths of Earth's surface. The study of Earth's oceans is called **oceanography.** Some oceanographers work on research ships that are equipped with special instruments for studying the sea. Other oceanographers study waves, tides, and ocean currents. Some oceanographers explore the ocean floor to obtain clues to Earth's history or to locate mineral deposits.

geology the scientific study of the origin, history, and structure of Earth and the processes that shape Earth

oceanography the scientific study of the ocean, including the properties and movements of ocean water, the characteristics of the ocean floor, and the organisms that live in the ocean

Figure 2 ▶ Fields of Study in Earth Science

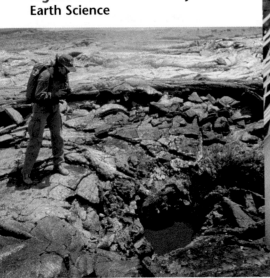

Geologists who study volcanoes are called *volcanologists*. This volcanologist is measuring the magnetic and electric properties of moving lava.

This astronomer is linking a telescope with a specialized instrument called a *spectrograph*. Information gathered will help her catalog the composition of more than 100 galaxies.

This meteorologist is studying ice samples to learn about past climate. Studying past climate patterns gives scientists information about possible future changes in climate.

Connection to HISTORY

Scientific Revolutions

Throughout history, many cultures have added to scientific knowledge. Over the last few centuries, global exploration and cultural exchanges have helped modern science change very quickly. During this time, science has aided the industrialization of countries around the world. Technology has also allowed humans to explore areas from the deep-ocean basins to the universe beyond Earth.

Advances in science usually occur through small additions to existing knowledge. The daily work of scientists and engineers normally results in step-by-step increases of understanding and improvements in the ability to meet human needs. In this way, scientists add knowledge, invent new technologies, and educate future generations of scientists.

However, some advances in science and technology occur very quickly and have effects that ripple through science and society. When a scientific advance completely changes the way that scientists think about the universe, a *scientific revolution* occurs. Scientific revolutions cause long-held ideas to be challenged and put aside for new ways of thinking and viewing the universe. Examples of recent scientific revolutions include Darwin's theory of evolution, the concept of quantum mechanics, and Einstein's general theory of relativity.

Progress in science and technology can be affected by social issues and challenges. In some cases, both scientists and nonscientists resist letting go of long-held beliefs. Many of the ideas that Einstein replaced with his theory of relativity had been in place for hundreds of years. Through many years of continued research and education, revolutionary ideas often become accepted by the scientific community and by society as a whole.

But even revolutionary ideas are continuously being tested. In 2002, experiments were performed aboard NASA's *Cassini* spacecraft to test a part of Einstein's theory of relativity. Using new technologies, scientists were able to verify Einstein's theory, which had been proposed almost 100 years earlier.

Meteorology

The study of Earth's atmosphere is called **meteorology.** Using satellites, radar, and other technologies, meteorologists study the atmospheric conditions that produce weather. Many meteorologists work as weather observers and measure factors such as wind speed, temperature, and rainfall. This weather information is then used to prepare detailed weather maps. Other meteorologists use weather maps, satellite images, and computer models to make weather forecasts. Some meteorologists study *climate,* the patterns of weather that occur over long periods of time.

meteorology the scientific study of Earth's atmosphere, especially in relation to weather and climate

astronomy the scientific study of the universe

Astronomy

The study of the universe beyond Earth is called **astronomy.** Astronomy is one of the oldest branches of Earth science. In fact, the ancient Babylonians charted the positions of planets and stars nearly 4,000 years ago. Modern astronomers use Earth-based and space-based telescopes as well as other instruments to study the sun, the moon, the planets, and the universe. Technologies such as rovers and space probes have also provided astronomers with new information about the universe.

Reading Check How has technology affected astronomy? (See the Appendix for answers to Reading Checks.)

SCiLINKS.

Developed and maintained by the National Science Teachers Association

For a variety of links related to this subject, go to www.scilinks.org

Topic: Branches of Earth Science
SciLinks code: HQ60191

Environmental Science

 Other Earth scientists study the ways in which humans interact with their environment. This relatively new field of Earth science is called *environmental science*. Environmental scientists study many issues, such as the use of natural resources, pollution, and the health of plant and animal species on Earth. Some environmental scientists study the effects of industries and technologies on the environment.

The Importance of Earth Science

Natural forces not only shape Earth but also affect life on Earth. For example, a volcanic eruption may bury a town under ash. And an earthquake may produce huge ocean waves that destroy shorelines. By understanding how natural forces shape our environment, Earth scientists, such as those in **Figure 3**, can better predict potential disasters and help save lives and property.

The work of Earth scientists also helps us understand our place in the universe. Astronomers studying distant galaxies have come up with new ideas about the origins of our universe. Geologists studying rock layers have found clues to Earth's past environments and to the evolution of life on this planet.

Earth provides the resources that make life as we know it possible. Earth also provides the materials to enrich the quality of people's lives. The fuel that powers a jet, the metal used in surgical instruments, and the paper and ink in this book all come from Earth's resources. The study of Earth science can help people gain access to Earth's resources, but Earth scientists also strive to help people use those resources wisely.

Figure 3 ▶ These meteorologists are risking their lives to gather information about tornadoes. If scientists can better predict when tornadoes will occur, many lives may be saved each year.

Section 1 Review

1. **Discuss** how one culture contributed to modern science. IE.1k

2. **Name** the four major branches of Earth science. IE.1l

3. **Describe** two specialized fields of geology.

4. **Describe** the work of oceanographers and meteorologists.

5. **Explain** how the work of astronomers has been affected by technology. IE.1k

CRITICAL THINKING

6. **Analyzing Ideas** How have Earth scientists improved our understanding of the environment? IE.1k, IE.1l

7. **Analyzing Concepts** Give two examples of how exploring space and exploring the ocean depths are similar. IE.1d

CONCEPT MAPPING

8. Use the following terms to create a concept map: *Earth science, geology, meteorology, climate, environmental science, astronomy,* and *oceanography.*

Figure 3 ▶ Astronaut Shannon Lucid observes wheat plants that are a part of an experiment aboard the *Mir* space station.

Test the Hypothesis

After a hypothesis is proposed, it is often tested by performing experiments. An *experiment* is a procedure that is carried out according to certain guidelines. Factors that can be changed in an experiment are variables. **Independent variables** are factors that can be changed by the person performing the experiment. **Dependent variables** are variables that change as a result of a change in independent variables.

In most experiments, only one independent variable is tested. For example, to test how sunlight affects plants, a scientist would grow identical plants. The plants would receive the same amount of water and fertilizer but different amounts of sunlight. Thus, sunlight would be the independent variable. How the plants respond to the different amounts of sunlight would be the dependent variable. Most experiments include a control group. A *control group* is a group that serves as a standard of comparison with another group to which the control group is identical except for one factor. In this experiment, the plants that receive a natural amount of sunlight would be the control group. An experiment that contains a control is called a *controlled experiment*. Most scientific experiments are controlled experiments. The "zero gravity" experiment shown in **Figure 3** is a controlled experiment.

Draw Conclusions

After many experiments and observations, a scientist may reach conclusions about his or her hypothesis. If the hypothesis fits the known facts, it may be accepted as true. If the experimental results differ from what was expected, the hypothesis may be changed or discarded. Expected and unexpected results lead to new questions and further study. The results of scientific inquiry may also lead to new knowledge and new methods of inquiry that further scientific aims.

independent variable in an experiment, the factor that is deliberately manipulated

dependent variable in an experiment, the factor that changes as a result of manipulation of one or more other factors (the independent variables)

Making Observations IE.1d

Procedure

1. Get an ordinary **candle** of any shape and color.
2. Record all the observations you can make about the candle.
3. Light the candle with a **match**, and watch it burn for 1 min.
4. Record as many observations about the burning candle as you can. When you are finished, extinguish the flame. Record any observations.

Analysis

1. Share your results with your class. How many things that your classmates observed did you not observe? Explain this phenomenon.

Good accuracy and good precision

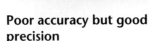
Poor accuracy but good precision

Good overall accuracy but poor precision

Figure 4 ▶ Accuracy and Precision

Scientific Measurements and Analysis

During an experiment, scientists must gather information. An important method of gathering information is measurement. Measurement is the comparison of some aspect of an object or event with a standard unit. Scientists around the world can compare and analyze each other's measurements because scientists use a common system of measurement called the *International System of Units,* or SI. This system includes standard measurements for length, mass, temperature, and volume. All SI units are based on intervals of 10. The Reference Tables section of the Appendix contains a chart of SI units.

Accuracy and Precision

Accuracy and precision are important in scientific measurements. *Accuracy* refers to how close a measurement is to the true value of the thing being measured. *Precision* is the exactness of the measurement. For example, a distance measured in millimeters is more precise than a distance measured in centimeters. Measurements can be precise and yet inaccurate. The relationship between accuracy and precision is shown in **Figure 4**.

Quick LAB 15 min

Sample Size and Accuracy ▦ IE.1c, IE.1d
Procedure
1. Shuffle a **deck of 52 playing cards** eight times.
2. Lay out 10 cards. Record the number of red cards.
3. Reshuffle, and repeat step 2 four more times.
4. Which trials showed the highest number and lowest number of red cards? Calculate the total range of red cards by finding the difference between the highest number and lowest number.
5. Determine the mean number of red cards per trial by adding the number of red cards in the five trials and then dividing by 5.

Analysis
1. A deck of cards has 50% red cards. How close is your average to the percentage of red cards in the deck?
2. Pool the results of your classmates. How close is the new average to the percentage of red cards in the deck?
3. How does changing the sample size affect accuracy?

Error

Error is an expression of the amount of imprecision or variation in a set of measurements. Error is commonly expressed as percentage error or as a confidence interval. Percentage error is the percentage of deviation of an experimental value from an accepted value. A *confidence interval* describes the range of values for a set percentage of measurements. For example, imagine that the average length of all of the ears of corn in a field is 23 cm, and 90% of the ears are within 3 cm of the average length. A scientist may report that the average length of all of the ears of corn in a field is 23 ± 3 cm with 90% confidence.

Observations and Models

In Earth science, using controlled experiments to test a hypothesis is often impossible. When experiments are impossible, scientists make additional observations to gather evidence. The hypothesis is then tested by examining how well the hypothesis fits or explains all of the known evidence.

Scientists also use models to simulate conditions in the natural world. A *model* is a description, representation, or imitation of an object, system, process, or concept. Scientists use several types of models, two of which are shown in **Figure 5.** Physical models are three-dimensional models that can be touched. Maps and charts are examples of graphical models.

Conceptual models are verbal or graphical models that represent how a system works or is organized. Mathematical models are mathematical equations that represent the way a system or process works. Most recently, scientists have developed computer models, which can be used to represent simple processes or complex systems. After a good computer model has been created, scientists can perform experiments by manipulating variables much as they would when performing a physical experiment.

Reading Check Name three types of models. (See the Appendix for answers to Reading Checks.)

Figure 5 ▶ Two models of Mount Everest are shown below. The computer model on the right is used to track erosion along the Tibetan Plateau. The model on the left is a physical model.

Mt. Everest

Figure 6 ▶ Meteorologists at a conference in California are watching the newly introduced "Science On a Sphere™" exhibit. They are wearing 3-D glasses to better see the complex and changing three-dimensional display of global temperatures.

Graphic Organizer **Chain-of-Events Chart**

Create the Graphic Organizer entitled "Chain-of-Events Chart" described in the Skills Handbook section of the Appendix. Then, fill in the chart with details about each step of how a hypothesis becomes an accepted scientific idea.

peer review the process in which experts in a given field examine the results and conclusions of a scientist's study before that study is accepted for publication

Acceptance of Scientific Ideas

When scientists reach a conclusion, they introduce their findings to the scientific community. New scientific ideas undergo review and testing by other scientists before the ideas are accepted.

Publication of Results and Conclusions

Scientists commonly present the results of their work in scientific journals or at professional meetings, such as the one shown in **Figure 6.** Results published in journals are usually written in a standard scientific format. Many journals are now being published online to allow scientists quicker access to the results of other scientists.

Peer Review

Scientists in any one research group tend to view scientific ideas similarly. Therefore, they may be biased in their experimental design or data analysis. To reduce bias, scientists submit their ideas to other scientists for peer review. **Peer review** is the process in which several experts on a given topic review another expert's work on that topic before the work gets published. These experts determine if the results and conclusions of the study merit publication. Peer reviewers commonly suggest improvements to the study, or they may determine that the results or conclusions are flawed and recommend that the study not be published. Scientists follow an ethical code that states that only valid experimental results should be published. The peer review process serves as a filter, which allows only well-supported ideas to be published.

✔ **Reading Check** Name two places scientists present the results of their work. (See the Appendix for answers to Reading Checks.)

Formulating a Theory

After results are published, they usually lead to more experiments, which are designed to test and expand the original idea. This process may continue for years until the original idea is disproved, is modified, or becomes generally accepted. Sometimes, elements of different ideas are combined to form concepts that are more complete.

When an idea has undergone much testing and reaches general acceptance, that idea may help form a theory. A **theory** is an explanation that is consistent with all existing tests and observations. Theories are often based on scientific laws. A *scientific law* is a general statement that explains how the natural world behaves under certain conditions and for which no exceptions have been found. Like theories, laws are discovered through scientific research. Theories and scientific laws can be changed if conflicting information is discovered in the future.

theory the explanation for some phenomenon that is based on observation, experimentation, and reasoning; that is supported by a large quantity of evidence; and that does not conflict with any existing experimental results or observations

The Importance of Interdisciplinary Science

Scientists from many disciplines commonly contribute the information necessary to support an idea. The free exchange of ideas between fields of science allows scientists to identify explanations that fit a wide range of scientific evidence. When an explanation is supported by evidence from a variety of fields, the explanation is more likely to be accurate. New disciplines of science sometimes emerge as a result of new connections that are found between more than one branch of science. An example of the development of a widely accepted hypothesis that is based on interdisciplinary evidence is shown in **Figure 7.**

Figure 7 ▶ The hypothesis that the dinosaurs were killed by an asteroid impact was developed over many years and through the work of many scientists from different disciplines.

Impact Hypothesis of Extinction of the Dinosaurs

Paleontology
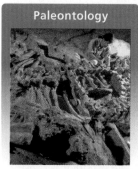
No dinosaur fossils exist in rock layers younger than 65 million years old.

Geology

A large impact crater about 65 million years old exists in the ocean near the Yucatan peninsula.

Astronomy

A layer of iridium occurs in rocks about 65 million years old all around Earth. Iridium is rare on Earth, but is common in meteoroids.

Climatology
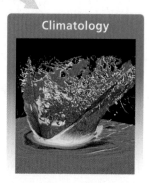
Climate models predict that a large impact would change Earth's climate and affect life on Earth.

Science and Society

Scientific knowledge helps us understand our world. The work of people, including scientists, is influenced by their cultural and personal beliefs. Science is a part of society, and advances in science can have important and long-lasting effects on both science and society. Examples of these far-reaching advances include the theory of plate tectonics, quantum mechanics, and the theory of evolution.

Science is also used to develop new technology, including new tools, machines, materials, and processes. Sometimes, technologies are designed to address a specific human need. In other cases, technology is an indirect result of science that was directed at another goal. For example, technology that was designed for space exploration has been used to improve computers, cars, medical equipment, and airplanes.

However, new technology may also create new problems. Scientists involved in research that leads to new technologies have an obligation to consider the possible negative effects of their work. Before making decisions about technology, people should consider the alternatives, risks, and costs and benefits to humans and to Earth. Even after such decisions are made, society often continues to debate them. For example, the Alaskan pipeline, part of which is shown in **Figure 8,** transports oil. But the transport of oil in the United States is part of an ongoing debate about how we use oil resources and how these uses affect our natural world.

Figure 8 ▶ The Alaskan pipeline has carried more than 13 billion barrels of oil since it was built in 1977. The pipeline has also sparked controversy about the potential dangers to nearby Alaskan wildlife.

Section 2 Review

1. **Describe** one reason that a scientist might conduct research. IE.1d

2. **Identify** the steps that make up scientific methods. IE.1a, IE.1d, IE.1j

3. **Compare** a hypothesis with a theory. IE.1f

4. **Describe** how scientists test hypotheses.

5. **Describe** the difference between a dependent variable and an independent variable.

6. **Explain** why scientific ideas that have been subject to many tests are still considered theories and not scientific laws.

7. **Summarize** how scientific methods contribute to the development of modern science. IE.1k

8. **Explain** how technology can affect scientific research. IE.1k

CRITICAL THINKING

9. **Analyzing Ideas** An observation can be precise but inaccurate. Do you think it is possible for an observation to be accurate but not precise? Explain. IE.1n

10. **Making Comparisons** When an artist paints a picture of a natural scene, what aspects of his or her work are similar to the methods of a scientist? What aspects are different? IE.1d

11. **Demonstrating Reasoned Judgment** A new technology is known to be harmful to a small group of people. How does this knowledge affect whether you would use this new technology? Explain. IE.1m

CONCEPT MAPPING

12. Use the following terms to create a concept map: *independent variable, observation, experiment, dependent variable, hypothesis, scientific methods,* and *conclusion.*

Sections

1 What Is Earth Science?

Key Terms

Earth science, 5
geology, 6
oceanography, 6
meteorology, 7
astronomy, 7

Key Concepts

▶ Many cultures have contributed to the development of science over thousands of years.

▶ The four main branches of Earth science are geology, oceanography, meteorology, and astronomy.

▶ Earth scientists help us understand how Earth formed and the natural forces that affect human society.

2 Science as a Process

Key Terms

observation, 10
hypothesis, 10
independent variable, 11
dependent variable, 11
peer review, 14
theory, 15

Key Concepts

▶ Scientific research attempts to solve problems logically through scientific methods.

▶ Science differs from other human endeavors by following a procedure of testing to help understand natural phenomena.

▶ Using scientific methods, scientists develop hypotheses and theories to describe natural phenomena.

▶ Scientific methods include observation and experimentation.

▶ Science aids in the development of technology. The main aim of technology is to solve human problems.

Using Key Terms

Use each of the following terms in a separate sentence.

1. *observation*
2. *peer review*
3. *theory*

For each pair of terms, explain how the meanings of the terms differ.

4. *hypothesis* and *theory* ▪ IE.1f
5. *geology* and *astronomy*
6. *oceanography* and *meteorology*
7. *dependent variable* and *independent variable*
8. *Earth science* and *geology*

Understanding Key Concepts

9. The study of solid Earth is called
   a. geology.
   c. oceanography.
   b. meteorology.
   d. astronomy.

10. The Earth scientist most likely to study storms is a(n)
    a. geologist.
    c. oceanographer.
    b. meteorologist.
    d. astronomer.

11. The study of the origin of the solar system and the universe in general is
    a. geology.
    c. meteorology.
    b. ecology.
    d. astronomy.

12. How long ago were the first scientific observations about Earth made? ▪ IE.1k
    a. a few years ago
    b. a few decades ago
    c. hundreds of years ago
    d. several thousand years ago

13. The Earth scientist most likely to study volcanoes is a(n)
    a. geologist.
    c. oceanographer.
    b. meteorologist.
    d. astronomer.

14. One possible first step in scientific problem solving is to
    a. form a hypothesis.
    b. ask a question.
    c. test a hypothesis.
    d. state a conclusion.

15. A possible explanation for a scientific problem is called a(n) ▪ IE.1f
    a. experiment.
    c. observation.
    b. theory.
    d. hypothesis.

16. A statement that consistently and correctly describes a natural phenomenon is a scientific ▪ IE.1f
    a. hypothesis.
    c. observation.
    b. theory.
    d. control.

17. When scientists pose questions about how nature operates and attempt to answer those questions through testing and observation, they are conducting
    a. research.
    c. examinations.
    b. predictions.
    d. peer reviews.

Short Answer

18. How does accuracy differ from precision in a scientific measurement? ▪ IE.1b, IE.1c

19. Why do scientists use control groups in experiments? ▪ IE.1j

20. A meteorite lands in your backyard. What two branches of Earth science would help you explain that natural event? ▪ IE.1l

21. Write a short paragraph about the relationship between science and technology. ▪ IE.1k

22. Give two reasons why interdisciplinary science is important to society. ▪ IE.1l

23. Explain how peer review affects scientific knowledge. ▪ IE.1k

24. How did some ancient cultures explain natural phenomena? ▪ IE.1k

Critical Thinking

25. Making Connections How could knowing how our solar system formed affect how we see the world? 🐾 IE.1k

26. Evaluating Hypotheses Some scientists have hypothesized that meteorites have periodically bombarded Earth and caused mass extinctions every 26 million years. How might this hypothesis be tested? 🐾 IE.1a, IE.1d, IE.1g

27. Determining Cause and Effect Name some possible negative effects of a new technology that uses nuclear fuel to power cars. 🐾 IE.1m

28. Analyzing Ideas A scientist observes that each eruption of a volcano is preceded by a series of small earthquakes. The scientist then makes the following statement: "Earthquakes cause volcanic eruptions." Is the scientist's statement a hypothesis or a theory? Why? 🐾 IE.1f

29. Forming a Hypothesis You find a yellow rock and wonder if it is gold. How could you apply scientific methods to this problem? 🐾 IE.1d

Concept Mapping

30. Use the following terms to create a concept map: *control group, accuracy, precision, variable, technology, Earth science, experiment,* and *error.* 🐾 IE.1j

Math Skills

31. Making Calculations One kilogram is equal to 2.205 lb at sea level. At the same location, how many kilograms are in 100 lb?

32. Making Calculations One meter is equal to 3.281 ft. How many meters are in 5 ft?

33. Making Calculations The accepted value of the average distance between Earth and the moon is 384,467 km. If a scientist measures that the moon is 384,476 km from Earth, what is the measurement's percentage error?

Writing Skills

34. Expressing Original Ideas Imagine that you must live in a place that has all the benefits of only one of the Earth sciences. Which branch would you choose? Defend your choice in an essay. 🐾 IE.1d

35. Outlining Topics Explain the sequence of events that happens as a scientific hypothesis becomes a theory. 🐾 IE.1f

Interpreting Graphics

The graph below shows error in measuring tectonic plate movements. The blue bars represent confidence intervals. Use this graph to answer the questions that follow.

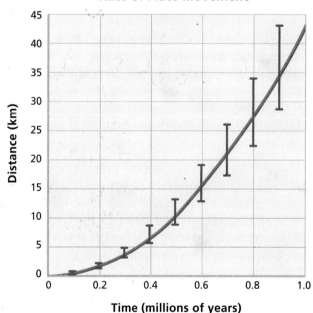

Rate of Plate Movement

36. How much error is there in the smallest measurement of plate movement?

37. How much error is there in the largest measurement of plate movement?

38. How would you explain the difference between the error in the smallest measurement and the error in the largest measurement? 🐾 IE.1c, IE.1d

Understanding Concepts

Directions (1–9): For *each* question, write on a separate sheet of paper the letter of the correct answer.

1 What is the difference between a theory and a hypothesis?
   A. A hypothesis is a possible explanation for a problem, and a theory is an explanation that is consistent with all existing tests.
   B. A hypothesis is an explanation that is consistent with all existing tests, and a theory is a general statement about the natural world for which no exceptions have been found.
   C. A hypothesis changes during an experiment, which results in a change in a theory.
   D. A hypothesis never changes during an experiment, while a theory is often changed as observations produce new data.

2 If experimental results do not match their predictions, scientists generally will
   A. repeat the experiment until the results match.
   B. make the measurements more precise.
   C. revise their working hypothesis.
   D. change their experimental results.

3 Earth scientists study various characteristics of Earth and the solar system. Which of the following statements describes the role of a meteorologist?
   A. a scientist who studies stars
   B. a scientist who studies the impact of human activities on the environment
   C. a scientist who studies rock layers
   D. a scientist who studies weather patterns

4 Which of the following is an example of a new technology?
   A. a tool that is designed to help a doctor better diagnose patients
   B. a previously unknown element that is discovered in nature
   C. a law that is passed to fund scientists conducting new experiments
   D. scientists that record observations on the movement of a star

5 Which of the following statements describes an example of a physical model?
   A. a model that consists of a graph
   B. a model made up of molded clay, soil, and chemicals
   C. a model that includes equations
   D. a model created using a program

6 During an experiment, scientists control conditions to avoid error. In a controlled experiment, which of the following factors is changed by the scientist?
   A. control group
   B. dependent variable
   C. independent variable
   D. observation

7 Which of the following describes a relationship between accuracy and precision that most likely would NOT result in experimental error?
   A. Measurements are precise, but inaccurate.
   B. Measurements are both accurate and precise.
   C. Measurements are imprecise and inaccurate.
   D. Measurements are accurate, but imprecise.

8 A scientist has developed a new technology that may benefit humans. Before the scientist introduces the new technology in society, the scientist should
   A. consider the possible negative effects of the technology.
   B. develop a new scientific theory.
   C. run an experiment that involves humans.
   D. address a specific human need.

9 If scientists make an observation that does not agree with an accepted scientific theory, the scientists should
   A. assume that their observations are incorrect.
   B. conclude that the theory is wrong.
   C. perform more experiments to determine if the observation is the result of error or if the theory is wrong.
   D. publish their results so other scientists can test the theory.

Interpreting Graphics

Directions (10–11): **For** *each* **question below, record the correct answer on a separate sheet of paper.**

Branches of Earth Science

10 The diagram above shows the four major areas studied by Earth scientists. A scientist studying the events that take place in area C would be primarily concerned with which of the following?

A. Earth's age
B. Earth's weather
C. movement of waves and tides
D. movement of the stars across the sky

Scientific Methods

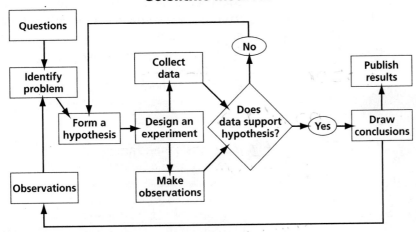

11 In the illustration above, during which step do scientists develop a possible explanation for a problem?

A. collect data
B. form a hypothesis
C. make observations
D. draw conclusions

Objectives

▶ **Observe** natural phenomena.
▶ **Propose** hypotheses to explain natural phenomena.
▶ **Evaluate** hypotheses.

Materials

hand lens

meterstick

Scientific Methods   IE.1a, IE.1c, IE.1d, IE.1n

Not all scientists think alike, and scientists don't always agree about various concepts. However, all scientists use scientific methods, part of which are the skills of observing, inferring, and predicting. In this lab, you will apply scientific methods as you examine a place where puddles often form after rainstorms. You can study the puddle area even when the ground is dry, but it would be best to observe the area again when it is wet. Because water is one of the most effective agents of change in our environment, you should be able to make many observations.

MAKE OBSERVATIONS

1 Examine the area of the puddle and the surrounding area carefully. Make a numbered list of what can be seen, heard, smelled, or felt. Sample observations are as follows: "The ground where the puddle forms is lower than the surrounding area, and there are cracks in the soil." Remember to avoid making any suggestions of causes.

FORM A HYPOTHESIS

2 Review your observations, and write possible causes for those observations. Sample causes are as follows: "Cracks in the soil (Observation 2) may have been caused by a lack of rain (Observation 5)."

Step 1

3. Review your observations and possible causes, and place them into similar groups, if possible. Can one cause or set of causes explain several observations? Is each cause reasonable when compared with the others? Does any cause contradict any of the other observations?

Step 2

TEST THE HYPOTHESIS

4. Based only on your hypotheses, make some predictions about what will happen at the puddle as conditions change. Describe the changes you expect and your reasoning. A sample prediction is the following: "If the puddle dries out, the crack will grow wider because of the loss of water."

5. Revisit the puddle several times to see if the changes that you observe match your predictions.

ANALYZE THE RESULTS

1. **Evaluating Results** Which of your predictions were correct, and which predictions were incorrect?

2. **Analyzing Methods** Which of your senses did you use most to make your observations? How could you improve your observations by using this sense? by using other senses?

3. **Evaluating Methods** What could you have used to measure, or quantify, many of your observations? Is quantitative observation better than qualitative observation? Explain your answer.

DRAW CONCLUSIONS

4. **Drawing Conclusions** Examine your incorrect predictions. What new knowledge have you gained from this new evidence?

5. **Analyzing Results** Reexamine your hypotheses. What can you say now about the ones that were correct?

6. **Drawing Conclusions** When knowledge is derived from observation and prediction, this process is called a *scientific method*. After reporting the results of a prediction, how might a scientist continue his or her research?

Extension

1. **Designing Experiments** Choose another small area to examine, but look for changes caused by a different factor, such as wind. Follow the steps outlined in this lab to predict changes that will occur in the area. Use scientific methods to design an experiment. Briefly describe your experiment, including how you would perform it.

Geologic Features and Political Boundaries in Europe

Map Skills Activity

This map shows the political boundaries of a part of Europe. The map also shows some surface features. Use the map to answer the questions below.

1. **Using the Key** What do the blue lines represent?

2. **Analyzing Data** How many countries are represented on the map?

3. **Examining Data** What country has two smaller countries within its borders?

4. **Applying Ideas** What type of surface features define the political boundary between Romania and Moldova and the political boundary between Switzerland and Germany?

5. **Applying Ideas** What type of surface feature defines the political boundary between Poland and the Czech Republic?

6. **Making Inferences** Why do you think that political boundaries commonly correspond with surface features?

Field Geologist

Imagine a summer visit to a meadow in Yellowstone National Park. Against blue skies, lush and grass-covered fields are dotted with grazing bison and elk. Field geologist Ken Pierce knows that there is more to this view than meets the eye. "Meadow areas, such as Hayden Valley," says Pierce, "are underlain by lake sediments deposited by glaciers thousands of years ago. This is why their soils hold a great deal of water and are great for plants—and for the animals that live there."

Earth's Past and Present

Pierce works in Montana for the United States Geological Survey. Pierce finds that connecting geology to biology is rewarding. "It's important to understand the geological history of the park. That's because the geology has important controls on the ecology. For example, the rock in the central part of Yellowstone is rhyolite, which forms nutrient-poor soils. This kind of rock almost always supports a desert-like ecology of lodgepole pine forests—thus, there are no bears in these areas because there's not much for bears to eat."

Geology—The Key

Like other geologists, Pierce studies the composition, structure, and history of Earth's crust. For Pierce, it was easy to see the career advantages. "You're outdoors when you're doing field geology!" says Pierce. While in the field, he observes, takes measurements, and collects samples that will later be studied in the lab. Pierce uses his observations, measurements, and samples to study the geological and biological history of the park.

Looking Ahead to the Future

Studying past events helps geologists better understand current events and sometimes

"A geologist is like a detective—he or she uses clues left in the natural world to determine what has happened in the past."

—Ken Pierce, Ph.D.

predict future ones. For example, Pierce uses the data he collects to determine when the land surface was offset by faulting during past earthquakes. He uses this information to estimate the risk of future earthquakes. His research also helps predict landslides or mudflows after natural events such as wildfires. Knowing where and how often such hazards may occur helps reduce the risk to humans who visit Yellowstone National Park.

Yellowstone National Park

◄ Yellowstone was the first national park established in the United States.

SciLINKS®

NSTA
Developed and maintained by the National Science Teachers Association

For a variety of links related to this subject, go to www.scilinks.org

Topic: Careers in Earth Science
SciLinks code: HQ60222

Earth as a System

Sections

1 Earth: A Unique Planet

2 Energy in the Earth System

3 Ecology

What You'll Learn

- How Earth is structured
- How energy and matter cycle through the Earth system
- Why living organisms are important to the Earth system

Why It's Relevant

The systems approach to studying Earth provides a way to understand the interrelated nature of the physical, chemical, and biological forces that shape the planet.

PRE-READING ACTIVITY

Table Fold
Before you read this chapter, create the FoldNote entitled "Table Fold" described in the Skills Handbook section of the Appendix. Label the columns of the table "Earth's structure," "Earth's cycles and systems," and "Ecosystems." As you read the chapter, write examples of each topic under the appropriate column.

▶ This brown bear gains energy and nutrients from eating salmon. Energy and matter move through Earth's systems in many ways, including through the eating of prey by predators.

 California Content Standards

4a Students know the relative amount of incoming solar energy compared with Earth's internal energy and the energy used by society.

4b Students know the fate of incoming solar radiation in terms of reflection, absorption, and photosynthesis.

7a Students know the carbon cycle of photosynthesis and respiration and the nitrogen cycle.

7b Students know the global carbon cycle: the different physical and chemical forms of carbon in the atmosphere, oceans, biomass, fossil fuels, and the movement of carbon among these reservoirs.

7c Students know the movement of matter among reservoirs is driven by Earth's internal and external sources of energy.

7d* Students know the relative residence times and flow characteristics of carbon in and out of its different reservoirs.

IE.1a Students will select and use appropriate tools and technology (such as computer-linked probes, spreadsheets, and graphing calculators) to perform tests, collect data, analyze relationships and display data.

IE.1d Students will formulate explanations using logic and evidence.

IE.1l Students will analyze situations and solve problems that require combining and applying concepts from more than one area of science.

IE.1m Students will investigate a science-based societal issue by researching the literature, analyzing data, and communicating the findings. Examples of issues include irradiation of food, cloning of animals by somatic cell nuclear transfer, choice of energy sources, and land and water use decisions in California.

Earth is unique for several reasons. It is the only known planet in the solar system that has liquid water on its surface and an atmosphere that contains a large proportion of oxygen. Earth is also the only planet—in our solar system or in any other solar system—that is known to support life. Scientists study the characteristics of Earth that make life possible in order to know what life-supporting conditions to look for on other planets.

Earth Basics

Earth is the third planet from the sun in our solar system. Earth formed about 4.6 billion years ago and is made mostly of rock. Approximately 71% of Earth's surface is covered by a relatively thin layer of water called the *global ocean*.

As viewed from space, Earth is a blue sphere covered with white clouds. Earth appears to be a perfect sphere but is actually an *oblate spheroid,* or slightly flattened sphere, as **Figure 1** shows. The spinning of Earth on its axis makes the polar regions flatten and the equatorial zone bulge. Earth's pole-to-pole circumference is 40,007 km. Its equatorial circumference is 40,074 km.

Earth's surface is relatively smooth. That is, distances between surface high points and low points are small relative to Earth's size. The difference between the height of the tallest mountain and the depth of the deepest ocean trench is about 20 km. This distance is small compared with Earth's average diameter of 12,756 km.

IE.1d Students will formulate explanations using logic and evidence.

OBJECTIVES

▶ **Describe** the size and shape of Earth.

▶ **Describe** the compositional and structural layers of Earth's interior.

▶ **Identify** the possible source of Earth's magnetic field.

▶ **Summarize** Newton's law of gravitation.

KEY TERMS

crust
mantle
core
lithosphere
asthenosphere
mesosphere

Figure 1 ▶ Although from afar Earth looks like a sphere (left), it is an oblate spheroid. In this illustration, Earth's shape has been exaggerated to show that Earth bulges at the equator.

Perfect sphere   Oblate spheroid

Equator

Axis of rotation

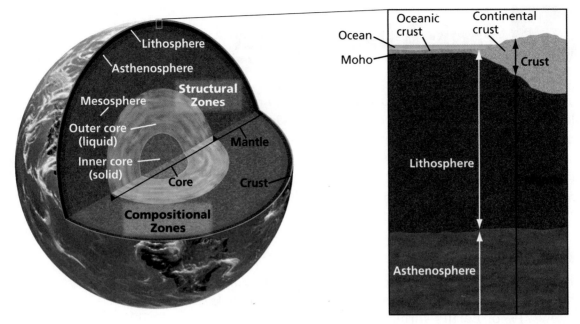

Figure 2 ▶ Changes in the speed and direction of seismic waves were used to determine the locations and properties of Earth's interior zones.

MATHPRACTICE

Speeding Waves

Earth's layers are of the following average thicknesses: crust, 35 km; mantle, 2,900 km; outer core, 2,250 km; and inner core, 1,228 km. Estimate how long a seismic wave would take to reach Earth's center if the wave's average rate of travel was 8 km/s through the crust, 12 km/s through the mantle, 9.5 km/s through the outer core, and 10.5 km/s through the inner core.

crust the thin and solid outermost layer of the Earth above the mantle

mantle in Earth science, the layer of rock between Earth's crust and core

core the central part of the Earth below the mantle

Earth's Interior

Direct observation of Earth's interior has been limited to the upper few kilometers that can be reached by drilling. So, scientists rely on indirect methods to study Earth at greater depths. For example, scientists have made important discoveries about Earth's interior through studies of seismic waves. *Seismic waves are vibrations that travel through Earth.* Earthquakes and explosions near Earth's surface produce seismic waves. By studying these waves as they travel through Earth, scientists have determined that Earth is made up of three major compositional zones and five major structural zones, as shown in **Figure 2.**

Compositional Zones of Earth's Interior

The thin, solid, outermost zone of Earth is called the **crust.** The crust makes up only 1% of Earth's mass. The crust beneath the oceans is called *oceanic crust.* Oceanic crust is only 5 to 10 km thick. The part of the crust that makes up the continents is called *continental crust.* The continental crust varies in thickness and is generally between 15 to 80 km thick. Continental crust is thickest beneath high mountain ranges.

The lower boundary of the crust, which was named for its discoverer, is called the *Mohorovičić* (MOH hoh ROH vuh CHICH) *discontinuity,* or *Moho.* The **mantle,** the layer that underlies the crust, is denser than the crust. The mantle is nearly 2,900 km thick and makes up almost two-thirds of Earth's mass.

The center of Earth is a sphere whose radius is about 3,500 km. Scientists think that this center sphere, called the **core,** is composed mainly of iron and nickel.

✓ Reading Check Explain why scientists have to rely on indirect observations to study Earth's interior. (See the Appendix for answers to Reading Checks.)

Structural Zones of Earth's Interior

The three compositional zones of Earth's interior are divided into five structural zones. The uppermost part of the mantle is cool and brittle. This part of the mantle and the crust above it make up the **lithosphere,** a rigid layer 15 to 300 km thick. Below the lithosphere is a less rigid layer, known as the **asthenosphere.** The asthenosphere is about 200 to 250 km thick. Because of enormous heat and pressure, the solid rock of the asthenosphere has the ability to flow. The ability of a solid to flow is called *plasticity*. Below the asthenosphere is a layer of solid mantle rock called the **mesosphere.**

At a depth of about 2,900 km lies the boundary between the mantle and the *outer core*. Scientists think that the outer core is a dense liquid. The inner core begins at a depth of 5,150 km. The inner core is a dense, rigid solid. The inner and outer core together make up nearly one-third of Earth's mass.

lithosphere the solid, outer layer of Earth that consists of the crust and the rigid upper part of the mantle

asthenosphere the solid, plastic layer of the mantle beneath the lithosphere; made of mantle rock that flows very slowly, which allows tectonic plates to move on top of it

mesosphere literally, the "middle sphere"; the strong, lower part of the mantle between the asthenosphere and the outer core

Earth as a Magnet

Earth has two magnetic poles. The lines of force of Earth's magnetic field extend between the North geomagnetic pole and the South geomagnetic pole. Earth's magnetic field, shown in **Figure 3,** extends beyond the atmosphere and affects a region of space called the *magnetosphere*.

The source of Earth's magnetic field may be the liquid iron in Earth's outer core. Scientists hypothesize that motions within the core produce electric currents that in turn create Earth's magnetic field. However, recent research indicates that the magnetic field may have another source. Scientists have learned that the sun and moon also have magnetic fields. Because the sun contains little iron and the moon does not have a liquid outer core, discovering the sources of the magnetic fields of the sun and moon may help identify the source of Earth's magnetic field.

Solar wind

Magnetic field lines

Figure 3 ▶ The magnetic field lines around Earth show the shape of Earth's magnetosphere. Earth's magnetosphere is compressed and shaped by solar wind, which is the flow of charged particles from the sun.

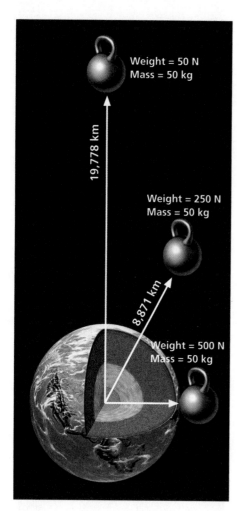

Weight = 50 N
Mass = 50 kg

19,778 km

Weight = 250 N
Mass = 50 kg

8,871 km

Weight = 500 N
Mass = 50 kg

Figure 4 ▶ As the distance between an object and Earth's center increases, the weight of the object decreases. An object's mass is constant as its distance from Earth's center changes.

Earth's Gravity

Earth, like all objects in the universe, is affected by gravity. *Gravity* is the force of attraction that exists between all matter in the universe. The 17th-century scientist Isaac Newton was the first to explain the phenomenon of gravity. Newton described the effects of gravity in his *law of gravitation*. According to the law of gravitation, the force of attraction between any two objects depends on the masses of the objects and the distance between the objects. The larger the masses of two objects and the closer together the objects are, the greater the force of gravity between the objects will be.

Weight and Mass

Earth exerts a gravitational force that pulls objects toward the center of Earth. Weight is a measure of the strength of the pull of gravity on an object. The newton (N) is the SI unit used to measure weight. On Earth's surface, a kilogram of mass weighs about 10 N. The mass of an object does not change with location, but the weight of the object does. An object's weight depends on its mass and its distance from Earth's center. According to the law of gravitation, the force of gravity decreases as the distance from Earth's center increases, as shown in **Figure 4.**

Weight and Location

Weight varies according to location on Earth's surface. As you may recall, Earth spins on its axis, and this motion causes Earth to bulge near the equator. Therefore, the distance between Earth's surface and its center is greater at the equator than at the poles. This difference in distance means that your weight at the equator would be about 0.3% less than your weight at the North Pole.

1. **Describe** the size and shape of Earth.

2. **Describe** two characteristics that make Earth unique in our solar system.

3. **Summarize** how scientists learn about Earth's interior.

4. **Compare** Earth's compositional layers with its structural layers.

5. **Identify** the possible source of Earth's magnetic field.

6. **Summarize** Newton's law of gravitation.

CRITICAL THINKING

7. **Making Inferences** What does the difference between your weight at the equator and your weight at the poles suggest about the shape of Earth? ▨IE.1d

8. **Making Comparisons** How does the asthenosphere differ from the mesosphere?

9. **Analyzing Ideas** Why would you weigh less on a high mountain peak than you would at sea level? ▨IE.1d

CONCEPT MAPPING

10. Use the following terms to create a concept map: *crust, mantle, core, lithosphere, asthenosphere, mesosphere, inner core,* and *outer core.*

Section 2 — Energy in the Earth System

California Content Standards

4a Students know the relative amount of incoming solar energy compared with Earth's internal energy and the energy used by society.

7a Students know the carbon cycle of photosynthesis and respiration and the nitrogen cycle.
7b Students know the global carbon cycle: the

different physical and chemical forms of carbon in the atmosphere, oceans, biomass, fossil fuels, and the movement of carbon among these reservoirs.

Traditionally, different fields of Earth science, such as geology, oceanography, and meteorology, have been studied separately. Geologists studied Earth's rocks and interior, oceanographers studied the oceans, and meteorologists studied the atmosphere. But now, some scientists are approaching the study of Earth in a new way. They are combining knowledge of several fields of Earth science in order to study Earth as a system.

Earth-System Science

An organized group of related objects or components that interact to create a whole is a **system.** Systems vary in size from subatomic to the size of the universe. All systems have boundaries, and many systems have matter and energy that flow through them. Even though each system can be described separately, all systems are linked. A large and complex system, such as the Earth system, operates as a result of the combination of smaller, interrelated systems, as shown in **Figure 1.**

The operation of the Earth system is a result of interaction between the two most basic components of the universe: matter and energy. *Matter* is anything that has mass and takes up space. Matter can be subatomic particles, such as protons, electrons, and neutrons. Matter can be atoms or molecules, such as oxygen atoms or water molecules, and matter can be larger objects, such as rocks, living organisms, or planets. *Energy* is defined as the ability to do work. Energy can be transferred in a variety of forms, including heat, light, vibrations, or electromagnetic waves. A system can be described by the way that matter and energy are transferred within the system or to and from other systems. Transfers of matter and energy are commonly accompanied by changes in the physical or chemical properties of the matter.

OBJECTIVES

▶ **Compare** an open system with a closed system.

▶ **List** the characteristics of Earth's four major spheres.

▶ **Identify** the two main sources of energy in the Earth system. ▦ 4a

▶ **Identify** four processes in which matter and energy cycle on Earth. ▦ 7a, 7b, 7c, 7d*

KEY TERMS

system
atmosphere
hydrosphere
geosphere
biosphere

system a set of particles or interacting components considered to be a distinct physical entity for the purpose of study

Figure 1 ▶ This threadfin butterflyfish is part of a system that includes other living organisms, such as coral. Together, the organisms are part of a larger system, a coral reef system in Micronesia.

Solar energy enters system.

Heat exits system.

Matter enters system.

Solar energy enters system.

Heat exits system.

Matter exits system.

Figure 2 ▶ Energy is exchanged in both the closed system (left) and the open system (right). In the open system, matter is also exchanged.

Closed Systems

A *closed system* is a system in which energy, but not matter, is exchanged with the surroundings. **Figure 2** shows a sealed jar, which is a closed system. Energy in the form of light and heat can be exchanged through the jar's sides. But because the jar is sealed, matter cannot exit or enter the system. Most aquariums are open systems because oxygen and food must be added to them, but some are closed systems. Closed-system aquariums contain a variety of organisms: plants, which produce oxygen, and aquatic animals, some of which are food for others. Some of the animals feed on the plants. Animal wastes and organic matter nourish the plants. Only sunlight enters from the surroundings.

Open Systems

An *open system* is a system in which both energy and matter are exchanged with the surroundings. The open jar in **Figure 2** is an open system. A lake is also an open system. Water molecules enter a lake through rainfall and streams. Water exits a lake through streams, evaporation, and absorption by the ground. Sunlight and air exchange heat with the lake. Wind's energy is transferred to the lake as waves.

The Earth System

Technically, all systems that make up the Earth system are open. But the Earth system is almost a closed system because matter exchange is limited. Energy enters the system in the form of sunlight and is released into space as heat. Only a small amount of dust and rock from space enters the system, and only a fraction of the hydrogen atoms in the atmosphere escape into space.

Reading Check What types of matter and energy are exchanged between Earth and space? (See the Appendix for answers to Reading Checks.)

SCi LINKS®

NSTA

Developed and maintained by the National Science Teachers Association

For a variety of links related to this subject, go to www.scilinks.org

Topic: Scientists in California
SciLinks code: HQ7C11

Earth's Four Spheres

Matter on Earth is in solid, liquid, and gaseous states. The Earth system is composed of four "spheres" that are storehouses of all of the planet's matter. These four spheres are shown in **Figure 3.**

The Atmosphere

The blanket of gases that surrounds Earth's surface is called the **atmosphere.** The atmosphere provides the air that you breathe and shields Earth from the sun's harmful radiation. Earth's atmosphere is made up of 78% nitrogen and 21% oxygen. The remaining 1% includes other gases, such as argon, carbon dioxide, water vapor, and helium.

The Hydrosphere

Water covers 71% of Earth's surface area, and 97% of surface water is contained in the salty oceans. The remaining 3% is fresh water. Fresh water can be found in lakes, rivers, and streams, frozen in glaciers and the polar ice sheets, and underground in soil and bedrock. All of Earth's water except the water that is in gaseous form in the atmosphere makes up the **hydrosphere.**

The Geosphere

The mostly solid part of Earth is known as the **geosphere.** This sphere includes all of the rock and soil on the surface of the continents and on the ocean floor. The geosphere also includes the solid and molten interior of Earth, which makes up the largest volume of matter on Earth. Natural processes, such as volcanism, bring matter from deep inside Earth's interior to the surface. Other processes move surface matter back into Earth's interior.

The Biosphere

Another one of the four subdivisions of the Earth system is the biosphere. The **biosphere** is composed of all of the forms of life in the geosphere, in the hydrosphere, and in the atmosphere. The biosphere also contains any organic matter that has not decomposed. Once organic matter has completely decomposed, it becomes a part of the other three spheres. The biosphere extends from the deepest parts of the ocean to the atmosphere a few kilometers above Earth's surface.

atmosphere a mixture of gases that surrounds a planet or moon

hydrosphere the portion of the Earth that is water

geosphere the mostly solid, rocky part of the Earth; extends from the center of the core to the surface of the crust

biosphere the part of Earth where life exists; includes all of the living organisms on Earth

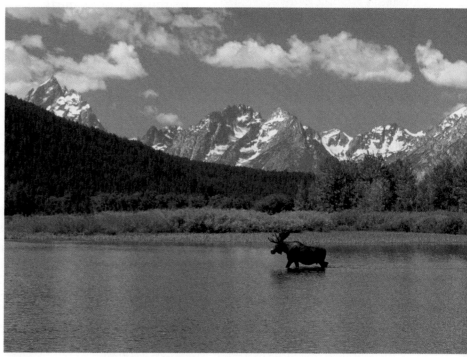

Figure 3 ▶ The Earth system is composed of the atmosphere, hydrosphere, geosphere, and biosphere. *Can you identify elements of the four spheres in this photo?*

Figure 4 ▶ Incoming solar energy is balanced by solar energy reflected or reradiated by several of Earth's systems.

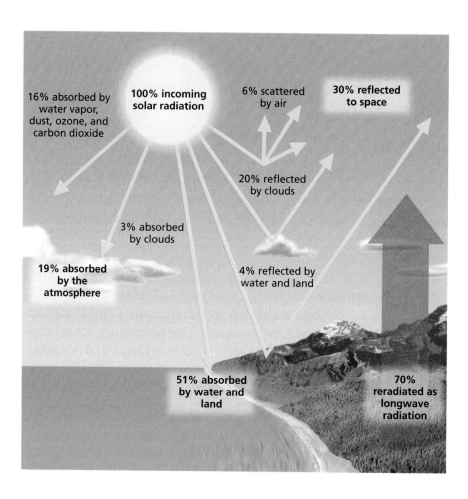

16% absorbed by water vapor, dust, ozone, and carbon dioxide

100% incoming solar radiation

6% scattered by air

30% reflected to space

20% reflected by clouds

3% absorbed by clouds

19% absorbed by the atmosphere

4% reflected by water and land

51% absorbed by water and land

70% reradiated as longwave radiation

Graphic Organizer Comparison Table

Create the **Graphic Organizer** entitled "Comparison Table" described in the Skills Handbook section of the Appendix. Label the columns with "Type of Source," and "Use of Source." Label the rows with "Radiactive decay," "Convection," "Sun," and "Moon." Then, fill in the table with details of the type and use of each energy source in Earth's system.

Earth's Energy Budget

Exchanges and flow of energy on Earth happen in predictable ways. According to the *first law of thermodynamics,* energy is transferred between systems, but it cannot be created or destroyed. The transfers of energy between Earth's spheres can be thought of as parts of an *energy budget,* in which additions in energy are balanced by subtractions. This concept is shown in **Figure 4,** which shows how solar energy is transferred through Earth's systems. Solar energy is absorbed and reflected in such a way that the solar energy input is balanced by the solar energy output. Like energy, matter can be transferred but cannot be created or destroyed.

The *second law of thermodynamics* states that when energy transfer takes place, matter becomes less organized with time. The overall effect of this natural law is that the universe's energy is spread out more and more uniformly over time.

Earth's four main spheres are open systems that can be thought of as huge storehouses of matter and energy. Matter and energy are constantly being exchanged between the spheres. This constant exchange happens through chemical reactions, radioactive decay, the radiation of energy (including light and heat), and the growth and decay of organisms.

✓ **Reading Check** Define *energy budget.* (See the Appendix for answers to Reading Checks.)

Internal Sources of Energy

When Earth formed about 4.6 billion years ago, its interior was heated by radioactive decay and gravitational contraction. Since that time, the amount of heat generated by radioactive decay has declined. But the decay of radioactive atoms still generates enough heat to keep Earth's interior hot. Earth's interior also retains much of the energy from the planet's formation.

Because Earth's interior is warmer than its surface layers, hot materials move toward the surface in a process called *convection.* As material is heated, the material's density decreases, and the hot material rises and releases heat. Cooler, denser material sinks and displaces the hot material. As a result, the heat in Earth's interior is transferred through the layers of Earth and is released at Earth's surface. On a large scale, this process drives the plate motions in the surface layers of the geosphere that create mountain ranges and ocean basins.

External Energy Sources

In order for the life-supporting processes on Earth to continue operating for billions of years, energy must be added to the Earth system. Earth's most important external energy source is the sun. Solar radiation warms Earth's atmosphere and surface. This heating causes the movement of air masses, which generates winds and ocean currents. Plants, such as the wheat shown in **Figure 5,** use solar energy to fuel their growth. Because many animals feed on plants, plants provide the energy that acts as a base for the energy flow through the biosphere. Even the chemical reactions that break down rock into soil require solar energy. Another important external source of energy is gravitational energy from the moon and sun. The pull of the sun and the moon on the oceans, combined with Earth's rotation, generates tides that cause currents and drive the mixing of ocean water.

QuickLAB 10 min

Effects of Solar Energy

Procedure 4a, IE.1d, IE.1l

1. Wrap one **small glass jar** with **black construction paper** so that no light can enter it. Get a **second glass jar.** Make sure that the second jar has a clean, transparent surface.

2. Use a **hammer** and **large nail** to punch a hole in each jar lid.

3. Place a **thermometer** through the hole in each jar lid. Place the lids tightly onto the jars.

4. Place the jars on the windowsill. Wait 5 min. Then, read the temperature from each jar's thermometer.

Analysis

1. Which jar had the higher temperature?

2. Which jar represents a system in which energy enters from outside the system?

Figure 5 ▶ Solar energy is changed into stored energy in the wheat kernels by chemical processes in the wheat plant. When the wheat is eaten, the stored energy is released from the wheat and used or stored by the consumer.

Cycles in the Earth System

A *reservoir* is a place where matter or energy is stored. A *cycle* is a group of processes in which matter and energy repeatedly move through a series of reservoirs. Many elements on Earth cycle between reservoirs. These cycles rely on energy sources to drive them. The length of time that energy or matter spends in a reservoir can vary from a few hours to several million years.

The Nitrogen Cycle

Organisms on Earth use the element nitrogen to build proteins, which are then used to build cells. Nitrogen gas makes up 78% of the atmosphere, but most organisms cannot use the atmospheric form of nitrogen. The nitrogen must be altered, or *fixed,* before organisms can use it. Nitrogen fixing is an important step in the *nitrogen cycle,* which is shown in **Figure 6.**

In the nitrogen cycle, nitrogen moves from air to soil, from soil to plants and animals, and back to air again. Nitrogen is removed from air mainly by the action of nitrogen-fixing bacteria. These bacteria live in soil and on the roots of certain plants. The bacteria chemically change nitrogen from air into nitrogen compounds, which are vital to the growth of all plants. When animals eat plants, nitrogen compounds in the plants become part of the animals' bodies. These compounds are returned to the soil by the decay of dead animals and in animals' excretions. After nitrogen compounds enter the soil, chemical processes release nitrogen back into the atmosphere. Water-dwelling plants and animals take part in a similar nitrogen cycle.

Figure 6 ▶ The balance of nitrogen in the atmosphere and biosphere is maintained through the nitrogen cycle. *What role do animals play in the nitrogen cycle?*

✔ **Reading Check** Identify two nitrogen reservoirs on Earth. (See the Appendix for answers to Reading Checks.)

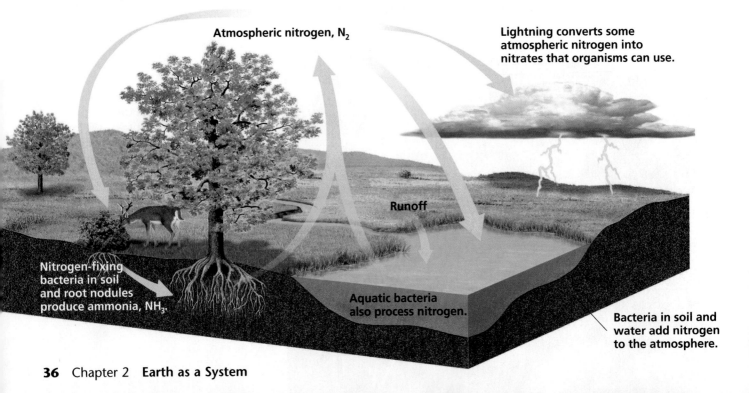

Atmospheric nitrogen, N_2

Lightning converts some atmospheric nitrogen into nitrates that organisms can use.

Runoff

Nitrogen-fixing bacteria in soil and root nodules produce ammonia, NH_3.

Aquatic bacteria also process nitrogen.

Bacteria in soil and water add nitrogen to the atmosphere.

Figure 7 ▶ Carbon moves through Earth's four spheres in a combination of short-term and long-term cycles.

The Carbon Cycle

Carbon is an essential substance in the fuels used for life processes. Carbon moves through all four spheres in a process called the *carbon cycle,* as **Figure 7** shows. Part of the carbon cycle is a short-term cycle. In this short-term cycle, plants convert carbon dioxide, CO_2, from the atmosphere into carbohydrates, such as glucose, $C_6H_{12}O_6$. Then, organisms eat the plants and obtain the carbon from the carbohydrates. Next, organisms' bodies break down the carbohydrates and release some of the carbon back into the air as CO_2. Organisms also release carbon into the air through their organic wastes and by the decay of their remains, which release carbon into the air as CO_2 or as methane, CH_4.

Part of the carbon cycle is a long-term cycle in which carbon moves through Earth's four spheres over a very long time period. Carbon is stored in the geosphere in buried plant or animal remains and in a type of rock called a *carbonate.* Carbonate forms from shells and bones of once-living organisms.

The Phosphorus Cycle

The element phosphorus is part of some molecules that organisms need to build cells. During the *phosphorus cycle,* phosphorus moves through every sphere except the atmosphere, because phosphorus is rarely a gas. Phosphorus enters soil and water when rock breaks down and when phosphorus dissolves in water. Some organisms excrete their excess phosphorus in their waste, and this phosphorus may enter soil and water. Plants absorb this phosphorus through their roots. The plants then incorporate the phosphorus into their tissues. Animals absorb the phosphorus when they eat the plants. When the animals die, the phosphorus returns to the environment through decomposition.

CONDENSATION

EVAPORATION

PRECIPITATION

Figure 8 ▶ The water cycle is the continuous movement of water from the atmosphere to Earth's surface and back to the atmosphere.

The Water Cycle

The movement of water from the atmosphere to Earth's surface and back to the atmosphere is always taking place. This continuous movement of water is called the *water cycle*, which is shown in **Figure 8.** In the water cycle, water changes from liquid water to water vapor through the energy transfers involved in evaporation and transpiration. Evaporation occurs when energy is absorbed by liquid water and the energy changes the water into water vapor. Transpiration is the release of moisture from plant leaves. During these processes, water absorbs heat and changes state. When the water loses energy, it condenses to form water droplets, such as those that form clouds. Eventually, water falls back to Earth's surface as precipitation, such as rain, snow, or hail.

Humans and the Earth System

All natural cycles can be altered by human activities. The carbon cycle is affected when humans use fossil fuels. Fossil fuels form over millions of years. Carbon dioxide is returned to the atmospheric reservoir rapidly when humans burn these fuels. Also, both the nitrogen and phosphorus cycles are affected by agriculture. Some farming techniques can strip the soil of nitrogen and phosphorus. Many farmers replace these nutrients by using fertilizers, which can upset the balance of these elements in nature.

Section 2 Review

1. **Explain** how Earth can be considered a system.

2. **Compare** an open system with a closed system.

3. **List** two characteristics of each of Earth's four major spheres.

4. **Identify** the two main sources of energy in Earth's system. 🐾 4a

5. **Identify** four processes in which matter and energy cycle on Earth. 🐾 7a, 7b, 7c

6. **Explain** how carbon cycles in Earth's system. 🐾 7a, 7b, 7c, 7d*

7. **Explain** how nitrogen cycles in Earth's system. 🐾 7a, 7c

CRITICAL THINKING

8. **Identifying Relationships** For each of Earth's four spheres, describe one way that the water cycle affects the sphere.

9. **Determining Cause and Effect** What effect, if any, would you expect a massive forest fire to have on the amount of carbon dioxide in the atmosphere? Explain your answer. 🐾 7a, 7b, 7c, IE.1d

10. **Analyzing Ideas** Early Earth was constantly being bombarded by meteorites, comets, and asteroids. Was early Earth an open system or a closed system? Explain your answer. 🐾 IE.1d

11. **Analyzing Relationships** Explain the role of energy in the carbon cycle. 🐾 7c

CONCEPT MAPPING

12. Use the following terms to create a concept map: *closed system, system, open system, matter, atmosphere, biosphere, energy, geosphere,* and *hydrosphere.*

Section 3 Ecology

California Content Standards

4b Students know the fate of incoming solar radiation in terms of reflection, absorption, and photosynthesis.

IE.1d Students will formulate explanations using logic and evidence.

IE.1l Students will analyze situations and solve

problems that require combining and applying concepts from more than one area of science.

One area of science in which life science and Earth science are closely linked is called *ecology*. Ecology is the study of the complex relationships between living things and their nonliving, or abiotic, environment. Some ecologists also investigate how communities of organisms change over time.

Ecosystems

Organisms on Earth inhabit many different environments. A community of organisms and the environment that the organisms inhabit is called an **ecosystem.** The terms *ecology* and *ecosystem* come from the Greek word *oikos*, which means "house." Each ecosystem on Earth is a distinct, self-supporting system. An ecosystem may be as large as an ocean or as small as a rotting log. The largest ecosystem is the entire biosphere.

Most of Earth's ecosystems contain a variety of plants and animals. Plants are important to an ecosystem because they use energy from the sun to produce their own food. Organisms that make their own food are called *producers*. Producers are a source of food for other organisms. *Consumers* are organisms that get their energy by eating other organisms. Consumers may get energy by eating producers or by eating other consumers, as the consumers shown in **Figure 1** are doing. Some consumers get energy by breaking down dead organisms. These consumers are called *decomposers*. To remain healthy, an ecosystem needs to have a balance of producers, consumers, and decomposers.

OBJECTIVES

▶ **Define** *ecosystem*.

▶ **Identify** three factors that control the balance of an ecosystem.

▶ **Summarize** how energy is transferred through an ecosystem. 🔲 4b

▶ **Describe** one way that ecosystems respond to environmental change.

KEY TERMS

ecosystem
carrying capacity
food web

ecosystem a community of organisms and their abiotic environment

Figure 1 ▶ Vultures and a spotted hyena are feeding on an elephant carcass in Chobe National Park in Botswana. *Name two consumers that are shown in this photo.*

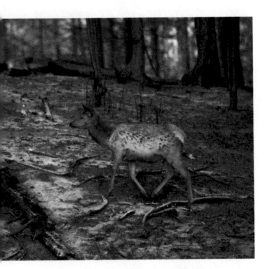

Figure 2 ▶ The fur of this elk calf was singed in a forest fire in Yellowstone National Park. Not enough food resources remain to allow the calf to stay in this area, but the calf may return here when the area has recovered.

carrying capacity the largest population that an environment can support at any given time

Balancing Forces in Ecosystems

Organisms in an ecosystem use matter and energy. Because amounts of matter and energy in an ecosystem are limited, population growth within the ecosystem is limited, too. The largest population that an environment can support at any given time is called the **carrying capacity.** Carrying capacity depends on available resources. The carrying capacity of an ecosystem is also affected by how easily matter and energy cycle between life-forms and the environment in that ecosystem. So, a given ecosystem can support only the number of organisms that allows matter and energy to cycle efficiently through the ecosystem.

Ecological Responses to Change

Changes in any one part of an ecosystem may affect the entire system in unpredictable ways. However, in general, ecosystems react to changes in ways that maintain or restore balance in the ecosystem.

Environmental change in the form of a sudden disturbance, such as a forest fire, can greatly damage and disrupt ecosystems, as shown in **Figure 2.** But over time, organisms will migrate back into damaged areas in predictable patterns. First, grasses and fast-growing plants will start to grow. Then, shrubs and small animal species will return. Eventually, larger tree species and larger animals will return to the area. Ecosystems are resilient and tend to restore a community of organisms to its original state unless the physical environment is permanently altered.

✓ Reading Check **Explain the relationship between carrying capacity and the amount of matter and energy in an ecosystem. (See the Appendix for answers to Reading Checks.)**

Connection to ENVIRONMENTAL SCIENCE

Lemmings

Lemmings are small arctic rodents. Lemmings play an important role in their ecosystem because they are the major food source for snowy owls and arctic foxes. While most animal species have a relatively constant population size, lemming populations vary greatly over a three- or four-year cycle.

When a lemming population is at its smallest, very few lemmings may be in an area. But lemmings can reproduce very quickly, and they produce large litters of up to 11 young. A female lemming can begin to produce offspring when she is only one month old. So, a very small population of lemmings can give rise to a large population in a short period of time. After a few years, the growing population of lemmings begins to use up available food resources. Eventually, lemmings begin to starve. When this happens, lemmings fight each other, and many migrate to other areas.

These mass migrations have given rise to myths that lemmings throw themselves off cliffs. Lemmings have been seen diving into the ocean, but scientists believe that lemmings do this because lemmings can swim. When lemmings swim across a stream, they can reach and populate new areas of land. When they dive into the ocean, however, they cannot reach land and often drown. When starvation, fighting, or drowning reduces a lemming population to very few members, the cycle of population growth repeats.

Energy Transfer

The ultimate source of energy for almost every ecosystem is the sun. Plants capture solar energy by a chemical process called *photosynthesis*. This captured energy then flows through ecosystems from the plants, to the animals that feed on the plants, and finally to the decomposers of animal and plant remains. Matter also cycles through an ecosystem by this process.

As matter and energy cycle through an ecosystem, chemical elements are combined and recombined. Each chemical change results in either the temporary storage of energy or the loss of energy. One way to see how energy is lost as it moves through the ecosystem is to draw an energy pyramid. Producers form the base of the pyramid. Consumers that eat producers are the next level of the pyramid. Animals that eat those consumers form the upper levels of the pyramid. As you move up the pyramid, more energy is lost at each level. Therefore, the least amount of total energy is available to organisms at the top of the pyramid.

Food Chains and Food Webs

The sequence in which organisms consume other organisms can be represented by a *food chain*. However, ecosystems are complex and generally contain more organisms than are on a single food chain. In addition, many organisms eat more than just one other species. Therefore, a **food web**, such as the one shown in **Figure 3**, is used to represent the relationships between multiple food chains. Each arrow points to the organism that eats the organism at the base of the arrow.

QuickLAB ⏱ 20 min

Studying Ecosystems

Procedure 🧪 4b, IE.1a, IE.1l

1. Find a **small natural area** near your school.

2. Choose a 5 m by 5 m section of the natural area to study. This area may include the ground or vegetation such as trees or bushes.

3. Spend 10 min documenting the number and types of organisms that live in the area.

Analysis

1. How many kinds of organisms live in the area that you studied?

2. Draw a food web that describes how energy may flow through the ecosystem that you studied.

food web a diagram that shows the feeding relationships among organisms in an ecosystem

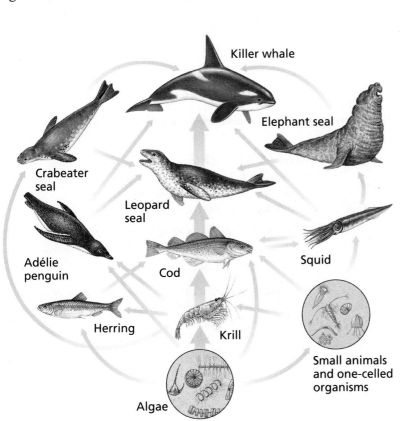

Killer whale

Elephant seal

Crabeater seal

Leopard seal

Adélie penguin

Cod

Squid

Herring

Krill

Small animals and one-celled organisms

Algae

Figure 3 ▶ This food web shows how, in an ocean ecosystem, the largest organisms, such as killer whales, depend on the smallest organisms, such as algae. *Which organisms would be near the top of a food pyramid?*

Human Stewardship of the Environment

All of Earth's systems are interconnected, and changes in one system may affect the operation of other systems. Earth's ecosystems provide a wide variety of resources on which people depend. People need water and air to survive. Changes in ecosystems can affect the ability of an area to sustain a human population. For example, the quality of the atmosphere, the productivity of soils, and the availability of natural resources can affect the availability of food.

Figure 4 ▶ These hikers are acting responsibly by choosing to remain on marked trails in the rain forest. In this way, they are helping prevent ecological damage to the area.

Ecological balances can be disrupted by human activity. Populations of plants and animals can be destroyed through overconsumption of resources. When humans convert large natural areas to agricultural or urban areas, natural ecosystems are often destroyed. Another serious threat to ecosystems is pollution. *Pollution* is the contamination of the environment with harmful waste products or impurities.

When people, such as those in **Figure 4,** strive to prevent ecological damage to an area, they are trying to be responsible stewards of Earth. To help ensure the ongoing health and productivity of the Earth system, many people work to use Earth's resources wisely. By using fossil fuels, land and water resources, and other natural resources wisely, many people are helping keep Earth's ecosystems in balance. ✦

Section 3 Review

1. **Define** ecosystem.

2. **Explain** why the entire biosphere is an ecosystem.

3. **Identify** three factors that control the balance of an ecosystem.

4. **Summarize** how energy is transferred between the sun and consumers in an ecosystem. 🐜 4b

5. **Describe** one way that ecosystems respond to environmental change.

6. **Compare** a food chain with a food web.

7. **Summarize** the importance of good stewardship of Earth's resources. 🐜 IE.1m

CRITICAL THINKING

8. **Making Inferences** Discuss two ways that the expansion of urban areas might be harmful to nearby ecosystems. 🐜 IE.1m, IE.1d, IE.1l

9. **Analyzing Ideas** Why would adapting to a gradual change in environment be easier for an ecosystem than adapting to a sudden disturbance would be? 🐜 IE.1d

10. **Making Inferences** Why does energy flow in only one direction in a given food chain of an ecosystem? 🐜 4b, IE.1d

CONCEPT MAPPING

11. Use the following terms to create a concept map: *ecology, ecosystem, producer, decomposer, carrying capacity, consumer,* and *food web*.

Chapter 2 Highlights

Sections

1 Earth: A Unique Planet

Key Terms

crust, 28
mantle, 28
core, 28
lithosphere, 29
asthenosphere, 29
mesosphere, 29

Key Concepts

▶ Earth is an oblate spheroid that has an average diameter of 12,756 km. About 71% of Earth's surface is covered by a relatively thin layer of water.

▶ Seismic waves have revealed that Earth's interior is composed of a series of layers of various densities.

▶ Earth has a magnetic field that extends into space in a region known as the *magnetosphere*.

2 Energy in the Earth System

Key Terms

system, 31
atmosphere, 33
hydrosphere, 33
geosphere, 33
biosphere, 33

Key Concepts

▶ A closed system is a system in which energy enters and exits but matter remains static—neither enters nor exits. An open system is a system in which both energy and matter enter and leave.

▶ The Earth system can be thought of as consisting of four spheres—the geosphere, the hydrosphere, the atmosphere, and the biosphere—that influence the operation of one another.

▶ Matter and energy are not created or destroyed. Matter and energy cycle between Earth's systems. Energy, most of which is solar, is required to maintain this cycling.

3 Ecology

Key Terms

ecosystem, 39
carrying capacity, 40
food web, 41

Key Concepts

▶ An ecosystem is a community of organisms and the environment that they inhabit.

▶ When sudden disturbances disrupt the health of an ecosystem, the components of the ecosystem respond in ways that return the ecosystem to a balanced condition.

▶ One way that energy moves through ecosystems is through the eating of organisms by other organisms.

▶ Humans are part of the global ecosystem. Stewardship of Earth's resources is important to maintaining healthy ecosystems.

Using Key Terms

Use each of the following terms in a separate sentence.

1. *system*
2. *carrying capacity*
3. *lithosphere*

For each pair of terms, explain how the meanings of the terms differ.

4. *system* and *ecosystem*
5. *biosphere* and *geosphere*
6. *hydrosphere* and *atmosphere*
7. *mantle* and *asthenosphere*
8. *energy pyramid* and *food web*

Understanding Key Concepts

9. The diameter of Earth is greatest at the
   a. poles.
   c. oceans.
   b. equator.
   d. continents.

10. The element that makes up the largest percentage of the atmosphere is 🐘 7a
    a. oxygen.
    b. nitrogen.
    c. carbon dioxide.
    d. ozone.

11. The gravitational attraction between two objects is determined by the mass of the two objects and the
    a. distance between the objects.
    b. weight of the objects.
    c. diameter of the objects.
    d. density of the objects.

12. Energy can enter the Earth system from internal sources through convection and from external sources through 🐘 4a
    a. radioactive decay.
    b. wave energy.
    c. wind energy.
    d. solar energy.

13. Closed systems exchange energy but do *not* exchange
    a. gravity.
    c. sunlight.
    b. matter.
    d. heat.

14. Which of the following is *not* an ecosystem?
    a. a lake
    c. a tree
    b. an ocean
    d. an atom

15. Which of the following processes is *not* involved in the water cycle?
    a. evaporation
    b. transpiration
    c. nitrogen fixing
    d. precipitation

16. A jar with its lid on tightly is one example of a(n)
    a. open system.
    c. closed system.
    b. biosphere.
    d. ecosystem.

17. Phosphorus cycles through all spheres except the
    a. geosphere.
    c. biosphere
    b. atmosphere.
    d. hydrosphere.

Short Answer

18. What characteristic of Earth's interior is likely to be responsible for Earth's magnetic field?

19. What is the role of decomposers in the cycling of matter in the biosphere? 🐘 7a, 7b, 7c

20. Compare the three compositional zones of Earth with the five structural zones of Earth.

21. Restate the first and second laws of thermodynamics, and explain how they relate to ecosystems on Earth. 🐘 IE.1l

22. Describe two ways that your daily activities affect the water cycle.

23. Explain three reasons that stewardship of Earth's resources is important. 🐘 IE.1m

	Initial mass (g)	Final mass (g)	Change in mass (g)
Trial 1			
Trial 2			

DO NOT WRITE IN THIS BOOK

6 When the reaction has finished, place both cups back on the balance. Determine the combined mass to the nearest 0.01 g. Record the combined mass in the first row of your table under "Final mass."

7 Subtract final mass from initial mass, and record the difference in the first row of your table under "Change in mass."

8 Repeat step 2, but carefully transfer the baking soda to one corner of a plastic bag rather than the cup.

9 To seal the baking soda in the corner of the bag, twist the corner of the bag above the baking soda and wrap the twist tie tightly around the twisted part of the bag.

10 Add 50 mL of vinegar to the bag. Zipper-close the bag so that the vinegar cannot leak out and the bag is airtight.

11 Place the bag in the beaker, and measure the mass of the beaker, the bag, and the reactants. Record the combined mass in the second row of your table under "Initial mass."

12 Remove the twist tie from the bag, and mix the reactants.

13 When the reaction has finished, repeat steps 6 and 7 by using the beaker, bag, twist tie, and products. Record the final mass and change in mass in the table's second row.

Step 11

ANALYSIS AND CONCLUSION

1 **Analyzing Data** Compare the change in mass that you calculated for the first trial with the change in mass that you calculated for the second trial. What evidence of the conservation of mass does the second trial show?

2 **Analyzing Results** Was the law of conservation of mass violated in the first trial? Explain your answer.

3 **Drawing Conclusions** Was the first trial an example of a closed system or an open system? Which type of system was the second trial? Explain your answer.

Extension

1 **Designing an Experiment** Brainstorm other ways to demonstrate the law of conservation of energy in a laboratory. Describe the materials that you would need, and describe any difficulties that you foresee.

MAPS *in Action*

Concentration of Plant Life on Earth

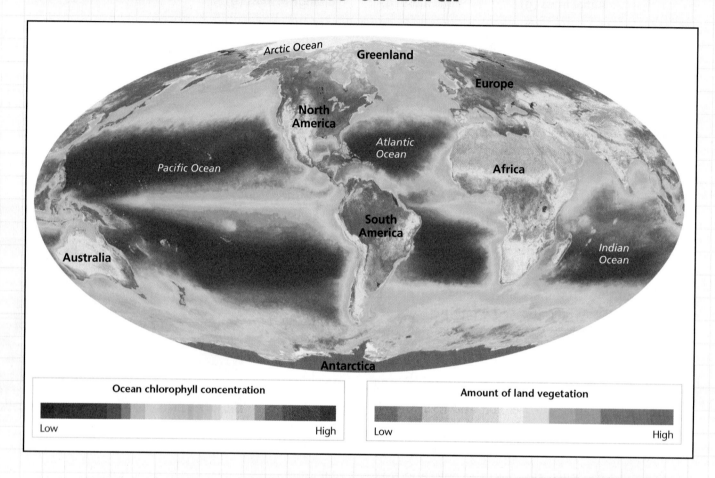

Ocean chlorophyll concentration
Low   High

Amount of land vegetation
Low   High

Map Skills Activity

This map shows the concentration of plant life on land and in the oceans. Each color in the key represents a concentration of plant life as indicated by the concentration of chlorophyll. The higher the concentration of chlorophyll is, the higher the concentration of plant life is. Use the map to answer the questions below.

1. **Using a Key** How can you distinguish between high chlorophyll concentration in the ocean and high chlorophyll concentration on land?

2. **Comparing Areas** List three areas that have very low chlorophyll concentration on land. What characteristics of these areas cause such low chlorophyll concentrations?

3. **Comparing Areas** Why do you think Antarctica, Greenland, and the Arctic Ocean lack chlorophyll?

4. **Identifying Trends** Where are the highest chlorophyll concentrations in the ocean located? Why do you think that these locations have high chlorophyll concentrations?

5. **Identifying Trends** Plants use sunlight and chlorophyll to produce energy. What can you infer about the amount of sunlight around the equator that could help explain why areas along the equator tend to have higher concentrations of chlorophyll than surrounding areas do?

Biological Clocks

Humans are affected by cycles in the Earth system. Scientists think that our ancestors arranged their daily activities to correspond with daylight. They were probably awakened by sunrise and ended their workday at sunset. With the development of artificial light sources, however, humans have become less dependent on sunlight to set their daily routines. Recent research reveals surprising evidence that our bodies are still closely tied to natural, daily rhythms.

Feeling the Rhythm

Scientists have discovered that many body processes occur in 24-hour cycles called *circadian rhythms*. No one understands exactly what controls circadian rhythms, but the human body seems to have a number of internal clocks. These "biological clocks" regulate patterns of sleeping and waking, daily changes in body temperature, hormone secretions, heart rate, and blood pressure. Even moods, coordination, and memory are thought to be affected by circadian rhythms.

Broken Clocks?

Studies indicate that the cycle of darkness and light caused by Earth's rotation sets many of our biological clocks. When biological clocks get out of sync with the sun's 24-hour cycle because of long-distance travel or unusual work hours, problems may arise.

One problem is jet lag. Jet lag is the exhaustion, irritability, and insomnia that travelers suffer after a flight across several time zones. The human body may take days or weeks to reset its biological clock.

People living in areas near the poles can experience adverse effects of long periods of seasonal darkness. Extended periods of little sunlight can cause hormonal changes and

▲ Nocturnal animals are awake at night and sleep during the day. These animals have circadian rhythms opposite those of diurnal organisms, such as humans.

mood disorders. Scientists are also beginning to understand how such mood and hormonal changes occur in people who work through the night and sleep during the day.

◄ Traveling over many time zones can interfere with natural patterns of sleep.

Extension

1. **Researching Information** When people travel to another time zone, their bodies stay synchronized with the cycle of the sun in the place that they left. Research ways in which travel affects circadian rhythms. Then, write a short brochure that explains how to reduce the effects of traveling across time zones.

Sections

1 Finding Locations on Earth

2 Mapping Earth's Surface

3 Types of Maps

What You'll Learn

- How people determine location on Earth's surface
- How people make maps
- How various types of maps are used

Why It's Relevant

Maps help people navigate and find locations on Earth's surface. Maps also help scientists study changes in Earth's surface.

PRE-READING ACTIVITY

Three-Panel Flip Chart

Before you read this chapter, create the FoldNote entitled "Three-Panel Flip Chart" described in the Skills Handbook section of the Appendix. Label the flaps of the three-panel flip chart with "Topographic maps," "Geologic maps," and "Other types of maps." As you read the chapter, write information you learn about each category under the appropriate flap.

▶ By using advanced technology, scientists can create highly accurate models of Earth. This image of India, taken from space, uses color to show the height of different land features and the depths of the ocean floor.

California Content Standards

IE.1a Students will select and use appropriate tools and technology (such as computer-linked probes, spreadsheets, and graphing calculators) to perform tests, collect data, analyze relationships and display data.
IE.1d Students will formulate explanations using logic and evidence.
IE.1g Students will recognize the usefulness and limitations of models and theories as scientific representations of reality.
IE.1h Students will read and interpret topographic and geologic maps.

Mapping Life on Earth

In 1992, researchers working in a forest in Southeast Asia made some amazing discoveries. They identified two species of deer and a species of oxen that scientists had never seen before! The researchers reported their findings and made plans for further study. Unfortunately, the forest was being cut down at an incredibly fast rate. Luckily, citizens, other scientists, and politicians got involved in trying to protect forests. Thanks to their efforts, Vietnam and Laos have begun measures to protect the remaining forests in the region.

Why All the Fuss?

The biosphere, which includes only a thin slice of Earth and its atmosphere, is the area where all life on our planet exists. For every known species, scientists estimate that there are at least eight others (mostly insects and microorganisms) that have never been identified. As forests and other natural areas are destroyed, many of these unknown species are becoming extinct.

Help from Above

Given the amount of the biosphere that has never been thoroughly studied, how do scientists identify ecosystems that are endangered? Using satellite images, scientists can identify the makeup and size of Earth's remaining unexplored natural areas. Scientists can also conduct ground surveys. By pooling their data, they can create a biodiversity map.

Biodiversity is the term used to describe the range of different organisms that live in an area. In locations that have a very high biodiversity, the variety of organisms living in a small area is large. Biodiversity

▲ Before 1992, scientists had never seen the Vu Quang Ox.

maps often use color to show which parts of a region have the highest biodiversity.

Short-Term Success Story

Making and using biodiversity maps has already proven successful. In Jamaica, for example, such maps helped identify areas that may benefit from being turned into national parks. The maps also highlighted some offshore areas of high biodiversity, and officials were able to close some of these areas to fishing.

◄ This satellite image of southeast Asia shows various densities of vegetation. The redder an area is, the denser the vegetation in that area is.

Extension

1. **Making Comparisons** How does creating a biodiversity map differ from creating a topographic map? Could you create a biodiversity map that is also topographic? Explain your answer.

Unit 2 Outline

CHAPTER 4
Earth Chemistry

CHAPTER 5
Minerals of Earth's Crust

CHAPTER 6
Rocks

CHAPTER 7
Resources and Energy

▶ The Fly Geysers of the Black Rock Desert in Nevada are surrounded by a pool of water in which many different types of minerals are dissolved. Hot, mineral-rich water periodically erupts from springs deep within Earth to create these formations.

Chapter 4

Earth Chemistry

Sections

1 Matter

2 Combinations of Atoms

What You'll Learn

- How chemical structure affects physical and chemical properties of substances
- How elements combine to form compounds

Why It's Relevant

Understanding the chemical structure of substances will help you to understand the properties of the different materials that make up Earth.

PRE-READING ACTIVITY

Double Door
Before you read this chapter, create the **FoldNote** entitled "Double Door" described in the Skills Handbook section of the Appendix. Write "Element" on one flap of the double door and "Compound" on the other flap. As you read the chapter, compare the two topics, and write characteristics of each on the inside of the appropriate flap.

▶ New Zealand's Champagne Pool is a geothermal pool that has a temperature of 74°C! Its water contains dissolved elements such as gold, silver, mercury, sulfur, antimony, and arsenic.

 California Content Standards

9a Students know the resources of major economic importance in California and their relation to California's geology.
IE.1a Students will select and use appropriate tools and technology (such as computer-linked probes, spreadsheets, and graphing calculators) to perform tests, collect data, analyze relationships and display data.
IE.1d Students will formulate explanations using logic and evidence.
IE.1l Students will analyze situations and solve problems that require combining and applying concepts from more than one area of science.

Matter

California
Content
Standards

IE.1d Students will formulate explanations using logic and evidence.
IE.1l Students will analyze situations and solve problems that require combining and applying concepts from more than one area of science.

Every object in the universe is made of particles of some kind of substance. Scientists use the word *matter* to describe the substances of which objects are made. **Matter** is anything that takes up space and has mass. The amount of matter in any object is the *mass* of that object. All matter has observable and measurable properties. Scientists can observe the properties of a substance to identify the kind of matter that makes up that substance.

Properties of Matter

All matter has two types of distinguishing properties—physical properties and chemical properties. *Physical properties* are characteristics that can be observed without changing the composition of the substance. For example, physical properties include density, color, hardness, freezing point, boiling point, and the ability to conduct an electric current.

Chemical properties are characteristics that describe how a substance reacts with other substances to produce different substances. For example, a chemical property of iron is that iron reacts with oxygen to form rust. A chemical property of helium is that helium does not react with other substances to form new substances. Understanding the chemical properties of a substance requires knowing some basic information about the particles that make up all substances.

Elements

An **element** is a substance that cannot be broken down into simpler, stable substances by chemical means. Each element has a characteristic set of physical and chemical properties that can be used to identify it. **Figure 1** shows the most common elements in Earth's continental crust. More than 90 elements occur naturally on Earth. About two dozen other elements have been created in laboratories. Of the natural elements, eight make up more than 98% of Earth's crust. Every known element is represented by a symbol of one or two letters.

OBJECTIVES

▶ **Compare** chemical properties and physical properties of matter.

▶ **Describe** the basic structure of an atom.

▶ **Compare** atomic number, mass number, and atomic mass.

▶ **Define** *isotope*.

▶ **Describe** the arrangement of elements in the periodic table.

KEY TERMS

matter
element
atom
proton
electron
neutron
isotope

matter anything that has mass and takes up space

element a substance that cannot be separated or broken down into simpler substances by chemical means; all atoms of an element have the same atomic number

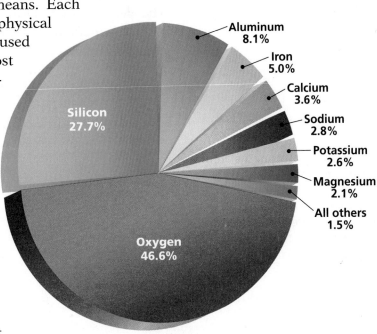

Figure 1 ▶ This graph shows the percentage of total mass that each common element makes up in Earth's continental crust.

Atoms

Elements consist of atoms. An **atom** is the smallest unit of an element that has the chemical properties of that element. Atoms cannot be broken down into smaller particles that will have the same chemical and physical properties as the atom. A single atom is so small that its size is difficult to imagine. To get an idea of how small it is, look at the thickness of this page. More than a million atoms lined up side by side would be equal to that thickness.

Atomic Structure

Even though atoms are very tiny, they are made up of smaller parts called *subatomic particles*. The three major kinds of subatomic particles are protons, electrons, and neutrons. **Protons** are subatomic particles that have a positive charge. **Electrons** are subatomic particles that have a negative charge. **Neutrons** are subatomic particles that have no charge.

The Nucleus

As shown in **Figure 2,** the protons and neutrons of an atom are packed close to one another. Together they form the *nucleus,* which is a small region in the center of an atom. The nucleus has a positive charge because protons have a positive charge and neutrons have no charge.

The nucleus makes up most of an atom's mass but very little of an atom's volume. If an atom's nucleus were the size of a gumdrop, the atom itself would be as big as a football stadium. Because electrons are even smaller than protons and neutrons, the volume of an atom is mostly empty space.

The Electron Cloud

The electrons of an atom move in a certain region of space called an *electron cloud* that surrounds the nucleus. Because opposite charges attract each other, the negatively charged electrons are attracted to the positively charged nucleus. This attraction is what holds electrons in the atom.

atom the smallest unit of an element that maintains the chemical properties of that element

proton a subatomic particle that has a positive charge and that is located in the nucleus of an atom; the number of protons of the nucleus is the atomic number, which determines the identity of an element

electron a subatomic particle that has a negative charge

neutron a subatomic particle that has no charge and that is located in the nucleus of an atom

Figure 2 ▶ The nucleus of the atom is made up of protons and neutrons. The protons give the nucleus a positive charge. The negatively charged electrons are in the electron cloud that surrounds the nucleus.

Nucleus made up of protons and neutrons

Electron cloud

Hydrogen
1 proton
1 electron
0 neutrons
Atomic number 1
Mass number 1

Helium
2 protons
2 electrons
2 neutrons
Atomic number 2
Mass number 4

Lithium
3 protons
3 electrons
4 neutrons
Atomic number 3
Mass number 7

Figure 3 ▶ Hydrogen, helium, and lithium are different elements because their atoms have different atomic numbers, or different numbers of protons.

Atomic Number

The number of protons in the nucleus of an atom is called the *atomic number*. All atoms of any given element have the same atomic number. An element's atomic number sets the atoms of that element apart from the atoms of all other kinds of elements, as shown in **Figure 3**. Because an uncharged atom has an equal number of protons and electrons, the atomic number is also equal to the number of electrons in an atom of any given element.

Elements on the periodic table are ordered according to their atomic numbers. The *periodic table,* shown on the following pages, is a system for classifying elements. Elements in the same column on the periodic table have similar arrangements of electrons in their atoms. Elements that have similar arrangements of electrons have similar chemical properties.

Atomic Mass

The sum of the number of protons and neutrons in an atom is the *mass number*. The mass of a subatomic particle is too small to be expressed easily in grams. So, a special unit called the *atomic mass unit* (amu) is used. Protons and neutrons each have an atomic mass that is close to 1 amu. In contrast, electrons have much less mass than protons and neutrons do. The mass of 1 proton is equal to the combined mass of about 1,840 electrons. Because electrons add little to an atom's total mass, their mass can be ignored when calculating an atom's approximate mass.

✓ **Reading Check** What is the difference between atomic number, mass number, and atomic mass unit? (See the Appendix for answers to Reading Checks.)

Isotopes

Although all atoms of a given element contain the same number of protons, the number of neutrons may differ. For example, while most helium atoms have two neutrons, some helium atoms have only one neutron. An atom that has the same number of protons (or the same atomic number) as other atoms of the same element do but has a different number of neutrons (and thus a different atomic mass) is called an **isotope** (IE suh TOHP).

A helium atom that has two neutrons is more massive than a helium atom that has only one neutron. Because of their different number of neutrons and their different masses, different isotopes of the same element have slightly different properties.

Quick LAB 🕙 10 min

Using the Periodic Table 🔖 IE.1d, IE.1l

Procedure

1. Use the **periodic table** to find the atomic numbers of the following elements: carbon, iron, molybdenum, and iodine.
2. Determine the number of protons and electrons that are in each neutral atom of the elements listed in step 1.
3. Find the average atomic masses of the elements listed in step 1.

Analysis

1. Use the atomic number and average atomic mass of each element to estimate the average number of neutrons in each atom of the elements listed in step 1 of this activity.
2. Which element has the largest difference between its average number of neutrons and the number of protons? Describe any trends that you observe.

isotope an atom that has the same number of protons (or the same atomic number) as the other atoms of the same element do but that has a different number of neutrons (and thus a different atomic mass)

The Periodic Table of Elements

Key:

Atomic number —— 6

Symbol —— **C**

Name —— Carbon

Average atomic mass —— 12.0107

Period

Group 1

1	
H	
Hydrogen	
1.007 94	

3	4
Li	**Be**
Lithium	Beryllium
6.941	9.012 182

11	12
Na	**Mg**
Sodium	Magnesium
22.989 770	24.3050

Group 2

Group 3	Group 4	Group 5	Group 6	Group 7	Group 8	Group 9
19 **K** Potassium 39.0983	20 **Ca** Calcium 40.078	21 **Sc** Scandium 44.955 910	22 **Ti** Titanium 47.867	23 **V** Vanadium 50.9415	24 **Cr** Chromium 51.9961	25 **Mn** Manganese 54.938 049	26 **Fe** Iron 55.845	27 **Co** Cobalt 58.933 200
37 **Rb** Rubidium 85.4678	38 **Sr** Strontium 87.62	39 **Y** Yttrium 88.905 85	40 **Zr** Zirconium 91.224	41 **Nb** Niobium 92.906 38	42 **Mo** Molybdenum 95.94	43 **Tc** Technetium (98)	44 **Ru** Ruthenium 101.07	45 **Rh** Rhodium 102.905 50
55 **Cs** Cesium 132.905 43	56 **Ba** Barium 137.327	57 **La** Lanthanum 138.9055	72 **Hf** Hafnium 178.49	73 **Ta** Tantalum 180.9479	74 **W** Tungsten 183.84	75 **Re** Rhenium 186.207	76 **Os** Osmium 190.23	77 **Ir** Iridium 192.217
87 **Fr** Francium (223)	88 **Ra** Radium (226)	89 **Ac** Actinium (227)	104 **Rf** Rutherfordium (261)	105 **Db** Dubnium (262)	106 **Sg** Seaborgium (266)	107 **Bh** Bohrium (264)	108 **Hs** Hassium (277)	109 **Mt** Meitnerium (268)

* The systematic names and symbols for elements greater than 110 will be used until the approval of trivial names by IUPAC.

58 **Ce** Cerium 140.116	59 **Pr** Praseodymium 140.907 65	60 **Nd** Neodymium 144.24	61 **Pm** Promethium (145)	62 **Sm** Samarium 150.36
90 **Th** Thorium 232.0381	91 **Pa** Protactinium 231.035 88	92 **U** Uranium 238.028 91	93 **Np** Neptunium (237)	94 **Pu** Plutonium (244)

internet connect

go.hrw.com

Topic: Periodic Table
Go To: go.hrw.com
Keyword: Holt Periodic

Visit the HRW Web site for updates on the periodic table.

Hydrogen
Semiconductors
(also known as *metalloids*)

Metals
Alkali metals
Alkaline-earth metals
Transition metals
Other metals

Nonmetals
Halogens
Noble gases
Other nonmetals

Group 18

2
He
Helium
4.002 602

Group 13	Group 14	Group 15	Group 16	Group 17
5	6	7	8	9	10
B	**C**	**N**	**O**	**F**	**Ne**
Boron	Carbon	Nitrogen	Oxygen	Fluorine	Neon
10.811	12.0107	14.0067	15.9994	18.998 4032	20.1797
13	14	15	16	17	18
Al	**Si**	**P**	**S**	**Cl**	**Ar**
Aluminum	Silicon	Phosphorus	Sulfur	Chlorine	Argon
26.981 538	28.0855	30.973 761	32.065	35.453	39.948

Group 10	Group 11	Group 12					
28	29	30	31	32	33	34	35	36
Ni	**Cu**	**Zn**	**Ga**	**Ge**	**As**	**Se**	**Br**	**Kr**
Nickel	Copper	Zinc	Gallium	Germanium	Arsenic	Selenium	Bromine	Krypton
58.6934	63.546	65.409	69.723	72.64	74.921 60	78.96	79.904	83.798
46	47	48	49	50	51	52	53	54
Pd	**Ag**	**Cd**	**In**	**Sn**	**Sb**	**Te**	**I**	**Xe**
Palladium	Silver	Cadmium	Indium	Tin	Antimony	Tellurium	Iodine	Xenon
106.42	107.8682	112.411	114.818	118.710	121.760	127.60	126.904 47	131.293
78	79	80	81	82	83	84	85	86
Pt	**Au**	**Hg**	**Tl**	**Pb**	**Bi**	**Po**	**At**	**Rn**
Platinum	Gold	Mercury	Thallium	Lead	Bismuth	Polonium	Astatine	Radon
195.078	196.966 55	200.59	204.3833	207.2	208.980 38	(209)	(210)	(222)
110	111	112	113	114	115			
Ds	**Uuu***	**Uub***	**Uut***	**Uuq***	**Uup***			
Darmstadtium	Unununium	Ununbium	Ununtrium	Ununquadium	Ununpentium			
(281)	(272)	(285)	(284)	(289)	(288)			

A team at Lawrence Berkeley National Laboratories reported the discovery of elements 116 and 118 in June 1999. The same team retracted the discovery in July 2001. The discovery of elements 113, 114, and 115 has been reported but not confirmed.

63	64	65	66	67	68	69	70	71
Eu	**Gd**	**Tb**	**Dy**	**Ho**	**Er**	**Tm**	**Yb**	**Lu**
Europium	Gadolinium	Terbium	Dysprosium	Holmium	Erbium	Thulium	Ytterbium	Lutetium
151.964	157.25	158.925 34	162.500	164.930 32	167.259	168.934 21	173.04	174.967
95	96	97	98	99	100	101	102	103
Am	**Cm**	**Bk**	**Cf**	**Es**	**Fm**	**Md**	**No**	**Lr**
Americium	Curium	Berkelium	Californium	Einsteinium	Fermium	Mendelevium	Nobelium	Lawrencium
(243)	(247)	(247)	(251)	(252)	(257)	(258)	(259)	(262)

The atomic masses listed in this table reflect the precision of current measurements. (Values listed in parentheses are those of the element's most stable or most common isotope.)

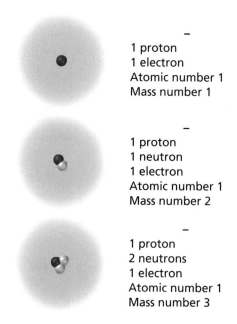

1 proton
1 electron
Atomic number 1
Mass number 1

1 proton
1 neutron
1 electron
Atomic number 1
Mass number 2

1 proton
2 neutrons
1 electron
Atomic number 1
Mass number 3

Figure 4 ▶ There are three naturally occurring isotopes of hydrogen. The main difference between these isotopes is their mass numbers.

For a variety of links related to this subject, go to www.scilinks.org

Topic: Valence Electrons
SciLinks code: HQ61591

Average Atomic Mass

Because the isotopes of an element have different masses, the periodic table uses an average atomic mass for each element. The *average atomic mass* is the weighted average of the atomic masses of the naturally occurring isotopes of an element.

As shown in **Figure 4,** hydrogen has three isotopes. Each isotope has a different mass because each has a different number of neutrons. By calculating the weighted average of the atomic masses of the three naturally occurring hydrogen isotopes, you can determine the average atomic mass. As noted on the periodic table, the average atomic mass of hydrogen is 1.007 94 amu.

Valence Electrons and Periodic Properties

Based on similarities in their chemical properties, elements on the periodic table are arranged in columns, which are called *groups*. An atom's chemical properties are largely determined by the number of the outermost electrons in an atom's electron cloud. These electrons are called *valence* (VAY luhns) electrons.

Within each group, the atoms of each element generally have the same number of valence electrons. For Groups 1 and 2, the number of valence electrons in each atom is the same as that atom's group number. Atoms of elements in Groups 3–12 have 2 or more valence electrons. For Groups 13–18, the number of valence electrons in each atom is the same as that atom's group number minus 10, except for helium, He. It has only two valence electrons. Atoms in Group 18 have 8 valence electrons. When an atom has 8 valence electrons, it is considered stable, or chemically unreactive. Unreactive atoms do not easily lose or gain electrons.

Elements whose atoms have only one, two, or three valence electrons tend to lose electrons easily. These elements have metallic properties and are generally classified as *metals*. Elements whose atoms have from four to seven valence electrons are more likely to gain electrons. Many of these elements, which are in Groups 13–17, are classified as *nonmetals*.

Section 1 Review

1. **Compare** the physical properties of matter with the chemical properties of matter.

2. **Describe** the basic structure of an atom.

3. **Name** the three basic subatomic particles.

4. **Compare** atomic number, mass number, and atomic mass.

5. **Explain** how isotopes of an element differ from each other.

CRITICAL THINKING

6. **Evaluating Data** Oxygen combines with hydrogen and becomes water. Is this combination a result of the physical or chemical properties of hydrogen? IE.1d

7. **Making Comparisons** What sets an atom of one element apart from atoms of all other elements? IE.1d

CONCEPT MAPPING

8. Use the following terms to create a concept map: *matter, element, atom, electron, proton, neutron, atomic number,* and *periodic table.*

Combinations of Atoms

California Content Standards

IE.1d Students will formulate explanations using logic and evidence.
IE.1l Students will analyze situations and solve problems that require combining and applying concepts from more than one area of science.

Elements rarely occur in pure form in Earth's crust. They generally occur in combination with other elements. A substance that is made of two or more elements that are joined by chemical bonds between the atoms of those elements is called a **compound**. The properties of a compound differ from those of the elements that make up the compound, as shown in **Figure 1**.

Molecules

The smallest unit of matter that can exist by itself and retain all of a substance's chemical properties is a **molecule.** In a molecule of two or more atoms, the atoms are chemically bonded together. Some molecules consist entirely of atoms of the same element.

Some elements occur naturally as *diatomic molecules*, which are molecules that are made up of only two atoms. For example, the oxygen in the air you breathe is the diatomic molecule O_2. The O in this notation is the symbol for oxygen. The subscript 2 indicates the number of oxygen atoms that are bonded together.

Chemical Formulas

In any given compound, the elements that make up the compound occur in the same relative proportions. Therefore, a compound can be represented by a chemical formula. A *chemical formula* is a combination of letters and numbers that shows which elements make up a compound. It also shows the number of atoms of each element that are required to make a molecule of a compound.

The chemical formula for water is H_2O, which indicates that each water molecule consists of two atoms of hydrogen and one atom of oxygen. In a chemical formula, the subscript that appears after the symbol for an element shows the number of atoms of that element that are in a molecule. For example, in the chemical formula for water, the subscript 2 and the symbol *H* mean that two atoms of hydrogen are in each molecule of water.

OBJECTIVES

▶ **Define** *compound* and *molecule*.

▶ **Interpret** chemical formulas.

▶ **Describe** two ways that electrons form chemical bonds between atoms.

▶ **Explain** the differences between compounds and mixtures.

KEY TERMS

compound
molecule
ion
ionic bond
covalent bond
mixture
solution

compound a substance made up of atoms of two or more different elements joined by chemical bonds

molecule a group of atoms that are held together by chemical forces; a molecule is the smallest unit of matter that can exist by itself and retain all of a substance's chemical properties

Figure 1 ▶ The silvery metal sodium combines with the poisonous, greenish-yellow gas chlorine to form white granules of table salt, which you can eat.

Sodium, Na   +   Chlorine, Cl_2 →   Table salt, NaCl

Methane
CH_4

Oxygen
$2O_2$

Carbon dioxide
CO_2

Water
$2H_2O$

Figure 2 ▶ Methane, CH_4, and oxygen gas, O_2, react during combustion to form the products carbon dioxide, CO_2, and water, H_2O. *How many hydrogen atoms are on each side of this reaction?*

Chemical Equations

Elements and compounds often combine through chemical reactions to form new compounds. The reaction of these elements and compounds can be described in a formula called a *chemical equation*.

Equation Structure

In a chemical equation, such as the one shown below, the *reactants*, which are on the left-hand side of the arrow, form the *products*, which are on the right-hand side of the arrow. When chemical equations are written, the arrow means "gives" or "yields."

$$CH_4 + 2O_2 \rightarrow CO_2 + 2H_2O$$

In this equation, one molecule of methane, CH_4, reacts with two molecules of oxygen, O_2, to yield one molecule of carbon dioxide, CO_2, and two molecules of water, H_2O, as shown in **Figure 2**.

Balanced Equations

Chemical equations are useful for showing the types and amounts of the products that could form from a particular set of reactants. However, the equation must be balanced to show this information. A chemical equation is balanced when the number of atoms of each element on the right side of the equation is equal to the number of atoms of the same element on the left side.

To balance an equation, you cannot change chemical formulas. Changing the formulas would mean that different substances were in the reaction. To balance an equation, you must put numbers called *coefficients* in front of chemical formulas.

On the left side of the equation above, the methane molecule has four hydrogen atoms, which are indicated by the subscript 4. On the right side, each water molecule has two hydrogen atoms, which are indicated by the subscript 2. A coefficient of 2 is placed in front of the formula for water to balance the number of hydrogen atoms. A coefficient multiplies the subscript in an equation. For example, four hydrogen atoms are in the formula $2H_2O$.

A coefficient of 2 is also placed in front of the oxygen molecule on the left side of the equation so that both sides of the equation have four oxygen atoms. When the number of atoms of each element on either side of the equation is the same, the equation is balanced.

MATHPRACTICE

Balancing Equations
Magnesium, Mg, reacts with oxygen gas, O_2, to form magnesium oxide, MgO. Write a balanced chemical equation for this reaction by placing the coefficients that are needed to obtain an equal number of magnesium and oxygen atoms on either side of the equation.

Chemical Bonds

The forces that hold together the atoms in molecules are called *chemical bonds*. Chemical bonds form because of the attraction between positive and negative charges. Atoms form chemical bonds by either sharing or transferring valence electrons from one atom to another. Transferring or sharing valence electrons from one atom to another changes the properties of the substance. Variations in the forces that hold molecules together are responsible for a wide range of physical and chemical properties.

As shown in **Figure 3**, scientists can study interactions of atoms to predict which kinds of atoms will form chemical bonds together. Scientists do this by comparing the number of valence electrons that are present in a particular atom with the maximum number of valence electrons that are possible. For example, a hydrogen atom has only one valence electron. But because hydrogen can have two valence electrons, it will give up or accept another electron to reach a more chemically unreactive state.

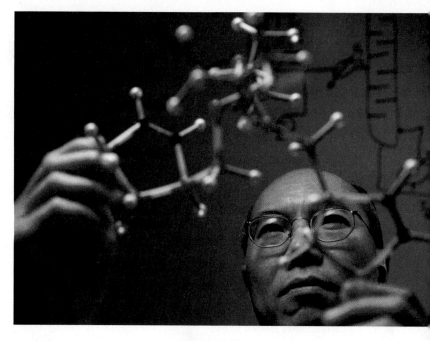

Figure 3 ▶ Scientists sometimes make physical models of molecules to better understand how chemical bonds affect the properties of compounds.

✓ Reading Check In what two ways do atoms form chemical bonds?
(See the Appendix for answers to Reading Checks.)

Connection to CHEMISTRY

States of Matter

Most matter on Earth can be classified into three states—solid, liquid, and gas. The speed at which the particles of matter move and the distance between the particles of matter determine the state of matter.

The particles that make up solids are packed tightly together in relatively fixed positions and are not free to move much in relation to each other. So, a *solid* has a definite shape and volume. A *liquid* has a definite volume but does not have a definite shape. Instead, a liquid takes the shape of the container that holds it. The particles that make up a liquid are also tightly packed, but they are more free to move than those in a solid are. A *gas* does not have a definite volume or shape. The particles of a gas are much farther apart and move faster and more freely than those of a liquid do. Thus, a gas is a formless collection of particles that tends to expand in all directions. If a gas is not confined, the space between its particles will continue to increase.

To melt a solid, you must add heat energy. The addition of energy causes the particles to move faster. When enough energy has been added, the individual particles break away from their fixed positions. When the particles break away, the material becomes a liquid. If enough energy is added, the particles move even faster and form a gas.

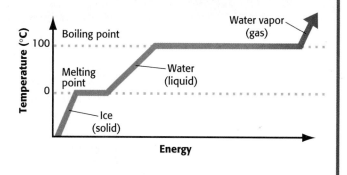

Ions

When an electron is transferred from one atom to another, both atoms become charged. A particle, such as an atom or molecule, that carries a charge is called an **ion**.

Neutral sodium atoms have 11 electrons. And because a sodium atom has 1 valence electron, sodium is a Group 1 element on the periodic table. If a sodium atom loses its outermost electron, the next 8 electrons in the atom's electron cloud become the outermost electrons. Because the sodium atom now has 8 valence electrons, it is unlikely to share or transfer electrons and therefore, is stable.

However, the sodium atom is missing the 1 electron that was needed to balance the number of protons in the nucleus. When an atom no longer has a balance between positive and negative charges, it becomes an ion. The sodium atom became a positive sodium ion, Na^+, when the atom released its valence electron.

Suppose a chlorine atom accepts the electron that the above sodium atom lost. A chlorine atom has a total of 17 electrons, 7 of which are valence electrons. This chlorine atom now has a complete set of 8 valence electrons and is chemically stable. The extra electron, however, changes the neutral chlorine atom into a negatively charged chloride ion, Cl^-.

Ionic Bonds

The attractive force between oppositely charged ions that result from the transfer of electrons from one atom to another is called an **ionic bond**. A compound that forms through the transfer of electrons is called an *ionic compound*. Most ionic compounds form when electrons are transferred between the atoms of metallic and nonmetallic elements.

Sodium chloride, or common table salt, is an ionic compound. The positively charged sodium ions and negatively charged chloride ions attract one another because of their opposite charges. This attraction between the positive sodium ions and the negative chloride ions is an ionic bond. The attraction creates cube-shaped crystals, such as the table salt shown in **Figure 4**.

ion an atom or molecule that has gained or lost one or more electrons and has a negative or positive charge

ionic bond the attractive force between oppositely charged ions, which form when electrons are transferred from one atom or molecule to another

Figure 4 ▼

Ionic Bonds

A sodium atom, Na, transfers an electron to a chlorine atom, Cl, to form table salt, NaCl. The chlorine atom with the added electron becomes a negatively charged ion, Cl^-, and the sodium atom, which lost the electron, becomes a positively charged ion, Na^+. The oppositely charged ions attract each other and form an ionic bond.

Table salt, NaCl

Figure 5 ▼

Covalent Bonds		
	Covalent bonds form when atoms share one or more pairs of electrons. In a covalent compound, pairs of electrons are shared between most of the atoms that make up the compound. Chlorine gas is an example of a covalent compound in which pairs of chlorine atoms are bonded together by sharing electrons.	Chlorine gas, Cl_2

Covalent Bonds

A bond that is formed by the attraction between atoms that share electrons is a **covalent bond.** When atoms share electrons, the positive nucleus of each atom is attracted to the shared negative electrons, as shown in **Figure 5.** The pull between the positive and negative charges is the force that keeps these atoms joined.

Water is an example of a *covalent compound*—that is, a compound formed by the sharing of electrons. Two hydrogen atoms can share their single valence electrons with an oxygen atom that has six valence electrons. The sharing of electrons creates a bond and gives oxygen a stable number of eight outermost electrons. At the same time, the oxygen atom shares two of its electrons—one for each hydrogen atom—which gives each hydrogen atom a more stable number of two electrons. Thus, a water molecule consists of two atoms of hydrogen combined with one atom of oxygen.

Polar Covalent Bonds

In many cases, atoms that are covalently bonded do not equally share electrons. The reason for this is that the ability of atoms of some elements to attract electrons from atoms of other elements differs. A covalent bond in which the bonded atoms have an unequal attraction for the shared electrons is called a *polar covalent bond.* Water is an example of a molecule that forms as a result of polar covalent bonds. Two hydrogen atoms bond covalently with an oxygen atom and form a water molecule. Because the oxygen atom has more ability to attract electrons than the hydrogen atoms do, the electrons are not shared equally between the oxygen and hydrogen atoms. Instead, the electrons remain closer to the oxygen nucleus, which has the greater pull. As a result, the water molecule as a whole has a slightly negative charge at its oxygen end and slightly positive charges at its hydrogen ends. The slightly positive ends of a water molecule attract the slightly negative ends of other water molecules.

✓ Reading Check Why do water molecules form from polar covalent bonds? (See the Appendix for answers to Reading Checks.)

covalent bond a bond formed when atoms share one or more pairs of electrons

Quick LAB ⏱ 10 min

Compounds

Procedure 📖 IE.1d

1. Place **4 g** of compound A in a clear plastic cup.
2. Place **4 g** of compound B in a second clear plastic cup.
3. Observe the color and texture of each compound. Record your observations.
4. Add **5 mL** of vinegar to each cup. Record your observations.

Analysis

1. What physical and chemical differences between the two compounds did you record? How do physical properties and chemical properties differ?
2. Vinegar reacts with baking soda but not with powdered sugar. Which of these compounds is compound A, and which is compound B?

Mixtures

On Earth, elements and compounds are generally mixed together. A **mixture** is a combination of two or more substances that are not chemically combined. The substances that make up a mixture keep their individual properties. Therefore, unlike a compound, a mixture can be separated into its parts by physical means. For example, you can use a magnet to separate a mixture of powdered sulfur, S, and iron, Fe, filings. The magnet will attract the iron, which is magnetic, and leave behind the sulfur, which is not magnetic.

Heterogeneous Mixtures

Mixtures in which two or more substances are not uniformly distributed are called *heterogeneous mixtures*. For example, the igneous rock granite is a heterogeneous mixture of crystals of the minerals quartz, feldspar, hornblende, and biotite.

Homogeneous Mixtures

In chemistry, the word *homogeneous* means "having the same composition and properties throughout." A homogeneous mixture of two or more substances that are uniformly dispersed throughout the mixture is a **solution.**

Any part of a given sample of the solution known as sea water, for example, will have the same composition. Sodium chloride, NaCl, (along with many other ionic compounds) is dissolved in sea water. The positive ends of water molecules attract negative chloride ions. And the negative end of water molecules attracts positive sodium ions. Eventually, all of the sodium and chloride ions become uniformly distributed among the water molecules.

Gases and solids can also be solutions. An *alloy* is a solution composed of two or more metals. The steel shown in **Figure 6** is an example of such a solution.

Figure 6 ▶ The steel that is being smelted in this steel mill in Iowa is a solution of iron, carbon, and various other metals such as nickel, chromium, and manganese.

mixture a combination of two or more substances that are not chemically combined

solution a homogeneous mixture of two or more substances that are uniformly dispersed throughout the mixture

---

Section 2 Review

1. **Define** *compound* and *molecule*.

2. **Determine** the number of each type of atom in the following chemical formula: $C_6H_{12}O_6$.

3. **Explain** why atoms join to form molecules.

4. **Describe** the difference between ionic and covalent bonds.

5. **Explain** why a water molecule has polar covalent bonds.

6. **Compare** compounds with mixtures.

7. **Identify** two common solutions.

CRITICAL THINKING

8. **Applying Ideas** What happens to the chemical properties of a substance when it becomes part of a mixture? IE.1d

9. **Evaluating Data** If you were given two mixtures and told that one is a solution, how might you determine which one is the solution? IE.1d

CONCEPT MAPPING

10. Use the following terms to create a concept map: *compound, molecule, ionic compound, ionic bond, ion, covalent compound,* and *covalent bond.*

Sections

1 Matter

Key Terms

matter, 81
element, 81
atom, 82
proton, 82
electron, 82
neutron, 82
isotope, 83

Key Concepts

▶ An element is a substance that has a characteristic set of physical and chemical properties and that cannot be separated into simpler substances by chemical means.

▶ An atom consists of electrons surrounding a nucleus that is made up of protons and neutrons.

▶ The atomic number of an atom is equal to the number of protons in the atom. The mass number is equal to the sum of the protons and neutrons in the atom.

▶ Isotopes are atoms that have different numbers of neutrons than other atoms of the same element do.

▶ Elements on the periodic table are arranged in groups that are based on similarities in the chemical properties of the elements.

2 Combinations of Atoms

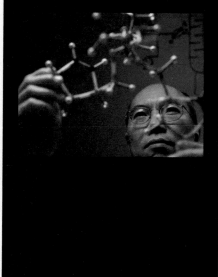

compound, 87
molecule, 87
ion, 90
ionic bond, 90
covalent bond, 91
mixture, 92
solution, 92

▶ A compound is a substance that is made up of two or more different elements that are joined by chemical bonds between the atoms of those elements.

▶ A chemical formula describes which elements and how many atoms of each of those elements make up a molecule of a compound.

▶ Chemical bonds between atoms form when electrons are shared or transferred between the atoms.

▶ A mixture consists of two or more substances that are not chemically bonded. A solution is a mixture in which one substance is uniformly dispersed in another substance.

Using Key Terms

Use each of the following terms in a separate sentence.

1. *matter*
2. *neutron*
3. *ion*

For each pair of terms, explain how the meanings of the terms differ.

4. *atom* and *molecule*
5. *element* and *compound*
6. *proton* and *electron*
7. *compound* and *mixture*
8. *covalent bond* and *ionic bond*

Understanding Key Concepts

9. Color and hardness are examples of a substance's
   a. physical properties.
   b. chemical properties.
   c. atomic structure.
   d. molecular properties.

10. Subatomic particles in atoms that do not carry an electric charge are called
    a. neutrons.   c. nuclei.
    b. protons.   d. ions.

11. Atoms of the same element that differ in mass are
    a. ions.   c. isotopes.
    b. neutrons.   d. molecules.

12. A combination of letters and numbers that indicates which elements make up a compound is a
    a. coefficient.
    b. reactant.
    c. chemical bond.
    d. chemical formula.

13. The type of chemical bond that forms between oppositely charged ions is a(n)
    a. covalent bond.
    b. mixture.
    c. ionic bond.
    d. solution.

14. Two or more elements whose atoms are chemically bonded form a(n)
    a. mixture.   c. nucleus.
    b. ion.   d. compound.

15. The outermost electrons in an atom's electron cloud are called
    a. ions.
    b. isotopes.
    c. valence electrons.
    d. neutrons.

16. A molecule of water, or H_2O, has one atom of
    a. hydrogen.   c. helium.
    b. oxygen.   d. osmium.

Short Answer

17. How do chemical properties differ from physical properties? IE.1d

18. Define the term *element*.

19. Name three basic subatomic particles.

20. In terms of valence electrons, what is the difference between metallic elements and nonmetallic elements?

21. Which type of bonding includes the sharing of electrons?

22. Using the periodic table to help you to understand the following chemical formulas, list the name and number of atoms of each element in each compound: NaCl, H_2O_2, Fe_3O_4, and SiO_2.

23. What sets an atom of one element apart from the atoms of all other elements? IE.1d

Critical Thinking

24. Applying Ideas Is a diatomic molecule more likely to be held together by a covalent bond or by an ionic bond? Explain your answer. **IE.1d**

25. Making Inferences Calcium chloride is an ionic compound. Carbon dioxide is a covalent compound. Which of these compounds forms as a result of the transfer of electrons from one atom to another? Explain your answer. **IE.1d**

26. Analyzing Relationships What happens to the chemical properties of a substance when it becomes part of a mixture? Explain your answer. **IE.1d**

27. Classifying Information Oxygen combines with hydrogen to form water. Is this process due to the physical or chemical properties of oxygen and hydrogen? **IE.1d**

Concept Mapping

28. Use the following terms to create a concept map: *chemical property, element, atom, electron, proton, neutron, atomic number, mass number, isotope, compound,* and *chemical bond.*

Math Skills

29. Making Calculations How many neutrons does a potassium atom have if its atomic number is 19 and its mass number is 39?

30. Using Formulas The covalent compound formaldehyde forms when one carbon atom, two hydrogen atoms, and one oxygen atom bond. Write a chemical formula for formaldehyde.

31. Balancing Equations Zinc metal, Zn, will react with hydrochloric acid, HCl, to produce hydrogen gas, H_2, and zinc chloride, $ZnCl_2$. Write and balance the chemical equation for this reaction.

Writing Skills

32. Organizing Data Choose one of the eight most common elements in Earth's crust, and write a brief report on the element's atomic structure, its chemical properties, and its economic importance. **9a, IE.1d, IE.1l**

33. Communicating Main Ideas Write a brief essay that describes how an element's chemical properties determine what other elements are likely to bond with that element. **IE.1d**

34. Making Comparisons Write a brief essay that describes the differences between atoms, elements, ions, and isotopes. **IE.1d**

Interpreting Graphics

The table below shows the average atomic masses and the atomic numbers of five elements. Use this table to answer the questions that follow.

Element	Symbol	Average atomic mass	Atomic number
Magnesium	Mg	24.3050	12
Tungsten	W	183.84	74
Copper	Cu	63.546	29
Silicon	Si	28.0855	14
Bromine	Br	79.904	35

35. If an atom of magnesium has 12 neutrons, what is its mass number?

36. Estimate the average number of neutrons in an atom of tungsten and in an atom of silicon.

37. Which element has the largest difference between the number of protons and the number of neutrons in the nucleus of one of its atoms? Explain your answer. **IE.1d**

Understanding Concepts

Directions (1–9): **For** *each* **question, write on a separate sheet of paper the number of the correct answer.**

1 Why is soil described as a mixture?
 A. Soil is made up of different substances that are uniformly dispersed.
 B. Soil is made up of two or more elements that are joined by chemical bonds between them.
 C. Soil is a combination of different substances that are not chemically combined.
 D. Soil is made up of the smallest units of matter, which cannot be broken down without changing their properties.

2 Isotopes are atoms of the same element that has different mass numbers. This difference is caused by
 A. a different number of electrons in the atoms.
 B. a different number of protons in the atoms.
 C. a different number of neutrons in the atoms.
 D. a different number of nuclei in the atoms.

3 One of the most economically important elements in California is gold, which has the chemical symbol Au. The atomic number of gold is 79 and its atomic mass is 197. Which of the following describes the electron, proton, and neutron makeup of gold?
 A. 79 electrons, 79 protons, 118 neutrons
 B. 197 electrons, 79 protons, 118 neutrons
 C. 118 electrons, 118 protons, 79 neutrons
 D. 118 electrons, 79 protons, 197 neutrons

4 An element is located on the periodic table according to
 A. when the element was discovered.
 B. the letters of the element's chemical symbol.
 C. the element's chemical name.
 D. the element's physical and chemical properties.

5 A scientist is studying a compound in which the chemical bonds are characterized by unequally shared electrons. Which type of substance is the scientist studying?
 A. ionic compound
 B. covalent compound
 C. polar covalent compound
 D. homogeneous mixture

6 A typical balanced chemical equation has coefficients, products, reactants, and subscripts, all of which show the elements and molecules that are broken down, joined, and formed during a chemical reaction. To show the conversion from one substance to another, the equation is separated by an arrow. Which parts of a chemical equation always follow the arrow?
 A. coefficients
 B. products
 C. reactants
 D. subscripts

7 What does a subscript in a chemical formula represent?
 A. Subscripts represent the number of atoms of the chemical symbol that they directly follow that are present in the molecule.
 B. Subscripts represent the number of atoms of the chemical symbol that they directly precede that are present in the molecule.
 C. Subscripts represent the number of protons that are present in each atom's nucleus.
 D. Subscripts represent the total number of atoms that are present in a molecule.

8 A material has different substances and different crystals. Which of the following statements best describes this material?
 A. a homogenous mixture, which contains substances that are uniformly distributed
 B. a compound, which has two or more elements that are chemically bonded
 C. a heterogenous mixture, which contains substances that are unevenly distributed
 D. a molecule, which cannot retain all of its characteristics if it is broken down

9 In California, silver is produced as a byproduct of gold production. Gold and silver are part of Group 11 on the periodic table. What does this indicate about silver?
 A. Silver has fewer valence electrons than gold does.
 B. Silver is a metal, but gold is not.
 C. Silver and gold have the same number of valence electrons.
 D. Silver has eight valence electrons.

The Smallest Particles

Matter is made of atoms. For a long time, scientists thought that atoms were the smallest particles of matter. Then, when protons, neutrons, and electrons were discovered, these particles were thought to be the smallest particles. Now, the honor goes to particles called *quarks* and *leptons*. But recent evidence suggests that quarks may be composed of smaller particles.

Energy to See

A fundamental principle of physics is that the smaller an object is, the greater the amount of energy is required to see it. Because the amount of energy needed to see subatomic particles does not exist naturally on Earth, scientists have to build up enough energy to break apart these particles so that individual parts can be isolated for study. Tevatron, a huge particle accelerator shown at right, is an underground, ring-shaped tunnel that has a 6.4 km circumference. It contains 1,000 superconducting magnets that move beams of particles at increasingly higher speeds. As the particles gain speed, they build up energy.

▶ Particle accelerators, such as this one in Illinois, are so expensive to build and operate that they require international cooperation.

When the energized particles are moving near the speed of light (299,792,458 m/s), they are directed to hit either a fixed target or particles moving in an opposite direction. On impact, the particles split. The byproducts of the particles separate and scatter. The smaller particles, including quarks and leptons, are measured by a collider detector.

Applying the Results

For now, the nature of subatomic particles may seem far removed from Earth science. However, research on the most basic particles of matter may one day influence the work of Earth scientists by changing basic theories that range from the ultimate structure of matter to the origin of the universe.

Extension

1. **Research** Find out more about quarks and leptons. Then, write a short report that describes their characteristics and where they are found in an atom.

▼ This image shows the paths of the subatomic particles created by collisions in a particle accelerator. The shape and location of each path indicates the type of particle that formed the path.

Chapter 5

Minerals of Earth's Crust

Sections

1 What Is a Mineral?

2 Identifying Minerals

What You'll Learn

- What the characteristics of minerals are
- Why minerals have certain properties
- How to identify minerals

Why It's Relevant

Minerals are valued for their use in making everything from airplanes to cookware. Understanding the characteristics of minerals is also an important way to understand how Earth's processes form minerals.

PRE-READING ACTIVITY

Double Door
Before you read this chapter, create the **FoldNote** entitled "Double Door" described in the Skills Handbook section of the Appendix. Write "Silicate minerals" on one flap of the double door and "Nonsilicate minerals" on the other flap. As you read the chapter, compare the two topics, and write characteristics of each on the inside of the appropriate flap.

▶ Agates are a form of the mineral chalcedony, which is a type of quartz. This agate was dyed a brilliant blue to show its internal structure.

California Content Standards

9a Students know the resources of major economic importance in California and their relation to California's geology.

IE.1a Students will select and use appropriate tools and technology (such as computer-linked probes, spreadsheets, and graphing calculators) to perform tests, collect data, analyze relationships and display data.

IE.1d Students will formulate explanations using logic and evidence.

IE.1g Students will recognize the usefulness and limitations of models and theories as scientific representations of reality.

IE.1l Students will analyze situations and solve problems that require combining and applying concepts from more than one area of science.

California Content Standards

IE.1d Students will formulate explanations using logic and evidence.
IE.1g Students will recognize the usefulness and limitations of models and theories as scientific representations of reality.
IE.1l Students will analyze situations and solve problems that require combining and applying concepts from more than one area of science.

A ruby, a gold nugget, and a grain of salt look very different from one another, but they have one thing in common. They are minerals, the basic materials of Earth's crust. A **mineral** is a natural, usually inorganic solid that has a characteristic chemical composition, an orderly internal structure, and a characteristic set of physical properties.

Characteristics of Minerals

To determine whether a substance is a mineral or a nonmineral, scientists ask four basic questions, as shown in **Table 1.** If the answer to all four questions is yes, the substance is a mineral.

First, is the substance inorganic? An inorganic substance is one that is not made up of living things or the remains of living things. Coal, for example, is organic—it is composed of the remains of ancient plants. Thus, coal is not a mineral.

Second, does the substance occur naturally? Minerals form and exist in nature. Thus, a manufactured substance, such as steel or brass, is not a mineral.

Third, is the substance a solid in crystalline form? The volcanic glass obsidian is a naturally occurring substance. However, the atoms in obsidian are not arranged in a regularly repeating crystalline structure. Thus, obsidian is not a mineral.

Finally, does the substance have a consistent chemical composition? The mineral fluorite has a consistent chemical composition of one calcium ion for every two fluoride ions. Basalt, however, can have a variety of substances. The ratio of these substances commonly varies in each sample of basalt.

OBJECTIVES

▶ **Define** *mineral.*

▶ **Compare** the two main groups of minerals.

▶ **Identify** the six types of silicate crystalline structures.

▶ **Describe** three common nonsilicate crystalline structures.

KEY TERMS

mineral
silicate mineral
nonsilicate mineral
crystal
silicon-oxygen tetrahedron

mineral a natural, usually inorganic solid that has a characteristic chemical composition, an orderly internal structure, and a characteristic set of physical properties

Table 1 ▶

Four Criteria for Minerals					
Questions to Identify a Mineral	**Coal**	**Brass**	**Obsidian**	**Basalt**	**Fluorite**
Is it inorganic?	No	Yes	Yes	Yes	Yes
Does it occur naturally?		No	Yes	Yes	Yes
Is it a crystalline solid?			No	Yes	Yes
Does it have a consistent chemical composition?				No	Yes

Kinds of Minerals

Earth scientists have identified more than 3,000 minerals, but fewer than 20 of the minerals are common. The common minerals are called *rock-forming minerals* because they form the rocks that make up Earth's crust. Three of these minerals are shown in **Figure 1.** Of the 20 rock-forming minerals, 10 are so common that they make up 90% of the mass of Earth's crust. These minerals are quartz, orthoclase, plagioclase, muscovite, biotite, calcite, dolomite, halite, gypsum, and ferromagnesian minerals. All minerals, however, can be classified into two main groups—silicate minerals and nonsilicate minerals—based on the chemical compositions of the minerals.

Figure 1 ▶ Plagioclase feldspar (left), muscovite mica (center), and orthoclase feldspar (right) are 3 of the 20 common rock-forming minerals.

silicate mineral a mineral that contains a combination of silicon and oxygen, and that may also contain one or more metals

Silicate Minerals

A mineral that contains a combination of silicon, Si, and oxygen, O, is a **silicate mineral.** The mineral quartz has only silicon and oxygen atoms. However, other silicate minerals have one or more additional elements. Feldspars are the most common silicate minerals. The type of feldspar that forms depends on which metal combines with the silicon and oxygen atoms. Orthoclase forms when the metal is potassium, K. Plagioclase forms when the metal is sodium, Na, calcium, Ca, or both.

In addition to quartz and the feldspars, ferromagnesian minerals—which are rich in iron, Fe, and magnesium, Mg—are silicates. These minerals include olivines, pyroxenes, amphiboles, and biotite. Silicate minerals make up 96% of Earth's crust. Feldspar and quartz alone make up more than 50% of the crust.

Connection to CHEMISTRY

Ions and Bonds

An atom that has a positive or negative charge is called an *ion*. When an atom loses one or more electrons, the atom has more protons than it has electrons. Thus, the atom acquires a positive charge. An ion that has a positive charge is called a *cation*. All of the most abundant elements in Earth's crust except oxygen release electrons and form cations. For example, sodium, Na, atoms generally lose one electron to form a cation that has a charge of +1.

An atom that gains one or more electrons acquires a negative charge because the atom has more electrons than protons. An ion that has a negative charge is called an *anion*. Chlorine, Cl, which generally gains one electron and thus has a charge of –1, forms an anion.

Atoms and ions rarely exist alone. Most atoms and ions combine to form *compounds*. Forces called *chemical bonds* hold atoms and ions together in these

Cation   Anion   Neutral compound

compounds. When ions combine to form compounds, the ions combine in proportions that allow all of the positive charges to equal and cancel out all of the negative charges. Thus, the compound is electrically neutral. The mineral halite is a good example of this relationship. Because sodium ions have +1 charges and chlorine ions have –1 charges, one sodium ion bonds with one chlorine ion to form the compound sodium chloride, NaCl, which is the mineral halite. Thus, $1 - 1 = 0$, and the compound is neutral.

Table 2 ▼

Major Classes of Nonsilicate Minerals

Carbonates

compounds that contain a carbonate group (CO_3)

Dolomite, $CaMg(CO_3)_2$

Calcite, $CaCO_3$

Halides

compounds that consist of chlorine or fluorine combined with sodium, potassium, or calcium

Halite, $NaCl$

Fluorite, CaF_2

Native elements

elements uncombined with other elements

Silver, Ag

Copper, Cu

Oxides

compounds that contain oxygen and an element other than silicon

Corundum, Al_2O_3

Hematite, Fe_2O_3

Sulfates

compounds that contain a sulfate group (SO_4)

Gypsum, $CaSO_4 \cdot 2H_2O$

Anhydrite, $CaSO_4$

Sulfides

compounds that consist of one or more elements combined with sulfur

Galena, PbS

Pyrite, FeS_2

Nonsilicate Minerals

Approximately 4% of Earth's crust is made up of minerals that do not contain compounds of silicon and oxygen, or **nonsilicate minerals. Table 2** organizes the six major groups of nonsilicate minerals by their chemical compositions: carbonates, halides, native elements, oxides, sulfates, and sulfides.

nonsilicate mineral a mineral that does not contain compounds of silicon and oxygen

✔ **Reading Check** What compound of elements will you never find in a nonsilicate mineral? (See the Appendix for answers to Reading Checks.)

Crystalline Structure

All minerals in Earth's crust have a crystalline structure. Each type of mineral crystal is characterized by a specific geometric arrangement of atoms. A **crystal** is a solid whose atoms, ions, or molecules are arranged in a regular, repeating pattern. A large mineral crystal displays the characteristic geometry of that crystal's internal structure. The conditions under which minerals form, however, often hinder the growth of single, large crystals. As a result, minerals are commonly made up of masses of crystals that are so small that you can see them only with a microscope. But, if a crystal forms where the surrounding material is not restrictive, the mineral will develop as a single, large crystal that has one of six basic crystal shapes. Knowing the crystal shapes is helpful in identifying minerals.

One way that scientists study the structure of crystals is by using X rays. X rays that pass through a crystal and strike a photographic plate produce an image that shows the geometric arrangement of the atoms that make up the crystal.

Crystalline Structure of Silicate Minerals

Even though there are many kinds of silicate minerals, their crystalline structure is made up of the same basic building blocks. Each building block has four oxygen atoms arranged in a pyramid with one silicon atom in the center. **Figure 2** shows this four-sided structure, which is known as a **silicon-oxygen tetrahedron.**

Silicon-oxygen tetrahedra combine in different arrangements to form different silicate minerals. The various arrangements are the result of the kinds of bonds that form between the oxygen atoms of the tetrahedra and other atoms. The oxygen and silicon atoms of tetrahedra may bond with those of neighboring tetrahedra. Bonds may also form between the oxygen atoms in the tetrahedra and other elements' atoms outside of the tetrahedra.

✔ **Reading Check** What is the building block of the silicate crystalline structure? (See the Appendix for answers to Reading Checks.)

crystal a solid whose atoms, ions, or molecules are arranged in a regular, repeating pattern

silicon-oxygen tetrahedron the basic unit of the structure of silicate minerals; a silicon ion chemically bonded to and surrounded by four oxygen ions

---

QuickLAB   5 min

Modeling Tetrahedra

Procedure   IE.1d, IE.1g

1. Place **four toothpicks** in a small marshmallow. Evenly space the toothpicks as far from each other as possible.
2. Place **four large marshmallows** on the ends of the toothpicks.

Analysis

1. In your model, what do the toothpicks represent?
2. When tetrahedra form chains or rings, the tetrahedra share electrons. If you wanted to build a chain of tetrahedra, how would you connect two tetrahedra together?

Figure 2 ▶ The structure of a silicon-oxygen tetrahedron can be shown by two different models. The model on the left represents the relative size and proximity of the atoms to one another in the molecule. The model on the right shows the tetrahedral shape of the molecule.

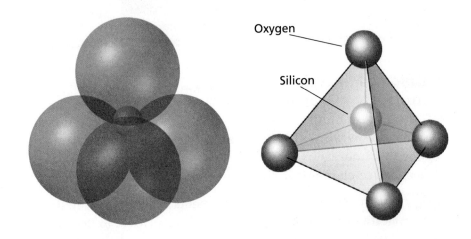

Oxygen

Silicon

Isolated Tetrahedral Silicates and Ring Silicates

The six kinds of arrangements that tetrahedra form are shown in **Figure 3.** In minerals that have *isolated tetrahedra*, only atoms other than silicon and oxygen atoms link silicon-oxygen tetrahedra. For example, olivine is a mineral that forms when the oxygen atoms of tetrahedra bond to magnesium, Mg, and iron, Fe, atoms.

Ring silicates form when shared oxygen atoms join the tetrahedra to form three-, four-, or six-sided rings. Ionic bonds hold the rings together, and the rings align to create channels that can contain a variety of ions, molecules, and neutral atoms. Beryl and tourmaline are minerals that have ring-silicate structures.

Single-Chain Silicates and Double-Chain Silicates

In *single-chain silicates*, each tetrahedron is bonded to two others by shared oxygen atoms. In *double-chain silicates*, two single chains of tetrahedra bond to each other. Most single-chain silicate minerals are called *pyroxenes*, and those made up of double chains are called *amphiboles*.

Sheet Silicates and Framework Silicates

In the *sheet silicates*, each tetrahedron shares three oxygen atoms with other tetrahedra. The fourth oxygen atom bonds with an atom of aluminum, Al, or magnesium, Mg, which joins one sheet to another. The mica minerals, such as muscovite and biotite, are examples of sheet silicates.

In the *framework silicates*, each tetrahedron is bonded to four neighboring tetrahedra to form a three-dimensional network. Frameworks that contain only silicon-oxygen tetrahedra form the mineral quartz. The chemical formula for quartz is SiO_2. Other framework silicates, such as the feldspars, contain some tetrahedra in which atoms of aluminum or other metals substitute for some of the silicon atoms.

Figure 3 ▶ Six Kinds of Silicate-Mineral Arrangements

1 **Isolated tetrahedra** do not link with other silicon or oxygen atoms.

2 **Ring silicates** form rings by sharing oxygen atoms.

3 **Single-chain silicates** form a chain by sharing oxygen atoms.

4 **Double-chain silicates** form when two single-chains of tetrahedra bond to each other.

5 **Sheet silicates** form when each tetrahedron shares three of its oxygen atoms with other tetrahedra.

6 **Framework silicates** form when each tetrahedron is bonded to four other tetrahedra.

Figure 4 ▶ Gold (left) commonly has a dendritic shape. Halite (center) commonly has cubic crystals. Diamond (right) commonly has an octahedral crystal shape. All three of these minerals are nonsilicates.

The Crystalline Structure of Nonsilicate Minerals

Because nonsilicate minerals have diverse chemical compositions, nonsilicate minerals display a vast variety of crystalline structures. Common crystal structures for nonsilicate minerals include cubes, hexagonal prisms, and irregular masses. Some of these structures are shown in **Figure 4.**

Nonsilicates may form tetrahedra that are similar to those in silicates. However, the ions at the center of these tetrahedra are not silicon. Minerals that have the same ion at the center of the tetrahedron commonly share similar crystal structures. Thus, the classes of nonsilicate minerals can be divided into smaller groups based on the structural similarities of the minerals' crystals.

The structure of a nonsilicate crystal determines the nonsilicate's characteristics. For example, the native elements have very high densities because their crystal structures are based on the packing of atoms as close together as possible. This crystal structure is called *closest packing.* In this crystal structure, each metal atom is surrounded by 8 to 12 other metal atoms that are as close to each other as the charges of the atomic nuclei will allow.

Section 1 Review

1. **Define** *mineral.*

2. **Summarize** the characteristics that are necessary to classify a substance as a mineral.

3. **Compare** the two main groups of minerals.

4. **Identify** the two elements that are in all silicate minerals.

5. **Name** six types of nonsilicate minerals.

6. **Describe** the six main crystalline structures of silicate minerals.

7. **Explain** why nonsilicate minerals have a wider variety of crystalline structures than silicate minerals do. IE.1d

CRITICAL THINKING

8. **Predicting Consequences** If silicon bonded with three oxygen atoms, how might the crystalline structures of silicate minerals be different? IE.1d

9. **Applying Ideas** Gold is an inorganic substance that forms naturally in Earth's crust. Gold is also a solid and has a definite chemical composition. Is gold a mineral? Explain your answer. IE.1d

CONCEPT MAPPING

10. Use the following terms to create a concept map: *mineral, crystal, silicate mineral, nonsilicate mineral, ring silicate, framework silicate, single-chain silicate,* and *silicon-oxygen tetrahedron.*

Identifying Minerals

California Content Standards

IE.1a Students will select and use appropriate tools and technology (such as computer-linked probes, spreadsheets, and graphing calcula- | tors) to perform tests, collect data, analyze relationships, and display data.
IE.1l Students will analyze situations and solve | problems that require combining and applying concepts from more than one area of science.

Earth scientists called **mineralogists** examine, analyze, and classify minerals. To identify minerals, mineralogists study the properties of the minerals. Some properties are simple to study, while special equipment may be needed to study other properties.

Physical Properties of Minerals

Each mineral has specific properties that are a result of its chemical composition and crystalline structure. These properties provide useful clues for identifying minerals. Many of these properties can be identified by simply looking at a sample of the mineral. Other properties can be identified through simple tests.

Color

One property of a mineral that is easy to observe is the mineral's color. Some minerals have very distinct colors. For example, sulfur is bright yellow, and azurite is deep blue. Color alone, however, is generally not a reliable clue for identifying a mineral sample. Many minerals are similar in color, and very small amounts of certain elements may greatly affect the color of a mineral. For example, corundum is a colorless mineral composed of aluminum and oxygen atoms. However, corundum that has traces of chromium, Cr, forms the red gem called *ruby*. Sapphire, which is a type of corundum, gets its blue color from traces of iron, Fe, and titanium, Ti. **Figure 1** compares colorless, pure quartz with purple amethyst. Amethyst is quartz that has manganese, Mn, and iron, Fe, which cause the purple color.

Color is also an unreliable identification clue because weathered surfaces may hide the color of minerals. For example, the golden color of iron pyrite ranges from dark yellow to black when iron pyrite is weathered. When examining a mineral for color, you should inspect only the mineral's freshly exposed surfaces.

OBJECTIVES

▶ **Describe** seven physical properties that help distinguish one mineral from another.

▶ **List** five special properties that may help identify certain minerals.

KEY TERMS

mineralogist
streak
luster
cleavage
fracture
Mohs hardness scale
density

mineralogist a person who examines, analyzes, and classifies minerals

SCiLINKS®

Developed and maintained by the National Science Teachers Association

For a variety of links related to this subject, go to www.scilinks.org

Topic: Minerals
SciLinks code: HQ60966
Topic: Mineral Identification
SciLinks code: HQ60965

Figure 1 ▶ Pure quartz (left) is colorless. Amethyst (right) is a variety of quartz that is purple because of the presence of small amounts of manganese and iron.

Figure 2 ▶ All minerals have either a metallic luster, as platinum does (top), or a nonmetallic luster, as talc does (bottom).

streak the color of a mineral in powdered form

luster the way in which a mineral reflects light

cleavage in geology, the tendency of a mineral to split along specific planes of weakness to form smooth, flat surfaces

fracture the manner in which a mineral breaks along either curved or irregular surfaces

Streak

A more reliable clue to the identity of a mineral is the color of the mineral in powdered form, which is called the mineral's **streak.** The easiest way to observe the streak of a mineral is to rub some of the mineral against a piece of unglazed ceramic tile called a *streak plate.* The streak's color may differ from the color of the solid form of the mineral. Metallic minerals generally have a dark streak. For example, the streak of gold-colored pyrite is black. For most nonmetallic minerals, however, the streak is either colorless or a very light shade of the mineral's standard color. Minerals that are harder than the ceramic plate will leave no streak.

Luster

Light that is reflected from a mineral's surface is called **luster.** A mineral is said to have a *metallic luster* if the mineral reflects light as a polished metal does, as shown in **Figure 2.** All other minerals have a *nonmetallic luster.* Mineralogists distinguish several types of nonmetallic luster. Transparent quartz and other minerals that look like glass have a glassy luster. Minerals that have the appearance of candle wax have a waxy luster. Some minerals, such as the mica minerals, have a pearly luster. Diamond is an example of a mineral that has a brilliant luster. A mineral that lacks any shiny appearance has a dull or earthy luster.

Cleavage and Fracture

The tendency of a mineral to split along specific planes of weakness to form smooth, flat surfaces is called **cleavage.** When a mineral has cleavage, as shown in **Figure 3,** it breaks along flat surfaces that generally run parallel to planes of weakness in the crystal structure. For example, the mica minerals, which are sheet silicates, tend to split into parallel sheets.

Many minerals, however, do not break along cleavage planes. Instead, they **fracture,** or break unevenly, into pieces that have curved or irregular surfaces. Mineralogists describe a fracture according to the appearance of the broken surface. For example, a rough surface has an *uneven* or *irregular fracture.* A broken surface that looks like a piece of broken wood has a *splintery* or *fibrous fracture.* Curved surfaces are *conchoidal fractures* (kahng KOYD uhl FRAK chuhr), as shown in **Figure 3.**

Figure 3 ▶ Calcite is a mineral that cleaves in three directions. Quartz tends to have a conchoidal fracture.

Table 1 ▼

Mohs Hardness Scale					
Mineral	Hardness	Common test	Mineral	Hardness	Common test
Talc	1	easily scratched by fingernail	Feldspar	6	scratches glass, but does not scratch steel
Gypsum	2	can be scratched by fingernail	Quartz	7	easily scratches both glass and steel
Calcite	3	barely can be scratched by copper penny	Topaz	8	scratches quartz
Fluorite	4	easily scratched with steel file or glass	Corundum	9	scratches topaz
Apatite	5	can be scratched by steel file or glass	Diamond	10	scratches everything

Hardness

The measure of the ability of a mineral to resist scratching is called *hardness*. Hardness does not mean "resistance to cleavage or fracture." A diamond, for example, is extremely hard but can be split along cleavage planes more easily than calcite, a softer mineral, can be split.

To determine the hardness of an unknown mineral, you can scratch the mineral against those on the **Mohs hardness scale,** which is shown in **Table 1.** This scale lists 10 minerals in order of increasing hardness. The softest mineral, talc, has a hardness of 1. The hardest mineral, diamond, has a hardness of 10. The difference in hardness between two consecutive minerals is about the same throughout the scale except for the difference between the two hardest minerals. Diamond (10) is much harder than corundum (9), which is listed on the scale before diamond.

To test an unknown mineral for hardness, you must determine the hardest mineral on the scale that the unknown mineral can scratch. For example, galena can scratch gypsum but not calcite. Thus, galena has a hardness that ranges between 2 and 3 on the Mohs hardness scale. If neither of two minerals scratches the other, the minerals have the same hardness.

The strength of the bonds between the atoms that make up a mineral's internal structure determines the hardness of that mineral. Both diamond and graphite consist only of carbon atoms. However, diamond has a hardness of 10, while the hardness of graphite is between 1 and 2. A diamond's hardness results from a strong crystalline structure in which each carbon atom is firmly bonded to four other carbon atoms. In contrast, the carbon atoms in graphite are arranged in layers that are held together by much weaker chemical bonds.

Reading Check What determines the hardness of a mineral? (See the Appendix for answers to Reading Checks.)

Mohs hardness scale the standard scale against which the hardness of minerals is rated

Graphic Organizer Comparison Table

Create the **Graphic Organizer** entitled "Comparison Table" described in the Skills Handbook section of the Appendix. Label the columns with "Diamond," "Corundum," "Graphite," and "Galena." Label the rows with "Hardness" and "Description." Then, fill in the table with details about the hardness and a description of each mineral.

Table 2 ▼

The Six Basic Crystal Systems	
Isometric or Cubic System Three axes of equal length intersect at 90° angles.	**Orthorhombic System** Three axes of unequal length intersect at 90° angles.
Tetragonal System Three axes intersect at 90° angles. The two horizontal axes are of equal length. The vertical axis is longer or shorter than the horizontal axes.	**Hexagonal System** Three horizontal axes of the same length intersect at 120° angles. The vertical axis is longer or shorter than the horizontal axes.
Monoclinic System Two of the three axes of unequal length intersect at 90° angles. The third axis is oblique to the others.	**Triclinic System** Three axes of unequal length are oblique to one another.

MATHPRACTICE

Calculating Density
A mineral sample has a mass (*m*) of 85 g and a volume (*V*) of 34 cm³. Use the equation below to calculate the sample's density (*D*).

$$D = \frac{m}{V}$$

density the ratio of the mass of a substance to the volume of the substance; commonly expressed as grams per cubic centimeter for solids and liquids and as grams per liter for gases

Crystal Shape
A mineral crystal forms in one of six basic shapes, as shown in **Table 2**. A certain mineral always has the same general shape because the atoms that form the mineral's crystals always combine in the same geometric pattern. But the six basic shapes can become more complex as a result of environmental conditions, such as temperature and pressure, during crystal growth.

Density
When handling equal-sized specimens of various minerals, you may notice that some feel heavier than others do. For example, a piece of galena feels heavier than a piece of quartz of the same size does. However, a more precise comparison can be made by measuring the density of a sample. **Density** is the ratio of the mass of a substance to the volume of the substance.

The density of a mineral depends on the kinds of atoms that the mineral has and depends on how closely the atoms are packed. Most of the common minerals in Earth's crust have densities between 2 and 3 g/cm³. However, the densities of minerals that contain heavy metals, such as lead, uranium, gold, and silver, range from 7 to 20 g/cm³. Thus, density helps identify heavier minerals more readily than it helps identify lighter ones.

Special Properties of Minerals

All minerals exhibit the properties that were described earlier in this section. However, a few minerals have some additional, special properties that can help identify those minerals.

Fluorescence and Phosphorescence

The mineral calcite is usually white in ordinary light, but in ultraviolet light, calcite often appears red. This ability to glow under ultraviolet light is called *fluorescence*. Fluorescent minerals absorb ultraviolet light and then produce visible light of various colors, as shown in **Figure 4**.

When subjected to ultraviolet light, some minerals will continue to glow after the ultraviolet light is turned off. This property is called *phosphorescence*. It is useful in the mining of phosphorescent minerals such as eucryptite, which is an ore of lithium.

Chatoyancy and Asterism

In reflected light, some minerals display a silky appearance that is called *chatoyancy* (shuh TOY uhn see). This effect is also called the *cat's-eye effect*. The word *chatoyancy* comes from the French word *chat*, which means "cat," and from *oeil*, which means "eye." Chatoyancy is the result of closely packed parallel fibers within the mineral. A similar effect called *asterism* is the phenomenon in which a six-sided star shape appears when a mineral reflects light.

 Reading Check What is the difference between chatoyancy and asterism? (See the Appendix for answers to Reading Checks.)

Figure 4 ▶ The fluorescent minerals calcite and willemite within this rock change colors as they are exposed to ordinary light (top) and ultraviolet light (bottom).

QuickLAB 10 min

Determining Density
Procedure IE.1d

1. Use a **triple-beam balance** to determine the mass of three similarly-sized **mineral samples** that have different masses. Record the mass of each mineral sample.
2. Fill a **graduated cylinder** with **70 mL of water.**
3. Add one mineral sample to the water in the graduated cylinder. Record the new volume after the mineral sample is added to the water.
4. Calculate the volume of the mineral sample by subtracting the 70 mL from the new volume.
5. Repeat steps 3 and 4 for the other two mineral samples.
6. Convert the volume of the mineral samples that you calculated in step 4 from milliliters to cubic centimeters by using the conversion: $1 \text{ mL} = 1 \text{ cm}^3$.

Analysis

1. Calculate the density of each mineral sample by using the following equation:
$$density = mass/volume$$
2. Compare the density of each mineral sample with the density of common minerals in Earth's crust. Compare the density of each mineral sample with minerals that contain a high percentage of heavy metals.
3. Do any of the mineral samples contain a high percentage of heavy metals? Explain your answer.

Figure 5 ▶ Some forms of the mineral calcite exhibit double refraction when light rays enter the crystal and split.

Double Refraction

Light rays bend as they pass through transparent minerals. This bending of light rays as they pass from one substance, such as air, to another, such as a mineral, is called *refraction*. Crystals of calcite and some other transparent minerals bend light in such a way that they produce a double image of any object viewed through them, as shown in **Figure 5**. This property is called *double refraction*. Double refraction takes place because light rays are split into two parts as they enter the crystal.

Magnetism

Magnets may attract small particles of some minerals that contain iron. Those minerals are also sometimes magnetic. In general, nonsilicate minerals that contain iron, such as magnetite, are more likely to be magnetic than other nonsilicate minerals are. Lodestone is a form of magnetite. Like a bar magnet, some pieces of lodestone have a north pole at one end and a south pole at the other. The needles of the first magnetic compasses were made of tiny slivers of lodestone.

Radioactivity

Some minerals have a property known as *radioactivity*. The arrangement of protons and neutrons in the nuclei of some atoms is unstable. Radioactivity results as unstable nuclei decay over time into stable nuclei by releasing particles and energy. A *Geiger counter* can be used to detect the released particles and, thus, to identify minerals that are radioactive. Uranium, U, and radium, Ra, are examples of radioactive elements. Pitchblende is the most common mineral that contains uranium. Other uranium-bearing minerals are carnotite, uraninite, and autunite.

Section 2 Review

1. **Describe** seven physical properties that help distinguish one mineral from another.

2. **Identify** the two main types of luster.

3. **Summarize** how you would determine the hardness of an unidentified mineral sample.

4. **Explain** why color is an unreliable clue to the identity of a mineral.

5. **List** five special properties that may help identify certain minerals.

6. **Explain** how magnetism can be useful for identifying minerals.

CRITICAL THINKING

7. **Evaluating Data** An unknown metal has a black streak and a density of 18 g/cm^3. Is the mineral more likely to be metallic or nonmetallic? IE.1d

8. **Analyzing Methods** Explain how phosphorescence is helpful in mining eucryptite. Describe other ways in which phosphorescent minerals might be used. IE.1d, IE.1l

CONCEPT MAPPING

9. Use the following terms to create a concept map: *luster, streak, fracture, hardness, Mohs hardness scale, streak plate, nonmetallic luster, metallic luster,* and *conchoidal fracture.*

Highlights

Sections

1 What Is a Mineral?

Key Terms

mineral, 103
silicate mineral, 104
nonsilicate mineral, 105
crystal, 106
silicon-oxygen tetrahedron, 106

Key Concepts

▶ A mineral is a natural, usually inorganic, crystalline solid that has a characteristic chemical composition, a regularly repeating internal structure, and a characteristic set of physical properties.

▶ The two main groups of minerals are silicate minerals and nonsilicate minerals.

▶ The six major groups of nonsilicate minerals are carbonates, halides, native elements, oxides, sulfates, and sulfides.

▶ Silicate minerals have six types of crystalline structures based on the arrangement of the silicon-oxygen tetrahedra.

2 Identifying Minerals

mineralogist, 109
streak, 110
luster, 110
cleavage, 110
fracture, 110
Mohs hardness scale, 111
density, 112

▶ Seven physical properties that help distinguish one mineral from another are color, streak, luster, cleavage and fracture, hardness, crystal shape, and density.

▶ Special properties such as fluorescence and phosphorescence, chatoyancy and asterism, double refraction, magnetism, and radioactivity can aid in the identification of certain minerals.

Using Key Terms

Use each of the following terms in a separate sentence.

1. *silicon-oxygen tetrahedron*
2. *mineral*
3. *Mohs hardness scale*
4. *cleavage*

For each pair of terms, explain how the meanings of the terms differ.

5. *mineral* and *crystal*
6. *silicate mineral* and *nonsilicate mineral*
7. *luster* and *streak*
8. *fluorescence* and *phosphorescence*

Understanding Key Concepts

9. The most common silicate minerals are the
   a. feldspars.
   b. halides.
   c. carbonates.
   d. sulfates.

10. Ninety-six percent of Earth's crust is made up of
    a. sulfur and lead.
    b. silicate minerals.
    c. copper and aluminum.
    d. nonsilicate minerals.

11. An example of a mineral that has a basic structure consisting of isolated tetrahedra linked by atoms of other elements is
    a. mica.
    b. olivine.
    c. quartz.
    d. feldspar.

12. When two single chains of tetrahedra bond to each other, the result is called a
    a. single-chain silicate.
    b. sheet silicate.
    c. framework silicate.
    d. double-chain silicate.

13. The words *waxy, pearly,* and *dull* describe a mineral's
    a. luster.
    b. hardness.
    c. streak.
    d. fluorescence.

14. The words *uneven* and *splintery* describe a mineral's
    a. cleavage.
    b. fracture.
    c. hardness.
    d. luster.

15. The ratio of a mineral's mass to its volume is the mineral's
    a. atomic weight.
    b. density.
    c. mass.
    d. weight.

16. Double refraction is a property of some crystals of
    a. mica.
    b. feldspar.
    c. calcite.
    d. galena.

Short Answer

17. Describe the six major classes of nonsilicate minerals.

18. List the 10 most common rock-forming minerals.

19. Why do minerals that have the nonsilicate crystalline structure called *closest packing* have high density?

20. Which of the two main groups of minerals is more abundant in Earth's crust?

21. Which of the following mineral groups, if any, contain silicon: carbonates, halides, or sulfides?

22. Describe the tetrahedral arrangement of olivine.

23. Summarize the characteristics that a substance must have to be classified as a mineral.

24. How many oxygen ions and silicon ions are in a silicon-oxygen tetrahedron?

Mining Engineer

"At first, I wasn't interested in being a mining engineer," remembers Jami Girard-Dwyer. "I wanted to get a degree in computer science and write programs. Then, I took a course entitled 'Introduction to Mining Engineering' and got a summer job at a nearby gold mine. I became fascinated with the process of extracting ore from Earth and coming up with a finished product."

Computers and Mining

Girard-Dwyer realized that her knowledge of computers had many applications in the mining industry. "I began writing computer programs to help mining operations work more efficiently," she recalls. "I became very interested in learning how mine openings could be designed to ensure that they wouldn't collapse on workers or equipment."

Rewards

Now a mining engineer for the National Institute for Occupational Safety and Health (NIOSH), Girard-Dwyer helps keep miners safe. "The most rewarding part of my job is helping mines develop safer environments so that nobody gets hurt," she says. "I study the health and safety of the mine workers. I also do research to help prevent accidents, injuries, and fatalities." Her work frequently requires her to travel to visit mines. She says, "At a mine site, I will install monitoring equipment and computers to collect data about a particular type of problem."

"Without mining, we would not have cars, electricity, computers, . . . or any of the items that we often take for granted in today's society."

—Jami Girard-Dwyer

I will then use computers to analyze the data and make recommendations to the mining company based on the results."

Mines may be located on the surface of Earth (open-pit or strip mines) or thousands of feet underground. "Metals such as gold or silver often come to mind when people think of mining," says Girard-Dwyer. "But there are also mines that recover coal for creating energy, silica for making glass, and special industrial minerals for manufacturing everything from kitty litter to toothpaste!" Each mining operation uses unique methods to recover the minerals.

◀ Miners, such as this one drilling for coal in Utah, rely on mining engineers like Girard-Dwyer to help develop safe working environments.

SCiLINKS®

NSTA
Developed and maintained by the National Science Teachers Association

For a variety of links related to this subject, go to www.scilinks.org

Topic: Careers in Earth Science
SciLinks code: HQ60222

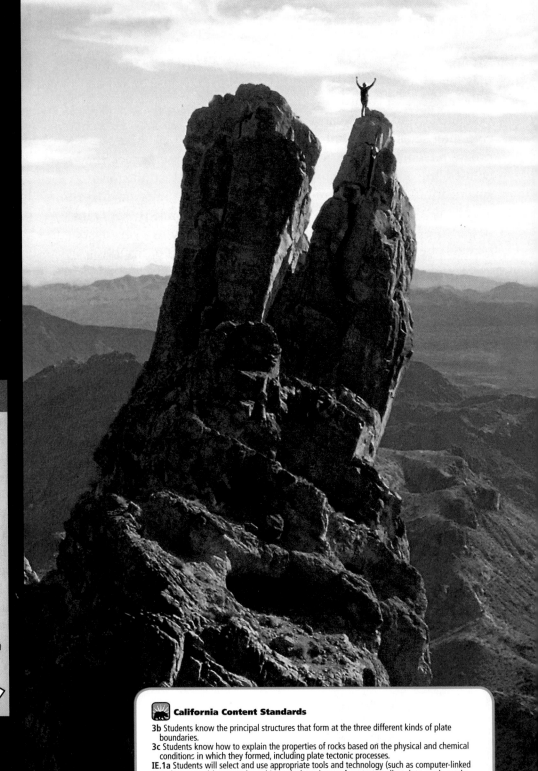

Chapter 6   Rocks

Sections

1 Rocks and the Rock Cycle

2 Igneous Rock

3 Sedimentary Rock

4 Metamorphic Rock

What You'll Learn

- How the processes that form rock determine the properties of rocks
- How scientists classify rocks

Why It's Relevant

Understanding how rocks form provides a basis for understanding the properties of different types of rocks.

PRE-READING ACTIVITY

Pyramid
Before you read this chapter, create the **FoldNote** entitled "Pyramid" described in the Skills Handbook section of the Appendix. Label the sides of the pyramid with "Igneous rock," "Sedimentary rock," and "Metamorphic rock." As you read the chapter, define each type of rock, and write characteristics of each type of rock on the appropriate pyramid side.

▶ Eagletail Peak stands more than 1005 m above Sonoran Desert in Arizona and is composed of sedimentary rock. Sedimentary rock is one of the three major types of rock.

California Content Standards

3b Students know the principal structures that form at the three different kinds of plate boundaries.
3c Students know how to explain the properties of rocks based on the physical and chemical conditions in which they formed, including plate tectonic processes.
IE.1a Students will select and use appropriate tools and technology (such as computer-linked probes, spreadsheets, and graphing calculators) to perform tests, collect data, analyze relationships and display data.
IE.1d Students will formulate explanations using logic and evidence.
IE.1h Students will read and interpret topographic and geologic maps.
IE.1i Students will analyze the locations, sequences, or time intervals that are characteristic of natural phenomena (e.g., relative ages of rocks, locations of planets over time, and succession of species in an ecosystem).

Igneous Rock

California
Content
Standards

3c Students know how to explain the properties of rocks based on the physical and chemical conditions in which they formed, including plate tectonic processes.
IE.1d Students will formulate explanations using logic and evidence.

When magma cools and hardens, it forms **igneous rock.** Because minerals crystallize as igneous rock forms from magma, most igneous rock can be identified as *crystalline,* or made of crystals. The chemical composition of minerals in the rock and the rock's texture determine the identity of the igneous rock.

The Formation of Magma

Magma forms when rock melts. The three factors that affect whether rock melts include temperature, pressure, and the presence of fluids in the rock. Rock melts when the temperature of the rock increases to above the melting point of minerals in the rock. The melting temperature is determined by the chemical composition of the minerals in the rock. Rock also melts when excess pressure is removed from rock that is hotter than its melting point. Rock may melt when fluids such as water are added to hot rock. The addition of fluids generally decreases the melting point of certain minerals in the rock, which can cause those minerals to melt.

Partial Melting

Different minerals have different melting points, and minerals that have lower melting points are the first minerals to melt. When the first minerals melt, the magma that forms has a specific composition. As the temperature increases and as other minerals melt, the magma's composition changes. The process by which different minerals in rock melt at different temperatures is called *partial melting.* Partial melting is shown in **Figure 1.**

OBJECTIVES

▶ **Summarize** three factors that affect whether rock melts. 🐾 3c

▶ **Describe** how the cooling rate of magma and lava affects the texture of igneous rocks. 🐾 3c

▶ **Classify** igneous rocks according to their composition and texture. 🐾 3c

▶ **Describe** intrusive and extrusive igneous rock structures. 🐾 3b

KEY TERMS

igneous rock
intrusive igneous rock
extrusive igneous rock
felsic
mafic

igneous rock rock that forms when magma cools and solidifies

Figure 1 ▶ How Magma Forms by Partial Melting

This solid rock contains the minerals quartz (yellow), feldspar (gray), biotite (brown), and hornblende (green).

The first minerals that melt are quartz and some types of feldspars. The orange background represents magma.

Minerals such as biotite and hornblende generally melt last, which changes the composition of the magma.

Figure 2 ▶ As the temperature decreases, the first minerals to crystallize from magma are minerals that have the highest freezing points, such as biotite and hornblende. As the magma changes composition and cools, minerals that have lower freezing points form.

Fractional Crystallization

When magma cools, the cooling process is the reverse of the process of partial melting. Chemicals in magma combine to form minerals, and each mineral has a different freezing point. Minerals that have the highest freezing points crystallize first. As those minerals crystallize, they remove specific chemicals from the magma and change the composition of the magma. As the composition changes, new minerals begin to form. The crystallization and removal of different minerals from the cooling magma is called *fractional crystallization* and is shown in **Figure 2.**

Minerals that form during fractional crystallization tend to settle to the bottom of the magma chamber or to stick to the ceiling and walls of the magma chamber. Crystals that form early in the process are commonly the largest because they have the longest time to grow. In some crystals, the chemical composition of the inner part of the crystal differs from the composition of the outer parts of the crystal. This difference occurs because the magma's composition changed while the crystal was growing.

QuickLAB   20 min

Crystal Formation
Procedure 3c, IE.1d

1. Add the following until **three glass jars** are 2/3 full: glass 1—water and **ice cubes**; glass 2—water at room temperature; and glass 3—**hot tap water**.

2. In a small **sauce pan**, mix **120 mL of Epsom salts** in **120 mL of water**. Heat the mixture on a **hot plate** over low heat. Do not let the mixture boil. Stir the mixture with a **spoon or stirring rod** until no more crystals dissolve.

3. Using a **funnel**, carefully pour equal amounts of the Epsom salts mixture into **three test tubes**. Use **tongs** to steady the test tubes as you pour. Drop a few crystals of Epsom salt into each test tube, and gently shake each one. Place one test tube into each glass jar.

4. Observe the solutions as they cool for 15 minutes. Let the glasses sit overnight, and examine the solutions again after 24 hours.

Analysis

1. In which test tube are the crystals the largest?
2. In which test tube are the crystals the smallest?
3. How does the rate of cooling affect the size of the crystals that form? Explain your answer.
4. How are the differing rates of crystal formation you observed related to igneous rock formation?
5. How would you change the procedure to obtain larger crystals of Epsom salts? Explain your answer.

Textures of Igneous Rocks

Igneous rocks are classified according to where magma cools and hardens. Magma that cools deep inside the crust forms **intrusive igneous rock.** The magma that forms these rocks intrudes, or enters, into other rock masses beneath Earth's surface. The magma then slowly cools and hardens. Lava that cools at Earth's surface forms **extrusive igneous rock.**

Intrusive and extrusive igneous rocks differ from each other not only in where they form but also in the size of their crystals or grains. The texture of igneous rock is determined by the size of the crystals in the rock. The size of the crystals is determined mainly by the cooling rate of the magma. Examples of different textures of igneous rocks are shown in **Figure 3.**

Coarse-Grained Igneous Rock

Intrusive igneous rocks commonly have large mineral crystals. The slow loss of heat allows the minerals in the cooling magma to form large, well-developed crystals. Igneous rocks that are composed of large mineral grains are described as having a *coarse-grained texture.* An example of a coarse-grained igneous rock is granite. The upper part of the continental crust is made mostly of granite.

Fine-Grained Igneous Rock

Many extrusive igneous rocks are composed of small mineral grains that cannot be seen by the unaided eye. Because these rocks form when magma cools rapidly, large crystals are unable to form. Igneous rocks that are composed of small crystals are described as having a *fine-grained texture.* Examples of common fine-grained igneous rocks are basalt and rhyolite (RIE uh LIET).

Other Igneous Rock Textures

Some igneous rock forms when magma cools slowly at first but then cools more rapidly as it nears Earth's surface. This type of cooling produces large crystals embedded within a mass of smaller ones. Igneous rock that has a mixture of large and small crystals has a *porphyritic texture* (POHR fuh RIT ik TEKS chuhr).

When a highly viscous magma cools quickly, few crystals are able to grow. If such magma contains a very small percentage of dissolved gases, a rock that has a *glassy* texture, such as obsidian forms. When this type of magma contains a large percentage of dissolved gases and cools rapidly, the gases become trapped as bubbles in the rock that forms. The rapid cooling process produces a rock full of holes called *vesicles,* such as those in pumice. This type of rock is said to have a *vesicular texture.*

✔ **Reading Check** What is the difference between fine-grained and coarse-grained igneous rock? (See the Appendix for answers to Reading Checks.)

intrusive igneous rock rock formed from the cooling and solidification of magma beneath Earth's surface

extrusive igneous rock rock that forms from the cooling and solidification of lava at Earth's surface

Figure 3 ▶ Igneous Rock Textures

Coarse-grained (granite)

Fine-grained (rhyolite)

Porphyritic (granite)

Glassy (obsidian)

Vesicular (pumice)

Figure 4 ▶ Felsic rocks, such as the outcropping and hand sample shown above (left), have light coloring. Mafic rocks (right) are usually darker in color.

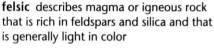

felsic describes magma or igneous rock that is rich in feldspars and silica and that is generally light in color

mafic describes magma or igneous rock that is rich in magnesium and iron and that is generally dark in color

Composition of Igneous Rocks

The mineral composition of an igneous rock is determined by the chemical composition of the magma from which the rock formed. Each type of igneous rock has a specific mineral composition. Geologists divide igneous rock into three families—felsic, mafic (MAF ik), and intermediate. Each of the three families has a different mineral composition. Examples of rock from the felsic and mafic families are shown in **Figure 4.**

Felsic Rock

Rock in the **felsic** family forms from magma that contains a large proportion of silica. Felsic rock generally has the light coloring of its main mineral components, potassium feldspar and quartz. Felsic rock commonly also contains plagioclase feldspar, biotite mica, and muscovite mica. The felsic family includes many common rocks, such as granite, rhyolite, obsidian, and pumice.

Mafic Rock

Rock in the **mafic** family forms from magma that contains lower proportions of silica than felsic rock does and that is rich in iron and magnesium. The main mineral components of rock in this family are plagioclase feldspar and pyroxene minerals. Mafic rock may also include dark-colored *ferromagnesian minerals,* such as hornblende. These ferromagnesian components, as well as the mineral olivine, give mafic rock a dark color. The mafic family includes the common rocks basalt and gabbro.

Intermediate Rocks

Rocks of the intermediate family are made up of the minerals plagioclase feldspar, hornblende, pyroxene, and biotite mica. Rocks in the intermediate family contain lower proportions of silica than rocks in the felsic family do but contain higher proportions of silica than rocks in the mafic family contain. Rocks in the intermediate family include diorite and andesite.

Intrusive Igneous Rock Structures

Igneous rock masses that form underground are called *intrusions*. Intrusions form when magma intrudes, or enters, into other rock masses and then cools deep inside Earth's crust. A variety of intrusions are shown in **Figure 5.**

Batholiths and Stocks

The largest of all intrusions are called *batholiths*. Batholiths are intrusive formations that spread over at least 100 km² when they are exposed on Earth's surface. The word *batholith* means "deep rock." Batholiths were once thought to extend to great depths beneath Earth's surface. However, studies have determined that many batholiths extend only several thousand meters below the surface. Batholiths form the cores of many mountain ranges, such as the Sierra Nevadas in California. The largest batholith in North America forms the core of the Coast Range in British Columbia. Another type of intrusion is called a *stock*. Stocks are similar to batholiths but cover less than 100 km² at the surface.

Laccoliths

When magma flows between rock layers and spreads upward, it sometimes pushes the overlying rock layers into a dome. The base of the intrusion is parallel to the rock layer beneath it. This type of intrusion is called a *laccolith*. The word *laccolith* means "lake of rock." Laccoliths commonly occur in groups and can sometimes be identified by the small dome-shaped mountains they form on Earth's surface. Many laccoliths are located beneath the Black Hills of South Dakota.

Reading Check What is the difference between stocks and batholiths? (See the Appendix for answers to Reading Checks.)

Sills and Dikes

When magma flows between the layers of rock and hardens, a *sill* forms. A sill lies parallel to the layers of rock that surround it, even if the layers are tilted. Sills vary in thickness from a few centimeters to hundreds of meters.

Magma sometimes forces through rock layers by following existing vertical fractures or by creating new ones. When the magma solidifies, a *dike* forms. Dikes cut across rock layers rather than lying parallel to the rock layers. Dikes are common in areas of volcanic activity.

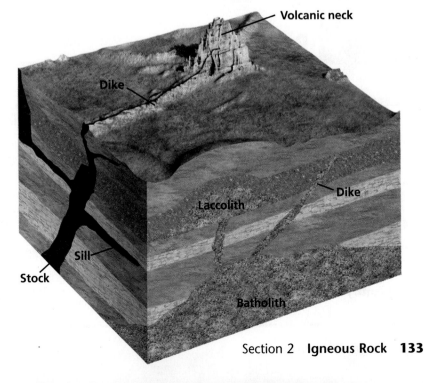

Figure 5 ▶ Igneous intrusions create a number of unique landforms. *What is the difference between a dike and a sill?*

Volcanic neck

Dike

Dike

Laccolith

Sill

Stock

Batholith

Figure 6 ▶ Shiprock, in New Mexico, is an example of a volcanic neck that was exposed by erosion.

Extrusive Igneous Rock Structures

Igneous rock masses that form on Earth's surface are called *extrusions*. A *volcano* is a vent through which magma, gases, or volcanic ash is expelled. When a volcanic eruption stops, the magma in the vent may cool to form rock. Eventually, the soft parts of the volcano are eroded by wind and water, and only the hardest rock in the vent remains. The solidified central vent is called a *volcanic neck*. Narrow dikes that sometimes radiate from the neck may also be exposed. A dramatic example of a volcanic neck called Shiprock is shown in **Figure 6.**

Extrusive igneous rock may also take other forms. Many extrusions are simply flat masses of rock called *lava flows*. A series of lava flows that cover a vast area with thick rock is known as a *lava plateau*. Volcanic ash deposits, also commonly called *tuff*, form when a volcano releases ash and other solid particles during an eruption. Tuff deposits can be several hundred meters thick and can cover areas of several hundred kilometers.

Section 2 Review

1. **Summarize** three factors that affect the melting of rock. 🐾 3c

2. **Contrast** partial melting and fractional crystallization. 🐾 3c

3. **Describe** how the cooling rate of magma affects the texture of igneous rock. 🐾 3c

4. **Name** the three families of igneous rocks, and identify their specific mineral compositions. 🐾 3c

5. **Describe** five intrusive igneous rock structures. 🐾 3b

6. **Identify** four extrusive igneous rock structures. 🐾 3b

CRITICAL THINKING

7. **Applying Ideas** If you wanted to create a rock that has large crystals in a laboratory, what conditions would you have to control? Explain your answer. 🐾 3c, IE.1d

8. **Applying Ideas** An unidentified, light-colored igneous rock is made up of potassium feldspar and quartz. To what family of igneous rocks does the rock belong? Explain your answer. 🐾 3c, IE.1d

CONCEPT MAPPING

9. Use the following terms to create a concept map: *igneous rock, magma, coarse grained, fine grained, felsic, mafic,* and *intermediate.* 🐾 3c

Sedimentary Rock

3c Students know how to explain the properties of rocks based on the physical and chemical conditions in which they formed, including plate tectonic processes.
IE.1d Students will formulate explanations using logic and evidence.

California Content Standards

Loose fragments of rock, minerals, and organic material that result from natural processes, including the physical breakdown of rocks, are called *sediment*. Most sedimentary rock is made up of combinations of different types of sediment. The characteristics of sedimentary rock are determined by the source of the sediment, the way the sediment was moved, and the conditions under which the sediment was deposited.

Formation of Sedimentary Rocks

After sediments form, they are generally transported by wind, water, or ice to a new location. The source of the sediment determines the sediment's composition. As the sediment moves, its characteristics change as it is physically broken down or chemically altered. Eventually, the loose sediment is deposited.

Two main processes convert loose sediment to sedimentary rock—compaction and cementation. **Compaction,** as shown in **Figure 1,** is the process in which sediment is squeezed and in which the size of the pore space between sediment grains is reduced by the weight and pressure of overlying layers. **Cementation** is the process in which sediments are glued together by minerals that are deposited by water. As water moves through the sediment, minerals precipitate from the water, surround the sediment grains, and form a cement that holds the fragments together.

Geologists classify sedimentary rocks by the processes by which the rocks form and by the composition of the rocks. There are three main classes of sedimentary rocks— chemical, organic, and clastic. These classes contain their own classifications of sedimentary rocks that are grouped based on the shape, size, and composition of the sediments that form the rocks.

OBJECTIVES

▶ **Explain** the processes of compaction and cementation. 3c
▶ **Describe** how chemical and organic sedimentary rocks form. 3c
▶ **Describe** how clastic sedimentary rock forms. 3c
▶ **Identify** seven sedimentary rock features. 3c

KEY TERMS

compaction
cementation
chemical sedimentary rock
organic sedimentary rock
clastic sedimentary rock

compaction the process in which the volume and porosity of a sediment is decreased by the weight of overlying sediments as a result of burial beneath other sediments

cementation the process in which minerals precipitate into pore spaces between sediment grains and bind sediments together to form rock

Figure 1 ▶ Processes That Form Sedimentary Rock

When mud is deposited, there may be a lot of space between grains. During compaction, the grains are squeezed together, and the rock that forms takes up less space.

Overlying layers squeeze sediment.

50-60% water

10-20% water

When sand is deposited, there are many spaces between the grains. During cementation, water deposits minerals such as calcite or quartz in the spaces around the sand grains, which glues the grains together.

Pore spaces between sediment grains are empty.

Water moves through pore spaces.

Minerals deposited by water cement the grains together.

chemical sedimentary rock sedimentary rock that forms when minerals precipitate from a solution or settle from a suspension

organic sedimentary rock sedimentary rock that forms from the remains of plants or animals

Chemical Sedimentary Rock

Rock called **chemical sedimentary rock** forms from minerals that were once dissolved in water. Some chemical sedimentary rock forms when dissolved minerals precipitate out of water because of changing concentrations of chemicals.

One reason minerals precipitate is because of evaporation. When water evaporates, the minerals that were dissolved in the water are left behind. Eventually, the concentration of minerals in the remaining water becomes high enough to cause minerals to precipitate out of the water. The minerals left behind form rocks called *evaporites*. Gypsum and halite, or rock salt, are two examples of evaporites. The Bonneville Salt Flats near the Great Salt Lake in Utah are a good example of evaporite deposits.

Organic Sedimentary Rocks

The second class of sedimentary rock is **organic sedimentary rock**. Organic sedimentary rock is rock that forms from the remains of living things. Coal and some limestones are examples of organic sedimentary rocks. Coal forms from plant remains that are buried before they decay and are then compacted into matter that is composed mostly of carbon.

While chemical limestones precipitate from chemicals dissolved in water, organic limestones form when marine organisms, such as coral, clams, oysters, and plankton, remove the chemical components of the minerals calcite and aragonite from sea water. These organisms make their shells from aragonite. When they die, their shells eventually become limestone. This process of limestone formation is shown in **Figure 2.** Chalk is an example of limestone made up of the shells of tiny, one-celled marine organisms that settle to the ocean floor.

Figure 2 ▶ Organic Limestone Formation

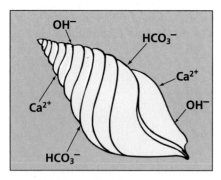

Organisms that live in lakes or oceans take chemicals from the water and produce the mineral calcium carbonate, $CaCO_3$. They use the $CaCO_3$ to build their shells or skeletons.

When the organisms die, the hard remains that are made of $CaCO_3$ settle to the lake or ocean floor.

The shells of the dead organisms pile up. Eventually, the layers are compacted and cemented to form limestone.

Figure 3 ▶ Types of Clastic Sedimentary Rock

Conglomerate is composed of rounded, pebble-sized fragments that are held together by a cement.

Breccia is similar to conglomerate, but breccia contains angular fragments.

Sandstone is made of small mineral grains that are cemented together.

Shale is made of flaky clay particles that compress into flat layers.

Clastic Sedimentary Rock

The third class of sedimentary rock is made of rock fragments that are carried away from their source by water, wind, or ice and left as deposits. Over time, the individual fragments may become compacted and cemented into solid rock. The rock formed from these deposits is called **clastic sedimentary rock.**

Clastic sedimentary rocks are classified by the size of the sediments they contain, as shown in **Figure 3.** One group consists of large fragments that are cemented together by finer sediments or by minerals. Rock that is composed of rounded fragments that range in size from fine mud to boulders is called a *conglomerate.* If the fragments are angular and have sharp corners, the rock is called a *breccia* (BRECH ee uh). In conglomerates and breccias, the individual pieces of sediment can be easily seen.

Another group of clastic sedimentary rocks is made up of sand-sized grains that have been cemented together. These rocks are called *sandstone.* Because quartz is one of the hardest common minerals, quartz is the major component of most sandstones. Many sandstones have pores between the sand grains through which fluids, such as groundwater, natural gas, and crude oil, can move.

A third group of clastic sedimentary rocks, called *shale,* consists of clay-sized particles that are cemented and compacted. The flaky clay particles are usually pressed into flat layers that will easily split apart.

✓ **Reading Check** Name three groups of clastic sedimentary rock. (See the Appendix for answers to Reading Checks.)

clastic sedimentary rock sedimentary rock that forms when fragments of preexisting rocks are compacted or cemented together

MATHPRACTICE

Sedimentation Rates The rate at which sediment accumulates is called the *sedimentation rate*. The sedimentation rate of an area is 1.5 mm per year. At this rate, how many years must pass for 10 cm of sediment to be deposited?

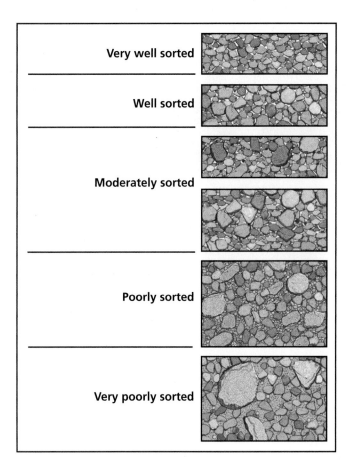

Very well sorted	
Well sorted	
Moderately sorted	
Poorly sorted	
Very poorly sorted	

Figure 4 ▶ Sorting of Sediments

Characteristics of Clastic Sediments

The physical characteristics of sediments are determined mainly by the way sediments were transported to the place where they are deposited. Sediments are transported by four main agents: water, ice, wind, and the effects of gravity. The speed with which the agent of erosion moves affects the size of sediment particles that can be carried and the distance that the particles will move. In general, both the distance the sediment is moved and the agent that moves the sediment determine the characteristics of that sediment.

Sorting

The tendency for currents of air or water to separate sediments according to size is called *sorting*. Sediments can be well sorted, poorly sorted, or somewhere in between, as shown in **Figure 4.** In well-sorted sediments, all of the grains are roughly the same size and shape. Poorly sorted sediment consists of grains that are many different sizes. The sorting of a sediment is the result of changes in the speed of the agent that is moving the sediment. For example, when a fast-moving stream enters a lake, the speed of the water decreases sharply. Because large grains are too heavy for the current to carry, these grains are deposited first. Fine grains can stay suspended in the water for much longer than large grains can. So, fine particles are commonly deposited farther from shore or on top of coarser sediments.

Angularity

As sediment is transported from its source to where it is deposited, the particles collide with each other and with other objects in their path. These collisions can cause the particles to change size and shape. When particles first break from the source rock, they tend to be angular and uneven. Particles that have moved long distances from the source tend to be more rounded and smooth. In general, the farther sediment travels from its source, the finer and smoother the particles of sediment become.

Sedimentary Rock Features

The setting in which sediment is deposited is called a *depositional environment*. Common depositional environments include rivers, deltas, beaches, and oceans. Each depositional environment has different characteristics that create specific structures in sedimentary rock. These features allow scientists to identify the depositional environment in which the rock formed.

Stratification

Layering of sedimentary rock, as shown in **Figure 5**, is called *stratification*. Stratification occurs when the conditions of sediment deposition change. The conditions may vary when there is a change in sediment type or of depositional environment. For example, a rise in sea level may cause an area that was once a beach to become a shallow ocean, which changes the type of sediment that is deposited in the area.

Stratified layers, or *beds*, vary in thickness depending on the length of time during which sediment is deposited and how much sediment is deposited. *Massive beds*, or beds that have no internal structures, form when similar sediment is deposited for long periods of time or when a large amount of sediment is deposited at one time.

Cross-beds and Graded Bedding

Some sedimentary rocks are characterized by slanting layers called *cross-beds* that form within beds. Cross-beds, which generally form in sand dunes or river beds, are shown in **Figure 5**.

When various sizes and kinds of materials are deposited within one layer, a type of stratification called *graded bedding* may occur. Graded bedding occurs when different sizes and shapes of sediment settle to different levels. Graded beds commonly transition from largest grains on the bottom to smallest grains on the top. However, certain depositional events, such as some mudflows, may cause *reverse grading*, in which the smallest grains are on the bottom and the largest grains are on top.

✓ **Reading Check** What is graded bedding? (See the Appendix for answers to Reading Checks.)

Quick LAB 10 min

Graded Bedding

Procedure 3c, IE.1d

1. Place **20 mL of water** into a small glass jar.
2. Pour **10 mL of poorly sorted sediment** into the jar. Place a **lid** securely on the jar.
3. Shake the jar vigorously for 1 min, and then let it sit still for 5 min.
4. Observe the settled sediment.

Analysis

1. Describe any sedimentary structures you observed.
2. Name two factors responsible for the sedimentary structures you observed.

Figure 5 ▶ Examples of Sedimentary Rock Structures

Stratification

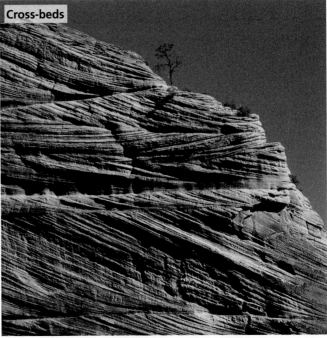

Cross-beds

Ripple Marks

Some sedimentary rocks clearly display *ripple marks*. Ripple marks are caused by the action of wind or water on sand. When the sand becomes sandstone, the ripple marks may be preserved. When scientists find ripple marks in sedimentary rock, the scientists know that the sediment was once part of a beach or a river bed.

Mud Cracks

The ground in **Figure 6** shows mud cracks, which are another feature of sedimentary rock. Mud cracks form when muddy deposits dry and shrink. The shrinking causes the drying mud to crack. A river's flood plain or a dry lake bed is a common place to find mud cracks. Once the area is flooded again, new deposits may fill in the cracks and preserve their features when the mud hardens to solid rock.

Fossils and Concretions

The remains or traces of ancient plants and animals, called *fossils,* may be preserved in sedimentary rock. As sediments pile up, plant and animal remains are buried. Hard parts of these remains may be preserved in the rock. More often, even the hard parts dissolve and leave only impressions in the rock. Sedimentary rocks sometimes contain lumps of rock that have a composition that is different from that of the main rock body. These lumps are known as *concretions*. Concretions form when minerals precipitate from fluids and build up around a nucleus. Groundwater sometimes deposits dissolved minerals inside cavities in sedimentary rock. The minerals may crystallize inside the cavities to form a special type of rock called a *geode*.

Figure 6 ▶ This dry and mud-cracked river bed is in Nagasaki, Japan. This river bed is the site of a future dam project.

Section 3 Review

1. **Explain** how the processes of compaction and cementation form sedimentary rock. 3c

2. **Describe** how chemical and organic sedimentary rocks form, and give two examples of each. 3c

3. **Describe** how clastic sedimentary rock differs from chemical and organic sedimentary rock. 3c

4. **Explain** how the physical characteristics of sediments change during transport. 3c

5. **Identify** seven features that you can use to identify the depositional environment in which sedimentary rocks formed. 3c

CRITICAL THINKING

6. **Making Comparisons** Compare the histories of rounded, smooth rocks and angular, uneven rocks. 3c, IE.1d

7. **Identifying Relationships** Which of the following would most effectively sort sediments: a fast-moving river or a small, slow-moving stream? Explain your answer. 3c, IE.1d

CONCEPT MAPPING

8. Use the following terms to create a concept map: *cementation, clastic sedimentary rock, sedimentary rock, chemical sedimentary rock, compaction,* and *organic sedimentary rock.* 3c

Section 4 — Metamorphic Rock

3c Students know how to explain the properties of rocks based on the physical and chemical conditions in which they formed, including plate tectonic processes.
IE.1d Students will formulate explanations using logic and evidence.

The process by which heat, pressure, or chemical processes change one type of rock to another is called **metamorphism.** Most metamorphic rock, or rock that has undergone metamorphism, forms deep within Earth's crust. All metamorphic rock forms from existing igneous, sedimentary, or metamorphic rock.

Formation of Metamorphic Rocks

During metamorphism, heat, pressure, and hot fluids cause some minerals to change into other minerals. Minerals may also change in size or shape, or they may separate into parallel bands that give the rock a layered appearance. Hot fluids from magma may circulate through the rock and change the mineral composition of the rock by dissolving some materials and by adding others. All of these changes are part of metamorphism.

The type of rock that forms because of metamorphism can indicate the conditions that were in place when the original rock changed, as shown in **Figure 1.** The composition of the rock being metamorphosed, the amount and direction of heat and pressure, and the presence or absence of certain fluids cause different combinations of minerals to form.

Two types of metamorphism occur in Earth's crust. One type occurs when small volumes of rock come into contact with magma. The second type occurs when large areas of Earth's crust are affected by the heat and pressure that is caused by the movement and collisions of Earth's giant tectonic plates.

OBJECTIVES

▶ **Describe** the process of metamorphism. 3c
▶ **Explain** the difference between regional and contact metamorphism. 3c
▶ **Distinguish** between foliated and nonfoliated metamorphic rocks, and give an example of each. 3c

KEY TERMS

metamorphism
contact metamorphism
regional metamorphism
foliation
nonfoliated

metamorphism the process in which one type of rock changes into metamorphic rock because of chemical processes or changes in temperature and pressure

Figure 1 ▶ Indicators of Metamorphic Conditions

Slate is a metamorphic rock that commonly forms in the outer zone of metamorphism around a body of magma where clay-rich rock is exposed to relatively small amounts of heat.

Hornfels is a metamorphic rock that forms in the innermost zone of metamorphism, where clay-rich rock is exposed to large amounts of heat from the magma.

Magma

Contact Metamorphism

When magma comes into contact with existing rock, heat from the magma can change the structure and mineral composition of the surrounding rock by a process called **contact metamorphism.** During contact metamorphism only a small area of rock that surrounds the hot magma is changed by the magma's heat. Hot chemical fluids moving through fractures may also cause changes in the surrounding rock during contact metamorphism.

Regional Metamorphism

Metamorphism sometimes occurs over an area of thousands of square kilometers during periods of high tectonic activity, such as when mountain ranges form. The type of metamorphism that occurs over a large area is called **regional metamorphism.**

The movement of one tectonic plate against another generates tremendous heat and pressure in the rocks at the edges of the tectonic plates. The heat and pressure cause chemical changes in the minerals of the rock. Most metamorphic rock forms as a result of regional metamorphism. However, volcanism and movement of magma often accompany tectonic activity. Thus, rocks that are formed by contact metamorphism are also commonly discovered where regional metamorphism has occurred.

✓ Reading Check How are minerals affected by regional metamorphism? (See the Appendix for answers to Reading Checks.)

> **contact metamorphism** a change in the texture, structure, or chemical composition of a rock due to contact with magma
>
> **regional metamorphism** a change in the texture, structure, or chemical composition of a rock due to changes in temperature and pressure over a large area, generally as a result of tectonic forces

---

Connection to PHYSICS

Directed Stress

The agents that cause metamorphism are temperature, pressure, chemically active fluids, and directed stress. When one of these conditions changes in a rock's environment, the minerals in the rock move from a stable state to an unstable state. This instability causes the rock to change, or metamorphose, to reach a more stable state in the new conditions.

Stress is the amount of force per unit area.

$$\sigma = \frac{Force}{Area}$$

Stress can be caused by fluids that are trapped in the rock or by the load of overlying and surrounding rock. At about 3.3 km below the surface of Earth's crust, the pressure of overlying rock is great enough to metamorphose rock.

In general, stress affects rock equally in all directions. However, sometimes, stresses acting in particular directions exceed the mean stress on the rock. This type of stress is called *directed stress*, and it can act in three ways. *Tension* is stress that expands the rock or pulls the rock apart. *Compression* is stress that squeezes the rock. *Shear stress* is stress that pushes different parts of a body of rock in different directions.

Compression of rock during metamorphism may form tiny folds, like the ones shown here.

Classification of Metamorphic Rocks

Minerals in the original rock help determine the mineral composition of the metamorphosed rock. As the original rock is exposed to changes in heat and pressure, the minerals in the original rock often combine chemically to form new minerals. While metamorphic rocks are classified by chemical composition, they are first classified according to their texture. Metamorphic rocks have either a foliated texture or a nonfoliated texture.

Foliated Rocks

The metamorphic rock texture in which minerals are arranged in planes or bands is called **foliation.** Foliated rock can form in one of two ways. Extreme pressure may cause the mineral crystals in the rock to realign or regrow to form parallel bands. Foliation also occurs as minerals that have different compositions separate to produce a series of alternating dark and light bands.

Foliated metamorphic rocks include the common rocks slate, schist, and gneiss (NIES). Slate forms when pressure is exerted on the sedimentary rock shale, which contains clay minerals that are flat and thin. The fine-grained minerals in slate are compressed into thin layers, which split easily into flat sheets. Flat sheets of slate are used in building materials, such as roof tiles or walkway stones.

When large amounts of heat and pressure are exerted on slate, a coarse-grained metamorphic rock known as *schist* may form. Deep underground, intense heat and pressure may cause the minerals in schist to separate into bands as the minerals recrystallize. The metamorphosed rock that has bands of light and dark minerals is called *gneiss*. Gneiss is shown in **Figure 2.**

foliation the metamorphic rock texture in which mineral grains are arranged in planes or bands

For a variety of links related to this subject, go to www.scilinks.org

Topic: Metamorphic Rock
SciLinks code: HQ60949

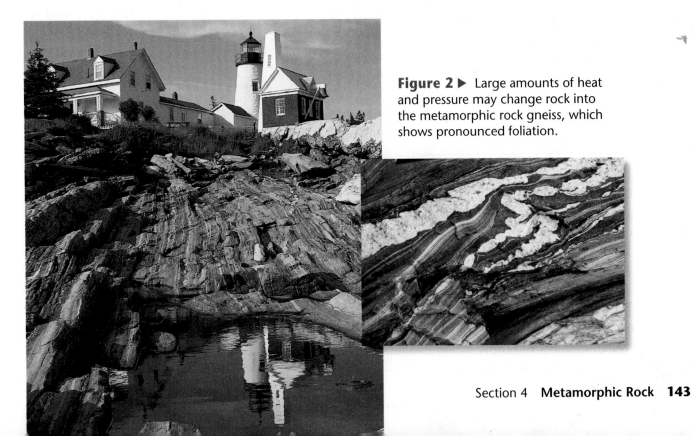

Figure 2 ▶ Large amounts of heat and pressure may change rock into the metamorphic rock gneiss, which shows pronounced foliation.

Nonfoliated Rocks

Rocks that do not have bands or aligned minerals are **nonfoliated**. Most nonfoliated metamorphic rocks share at least one of two main characteristics. First, the original rock that is metamorphosed may contain grains of only one mineral or contains very small amounts of other minerals. Thus, the rock does not form compositional bands when it is metamorphosed. Second, the original rock may contain grains that are round or square. Because the grains do not have some long and some short sides, these grains do not change position when exposed to pressure in one direction.

Quartzite is one common nonfoliated rock. Quartzite forms when quartz sandstone is metamorphosed. Because quartzite is very hard and durable, it is resistant to weathering. For this reason, quartzite remains after weaker rocks around it have eroded and may form hills or mountains.

Marble, the beautiful stone that is used for building monuments and statues, is a metamorphic rock that forms from the compression of limestone. The Parthenon, which is shown in **Figure 3,** has been standing in Greece for more than 1,400 years. However, the calcium carbonate in marble is susceptible to accelerated chemical weathering by acid rain, which is caused by air pollution. Many ancient marble structures and sculptures are being damaged by acid rain.

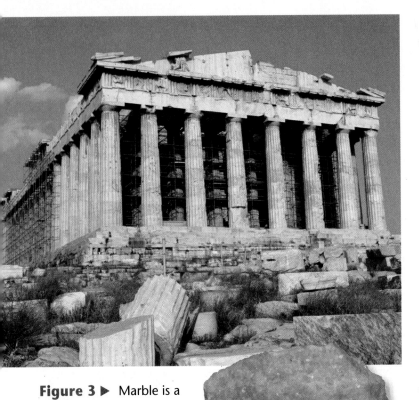

Figure 3 ▶ Marble is a nonfoliated metamorphic rock that is used as building and sculpting material.

nonfoliated the metamorphic rock texture in which mineral grains are not arranged in planes or bands

---

Section 4 Review

1. **Describe** the process of metamorphism. 3c

2. **Explain** the difference between regional and contact metamorphism. 3c

3. **Distinguish** between foliated and nonfoliated metamorphic rocks. 3c

4. **Identify** two foliated metamorphic rocks and two nonfoliated metamorphic rocks. 3c

CRITICAL THINKING

5. **Analyzing Relationships** What do a butterfly and metamorphic rock have in common? IE.1d

6. **Making Comparisons** If you have samples of the two metamorphic rocks slate and hornfels, what can you say about the history of each rock? 3c

7. **Identifying Relationships** The Himalaya Mountains are located on a boundary between two colliding tectonic plates. Would most of the metamorphic rock in that area occur in small patches or in wide regions? Explain your answer. 3c, IE.1d

CONCEPT MAPPING

8. Use the following terms to create a concept map: *contact metamorphism, foliated, regional metamorphism, metamorphic rock,* and *nonfoliated.* 3c

---

Sections

1 Rocks and the Rock Cycle

2 Igneous Rock

3 Sedimentary Rock

4 Metamorphic Rock

Key Terms

rock cycle, 126
Bowen's reaction series, 127

igneous rock, 129
intrusive igneous rock, 131
extrusive igneous rock, 131
felsic, 132
mafic, 132

compaction, 135
cementation, 135
chemical sedimentary rock, 136
organic sedimentary rock, 136
clastic sedimentary rock, 137

metamorphism, 141
contact metamorphism, 142
regional metamorphism, 142
foliation, 143
nonfoliated, 144

Key Concepts

▶ Rocks are classified into three major types based on how they form. These types are igneous rock, sedimentary rock, and metamorphic rock.

▶ In the rock cycle, rocks change from one type into another.

▶ The different minerals in igneous rocks form in a specific order as represented in Bowen's reaction series.

▶ The rate at which magma and lava cool determines the texture of igneous rock.

▶ Igneous rocks are divided into three families based on their mineral composition. These families are felsic, mafic, and intermediate.

▶ Igneous rock structures take two basic forms. They are intrusions and extrusions.

▶ Sedimentary rock forms in one of three ways. It may form from minerals once dissolved in water, from the remains of organisms, or from rock fragments.

▶ Sedimentary rocks have a number of identifiable features, including stratification, ripple marks, mud cracks, fossils, and concretions.

▶ Metamorphic rock forms as a result of heat and pressure caused by hot magma or tectonic plate movement.

▶ Metamorphic rocks can have a foliated or nonfoliated texture.

Using Key Terms

Use each of the following terms in a separate sentence.

1. *rock cycle* 🔳 3c
2. *Bowen's reaction series* 🔳 IE.1i
3. *sediment* 🔳 3c

For each pair of terms, explain how the meanings of the terms differ.

4. *igneous rock* and *metamorphic rock* 🔳 3c
5. *intrusive igneous rock* and *extrusive igneous rock* 🔳 3b, 3c
6. *chemical sedimentary rock* and *organic sedimentary rock* 🔳 3c
7. *contact metamorphism* and *regional metamorphism* 🔳 3c
8. *foliated* and *nonfoliated* 🔳 3c

Understanding Key Concepts

9. Intrusive igneous rocks are characterized by a coarse-grained texture because they contain 🔳 3b, 3c
   a. heavy elements.
   b. small crystals.
   c. large crystals.
   d. fragments of different sizes and shapes.

10. Light-colored igneous rocks are generally part of the 🔳 3c
    a. basalt family.
    b. intermediate family.
    c. felsic family.
    d. mafic family.

11. Magma that solidifies underground forms rock masses that are known as 🔳 3b
    a. extrusions.
    b. volcanic cones.
    c. lava plateaus.
    d. intrusions.

12. One example of an extrusion is a 🔳 3b
    a. stock.
    c. batholith.
    b. dike.
    d. lava plateau.

13. Sedimentary rock formed from rock fragments is called 🔳 3c
    a. organic.
    c. clastic.
    b. chemical.
    d. granite.

14. One example of chemical sedimentary rock is 🔳 3c
    a. an evaporite.
    c. sandstone.
    b. coal.
    d. breccia.

15. The splitting of slate into flat layers illustrates its 🔳 3c
    a. contact metamorphism.
    b. formation.
    c. sedimentation.
    d. foliation.

Short Answer

16. Describe partial melting and fractional crystallization. 🔳 3c

17. Name and define the three main types of rock. 🔳 3c

18. How do clastic sedimentary rocks differ from chemical and organic sedimentary rocks? 🔳 3c

19. What is Bowen's reaction series? 🔳 IE.1i

20. What factors affect the chemical and physical stability of rock? 🔳 3c

21. Describe three factors that affect whether rock melts. 🔳 3c

22. Why are some metamorphic rocks foliated while others are not? 🔳 3c

23. How does transport affect the size and shape of sediment particles? 🔳 3c

24. **Making Inferences** A certain rock is made up mostly of plagioclase feldspar and pyroxene minerals. It also includes olivine and hornblende. Will the rock have a light or dark coloring? Explain your answer. 3c, IE.1d

25. **Classifying Information** Explain how metamorphic rock can change into either of the other two types of rock through the rock cycle. 3c, IE.1d

26. **Applying Ideas** Imagine that you have found a piece of limestone, which is a sedimentary rock, that has strange-shaped lumps on it. Will the lumps have the same composition as the limestone? Explain your answer. 3c, IE.1d

27. **Analyzing Ideas** Which would be easier to break, the foliated rock slate or the nonfoliated rock quartzite? Explain your answer. 3c, IE.1d

Concept Mapping

28. Use the following terms to create a concept map: *rock cycle, foliated, igneous rock, intrusive, sedimentary rock, clastic sedimentary rock, metamorphic rock, chemical sedimentary rock, extrusive, organic sedimentary rock,* and *nonfoliated.* 3c

Math Skills

29. **Making Calculations** The gram formula weight (weight of one mole) of the mineral quartz is 60.1 g, and the gram formula weight of magnetite is 231.5 g. If you had 4 moles of magnetite, how many moles of quartz would be equal to the weight of the magnetite?

30. **Making Calculations** The gram formula weight (weight of one mole) of the mineral hematite, Fe_2O_3, is 159.7 g, and the gram formula weight of magnetite, Fe_3O_4, is 231.5 g. Which of the following would weigh more: half a mole of hematite or one-third of a mole of magnetite?

Writing Skills

31. **Outlining Topics** Outline the essential steps in the rock cycle. 3c

32. **Writing from Research** Find out what types of rock are most abundant in your state. Research the geologic processes that form those types of rock, and write a brief report that describes how the rocks in your state most likely formed. IE.1d

Interpreting Graphics

The graph below is a ternary diagram that shows the classification of some igneous rocks. Refer to the Skills Handbook in the Appendix for instructions on how to read a ternary diagram. Use the diagram to answer the questions that follow.

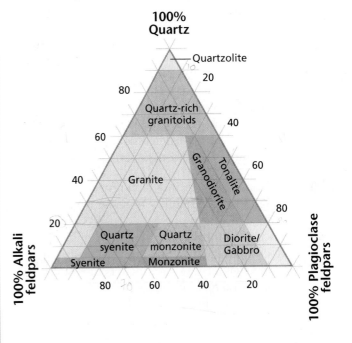

33. What is the maximum amount of quartz in a quartz syenite?

34. What would a rock that contains 30% quartz, 20% alkali feldspar, and 50% plagioclase feldspar be called? 3c

Understanding Concepts

Directions (1–10): For *each* question, write on a sheet of paper the number of the correct answer.

1 Which of the following statements best describes the formation of fossils?
A. An organism is caught in a lava flow.
B. An organism is covered by layers of sediment.
C. An organism is enveloped in magma that contains a high level of silica.
D. An organism is covered by rock during a landslide.

2 The large, well-developed crystals found in some samples of granite are a sign that
A. the lava from which it formed cooled rapidly.
B. the magma contained a lot of dissolved gases.
C. the lava from which it formed cooled slowly.
D. water deposited minerals in the rock cavities.

3 How does coal differ from breccia?
A. Coal is an example of sedimentary rock, and breccia is an example of metamorphic rock.
B. Coal is an example of metamorphic rock, and breccia is an example of igneous rock.
C. Coal is an example of organic rock, and breccia is an example of clastic rock.
D. Coal is an example of clastic rock, and breccia is an example of a conglomerate.

4 How does the order in which igneous rocks form relate to their ability to resist weathering agents?
A. Rocks that form last weather faster.
B. Rocks that form first are the most resistant.
C. Rocks that form last are the most resistant.
D. There is no relationship between the order of igneous rock formation and weathering.

5 To make a statue, an artist uses a stone that formed from another type of stone by compression and that lacks bands. Which type of rock is the artist using?
A. sedimentary
B. igneous
C. foliated metamorphic
D. nonfoliated metamorphic

6 Igneous rock forms many intrusive structures. Which of the following statements describes a large igneous structure that forms on Earth's surface?
A. a batholith, which spreads over at least 100 km^2
B. a stock, which covers less than 100 km^2
C. a laccolith, which forms when lava flows up between layers and forms a dome
D. a sill, which lies parallel to the layers of rock around it

7 Dikes and sills are two types of igneous intrusions. What is the difference between dikes and sills?
A. A dike is larger than a sill is.
B. A sill is larger than 100 km^2 while a dike is smaller than 100 km^2.
C. A dike cuts across rock layers while a sill lies between rock layers.
D. A sill forms on Earth's surface while a dike forms beneath Earth's surface.

8 What occurs when heat from nearby magma causes changes in the surrounding rocks?
A. contact metamorphism
B. fluid metamorphism
C. intrusive metamorphism
D. regional metamorphism

9 A mountain in the desert is found to be made from the remains of ancient ocean organisms. Which type of rock makes up the mountain?
A. chemical sedimentary rock
B. clastic sedimentary rock
C. organic sedimentary rock
D. fossilized sedimentary rock

10 Which of the following statements about the texture of sedimentary rock is most likely true?
A. Sedimentary rocks are always lumpy and made up of large pieces of older rocks.
B. Sedimentary rocks all contain alternating bands of lumpy and smooth textures.
C. Sedimentary rocks are always smooth and made up of small pieces of older rocks.
D. Sedimentary rocks have a variety of textures that depend on the size and type of pieces that make up the rock.

Moon Rock

NASA's Apollo missions brought 382 kg of lunar rock and soil back to Earth. In fact, moments after *Apollo 11* astronauts set foot on the moon in 1969, they began to fill two boxes with brown and gray moon rock. Later expeditions to the moon included vehicles that allowed a total of about 2,000 specimens to be collected.

Back on Earth

Geologists on Earth discovered that moon rocks are similar to Earth rocks in composition and in the way they formed. Geologists used their knowledge of Earth rock to analyze the moon rock and to learn about the geologic history of the moon.

Much of the rock material that was brought back from the moon was in a powdery form. This pulverized rock, called *regolith* (REG uh lith), covers much of the surface of the moon. Rock-dating methods show that regolith is one of the oldest materials on the moon's surface. From this information, geologists concluded that during the first billion years of the moon's existence, a shower of meteorites pulverized most of the moon's existing surface rock.

The Moon's History

The solid rocks on the moon are of two types—highland rocks and mare (MAW RAY) rocks. The highland rocks are igneous rocks that contain a large amount of plagioclase feldspar.

▶ This false-color image shows differences in the moon's composition. The blue areas have rock that contains large amounts of titanium.

Mare, which is Latin for "sea," refers to the dark areas on the lunar surface. Scientists discovered that mare rock formed after meteor showers made craters on the moon. Lava from inside the moon then poured onto the crater floors and covered large areas of the lunar surface. The lava then cooled and hardened into basalt about 4 billion years ago.

▲ *Apollo 12* astronaut Alan Bean holds a container designed to hold lunar soil (above). NASA scientist Andrea Mosie examines a volcanic moon rock (left).

Extension

1. **Making Inferences** Is mare rock classified as igneous, metamorphic, or sedimentary rock? Explain.

Chapter 7

Resources and Energy

Sections

1 **Mineral Resources**

2 **Nonrenewable Energy**

3 **Renewable Energy**

4 **Resources and Conservation**

What You'll Learn

- Which of Earth's resources humans use
- How resources are obtained
- How resource use affects the environment

Why It's Relevant

Supplies of some resources are diminishing. By understanding how these resources are used, scientists can search for sustainable, alternative resources.

PRE-READING ACTIVITY

Four-Corner Fold

Before you read this chapter, create the **FoldNote** entitled "Four-Corner Fold" described in the Skills Handbook section of the Appendix. Label each flap of the four-corner fold with a topic from the chapter. Write what you know about each topic under the appropriate flap. As you read the chapter, add other information that you learn.

▶ Hoover Dam generates hydroelectric power. Its construction also created Lake Mead, whose water is used to irrigate more than a million acres of land in California, Arizona, and Mexico.

Section 1 Mineral Resources

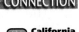
California Content Standards

7c Students know the movement of matter among reservoirs is driven by Earth's internal and external sources of energy.

IE.1d Students will formulate explanations using logic and evidence.

Earth's crust contains useful mineral resources. The processes that formed many of these resources took millions of years. Scientists have identified more than 3,000 different minerals in Earth's crust. Many of these mineral resources are mined for human use.

Mineral resources can be either *metals,* such as gold, Au, silver, Ag, and aluminum, Al, or *nonmetals,* such as sulfur, S, and quartz, SiO_2. Metals can be identified by their shiny surfaces. Metals are also good conductors of heat and electricity, and they tend to bend easily when in thin sheets. Most nonmetals have a dull surface and are poor conductors of heat and electricity.

OBJECTIVES

▶ **Explain** what ores are and how they form. 7c

▶ **Identify** four uses for mineral resources.

▶ **Summarize** two ways humans obtain mineral resources.

KEY TERMS

ore
lode
placer deposit
gemstone

Ores

Metallic minerals such as gold, silver, and copper, Cu, are called *native elements* and can exist in Earth's crust as nuggets of pure metal. But most other minerals in Earth's crust are *compounds* of two or more elements. Mineral deposits from which metals and nonmetals can be removed profitably are called **ores.** For example, the metal iron, Fe, can be removed from naturally occurring deposits of the minerals magnetite and hematite. Mercury, Hg, can be separated from cinnabar, and aluminum, Al, can be separated from the ore bauxite.

ore a natural material whose concentration of economically valuable minerals is high enough for the material to be mined profitably

Ores Formed by Cooling Magma

Ores form in a variety of ways, as shown in **Figure 1.** Some ores, such as chromium, Cr; nickel, Ni; and lead, Pb, ores form within cooling magma. As the magma cools, dense metallic minerals sink. As the minerals sink, layers of these minerals accumulate at the bottom of the magma chamber to form ore deposits.

Figure 1 ▶ **The Formation of Ores**

Groundwater moving downward through rock is heated by magma. Dissolved metals crystallize out of the hot fluid to form new minerals.

When a body of water evaporates, minerals such as halite (rock salt) and gypsum crystallize.

Dissolved minerals that are carried into bodies of water crystallize on the bottom.

Magma

As magma moves upward through the crust, minerals form from the slow-cooling liquid.

Ores Formed by Contact Metamorphism

Some lead, Pb; copper, Cu; and zinc, Zn, ores form through the process of contact metamorphism. *Contact metamorphism* is a process that occurs when magma comes into contact with existing rock. Heat and chemical reactions with hot fluids from the magma can change the composition of the surrounding rock. These changes sometimes form ores.

Contact metamorphism can also form ore deposits when hot fluids called *hydrothermal solutions* move through small cracks in a large mass of rock. In this process, minerals from the surrounding rock dissolve into the hydrothermal solution. Over time, new minerals precipitate from the solution and form narrow zones of rock called *veins*. Veins commonly consist of ores of valuable heavy minerals, such as gold, Au; tin, Sn; lead, Pb; and copper, Cu. When many thick mineral veins form in a relatively small region, the ore deposit is called a **lode.** Stories of a "Mother Lode" kept people coming to California during the California gold rush in the late 1840s.

lode a mineral deposit within a rock formation

placer deposit a deposit that contains a valuable mineral that has been concentrated by mechanical action

Ores Formed by Moving Water

The movement of water helps to form ore deposits. First, tiny fragments of native elements, such as gold, Au, are released from rock as it breaks down by weathering. Then, streams carry the fragments until the currents become too weak to carry these dense metals. Finally, because of the mechanical action of the stream, the fragments become concentrated at the bottom of stream beds in **placer deposits.** A placer deposit is shown in **Figure 2.**

> **Reading Check** Name two ways water creates ore deposits. (See the Appendix for answers to Reading Checks.)

Figure 2 ▶ Placer deposits may occur at a river bend (left) or in holes downstream from a waterfall (right). Gold is a mineral that is commonly found in placer deposits. A stream carries heavy gold grains and nuggets and drops them where the current is weak.

Placer deposits

Placer deposits

Table 1

Minerals and Their Uses	
Metallic minerals	**Uses**
Hematite and magnetite (iron)	in making steel
Galena (lead)	in car batteries; in solder
Gold, silver, and platinum	in electronics and dental work; as objects such as coins, jewelry, eating utensils, and bowls
Chalcopyrite (copper)	as wiring, in coins and jewelry, and as building ornaments
Sphalerite (zinc)	in making brass and galvanized steel
Nonmetallic minerals	**Uses**
Diamond (carbon)	in drill bits and saws (industrial grade) and in jewelry (gemstone quality)
Graphite (carbon)	in pencils, paint, lubricants, and batteries
Calcite	in cement; as building stone
Halite (salt)	in food preparation and preservation
Kaolinite (clay)	in ceramics, cement, and bricks
Quartz (sand)	as glass
Sulfur	in gunpowder, medicines, and rubber
Gypsum	in plaster and wallboard

Uses of Mineral Resources

Some metals, such as gold, Au, platinum, Pt, and silver, Ag, are prized for their beauty and rarity. Metallic ores are sources of these valuable minerals and elements. Certain rare nonmetallic minerals called **gemstones** display extraordinary brilliance and color when they are specially cut for jewelry. Other nonmetallic minerals, such as calcite and gypsum, are used as building materials. **Table 1** shows some metallic and nonmetallic minerals and their common uses.

gemstone a mineral, rock, or organic material that can be used as jewelry or an ornament when it is cut and polished

Mineral Exploration and Mining

Companies that mine and recover minerals are often looking for new areas to mine. These companies identify areas that may contain enough minerals for economic recovery through mineral exploration. In general, an area is considered for mining if it has at least 100 to 1,000 times the concentration of minerals that are found elsewhere.

During mineral exploration, people search for mineral deposits by studying local geology. Airplanes that carry special equipment are used to measure and identify patterns in magnetism, gravity, radioactivity, and rock color. Exploration teams also collect and test rock samples to determine whether the rock contains enough metal to make a mine profitable.

SCiLINKS®

NSTA
Developed and maintained by the
National Science Teachers Association

For a variety of links related to this subject, go to www.scilinks.org

Topic: Using Mineral Resources
SciLinksCode: HQ61587
Topic: Mining Minerals
SciLinksCode: HQ60968

Subsurface Mining

Many mineral deposits are located below Earth's surface. These minerals are mined by miners who work underground to recover mineral deposits. These mining techniques are called *subsurface mining*.

Surface Mining

When mineral deposits are located close to Earth's surface, they may be mined by using *surface mining* methods. In these methods, the overlying rock material is stripped away to reveal the mineral deposits. A very large open-pit copper mine is shown in **Figure 3.**

Placer Mining

Minerals in placer deposits are mined by dredging. In placer mining, large buckets are attached to a floating barge. The buckets scoop up the sediments in front of the barge. Dense minerals from placer deposits are separated from the surrounding sediment. Then, the remaining sediments are released into the water.

Undersea Mining

The ocean floor also contains mineral resources. *Nodules* are lumps of minerals on the deep-ocean floor that contain iron, Fe; manganese, Mn; and nickel, Ni, and that could become economically important if they could be recovered efficiently. However, because of their location, these deposits are very difficult to mine. Mineral deposits on land can be mined less expensively than deposits on the deep-ocean floor can.

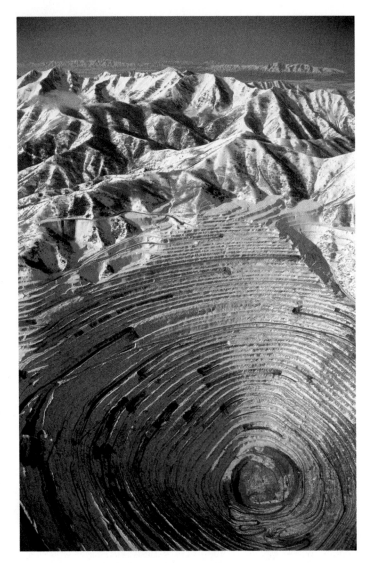

Figure 3 ▶ With a rim diameter of 4 km and a depth of almost 1 km, the Bingham Canyon Mine in Utah is the largest copper mine in the world.

Section 1 Review

1. **Define** *ore*.

2. **Describe** three ways that ore deposits form. 7c

3. **Identify** two uses for each of the following minerals: sulfur, copper, and diamond.

4. **Summarize** the four main types of mining.

CRITICAL THINKING

5. **Applying Ideas** Which would be a better insulator for a hot-water pipe, a metal or a nonmetal? Explain your answer. IE.1d

6. **Understanding Relationships** Why are dense minerals more likely to form placer deposits than less dense minerals are? IE.1d

7. **Making Inferences** Why do you think that mining on land is less costly than mining in the deep ocean is? IE.1d

CONCEPT MAPPING

8. Use the following terms to create a concept map: *mineral, ore, magma, contact metamorphism, vein, lode, placer deposit,* and *mine.*

Section 2 Nonrenewable Energy

California Content Standards

7b Students know the global carbon cycle: the different physical and chemical forms of carbon in the atmosphere, oceans, biomass, fossil fuels, and the movement of carbon among these reservoirs.
7d* Students know the relative residence times and flow characteristics of carbon in and out of its different reservoirs.
IE.1d Students will formulate explanations using logic and evidence.

Many of Earth's resources are used to generate energy. Energy is used for transportation, manufacturing, and countless other things that are important to life as we know it. Energy resources that exist in limited amounts and that cannot be replaced quickly once they are used are examples of **nonrenewable resources.**

Fossil Fuels

Some of the most important nonrenewable resources are buried within Earth's crust. These natural resources—coal, petroleum, and natural gas—formed from the remains of living things. Because of their organic origin, coal, petroleum, and natural gas are called **fossil fuels.** Fossil fuels consist primarily of compounds of carbon and hydrogen called *hydrocarbons*. These compounds contain stored energy originally obtained from sunlight by plants and animals that lived millions of years ago. When hydrocarbons are burned, the breaking of chemical bonds releases energy as heat and light. Much of the energy humans use every day comes from the burning of the hydrocarbons that make up fossil fuels.

Formation of Coal

The most commonly burned fossil fuel is coal. The coal deposits of today are the remains of plants that have undergone a complex process called carbonization. *Carbonization* occurs when partially decomposed plant material is buried in swamp mud and becomes peat. Bacteria consume some of the peat and release the gases methane, CH_4, and carbon dioxide, CO_2. As gases escape, the chemical content of the peat gradually changes until mainly carbon remains. The complex chemical and physical changes that produce coal happen only if oxygen in a swamp is absent. When the conditions are not right for carbonization or if the time required for coal formation has not elapsed, peat remains. Peat may be used as an energy source, as shown in **Figure 1.**

OBJECTIVES

▶ **Explain** why coal is a fossil fuel. **7b**

▶ **Describe** how petroleum and natural gas form and how they are removed from Earth. **7d*, 7b**

▶ **Summarize** the processes of nuclear fission and nuclear fusion. **1e**

▶ **Explain** how nuclear fission generates electricity.

KEY TERMS

nonrenewable resource
fossil fuel
nuclear fission
nuclear fusion

nonrenewable resource a resource that forms at a rate that is much slower than the rate at which it is consumed

fossil fuel a nonrenewable energy resource that formed from the remains of organisms that lived long ago; examples include oil, coal, and natural gas

Figure 1 ▶ Peat deposits are still forming today. Some people in Ireland and Scotland heat their houses with peat. In Ireland and Russia, peat is used to fuel some electric power plants.

Figure 2 ▶ Types of Coal

Stage 1: Peat
The partial decomposition of plant remains forms a brownish-black material called *peat*.

Stage 2: Lignite
Peat is buried by other sediment. As heat and pressure increase, peat becomes lignite. Lignite is also called *brown coal*.

Stage 3: Bituminous Coal
Increased temperature and pressure turn lignite into bituminous coal, which is 80% carbon. Bituminous coal is also called *soft coal*.

Stage 4: Anthracite
Under high temperature and pressure conditions, bituminous coal eventually becomes anthracite, which is the hardest form of coal.

Types of Coal Deposits

As peat is covered by layers of sediments, the weight of these sediments squeezes out water and gases. A denser material called *lignite* forms, as shown in the second step of **Figure 2.** The increased temperature and pressure of more sediments compacts the lignite and forms *bituminous coal*. Bituminous coal is the most abundant type of coal. Where the folding of Earth's crust produces high temperatures and pressure, bituminous coal changes into *anthracite*, the hardest form of coal. Bituminous coal is made of 80% carbon, and anthracite is made of 90% carbon. Both release a large amount of heat when they burn.

Formation of Petroleum and Natural Gas

When microorganisms and plants died in shallow prehistoric oceans and lakes, their remains accumulated on the ocean floor and lake bottoms and were buried by sediment. As more sediments accumulated, heat and pressure increased. Over millions of years, the heat and pressure caused chemical changes to convert the remains into petroleum and natural gas.

Petroleum and natural gas are mixtures of hydrocarbons. Petroleum, which is also called *oil*, is made of liquid hydrocarbons. Natural gas is made of hydrocarbons in the form of gas.

MATHPRACTICE

Coal Reserves
There are thought to be more than 1,000 billion tons of coal on Earth that can be mined. If 4.5 billion tons are used worldwide every year, for how many years will Earth's coal reserves last? If coal use increases to 10 billion tons per year, for how many years will Earth's coal reserves last?

Petroleum and Natural Gas Deposits

Petroleum and natural gas are very important sources of energy for transportation, farming, and many other industries. Because of their importance, petroleum and natural gas deposits are valuable and are highly sought after. Petroleum and natural gas are most often mined from permeable sedimentary rock. *Permeable rocks* have interconnected spaces through which liquids can easily flow.

As sediments accumulate and sedimentary rock forms, pressure increases. This pressure forces fluids, including water, oil, and gas, out of the pores and up through the layers of permeable rock. The fluids move upward until they reach a layer of *impermeable rock*, or rock through which liquids cannot flow, called *cap rock*. Petroleum that accumulates beneath the cap rock fills all the spaces to form an oil reservoir. Because petroleum is less dense than water, petroleum rises above any trapped water. Similarly, natural gas rises above petroleum, because natural gas is less dense than both oil and water.

Oil Traps

Geologists explore Earth's crust to discover the kinds of rock structures that may trap oil or gas. They look for oil trapped in places such as the ones shown in **Figure 3.** When a well is drilled into an oil reservoir, the petroleum and natural gas often flow to the surface. When the pressure of the overlying rock is removed, fluids rise up and out through the well.

Figure 3 ▶ Oil Traps

Many oil traps are anticlines, or upward folds in rock layers.

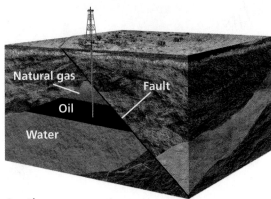

Another common type of oil trap is a fault, or crack, in Earth's crust that seals the oil- or gas-bearing formation.

Fossil-Fuel Supplies

Fossil fuels, like minerals, are nonrenewable resources. Globally, fossil fuels are one of the main sources of energy. *Crude oil*, or unrefined petroleum, is also used in the production of plastics, synthetic fabrics, medicines, waxes, synthetic rubber, insecticides, chemical fertilizers, detergents, shampoos, and many other products.

Coal is the most abundant fossil fuel in the world. Every continent has coal, but almost two-thirds of known deposits occur in three countries—the United States, Russia, and China. Scientists estimate that most of the petroleum reserves in the world have been discovered. However, scientists think that there are undiscovered natural gas reserves. There is also a relatively abundant material called *oil shale* that contains petroleum. But the cost of mining oil from shale is far greater than the present cost of recovering oil from other sedimentary rocks.

For a variety of links related to this subject, go to www.scilinks.org

Topic: Nonrenewable Resources
SciLinksCode: HQ61044
Topic: Fossil Fuels
SciLinksCode: HQ60614

Reading Check What is cap rock? (See the Appendix for answers to Reading Checks.)

Nuclear Energy

When scientists discovered that atoms had smaller fundamental parts, scientists wondered if atoms could be split. In 1919, Ernest Rutherford first studied and explained the results of bombarding atomic nuclei with high-energy particles. In the 30 years that followed his research, nuclear (NOO klee uhr) technologies were developed that allowed atomic weapons to be made and allowed nuclear reactions to be used to generate electricity. Energy that is produced by using these technologies is called *nuclear energy*.

Nuclear Fission

One form of nuclear energy is produced by splitting the nuclei of heavy atoms. This splitting of the nucleus of a large atom into two or more smaller nuclei is called **nuclear fission**. The process of nuclear fission is shown in **Figure 4**.

The forces that hold the nucleus of an atom together are more than 1 million times stronger than the strongest chemical bonds between atoms. If a nucleus is struck by a free neutron, however, the nucleus of the atom may split. When the nucleus splits, it releases additional neutrons as well as energy. The newly released neutrons strike other nearby nuclei, which causes those nuclei to split and to release more neutrons and more energy. A chain reaction occurs as more neutrons strike neighboring atoms. If a fission reaction is allowed to continue uncontrolled, the reaction will escalate quickly and may result in an explosion. However, controlled fission produces heat that can be used to generate electricity.

✓ Reading Check What causes a chain reaction during nuclear fission? (See the Appendix for answers to Reading Checks.)

nuclear fission the process by which the nucleus of a heavy atom splits into two or more fragments; the process releases neutrons and energy

Figure 4 ▶ An Example of a Nuclear Fission Reaction

Neutron

Proton

Fission product

ENERGY

ENERGY

ENERGY

❶ An intact nucleus is about to be struck by a neutron.

❷ When struck by a neutron, the nucleus splits, forms new elements, and releases neutrons plus energy.

❸ The released neutrons strike other nuclei.

❹ The nuclei split and release more neutrons and energy.

Figure 5 ▶ How a Nuclear Power Plant Generates Electricity

❷ The superheated water is pumped into a heat exchanger, which transfers the heat of the first circuit to the second circuit. Water in the second circuit flashes into high-pressure steam.

❸ Steam is directed against a turbine, setting it in motion. The turbine sets the generator in motion, generating electricity.

Control rod

Steam

Cooling tower

Electric current from generator

Second circuit

Water

Pump

Fuel rod

First circuit

Third circuit

❶ Energy released by the nuclear reaction heats water in the pressurized first circuit to a high temperature.

❹ A third circuit cools the steam from the turbine and the waste heat is released from the cooling tower in the form of steam.

How Fission Generates Electricity

When a nuclear power plant is working correctly, the chain reaction that occurs during nuclear fission is controlled. The flow of neutrons into the fission reaction is regulated so that the reaction can be slowed down, speeded up, or stopped as needed. The specialized equipment in which controlled nuclear fission is carried out is called a *nuclear reactor*.

During fission, a tremendous amount of heat energy is released. This heat energy can in turn be used to generate electricity. **Figure 5** shows how nuclear fission inside a nuclear reactor can be used to generate electricity. Currently, only one kind of naturally occurring element is used for nuclear fission. It is a rare isotope of the element uranium called *uranium-235*, or ^{235}U. Because ^{235}U is rare, the ore that is mined is processed into fuel pellets that have a high ^{235}U content. After this process is complete, the fuel pellets are said to be uranium-enriched pellets.

These enriched fuel pellets are placed into rods to make *fuel rods*. Bundles of these fuel rods are then bombarded by neutrons. When struck by a neutron, the ^{235}U nuclei in the fuel rods split and release neutrons and energy. The resulting chain reaction causes the fuel rods to become very hot.

Water is pumped around the fuel rods to absorb and remove the heat energy. The water is then pumped into a second circuit, where the water becomes steam. The steam turns the turbines that provide power for electric generators. A third water circuit carries away excess heat and releases it into the environment.

Graphic Organizer Chain-of-Events Chart

Create the **Graphic Organizer** entitled "Chain-of-Events Chart" described in the Skills Handbook section of the Appendix. Then, fill in the chart with details about each step of how electricity is generated by fission.

Advantages and Disadvantages of Nuclear Fission

Nuclear power plants burn no fossil fuels and produce no air pollution. But because nuclear fission uses and produces radioactive materials that have very long half-lives, wastes must be safely stored for thousands of years. These waste products give off high doses of radiation that can destroy plant and animal cells and can cause harmful changes in the genetic material of living cells.

Currently, nuclear power plants store their nuclear wastes in dry casks or in onsite water pools, as shown in **Figure 6.** Other wastes are either stored onsite or transported to one of three disposal facilities in the United States. The U.S. Department of Energy has plans for a permanent disposal site for highly radioactive nuclear wastes.

Nuclear Fusion

All of the energy that reaches Earth from the sun is produced by a kind of nuclear reaction, called nuclear fusion. During **nuclear fusion**, the nuclei of hydrogen atoms combine to form larger nuclei of helium. This process releases energy. Fusion reactions occur only at temperatures of more than 15,000,000°C.

For more than 40 years, scientists have been trying to harness the energy released by nuclear fusion to produce electricity. More research is needed before a commercial fusion reactor can be built. If such a reactor could be built in the future, hydrogen atoms from ocean water might be used as the fuel. With ocean water as fuel, the amount of energy available from nuclear fusion would be almost limitless. Scientists also think that wastes from fusion would be much less dangerous than wastes from fission. The only byproducts of fusion are helium nuclei, which are harmless to living cells.

Figure 6 ▶ These water pools store radioactive wastes. The blue glow indicates that the waste products are highly radioactive.

nuclear fusion the process by which nuclei of small atoms combine to form new, more massive nuclei; the process releases energy

---

Section 2 Review

1. **Explain** why coal, petroleum, and natural gas are called *fossil fuels*. 7b

2. **Compare** how coal, petroleum, and natural gas form. 7b, 7d*

3. **Describe** the kind of rock structures in which petroleum reservoirs form. 7b

4. **Identify** the naturally occurring element that is used for nuclear fission.

5. **Explain** how nuclear fission generates electricity.

6. **Summarize** the process of nuclear fusion. 1e

CRITICAL THINKING

7. **Analyzing Relationships** Why have we been able to build nuclear power plants for only the last 50 years? IE.1d

8. **Recognizing Relationships** Can the waste products of nuclear fission be safely disposed of in rivers or lakes? Explain your answer. IE.1d

9. **Making Comparisons** How do the processes of nuclear fusion and nuclear fission differ? 1e, IE.1d

CONCEPT MAPPING

10. Use the following terms to create a concept map: *nonrenewable resource, fossil fuel, coal, carbonization, peat, lignite, bituminous coal, anthracite coal, petroleum,* and *natural gas.*

▶ Scientists learn about Earth's past by studying rocks and fossils. This fossil from the Green River formation in Wyoming is a fossilized predatory fish called *Mioplosus*. In this extraordinary fossil, was preserved a *Mioplosus* in the act of devouring a small fish.

The Rock Record

Sections

1 Determining Relative Age

2 Determining Absolute Age

3 The Fossil Record

What You'll Learn

- How scientists determine relative age
- How scientists determine absolute age
- How fossils form

Why It's Relevant

To study Earth's 4.6 billion year history, scientists look to the information stored in rocks. Scientists must determine the age of rocks to put the events of Earth's history in order.

PRE-READING ACTIVITY

Table Fold Before you read this chapter, create the **FoldNote** entitled "Table Fold" described in the Skills Handbook section of the Appendix. Label the columns of the table fold with "Absolute age" and "Relative age." As you read the chapter, write examples of each topic under the appropriate column.

▶ This slab of beautifully preserved crinoids shows each organism's 10 radial arms. Crinoids have been inhabiting aquatic environments on Earth for almost 490 million years.

California Content Standards

IE.1a Students will select and use appropriate tools and technology (such as computer-linked probes, spreadsheets, and graphing calculators) to perform tests, collect data, analyze relationships and display data.

IE.1d Students will formulate explanations using logic and evidence.

IE.1g Students will recognize the usefulness and limitations of models and theories as scientific representations of reality.

IE.1h Students will read and interpret topographic and geologic maps.

IE.1i Students will analyze the locations, sequences, or time intervals that are characteristic of natural phenomena (e.g., relative ages of rocks, locations of planets over time, and succession of species in an ecosystem).

IE.1k Students will recognize the cumulative nature of scientific evidence.

California Content Standards

IE.1d Students will formulate explanations using logic and evidence.
IE.1i Students will analyze the locations, sequences, or time intervals that are characteristic of natural phenomena (e.g., relative ages of rocks, locations of planets over time, and succession of species in an ecosystem).
IE.1k Students will recognize the cumulative nature of scientific evidence.

Geologists estimate that Earth is about 4.6 billion years old. The idea that Earth is billions of years old originated with the work of James Hutton, an 18th-century Scottish physician and farmer. Hutton, who is shown in **Figure 1,** wrote about agriculture, weather, climate, physics, and even philosophy. Hutton was also a keen observer of the geologic changes taking place on his farm. Using scientific methods, Hutton drew conclusions based on his observations. Today, he is most famous for his ideas and writings about geology.

Uniformitarianism

Hutton theorized that the same forces that changed the landscape of his farm had changed Earth's surface in the past. He thought that by studying the present, people could learn about Earth's past. Hutton's principle of **uniformitarianism** is that current geologic processes, such as volcanism and erosion, are the same processes that were at work in the past. This principle is one of the basic foundations of the science of geology. Geologists later refined Hutton's ideas by pointing out that although the processes of the past and present are the same, the rates of the processes may vary over time.

OBJECTIVES

▶ **State** the principle of uniformitarianism. IE.1k

▶ **Explain** how the law of superposition can be used to determine the relative age of rocks. IE.1k, IE.1i

▶ **Compare** three types of unconformities. IE.1i

▶ **Apply** the law of crosscutting relationships to determine the relative age of rocks. IE.1i, IE.1k

KEY TERMS

uniformitarianism
relative age
law of superposition
unconformity
law of crosscutting relationships

---

uniformitarianism a principle that geologic processes that occurred in the past can be explained by current geologic processes

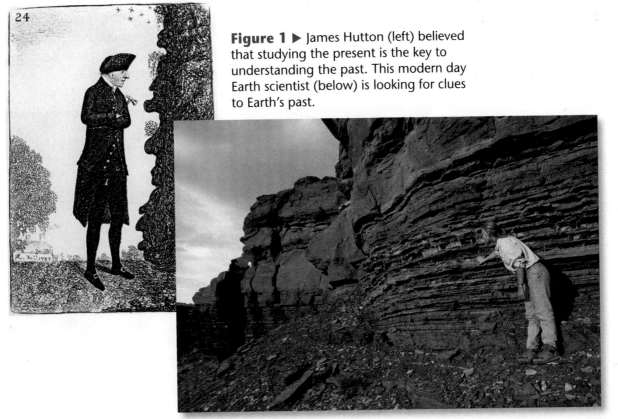

Figure 1 ▶ James Hutton (left) believed that studying the present is the key to understanding the past. This modern day Earth scientist (below) is looking for clues to Earth's past.

What's Your Relative Age? IE.1d, IE.1i

Procedure

1. Form a group with 5 to 10 of your classmates.

2. Work together to arrange group members in order from oldest to youngest.

Analysis

1. How did you determine your classmates' relative ages?

2. How did the relative ages compare to the absolute ages of your classmates?

3. How is this process of determining relative and absolute age different from the way scientists date rocks?

relative age the age of an object in relation to the ages of other objects

Earth's Age

Before Hutton's research was completed, many people thought that Earth was only about 6,000 years old. They also thought that all geologic features had formed at the same time. Hutton's principle of uniformitarianism raised some serious questions about Earth's age. Hutton observed that the forces that changed the land on his farm operated very slowly. He reasoned that millions of years must be needed for those same forces to create the complicated rock structures observed in Earth's crust. He concluded that Earth must be much older than previously thought. Hutton's observations and conclusions about the age of Earth encouraged other scientists to learn more about Earth's history. One way to learn about Earth's past is to determine the order in which rock layers and other rock structures formed.

✓ **Reading Check** What evidence did Hutton propose to show that Earth is very old? (See the Appendix for answers to Reading Checks.)

Relative Age

In the same way that a history book shows an order of events, layers of rock, called *strata*, show the sequence of events that took place in the past. Using a few basic principles, scientists can determine the order in which rock layers formed. Once they know the order, a relative age can be determined for each rock layer. **Relative age** indicates that one layer is older or younger than another layer but does not indicate the rock's age in years.

Various types of rock form layers. Igneous rocks form layers when successive lava flows stack on top of each other. Some types of metamorphic rock, such as marble, also have layers. To determine the relative age of rocks, however, scientists commonly study the layers in sedimentary rocks, such as those shown in **Figure 2.**

Figure 2 ▶ The layers of sedimentary rock that make up Canyon de Chelly in Arizona were deposited over millions of years.

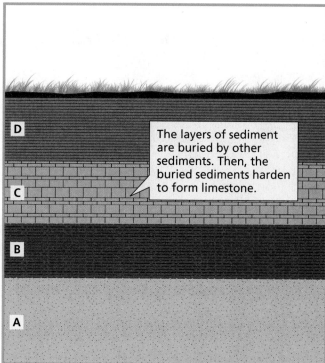

Law of Superposition

Sedimentary rocks form when new sediments are deposited on top of old layers of sediment. As the sediments accumulate, they are compressed and harden into sedimentary rock layers which are called *beds*. The boundary between two beds is called a *bedding plane*.

Scientists use a basic principle called the law of superposition to determine the relative age of a layer of sedimentary rock. The **law of superposition** is that an undeformed sedimentary rock layer is older than the layers above it and younger than the layers below it. According to the law of superposition, layer A, shown in **Figure 3,** was the first layer deposited, and thus it is the oldest layer. The last layer deposited was layer D, and thus it is the youngest layer.

Principle of Original Horizontality

Scientists also know that sedimentary rock generally forms in horizontal layers. The *principle of original horizontality* is that sedimentary rocks left undisturbed will remain in horizontal layers. Therefore, scientists can assume that sedimentary rock layers that are not horizontal have been tilted or deformed by crustal movements that happened after the layers formed.

In some cases, tectonic forces push older layers on top of younger ones or overturn a group of rock layers. In such cases, the law of superposition cannot be easily applied. So, scientists must look for clues to the original position of layers and then apply the law of superposition.

Figure 3 ▶ By applying the law of superposition, geologists are able to determine that layer D is the youngest bed in this rock section. *According to the law of superposition, is layer B older or younger than layer C?*

law of superposition the law that a sedimentary rock layer is older than the layers above it and younger than the layers below it if the layers are not disturbed

For a variety of links related to this subject, go to www.scilinks.org

Topic: Law of Superposition
SciLinks code: HQ60858

Figure 4 ▶ Sedimentary Rock Structures

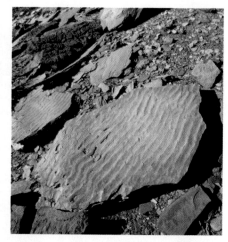

Graded Bedding Heavy particles settle to the bottom of a lake or river faster than smaller particles do and create graded beds like this one.

Cross-beds As sand slides down the slope of a large sand dune, the sand forms slanting layers like the ones shown here.

Ripple Marks When waves move back and forth on a beach, ripple marks like these commonly form.

Graphic Organizer Spider Map

Create the **Graphic Organizer** entitled "Spider Map" described in the Skills Handbook section of the Appendix. Label the circle "Unconformities." Create a leg for each type of unconformity. Then, fill in the map with details about each type of unconformity.

Graded Bedding

One possible clue to the original position of rock layers is the size of the particles in the layers. In some depositional environments, the largest particles of sediment are deposited in the bottom layers, as shown in **Figure 4.** The arrangement of layers in which coarse and heavy particles are located in the bottom layers is called *graded bedding.* If larger particles are located in the top layers, the layers may have been overturned by tectonic forces.

Cross-Beds

Another clue to the original position of rock layers is in the shape of the bedding planes. When sand is deposited, sandy sediment forms curved beds at an angle to the bedding plane. These beds are called *cross-beds* and are shown in **Figure 4.** The tops of these layers commonly erode before new layers are deposited. So, the sediment appears to be curved at the bottom of the layer and to be cut off at the top. By studying the shape of the cross-beds, scientists can determine the original position of these layers.

Ripple Marks

Ripple marks are small waves that form on the surface of sand because of the action of water or wind. When the sand becomes sandstone, the ripple marks may be preserved, as shown in **Figure 4.** In undisturbed sedimentary rock layers, the crests of the ripple marks point upward. By examining the orientation of ripple marks, scientists can establish the original arrangement of the rock layers. The relative ages of the rocks can then be determined by using the law of superposition.

✓ **Reading Check** How can ripple marks indicate the original position of rock layers? (See the Appendix for answers to Reading Checks.)

Unconformities

Movements of Earth's crust can lift up rock layers that were buried and expose them to erosion. Then, if sediments are deposited, new rock layers form in place of the eroded layers. The missing rock layers create a break in the geologic record in the same way that pages missing from a book create a break in a story. A break in the geologic record is called an **unconformity.** An unconformity shows that deposition stopped for a period of time, and rock may have been removed by erosion before deposition resumed.

As shown in **Table 1,** there are three types of unconformities. An unconformity in which stratified rock rests upon unstratified rock is called a *nonconformity*. The boundary between a set of tilted layers and a set of horizontal layers is called an *angular unconformity*. The boundary between horizontal layers of old sedimentary rock and younger, overlying layers that are deposited on an eroded surface is called a *disconformity*. According to the law of superposition, all rocks beneath an unconformity are older than the rocks above the unconformity.

unconformity a break in the geologic record created when rock layers are eroded or when sediment is not deposited for a long period of time

Table 1 ▼

Types of Unconformities		
Type	**Example**	**Description**
Nonconformity		Unstratified igneous or metamorphic rock may be uplifted to Earth's surface by crustal movements. Once the rock is exposed, it erodes. Sediments may then be deposited on the eroded surface. The boundary between the new sedimentary rock and the igneous or metamorphic rock is a *nonconformity*. The boundary represents an unknown period of time during which the older rock was eroded.
Angular unconformity		An *angular unconformity* forms when rock deposited in horizontal layers is folded or tilted and then eroded. When erosion stops, a new horizontal layer is deposited on top of a tilted layer. When the bedding planes of the older rock layers are not parallel to those of the younger rock layers deposited above them, an angular unconformity results.
Disconformity		Sometimes, layers of sediments are uplifted without folding or tilting and are eroded. Eventually, the area subsides and deposition resumes. The layers on either side of the boundary are nearly horizontal. Although the rock layers look as if they were deposited continuously, a large time gap exists where the upper and lower layers meet. This gap is known as a *disconformity*.

Figure 5 ▶ The law of crosscutting relationships can be used to determine the relative ages of rock layers and the faults and intrusions within them.

Igneous intrusion   Fault

law of crosscutting relationships the principle that a fault or body of rock is younger than any other body of rock that it cuts through

Crosscutting Relationships

When rock layers have been disturbed by faults or intrusions, determining relative age may be difficult. A *fault* is a break or crack in Earth's crust along which rocks shift their position. An *intrusion* is a mass of igneous rock that forms when magma is injected into rock and then cools and solidifies. In such cases, scientists may apply the law of crosscutting relationships. The **law of crosscutting relationships** is that a fault or igneous intrusion is always younger than the rock layers it cuts through. If a fault or intrusion cuts through an unconformity, the fault or intrusion is younger than all the rocks it cuts through above and below the unconformity.

Figure 5 shows a series of rock layers that contains both a fault and an igneous intrusion. As you can see, an intrusion cuts across layers A, B, and C. According to the law of crosscutting relationships, the intrusion is younger than layers A, B, and C. The fault is younger than the intrusion and all four layers.

Section 1 **Review**

1. **Explain** why it is important for scientists to be able to determine the relative age of rocks. IE.1i

2. **State** the principle of uniformitarianism in your own words. IE.1k

3. **Explain** how the law of superposition can be used to determine the relative age of sedimentary rock. IE.1i, IE.1k

4. **Explain** the difference between an unconformity and a nonconformity. IE.1i

5. **Compare** an angular unconformity with a disconformity. IE.1i

6. **Describe** how the law of crosscutting relationships helps scientists determine the relative ages of rocks. IE.1i, IE.1k

CRITICAL THINKING

7. **Making Comparisons** Which would be more difficult to recognize: a nonconformity or a disconformity? Explain your answer. IE.1d

8. **Analyzing Relationships** Suppose that you find a series of rock layers in which a fault ends at an unconformity. Explain how you could apply the law of crosscutting relationships to determine the relative age of the fault and of the rock layers that were deposited above the unconformity. IE.1d, IE.1i, IE.1k

CONCEPT MAPPING

9. Use the following terms to create a concept map: *principle of original horizontality, relative age, graded bedding, law of superposition, cross-bed,* and *ripple mark.* IE.1i, IE.1k

Determining Absolute Age

California Content Standards

IE.1d Students will formulate explanations using logic and evidence.
IE.1i Students will analyze the locations, sequences, or time intervals that are characteristic of natural phenomena (e.g., relative ages of rocks, locations of planets over time, and succession of species in an ecosystem).

Relative age indicates only that one rock formation is younger or older than another rock formation. To learn more about Earth's history, scientists often need to determine the numeric age, or **absolute age,** of a rock formation.

Absolute Dating Methods

Scientists use a variety of methods to measure absolute age. Some methods use geologic processes that can be observed and measured over time. Other methods measure the chemical composition of certain materials in rock.

Rates of Erosion

One way to estimate absolute age is to study rates of erosion. For example, if scientists measure the rate at which a stream erodes its bed, they can estimate the age of the stream. But determining absolute age by using the rate of erosion is practical only for geologic features that formed within the past 10,000 to 20,000 years. One example of such a feature is Niagara Falls, which is shown in **Figure 1.** For older surface features, such as the Grand Canyon, which formed over millions of years, the method is less dependable because rates of erosion may vary greatly over millions of years.

OBJECTIVES

▶ **Summarize** the limitations of using the rates of erosion and deposition to determine the absolute age of rock formations. IE.1i

▶ **Describe** the formation of varves. IE.1i

▶ **Explain** how the process of radioactive decay can be used to determine the absolute age of rocks. IE.1i

KEY TERMS

absolute age
varve
radiometric dating
half-life

absolute age the numeric age of an object or event, often stated in years before the present, as established by an absolute-dating process, such as radiometric dating

Figure 1 ▶ The rocky ledge above Niagara Falls has been eroding at a rate of about 1.3 m per year for nearly 9,900 years. *How many kilometers has the ledge been eroded in the last 9,900 years?*

varve a banded layer of sand and silt that is deposited annually in a lake, especially near ice sheets or glaciers, and that can be used to determine absolute age

Rates of Deposition

Another way to estimate absolute age is to calculate the rate of sediment deposition. By using data collected over a long period of time, geologists can estimate the average rates of deposition for common sedimentary rocks such as limestone, shale, and sandstone. In general, about 30 cm of sedimentary rock are deposited over a period of 1,000 years. However, any given sedimentary layer that is being studied may not have been deposited at an average rate. For example, a flood can deposit many meters of sediment in just one day. In addition, the rate of deposition may change over time. Therefore, this method of determining absolute age is not always accurate; it merely provides an estimate.

Varve Count

You may know that a tree's age can be estimated by counting the growth rings in its trunk. Scientists have devised a similar method for estimating the age of certain sedimentary deposits. Some sedimentary deposits show definite annual layers, called **varves**, that consist of a light-colored band of coarse particles and a dark band of fine particles.

Varves generally form in glacial lakes. During the summer, when snow and ice melt rapidly, a rush of water can carry large amounts of sediment into a lake. Most of the coarse particles settle quickly to form a layer on the bottom of the lake. With the coming of winter, the surface of the lake begins to freeze. Fine clay particles still suspended in the water settle slowly to form a thin layer on top of the coarse sediments. A coarse summer layer and the overlying, fine winter layer make up one varve. Thus, each varve represents one year of deposition. Some varves are shown in **Figure 2.** By counting the varves, scientists can estimate the age of the sediments.

Reading Check How are varves like tree rings? (See the Appendix for answers to Reading Checks.)

Figure 2 ▶ Varves (below), which form in glacial lakes (right), can be counted to determine the absolute age of sediments.

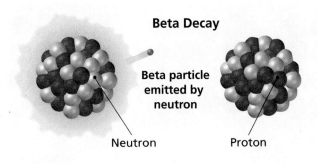

Beta Decay

Beta particle
emitted by
neutron

Neutron   Proton

Alpha Decay

**Alpha particle (two protons and two
neutrons) emitted by nucleus**

Radiometric Dating

Rocks generally contain small amounts of radioactive material that can act as natural clocks. Atoms of the same element that have different numbers of neutrons are called *isotopes*. *Radioactive isotopes* have nuclei that emit particles and energy at a constant rate regardless of surrounding conditions. **Figure 3** shows two of the ways that radioactive isotopes decay. During the emission of the particles, large amounts of energy are released. Scientists use this natural breakdown of isotopes to accurately measure the absolute age of rocks. The method of using radioactive decay to measure absolute age is called **radiometric dating.**

As an atom emits particles and energy, the atom changes into a different isotope of the same element or an isotope of a different element. Scientists measure the concentrations of the original radioactive isotope, or *parent isotope,* and of the newly formed isotopes, or *daughter isotopes*. Using the known decay rate, the scientists compare the proportions of the parent and daughter isotopes to determine the absolute age of the rock.

Figure 3 ▶ Beta decay and alpha decay are two forms of radioactive decay. In all forms of radioactive decay, an atom emits particles and energy.

radiometric dating a method of determining the absolute age of an object by comparing the relative percentages of a radioactive (parent) isotope and a stable (daughter) isotope

---

Connection to CHEMISTRY

Radioactive Decay of Uranium

Uranium is a radioactive element that occurs in some rocks. One form of uranium, which is represented by the symbol ^{238}U, has a mass number of 238 and an atomic number of 92. The atomic number is the number of protons in the nucleus. The mass number is the sum of the number of protons and neutrons in the nucleus. Uranium-238 is particularly useful in establishing the absolute ages of rocks.

The highly radioactive nucleus of ^{238}U spontaneously emits two protons and two neutrons in a process called *alpha decay* or alpha particle emission. The loss of protons and neutrons from the nucleus decreases both the atomic number and the mass number. After the first decay of ^{238}U, the new nucleus has a mass number of 234 and an atomic number of 90. The atom has changed into an isotope of thorium, ^{234}Th.

The ^{234}Th nucleus is also radioactive, and one of its neutrons changes into a proton and an electron in a process called *beta decay*. The change of the neutron to a proton increases the atomic number by one, and the thorium isotope then becomes an isotope of protactinium, ^{234}Pa, which is also radioactive.

The cycle of radioactive decay continues until a stable, or nonradioactive, form of lead is produced. A form of lead that has a mass number of 206, ^{206}Pb, is the final product of this radioactive-decay chain. In this chain of decay, ^{238}U is the parent isotope and ^{206}Pb is a daughter isotope. The time required for half of any given amount of ^{238}U to decay into ^{206}Pb is 4.5 billion years. Thus, 4.5 billion years is the half-life of ^{238}U.

Figure 4 ▶ After each half-life, one-half of the parent isotope is converted into a daughter isotope. After four half-lives, only 1/16 of the parent isotope remains.

half-life the time required for half of a sample of a radioactive isotope to break down by radioactive decay to form a daughter isotope

Half-Life

Radioactive decay happens at a relatively constant rate that is not changed by temperature, pressure, or other environmental conditions. Scientists have determined that the time required for half of any amount of a particular radioactive isotope to decay is always the same and can be determined for any isotope. Therefore, a **half-life** is the time it takes half the mass of a given amount of a radioactive isotope to decay into its daughter isotopes. If you began with 10 g of a parent isotope, you would have 5 g of that isotope after one half-life of that isotope. At the end of a second half-life, one-fourth, or 2.5 g, of the original isotope would remain. Three-fourths of the sample would now be the daughter isotope. This process is shown in **Figure 4.**

By comparing the amounts of parent and daughter isotopes in a rock sample, scientists can determine the age of the sample. The greater the percentage of daughter isotopes present in the sample, the older the rock is. But comparing parent to daughter isotopes works only when the sample has not gained or lost either parent or daughter isotopes through leaking or contamination.

QuickLAB 10 min

Radioactive Decay
Procedure 🔬 IE.1i, IE.1d

1. Use a **clock or watch that has a second hand** to record the time.
2. Wait 20 s, and then use **scissors** to carefully cut a **sheet of paper** in half. Select one piece, and set the other piece aside.
3. Repeat step 2 until nine 20 s intervals have elapsed.

Analysis

1. What does the whole piece of paper used in this investigation represent?
2. What do the pieces of paper that you set aside in each step represent?
3. What is the half-life of your paper isotope?

4. How much of your paper isotope was left after the first three intervals? after six intervals? after nine intervals? Express your answers as percentages.
5. What two factors in your model must remain constant so that your model is accurate? Explain your answer.

Table 1 ▼

Radiometric Dating Methods				
Radiometric dating method	Parent Isotope	Daughter isotope	Half-life	Effective dating range
Radiocarbon dating	carbon-14, ^{14}C	nitrogen-14, 14N	5,730 years	less than 70,000 years
Argon-argon dating, $^{39}Ar/^{40}Ar$	potassium-40, ^{40}K irradiated to form argon-39, ^{39}Ar	argon-40, ^{40}Ar	1.25 billion years	10,000 to 4.6 billion years
Potassium-argon dating, $^{40}K/^{40}Ar$	potassium-40, ^{40}K	Argon-40, ^{40}Ar	1.25 billion years	50,000 to 4.6 billion years
Rubidium-strontium dating, $^{87}Rb/^{87}Sr$	rubidium-87, ^{87}Rb	strontium-87, ^{87}Sr	48.8 billion years	10 million to 4.6 billion years
Uranium-lead dating, $^{235}U/^{207}Pb$	uranium-235, ^{235}U	lead-207, ^{207}Pb	704 million years	10 million to 4.6 billion years
Uranium-lead dating, $^{238}U/^{206}Pb$	uranium-238, ^{238}U	lead-206, ^{206}Pb	4.5 billion years	10 million to 4.6 billion years
Thorium-lead dating	thorium-232, ^{232}Th	lead-208, ^{208}Pb	14.0 billion years	greater than 200 million years

Radioactive Isotopes

The amount of time that has passed since a rock formed determines which radioactive element will give a more accurate age measurement. If too little time has passed since radioactive decay began, there may not be enough of the daughter isotope for accurate dating. If too much time has passed, there may not be enough of the parent isotope left for accurate dating.

Uranium-238, ^{238}U (which is read as "U two thirty-eight"), has an extremely long half-life of 4.5 billion years. ^{238}U is most useful for dating geologic samples that are more than 10 million years old, as long as they contain uranium. In addition to ^{238}U, several other radioactive isotopes are used to date rock samples. One such isotope is potassium-40, ^{40}K, which has a half-life of 1.25 billion years. ^{40}K occurs in mica, clay, and feldspar and is used to date rocks that are between 50,000 and 4.6 billion years old. Rubidium-87, ^{87}Rb, has a half-life of about 49 billion years. ^{87}Rb, which commonly occurs in minerals that contain ^{40}K, can be used to verify the age of rocks previously dated by using ^{40}K. **Table 1** provides a list of other radiometric dating methods.

SCiLINKS®

NSTA
Developed and maintained by the National Science Teachers Association

For a variety of links related to this subject, go to www.scilinks.org

Topic: Radiometric Dating
SciLinks code: HQ61261

✔ **Reading Check** How does the half-life of an isotope affect the accuracy of the radiometric dating method? (See the Appendix for answers to Reading Checks.)

Figure 5 ▶ This scientist is preparing a mammoth's tooth for carbon-14 dating, which will determine the tooth's absolute age.

Carbon Dating

Younger rock layers may be dated indirectly by dating organic material found within the rock. The ages of wood, bones, shells, and other organic remains that are included in the layers and that are less than 70,000 years old can be determined by using a method known as *carbon-14 dating*, or *radiocarbon dating*, as shown in **Figure 5**. The isotope carbon-14, ^{14}C, combines with oxygen to form radioactive carbon dioxide, CO_2. Most CO_2 in the atmosphere contains nonradioactive carbon-12, ^{12}C. Only a small amount of CO_2 in the atmosphere contains ^{14}C.

Plants absorb CO_2, which contains either ^{12}C or ^{14}C during photosynthesis. Then, when animals eat the plants or the plant-eating animals, the ^{12}C and ^{14}C become part of the animals' body tissues. Thus, all living organisms contain both ^{12}C and ^{14}C.

To find the age of a small amount of organic material, scientists first determine the ratio of ^{14}C to ^{12}C in the sample. Then, they compare that ratio with the ratio of ^{14}C to ^{12}C known to exist in a living organism. While organisms are alive, the ratio of ^{12}C to ^{14}C remains relatively constant. When a plant or an animal dies, however, the ratio begins to change. The half-life of ^{14}C is only about 5,730 years. Because the organism is dead, it no longer absorbs ^{12}C and ^{14}C, and the amount of ^{14}C in the organism's tissues decreases steadily as the radioactive ^{14}C decays to nonradioactive nitrogen-14, ^{14}N.

Section 2 Review

1. **Differentiate** between relative and absolute age. IE.1i
2. **Summarize** why calculations of absolute age based on rates of erosion and deposition can be inaccurate. IE.1i
3. **Describe** varves, and describe how and where they form. IE.1i
4. **Explain** how radiometric dating is used to estimate absolute age. IE.1i
5. **Define** half-life, and explain how it helps determine an object's absolute age. IE.1i
6. **List** three methods of radiometric dating, and explain the age range for which they are most effective. IE.1i

CRITICAL THINKING

7. **Demonstrating Reasoned Judgment** Suppose you have a shark's tooth that you suspect is about 15,000 years old. Would you use ^{238}U or ^{14}C to date the tooth? Explain your answer. IE.1i, IE.1d

8. **Making Inferences** You see an advertisement for an atomic clock. You also know that radioactive decay emits harmful radiation. Do you think the atomic clock contains decaying isotopes? Explain. IE.1i, IE.1d

CONCEPT MAPPING

9. Use the following terms to create a concept map: *absolute age, varve, radiometric dating, parent isotope, daughter isotope,* and *carbon dating.* IE.1i

Highlights

Sections

1 Determining Relative Age

Key Terms

uniformitarianism, 185

relative age, 186

law of super-position, 187

unconformity, 189

law of crosscutting relationships, 190

Key Concepts

▶ According to the principle of uniformitarianism, the forces that are changing Earth's surface today are the same forces that changed Earth's surface in the past.

▶ Scientists use the law of superposition to determine the relative ages of rock layers.

▶ Nonconformities, angular unconformities, and disconformities are interruptions in the sequence of rock layers and are collectively known as unconformities.

▶ Scientists use the law of crosscutting relationships to determine the relative ages of rock layers.

2 Determining Absolute Age

absolute age, 191

varve, 192

radiometric dating, 193

half-life, 194

▶ Absolute age is the numeric age of an object given in years.

▶ Because they can change over time, the rates of erosion and deposition are imprecise methods for determining absolute age of rocks.

▶ Varves are layers of sediment that form in glacial lakes as a result of the annual cycle of freezing and thawing of the glacier.

▶ Radioactive elements decay at constant and measurable rates and can be used to determine absolute age.

3 The Fossil Record

fossil, 197

paleontology, 197

trace fossil, 199

index fossil, 200

▶ Entire organisms may be preserved in amber, in tar seeps, or through freezing or mummification.

▶ Fossilized evidence of organisms includes trace fossils, imprints, molds, casts, coprolites, and gastroliths.

▶ Index fossils occur only in rock layers of a particular geologic age.

Using Key Terms

Use each of the following terms in a separate sentence.

1. *uniformitarianism* IE.1i, IE.1k
2. *varve* IE.1i
3. *radiometric dating* IE.1i
4. *half-life* IE.1i

For each pair of terms, explain how the meanings of the terms differ.

5. *relative age* and *absolute age* IE.1i
6. *law of superposition* and *law of crosscutting relationships* IE.1i, IE.1k
7. *trace fossil* and *index fossil* IE.1i

Understanding Key Concepts

8. Varves are layers of IE.1i
   a. limestone mixed with coarse sediments.
   b. alternating coarse and fine sediments.
   c. fossils.
   d. sediments that have gaps that represent missing time in the rock sequence.

9. An unconformity that results when new sediments are deposited on eroded horizontal layers is a(n) IE.1i
   a. angular unconformity.
   b. disconformity.
   c. crosscut unconformity.
   d. nonconformity.

10. A fault or intrusion is younger than the rock it cuts through, according to the IE.1i
    a. type of unconformity.
    b. law of superposition.
    c. law of crosscutting relationships.
    d. principle of uniformitarianism.

11. The age of a rock in years is the rock's numerical age, or IE.1i
    a. index age.
    c. half-life age.
    b. relative age.
    d. absolute age.

12. A gap in the sequence of rock layers is a(n) IE.1i
    a. bedding plane.
    b. varve.
    c. unconformity.
    d. uniformity.

13. The process by which the remains of an organism are preserved by drying is called
    a. petrification.
    c. erosion.
    b. mummification.
    d. superposition.

14. Molds that fill with sediment sometimes produce
    a. casts.
    c. coprolites.
    b. gastroliths.
    d. imprints.

Short Answer

15. What prompted James Hutton to formulate the principle of uniformitarianism? IE.1i, IE.1k

16. Describe how the law of superposition helps scientists determine relative age. IE.1i, IE.1k

17. Compare and contrast the three types of unconformities. IE.1i

18. How do scientists use radioactive decay to determine absolute age? IE.1i

19. Besides radiometric dating, what are three other methods of estimating absolute age? IE.1i

20. List and describe five ways that organisms can be preserved.

21. List the four characteristics that define an index fossil. IE.1i

CT Scanning Fossils

Paleontologists studying dinosaur bones want to learn as much as possible from the fossils they find. However, scientists often have to destroy a fossil to look inside it.

The Price of Discovery

Usually, paleontologists examine the inside of a fossil by grinding away the specimen layer by layer. Unfortunately, by the time all of the fossil's internal structures are revealed, the specimen is completely destroyed.

Sectioning a fossil by layers also takes a lot of time. Scientists must carefully document each fresh surface because it will be destroyed later to uncover the next surface. Scientists record their observations by measuring, drawing, photographing, and making an imprint of each new surface.

▼ This fossil is the skull of a *Nanotyrannus lancensis.*

▲ This CT image shows the size and location of the dinosaur's brain.

New Uses for Technology

But now, some paleontologists can use *computerized axial tomography,* or CT scanning, to examine certain fossils without destroying them. CT scanning was originally developed for diagnosing illnesses in people. A CT scanner bombards an object with X rays from all angles within a single plane. The scanner measures the absorption of this radiation to create a map of the different densities within the object. Denser areas absorb more of the X rays' energy and appear white or light gray. Less dense areas appear dark gray or black. Once the object has been scanned in one plane, it is moved less

than a millimeter and another scan is performed. This process is repeated until the entire object has been scanned. A computer imaging program then assembles the cross sections into a picture that can be viewed from any angle.

CT scanning allows scientists to study some extremely fragile fossils that cannot be studied by using traditional methods. It also allows scientists to study rare or unique fossils that must be preserved. Using CT scans, paleontologists can study the interior of fossils in a much less destructive way and in much less time.

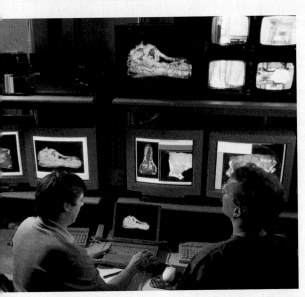

◄ High-resolution CT scanners provide unparalleled views of the internal structures of fossils.

Extension

1. **Making Comparisons**
   Research another use of CT scans. Write a brief report about your findings.

▶ This photo was taken from the space shuttle *Endeavor* as Russia's Kliuchevskoi volcano erupted on September 30, 1994. The volcanic cloud reached 60,000 ft into the atmosphere, and wind carried the ash as far as 640 mi.

Plate Tectonics

Sections

1 Continental Drift

2 The Theory of Plate Tectonics

3 The Changing Continents

What You'll Learn

- How scientists developed the theory of plate tectonics
- Why tectonic plates move
- How Earth's geography has changed

Why It's Relevant

Understanding why and how tectonic plates move provides a basis for understanding other concepts of Earth science.

PRE-READING ACTIVITY

Tri-Fold
Before you read this chapter, create the **FoldNote** entitled "TriFold" described in the Skills Handbook section of the Appendix. Write what you know about plate tectonics in the column labeled "Know." Then, write what you want to know in the column labeled "Want." As you read the chapter, write what you learn in the column labeled "Learn."

▶ The island of Iceland is being torn into two pieces as two tectonic plates pull apart. Iceland is one of only a few places on Earth where this process can be seen on land.

 California Content Standards

3a Students know features of the ocean floor (magnetic patterns, age, and sea-floor topography) provide evidence of plate tectonics.

3b Students know the principal structures that form at the three different kinds of plate boundaries.

3c Students know how to explain the properties of rocks based on the physical and chemical conditions in which they formed, including plate tectonic processes.

6c Students know how Earth's climate has changed over time, corresponding to changes in Earth's geography, atmospheric composition, and other factors, such as solar radiation and plate movement.

9b Students know the principal natural hazards in different California regions and the geologic basis of those hazards.

IE.1a Students will select and use appropriate tools and technology (such as computer-linked probes, spreadsheets, and graphing calculators) to perform tests, collect data, analyze relationships and display data.

IE.1d Students will formulate explanations using logic and evidence.

IE.1g Students will recognize the usefulness and limitations of models and theories as scientific representations of reality.

IE.1i Students will analyze the locations, sequences, or time intervals that are characteristic of natural phenomena (e.g., relative ages of rocks, locations of planets over time, and succession of species in an ecosystem).

IE.1k Students will recognize the cumulative nature of scientific evidence.

IE.1l Students will analyze situations and solve problems that require combining and applying concepts from more than one area of science.

California Content Standards

3a Students know features of the ocean floor (magnetic patterns, age, and sea floor topography) provide evidence of plate tectonics.

IE.1g Students will recognize the usefulness and limitations of models and theories as scientific representations of reality.

IE.1k Students will recognize the cumulative nature of scientific evidence.

One of the most exciting recent theories in Earth science began with observations made more than 400 years ago. As early explorers sailed the oceans of the world, they brought back information about new continents and their coastlines. Mapmakers used the information to chart the new discoveries and to make the first reliable world maps.

As people studied the maps, they were impressed by the similarity of the continental shorelines on either side of the Atlantic Ocean. The continents looked as though they would fit together like parts of a giant jigsaw puzzle. The east coast of South America, for example, seemed to fit perfectly into the west coast of Africa, as shown in **Figure 1.**

Wegener's Hypothesis

In 1912, a German scientist named Alfred Wegener (VAY guh nuhr) proposed a hypothesis that is now called **continental drift.** Wegener hypothesized that the continents once formed part of a single landmass called a *supercontinent.* According to Wegener, this supercontinent began breaking up into smaller continents about 250 million years ago (during the Mesozoic Era). Over millions of years, these continents drifted to their present locations. Wegener speculated that the crumpling of the crust in places may have produced mountain ranges such as the Andes on the western coast of South America.

OBJECTIVES

▶ **Summarize** Wegener's hypothesis of continental drift. 🐾 IE.1k

▶ **Describe** the process of sea-floor spreading. 🐾 3a

▶ **Identify** how paleomagnetism provides support for the idea of sea-floor spreading. 🐾 3a

▶ **Explain** how sea-floor spreading provides a mechanism for continental drift. 🐾 3a

KEY TERMS

continental drift
mid-ocean ridge
sea-floor spreading
paleomagnetism

---

continental drift the hypothesis that states that the continents once formed a single landmass, broke up, and drifted to their present locations

TYPVS ORBIS TERRARVM.

Figure 1 ▶ Early explorers noticed that the coastlines of Africa and South America could fit together like puzzle pieces. *Can you identify any other continents that could fit together like puzzle pieces?*

Figure 2 ▶ Fossils of *Mesosaurus*, such as the one shown below, were found in both South America and western Africa. Mountain chains of similar ages also exist on different continents, as shown in the map at right.

NORTH AMERICA

ATLANTIC OCEAN

EUROPE

ASIA

AFRICA

SOUTH AMERICA

PACIFIC OCEAN

INDIAN OCEAN

- ▨ Mountains formed ~ 410 million years ago
- ▨ Mountains formed ~ 250 million years ago
- ▨ Distribution of *Mesosaurus* fossils
- ▨ Distribution of *Glossopteris* fossils

Fossil Evidence

In addition to seeing the similarities in the coastlines of the continents, Wegener found other evidence to support his hypothesis. He reasoned that if the continents had once been joined, fossils of the same plants and animals should be found in areas that had once been connected. Wegener knew that identical fossils of *Mesosaurus*, a small, extinct land reptile, had been found in both South America and western Africa. *Mesosaurus*, a fossil of which is shown in **Figure 2,** lived 270 million years ago (during the Paleozoic Era). Wegener knew that it was unlikely that these reptiles had swum across the Atlantic Ocean. He also saw no evidence that land bridges had once connected the continents. So, he concluded that South America and Africa had been joined at one time in the past.

Evidence from Rock Formations

Geologic evidence also supported Wegener's hypothesis of continental drift. The ages and types of rocks in the coastal regions of widely separated areas, such as western Africa and eastern South America, matched closely. Mountain chains that ended at the coastline of one continent seemed to continue on other continents across the ocean, as shown in **Figure 2.** The Appalachian Mountains, for example, extend northward along the eastern coast of North America, and mountains of similar age and structure are found in Greenland, Scotland, and northern Europe. If the continents are assembled into a model supercontinent, the mountains of similar age fit together in continuous chains.

Climatic Evidence

Changes in climatic patterns also suggest that the continents have not always been located where they are now. Geologists discovered layers of debris from ancient glaciers in southern Africa and South America. Today, those areas have climates that are too warm for glaciers to form. Other fossil evidence—such as the plant fossil shown in **Figure 3**—indicated that tropical or subtropical swamps covered areas that now have much colder climates. Wegener suggested that if the continents were once joined and positioned differently, evidence of climatic differences would be easy to explain.

Missing Mechanisms

Despite the evidence that supports the hypothesis of continental drift, Wegener's ideas were strongly opposed. Other scientists of the time rejected the mechanism by which Wegener proposed that the continents moved. Wegener suggested that the continents plowed through the rock of the ocean floor. However, this idea was easily disproved by geologic evidence. Wegener spent the rest of his life searching for a mechanism that would gain scientific consensus. Unfortunately, Wegener died in 1930 before he identified a plausible explanation.

Reading Check Why did many scientists reject Wegener's hypothesis of continental drift? (See the Appendix for answers to Reading Checks.)

Figure 3 ▶ The climate of Antarctica was not always as harsh and cold as it is today. When the plant that became this fossil lived, the climate of Antarctica was warm and tropical.

Mid-Ocean Ridges

The evidence that Wegener needed to support his hypothesis was discovered nearly two decades after his death. The evidence lay on the ocean floor. In 1947, a group of scientists set out to map the Mid-Atlantic Ridge. The Mid-Atlantic Ridge is part of a system of **mid-ocean ridges,** which are undersea mountain ranges through the center of which run steep, narrow valleys. A special feature of mid-ocean ridges is shown in **Figure 4.** While studying the Mid-Atlantic Ridge, scientists noticed two surprising trends. First, they noticed that the sediment that covers the sea floor is thinner closer to a ridge than it is farther from the ridge, as shown in **Figure 5.**

Figure 4 ▶ Black smokers are vents on the sea floor that form as hot, mineral-rich water rushes from the hot rock at mid-ocean ridges and mixes with the surrounding cold ocean water. This photo was taken from a submersible.

This evidence suggests that sediment has been settling on the sea floor farther from the ridge for a longer time than it has been settling near the ridge. Scientists then examined the remains of tiny ocean organisms found in the sediment to date the sediment. The distribution of these organisms showed that the closer the sediment is to a ridge, the younger the sediment is. This evidence indicates that rocks closer to the ridge are younger than rocks farther from the ridge.

mid-ocean ridge a long, undersea mountain chain that has a steep, narrow valley at its center, that forms as magma rises from the asthenosphere, and that creates new oceanic lithosphere (sea floor) as tectonic plates move apart

Second, scientists learned that the ocean floor is very young. While rocks on land are as old as 3.8 billion years, none of the oceanic rocks are more than 175 million years old. Radiometric dating also showed evidence that sea-floor rocks closer to a mid-ocean ridge are younger than sea-floor rocks farther from a ridge.

Figure 5 ▶ Rocks closer to a mid-ocean ridge are younger than rocks farther from the ridge. In addition, rocks closer to the ridge are covered with less sediment, which indicates that sediment has had less time to settle on them.

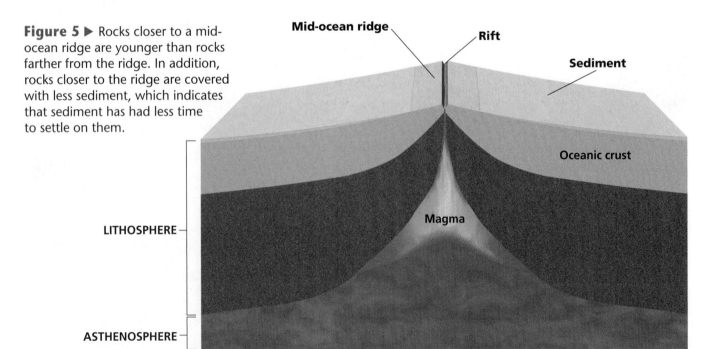

Sea-Floor Spreading

In the late 1950s, a geologist named Harry Hess suggested a new hypothesis. He proposed that the valley at the center of the ridge was a crack, or *rift*, in Earth's crust. At this rift, molten rock, or *magma*, from deep inside Earth rises to fill the crack. As the ocean floor moves away from the ridge, rising magma cools and solidifies to form new rock that replaces the ocean floor. This process is shown in **Figure 6.** Robert Dietz, another geologist, named this process by which new ocean lithosphere (sea floor) forms as magma rises to Earth's surface and solidifies at a mid-ocean ridge as **sea-floor spreading.** Hess suggested that if the ocean floor is moving, the continents might be moving, too. Hess thought that sea-floor spreading was the mechanism that Wegener had failed to find.

Still, Hess's ideas were only hypotheses. More evidence for sea-floor spreading would come years later, in the mid-1960s. This evidence would be discovered through **paleomagnetism,** the study of the magnetic properties of rocks.

✔ Reading Check How does new sea floor form? (See the Appendix for answers to Reading Checks.)

sea-floor spreading the process by which new oceanic lithosphere (sea floor) forms as magma rises to Earth's surface and solidifies at a mid-ocean ridge

paleomagnetism the study of the alignment of magnetic minerals in rock, specifically as it relates to the reversal of Earth's magnetic poles; also the magnetic properties that rock acquires during formation

Graphic Organizer Chain-of-Events Chart

Create the **Graphic Organizer** entitled "Chain-of-Events Chart" described in the Skills Handbook section of the Appendix. Then, fill in the chart with details about each step of sea-floor spreading.

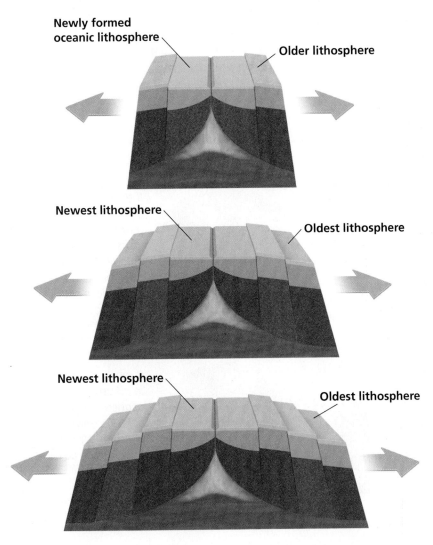

Newly formed oceanic lithosphere

Older lithosphere

Newest lithosphere

Oldest lithosphere

Newest lithosphere

Oldest lithosphere

Figure 6 ▶ As the ocean floor spreads apart at a mid-ocean ridge, magma rises to fill the rift and then cools to form new rock. As this process is repeated over millions of years, new sea floor forms.

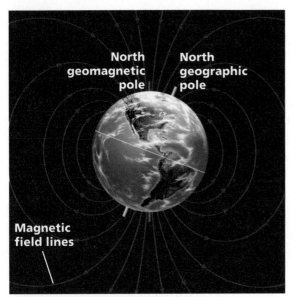

Figure 7 ▶ Earth acts as a giant magnet because of currents in Earth's core.

Paleomagnetism

If you have ever used a compass to determine direction, you know that Earth acts as a giant magnet. Earth has north and south geomagnetic poles, as shown in **Figure 7.** The compass needle aligns with the field of magnetic force that extends from one pole to the other.

As magma solidifies to form rock, iron-rich minerals in the magma align with Earth's magnetic field in the same way that a compass needle does. When the rock hardens, the magnetic orientation of the minerals becomes permanent. This residual magnetism of rock is called *paleomagnetism*.

Magnetic Reversals

Geologic evidence suggests that Earth's magnetic field has not always pointed north, as it does now. Scientists have discovered rocks whose magnetic orientations point opposite of Earth's current magnetic field. Scientists have dated rocks of different magnetic polarities. All rocks with magnetic fields that point north, or *normal polarity*, are classified in the same time periods. All rocks with magnetic fields that point south, or *reversed polarity*, also fell into specific time periods. When scientists placed these periods of normal and reverse polarity in chronological order, they discovered a pattern of alternating normal and reversed polarity in the rocks. Scientists used this pattern to create the *geomagnetic reversal time scale*.

Connection to PHYSICS

What Makes Materials Magnetic?

Some materials are magnetic, while others are not. So, what makes a material magnetic? All matter is composed of atoms. In atoms, electrons are the negatively charged particles that move around the nucleus. The motion of electrons in an atom produces magnetic fields that can give the atom a north pole and a south pole.

In most materials, the magnetic fields of individual atoms are not aligned, so the materials are not magnetic. However, in some materials, such as the iron in some rocks, the atoms group together in tiny regions called *domains*. The atoms in a domain are arranged so that the north and south poles of the atoms are aligned to create a stronger magnetic field than that of a single atom. If most of the domains in an object are also aligned, their magnetic fields combine to make the whole object magnetic.

If the domains in an object are randomly arranged, the magnetic fields of individual domains cancel each other out and the object does not have magnetic properties.

If most of the domains in an object are aligned, the magnetic fields of individual domains combine to make the object magnetic.

Magnetic Symmetry

As scientists were learning about the age of the sea floor, they also were finding puzzling magnetic patterns on the ocean floor. The scientists used the geomagnetic reversal time scale to help them unravel the mystery of these magnetic patterns.

Scientists noticed that the striped magnetic pattern on one side of a mid-ocean ridge is a mirror image of the striped pattern on the other side of the ridge. These patterns are shown in **Figure 8.** When drawn on maps of the ocean floor, these patterns showed alternating bands of normal and reversed polarity that match the geomagnetic reversal time scale. Scientists suggested that as new sea floor forms at a mid-ocean ridge, the new sea floor records reversals in Earth's magnetic field.

By matching the magnetic patterns on each side of a mid-ocean ridge to the geomagnetic reversal time scale, scientists could assign ages to the sea-floor rocks. The scientists found that the ages of sea-floor rocks were also symmetrical. The youngest rocks were at the center, and older rocks were farther away on either side of the ridge. The only place on the sea floor that new rock forms is at the rift in a mid-ocean ridge. Thus, the patterns indicate that new rock forms at the center of a ridge and then moves away from the center in opposite directions. Thus, the symmetry of magnetic patterns—and the symmetry of ages of sea-floor rocks—supports Hess's idea of sea-floor spreading.

Reading Check How are magnetic patterns in sea-floor rock evidence of sea-floor spreading? (See the Appendix for answers to Reading Checks.)

Quick LAB 10 min

Making Magnets IE.1d, IE.1g

Procedure

1. Slide one end of a **bar magnet** down the side of a **5 inch iron nail** 10 times. Always slide the magnet in the same direction.
2. Hold the nail over a small pile of **steel paperclips.** Record what happens.
3. Slide the bar magnet back and forth 10 times down the side of the nail. Repeat step 2.

Analysis

1. What was the effect of sliding the magnet down the nail in one direction? in different directions?
2. How does this lab demonstrate the idea of domains?

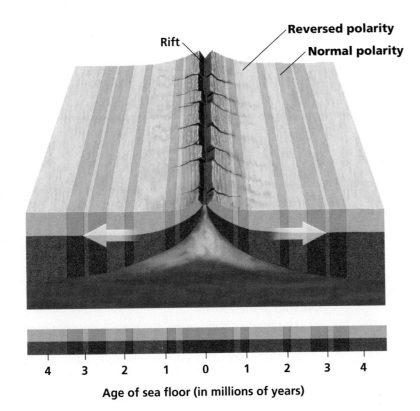

Reversed polarity

Normal polarity

Rift

4 3 2 1 0 1 2 3 4

Age of sea floor (in millions of years)

Figure 8 ▶ The stripes in the sea floor shown here illustrate Earth's alternating magnetic field. Dark stripes represent normal polarity, while the lighter stripes represent reversed polarity. *What is the polarity of the rocks closest to the rift?*

Figure 9 ▶ Scientists collected samples of these sedimentary rocks in California and used the magnetic properties of the samples to date the rocks by using the geomagnetic reversal time scale.

Wegener Redeemed

Another group of scientists discovered that the reversal patterns seen in rocks on the sea floor also appeared in rocks on land, such as those shown in **Figure 9.** The reversals in the land rocks matched the geomagnetic reversal time scale. Because the same pattern occurs in rocks of the same ages on both land and the sea floor, scientists became confident that magnetic patterns show changes over time. Thus, the idea of sea-floor spreading gained further favor in the scientific community.

Scientists reasoned that sea-floor spreading provides a way for the continents to move over Earth's surface. Continents are carried by the widening sea floor in much the same way that objects are moved by a conveyer belt. The molten rock from a rift cools, hardens, and then moves away in the opposite direction on both sides of the ridge. Here, at last, was the mechanism that verified Wegener's hypothesis of continental drift.

Section 1 Review

1. **Describe** the observation that first led to Wegener's hypothesis of continental drift. 🐻 IE.1k

2. **Summarize** the evidence that supports Wegener's hypothesis. 🐻 3a, IE.1k

3. **Compare** sea-floor spreading and the formation of mid-ocean ridges. 🐻 3a

4. **Explain** how scientists know that Earth's magnetic poles have reversed many times during Earth's history.

5. **Identify** how magnetic symmetry can be used as evidence of sea-floor spreading. 🐻 3a

6. **Explain** how scientists date sea-floor rocks. 🐻 IE.1i

CRITICAL THINKING

7. **Making Inferences** How does evidence that sea-floor rocks farther from a ridge are older than rocks closer to the ridge support the idea of sea-floor spreading? 🐻 3a, IE.1d, IE.1i

8. **Analyzing Ideas** Explain how sea-floor spreading provides an explanation for how continents may move over Earth's surface. 🐻 3a, IE.1d

CONCEPT MAPPING

9. Use the following terms to create a concept map: *continental drift, paleomagnetism, fossils, climate, sea-floor spreading, geologic evidence, supercontinent,* and *mid-ocean ridge.* 🐻 3a

3b Students know the principal structures that form at the three different kinds of plate boundaries.

3c Students know how to explain the properties of rocks based on the physical and chemical conditions in which they formed, including plate tectonic processes.

IE.1g Students will recognize the usefulness and limitations of models and theories as scientific representations of reality.

By the 1960s, evidence supporting continental drift and sea-floor spreading led to the development of a theory called *plate tectonics*. **Plate tectonics** is the theory that explains why and how continents move and is the study of the formation of features in Earth's crust.

How Continents Move

Earth's crust and the rigid, upper part of the mantle form a layer of Earth called the **lithosphere.** The lithosphere forms the thin outer shell of Earth. It is broken into several blocks, called *tectonic plates*, that ride on a deformable layer of the mantle called the *asthenosphere* in much the same way that blocks of wood float on water. The **asthenosphere** (as THEN uh sfir) is a layer of "plastic" rock just below the lithosphere. Plastic rock is solid rock that is under great pressure and that flows very slowly, like putty does. **Figure 1** shows what tectonic plates may look like.

Earth's crust is classified into two types—*oceanic crust* and *continental crust.* Oceanic crust is dense and is made of rock that is rich in iron and magnesium. Continental crust has a low density and is made of rock that is rich in silica. Tectonic plates can include continental crust, oceanic crust, or both. The continents and oceans are carried along on the moving tectonic plates in the same way that passengers are carried by a bus.

OBJECTIVES

▶ **Summarize** the theory of plate tectonics. 🐻 IE.1g

▶ **Identify** and describe the three types of plate boundaries. 🐻 3b

▶ **List** and describe three causes of plate movement. 🐻 3c

KEY TERMS

plate tectonics
lithosphere
asthenosphere
divergent boundary
convergent boundary
transform boundary

plate tectonics the theory that explains how large pieces of the lithosphere, called *plates,* move and change shape

lithosphere the solid, outer layer of Earth that consists of the crust and the rigid upper part of the mantle

asthenosphere the solid, plastic layer of the mantle beneath the lithosphere; made of mantle rock that flows very slowly, which allows tectonic plates to move on top of it

South American plate

Nazca plate

Pacific plate

Antarctic plate

Figure 1 ▶ Tectonic plates fit together on Earth's surface like three-dimensional puzzle pieces.

Tectonic Plates

Scientists have identified about 15 major tectonic plates. While many plates are bordered by major surface features, such as mountain ranges or deep trenches in the oceans, the boundaries of the plates are not always easy to identify. As shown in **Figure 2**, the familiar outlines of the continents and oceans do not always match the outlines of plate boundaries. Some plate boundaries are located within continents far from mountain ranges.

Earthquakes

Scientists identify plate boundaries primarily by studying data from earthquakes. When tectonic plates move, sudden shifts can occur along their boundaries. These sudden movements are called *earthquakes*. Frequent earthquakes in a given zone are evidence that two or more plates may meet in that area.

Volcanoes

The locations of volcanoes can also help identify the locations of plate boundaries. Some volcanoes form when plate motions generate magma that erupts on Earth's surface. For example, the Pacific Ring of Fire is a zone of active volcanoes that encircles the Pacific Ocean. This zone is also one of Earth's major earthquake zones. The characteristics of this zone indicate that the Pacific Ocean is surrounded by plate boundaries.

✔ **Reading Check** How do scientists identify locations of plate boundaries? (See the Appendix for answers to Reading Checks.)

Figure 2 ▶ Tectonic plates may contain both oceanic and continental crust. Notice that the boundaries of plates do not always match the outlines of continents.

Ridge Push

Newly formed rock at a mid-ocean ridge is warm and less dense than older rock nearby. The warm, less dense rock is elevated above nearby rock, and older, denser rock slopes downward away from the ridge. As the newer, warmer rock cools and becomes denser, it begins to sink into the mantle and pull away from the ridge.

As the cooling rock sinks, the asthenosphere below it exerts force on the rest of the plate. This force is called *ridge push*. This force pushes the rest of the plate away from the mid-ocean ridge. Ridge push is illustrated in **Figure 7**.

Scientists think that ridge push may help drive plate motions. However, most scientists agree that ridge push is not the main driving force of plate motion. So, scientists looked to convergent boundaries for other clues to the forces that drive plate motion.

Figure 7 ▶ As the cooling lithosphere sinks, the asthenosphere moves away from the sinking lithosphere and pushes on the bottom of the plate. The plate moves in the direction that it is pushed by the asthenosphere.

 Reading Check How may density differences in the rock at a mid-ocean ridge help drive plate motion? (See the Appendix for answers to Reading Checks.)

QuickLAB

30 min

Tectonic Plate Boundaries

Procedure 3b, 3c, IE.1d

1. Using a **ruler**, draw two 7 cm × 12 cm rectangles on a **piece of paper**. Cut them out with **scissors**.

2. Use a rolling pin to flatten **two different colored pieces of clay** to about 1/2 cm thick.

3. Use a **plastic knife** to cut each piece of clay into a 7 cm × 12 cm rectangle. Place a paper rectangle on each piece of clay.

4. Place the two clay models side by side on a flat surface and paper side down.

5. Place one hand on each piece of clay, and slowly push the blocks together until the edges begin to buckle and rise off the surface of the table.

6. Turn the clay models around so that the unbuckled edges are touching each other.

7. Place one hand on each clay model. Apply slight pressure toward the plane where the two blocks meet. Slide one clay model forward 7 cm and the other model backward about 7 cm.

Analysis

1. What type of plate boundary are you modeling in step 5?

2. What type of plate boundary are you modeling in step 7?

3. How do you think the processes modeled in this activity might affect the appearance of Earth's surface?

Direction of plate motion

Resulting plate motion

Sinking due to density

Figure 8 ▶ The leading edge of the subducting plate pulls the rest of the subducting plate into the asthenosphere in a process called *slab pull*.

Slab Pull

Where plates pull away from each other at mid-ocean ridges, magma from the asthenosphere rises to the surface. The magma then cools to form new lithosphere. As the lithosphere moves away from the mid-ocean ridge, the lithosphere cools and becomes denser. Where the lithosphere is dense enough, it begins to subduct into the asthenosphere. As the leading edge of the plate sinks, it pulls the rest of the plate along behind it. The force exerted by the sinking plate is called *slab pull*. This process is shown in **Figure 8.** In general, plates that are subducting move faster than plates that are not subducting. This evidence indicates that the downward pull of the subducting lithosphere is a strong driving force for tectonic plate motion.

All three mechanisms of Earth's convecting system—drag on the bottoms of tectonic plates, ridge push, and slab pull—work together to drive plate motions. These mechanisms form a system that makes Earth's tectonic plates move constantly.

Section 2 Review

1. **Summarize** the theory of plate tectonics. 3c

2. **Explain** why most earthquakes and volcanoes happen along plate boundaries. 3b, 3c

3. **Identify and describe** the three major types of plate boundaries. 3b

4. **Compare** the changes in Earth's surface that happen at a convergent boundary with those that happen at a divergent boundary. 3b

5. **Describe** the role of convection currents in plate movement.

6. **Describe** how ridge push and slab pull contribute to the movement of tectonic plates. 3b, 3c

CRITICAL THINKING

7. **Making Inferences** How do convergent boundaries add material to Earth's surface? 3b, 3c, IE.1d

8. **Determining Cause and Effect** Explain how the outward transfer of heat energy from inside Earth drives the movement of tectonic plates. IE.1d

CONCEPT MAPPING

9. Use the following terms to create a concept map: *tectonic plate, divergent, convergent, convection, transform, ridge push, slab pull, subduction zone,* and *mid-ocean ridge.* 3b, 3c

The Changing Continents

3b Students know the principal structures that form at the three different kinds of plate boundaries.

6c Students know how Earth's climate has changed over time, corresponding to changes in Earth's geography, atmospheric composition, and other factors, such as solar radiation and plate movement.

IE.1k Students will recognize the cumulative nature of scientific evidence.

The continents did not always have the same shapes that they do today. And geologic evidence indicates that they will not stay the same shape forever. In fact, the continents are always changing. Slow movements of tectonic plates change the size and shape of the continents over millions of years.

Reshaping Earth's Crust

All of the continents that exist today contain large areas of stable rock, called *cratons,* that are older than 540 million years. Rocks within the cratons that have been exposed at Earth's surface are called *shields.* Cratons represent ancient cores around which the modern continents formed.

Rifting and Continental Reduction

One way that continents change shape is by breaking apart. **Rifting** is the process by which a continent breaks apart. New, smaller continents may form as a result of this process. The reason that continents rift is not entirely known. Because continental crust is thick and has a high silica content, continental crust acts as an insulator. This insulating property prevents heat in Earth's interior from escaping. Scientists think that as heat from the mantle builds up beneath the continent, continental lithosphere becomes thinner and begins to weaken. Eventually, a rift forms in this zone of weakness, and the continent begins to break apart, as shown in **Figure 1.**

OBJECTIVES

▶ **Identify** how movements of tectonic plates change Earth's surface.

▶ **Summarize** how movements of tectonic plates have influenced climates and life on Earth. **3b** **6c**

▶ **Describe** the supercontinent cycle. **IE.1k**

KEY TERMS

rifting
terrane
supercontinent cycle
Pangaea
Panthalassa

rifting the process by which Earth's crust breaks apart; can occur within continental crust or oceanic crust

Figure 1 ▶ The East African Rift Valley formed as Africa began rifting about 30 million years ago.

Terranes and Continental Growth

Continents change not only by breaking apart but also by gaining material. Most continents consist of cratons surrounded by a patchwork of terranes. A **terrane** is a piece of lithosphere that has a unique geologic history that differs from the histories of surrounding lithosphere. A terrane can be identified by three characteristics. First, a terrane contains rock and fossils that differ from the rock and fossils of neighboring terranes. Second, there are major faults at the boundaries of a terrane. Third, the magnetic properties of a terrane generally do not match those of neighboring terranes.

Terranes become part of a continent at convergent boundaries. When a tectonic plate carrying a terrane subducts under a plate made of continental crust, the terrane is scraped off the subducting plate, as shown in **Figure 2.** The terrane then becomes part of the continent. Some terranes may form mountains, while other terranes simply add to the surface area of a continent. The process in which a terrane becomes part of a continent is called *accretion* (uh KREE shuhn).

A variety of materials can form terranes. Terranes may be small volcanic islands or underwater mountains called *seamounts*. Small coral islands, or *atolls,* can also form terranes. And large chunks of continental crust can be terranes. When large terranes and continents collide, major mountain chains often form. For example, the Himalaya Mountains formed when India began colliding with Asia about 50 million years ago (during the Cenozoic Era).

✓ Reading Check Describe the process of accretion. (See the Appendix for answers to Reading Checks.)

terrane a piece of lithosphere that has a unique geologic history and that may be part of a larger piece of lithosphere, such as a continent

Figure 2 ▶ As oceanic crust subducts, a terrane is scraped off the ocean floor and becomes part of the continental crust. *What would you expect to happen to sediments on the sea floor when the plate they are on subducts?*

As the oceanic plate subducts, terranes are carried closer to the continent.

When the terrane reaches the subduction zone, the terrane is scraped off the subducting plate and is added to the continent's edge.

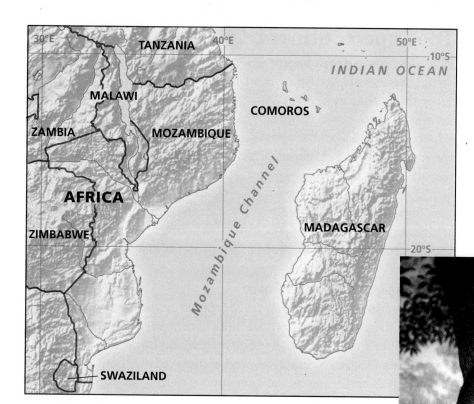

Figure 3 ▶ Madagascar separated from Africa about 165 million years ago and separated from India about 88 million years ago. This separation isolated the plants and animals on the island of Madagascar. As a result, unique species of plants and animals evolved on Madagascar. These species, such as the fossa (below), are found nowhere else on Earth.

Effects of Continental Change

Modern climates are a result of past movements of tectonic plates. A continent's location in relation to the equator and the poles affects the continent's overall climate. A continent's climate is also affected by the continent's location in relation to oceans and other continents. Mountain ranges affect air flow and wind patterns around the globe. Mountains also affect the amount of moisture that reaches certain parts of a continent. When continents move, the flow of air and moisture around the globe changes and causes climates to change.

Changes in Climate

Geologic evidence shows that ice once covered most of Earth's continental surfaces. Even the Sahara in Africa, one of the hottest places on Earth today, was once covered by a thick ice sheet. This ice sheet formed when all of the continents were close together and were located near the South Pole. As continents began to drift around the globe, however, global temperatures changed and much of the ice sheet melted.

Changes in Life

As continents rift or as mountains form, populations of organisms are separated. When populations are separated, new species may evolve from existing species. Sometimes, isolation protects organisms from competitors and predators and may allow the organismsm to evolve into unique organisms, as shown in **Figure 3.**

The Supercontinent Cycle

Using evidence from many scientific fields, scientists can construct a general picture of continental change throughout time. They think that at several times in the past, the continents were arranged into large landmasses called *supercontinents*. These supercontinents broke apart to form smaller continents that moved around the globe. Eventually, the smaller continents joined again to form another supercontinent. When the last supercontinent broke apart, the modern continents formed. A new supercontinent is likely to form in the future. The process by which supercontinents form and break apart over time is called the **supercontinent cycle** and is shown in **Figure 4.**

Why Supercontinents Form

The movement of plates toward convergent boundaries eventually causes continents to collide. Because continental lithosphere does not subduct, the convergent boundary between two continents becomes inactive, and a new convergent boundary forms. Over time, all of the continents collide to form a supercontinent. Then, heat from Earth's interior builds up under the supercontinent, and rifts form in the supercontinent. The supercontinent breaks apart, and plates carrying separate continents move around the globe.

Formation of Pangaea

The supercontinent **Pangaea** (pan JEE uh) formed about 300 million years ago (during the Paleozoic Era). As the continents collided to form Pangaea, mountains formed. The Appalachian Mountains of eastern North America and the Ural Mountains of Russia formed during these collisions. A body of water called the Tethys Sea cut into the eastern edge of Pangaea. The single, large ocean that surrounded Pangaea was called **Panthalassa.**

supercontinent cycle the process by which supercontinents form and break apart over millions of years

Pangaea the supercontinent that formed 300 million years ago and that began to break up beginning 250 million years ago

Panthalassa the single, large ocean that covered Earth's surface during the time the supercontinent Pangaea existed

Figure 4 ▶ Over millions of years, supercontinents form and break apart in a cycle known as the *supercontinent cycle.*

About 450 million years ago
Earth's continents were separated, as they are today.

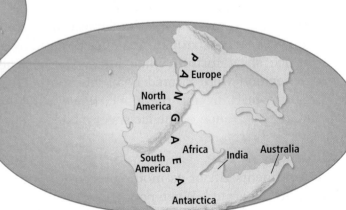

260 million to 240 million years ago
Pangaea had formed and was beginning to break apart.

Breakup of Pangaea

About 250 million years ago (during the Paleozoic Era), Pangaea began to break into two continents—*Laurasia* and *Gondwanaland*. A large rift split the supercontinent from east to west. Then, Laurasia began to drift northward and rotate slowly, and a new rift formed. This rift separated Laurasia into the continents of North America and Eurasia. The rift eventually formed the North Atlantic Ocean. The rotation of Laurasia also caused the Tethys Sea to close. The Tethys Sea eventually became the Mediterranean Sea.

As Laurasia began to break apart, Gondwanaland also broke into two continents. One continent broke apart to become the continents of South America and Africa. About 150 million years ago (during the Mesozoic Era), a rift between Africa and South America opened to form the South Atlantic Ocean. The other continent separated to form India, Australia, and Antarctica. As India broke away from Australia and Antarctica, it started moving northward, toward Eurasia. About 50 million years ago (during the Cenozoic Era), India collided with Eurasia, and the Himalaya Mountains began to form.

The Modern Continents

Slowly, the continents moved into their present positions. As the continents drifted, they collided with terranes and other continents. These collisions welded new crust onto the continents and uplifted the land. Mountain ranges, such as the Rocky Mountains, the Andes, and the Alps, formed. Tectonic plate motion also caused new oceans to open up and caused others to close.

Reading Check What modern continents formed from Gondwanaland? (See the Appendix for answers to Reading Checks.)

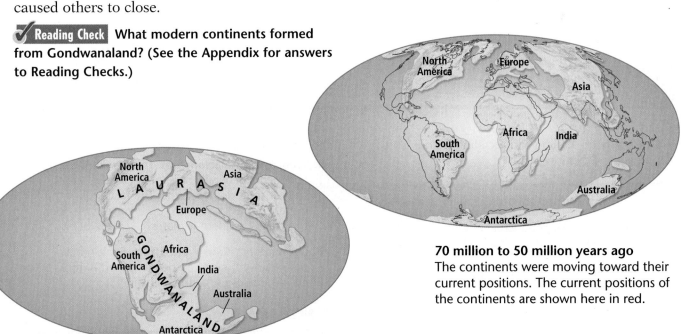

70 million to 50 million years ago
The continents were moving toward their current positions. The current positions of the continents are shown here in red.

160 million to 140 million years ago
Pangaea split into two continents—Laurasia to the north and Gondwanaland to the south.

Geography of the Future

As tectonic plates continue to move, Earth's geography will change dramatically. If plate movements continue at current rates, in about 150 million years, Africa will collide with Eurasia, and the Mediterranean Sea will close. A new ocean will form as east Africa separates from the rest of Africa and moves eastward. New subduction zones will form off the east coast of North and South America. North and South America will then move east across the Atlantic Ocean. The Atlantic Ocean will close as North and South America collide with Africa.

In North America, Mexico's Baja Peninsula and the part of California that is west of the San Andreas Fault will move to where Alaska is today. If this plate movement occurs as predicted, Los Angeles will be located north of San Francisco's current location. Scientists predict that in 250 million years, the continents will come together again to form a new supercontinent, as shown in **Figure 5.**

Figure 5 ▶ Scientists predict that movements of tectonic plates will cause a supercontinent to form in the future.

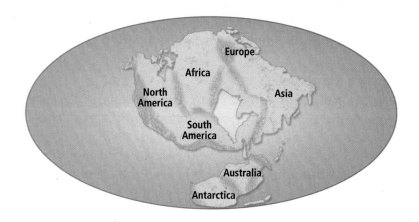

1. **Identify** how rifting and accretion change the shapes of continents. 🌐 3b

2. **Describe** why a terrane has a different geologic history from that of the surrounding area. 🌐 3b

3. **Summarize** how continental rifting may lead to changes in plants and animals. 🌐 6c

4. **Describe** the supercontinent cycle. 🌐IE.1k

5. **Explain** how the theory of plate tectonics relates to the formation and breakup of Pangaea. 🌐 6c, IE.1k

6. **Compare** Pangaea and Gondwanaland. 🌐 6c

7. **List** three changes in geography that are likely to happen in the future. 🌐 3b, 2c, 6c

CRITICAL THINKING

8. **Identifying Relationships** The interior parts of continents generally have drier climates than coastal areas do. How does this fact explain the evidence that the climate on Pangaea was drier than many modern climates? 🌐 6c, IE.1d

9. **Determining Cause and Effect** Explain how mountains on land can be composed of rocks that contain fossils of marine animals. 🌐 6c

CONCEPT MAPPING

10. Use the following terms to create a concept map: *supercontinent, rifting, atoll, continent, terrane, seamount, accretion,* and *Pangaea.* 🌐 6c

Sections

1 Continental Drift

Key Terms

continental drift, 239

mid-ocean ridge, 242

seafloor spreading, 243

paleomagnetism, 243

Key Concepts

▶ Fossil, rock, and climatic evidence supports Wegener's hypothesis of continental drift. However, Wegener could not explain the mechanism by which the continents move.

▶ New ocean floor is constantly being produced through sea-floor spreading, which creates mid-ocean ridges and changes the topography of the sea floor.

▶ Sea-floor spreading provides a mechanism for continental drift.

2 The Theory of Plate Tectonics

plate tectonics, 247

lithosphere, 247

asthenosphere, 247

divergent boundary, 249

convergent boundary, 250

transform boundary, 251

▶ The theory of plate tectonics proposes that changes in Earth's crust are caused by the very slow movement of large tectonic plates.

▶ Earthquakes, volcanoes, and young mountain ranges tend to be located in belts along the boundaries between tectonic plates.

▶ Tectonic plates meet at three types of boundaries—divergent, convergent, and transform. The geologic activity that occurs along the three types of plate boundaries differs according to the way plates move relative to each other.

▶ Tectonic plates may be part of a convecting system that is driven by differences in density and heat.

3 The Changing Continents

rifting, 255

terrane, 256

supercontinent cycle, 258

Pangaea, 258

Panthalassa, 258

▶ Continents grow through the accretion of terranes. Continents break apart through rifting.

▶ Movements of tectonic plates have altered climates on continents and have created conditions that lead to changes in plants and animals.

▶ Continents collide to form supercontinents and then break apart in a cycle called the *supercontinent cycle*.

▶ Earth's tectonic plates continue to move, and in the future, the continents will likely be in a different configuration.

Using Key Terms

Use each of the following terms in a separate sentence.

1. *sea-floor spreading* 🐘3a
2. *convection*
3. *divergent boundary* 🐘3b
4. *terrane* 🐘3b

For each pair of terms, explain how the meanings of the terms differ.

5. *convergent boundary* and *subduction zone* 🐘3b
6. *continental drift* and *plate tectonics* 🐘3a, 3b, 3c
7. *ridge push* and *slab pull* 🐘3b
8. *Pangaea* and *Panthalasa* 🐘6c

Understanding Key Concepts

9. Support for Wegener's hypothesis of continental drift includes evidence of changes in 🐘IE.1k
   a. climatic patterns.
   c. terranes.
   b. Panthalassa.
   d. subduction.

10. New ocean floor is constantly being produced through the process known as 🐘3a
    a. subduction.
    b. continental drift.
    c. sea-floor spreading.
    d. terranes.

11. An underwater mountain chain that formed by sea-floor spreading is called a 🐘3a
    a. divergent boundary.
    b. subduction zone.
    c. mid-ocean ridge.
    d. convergent boundary.

12. Scientists think that the upwelling of mantle material at mid-ocean ridges is caused by the motion of tectonic plates and comes from 🐘3a
    a. the lithosphere.   c. the asthenosphere.
    b. terranes.   d. rift valleys.

13. The layer of plastic rock that underlies the tectonic plates is the 🐘3a
    a. lithosphere.   c. oceanic crust.
    b. asthenosphere.   d. terrane.

14. The region along tectonic plate boundaries where one plate moves beneath another is called a 🐘3b
    a. rift valley.
    b. transform boundary.
    c. subduction zone.
    d. convergent boundary.

15. Two plates grind past each other at a 🐘3b
    a. transform boundary.
    b. convergent boundary.
    c. subduction zone.
    d. divergent boundary.

16. Convection occurs because heated material becomes
    a. less dense and rises.
    b. denser and rises.
    c. denser and sinks.
    d. less dense and sinks.

Short Answer

17. Explain the role of technology in the progression from the hypothesis of continental drift to the theory of plate tectonics. 🐘3a, 3b, 3c, IE.1k

18. Summarize how the continents moved from being part of Pangaea to their current locations. 🐘6c

19. Why do most earthquakes and volcanoes happen at or near plate boundaries? 🐘3b

20. Explain the following statement: "Because of sea-floor spreading, the ocean floor is constantly renewing itself." 🐘3a

21. Describe how rocks that form at a mid-ocean ridge become magnetized. 🐘3a

22. How may continental rifting influence the evolution of plants and animals? 🐘6c

Critical Thinking

23. Making Comparisons How are tectonic plates like the pieces of a jigsaw puzzle? IE.1d

24. Making Inferences If Alfred Wegener had found identical fossil remains of plants and animals that had lived no more than 10 million years ago in both eastern Brazil and western Africa, what might he have concluded about the breakup of Pangaea? 6c, IE.1d, IE.1k

25. Identifying Relationships Assume that the total surface area of Earth is not changing. If new material is being added to Earth's crust at one boundary, what would you expect to be happening at another boundary? 3b, 6c, IE.1d

26. Making Predictions One hundred fifty million years from now, the continents will have drifted to new locations. How might these changes affect life on Earth? 6c, IE.1d

Concept Mapping

27. Use the following terms to create a concept map: *asthenosphere, lithosphere, divergent boundary, convergent boundary, transform boundary, subduction zone, mid-ocean ridge, plates, convection, continental drift, theory of plate tectonics,* and *sea-floor spreading.* 3a, 3b, 3c

Math Skills

28. Making Calculations The coasts of Africa and South America began rifting about 150 million years ago. Today, the coast of South America is about 6,660 km from the coast of Africa. Using the equation *velocity = distance ÷ time*, determine how fast the continents moved apart in millimeters per year. 6c

29. Using Equations Assume that scientists know the rate at which the North American and Eurasian plates are moving away from each other. If t = time. d = distance, and v = velocity, what equation can they use to determine when North America separated from Eurasia during the breakup of Pangaea? 6c

Writing Skills

30. Writing Persuasively Imagine that you are Alfred Wegener. Write a persuasive essay to explain your idea of continental drift. Use only evidence originally used by Wegener to support his hypothesis. IE.1k

31. Communicating Main Ideas Explain how the research of Wegener, Hess, and others led to the theory of plate tectonics. IE.1k

Interpreting Graphics

The graph below shows the relationship between the age of sea floor rocks and the depth of the sea floor beneath the ocean surface. Use the graph to answer the questions that follow.

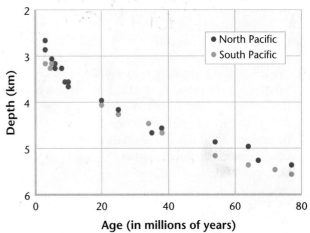

32. How old is the sea floor at a depth of 4 km? 3a

33. Approximately how deep is the sea floor when it is 55 million years old? 3a

34. What can you infer about the age of very deep sea floor from the data in the graph? 3a

35. The ridge in the South Pacific Ocean is spreading faster than the ridge in the North Pacific Ocean. If this graph showed the depth of the sea floor in relation to the distance from the ridge, how would the graphs of the North Pacific and South Pacific ridges differ? 3a, IE.1d

Understanding Concepts

Directions (1–10): **For *each* question, write on a separate sheet of paper the number of the correct answer.**

1 Which of the following factors is most important when determining the type of boundary that forms when two lithospheric plates collide?
A. the density of each plate
B. the size of each plate
C. the paleomagnetism of the rock
D. the length of the boundary

2 At locations where sea-floor spreading occurs, rock is moved away from a mid-ocean ridge. What replaces the rock as it moves away?
A. molten rock
B. older rock
C. continental crust
D. compacted sediment

3 Which of the following was a weakness of Wegener's proposal of continental drift when he first proposed the hypothesis?
A. an absence of fossil evidence
B. unsupported climatic evidence
C. unrelated continent features
D. a lack of proven mechanisms

4 Which of the following statements describes a specific type of continental growth?
A. Continents change not only by gaining material but also by losing material.
B. Terranes become part of a continent at convergent boundaries.
C. Ocean sediments move onto land because of sea-floor spreading.
D. Rifting adds new rock to a continent and causes the continent to become wider.

5 Modern climates result from
A. the past movements of tectonic plates.
B. changes in populations of organisms.
C. the flow of air in ancient times.
D. isolation.

6 Which of the following statements best describes magma formation at a divergent boundary?
A. One plate subducts under another as two plates collide, forming magma.
B. Magma rises as the plates move apart.
C. Magma forms as two plates slide against each other.
D. A plate subducts as two plates pull apart, forming magma.

7 The San Andreas Fault is a major boundary between the North American plate and Pacific plate. Earthquakes occur along this fault because
A. the plates are spreading.
B. one of the plates subducts under the other.
C. the plates slide against each other.
D. one plate is denser than the other.

8 Rocks on the ocean floor
A. are the same age as rocks on land.
B. are much younger than rocks on land.
C. are older the closer they are to mid-ocean ridges.
D. become magma as they get older.

9 Which of the following best describes the supercontinent cycle that resulted in the continents?
A. Pangaea→Gondwanaland and Laurasia→ separate continents
B. Pangaea→separate continents→ Gondwanaland and Laurasia
C. separate continents→Gondwanaland and Laurasia→Pangaea
D. Gondwanaland and Laurasia→ separate continents→Pangaea

10 Which of the following is NOT true of magnetic reversals?
A. They can be used to assign age to sea floor rocks.
B. They form mirror images on either side of a mid-ocean ridge.
C. They are rarely used to create a time scale.
D. They record changes in Earth's magnetic field.

Interpreting Graphics

Directions (11–13): For *each* question below, record the correct answer on a separate sheet of paper.

The map below shows the locations of the Earth's major tectonic plate boundaries.

Earth's Tectonic Plates

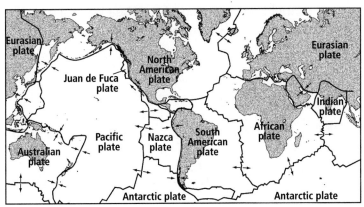

11 What type of boundary is found between the South American plate and the African plate?

A. convergent
B. divergent

C. transform
D. subduction

12 What surface features are most often found at boundaries such as those between the South American and African plates?

A. mountains
B. deep-ocean trenches
C. mid-ocean ridges
D. faults

Plate Boundaries

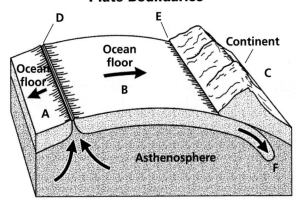

13 The illustration above shows a strike-slip fault that formed along a transform boundary. What type of crustal interaction is indicated by the letter E?

A. continental rifting
B. sea-floor spreading

C. divergence
D. subduction

Making Models Lab

Objectives

▶ **Model** the formation of sea floor.

▶ **Identify** how magnetic patterns are caused by sea-floor spreading.

Materials

marker

paper, unlined

ruler, metric

scissors or utility knife

shoebox

Safety

Sea-Floor Spreading 3a, 6c, IE.1a, IE.1d, IE.1g, IE.1i

The places on Earth's surface where plates pull apart have many names. They are called divergent boundaries, mid-ocean ridges, and spreading centers. The term *spreading center* refers to the fact that sea-floor spreading happens at these locations. In this lab, you will model the formation of new sea floor at a divergent boundary. You will also model the formation of magnetic patterns on the sea floor.

PROCEDURE

1 Cut two identical strips of unlined paper, each 7 cm wide and 30 cm long.

2 Cut a slit 8 cm long in the center of the bottom of a shoebox.

3 Lay the strips of paper together on top of each other end to end so that the ends line up. Push one end of the strips through the slit in the shoe box, so that a few centimeters of both strips stick out of the slit.

Step 3

④ Place the shoe box flat on a table open side down, and make sure the ends of the paper strips are sticking up.

⑤ Separate the strips, and hold one strip in each hand. Pull the strips apart. Then, push the strips down against the shoe box.

⑥ Use a marker to mark across the paper strips where they exit the box. One swipe with the marker should mark both strips.

⑦ Pull the strips evenly until about 2 cm have been pulled through the slit.

⑧ Mark the strips with the marker again.

⑨ Repeat steps 7 and 8, but vary the length of paper that you pull from the slit. Continue this process until both strips are pulled out of the box.

Step 6

ANALYSIS AND CONCLUSION

❶ **Evaluating Models** How does this activity model sea-floor spreading?

❷ **Analyzing Models** What do the marker stripes in this model represent?

❸ **Analyzing Methods** If each 2 cm marked on the paper is equal to 3 million years, how could you use your model to determine the age of certain points on the sea floor?

❹ **Applying Conclusions** You are given only the paper strips with marks already drawn on them. How would you use the paper strips to reconstruct the way in which the sea-floor was formed?

Extension

❶ **Making Models** Design a model that shows what happens at a convergent boundary and what happens at a transform boundary. Present these models to the class.

Locations of Earthquakes in South America, 2002–2003

Earthquake Depth (km)
- 0
- 25
- 75
- 150
- 300
- 600

Map Skills Activity

This map shows the locations and depths of earthquakes that registered magnitudes greater than 5 and that happened in South America in 2002 and 2003. Use the map to answer the questions below.

1. **Using the Key** How many earthquakes happened at a depth greater than 300 km?

2. **Analyzing Data** Deep earthquakes are earthquakes that happen at a depth greater than 300 km. Which earthquakes happen more frequently: deep earthquakes or shallow earthquakes?

3. **Making Comparisons** How does the earthquake activity on the eastern edge of South America differ from the earthquake activity on the western edge?

4. **Inferring Relationships** The locations of earthquakes and plate boundaries are related. Where would you expect to find a major plate boundary?

5. **Identifying Trends** In what part of South America do most deep earthquakes happen? What relationships do you see between the locations of shallow and deep earthquakes in South America?

6. **Analyzing Relationships** Most deep earthquakes happen where subducting plates move deep into the mantle. What type of plate boundary is indicated by the earthquake activity in South America? Explain your answer.

The Mid-Atlantic Ridge

Deep in the Atlantic Ocean lies a mountain range so vast that it dwarfs the Himalaya Mountains. This mountain range, called the *Mid-Atlantic Ridge,* is the mid-ocean ridge at the diverging boundary between the North American and Eurasian plates and also between the South American and African plates.

Sea-Floor Spreading on Land

Most of Earth's mid-ocean ridges are underwater, but part of the Mid-Atlantic Ridge rises above sea level just south of the Arctic Circle. The exposed section of the Mid-Atlantic Ridge forms the country of Iceland. Since Iceland was founded by Vikings more than 1,000 years ago, its inhabitants have contended with constant geologic activity associated with sea-floor spreading.

Lots and Lots of Lava

Separation of Earth's crust along the Mid-Atlantic Ridge affects Iceland's landscape in several ways. The movement of magma causes frequent earthquakes. Iceland is also one of the most volcanically active areas in the world. It contains about 200 volcanoes and averages one eruption every five years. Magma flowing up from the mantle creates numerous hot springs, geysers, and sulfurous gas vents. Scientists estimate that one-third of the total lava flow from Earth in the last 500 years has occurred on Iceland.

Despite Iceland's numerous volcanoes, much of its lava comes not from isolated eruptions but from cracks, or *fissures,* in the crust. In a recent rifting episode that lasted nearly 10 years, a series of fissures spit out enough molten basalt to cover 35 km² of land and individual fissures grew as much as 8 m in width. At present, sea-floor spreading adds an average of 2.5 cm of new material to Iceland each year. At this rate, Iceland will grow 25 km in width during the next million years.

Extension

1. **Making Inferences** If geologists want to locate the youngest rocks on Iceland, where should they look? Where should they look to find the oldest rocks? Explain your answers.

Greenland   Iceland

◄ The Helgafjell volcano erupted in a curtain of fire that rained black ash on the town of Reykjavik Iceland, in 1973.

SCILINKS®

NSTA
Developed and maintained by the National Science Teachers Association

For a variety of links related to this chapter, go to www.scilinks.org

Topic: Mid-Atlantic Ridge
SciLinks code: HQ60960

11

Deformation of the Crust

What You'll Learn

- How Earth's crust responds to stress
- What forms deformed rock takes
- How forces in the crust cause mountains to form

Why It's Relevant

Many of the most dramatic features of Earth's surface are the result of deformation of the crust. Knowing how rock responds to stress provides a strong basis for understanding why and how Earth's surface changes.

PRE-READING ACTIVITY

FOLDNOTES

Key-Term Fold
Before you read this chapter, create the FoldNote entitled "Key-Term Fold" described in the Skills Handbook section of the Appendix. Write a key term from the chapter on each tab of the key-term fold. Under each tab, write the definition of the key term.

▶ To build this portion of Highway 14 in California, construction crews had to cut through a hill. The exposed rock in the roadcut shows layers of sedimentary rock that have been folded by the stress caused by the nearby San Andreas fault.

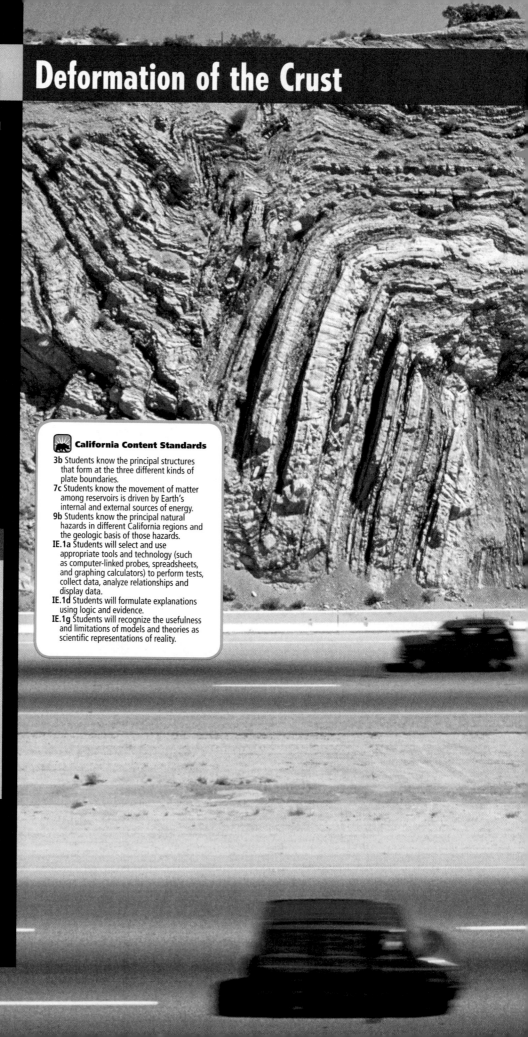

California Content Standards

3b Students know the principal structures that form at the three different kinds of plate boundaries.

7c Students know the movement of matter among reservoirs is driven by Earth's internal and external sources of energy.

9b Students know the principal natural hazards in different California regions and the geologic basis of those hazards.

IE.1a Students will select and use appropriate tools and technology (such as computer-linked probes, spreadsheets, and graphing calculators) to perform tests, collect data, analyze relationships and display data.

IE.1d Students will formulate explanations using logic and evidence.

IE.1g Students will recognize the usefulness and limitations of models and theories as scientific representations of reality.

7c Students know the movement of matter among reservoirs is driven by Earth's internal and external sources of energy.

IE.1d Students will formulate explanations using logic and evidence.
IE.1g Students will recognize the usefulness and

limitations of models and theories as scientific representations of reality.

The Himalayas, the Rockies, and the Andes are some of Earth's most majestic mountain ranges. Mountain ranges are visible reminders that the shape of Earth's surface changes constantly. These changes result from **deformation**, or the bending, tilting, and breaking of Earth's crust.

Isostasy

Deformation sometimes occurs because the weight of some part of Earth's crust changes. Earth's crust is part of the lithospheric plates that ride on top of the plastic part of the mantle called the *asthenosphere*. When parts of the lithosphere thicken and become heavier, they sink deeper into the asthenosphere. If parts of the lithosphere thin and become lighter, the lithosphere rises higher in the asthenosphere.

Vertical movement of the lithosphere depends on two opposing forces. One force is the force due to gravity, or weight, of the lithosphere pressing down on the asthenosphere. The other force is the buoyant force of the asthenosphere pressing up on the lithosphere. When these two forces are balanced, the lithosphere and asthenosphere are in a state called **isostasy**. However, when the weight of the lithosphere changes, the lithosphere sinks or rises until a balance of the forces is reached again. The movements of the lithosphere to reach isostasy are called *isostatic adjustments*. One type of isostatic adjustment is shown in **Figure 1**. As these isostatic adjustments occur, areas of the crust are bent up and down. This bending causes rock in that area to deform.

OBJECTIVES

▶ **Summarize** the principle of isostasy.

▶ **Identify** the three main types of stress.

▶ **Compare** folds and faults.

KEY TERMS

deformation
isostasy
stress
strain
fold
fault

deformation the bending, tilting, and breaking of Earth's crust; the change in shape or volume of rock in response to stress

isostasy a condition of gravitational and buoyant equilibrium between Earth's lithosphere and asthenosphere

Figure 1 ▶ Isostatic Adjustments as a Result of Erosion

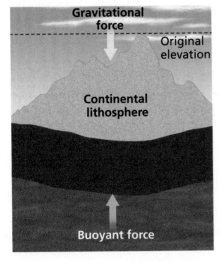

When the gravitational force equals the buoyant force, the lithosphere and asthenosphere are in isostasy.

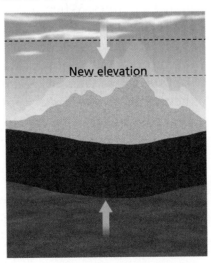

As erosion wears away the crust, the lithosphere becomes lighter and is pushed up by the asthenosphere.

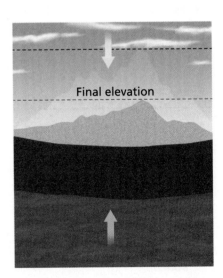

As erosion continues, the isostatic adjustment also continues.

Figure 2 ▶ Mt. Katahdin in Baxter State Park, Maine, has been worn down by weathering and erosion. As the mountain shrinks, the crust underneath it is uplifted.

QuickLAB 🕐 **5 min**

Modeling Isostasy 🖫 IE.1d, IE.1g

Procedure

1. Fill a **1 L beaker** with **500 mL** of water.

2. Place a **wooden block** in the water. Use a **grease pencil** to mark on the side of the beaker the levels of the top and the bottom of the block.

3. Place a **small mass**, of about 1 g, on the wooden block. Use a **second grease pencil** to mark the levels of the top and the bottom of the block.

Analysis

1. What happens to the block of wood when the weight is added?

2. What type of isostatic adjustment does this activity model?

Mountains and Isostasy

In mountainous regions, isostatic adjustments constantly occur. Over millions of years, the rock that forms mountains is worn away by the erosive actions of wind, water, and ice. This erosion can significantly reduce the height and weight of a mountain range, such as the one shown in **Figure 2.** As a mountain becomes smaller and lighter, the area may rise by isostatic adjustment in a process called *uplift.*

Deposition and Isostasy

Another type of isostatic adjustment occurs in areas where rivers carrying large amounts of mud, sand, and gravel flow into larger bodies of water. When a river flows into the ocean, most of the material that the river carries is deposited on the nearby ocean floor. The added weight of the deposited material causes the ocean floor to sink by isostatic adjustment in a process known as *subsidence.* This process is occurring in the Gulf of Mexico at the mouth of the Mississippi River, where a thick accumulation of deposited materials has formed.

Glaciers and Isostasy

Isostatic adjustments also occur as a result of the growth and retreat of glaciers and ice sheets. When a large amount of water is held in glaciers and ice sheets, the weight of the ice causes the lithosphere beneath the ice to sink. Simultaneously, the ocean floor rises because the weight of the overlying ocean water is less. When glaciers and ice sheets melt, the land that was covered with ice slowly rises as the weight of the crust decreases. As the water returns to the ocean, the ocean floor sinks.

Stress

As Earth's lithosphere moves, the rock in the crust is squeezed, stretched, and twisted. These actions exert force on the rock. The amount of force that is exerted on each unit of area is called **stress.** For example, during isostatic adjustments, the lithosphere sinks and rises atop the asthenosphere. As the lithosphere sinks, the rock in the crust is squeezed and the direction of stress changes. As the lithosphere rises, the rock in the crust is stretched and the direction of stress changes again. Similarly, stress occurs in Earth's crust when tectonic plates collide, separate, or scrape past each other. **Figure 3** shows the three main types of stress.

stress the amount of force per unit area that acts on a rock

Compression

The type of stress that squeezes and shortens a body is called *compression.* Compression commonly reduces the amount of space that rock occupies. In addition to reducing the volume of rock, compression pushes rocks higher up or deeper down into the crust. Much of the stress that occurs at or near convergent boundaries, where tectonic plates collide, is compression.

Tension

Another type of stress is tension. *Tension* is stress that stretches and pulls a body apart. When rocks are pulled apart by tension, they tend to become thinner. Much of the stress that occurs at or near divergent boundaries, where tectonic plates pull apart, is tension.

Shear Stress

The third type of stress is shear stress. *Shear stress* distorts a body by pushing parts of the body in opposite directions. Sheared rocks bend, twist, or break apart as they slide past each other. Shear stress is common at transform boundaries, where tectonic plates slide horizontally past each other. However, each type of stress occurs at or near all types of plate boundaries and in various other regions of the crust, too.

Reading Check Which two kinds of stress pull rock apart? (See the Appendix for answers to Reading Checks.)

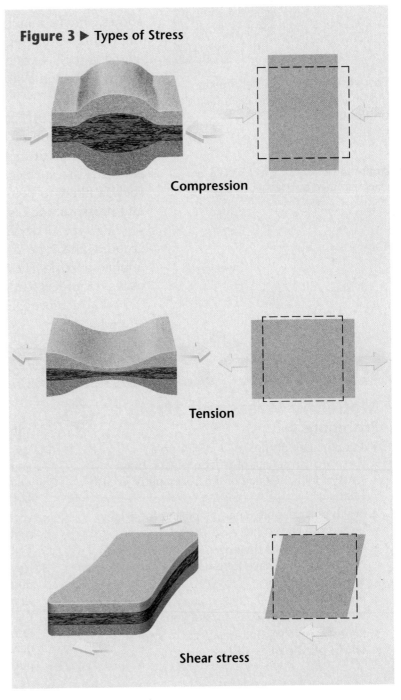

Figure 3 ▶ Types of Stress

Compression

Tension

Shear stress

Figure 4 ▶ This rock deformation in Kingman, Arizona, is an example of brittle strain.

strain any change in a rock's shape or volume caused by stress

Strain

When stress is applied to rock, rock may deform. Any change in the shape or volume of rock that results from stress is called **strain**. When stress is applied slowly, the deformed rock may regain its original shape when the stress is removed. However, the amount of stress that rock can withstand without permanently changing shape is limited. This limit varies with the type of rock and the conditions under which the stress is applied. If a stress exceeds the rock's limit, the rock's shape permanently changes.

Types of Permanent Strain

Materials that respond to stress by breaking or fracturing are *brittle*. Brittle strain appears as cracks or fractures, as **Figure 4** shows. *Ductile* materials respond to stress by bending or deforming without breaking. Ductile strain is a change in the volume or shape of rock in which the rock does not crack or fracture. Brittle strain and ductile strain are types of permanent strain.

Factors That Affect Strain

The composition of rock determines whether rock is ductile or brittle. Temperature and pressure also affect how rock deforms. Near Earth's surface, where temperature and pressure are low, rock is likely to deform in a brittle way. At higher temperature and pressure, rock is more likely to deform in a ductile way.

The type of strain that stress causes is determined by the amount and type of stress and by the rate at which stress is applied to rock. The greater the stress on rock is, the more likely rock is to undergo brittle strain. The more quickly stress is applied to rock, the more likely rock is to respond in a brittle way.

Quick LAB 15 min

Modeling Stress and Strain
Procedure IE.1d, IE.1g

1. Put on a pair of **gloves,** and pick up a 5 cm × 5 cm square of **frozen plastic play putty.** Hold one edge of the frozen putty in each hand.

2. Try to pull the putty apart by pulling the edges away from each other.

3. Push the edges of the frozen putty toward each other. (You may have to reshape the putty between steps.)

4. Push one edge of the frozen putty away from you, and pull the other edge toward you.

5. Repeat steps 2–4, but use a 5 cm × 5 cm square of **warm plastic play putty.**

Analysis

1. What types of stress did you model in steps 2, 3, and 4?

2. Make a table that lists the characteristics of the two substances that you modeled, the stresses that you modeled, and the resulting strain on each model.

3. How does the frozen putty respond to the stress? How does the warm putty's response to the stress differ from the frozen putty's response?

Folds

When rock responds to stress by deforming in a ductile way, folds commonly form. A **fold** is a bend in rock layers that results from stress. A fold is most easily observed where flat layers of rock were compressed or squeezed inward. As stress was applied, the rock layers bent and folded. Cracks sometimes appear in or near a fold, but most commonly the rock layers remain intact. Although a fold commonly results from compression, it can also form as a result of shear stress.

Anatomy of a Fold

Folds have features by which they can be identified. Scientists use these features to describe folds. The main features of a fold are shown by the illustration in **Figure 5.** The sloping sides of a fold are called *limbs*. The limbs meet at the bend in the rock layers, which is called the *hinge*. Some folds also contain an additional feature. If a fold's structure is such that a plane could slice the fold into two symmetrical halves, the fold is symmetrical. The plane is called the fold's *axial plane*. However, the two halves of a fold are rarely symmetrical.

Many folds bend vertically, but folds can have many other shapes, as shown by the photograph in **Figure 5.** Folds can be asymmetrical. Sometimes, one limb of a fold dips more steeply than the other limb does. If a fold is *overturned*, the fold appears to be lying on its side. Folds can have open shapes or be as tight as a hairpin. A fold's hinge can be a smooth bend or may come to a sharp point. Each fold is unique because the combination of stresses and conditions that caused the fold was unique.

Reading Check Name two features of a fold. (See the Appendix for answers to Reading Checks.)

fold a form of ductile strain in which rock layers bend, usually as a result of compression

MATHPRACTICE

Units of Stress

Two units are commonly used to describe stress or pressure. One unit is the pascal (Pa). A pascal is a measure of force (in newtons) divided by area (in square meters). The other unit of stress is the pound per square inch (psi). If the pressure in a region of Earth's crust is measured as 25 MPa (megapascals) and as 3,626 psi, how many pounds per square inch does 1 MPa equal? (Note: 1 MPa = 1,000,000 Pa)

Figure 5 ▶ Although not every fold is symmetrical, every fold has a hinge and limbs. *Can you identify the limbs and hinge of each fold in the photo?*

Axial plane

Hinge

Limb

Oldest rock

Youngest rock

Figure 6 ▶ The three major types of folds are anticlines (top), synclines (middle), and monoclines (bottom).

Types of Folds

To categorize a fold, scientists study the relative ages of the rocks in the fold. The rock layers of the fold are identified by age from youngest to oldest. An *anticline* is a fold in which the oldest layer is in the center of the fold. Anticlines are commonly arch shaped. A *syncline* is a fold in which the youngest layer is in the center of the fold. Synclines are commonly bowl shaped. A *monocline* is a fold in which both limbs are horizontal or almost horizontal. Monoclines form when one part of Earth's crust moves up or down relative to another part. The three major types of folds are shown in **Figure 6.**

Sizes of Folds

Folds, which appear as wavelike structures in rock layers, vary greatly in size. Some folds are small enough to be contained in a hand-held rock specimen. Other folds cover thousands of square kilometers and can be seen only from the air.

Sometimes, a large anticline forms a ridge. A *ridge* is a large, narrow strip of elevated land that can occur near mountains. Nearby, a large syncline may form a valley. The ridges and valleys of the Appalachian Mountains are examples of landforms that were formed by anticlines and synclines.

Connection to ENGINEERING

Oil Traps

Oil and natural gas form where the remains of organisms, especially marine plants, are buried in an environment that prevents the remains from rapidly decomposing. Over millions of years, chemical reactions slowly change the organic remains into oil and natural gas.

When prospecting for oil and natural gas, oil companies look for porous and permeable rock layers. Porous rock has spaces between rock particles. Permeable rock is rock in which the pore spaces are connected, so fluids can flow through the rock. When a rock layer is both porous and permeable and contains oil or gas, the layer is called a *reservoir*.

Because oil and natural gas are fluids that have low densities, they move upward through rock toward Earth's surface. Oil and gas move through rock layers until they meet an impermeable rock layer or structure, which then traps the oil and gas below it.

In addition to looking for porous and permeable rock layers, petroleum engineers look for rock layers that have been folded. Many folds are anticlines in which layers of impermeable rock overlay layers of permeable rock. Because the limbs of the fold slope upward, the oil and natural gas rise through the permeable layer to the crest of the anticline and are trapped there by the impermeable layer. Engineers can then drill through the impermeable layer to reach the oil or gas reservoir.

This oil pump brings oil and natural gas up to the surface.

Figure 7 ▶ Normal and Reverse Faults

Footwall

Hanging wall

Reverse fault

Normal fault

Thrust fault

Faults

Stress does not always cause rock to fold. Near Earth's surface, where temperatures and pressure are low, stresses may simply cause rock to break. Breaks in rock are divided into two categories. A break along which there is no movement of the surrounding rock is called a *fracture*. A break along which the surrounding rock moves is called a **fault**. The surface or plane along which the motion occurs is called the *fault plane*. In a nonvertical fault, the *hanging wall* is the rock above the fault plane. The *footwall* is the rock below the fault plane.

fault a break in a body of rock along which one block slides relative to another; a form of brittle strain

Normal Faults

As shown in **Figure 7,** a *normal fault* is a fault in which the hanging wall moves downward relative to the footwall. Normal faults commonly form at divergent boundaries, where the crust is being pulled apart by tension. Normal faults may occur as a series of parallel fault lines, forming steep, steplike landforms. The Great Rift Valley of East Africa formed by large-scale normal faulting.

Reverse Faults

When compression causes the hanging wall to move upward relative to the footwall, also shown in **Figure 7,** a *reverse fault* forms. A *thrust fault* is a special type of reverse fault in which the fault plane is at a low angle or is nearly horizontal. Because of the low angle of the fault plane, the rock of the hanging wall is pushed up and over the rock of the footwall. Reverse faults and thrust faults are common in steep mountain ranges, such as the Rockies and the Alps.

SCiLINKS®

NSTA
Developed and maintained by the National Science Teachers Association

For a variety of links related to this subject, go to www.scilinks.org

Topic: Folding and Faulting
SciLinks code: HQ60589

✓ Reading Check How does a thrust fault differ from a reverse fault? (See the Appendix for answers to Reading Checks.)

Strike-Slip Faults

In a *strike-slip fault,* the rock on either side of the fault plane slides horizontally in response to shear stress. Strike-slip faults got their name because they slide, or *slip,* parallel to the direction of the length, or *strike,* of the fault. Some strike-slip fault planes are vertical, but many are sloped.

Strike-slip faults commonly occur at transform boundaries, where tectonic plates grind past each other as they move in opposite directions. These motions cause shear stress on the rocks at the edges of the plates. Strike-slip faults also occur at fracture zones between offset segments of mid-ocean ridges. Commonly, strike-slip faults occur as groups of smaller faults in areas where large-scale deformation is happening.

Sizes of Faults

Like folds, faults vary greatly in size. Some faults are so small that they affect only a few layers of rock in a small region. Other faults are thousands of kilometers long and may extend several kilometers below Earth's surface. Generally, large faults that cover thousands of kilometers are composed of systems of many smaller, related faults, rather than of a single fault. The San Andreas fault in California, shown in **Figure 8,** is an example of a large fault system.

Figure 8 ▶ The San Andreas fault system stretches more than 1,200 km across California and is the result of two tectonic plates moving in different directions.

Section 1 Review

1. **Summarize** how isostatic adjustments affect isostasy.

2. **Identify and describe** three types of stress.

3. **Compare** stress and strain.

4. **Describe** one type of strain that results when rock responds to stress by permanently deforming without breaking.

5. **Identify** features that all types of folds share and features that only some types of folds have.

6. **Describe** four types of faults.

7. **Compare** folding and faulting as responses to stress.

CRITICAL THINKING

8. **Applying Ideas** Why is faulting most likely to occur near Earth's surface and not deep within Earth?

9. **Making Comparisons** How would the isostatic adjustment that results from the melting of glaciers differ from the isostatic adjustment that may occur when a large river empties into the ocean? IE.1d

10. **Analyzing Relationships** You are examining a rock outcrop that shows a fold in which both limbs are horizontal but occur at different elevations. What type of fold does this outcrop show, and what can you say about the type of stress that the rock underwent? IE.1d

11. **Predicting Consequences** You are watching a lab experiment in which a rock sample is being gently heated and slowly bent. Would you expect the rock to fold or to fracture? Explain your reasoning. IE.1d

CONCEPT MAPPING

12. Use the following terms to create a concept map: *stress, compression, strain, tension, shear stress, folds,* and *faults.*

How Mountains Form

California Content Standards

3b Students know the principal structures that form at the three different kinds of plate boundaries.
IE.1d Students will formulate explanations using logic and evidence.
IE.1g Students will recognize the usefulness and limitations of models and theories as scientific representations of reality.

A mountain is the most extreme type of deformation. Mount Everest, whose elevation is more than 8 km above sea level, is Earth's highest mountain. Forces inside Earth cause Mount Everest to grow taller every year. Mount St. Helens, a volcanic mountain, captured the world's attention in 1980 when its explosive eruption devastated the surrounding area.

Mountain Ranges and Systems

A group of adjacent mountains that are related to each other in shape and structure is called a **mountain range.** Mount Everest is part of the Great Himalaya Range, and Mount St. Helens is part of the Cascade Range. A group of mountain ranges that are adjacent is called a *mountain system.* In the eastern United States, for example, the Great Smoky, Blue Ridge, Cumberland, and Green mountain ranges make up the Appalachian mountain system.

The largest mountain systems are part of two larger systems called *mountain belts.* Earth's two major mountain belts, the circum-Pacific belt and the Eurasian-Melanesian belt, are shown in **Figure 1.** The circum-Pacific belt forms a ring around the Pacific Ocean. The Eurasian-Melanesian belt runs from the Pacific islands through Asia and southern Europe and into northwestern Africa.

OBJECTIVES

▶ **Identify** the types of plate collisions that form mountains. 🔲 **3b**
▶ **Identify** four types of mountains. 🔲 **3b**
▶ **Compare** how folded and fault-block mountains form. 🔲 **3b**

KEY TERMS

mountain range
folded mountain
fault-block mountain
dome mountain

mountain range a series of mountains that are closely related in orientation, age, and mode of formation

Figure 1 ▶ Most mountain ranges lie along either the Eurasian-Melanesian mountain belt or the circum-Pacific mountain belt.

◼ Eurasian-Melanesian mountain belt
◼ Circum-Pacific mountain belt

Plate Tectonics and Mountains

Both the circum-Pacific and the Eurasian-Melanesian mountain belts are located along convergent plate boundaries. Scientists think that the location of these two mountain belts provides evidence that most mountains form as a result of collisions between tectonic plates. Some mountains, such as the Appalachians, do not lie along active convergent plate boundaries. However, evidence indicates that the places at which these ranges formed were previously active plate boundaries.

Collisions Between Continental and Oceanic Crust

Some mountains form when oceanic lithosphere and continental lithosphere collide at convergent plate boundaries. When the moving plates collide, the oceanic lithosphere subducts beneath the continental lithosphere, as shown in **Figure 2.** This type of collision produces such large-scale deformation of rock that high mountains are uplifted. In addition, the subduction of the oceanic lithosphere causes partial melting of the overlying mantle and crust. This melting produces magma that may eventually erupt to form volcanic mountains on Earth's surface. The mountains of the Cascade Range in the northwest region of the United States formed in this way. The Andes mountains on the western coast of South America are another example of mountains that formed by this type of collision.

Some mountains at the boundary between continental lithosphere and oceanic lithosphere may form by a different process. As the oceanic lithosphere subducts, pieces of crust called *terranes* are scraped off. These terranes then become part of the continent and may form mountains.

Graphic

Organizer Cause-and-Effect Map

Create the **Graphic Organizer** entitled "Cause-and-Effect Map" described in the Skills Handbook section of the Appendix. Label the effect with "Mountain formation." Then, fill in the map with causes of mountain formation and details about why mountains form.

Figure 2 ▶ The Andes, shown below, are being uplifted as the Pacific plate subducts beneath the South American plate.

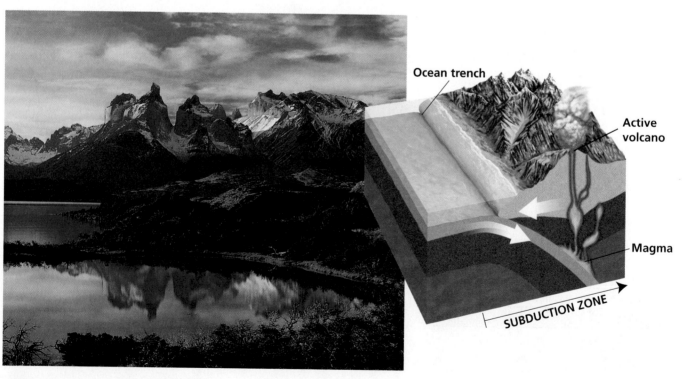

Ocean trench

Active volcano

Magma

SUBDUCTION ZONE

Sections

1 How Rock Deforms

Key Terms

deformation, 271
isostasy, 271
stress, 273
strain, 274
fold, 275
fault, 277

Key Concepts

▶ Tectonic plate movement and isostatic adjustments cause stress on the rock in Earth's crust.

▶ Stress can squeeze rock together, pull rock apart, and bend and twist rock.

▶ Stress on rock can cause strain, or the deformation of rock. Rock can deform by folding or by breaking to form fractures or faults.

▶ Three types of faults occur in rock: normal faults, reverse faults (including thrust faults), and strike-slip faults.

2 How Mountains Form

mountain range, 279
folded mountain, 282
fault-block mountain, 283
dome mountain, 283

▶ Mountains make up mountain ranges, which, in turn, make up mountain systems. The largest mountain systems form two major mountain belts.

▶ Four types of mountains are folded mountains, fault-block mountains, dome mountains, and volcanic mountains.

▶ Mountains commonly form as the result of the collision of tectonic plates.

▶ A mountain is classified according to the way in which the crust deforms when the mountain forms.

Using Key Terms

Use each of the following terms in a separate sentence.

1. *isostasy*
2. *compression*
3. *shear stress*

For each pair of terms, explain how the meanings of the terms differ.

4. *stress* and *strain*
5. *fold* and *fault*
6. *syncline* and *monocline*
7. *dome mountains* and *volcanic mountains* 3b
8. *folded mountains* and *fault-block mountains* 3b

Understanding Key Concepts

9. When the weight of an area of Earth's crust increases, the lithosphere
   a. sinks.   c. rises.
   b. melts.   d. collides.

10. The force per unit area that changes the shape and volume of rock is
    a. footwall.   c. rising.
    b. isostasy.   d. stress.

11. Shear stress
    a. bends, twists, or breaks rock.
    b. causes isostasy.
    c. causes rock to melt.
    d. causes rock to expand.

12. When stress is applied under conditions of high pressure and high temperature, rock is more likely to
    a. fracture.   c. fault.
    b. sink.   d. fold.

13. Folds in which both limbs remain horizontal are called
    a. monoclines.   c. synclines.
    b. fractures.   d. anticlines.

14. When a fault is not vertical, the rock above the fault plane makes up the
    a. tension.   c. hanging wall.
    b. footwall.   d. compression.

15. A fault in which the rock on either side of the fault plane moves horizontally in nearly opposite directions is called a
    a. normal fault.   c. strike-slip fault.
    b. reverse fault.   d. thrust fault.

16. The largest mountain systems are part of still larger systems called 3b
    a. continental margins.
    b. ranges.
    c. belts.
    d. synclines.

17. Large areas of flat-topped rock high above the surrounding landscape are
    a. grabens.   c. hanging walls.
    b. footwalls.   d. plateaus.

Short Answer

18. Name two types of deformation in Earth's crust, and explain how each type occurs.

19. Explain how to identify an anticline.

20. Identify the two major mountain belts on Earth. 3b

21. Describe how the various types of mountains are categorized.

22. Identify the two forces that are kept in balance by isostatic adjustments.

23. Compare the features of dome mountains with those of fault-block mountains. 3b

The Disappearing Mediterranean

Two of the most breathtaking regions of the world are the Alps and the Mediterranean. The Alps, considered to be among Earth's most beautiful mountains, have become a vast natural playground for skiers, hikers, and climbers. The Mediterranean plays host to travelers from around the world who wish to sample the diverse cultures, balmy climate, and famous beach resorts that surround the Mediterranean Sea. Local residents depend on the sea for their economic well-being.

Push and Pull

The same natural forces that uplifted the Alps are slowly swallowing up the Mediterranean. The Alps were formed—and are still being shaped—by the collision of two tectonic plates. Italy, part of which rides on the African plate, collided with Eurasia sometime in the past. The collision formed the Alps, but it did not stop the movement of the African plate.

The History of Tomorrow

The northern oceanic crust of the African plate, which is the sea floor of the Mediterranean, is still subducting beneath the continental crust of Eurasia. As more oceanic crust subducts, the Mediterranean Sea will become smaller. Italy, which continues to be pushed into Eurasia, will eventually cease to exist as we know it. When the northern coast of the African continent finally collides with Eurasia, the Mediterranean Sea will disappear completely. Of course, this process will take millions of years, because tectonic plates move so slowly.

▼ The Aegean Sea is part of the larger Mediterranean Sea, which is slowly disappearing.

Extension

1. **Applying Ideas** What do you think will happen to the Alps as the African plate continues to push northward?

▼ The Alps formed when the African plate collided with Eurasia.

◄ Santorini, Greece, is an island in the Aegean Sea.

293

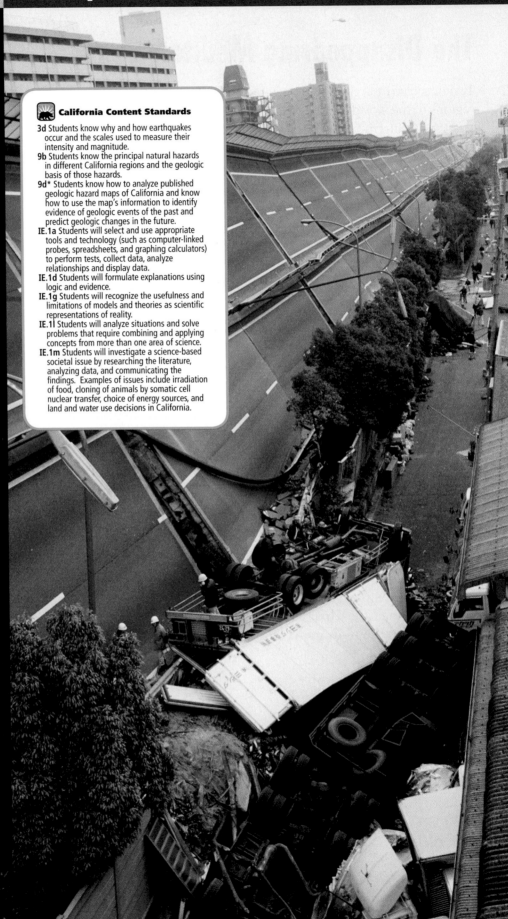

Chapter 12

Earthquakes

Sections

1 How and Where Earthquakes Happen

2 Studying Earthquakes

3 Earthquakes and Society

What You'll Learn

- What causes earthquakes
- How scientists measure earthquakes
- How earthquakes cause damage

Why It's Relevant

Understanding how, where, and why earthquakes happen can help scientists and engineers reduce earthquake damage and save lives. Studying earthquakes also helps scientists understand Earth's interior.

PRE-READING ACTIVITY

Pyramid
Before you read this chapter, create the **FoldNote** entitled "Pyramid" described in the Skills Handbook section of the Appendix. Label the sides of the pyramid with "How earthquakes happen," "How earthquakes are studied," and "How earthquakes affect society." As you read the chapter, write characteristics of each topic on the appropriate pyramid side.

▶ This expressway in Kobe, Japan, was toppled by the ground shaking of an earthquake that lasted 20 seconds and had a moment magnitude of 6.9.

3d Students know why and how earthquakes occur and the scales used to measure their intensity and magnitude.

IE.1d Students will formulate explanations using logic and evidence.
IE.1l Students will analyze situations and solve problems that require combining and applying concepts from more than one area of science.

Earthquakes are one of the most destructive natural disasters. A single earthquake can kill thousands of people and cause millions of dollars in damage. **Earthquakes** are defined as movements of the ground that are caused by a sudden release of energy when rocks along a fault move. Earthquakes usually occur when rocks under stress suddenly shift along a fault. A *fault* is a break in a body of rock along which one block slides relative to another.

Why Earthquakes Happen

The rocks along both sides of a fault are commonly pressed together tightly. Although the rocks may be under stress, friction prevents them from moving past each other. In this immobile state, a fault is said to be *locked*. Parts of a fault remain locked until the stress becomes so great that the rocks suddenly grind past each other. This slippage causes the trembling and vibrations of an earthquake.

Elastic Rebound

Geologists think that earthquakes are a result of elastic rebound. **Elastic rebound** is the sudden return of elastically deformed rock to its undeformed shape. In this process, the rocks on each side of a fault are moving slowly. If the fault is locked, stress in the rocks increases. When the rocks are stressed past the point at which they can maintain their integrity, they fracture. The rocks then separate at their weakest point and *rebound,* or spring back to their original shape. This process is shown in **Figure 1.**

OBJECTIVES

▶ **Describe** elastic rebound. **3d**
▶ **Compare** body waves and surface waves. **3d**
▶ **Explain** how the structure of Earth's interior affects seismic waves. **3d**
▶ **Explain** why earthquakes generally occur at plate boundaries. **3d**

KEY TERMS

earthquake
elastic rebound
focus
epicenter
body wave
surface wave
P wave
S wave
shadow zone
fault zone

---

earthquake a movement or trembling of the ground that is caused by a sudden release of energy when rocks along a fault move

elastic rebound the sudden return of elastically deformed rock to its undeformed shape

Figure 1 ▶ Elastic Rebound

Two blocks of crust pressed against each other at a fault are under stress but do not move because friction holds them in place.

As stress builds up at the fault, the crust deforms.

The rock fractures and then snaps back into its original shape, which causes an earthquake.

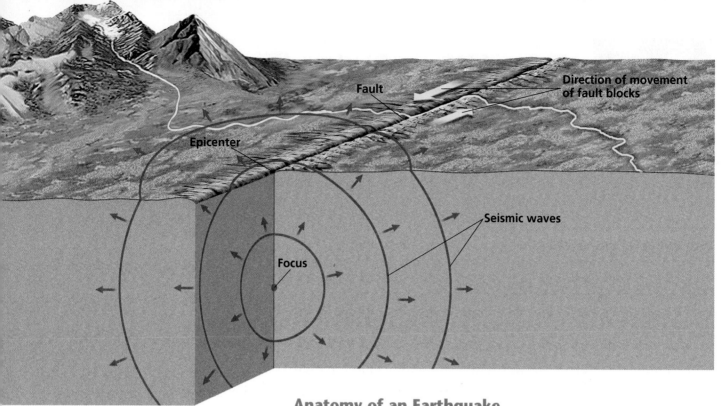

Fault

Direction of movement
of fault blocks

Epicenter

Seismic waves

Focus

Figure 2 ▶ The epicenter of an earthquake is the point on the surface directly above the focus.

focus the location within Earth along a fault at which the first motion of an earthquake occurs

epicenter the point on Earth's surface directly above an earthquake's starting point, or focus

body wave in geology, a seismic wave that travels through the body of a medium

surface wave in geology, a seismic wave that travels along the surface of a medium and that has a stronger effect near the surface of the medium than it has in the interior

Anatomy of an Earthquake

The location within Earth along a fault at which the first motion of an earthquake occurs is called the **focus** (plural, *foci*). The point on Earth's surface directly above the focus is called the **epicenter** (EP i SENT uhr), as shown in **Figure 2.**

Although the focus depths of earthquakes vary, about 90% of continental earthquakes have a shallow focus. Earthquakes that have shallow foci take place within 70 km of Earth's surface. Earthquakes that have intermediate foci occur at depths between 70 km and 300 km. Earthquakes that have deep foci take place at depths between 300 km and 650 km. Earthquakes that have deep foci usually occur in subduction zones and occur farther from the plate boundary than shallower earthquakes do.

By the time the vibrations from an earthquake that has an intermediate or deep focus reach the surface, much of their energy has dissipated. For this reason, the earthquakes that usually cause the most damage usually have shallow foci.

Seismic Waves

As rocks along a fault slip into new positions, the rocks release energy in the form of vibrations called *seismic waves*. These waves travel outward in all directions from the focus through the surrounding rock. This wave action is similar to what happens when you drop a stone into a pool of still water and circular waves ripple outward from the center.

Earthquakes generally produce two main types of waves. **Body waves** are waves that travel through the body of a medium. **Surface waves** travel along the surface of a body rather than through the middle. Each type of wave travels at a different speed and causes different movements in Earth's crust.

Body Waves

Body waves can be placed into two main categories: P waves and S waves. **P waves**, also called *primary waves* or *compression waves*, are the fastest seismic waves and are always the first waves of an earthquake to be detected. P waves cause particles of rock to move in a back-and-forth direction that is parallel to the direction in which the waves are traveling, as shown in **Figure 3**. P waves can move through solids, liquids, and gases. The more rigid the material is, the faster the P waves travel through it.

S waves, also called *secondary waves* or *shear waves*, are the second-fastest seismic waves and arrive at detection sites after P waves. S waves cause particles of rock to move in a side-to-side direction that is perpendicular to the direction in which the waves are traveling. Unlike P waves, however, S waves can travel through only solid material.

Surface Waves

Surface waves form from motion along a shallow fault or from the conversion of energy when P waves and S waves reach Earth's surface. Although surface waves are the slowest-moving waves, they may cause the greatest damage during an earthquake. The two types of surface waves are Love waves and Rayleigh waves. *Love waves* cause rock to move side-to-side and perpendicular to the direction in which the waves are traveling. *Rayleigh waves* cause the ground to move with an elliptical, rolling motion.

Reading Check Describe the two types of surface waves. (See the Appendix for answers to Reading Checks.)

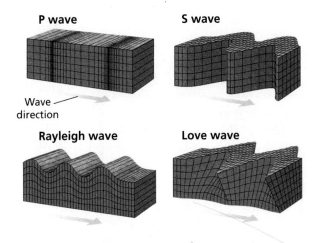

Figure 3 ▶ The different types of seismic waves cause different rock movements, which have different effects on Earth's crust.

P wave a primary wave, or compression wave; a seismic wave that causes particles of rock to move in a back-and-forth direction parallel to the direction in which the wave is traveling; P waves are the fastest seismic waves and can travel through solids, liquids, and gases

S wave a secondary wave, or shear wave; a seismic wave that causes particles of rock to move in a side-to-side direction perpendicular to the direction in which the wave is traveling; S waves are the second-fastest seismic waves and can travel only through solids

Connection to ENGINEERING

Seismic Reflection Surveying

Many surveying companies have discovered the usefulness of seismic waves in mapping underground features. These features can be used to identify possible mineral deposits and oil or natural gas reservoirs.

In seismic surveying, a seismic shock is generated by using explosives, air guns, or a mechanical thumper. The seismic waves produced by the shock travel through the ground and reflect off bedding planes or other features below the surface. The reflected waves travel back to the surface, where they are recorded by an array of geophones. *Geophones* are instruments that convert the motion of a seismic wave into an electrical signal.

The geophones are set up in a straight line to collect data that are used to construct a two-dimensional

profile of the underground layers. Scientists can also arrange the geophones in more-complex patterns to create three-dimensional images of the layers. Because each underground layer reflects waves at a different time, scientists can plot all of the data to construct an accurate picture of the underground layers.

Seismic reflection can be used to study phenomena at a variety of scales. It may be used to study just the top few tens of meters of soil and rock, or it may be used to study the structure of the deep crust. In particular, this technology has been adapted for use by oil and natural gas exploration companies to locate oil and gas reservoirs.

shadow zone an area on Earth's surface
where no direct seismic waves from a
particular earthquake can be detected

Figure 4 ▶ P waves and S waves
behave differently as they pass
through different structural layers
of Earth.

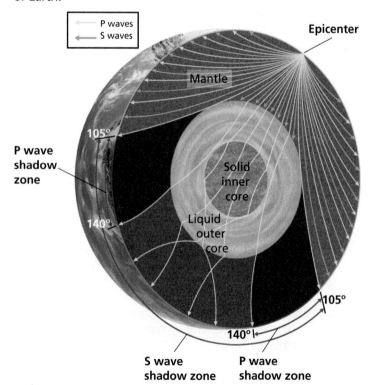

Seismic Waves and Earth's Interior

Seismic waves are useful to scientists in exploring Earth's interior. The composition of the material through which P waves and S waves travel affects the speed and direction of the waves. For example, P waves travel fastest through materials that are very rigid and are not easily compressed. By studying the speed and direction of seismic waves, scientists can learn more about the makeup and structure of Earth's interior.

Earth's Internal Layers

In 1909, Andrija Mohorovičić (MOH hoh ROH vuh CHICH), a Croatian scientist, discovered that the speed of seismic waves increases abruptly at about 30 km beneath the surface of continents. This increase in speed takes place because the mantle is denser than the crust. The location at which the speed of the waves increases marks the boundary between the crust and the mantle. The depth of this boundary varies from about 10 km below the oceans to about 30 km below continents. By studying the speed of seismic waves, scientists have been able to locate boundaries between other internal layers of Earth. The three main compositional layers of Earth are the *crust,* the *mantle,* and the *core.* Earth is also composed of five mechanical layers—the *lithosphere,* the *asthenosphere,* the *mesosphere,* the *outer core,* and the *inner core.*

Shadow Zones

Recordings of seismic waves around the world reveal shadow zones. **Shadow zones** are locations on Earth's surface where no body waves from a particular earthquake can be detected. Shadow zones exist because the materials that make up Earth's interior are not uniform in rigidity. When seismic waves travel through materials of differing rigidities, the speed of the waves changes. The waves will also bend and change direction as they pass through different materials.

As shown in **Figure 4,** a large S-wave shadow zone covers the side of Earth that is opposite an earthquake. S waves do not reach the S-wave shadow zone because they cannot pass through the liquid outer core. Although P waves can travel through all of the layers, the speed and direction of the waves change as the waves pass through each layer. The waves bend in such a way that a P-wave shadow zone forms.

✓ Reading Check What causes the speed of a seismic wave to change? (See the Appendix for answers to Reading Checks.)

Figure 5 ▶ Earthquakes are the result of tectonic stresses in Earth's crust and occur in three main tectonic settings—mid-ocean ridges, subduction zones, and continental collisions.

Earthquakes and Plate Tectonics

Earthquakes are the result of stresses in Earth's lithosphere. Most earthquakes occur in three main tectonic environments, as shown in **Figure 5**. These settings are generally located at or near tectonic plate boundaries, where stress on the rock is greatest.

Convergent Oceanic Environments

At convergent plate boundaries, plates move toward each other and collide. The plate that is denser subducts, or sinks into the asthenosphere below the other plate. As the plates move, the overriding plate scrapes across the top of the subducting plate, and earthquakes occur. Convergent oceanic boundaries can occur between two oceanic plates or between one oceanic plate and one continental plate.

Divergent Oceanic Environments

At the divergent plate boundaries that make up the mid-ocean ridges, plates are moving away from each other. Earthquakes occur along mid-ocean ridges because oceanic lithosphere is pulling away from both sides of each ridge. This spreading motion causes earthquakes along the ocean ridges.

Continental Environments

Earthquakes also occur at locations where two continental plates converge, diverge, or move horizontally in opposite directions. As the continental plates interact, the rock surrounding the boundary experiences stress. The stress may cause mountains to form and also causes frequent earthquakes.

Graphic Organizer Spider Map
Create the Graphic Organizer entitled "Spider Map" described in the Skills Handbook section of the Appendix. Label the circle "Major earthquake zones." Create a leg for each type of earthquake zone. Then, fill in the map with details about each type of earthquake zone.

Fault Zones

At some plate boundaries, there are regions of numerous, closely spaced faults called **fault zones.** Fault zones form at plate boundaries because of the intense stress that results when the plates separate, collide, subduct, or slide past each other. One such fault zone is the North Anatolian fault zone, shown in **Figure 6,** that extends almost the entire length of the country of Turkey. Where the edge of the Arabian plate pushes against the Eurasian plate, the small Turkish microplate is squeezed westward. When enough stress builds up, movement occurs along one or more of the individual faults in the fault zone and sometimes causes major earthquakes.

Figure 6 ▶ A series of parallel transform faults, seen in the center of this photo, make up part of the North Anatolian fault zone in Turkey.

fault zone a region of numerous, closely spaced faults

Earthquakes Away from Plate Boundaries

Not all earthquakes result from movement along plate boundaries. The most widely felt series of earthquakes in the history of the United States did not occur near an active plate boundary. Instead, these earthquakes occurred in the middle of the continent, near New Madrid, Missouri, in 1811 and 1812. The vibrations from the earthquakes that rocked New Madrid were so strong that they caused damage as far away as South Carolina.

It was not until the late 1970s that studies of the Mississippi River region revealed an ancient fault zone deep within Earth's crust. This zone is thought to be part of a major fault zone in the North American plate. Scientists have determined that the fault formed at least 600 million years ago and that it was later buried under many layers of sediment and rock.

Section 1 Review

1. **Describe** elastic rebound. 3d

2. **Explain** the difference between the epicenter and the focus of an earthquake. 3d

3. **Compare** body waves and surface waves. 3d

4. **Explain** how seismic waves help scientists learn about Earth's interior. 3d

5. **Explain** how the structure of Earth's interior affects seismic wave speed and direction. 3d

6. **Explain** why earthquakes generally take place at plate boundaries. 3d

7. **Describe** a fault zone, and explain how earthquakes occur along fault zones. 3d

CRITICAL THINKING

8. **Applying Ideas** In earthquakes that cause the most damage, at what depth would movement along a fault most likely occur? 3d, IE.1d

9. **Identifying Patterns** If a seismologic station measures P waves but no S waves from an earthquake, what can you conclude about the earthquake's location? 3d, IE.1d

10. **Making Inferences** If an earthquake occurs in the center of Brazil, what can you infer about the geology of that area? 3d, IE.1d

CONCEPT MAPPING

11. Use the following terms to create a concept map: *earthquake, seismic wave, body wave, surface wave, P wave, S wave, Rayleigh wave,* and *Love wave.* 3d

3d Students know why and how earthquakes occur and the scales used to measure their intensity and magnitude.

IE.1a Students will select and use appropriate tools and technology (such as computer-linked probes, spreadsheets, and graphing calcula-

tors) to perform tests, collect data, analyze relationships, and display data.
IE.1d Students will formulate explanations using logic and evidence.

The study of earthquakes and seismic waves is called *seismology*. Many scientists study earthquakes because earthquakes are the best tool Earth scientists have for investigating Earth's internal structure and dynamics. These scientists have developed special sensing equipment to record, locate, and measure earthquakes.

Recording Earthquakes

Vibrations in the ground can be detected and recorded by using an instrument called a **seismograph** (SIEZ MUH graf), such as the one shown in **Figure 1.** A modern three-component seismograph consists of three sensing devices. One device records the vertical motion of the ground. The other two devices record horizontal motion—one for east-west motion and the other for north-south motion. Seismographs record motion by tracing wave-shaped lines on paper or by translating the motion into electronic signals. The electronic signals can be recorded on magnetic tape or can be loaded directly into a computer that analyzes seismic waves. A tracing of earthquake motion that is recorded by a seismograph is called a **seismogram.**

Because they are the fastest-moving seismic waves, P waves are the first waves to be recorded by a seismograph. S waves travel much slower than P waves. Therefore, S waves are the second waves to be recorded by a seismograph. Surface waves, or Rayleigh and Love waves, are the slowest-moving waves. Thus, Rayleigh and Love waves are the last waves to be recorded by a seismograph.

OBJECTIVES

▶ **Describe** the instrument used to measure and record earthquakes. 3d

▶ **Summarize** the method scientists use to locate an epicenter. IE.1a, 3d

▶ **Describe** the scales used to measure the magnitude and intensity of earthquakes. 3d

KEY TERMS

seismograph
seismogram
magnitude
intensity

seismograph an instrument that records vibrations in the ground

seismogram a tracing of earthquake motion that is recorded by a seismograph

Figure 1 ▶ A seismograph station has banks of seismographs to record earthquakes. Each type of seismic wave leaves a unique "signature" on a seismogram (inset).

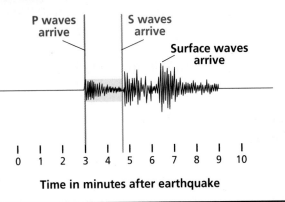

Locating an Earthquake

To determine the distance to an epicenter, scientists analyze the arrival times of the P waves and the S waves. The longer the lag time between the arrival of the P waves and the arrival of the S waves is, the farther away the earthquake occurred. To determine how far an earthquake is from a given seismograph station, scientists consult a lag-time graph. This graph translates the difference in arrival times of the P waves and S waves into distance from the epicenter to each station. The start time of the earthquake can also be determined by using this graph.

To locate the epicenter of the earthquake, scientists use computers to perform complex triangulations based on information from several seismograph stations. Before computers were widely available, scientists performed this calculation in a simpler and more imprecise way. On a map, they drew circles around at least three seismograph stations that recorded vibrations from the earthquake. The radius of each circle was equal to the distance from that station to the earthquake's epicenter. The point at which all of the circles intersected indicated the location of the epicenter of the earthquake.

QuickLAB 20 min

Seismographic Record
Procedure 3d, IE.1d

1. Line a shoe box with a plastic bag. Fill the box to the rim with sand. Put on the lid.
2. Mark an X near the center of the lid.
3. Fasten a felt-tip pen to the lid of the box with a tight rubber band so that the pen extends slightly beyond the edge of the box.
4. Have a partner hold a pad of paper so that the paper touches the pen.
5. Hold a ball over the X at a height of 30 cm. As your partner slowly moves the paper horizontally past the pen, drop the ball on the X.
6. Label the resulting line with the type of material in the box.
7. Replace about 2/3 of the sand with crumpled newspaper. Put on the lid, and fasten the pen to the lid with the rubber band.
8. Repeat steps 4–6.

Analysis
1. What do the lines on the paper represent?
2. What do the sand and newspaper represent?

3. Compare the lines made in steps 4–6 with those made in step 8. Which material vibrated more when the ball was dropped on it? Explain why one material might vibrate more than the other.
4. How might different types of crustal material affect seismic waves that pass through it?
5. How might the distance of the epicenter of an earthquake from a seismograph affect the reading of a seismograph?

Figure 2 ▶ The 1995 earthquake in Kobe, Japan, had a moment magnitude of 6.9, lasted 20 s, and killed 5,470 people.

Earthquake Measurement

Scientists who study earthquakes are interested in the amount of energy released by an earthquake. Scientists also study the amount of damage done by the earthquake. These properties are studied by measuring magnitude and intensity.

Magnitude

The measure of the strength of an earthquake is called **magnitude.** Magnitude is determined by measuring the amount of ground motion caused by an earthquake. Seismologists express magnitude by using a magnitude scale, such as the Richter scale or the moment magnitude scale.

The *Richter scale* measures the ground motion from an earthquake to find the earthquake's strength. While the Richter scale was widely used for most of the 20th century, scientists now prefer the moment magnitude scale. *Moment magnitude* is a measurement of earthquake strength based on the size of the area of the fault that moves, the average distance that the fault blocks move, and the rigidity of the rocks in the fault zone. Although the moment magnitude and the Richter scales provide similar values for small earthquakes, the moment magnitude scale is more accurate for large earthquakes.

The moment magnitude of an earthquake is expressed by a number. The larger the number, the stronger the earthquake. The largest earthquake that has been recorded registered a moment magnitude of 9.5. The earthquake in Kobe, Japan, in 1995 that caused the damage shown in **Figure 2** had a moment magnitude of 6.9. Earthquakes that have moment magnitudes of less than 2.5 usually are not felt by people.

✓ Reading Check What is the difference between the Richter scale and the moment magnitude scale? (See the Appendix for answers to Reading Checks.)

magnitude a measure of the strength of an earthquake

MATHPRACTICE

Magnitudes On both the moment magnitude scale and the Richter scale, the energy of an earthquake increases by a factor of about 30 for each increment on the scale. Thus, a magnitude 4 earthquake releases 30 times as much energy as a magnitude 3 earthquake does. How much more energy does a magnitude 6 earthquake release than a magnitude 3 earthquake does?

Table 1 ▼

	Modified Mercalli Intensity Scale
Intensity	**Description**
I	is not felt except by very few under especially favorable conditions
II	is felt by only few people at rest; delicately suspended items may swing
III	is felt by most people indoors; vibration is similar to the passing of a large truck
IV	is felt by many people; dishes and windows rattle; sensation is similar to a building being struck
V	is felt by nearly everyone; some objects are broken; and unstable objects are overturned
VI	is felt by all people; some heavy objects are moved; causes very slight damage to structures
VII	causes slight to moderate damage to ordinary buildings; some chimneys are broken
VIII	causes considerable damage (including partial collapse) to ordinary buildings
IX	causes considerable damage (including partial collapse) to earthquake-resistant buildings
X	destroys some to most structures, including foundations; rails are bent
XI	causes few structures, if any, to remain standing; bridges are destroyed and rails are bent
XII	causes total destruction; distorts lines of sight; objects are thrown into the air

Intensity

Before the development of magnitude scales, the size of an earthquake was determined based on the earthquake's effects. A measure of the effects of an earthquake is the earthquake's **intensity**. The modified *Mercalli scale*, shown in **Table 1,** expresses intensity in Roman numerals from I to XII and provides a description of the effects of each earthquake intensity. The highest-intensity earthquake is designated by Roman numeral XII and is described as total destruction. The intensity of an earthquake depends on the earthquake's magnitude, the distance between the epicenter and the affected area, the local geology, the earthquake's duration, and human infrastructure.

intensity in Earth science, the amount of damage caused by an earthquake

1. **Describe** the instrument that is used to record seismic waves. 🌐 3d

2. **Compare** a seismograph and a seismogram. 🌐 3d

3. **Summarize** the method that scientists used to identify the location of an earthquake before computers became widely used. 🌐 3d, IE.1a

4. **Describe** the scales that scientists use to measure the magnitude of an earthquake. 🌐 3d

5. **Explain** the difference between magnitude and intensity of an earthquake. 🌐 3d

CRITICAL THINKING

6. **Analyzing Methods** Explain why it would be difficult for scientists to locate the epicenter of an earthquake if they have seismic wave information from only two locations. 🌐 3d, IE.1a, IE.1d

7. **Evaluating Data** Explain why an earthquake with a moderate magnitude might have a high intensity? 🌐 3d, IE.1d

CONCEPT MAPPING

8. Use the following terms to create a concept map: *seismograph, seismogram, epicenter, P wave, S wave, magnitude,* and *intensity.* 🌐 3d

California Content Standards

9b Students know the principal natural hazards in different California regions and the geological basis of those hazards.

IE.1m Students will investigate a science-based societal issue by researching the literature, analyzing data, and communicating the find-

ings. Examples of issues include irradiation of food, cloning of animals by somatic cell nuclear transfer, choice of energy sources, and land and water use decisions in California.

Movement of the ground during an earthquake seldom directly causes many deaths or injuries. Instead, most injuries result from the collapse of buildings and other structures or from falling objects and flying glass. Other dangers include landslides, fires, explosions caused by broken electric and gas lines, and floodwaters released from collapsing dams.

Tsunamis

An earthquake whose epicenter is on the ocean floor may cause a giant ocean wave called a **tsunami** (tsoo NAH mee), which may cause serious destruction if it crashes into land. A tsunami may begin to form when a sudden drop or rise in the ocean floor occurs because of faulting associated with undersea earthquakes. The drop or rise of the ocean floor causes a large mass of sea water to also drop or rise. This mass of water moves up and down as it adjusts to the change in sea level. This movement sets into motion a series of long, low waves that increase in height as they near the shore. These waves are tsunamis. A tsunami may also be triggered by an underwater landslide caused by an earthquake.

Destruction to Buildings and Property

Most buildings are not designed to withstand the swaying motion caused by earthquakes. Buildings whose walls are weak may collapse completely. Very tall buildings may sway so violently that they tip over and fall onto lower neighboring structures, as shown in **Figure 1.**

The type of ground beneath a building can affect the way in which the building responds to seismic waves. A building constructed on loose soil and rock is much more likely to be damaged during an earthquake than a building constructed on solid ground is. During an earthquake, the loose soil and rock can vibrate like jelly. Buildings constructed on top of this kind of ground experience exaggerated motion and sway violently.

OBJECTIVES

▶ **Discuss** the relationship between tsunamis and earthquakes. **9b**

▶ **Describe** two possible effects of a major earthquake on buildings. **9b**

▶ **List** three safety techniques to prevent injury caused by earthquake activity. **IE.1m**

▶ **Identify** four methods scientists use to forecast earthquake risks. **9b**

KEY TERMS

tsunami

seismic gap

tsunami a giant ocean wave that forms after a volcanic eruption, submarine earthquake, or landslide

Figure 1 ▶ Rescue workers surround a building that collapsed in Taipei, Taiwan, during the earthquake of 1999.

Figure 2 ▶ In Tokyo, Japan—an area that has a high earthquake-hazard level—earthquake safety materials are available at disaster control centers.

Earthquake Safety

A destructive earthquake may take place in any region of the United States. However, destructive earthquakes are more likely to occur in certain geographic areas, such as California or Alaska. People who live near active faults should be ready to follow a few simple earthquake safety rules. These safety rules may help prevent death, injury, and property damage.

Before an Earthquake

Before an earthquake occurs, be prepared. Keep on hand a supply of canned food, bottled water, flashlights, batteries, and a portable radio. Some safety material is shown in **Figure 2.** Plan what you will do if an earthquake strikes while you are at home, in school, or in a car. Discuss these plans with your family. Learn how to turn off the gas, water, and electricity in your home.

During an Earthquake

When an earthquake occurs, stay calm. During the few seconds between tremors, you can move to a safer position. If you are indoors, protect yourself from falling debris by standing in a doorway or crouching under a desk or table. Stay away from windows, heavy furniture, and other objects that might topple over. If you are in school, follow the instructions given by your teacher or principal. If you are in a car, stop in a place that is away from tall buildings, tunnels, power lines, or bridges. Then, remain in the car until the tremors cease.

After an Earthquake

After an earthquake, be cautious. Check for fire and other hazards. Always wear shoes when walking near broken glass, and avoid downed power lines and objects touched by downed wires.

Earthquake Warnings and Forecasts

Humans have long dreamed of being able to predict earthquakes. Accurate earthquake predictions could help prevent injuries and deaths that result from earthquakes.

Today, scientists study past earthquakes to predict where future earthquakes are most likely to occur. Using records of past earthquakes, scientists can make approximate forecasts of future earthquake risks. However, there is currently no reliable way to predict exactly when or where an earthquake will occur. Even the best forecasts may be off by several years.

To make forecasts that are more accurate, scientists are trying to detect changes in Earth's crust that can signal an earthquake. Faults near many population centers have been located and mapped. Instruments placed along these faults measure small changes in rock movement around the faults and can detect an increase in stress. Currently, however, these methods cannot provide reliable or accurate predictions of earthquakes.

Seismic Gaps

Scientists have identified zones of low earthquake activity, or seismic gaps, along some faults. A **seismic gap** is an area along a fault where relatively few earthquakes have occurred recently but where strong earthquakes occurred in the past. Some scientists think that seismic gaps are likely locations of future earthquakes. Several gaps that exist along the San Andreas Fault zone may be sites of major earthquakes in the future. One of these locations, Loma Prieta, California, is shown in **Figure 3.**

Reading Check Why do scientists think that seismic gaps are areas where future earthquakes are likely to occur? (See the Appendix for answers to Reading Checks.)

seismic gap an area along a fault where relatively few earthquakes have occurred recently but where strong earthquakes are known to have occurred in the past

Figure 3 ▶ Each red dot in the cross section of the San Andreas Fault represents an earthquake or aftershock before the 1989 Loma Prieta earthquake. Note how seismic gap 2 was filled by the 1989 earthquake and its aftershocks, which are represented by the blue dots.

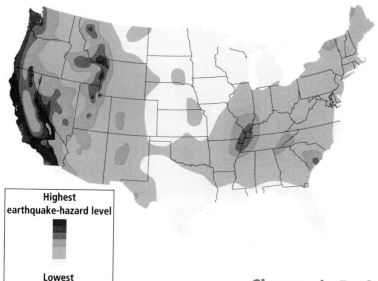

Highest earthquake-hazard level

Lowest earthquake-hazard level

Figure 4 ▶ California, which has experienced severe earthquakes recently, has the highest earthquake-hazard level of the contiguous United States.

Foreshocks

Some earthquakes are preceded by little earthquakes called *foreshocks*. Foreshocks can precede an earthquake by a few seconds or a few weeks. In 1975, geophysicists in China recorded foreshocks near the city of Haicheng, which had a history of earthquakes. The city was evacuated the day before a major earthquake. The earthquake caused widespread destruction, but few lives were lost thanks to the warning. However, the Haicheng earthquake is the only example of a successful prediction made by using this method.

Changes in Rocks

Scientists use a variety of sensors to detect slight tilting of the ground and to identify the strain and cracks in rocks caused by the stress that builds up in fault zones. When these cracks in the rocks are filled with water, the magnetic and electrical properties of the rocks may change. Scientists also monitor natural gas seepage from rocks that are strained or fractured from seismic activity. Scientists hope that they will one day be able to use these signals to predict earthquakes.

Reliability of Earthquake Forecasts

Unfortunately, not all earthquakes have foreshocks or other precursors. Earthquake prediction is mostly unreliable. However, scientists have been able to determine areas that have a high earthquake-hazard level, as shown in **Figure 4.** Scientists continue to study seismic activity so that they may one day make accurate forecasts and save more lives.

Section 3 Review

1. **Discuss** the relationship between tsunamis and earthquakes. 9b

2. **Describe** two possible effects of a major earthquake on buildings. 9b

3. **List** three safety rules to follow when an earthquake strikes. IE.1m

4. **Describe** how identifying seismic gaps may help scientists predict earthquakes. 9b

5. **Identify** changes in rocks that may signal earthquakes. 9b

CRITICAL THINKING

6. **Applying Concepts** What type of building construction and location regulations should be included in the building code of a city that is located near an active fault? 9b, IE.1d, IE.1m

7. **Applying Concepts** You are a scientist assigned to study an area that has a high earthquake-hazard level. Describe a program that you could set up to predict potential earthquakes. 9b, IE.1m

CONCEPT MAPPING

8. Use the following terms to create a concept map: *earthquake, earthquake-hazard level, damage, tsunami, safety,* and *prediction.* 9b

Sections

1 How and Where Earthquakes Happen

Key Terms

earthquake, 295
elastic rebound, 295
focus, 296
epicenter, 296
body wave, 296
surface wave, 296
P wave, 297
S wave, 297
shadow zone, 298
fault zone, 300

Key Concepts

▶ In the process of elastic rebound, stress builds in rocks along a fault until they break and spring back to their original shape.

▶ There are two major types of seismic waves: body waves and surface waves.

▶ Different seismic waves act differently depending on the material of Earth's interior through which they pass.

▶ Most earthquakes occur near tectonic plate boundaries.

2 Studying Earthquakes

seismograph, 301
seismogram, 301
magnitude, 303
intensity, 304

▶ Scientists use seismographs to record earthquake vibrations.

▶ The difference in the times that P waves and S waves take to arrive at a seismograph station helps scientists locate the epicenter of an earthquake.

▶ Earthquake magnitude scales describe the strength of an earthquake. Intensity is a measure of the effects of an earthquake.

3 Earthquakes and Society

tsunami, 305
seismic gap, 307

▶ Most earthquake damage is caused by the collapse of buildings and other structures.

▶ Tsunamis often are caused by ocean-floor earthquakes.

▶ People who follow safety guidelines are less likely to be harmed by an earthquake.

▶ Seismic gaps, tilting ground, and variations in rock properties are some of the changes in Earth's crust that scientists use when trying to predict earthquakes.

Using Key Terms

Use each of the following terms in a separate sentence.

1. *elastic rebound* 🐾3d

2. *fault zone* 🐾3d

3. *seismic gap* 🐾3d

For each pair of terms, explain how the meanings of the terms differ.

4. *focus* and *epicenter* 🐾3d

5. *body wave* and *surface wave* 🐾3d

6. *P wave* and *S wave* 🐾3d

7. *seismograph* and *seismogram* 🐾3d

8. *intensity* and *magnitude* 🐾3d

Understanding Key Concepts

9. Vibrations in Earth that are caused by the sudden movement of rock are called 🐾3d

  a. epicenters.   **c.** faults.

  b. earthquakes.   **d.** tsunamis.

10. In the process of elastic rebound, as a rock becomes stressed, it first 🐾3d

  a. deforms.   **c.** breaks.

  b. melts.   **d.** shrinks.

11. Earthquakes that cause severe damage are likely to have what characteristic? 🐾3d, 9b

  a. a deep focus

  b. an intermediate focus

  c. a shallow focus

  d. a deep epicenter

12. Most earthquakes occur 🐾3d

  a. in mountains.

  b. along major rivers.

  c. at plate boundaries.

  d. in the middle of tectonic plates.

13. P waves travel 🐾3d

  a. only through solids.

  b. only through liquids and gases.

  c. through solids, liquids, and gases.

  d. only through liquids.

14. S waves cannot pass through 🐾3d

  a. solids.   **c.** Earth's outer core.

  b. the mantle.   **d.** the asthenosphere.

15. Most injuries during earthquakes are caused by 🐾3d, 9b

  a. the collapse of buildings.

  b. cracks in Earth's surface.

  c. the vibration of S waves.

  d. the vibration of P waves.

16. Which of the following is *not* a method used to forecast earthquake risks? 🐾9b

  a. identifying seismic gaps

  b. determining moment magnitude

  c. recording foreshocks

  d. detecting changes in the rock

Short Answer

17. How do seismic waves help scientists understand Earth's interior? 🐾3d

18. Why is the S-wave shadow zone larger than the P-wave shadow zones are? 🐾3d

19. How do scientists determine the location of an earthquake's epicenter? 🐾3d

20. Why do scientists prefer the moment magnitude scale to the Richter scale? 🐾3d

21. How might tall buildings respond during a major earthquake? 🐾3d, 9b

22. What should you do if you are in a car when an earthquake happens? 🐾3d, 9b, IE.1m

23. List three changes in rock that may one day be used to help forecast earthquakes. 🐾3d

Critical Thinking

24. **Understanding Relationships** Why might surface waves cause the greatest damage during an earthquake? 3d, 9b, IE.1d

25. **Determining Cause and Effect** Two cities are struck by the same earthquake. The cities are the same size, are built on the same type of ground, and have the same types of buildings. The city in which the earthquake produced a maximum intensity of VI on the Mercalli scale suffered $1 million in damage. The city in which the earthquake produced a maximum intensity of VIII on the Mercalli scale suffered $50 million in damage. What might account for this great difference in the costs of the damage? 3d, 9b, IE.1d

26. **Recognizing Relationships** Would an earthquake in the Rocky Mountains in Colorado be likely to form a tsunami? Explain your answer. 3d

Concept Mapping

27. Use the following terms to create a concept map: *earthquake, elastic rebound, surface wave, body wave, seismic wave, tsunami, seismograph, magnitude, intensity, moment magnitude scale,* and *Richter scale.* 3d

Math Skills

28. **Making Calculations** If a P wave traveled 6.1 km/s, how long would the P wave take to travel 800 km? 3d

29. **Using Equations** An earthquake with a magnitude of 3 releases 30 times more energy than does an earthquake with a magnitude of 2. How much more energy does an earthquake with a magnitude of 8 release than an earthquake with a magnitude of 6 does? 3d

30. **Making Calculations** Of the approximately 420,000 earthquakes recorded each year, about 140 have a magnitude greater than 6. What percentage of all earthquakes have a magnitude greater than 6? 3d

Writing Skills

31. **Writing from Research** Find out how and why the worldwide network of seismograph stations was formed. Also, find out how all the stations in the network work together. Prepare a report about your findings. 3d, 9b, IE.1m

32. **Communicating Main Ideas** Find out which earthquake registered the highest intensity in history. Write a brief report that describes the effects of this earthquake. 3d, IE.1m

Interpreting Graphics

The graph below shows three seismograms from a single earthquake. Use the graph to answer the questions that follow.

Seismic Wave Lapse Time

33. How far from the epicenter is seismograph B? 3d

34. How far from the epicenter is seismograph C? 3d

35. Which seismograph is farthest from the epicenter? 3d

36. Why is there an 8 min interval between P waves and S waves in seismogram B but an 11 min interval between P waves and S waves in seismogram C? 3d

Understanding Concepts

Directions (1–9): For *each* question, write on a separate sheet of paper the letter of the correct answer.

1 Which of the following statements describes the relationship between the epicenter and focus of an earthquake?
A. The focus is the point on Earth's surface where the epicenter of an earthquake is located.
B. The epicenter is the point on Earth's surface that lies directly above the focus.
C. The epicenter is the point where an earthquake occurs, and the focus is where seismic waves reach Earth's surface.
D. The focus is deeper within the Earth than the epicenter is.

2 Earthquakes result from
A. the immobilization of faults.
B. the sudden return of elastically deformed rock to its undeformed shape.
C. zones where body waves cannot be detected.
D. movement between the layers that make up Earth.

3 Most earthquake-related injuries are caused by
A. tsunamis.
B. collapsing buildings.
C. rolling ground movements.
D. sudden cracks in the ground.

4 Which of the following is least likely to cause deaths during an earthquake?
A. floodwaters from collapsing dams
B. falling objects and flying glass
C. actual ground movement
D. fires from broken electric and gas lines

5 California has the highest earthquake hazard level in the United States, as indicated by geological hazard maps. Why might scientists use geologic hazard maps?
A. to determine areas that are at higher risk from a geologic hazard
B. to predict when an earthquake might occur
C. to identify stress-related strain in rocks
D. to monitor gas seepage from strained or fractured rocks

6 The magnitude of an earthquake can be expressed numerically by using
A. only the Richter scale.
B. only the Mercalli scale.
C. both the Mercalli scale and the moment magnitude scale.
D. both the Richter scale and the moment magnitude scale.

7 Which of the following statements about shadow zones is NOT true?
A. They are locations on Earth's surface where no body waves from a particular earthquake can be detected.
B. Waves bend and change directions as they pass through Earth.
C. They exist because the materials that make up Earth's interior have uniform rigidity.
D. A large S-wave shadow zone covers the side of Earth opposite an earthquake.

8 How is the intensity of an earthquake measured?
A. by measuring the amount of ground motion caused by the earthquake
B. by measuring the strength of the earthquake based on the size of the area of the fault that moves
C. by measuring the amount of destruction caused by the earthquake
D. by measuring the number of seismic waves that occur during the earthquake

9 What is the relationship between seismic gaps and earthquakes?
A. A seismic gap is the area where an earthquake originates.
B. A seismic gap is an area where numerous, closely-spaced faults produce earthquakes.
C. A seismic gap occurs because the interior of Earth is not uniformly rigid and seismic waves travel through Earth's core at varying speeds.
D. A seismic gap is an area along a fault where relatively few earthquakes have occurred recently but where strong earthquakes have occurred in the past.

Interpreting Graphics

Directions (10–12): **For *each* question below, record the correct answer on a separate sheet of paper.**

The diagram shows a recording of data by a seismograph.

Reading a Seismogram

Arrival time (sec)

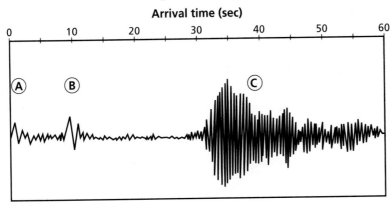

10 What type of seismic waves are indicated by the points on the seismogram marked by the letter A?
  A. Love waves
  B. Rayleigh waves
  C. P waves
  D. S waves

11 How are the waves at point C different from the waves at point B?
  A. The waves at point C are slower than the waves at point B are.
  B. The waves at point C are less damaging than the waves at point B are.
  C. The waves at point C are S waves, while the waves at point B are surface waves.
  D. The waves at point B get their energy from the waves at point C.

Earthquake Damage

12 Based on the illustration above, the people that lived in this area would be at most danger from what during an earthquake?
  A. tsunamis
  B. collapsing power lines
  C. surface waves
  D. aftershocks

Skills Practice Lab

Finding an Epicenter ⬛ 3d, 9b, IE.1d

Objectives

▶ **USING SCIENTIFIC METHODS**
Analyze P waves and S waves to determine the distance from a city to the epicenter of an earthquake.

▶ **Determine** the location of an earthquake epicenter by using the distance from three different cities to the epicenter of an earthquake.

Materials

calculator

drawing compass

ruler

An earthquake releases energy that travels through Earth in all directions. This energy is in the form of waves. Two kinds of seismic waves are P waves and S waves. P waves travel faster than S waves and are the first to be recorded at a seismograph station. The S waves arrive after the P waves. The time difference between the arrival of the P waves and the S waves increases as the waves travel farther from their origin. This difference in arrival time, called *lag time,* can be used to find the distance to the epicenter of the earthquake. Once the distance from three different locations is determined, scientists can find the approximate location of the epicenter.

PROCEDURE

1. The average speed of P waves is 6.1 km/s. The average speed of S waves is 4.1 km/s. Calculate the lag time between the arrival of P waves and S waves over a distance of 100 km.

2. The graph below shows seismic records made in three cities following an earthquake. These traces begin at the left. The arrows indicate the arrival of the P waves. The beginning of the next wave on each seismograph record indicates the arrival of the S wave. Use the time scale to find the lag time between the P wave and the S waves for each city. Draw a table similar to **Table 1.**

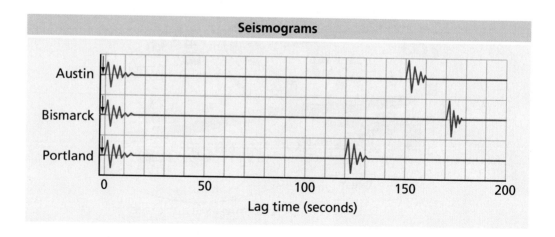

Seismograms

Austin

Bismarck

Portland

0   50   100   150   200

Lag time (seconds)

Table 1

City	Lag time (seconds)	Distance from city to epicenter
Austin		
Bismarck		
Portland		

DO NOT WRITE IN THIS BOOK

3 Record lag time for each city in the table.

4 Use the lag times found in step 2 and the lag time per 100 km found in step 1 to calculate the distance from each city to the epicenter of the earthquake by using the equation below.

$$distance = \frac{measured\ lag\ time\ (s) \times 100\ km}{lag\ time\ for\ 100\ km}$$

5 Record distances in the table.

6 Copy the map at right, which shows the location of the three cities. Using the map scale on your copy of the map, adjust the compass so that the radius of the circle with Austin at the center is equal to the calculation for Austin in step 2. Put the point of the compass on Austin. Draw a circle on your copy of the map.

7 Repeat step 6 for Bismarck and for Portland. The epicenter of the earthquake is located near the point at which the three circles intersect.

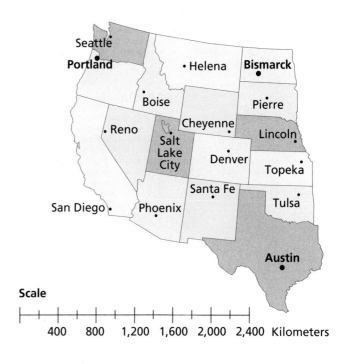

Scale

400   800   1,200 1,600 2,000 2,400 Kilometers

ANALYSIS AND CONCLUSION

1 **Evaluating Data** Describe the location of the earthquake's epicenter. To which city is the location of the earthquake's epicenter closest?

2 **Analyzing Processes** Why must measurements from three locations be used to find the epicenter of an earthquake?

Extension

1 **Evaluating Data** Research earthquakes in the United States. What is the probability of a major earthquake occurring in the area where you live? If an earthquake did occur in your area, what would most likely cause the earthquake?

Earthquake Hazard Map

Robinson Projection
Scale: 1:35,000,000 At The Equator

| LOW HAZARD | MODERATE HAZARD | HIGH HAZARD | VERY HIGH HAZARD |

Map Skills Activity

This map shows the earthquake-hazard levels for Europe, Asia, Africa, and Australia. Use the map to answer the questions below.

1. **Using a Key** Which areas of the map have a very high earthquake-hazard level?

2. **Using a Key** Determine which areas of the map have very low earthquake-hazard levels.

3. **Inferring Relationships** Most earthquakes take place near tectonic plate boundaries. Based on the hazard levels, describe the areas of the map where you think tectonic plate boundaries are located.

4. **Analyzing Relationships** In Asia, just below 60° north latitude, there are areas that have high earthquake-hazard levels but no plate boundaries. Explain why these areas might experience earthquakes.

5. **Forming a Hypothesis** There is a tectonic plate boundary between Africa and Saudi Arabia. However, the earthquake-hazard level in that region is low. Explain the low earthquake-hazard level.

6. **Analyzing Relationships** A divergent plate boundary began to tear apart the continent of Africa about 30 million years ago. Where on the continent of Africa would you expect to find landforms created by this boundary? Explain your answer.

Geophysicist

Earth's surface may appear solid and unmoving. But Wayne Thatcher sees daily evidence that Earth's surface is always changing. As a research geophysicist for the U.S. Geological Survey, Thatcher studies the forces that shape Earth's crust, such as earthquakes.

Tools of the Trade

To measure ground deformation, Thatcher and his colleagues use global positioning system (GPS) and radar satellite images. GPS is a network of satellites that is commonly used for navigation of ships and aircraft. Thatcher uses GPS to measure changes in Earth's crust. By measuring ground elevation changes of a few millimeters, GPS enables discoveries that would not have been made many years ago.

Thatcher also uses Interferometric Synthetic Aperture Radar (InSAR), a remote-sensing technique that uses satellite radio waves to create three-dimensional images of Earth's surface. In this way, InSAR is able to map ground displacement from one satellite pass to the next, which helps scientists form mappings of deformation over months or years.

Predicting Future Earthquakes

For Thatcher and other geophysicists, the ability to forecast an earthquake remains an ongoing research aim. "Prediction is one of our ultimate goals," he notes. "We can estimate the level of risk based on GPS or InSAR readings. For example, we can track fault movements and note that

"**Geophysics is a very international field of study. It's good to compare similarities and differences with other researchers who study earthquakes and volcanoes around the world.**"

—**Wayne Thatcher, Ph.D.**

'something's got to give' and a quake is due."

For his research, Thatcher travels to fault zones throughout the western United States, where he sets up GPS benchmark sites. Trips to the sites in later years enable scientists to measure the rate and extent of movement of Earth's crust. Thatcher also journeys to other geologically active parts of the world, such as Japan, New Zealand, and Greece.

◄ This colored satellite map shows the ground displacement after a 7.3 moment magnitude earthquake in Landers, California, on June 28, 1992.

SCiLINKS®

NSTA
Developed and maintained by the National Science Teachers Association

For a variety of links related to this subject, go to www.scilinks.org

Topic: Careers in Earth Science
SciLinks code: HQ60222

Sections

1 Volcanoes and Plate Tectonics

2 Volcanic Eruptions

What You'll Learn

- Where volcanoes are located
- What causes volcanic eruptions
- How lava affects the shape of volcanoes

Why It's Relevant

Volcanoes can form features such as mountains or islands. Volcanic eruptions can also endanger human life. Learning about volcanoes can help scientists better predict eruptions and can prepare people to evacuate dangerous areas.

 California Content Standards

3e Students know there are two kinds of volcanoes: one kind with violent eruptions producing steep slopes and the other kind with voluminous lava flows producing gentle slopes.

3f* Students know the explanation for the location and properties of volcanoes that are due to hot spots and the explanation for those that are due to subduction.

IE.1a Students will select and use appropriate tools and technology (such as computer-linked probes, spreadsheets, and graphing calculators) to perform tests, collect data, analyze relationships and display data.

IE.1d Students will formulate explanations using logic and evidence.

IE.1g Students will recognize the usefulness and limitations of models and theories as scientific representations of reality.

IE.1l Students will analyze situations and solve problems that require combining and applying concepts from more than one area of science.

PRE-READING ACTIVITY

Table Fold
Before you read this chapter, create the **FoldNote** entitled "Table Fold" described in the Skills Handbook section of the Appendix. Label the columns of the table fold with "Slope," "Lava," and "Eruption style." Label the rows with the three different types of volcanic cones. As you read the chapter, write examples of each topic under the appropriate column.

▶ Because volcanic eruptions add new material to Earth's surface, they have formed many islands, such as the Hawaiian Island chain. There, you can witness the volcanic processes that form islands, as shown in this photo.

Volcanoes and Plate Tectonics

California
Content
Standards

3f* Students know the explanation for the location and properties of volcanoes that are due to hot spots and the explanation for those

that are due to subduction.
IE.1d Students will formulate explanations using logic and evidence.

IE.1g Students will recognize the usefulness and limitations of models and theories as scientific representations of reality.

Volcanic eruptions can cause some of the most dramatic changes to Earth's surface. Some eruptions can be more powerful than the explosion of an atomic bomb. The cause of many of these eruptions is the movement of tectonic plates. The movement of tectonic plates is driven by Earth's internal heat.

By studying temperatures within Earth, scientists can learn more about volcanic eruptions. **Figure 1** shows estimates of Earth's inner temperatures and pressures. As the graph shows, the combined temperature and pressure in the lower part of the mantle keeps the rocks below their melting point.

Formation of Magma

Despite the high temperature in the mantle, most of this zone remains solid because of the large amount of pressure from the surrounding rock. Sometimes, however, solid mantle and crust melt to form **magma,** or liquid rock that forms under Earth's surface.

Magma can form under three conditions. First, if the temperature of rock rises above the melting point of the minerals the rock is composed of, the rock will melt. Second, if enough pressure is removed from the rock, the melting point will decrease and the rock will melt. Third, the addition of fluids, such as water, may decrease the melting point of some minerals in the rock and cause the rock to melt.

OBJECTIVES

▶ **Describe** the three conditions under which magma can form. 🐻 3f*

▶ **Explain** what volcanism is. 🐻 3f*

▶ **Identify** three tectonic settings where volcanoes form. 🐻 3f*

▶ **Describe** how magma can form plutons. 🐻 3f*

KEY TERMS

magma
volcanism
lava
volcano
hot spot

magma liquid rock produced under Earth's surface

Figure 1 ▶ Temperature and pressure increase as depth beneath Earth's surface increases. So, rock in the lower mantle stays below its melting point.

Volcanism

volcanism any activity that includes the movement of magma toward or onto Earth's surface

lava magma that flows onto Earth's surface; the rock that forms when lava cools and solidifies

volcano a vent or fissure in Earth's surface through which magma and gases are expelled

Any activity that includes the movement of magma onto Earth's surface is called **volcanism.** Magma rises upward through the crust because the magma is less dense than the surrounding rock. As bodies of magma rise toward the surface, they can become larger in two ways. First, because they are so hot, they can melt some of the surrounding rock. Second, as the magma rises, it is forced into cracks in the surrounding rock. This process causes large blocks of overlying rock to break off and melt. Both of these processes add material to the magma body.

When magma erupts onto Earth's surface, the magma is called **lava.** As lava flows from an opening, or *vent,* the material may build up as a cone of material that may eventually form a mountain. The vent in Earth's surface through which magma and gases are expelled is called a **volcano.**

Major Volcanic Zones

If you were to plot the locations of the volcanoes that have erupted in the past 50 years, you would see that the locations form a pattern across Earth's surface. Like earthquakes, most active volcanoes occur in zones near both convergent and divergent boundaries of tectonic plates, as shown in **Figure 2.**

A major zone of active volcanoes encircles the Pacific Ocean. This zone, called the Pacific Ring of Fire, is formed by the subduction of plates along the Pacific coasts of North America, South America, Asia, and the islands of the western Pacific Ocean. The Pacific Ring of Fire is also one of Earth's major earthquake zones.

Figure 2 ▶ This map shows the locations of major tectonic plate boundaries and of active volcanoes. *What is the relationship between the volcanoes and tectonic plate boundaries?*

— Plate boundary
• Active volcanoes

Subduction Zones

Many volcanoes are located along *subduction zones*, where one tectonic plate moves under another. When a plate that consists of oceanic lithosphere meets one that consists of continental lithosphere, the denser oceanic lithosphere moves beneath the continental lithosphere. A deep *trench* forms on the ocean floor along the edge of the continent where the plate is subducted. The plate that consists of continental lithosphere buckles and folds to form a line of mountains along the edge of the continent.

As the oceanic plate sinks into the asthenosphere, fluids such as water from the subducting plate combine with crust and mantle material. These fluids decrease the melting point of the rock and cause the rock to melt and form magma. When the magma rises through the lithosphere and erupts on Earth's surface, lines of volcanic mountains form along the edge of the tectonic plate.

If two plates that have oceanic lithosphere at their boundaries collide, one plate subducts, and a deep trench forms. As in the case of continental lithosphere colliding with oceanic lithosphere, magma also forms as fluids are introduced into the mantle during oceanic plate collisions. Some of the magma breaks through the overriding plate to Earth's surface. Over time, a string of volcanic islands, called an *island arc*, forms on the overriding plate, as shown in **Figure 3.** The early stages of this type of subduction produce an arc of small volcanic islands, such as the Aleutian Islands, which are in the North Pacific Ocean and between Alaska and Siberia. As more magma reaches the surface, the islands become larger and join to form one landmass, such as the volcanic islands that joined to form present-day Japan.

✔ **Reading Check** When a plate that consists of oceanic crust and one that consists of continental crust meet, which plate subducts beneath the other plate? (See the Appendix for answers to Reading Checks.)

Figure 3 ▶ The Aleutian Islands (below) formed when oceanic lithosphere subducted beneath oceanic lithosphere and caused magma to rise to the surface and erupt to form volcanic islands (left).

Island arc volcanoes

Trench

Oceanic lithosphere

Oceanic lithosphere

Asthenosphere

Subduction zone

Figure 4 ▶ When water rapidly cools hot lava, a hard, pillow-shaped crust forms. As the crust cools, it contracts and cracks. Hot lava flows through the cracks in the crust and then cools quickly to form another pillow-shaped structure.

Mid-Ocean Ridges

The largest amount of magma comes to the surface where plates are moving apart at mid-ocean ridges. Thus, the interconnected mid-ocean ridges that circle Earth form a major zone of volcanic activity. As plates pull apart, magma flows upward along the rift zone. The upwelling magma adds material to the mid-ocean ridge and creates new lithosphere along the rift. This magma erupts to form underwater volcanoes. **Figure 4** shows pillow lava, an example of volcanic rock that forms underwater at a mid-ocean ridge. Pillow lava is named for its pillow shape, which is caused by the water that rapidly cools the outer surface of the lava.

Most volcanic eruptions that happen along mid-ocean ridges are unnoticed by humans because the eruptions take place deep in the ocean. An exception is found on Iceland. Iceland is one part of the Mid-Atlantic Ridge that is above sea level. One-half of Iceland is on the North American plate and is moving westward. The other half is on the Eurasian plate and is moving eastward. The middle of Iceland is cut by large *fissures,* which are cracks through which lava flows to Earth's surface.

Connection to GEOLOGY

Sea-floor Formation

At mid-ocean ridges, magma moves upward from the asthenosphere. When the magma reaches the surface, the magma cools to form new sea-floor rock. When new sea floor forms at a mid-ocean ridge, a special sequence of rocks forms. This sequence forms because of the way the magma rises and cools. The thickness of the layers in this sequence varies greatly worldwide.

At the base of the new lithosphere, where the plates pull apart, a magma chamber forms. This chamber is cooled by circulating sea water. As the magma slowly cools, large crystals form. The crystals stick to the roof and sides of the magma chamber or sink to the bottom of the chamber and form a type of rock called *gabbro*. Gabbro forms the base layer in the rock sequence.

In the rift where the plates pull apart, the magma repeatedly intrudes. This repeated intrusion forms a series of vertical dikes called *sheeted dikes*. The structure of these dikes appears to be similar

to a deck of cards standing on end. The sheeted-dike complex forms the middle layer in the rock sequence.

At the top of the new lithosphere, where the magma comes into contact with the cold ocean water, the magma freezes rapidly. This rapid freezing causes pillow lava to form. Pillow lava forms the uppermost layer in the rock sequence.

Sea-floor rock that formed millions of years ago can be seen on land today. When one plate subducts under another plate, some of the subducting crust is scraped off and becomes part of the overriding plate. The crust that was scraped off is later uplifted and exposed on land, where geologists can study the rock to learn more about the formation of sea floor.

Ni'ihau (5 Ma)
Kauai (5 Ma)
Oahu (3 Ma)
Molokai (2 Ma)
Maui (0.75 Ma to 1.3 Ma)
Hawaii (currently active)
Direction of plate movement
Lanai (1.3 Ma)
Kahoolawe (1 Ma)
Hot spot
Mantle plume

Figure 5 ▶ As a tectonic plate moves over a stationary mantle plume, volcanic mountains form (above). The Hawaiian Islands (left) formed in this way.

Hot Spots

Not all volcanoes develop along plate boundaries. Areas of volcanism within the interiors of lithospheric plates are called **hot spots.** Most hot spots form where columns of solid, hot material from the deep mantle, called *mantle plumes*, rise and reach the lithosphere. When a mantle plume reaches the lithosphere, the plume spreads out. As magma rises to the surface, it breaks through the overlying crust. Volcanoes can then form in the interior of a tectonic plate, as shown in **Figure 5.**

Mantle plumes appear to remain nearly stationary. However, the lithospheric plate above a mantle plume continues to drift slowly. So, the volcano on the surface is eventually carried away from the mantle plume. The activity of the volcano stops because a hot spot that contains magma no longer feeds the volcano. However, a new volcano forms where the lithosphere has moved over the mantle plume.

Other scientists think that hot spots are the result of cracks in Earth's crust. The theory argues that hot-spot volcanoes occur in long chains because they form along cracks in Earth's crust. Both theories may be correct.

hot spot a volcanically active area of Earth's surface, commonly far from a tectonic plate boundary

✔ Reading Check Explain how one mantle plume can form several volcanic islands. (See the Appendix for answers to Reading Checks.)

Figure 6 ▶ Devils Tower in Wyoming is an example of a pluton called a *volcanic neck*, a formation caused by cooling of magma within the vent of a volcano. The outer part of the volcano eroded, and only the volcanic neck remains.

Intrusive Activity

Because magma is less dense than solid rock, magma rises through the crust toward the surface. As the magma moves upward, it comes into contact with, or *intrudes*, the overlying rock. Because of magma's high temperature, magma affects surrounding rock in a variety of ways. Magma may melt surrounding rock or may change the rock. Magma may also fracture surrounding rock and cause fissures to form or cause the surrounding rock to break apart and fall into the magma. Rock that falls into the magma may eventually melt, or the rock may combine with the new *igneous rock*, which is rock that forms when the magma cools.

When magma does not reach Earth's surface, the magma may cool and solidify inside the crust. This process results in large formations of igneous rock called *plutons*, as shown in **Figure 6.** Plutons can vary greatly in size and shape. Small plutons called *dikes* are tabular in shape and may be only a few centimeters wide. *Batholiths* are large plutons that cover an area of at least 100 km^2 when they are exposed on Earth's surface.

Section 1 **Review**

1. **Describe** three conditions that affect whether magma forms. 3f*

2. **Explain** how magma reaches Earth's surface. 3f*

3. **Compare** magma with lava. 3f*

4. **Describe** how subduction produces magma. 3f*

5. **Identify** three tectonic settings where volcanoes commonly occur. 3f*

6. **Summarize** the formation of hot spots. 3f*

7. **Describe** two igneous structures that form under Earth's surface. 3f*

CRITICAL THINKING

8. **Identifying Relationships** Describe how the presence of ocean water in crustal rocks might affect the formation of magma. IE.1d

9. **Applying Ideas** Yellowstone National Park in Wyoming is far from any plate boundary. How would you explain the volcanic activity in the park? 3f*, IE.1d

CONCEPT MAPPING

10. Use the following terms to create a concept map: *magma, volcanism, vent, volcano, subduction zone, hot spot, dike,* and *pluton.* 3f*

Volcanic Eruptions

California Content Standards

3e Students know there are two kinds of volcanoes: one kind with violent eruptions producing steep slopes and the other with voluminous lava flows producing gentle slopes.
IE.1d Students will formulate explanations using logic and evidence.
IE.1g Students will recognize the usefulness and limitations of models and theories as scientific representations of reality.

Volcanoes can be thought of as windows into Earth's interior. Lava that erupts from them provides an opportunity for scientists to study the nature of Earth's crust and mantle. By analyzing the composition of volcanic rocks, geologists have concluded that there are two general types of magma. **Mafic** (MAF ik) describes magma or rock that is rich in magnesium and iron and is commonly dark in color. **Felsic** (FEL sik) describes magma or rock that is rich in light-colored silicate materials. Mafic rock commonly makes up the oceanic crust, whereas felsic and mafic rock commonly make up the continental crust.

Types of Eruptions

The *viscosity*, or resistance to flow, of magma affects the force with which a particular volcano will erupt. The viscosity of magma is determined by the magma's composition. Because mafic magmas produce runny lava that has a low viscosity, they typically cause quiet eruptions. Because felsic magmas produce sticky lava that has a high viscosity, they typically cause explosive eruptions. Magma that contains large amounts of trapped, dissolved gases is more likely to produce explosive eruptions than is magma that contains small amounts of dissolved gases.

Quiet Eruptions

Oceanic volcanoes commonly form from mafic magma. Because of mafic magma's low viscosity, gases can easily escape from mafic magma. Eruptions from oceanic volcanoes, such as those in Hawaii, shown in **Figure 1,** are usually quiet.

OBJECTIVES

▶ **Explain** how the composition of magma affects volcanic eruptions and lava flow. **3e**

▶ **Describe** the five major types of pyroclastic material. **3e**

▶ **Identify** the three main types of volcanic cones. **3e**

▶ **Describe** how a caldera forms. **3e**

▶ **List** three events that may signal a volcanic eruption. **IE.1d**

KEY TERMS

mafic
felsic
pyroclastic material
caldera

mafic describes magma or igneous rock that is rich in magnesium and iron and that is generally dark in color

felsic describes magma or igneous rock that is rich in feldspar and silica and that is generally light in color

Figure 1 ▶ Lava flows from a quiet eruption like a red-hot river would flow. This lava flowed several miles from the Kilauea volcano to the sea.

Figure 2 ► Types of Mafic Lava Flow

Pahoehoe is the least viscous type of mafic lava. It forms wrinkly volcanic rock when it cools.

Aa lava is more viscous than pahoehoe lava and forms sharp volcanic rock when it cools.

Blocky lava is the most viscous type of mafic lava and forms chunky volcanic rock when it cools.

MATHPRACTICE

A Lot of Lava Since late 1986, Kilauea volcano in Hawaii has been erupting mafic lava. In 2003, the total volume of lava that had been produced by this eruption was 0.6 mi^3, or 2.5 km^3. Calculate the average amount of lava, in cubic meters, that erupts from Kilauea each year.

Lava Flows

When mafic lava cools rapidly, a crust forms on the surface of the flow. If the lava continues to flow after the crust forms, the crust wrinkles to form a volcanic rock called *pahoehoe* (pah HOH ee HOH ee), which is shown in **Figure 2.** Pahoehoe forms from hot, fluid lava. As it cools, it forms a smooth, ropy texture. Pahoehoe actually means "ropy" in Hawaiian.

If the crust deforms rapidly or grows too thick to form wrinkles, the surface breaks into jagged chunks to form *aa* (AH AH). Aa forms from lava that has the same composition as pahoehoe lava. Aa lava's texture results from differences in gas content and in the rate and slope of the lava flow.

Blocky lava has a higher silica content than aa lava does, which makes blocky lava more viscous than aa lava. The high viscosity causes the cooled lava at the surface to break into large chunks, while the hot lava underneath continues to flow. This process gives the lava flow a blocky appearance.

✓ **Reading Check** How do flow rate and gas content affect the appearance of lavas? (See the Appendix for answers to Reading Checks.)

Explosive Eruptions

Unlike the fluid lavas produced by oceanic volcanoes, the felsic lavas of continental volcanoes, such as Mount St. Helens, tend to be cooler and stickier. Felsic lavas also contain large amounts of trapped gases, such as water vapor and carbon dioxide. When a volcano erupts, the dissolved gases within the lava escape and send molten and solid particles shooting into the air. So, felsic lava tends to explode and throw pyroclastic material into the air. **Pyroclastic material** consists of fragments of rock that form during a volcanic eruption.

pyroclastic material fragments of rock that form during a volcanic eruption

Types of Pyroclastic Material

Some pyroclastic materials form when magma breaks into fragments during an eruption because of the rapidly expanding gases in the magma. Other pyroclastic materials form when fragments of erupting lava cool and solidify as they fly through the air.

Scientists classify pyroclastic materials according to the sizes of the particles, as shown in **Figure 3.** Pyroclastic particles that are less than 2 mm in diameter are called *volcanic ash*. Volcanic ash that is less than 0.25 mm in diameter is called *volcanic dust*. Most volcanic dust and ash settles on the land that immediately surrounds the volcano. However, some of the smallest dust particles may travel around Earth in the upper atmosphere.

Large pyroclastic particles that are less than 64 mm in diameter, are called *lapilli* (luh PIL IE), which is from a Latin word that means "little stones." Lapilli generally fall near the vent.

Large clots of lava may be thrown out of an erupting volcano while they are red-hot. As they spin through the air, they cool and develop a round or spindle shape. These pyroclastic particles are called *volcanic bombs*. The largest pyroclastic materials, known as *volcanic blocks*, form from solid rock that is blasted from the vent. Some volcanic blocks are the size of a small house.

Graphic
Organizer Spider Map

Create the **Graphic Organizer** entitled "Spider Map" described in the Skills Handbook section of the Appendix. Label the circle "Pyroclastic material." Create a leg for each type of pyroclastic material. Then, fill in the map with details about each type of pyroclastic material.

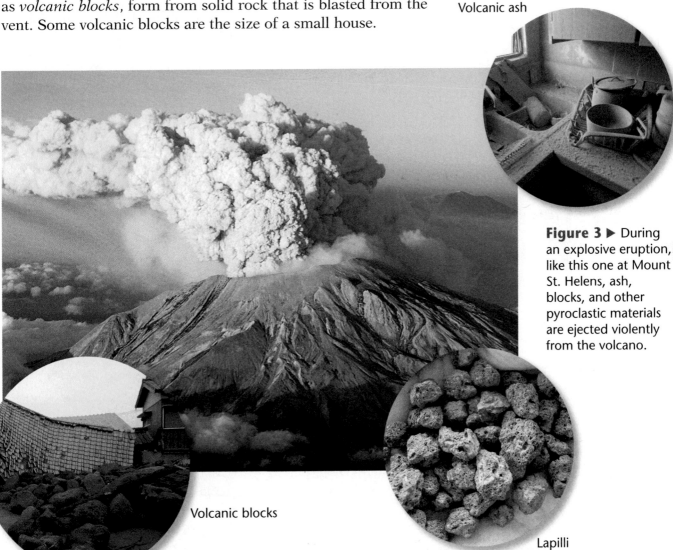

Volcanic ash

Volcanic blocks

Lapilli

Figure 3 ▶ During an explosive eruption, like this one at Mount St. Helens, ash, blocks, and other pyroclastic materials are ejected violently from the volcano.

Types of Volcanoes

Volcanic activity produces a variety of characteristic features that form during both quiet and explosive eruptions. The lava and pyroclastic material that are ejected during volcanic eruptions build up around the vent and form volcanic cones. Volcanic cones are classified as three main types, as described in **Table 1.**

The funnel-shaped pit at the top of a volcanic vent is known as a *crater.* The crater forms when material is blown out of the volcano by explosions. A crater usually becomes wider as weathering and erosion break down the walls of the crater and allow loose materials to collapse into the vent. Sometimes, a small cone forms within a crater. This formation occurs when subsequent eruptions cause material to build up around the vent.

Table 1 ▶ Volcanic cones are classified into three main categories. *Which type of volcano would form from lava that is highly viscous?*

Types of Volcanoes

Shield Volcanoes Volcanic cones that are broad at the base and have gently sloping sides are called *shield volcanoes.* A shield volcano covers a wide area and generally forms from quiet eruptions. Layers of hot, mafic lava flow out around the vent, harden, and slowly build up to form the cone. The Hawaiian Islands form a chain of shield volcanoes that built up from the ocean floor at a hot spot.

Cinder Cones A type of volcano that has very steep slopes is a cinder cone. The slope angles of the cinder cones can be close to 40°, and the slopes are rarely more than a few hundred meters high. Cinder cones form from explosive eruptions and are made of pyroclastic material.

Composite Volcanoes Composite volcanoes are made of alternating layers of hardened lava flows and pyroclastic material. During a quiet eruption, lava flows cover the sides of the cone. Then, when an explosive eruption occurs, large amounts of pyroclastic material are deposited around the vent. The explosive eruption is followed again by quiet lava flows. Composite volcanoes, also known as *stratovolcanoes,* commonly develop to form large volcanic mountains.

Figure 4 ▶ The Formation of a Caldera

Ground surface sinks.

Caldera

A cone forms from volcanic eruptions.

Volcanic eruptions partially empty the magma chamber.

The top of the cone collapses inward to form a caldera.

Calderas

When the magma chamber below a volcano empties, the volcanic cone may collapse and leave a large, basin-shaped depression called a **caldera** (kal DER uh). The process of caldera formation is shown in **Figure 4.**

Eruptions that discharge large amounts of magma can also cause a caldera to form. Krakatau, a volcanic island in Indonesia, is an example of this type of caldera. When the volcanic cone exploded in 1883, a caldera with a diameter of 6 km formed.

Calderas may later fill with water to form lakes. Thousands of years ago, the cone of Mount Mazama in Oregon collapsed and formed a caldera. The caldera eventually filled with water and is now called Crater Lake.

caldera a large, circular depression that forms when the magma chamber below a volcano partially empties and causes the ground above to sink

✔ **Reading Check** Describe two ways that calderas form. (See the Appendix for answers to Reading Checks.)

QuickLAB 25 min

Volcanic Cones
Procedure 3e, IE.1g
1. Pour 1/2 cup (about 4 oz) of dry plaster of Paris into a measuring cup.
2. Use a graduated cylinder to measure 60 mL of water, and add the water to the dry plaster in the measuring cup. Use a mixing spoon to blend the mixture until it is smooth.
3. Hold the measuring cup about 2 cm over a paper plate. Pour the contents slowly and steadily onto the center of the plate. Allow the plaster to dry.
4. On a clean paper plate, pour dry oatmeal or potato flakes slowly until the mound is approximately 5 cm high.

5. Without disturbing the mound, use a protractor to measure its slope.
6. When the plaster cone has hardened, remove it from the plate. Measure the average slope angle of the cone.

Analysis
1. Which cone represents a cinder cone? Which cone represents a shield volcano? Compare the slope angles formed by these cones.
2. How would the slope be affected if the oatmeal were rounder, and how would the slope be affected if the oatmeal were thicker?
3. How would you use the same supplies to model a composite volcano?

Predicting Volcanic Eruptions

A volcanic eruption can be one of Earth's most destructive natural phenomena. Scientists, such as those in **Figure 5**, look for a variety of events that may signal the beginning of an eruption.

Earthquake Activity

One of the most important warning signals of volcanic eruptions is changes in earthquake activity around the volcano. Growing pressure on the surrounding rocks from magma that is moving upward causes small earthquakes. Temperature changes within the rock and fracturing of the rock around a volcano also cause small earthquakes. An increase in the strength and frequency of earthquakes may be a signal that an eruption is about to occur.

Figure 5 ▶ These scientists are sampling gases emitted from the fumarole field on Vulcano Island in Italy.

Patterns in Activity

Before an eruption, the upward movement of magma beneath the surface may cause the surface of the volcano to bulge outward. Special instruments can measure small changes in the tilt of the ground surface on the volcano's slopes.

Predicting the eruption of a particular volcano also requires some knowledge of its previous eruptions. Scientists compare the volcano's past behavior with current daily measurements of earthquakes, surface bulges, and changes in the amount and composition of the gases that the volcano emits. Unfortunately, only a few of the active volcanoes in the world have been studied by scientists long enough to establish any activity patterns. Also, volcanoes that have been dormant for long periods of time may, with little warning, suddenly become active.

For a variety of links related to this subject, go to www.scilinks.org

Topic: Predicting Volcanic Eruptions
SciLinks code: HQ61209

Section 2 Review

1. **Summarize** the difference between mafic and felsic magma. 🐾3e

2. **Explain** how the composition of magma affects the force of volcanic eruptions. 🐾3e

3. **Compare** three major types of lava flows. 🐾3e

4. **Define** *pyroclastic material*, and list three examples. 🐾3e

5. **Identify** the three main types of volcanic cones. 🐾3e

6. **Describe** how calderas form. 🐾3e

7. **List** three events that may precede a volcanic eruption. 🐾IE.1d

CRITICAL THINKING

8. **Applying Ideas** Would quiet eruptions or explosive eruptions be more likely to increase the steepness of a volcanic cone? Explain your answer. 🐾3e, IE.1d

9. **Drawing Conclusions** Why would a sudden increase of earthquake activity around a volcano indicate a possible eruption? 🐾IE.1d

CONCEPT MAPPING

10. Use the following terms to create a concept map: *mafic lava, felsic lava, pahoehoe, aa, shield volcano, pyroclastic material, lapilli, volcanic bomb, volcanic block, volcanic ash,* and *volcanic dust.* 🐾3e

Highlights

Sections

1 Volcanoes and Plate Tectonics

Key Terms

magma, 319
volcanism, 320
lava, 320
volcano, 320
hot spot, 323

Key Concepts

▶ Magma can form when temperature or pressure changes in mantle rock. Magma also may form when water is added to hot rock.

▶ Volcanism is any activity that includes the movement of magma onto Earth's surface.

▶ Volcanism is common at convergent and divergent boundaries between tectonic plates.

▶ Hot spots are areas of volcanic activity that are located over rising mantle plumes that can exist far from tectonic plate boundaries.

▶ Magma that cools below Earth's surface forms intrusive igneous rock bodies called plutons.

2 Volcanic Eruptions

mafic, 325
felsic, 325
pyroclastic material, 326
caldera, 329

▶ Lava and magma can be described as mafic or felsic.

▶ Hot, less viscous, mafic lava commonly causes quiet eruptions. Cool, more viscous, felsic lava commonly causes explosive eruptions, especially if it contains trapped gases.

▶ Volcanic cones are classified into three categories based on composition and form.

▶ A caldera forms where a volcanic cone collapses and leaves a large, basin-shaped depression.

▶ Events that might signal a volcanic eruption include changes in earthquake activity, changes in the volcano's shape, changes in composition and amount of gases emitted, and changes in the patterns of the volcano's normal activity.

Using Key Terms

Use each of the following terms in a separate sentence.

1. *volcanism* ▣3f*

2. *hot spot* ▣3f*

3. *pyroclastic material* ▣3e

For each pair of terms, explain how the meanings of the terms differ.

4. *magma* and *lava* ▣3f*

5. *mafic* and *felsic* ▣3e

6. *shield volcano* and *composite volcano* ▣3e

7. *crater* and *caldera* ▣3e

Understanding Key Concepts

8. A characteristic of lava that determines the force of a volcanic eruption is ▣3e
a. color.
c. density.
b. viscosity.
d. age.

9. Island arcs form when oceanic lithosphere subducts under ▣3f*
a. continental lithosphere.
b. calderas.
c. volcanic bombs.
d. oceanic lithosphere.

10. Areas of volcanism within tectonic plates ▣3f* are called
a. hot spots.
c. calderas.
b. cones.
d. fissures.

11. Explosive volcanic eruptions commonly result from ▣3e
a. mafic magma.
c. aa lava.
b. felsic magma.
d. pahoehoe lava.

12. Pyroclastic materials that form rounded or spindle shapes as they fly through the air are called ▣3e
a. ash.
c. lapilli.
b. volcanic bombs.
d. volcanic blocks.

13. A cone formed by only solid fragments built up around a volcanic opening is a ▣3e
a. shield volcano.
b. cinder cone.
c. composite volcano.
d. stratovolcano.

14. The depression that results when a volcanic cone collapses over an emptying magma chamber is a ▣3e
a. crater.
c. vent.
b. caldera.
d. fissure.

15. Scientists have discovered that before an eruption, earthquakes commonly
a. stop.
b. increase in number.
c. have no relationship with volcanism.
d. decrease in number.

Short Answer

16. At what point does magma become lava? ▣3f*

17. Describe how tectonic movement can form volcanoes. ▣3f*

18. Name the process that includes the movement of magma onto Earth's surface. ▣3f*

19. What may happen to magma that does not reach Earth's surface? ▣IE.1d

20. How is the composition of magma related to the force of volcanic eruptions? ▣3e

21. List and describe the major types of pyroclastic material. ▣3e

22. Compare the three main types of volcanic cones. ▣3e

23. What signs can scientists study to try to predict volcanic eruptions?

4. Sprinkle 5 cm³ of baking soda along the center of a single section of bathroom tissue. Then, roll the tissue, and twist the ends so that the baking soda can't fall out.

5. Drop the tissue into the drink bottle, and immediately put the short end of the straw inside the bottle to make a seal with the clay.

6. Put the other end of the straw into the limewater.

7. Record your observations. You have just taken your first measurement of gas levels from the volcano.

8. Imagine that it is several days later and that you need to test the volcano again to collect more data. Before you continue, toss a coin. If it lands heads up, go to step 9. If it lands tails up, go to step 10. Write down the step that you follow.

9. Repeat steps 1–7. But use 2 cm³ of baking soda in the tissue in step 4 instead of 5 cm³. (Note: You must use fresh water, vinegar, and limewater.) Record your observations.

10. Repeat steps 1–7. But use 8 cm³ of baking soda in the tissue in step 4 instead of 5 cm³. (Note: You must use fresh water, vinegar, and limewater.) Record your observations.

Mount Usu, 770 kilometers from Tokyo in Japan, erupted on March 31, 2000.

ANALYSIS AND CONCLUSION

1. **Explaining Events** How do you explain the difference in the appearance of the limewater from one trial to the next?

2. **Recognizing Patterns** What does the data that you collected tell you about the activity in the volcano?

3. **Evaluating Results** Based on your results in step 9 or 10, do you think it would be necessary to evacuate the city?

4. **Applying Conclusions** How would a geologist use a gas-emissions tester to predict volcanic eruptions?

Extension

1. **Evaluating Data** Scientists base their predictions of eruptions on a variety of evidence before recommending an evacuation. What other forms of evidence would a scientist need to know to predict an eruption?

MAPS in Action

The Hawaiian-Emperor Seamount Chain

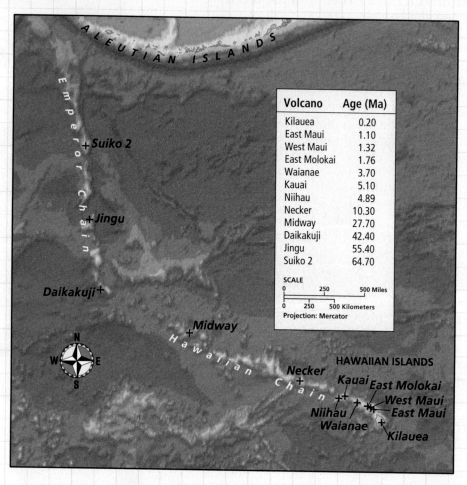

Volcano	Age (Ma)
Kilauea	0.20
East Maui	1.10
West Maui	1.32
East Molokai	1.76
Waianae	3.70
Kauai	5.10
Niihau	4.89
Necker	10.30
Midway	27.70
Daikakuji	42.40
Jingu	55.40
Suiko 2	64.70

SCALE

0   250   500 Miles

0   250   500 Kilometers

Projection: Mercator

Map Skills Activity

This map shows the locations and ages of islands and seamounts in the Hawaiian-Emperor seamount chain, which is located in the Pacific Ocean. Use the map to answer the questions below.

1. **Inferring Relationships** Under which volcano is the hot spot presently located?

2. **Using the Key** Which volcano is the oldest?

3. **Evaluating Data** A seamont is a submarine volcanic mountain. Would you expect older volcanoes to be seamounts or islands? Explain your answer.

4. **Analyzing Data** Which island signifies a change in direction of the movement of the Pacific plate? Explain your answer.

5. **Identifying Trends** In which direction has the Pacific plate been moving since the formation of the islands in the seamount chain changed direction?

6. **Analyzing Relationships** How many years ago did the Pacific plate change its direction?

7. **Analyzing Data** What is the average speed of the Pacific plate over the last 65 million years?

8. **Predicting Consequences** Where would you expect a new volcano to form 1 million years from now?

The Effects of Volcanoes on Climate

Some scientists think that average temperatures around the globe will rise by 2°C by the year 2050 because of the air pollution released by the use of fossil fuels by humans. To understand the possible effects of human activity on Earth's environment, scientists are studying another source of atmospheric pollution—volcanoes.

Volcanic Ash

The lava, gases, and ash that erupt into the atmosphere during a volcanic eruption can darken the skies for hundreds of kilometers. In the months after an eruption, some of this material settles to Earth, but much of it remains in the atmosphere, where wind currents disperse it around the world. While the dust and gases are not visible, they affect the climate of the entire planet.

Blocking the Sun's Energy

In June of 1991, Mount Pinatubo began a long series of eruptions. The resulting lava, ash, and mud flows devastated 20,000 km² of land. The eruption also released more than 18 million metric tons of sulfur dioxide into the atmosphere. Sulfur dioxide combines with water to become sulfuric acid, which reflects the sun's energy back into space. Scientists predicted that these large amounts of sulfur dioxide would have a cooling effect on Earth's surface. As predicted, average global surface temperatures dropped about 0.6°C by late 1992 and began to recover slowly after that.

By using data collected from several volcanic eruptions, scientists are developing computer models that may help them better understand and predict global climate changes.

Mount Pinatubo's Effect on Global Temperature

▲ The low average global temperatures in 1992 are most likely caused by Mount Pinatubo's eruption in 1991.

Learning how the atmosphere is affected by such natural events will also help scientists understand how pollution from human sources affects the atmosphere.

▼ During the 1991 eruption of Mount Pinatubo in the Philippines, ash fell like snow falls for several days.

Extension

1. **Applying Ideas** How would you determine if the 1991 eruption of Mount Pinatubo affected the average monthly temperatures in your community?
2. **Research** Find out how the 1980 eruption of Mount St. Helens changed nearby ecosystems, and identify which effects are still noticeable today.

▶ Earth's surface is constantly shaped by the action of wind and water. Winds in the Sahara move enormous amounts of sand and form huge sand dunes, such as these near the town

Sections

What You'll Learn

- How rock breaks down
- How soil forms
- What agents erode rock and soil

Why It's Relevant

Weathering and erosion change the shape of Earth's surface and are essential to the formation of soil, one of our most important natural resources.

PRE-READING ACTIVITY

FOLDNOTES

TriFold
Before you read this chapter, create the **FoldNote** entitled "TriFold" described in the Skills Handbook Section of the Appendix. Write what you know about weathering and erosion in the column labeled "Know." Then, write what you want to know in the column labeled "Want." As you read the chapter, write what you learn about weathering and erosion in the column labeled "Learn."

▶ Ayers Rock in Australia, also called *Uluru* by the aboriginal peoples of Australia, is gray under its red surface. The surface appears red because iron in the rock oxidizes when it is exposed to air and water.

California Content Standards

7c Students know the movement of matter among reservoirs is driven by Earth's internal and external sources of energy.

9b Students know the principal natural hazards in different California regions and the geologic basis of those hazards.

IE.1a Students will select and use appropriate tools and technology (such as computer-linked probes, spreadsheets, and graphing calculators) to perform tests, collect data, analyze relationships and display data.

IE.1d Students will formulate explanations using logic and evidence.

IE.1l Students will analyze situations and solve problems that require combining and applying concepts from more than one area of science.

Weathering Processes

California Content Standards

7c Students know the movement of matter among reservoirs is driven by Earth's internal and external sources of energy.

IE.1d Students will formulate explanations using logic and evidence.

Most rocks deep within Earth's crust formed under conditions of high temperature and pressure. When these rocks are uplifted to the surface, they are exposed to much lower temperature and pressure. Uplifted rock is also exposed to the gases and water in Earth's atmosphere.

Because of these environmental factors, surface rocks undergo changes in their appearance and composition. The physical break-down or chemical decomposition of rock materials exposed at Earth's surface is called **weathering.** There are two main types of weathering processes—mechanical weathering and chemical weathering. Each type of weathering has different effects on rock.

Mechanical Weathering

The process by which rock is broken down into smaller pieces by physical means is **mechanical weathering.** Mechanical weathering is strictly a physical process and does not change the composition of the rock. Common agents of mechanical weathering are ice, plants and animals, gravity, running water, and wind.

Physical changes within the rock also affect mechanical weathering. For example, when overlying rocks are eroded, granite that formed deep beneath Earth's surface can be exposed, decreasing the pressure on the granite. As a result of the decreasing pressure, the granite expands. Long, curved cracks, called *joints,* develop in the rock. When joints are parallel to the surface of the rock, the rock breaks into curved sheets that peel away from the underlying rock in a process called *exfoliation.* One example of granite exfoliation on a dome in Yosemite National Park is shown in **Figure 1.**

OBJECTIVES

▶ **Identify** three agents of mechanical weathering. 7c

▶ **Compare** mechanical and chemical weathering processes. 7c

▶ **Describe** four chemical reactions that decompose rock. 7c

KEY TERMS

weathering
mechanical weathering
abrasion
chemical weathering
oxidation
hydrolysis
carbonation
acid precipitation

weathering the natural process by which atmospheric and environmental agents, such as wind, rain, and temperature changes, disintegrate and decompose rocks

mechanical weathering the process by which rocks break down into smaller pieces by physical means

Figure 1 ▶ This area of Yosemite National Park is part of a dome of granite that is shedding large sheets of rock through the process of exfoliation.

Figure 2 ▶ Water flows into a crack in a rock's surface. When the water freezes, it expands and causes the crack to widen. Ice wedging is responsible for most of the cracks shown in the photograph.

Water

Ice

Water

Ice

abrasion the grinding and wearing away of rock surfaces through the mechanical action of other rock or sand particles

Ice Wedging

A type of mechanical weathering that occurs in cold climates is called *ice wedging*. Ice wedging occurs when water seeps into cracks in rock and then freezes. When the water freezes, its volume increases by about 10% and creates pressure on the surrounding rock. Every time the ice thaws and refreezes, cracks in the rock widen and deepen. This process eventually splits the rock apart, as shown in **Figure 2.** Ice wedging commonly occurs at high elevations and in cold climates. It also occurs in climates where the temperature regularly rises above and then falls below freezing, such as in the northern United States.

Abrasion

The collision of rocks that results in the breaking and wearing away of the rocks is a form of mechanical weathering called **abrasion.** Abrasion is caused by gravity, running water, and wind. Gravity causes loose soil and rocks to move down the slope of a hill or mountain. Rocks break into smaller pieces as they fall and collide. Running water can carry particles of sand or rock that scrape against each other and against stationary rocks. Thus, exposed surfaces are weathered by abrasion.

Wind is another agent of abrasion. When wind lifts and carries small particles, it can hurl them against surfaces, such as rocks. As the airborne particles strike the rock, they wear away the surface in the same way that a sandblaster would.

✓ **Reading Check** Describe two types of mechanical weathering. (See the Appendix for answers to Reading Checks.)

Figure 3 ▶ This gray wolf (left) is burrowing into soil to make a den. Prairie dogs (above) also dig into soil and rock to form extensive burrows, where an entire prairie dog community may live.

Organic Activity

Plants and animals are important agents of mechanical weathering. As plants grow, the roots grow and expand to create pressure that wedges rock apart. The roots of small plants cause small cracks to form in the rocks. Eventually, the roots of large plants and trees can fit in the cracks and make the cracks bigger.

The digging activities of burrowing animals, shown in **Figure 3,** also cause weathering. Common burrowing animals include ground squirrels, prairie dogs, ants, earthworms, coyotes, and rabbits. Earthworms and other animals that move soil expose new rock surfaces to both mechanical and chemical weathering. Animal activities and plants can weather rocks dramatically over a long period of time.

   15 min

Mechanical Weathering

Procedure 7c, IE.1d

1. Examine some **silicate rock chips** by using a **hand lens.** Observe the shape and surface texture.
2. Fill a **plastic container** that has a **tight-fitting lid** about half full of rock chips. Add **water** to just cover the chips.
3. Tighten the lid, and shake the container 100 times.
4. Hold a **strainer** over another container. Pour the water and rock chips into the strainer.
5. Move your finger around the inside of the empty container. Describe what you feel.
6. Use the hand lens to observe the rock chips.
7. Pour the water into a **glass jar,** and examine the water with the hand lens.
8. Put the rock chips and water back into the container that has the lid. Repeat steps 3–7.
9. Repeat step 8 two more times.

Analysis

1. Did the amount and particle size of the sediment that was left in the container change during your investigation? Explain your answer.
2. How did the appearance of the rock chips change? How did the appearance of the water change?
3. How does the transport of rock particles by water, such as in a river, affect the size and shape of the rock particles?

Chemical Weathering

The process by which rock is broken down because of chemical interactions with the environment is **chemical weathering.** Chemical weathering, or decomposition, occurs when chemical reactions act on the minerals in rock. Chemical reactions commonly occur between rock, water, carbon dioxide, oxygen, and acids. Acids are substances that form *hydronium ions,* or H_3O^+, in water. Hydronium ions are electrically charged and can pull apart the chemical bonds of the minerals in rock. Bases can also chemically weather rock. Bases are substances that form *hydroxide ions,* or OH^-, in water. Chemical reactions with either acids or bases can change the structure of minerals, which leads to the formation of new minerals. Chemical weathering changes both the chemical composition and physical appearance of the rock.

Oxidation

The process by which elements combine with oxygen is called **oxidation.** Oxidation commonly occurs in rock that has iron-bearing minerals, such as hematite and magnetite. Iron, Fe, in rocks and soil combines quickly with oxygen, O_2, that is dissolved in water to form rust, or iron oxide, Fe_2O_3:

$$4Fe + 3O_2 \rightarrow 2Fe_2O_3$$

The red color of much of the soil in the southeastern United States, as shown in **Figure 4,** is due to mainly the presence of iron oxide produced by oxidation. Similarly, the color of many red-colored rocks is caused by oxidized, iron-rich minerals.

> ✓ **Reading Check** Describe two effects of chemical weathering. (See the Appendix for answers to Reading Checks.)

chemical weathering the process by which rocks break down as a result of chemical reactions

oxidation a reaction that removes one or more electrons from a substance such that the substance's valence or oxidation state increases; in geology, the process by which a metallic element combines with oxygen

MATHPRACTICE

Rates of Weathering
Limestone is dissolved by chemical weathering at a rate of 0.2 cm every 100 years. At this rate, after how many years would a layer of limestone 15 m thick completely dissolve?

Figure 4 ▶ The red tint of the soil surrounding this farmhouse in Georgia is caused by the chemical interaction of iron-bearing minerals in the soil with oxygen in the atmosphere.

Rain, weak acids, and air chemically weather granite.

The bonds between mineral grains weaken as weathering proceeds.

Sediment forms from the weathered granite.

Figure 5 ▶ Thousands of years of chemical weathering processes, such as hydrolysis and carbonation, can turn even a hard rock such as granite into sediment.

Hydrolysis

Water plays a crucial role in chemical weathering, as shown in **Figure 5.** The change in the composition of minerals when they react chemically with water is called **hydrolysis.** For example, a type of feldspar combines with water and produces a common clay called *kaolin*. In this reaction, hydronium ions displace the potassium and calcium atoms in the feldspar crystals, which changes the feldspar into clay.

Minerals that are affected by hydrolysis often dissolve in water. Water can then carry the dissolved minerals to lower layers of rock in a process called *leaching*. Ore deposits, such as bauxite, the aluminum ore, sometimes form when leaching causes a mineral to concentrate in a thin layer beneath Earth's surface.

Carbonation

When carbon dioxide, CO_2, from the air dissolves in water, H_2O, a weak acid called *carbonic acid*, H_2CO_3, forms:

$$H_2O + CO_2 \quad H_2CO_3$$

Carbonic acid has a higher concentration of hydronium ions than pure water does, which speeds up the process of hydrolysis. When certain minerals come in contact with carbonic acid, they combine with the acid to form minerals called carbonates. The conversion of minerals into a carbonate is called **carbonation.**

One example of carbonation occurs when carbonic acid reacts with calcite, a major component of limestone, and converts the calcite into calcium bicarbonate. Calcium bicarbonate dissolves easily in water, so the limestone eventually weathers away.

Organic Acids

Acids are produced naturally by certain living organisms. Lichens and mosses grow on rocks and produce weak acids that can weather the surface of the rock. The acids seep into the rock and produce cracks that eventually cause the rock to break apart.

hydrolysis a chemical reaction between water and another substance to form two or more new substances

carbonation the conversion of a compound into a carbonate

Figure 6 ▶ This stone lion sits outside Leeds Town Hall in England. It was damaged by acid precipitation.

acid precipitation precipitation, such as rain, sleet, or snow, that contains a high concentration of acids, often because of the pollution of the atmosphere

Acid Precipitation

Natural rainwater is slightly acidic because it combines with small amounts of carbon dioxide. But when fossil fuels, especially coal, are burned, nitrogen oxides and sulfur dioxides are released into the air. These compounds combine with water in the atmosphere to produce nitric acid, nitrous acid, or sulfuric acid. When these acids fall to Earth, they are called **acid precipitation.**

Acid precipitation weathers some rock faster than ordinary precipitation does. In fact, many historical monuments and sculptures have been damaged by acid precipitation, as shown in **Figure 6.** Between 1940 and 1990, acid precipitation fell regularly in some cities in the United States. In 1990, the Acid Rain Control Program was added to the Clean Air Act of 1970. These regulations gave power plants 10 years to decrease sulfur dioxide emissions. The occurrence of acid precipitation has been greatly reduced since power plants have installed scrubbers that remove much of the sulfur dioxide before it can be released.

Section 1 Review

1. **Identify** three agents of mechanical weathering. 7c

2. **Describe** how ice wedging weathers rock. 7c

3. **Explain** how two activities of plants or animals help weather rocks or soil. 7c

4. **Compare** mechanical and chemical weathering processes. 7c

5. **Identify** and describe three chemical processes that weather rock. 7c

6. **Compare** hydrolysis, carbonation, and oxidation. 7c

7. **Summarize** how acid precipitation forms.

CRITICAL THINKING

8. **Making Connections** What two agents of weathering would be rare in a desert? Explain your reasoning. 7c, IE.1d

9. **Understanding Relationships** Automobile exhaust contains nitrogen oxides. How might these pollutants affect chemical weathering processes? 7c, IE.1d

CONCEPT MAPPING

10. Use the following terms to create a concept map: *weathering, oxidation, mechanical weathering, ice wedging, hydrolysis, abrasion, chemical weathering, carbonation,* and *acid precipitation.* 7c

IE.1d Students will formulate explanations using logic and evidence.

The processes of mechanical and chemical weathering generally work very slowly. For example, carbonation dissolves limestone at an average rate of only about one-twentieth of a centimeter (0.2 cm) every 100 years. At this rate, it could take up to 30 million years to dissolve a layer of limestone that is 150 m thick.

The pinnacles in Nambung National Park in Australia are shown in **Figure 1.** These large, jutting pieces of limestone are all that remains of a thick limestone formation that covered the area millions of years ago. Most of the limestone was weathered away by agents of both chemical and mechanical weathering until only the pinnacles remained. The rate at which rock weathers depends on a number of factors, including rock composition, climate, and topography.

Differential Weathering

The composition of rock greatly affects the rate at which rock weathers. The process by which softer, less weather-resistant rock wears away and leaves harder, more resistant rock behind is called **differential weathering.** When rocks that are rich in the mineral quartz are exposed on Earth's surface, they remain basically unchanged, even after all of the surrounding rock has weathered away. They remain unchanged because the chemical composition and crystal structure of quartz make quartz resistant to chemical weathering. These same characteristics make quartz a very hard mineral, so it also resists mechanical weathering.

Rock Composition

Limestone and other sedimentary rocks that contain calcite are weathered most rapidly. They weather rapidly because they commonly undergo carbonation. Other sedimentary rocks are affected mainly by mechanical weathering processes. The rates at which these rocks weather depend mostly on the material that holds the sediment grains together. For example, shales and sandstones that are not firmly cemented together gradually break up to become clay and sand particles. However, conglomerates and sandstones that are strongly cemented by silicates resist weathering. Some of these strongly cemented sedimentary rocks can resist weathering longer than some igneous rocks do.

OBJECTIVES

▶ **Explain** how rock composition affects the rate of weathering.

▶ **Discuss** how surface area affects the rate at which rock weathers.

▶ **Describe** the effects of climate and topography on the rate of weathering.

KEY TERM

differential weathering

differential weathering the process by which softer, less weather resistant rocks wear away at a faster rate than harder, more weather resistant rocks do

Figure 1 ▶ Differences in rock composition and structure are the reasons for the different rates of weathering that formed these limestone pinnacles at Nambung National Park in Australia.

Figure 2 ▶ The Ratio of Total Surface Area to Volume

All cubes have both volume and surface area. The total surface area is equal to the sum of the areas of each of the six sides, or the length of each side multiplied by the width of each side.

If you split the first cube into eight smaller cubes, you have the same amount of material (volume), but the surface area doubles. If you split the eight small cubes in the same way, the original surface area is doubled again.

Amount of Exposure

The more exposure to weathering agents a rock receives, the faster the rock will weather. The amount of time the rock is exposed and the amount of the rock's surface area that is available for weathering are important factors in determining the rate of weathering.

Surface Area

Both chemical and mechanical weathering may split rock into a number of smaller rocks. The part of a rock that is exposed to air, water, and other agents of weathering is called the rock's *surface area*. As a rock breaks into smaller pieces, the surface area that is exposed increases. For example, imagine a block of rock as a cube that has six sides exposed. Splitting the block into eight smaller blocks, as shown in **Figure 2,** doubles the total surface area available for weathering.

Fractures and Joints

Most rocks on Earth's surface contain natural fractures and joints. These structures are natural zones of weakness within the rock. Fractures and joints increase the surface area of a rock and allow weathering to take place more rapidly. They also form natural channels through which water flows. Water may penetrate the rock through these channels and break the rock by ice wedging. As water moves through these channels, it chemically weathers the rock that is exposed in the fracture or joint. The chemical weathering removes rock material and makes the jointed or fractured area weaker.

✓ **Reading Check** How do fractures and joints affect surface area? **(See the Appendix for answers to Reading Checks.)**

Quick LAB 10 min

Surface Areas ⬛ IE.1d

Procedure

1. Fill **two small containers** about half full with **water.**
2. Add **one sugar cube** to one container.
3. Add **1 tsp of granulated sugar** to the other container.
4. Use **two different spoons** to stir the water and sugar in each container at the same rate.
5. Use a **stopwatch** to measure how long the sugar in each container takes to dissolve.

Analysis

1. Did the sugar dissolve at the same rate in both containers?
2. Which do you think would wear away faster—a large rock or a small rock? Explain your answer.

Figure 3 ▶ The photo on the left shows Cleopatra's Needle before it was moved to New York City. The photograph on the right shows the 3,500 year old carving after only one century in New York City.

Climate

In general, climates that have alternating periods of hot and cold weather allow the fastest rates of weathering. Freezing and thawing can cause the mechanical breakdown of rock by ice wedging. Chemical weathering can then act quickly on the fractured rock. When temperatures rise, the rate at which chemical reactions occur also accelerates. In warm, humid climates, chemical weathering is also fairly rapid. The constant moisture is highly destructive to exposed surfaces.

The slowest rates of weathering occur in hot, dry climates. The lack of water limits many weathering processes, such as carbonation and ice wedging. Weathering is also slow in very cold climates.

The effects of climate on weathering rates can be seen on Cleopatra's Needle, which is shown in **Figure 3.** Cleopatra's needle is an obelisk that is made of granite. For 3,000 years, the obelisk stood in Egypt, where the hot, dry climate scarcely changed its surface. Then, in 1880, Cleopatra's Needle was moved to New York City. After the obelisk was exposed to more than 100 years of moisture, the pollution, ice wedging, and acid precipitation caused more weathering than was caused in the preceding 3,000 years in the Egyptian desert.

Topography and Elevation

Topography, or the elevation and slope of the land surface, also influences the rate of weathering. Because temperatures are generally cold at high elevations, ice wedging is more common at high elevations than at low elevations. On steep slopes, such as mountainsides, weathered rock fragments are pulled downhill by gravity and washed out by heavy rains. As the rocks slide down the mountain or are carried away by mountain streams, rocks smash against each other and break apart. As a result of the removal of these surface rocks, new surfaces of the mountain are continually exposed to weathering.

SCI**LINKS**®

NSTA
Developed and maintained by the National Science Teachers Association

For a variety of links related to this subject, go to www.scilinks.org

Topic: Rates of Weathering
SciLinksCode: HQ61269

Human Activities

Rock can be chemically and mechanically broken down by the action of humans. Mining and construction often expose rock surfaces to agents of weathering. Mining also often exposes rock to strong acids and other chemical compounds that are used in mining processes. Construction often removes soil and exposes previously unexposed rock surfaces. Recreational activities such as hiking or riding all-terrain vehicles, as shown in **Figure 4**, can also speed up weathering by exposing new rock surfaces. Rock that is disturbed or broken by human activities weathers more rapidly than undisturbed rock does.

Plant and Animal Activities

Rock that is disturbed or broken by plants or animals also weathers more rapidly than undisturbed rock does. The roots of plants and trees often break apart rock. Burrowing animals dig holes into rock and soil. Some biological wastes of animals can cause chemical weathering. For example, caves that have large populations of bats also have large amounts of bat guano on the cave floors. Bat guano attracts small animals such as millipedes and other insects. The presence of these insects speeds up mechanical weathering, and the presence of the guano speeds up certain chemical weathering processes.

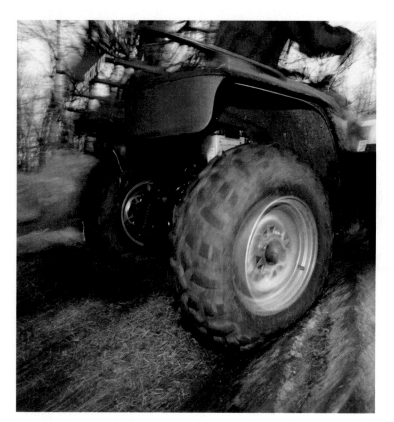

Figure 4 ▶ All-terrain vehicles cause mechanical weathering on exposed surfaces. Because of this weathering, these vehicles are banned from some areas where erosion is a concern.

Section 2 Review

1. **Explain** how rock composition affects the rate of weathering.

2. **Discuss** how the surface area of a rock can affect the rock's weathering rate.

3. **Identify** two ways that climate can influence weathering rates.

4. **Describe** two ways the topography of a region affects weathering rates.

5. **Summarize** three ways human actions can affect the rate of weathering.

6. **Explain** two ways that animals can affect the rate of weathering.

CRITICAL THINKING

7. **Applying Concepts** Imagine that there is an area of land where mechanical weathering has caused damage. Describe two ways to reduce the rate of mechanical weathering. IE.1d

8. **Identifying Relationships** How would Cleopatra's Needle probably have been affected if it had been in the cold, dry climate of Siberia for 100 years? IE.1d

CONCEPT MAPPING

9. Use the following terms to create a concept map: *composition, exposure, precipitation, surface area, climate, temperature, topography, weathering, elevation,* and *human activities.*

7c Students know the movement of matter among reservoirs is driven by Earth's internal and external sources of energy.

IE.1d Students will formulate explanations using logic and evidence.

One result of weathering is the formation of *regolith*, the layer of weathered rock fragments that covers much of Earth's surface. *Bedrock* is the solid, unweathered rock that lies beneath the regolith. The lower regions of regolith are partly protected by those above and thus do not weather as rapidly as the upper regions do. The uppermost rock fragments weather to form a layer of very fine particles. This layer of small rock particles provides the basic components of soil. **Soil** is a complex mixture of minerals, water, gases, and the remains of dead organisms.

Characteristics of Soil

The characteristics of soil depend mainly on the rock from which the soil was weathered, which is called the soil's *parent rock*. Soil that forms and stays directly over its parent rock is called *residual soil*. However, the weathered mineral grains that form soil may be carried away from the location of the parent rock by water, wind, or glaciers. Soil that results from the deposition of this material is called *transported soil*, and this soil may have different characteristics than the bedrock on which it rests.

Soil Composition

Parent rock that is rich in feldspar or other minerals that contain aluminum weathers to form soils that contain large amounts of clay. Rocks that contain large amounts of quartz, such as granite, weather to form sandy soils. Soil composition refers to the materials of which it is made. The color of soil is related to the composition of the soil. Black soils are commonly rich in organic material, while red soils may form from iron-rich parent rocks. Soil moisture can also affect color, as shown in **Figure 1.**

OBJECTIVES

▶ **Summarize** how soils form.

▶ **Explain** how the composition of parent rock affects soil composition.

▶ **Describe** the characteristic layers of mature residual soils.

▶ **Predict** the type of soil that will form in arctic and tropical climates.

KEY TERMS

soil
soil profile
horizon
humus

soil a loose mixture of rock fragments and organic material that can support the growth of vegetation

Figure 1 ▶ These soil scientists are testing soil moisture to determine whether irrigation will be needed. Moister soils are generally darker than drier soils are.

Soil Texture

Rock material in soil consists of three main types: clay, silt, and sand. Clay particles have a diameter of less than 0.004 mm. Silt particles have diameters from 0.004 to 0.06 mm. Silt particles are too small to be seen easily, but they make soil feel gritty. Sand particles have diameters from 0.06 to 2 mm. The proportion of clay, silt, and sand in soil depends on the soil's parent rock.

Soil Profile

Transported soils are commonly deposited in unsorted masses by water or wind. However, residual soils commonly develop distinct layers over time. To determine a soil's composition, scientists study a soil profile. A **soil profile** is a cross section of the soil and its bedrock. The different layers of soil are called **horizons.**

Residual soils generally consist of three main horizons. The *A horizon,* or *topsoil,* is a mixture of organic materials and small rock particles. Almost all organisms that live in soil inhabit the A horizon. As organisms die, their remains decay and produce **humus,** a dark, organic material. The A horizon is also the zone from which surface water leaches minerals. The *B horizon* or *subsoil,* contains the minerals leached from the topsoil, clay, and, sometimes, humus. In dry climates, the B horizon also may contain minerals that accumulate as water in the soil evaporates. The *C horizon* consists of partially-weathered bedrock. The first stages of mechanical and chemical change happen in this bottom layer. **Figure 2** shows the relationships between the three soil horizons.

soil profile a vertical section of soil that shows the layers of horizons

horizon a horizontal layer of soil that can be distinguished from the layers above and below it; *also* a boundary between two rock layers that have different physical properties

humus dark, organic material formed in soil from the decayed remains of plants and animals

Figure 2 ▶ Soil Horizons of Residual Soils

Surface litter fallen leaves and partially decomposed organic matter

Topsoil organic matter, living organisms, and rock particles

Zone of leaching dissolved or suspended materials moving downward

Subsoil larger rock particles with organic matter, and inorganic compounds

Rock particles rock that has undergone weathering

Bedrock solid rock layer

Horizon A

Horizon B

Horizon C

Soil and Climate

Climate is one of the most important factors that influences soil formation. Climate determines the weathering processes that occur in a region. These weathering processes, in turn, help determine the composition of soil.

Tropical Soils

In humid tropical climates, where much rain falls and where temperatures are high, chemical weathering causes thick soils to develop rapidly. These thick, tropical soils, called *laterites* (LAT uhr IETS), contain iron and aluminum minerals that do not dissolve easily in water. Leached minerals from the A horizon sometimes collect in the B horizon. Heavy rains, which are common in tropical climates, cause a lot of leaching of the topsoil, and thus keep the A horizon thin. But because of the dense vegetation in humid, warm climates, organic material is continuously added to the soil. As a result, a thin layer of humus usually covers the B horizon, as shown in **Figure 3.**

Temperate Soils

In temperate climates, where temperatures range between cool and warm and where rainfall is not excessive, both mechanical and chemical weathering occur. All three soil horizons in temperate soils may reach a thickness of several meters, as shown in **Figure 3.**

Two main soil types form in temperate climates. In areas that receive more than 65 cm of rain per year, a type of soil called *pedalfer* (pi DAL fuhr) forms. Pedalfer soils contain clay, quartz, and iron compounds. The Gulf Coast states and states east of the Mississippi River have pedalfer soils. In areas that receive less than 65 cm of rain per year, a soil called *pedocal* (PED oh KAL) forms. Pedocal soils contain large amounts of calcium carbonate, which makes pedocal soil very fertile and less acidic than pedalfer soil. The southwestern states and most states west of the Mississippi River have pedocal soils.

✔ Reading Check Compare the formation of tropical soils and temperate soils. (See the Appendix for answers to Reading Checks.)

Desert and Arctic Soils

In desert and arctic climates, rainfall is minimal and chemical weathering occurs slowly. As a result, the soil is thin and consists mostly of regolith—evidence that soil in these areas forms mainly by mechanical weathering. Desert and arctic climates are also often too warm or too cold to sustain life, so their soils have little humus.

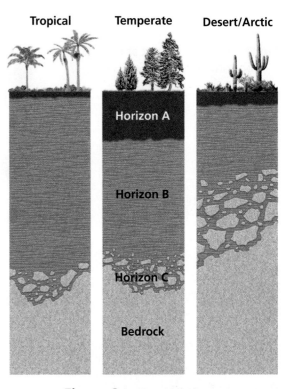

Tropical   Temperate   Desert/Arctic

Horizon A

Horizon B

Horizon C

Bedrock

Figure 3 ▶ Tropical climates produce thick, infertile soils. Temperate climates produce thick, fertile soils. Desert and arctic climates produce thin soils.

Figure 4 ▶ Soil is thick at the top and bottom of a slope. Soil is thin along the slope.

Thin soil

Thick soil

For a variety of links related to this subject, go to www.scilinks.org

Topic: Soil
SciLinksCode: HQ61407

Soil and Topography

The shape of the land, or topography, also affects soil formation. Because rainwater runs down slopes, much of the topsoil of the slope washes away. Therefore, as shown in **Figure 4,** the soil at the top and bottom of a slope tends to be thicker than the soil on the slope.

One study of soil in Canada showed that A horizons on flat areas were more than twice as thick as those on 10° slopes. Topsoil that remains on a slope is often too thin to support dense plant growth. The lack of vegetation contributes to the development of a poor-quality soil that lacks humus. The soils on the sides of mountains are commonly thin and rocky, and the soils have few nutrients. Lowlands that retain water tend to have thick, wet soils and a high concentration of organic matter, which forms humus. A fairly flat area that has good drainage provides the best surface for formation of thick, fertile layers of residual soil.

Section 3 Review

1. **Summarize** how soils form.

2. **Explain** how the composition of parent rock affects soil composition.

3. **Describe** the three horizons of a residual soil. 7c

4. **Predict** the type of soil that will form in arctic and tropical climates.

CRITICAL THINKING

5. **Applying Ideas** What combination of soil and climate would be ideal for growing deep-rooted crops? Explain your answer. IE.1d

6. **Analyzing Relationships** Would you expect crop growth to be more successful on a farm that has an uneven topography or on a farm that has level land? Explain your answer. IE.1d

7. **Analyzing Ideas** Why would tropical soil not be good for sustained farming? IE.1d

8. **Making Comparisons** Although desert and arctic climates are extremely different, their soils may be somewhat similar. Explain why. IE.1d

CONCEPT MAPPING

9. Use the following terms to create a concept map: *soil, bedrock, regolith, humus, parent rock, residual soil, transported soil, horizon, soil profile, climate,* and *topography.*

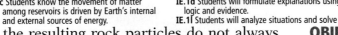
Section 4
Erosion

California Content Standards

7c Students know the movement of matter among reservoirs is driven by Earth's internal and external sources of energy.

IE.1d Students will formulate explanations using logic and evidence.
IE.1l Students will analyze situations and solve

problems that require combining and applying concepts from more than one area of science.

When rock weathers, the resulting rock particles do not always stay near the parent rock. Various forces may move weathered fragments of rock away from where the weathering occurred. The process by which the products of weathering are transported is called **erosion.** The most common agents of erosion are gravity, wind, glaciers, and water. Water can move weathered rock in several different ways including by ocean waves and currents, by streams and runoff, and by the movements of groundwater.

Soil Erosion

As rock weathers, it eventually becomes very fine particles that mix with water, air, and humus to form soil. The erosion of soil occurs worldwide and is normally a slow process. Ordinarily, new soil forms about as fast as existing soil erodes. However, some forms of land use and unusual climatic conditions can upset this natural balance. Once the balance is upset, soil erosion often accelerates.

Some farming and ranching practices increase soil erosion. For example, plants anchor soil with their roots and prevent wind and water from eroding the soil. Clearing plants or allowing animals to overgraze destroys this groundcover and increases erosion rates. Soil erosion is considered by some scientists to be the greatest environmental problem that faces the world today. As shown in **Figure 1,** vulnerability to erosion affects fertile topsoil around the world. This erosion prevents some countries from growing the crops needed to prevent widespread famine.

OBJECTIVES

▶ **Define** erosion, and list four agents of erosion. 7c

▶ **Identify** four farming methods that conserve soil. 7c, IE.1l

▶ **Discuss** two ways gravity contributes to erosion. 7c

▶ **Describe** the three major landforms shaped by weathering and erosion. 7c

KEY TERMS

erosion
sheet erosion
mass movement
solifluction
creep
landform

erosion a process in which the materials of Earth's surface are loosened, dissolved, or worn away and transported from one place to another by a natural agent, such as wind, water, ice, or gravity

Figure 1 ▶ This map shows the vulnerability of soils worldwide to erosion by water.

Vulnerability
Low
Moderate
High
Very high

30°N

Equator

30°S

Figure 2 ▶ This land in Madagascar can no longer be used for farming because of a form of rapid erosion called *gullying*.

sheet erosion the process by which water flows over a layer of soil and removes the topsoil

Gullying and Sheet Erosion

One farming technique that can accelerate soil erosion is the improper plowing of furrows, or long, narrow rows. Furrows that are plowed up and down slopes allow water to run swiftly over soil. As soil is washed away with each rainfall, a furrow becomes larger and forms a small gully. Eventually, land that is plowed in this way can become covered with deep gullies. This type of accelerated soil erosion is called *gullying*. The farmland shown in **Figure 2** has been ruined by gullying.

Another type of soil erosion strips away layers of topsoil. Eventually, erosion can expose the surface of the subsoil. This process is called **sheet erosion.** Sheet erosion may occur where continuous rainfall washes away layers of the topsoil. Wind also can cause sheet erosion during unusually dry periods. The soil, which is made dry and loose by a lack of moisture, is carried away by the wind as clouds of dust and drifting sand. These wind-borne particles may produce large dust storms.

✓ **Reading Check** Describe one way a dust storm may form, and explain how a dust storm can affect the fertility of land. (See the Appendix for answers to Reading Checks.)

Results of Soil Erosion

Constant erosion reduces the fertility of the soil by removing the A horizon, which contains the fertile humus. The B horizon, which does not contain much organic matter, is difficult to farm because it is much less fertile than the A horizon. Without plants, the B horizon has nothing to protect it from further erosion. So, within a few years, all of the soil layers could be removed by continuous erosion.

Soil Conservation

Erosion rates are affected not only by natural factors but also by human activities. Certain farming and grazing techniques and construction projects can also increase the rate of erosion. In developing urban areas, vegetation is removed to build houses and roads, such as those shown in **Figure 3.** This land clearing removes protective ground cover plants and accelerates topsoil erosion. In some areas, such as deserts or mountainous regions, it may take hundreds or thousands of years for the topsoil to be replenished.

But rapid, destructive soil erosion can be prevented by soil conservation methods. People, including city planners and some land developers, have begun to recognize the environmental impact of land development and are beginning to implement soil conservation measures. Some land development projects are leaving trees and vegetation in place whenever possible. Other projects are planting cover plants to hold the topsoil in place. Farmers are also looking for new ways to prevent soil erosion to preserve fertile topsoil.

Figure 3 ▶ This housing development in England is encroaching on cropland. The clearing of land for development can accelerate topsoil erosion.

Connection to ENVIRONMENTAL SCIENCE

Land Degradation

Soil that can support the growth of healthy plants is called *fertile soil.* Land that can be used to grow crops is called *arable land.* A limited area of arable land is available on Earth. As humans use this land for agriculture, they plow, fertilize, irrigate, and otherwise change the natural processes of soil formation.

Human activity and natural processes may damage land to the point that it can no longer support the local ecosystem. This process is called *land degradation.* Several activities may lead to land degradation. Three common factors in land degradation are urbanization, overgrazing, and deforestation.

Urbanization is the movement of people from rural areas to cities. As cities expand rapidly, people begin to develop the surrounding area, in a process called *urban sprawl.* As a result, arable land is paved and demand for resources may overwhelm the water and land resources in the area.

Overgrazing occurs when more animals are allowed to graze an area than the plants in that area can support. When animals overgraze, too many plants are eaten or trampled and too few plants are left to protect the soil from eroding.

If this clearcut in Willamette National Forest in Oregon was not reclaimed, the land may have continued to undergo degradation.

Deforestation is the clearing of trees from an area without replacing them. This process destroys wildlife habitat and results in accelerated soil erosion.

Extreme land degradation may cause desertification. *Desertification* is the process by which land in dry areas becomes more desertlike because of human activity or climate change. Desertification can cause land to become useless for farming or human habitation.

Many government and independent organizations are working to develop laws and guidelines to protect both wilderness and agricultural land. These groups hope that by protecting these lands now, the resources will be available for future generations.

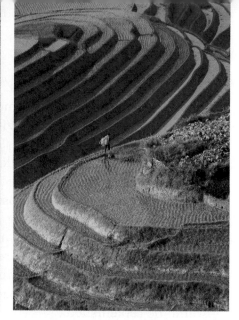

Contour Plowing These fields are plowed in contours (or curves) that follow the shape of the land.

Strip-Cropping These fields were planted with alternating strips of different crops.

Terracing These terraced fields help slow runoff and prevent rapid soil erosion.

Figure 4 ▶ Soil Conservation Methods

Graphic

Organizer Spider Map

Create the **Graphic Organizer** entitled "Spider Map" described in the Skills Handbook section of the Appendix. Label the circle "Soil conservation methods." Then, fill in the map with at least four methods for soil conservation.

Contour Plowing

Farmers in countries around the world use planting techniques to reduce soil erosion. In one method, called *contour plowing*, soil is plowed in curved bands that follow the contour, or shape, of the land. This method of planting, shown in **Figure 4,** prevents water from flowing directly down slopes, so the method prevents gullying.

Strip-Cropping

In *strip-cropping*, crops are planted in alternating bands, also shown in **Figure 4.** A crop planted in rows, such as corn, may be planted in one band, and another crop that fully covers the surface of the land, such as alfalfa, will be planted next to it. The *cover crop* protects the soil by slowing the runoff of rainwater. Strip-cropping is often combined with contour plowing. The combination of these two methods can reduce soil erosion by 75%.

Terracing

The construction of steplike ridges that follow the contours of a sloped field is called *terracing*, as shown in **Figure 4.** Terraces, especially those used for growing rice in Asia, prevent or slow the downslope movement of water and thus prevent rapid erosion.

Crop Rotation

In *crop rotation*, farmers plant one type of crop one year and a different type of crop the next. For example, crops that expose the soil to the full effects of erosion may be planted one year, and a cover crop will be planted the next year. Crop rotation stops erosion in its early stages, which allows small gullies that formed during one growing season to fill with soil during the next one.

Gravity and Erosion

Gravity causes rock fragments to move down inclines. This movement of fragments down a slope is called **mass movement**. Some mass movements occur rapidly, and others occur very slowly.

Rockfalls and Landslides

The most dramatic and destructive mass movements occur rapidly. The fall of rock from a steep cliff is called a *rockfall*. A rockfall is the fastest kind of mass movement. Rocks in rockfalls often range in size from tiny fragments to giant boulders.

When masses of loose rock combined with soil suddenly fall down a slope, the event is called a *landslide*. Large landslides, in which loosened blocks of bedrock fall, generally occur on very steep slopes. You may have seen a small landslide on cliffs and steep hills overlooking highways, such as the one shown in **Figure 5.** Heavy rainfall, spring thaws, volcanic eruptions, and earthquakes can trigger landslides.

✔ **Reading Check** What is the difference between a rockfall and a landslide? (See the Appendix for answers to Reading Checks.)

Mudflows and Slumps

The rapid movement of a large amount of mud creates a *mudflow*. Mudflows occur in dry, mountainous regions during sudden, heavy rainfall or as a result of volcanic eruptions. Mud churns and tumbles as it moves down slopes and through valleys, and it frequently spreads out in a large fan shape at the base of the slope. The mass movements that sometimes occur in hillside communities, such as the one shown in **Figure 5,** are often referred to as landslides, but they are actually mudflows.

Sometimes, a large block of soil and rock becomes unstable and moves downhill in one piece. The block of soil then slides along the curved slope of the surface. This type of movement is called a *slump*. Slumping occurs along very steep slopes. Saturation by water and loss of friction with underlying rock causes loose soil to slip downhill over the solid rock.

mass movement the movement of a large mass of sediment or a section of land down a slope

Figure 5 ▶ An earthquake in El Salvador caused this dramatic landslide (left). Heavy rains in the Philippines caused this destructive mudflow (right).

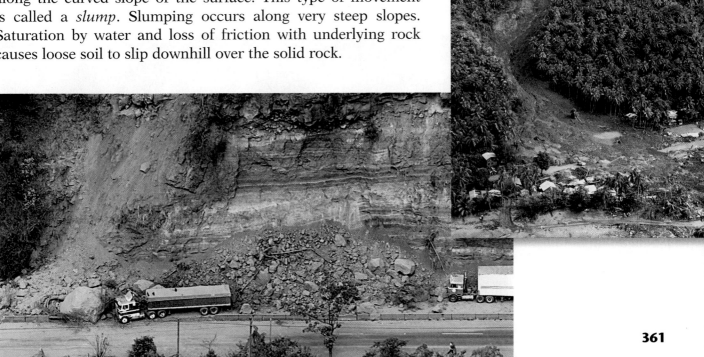

Solifluction

Although most slopes appear to be unchanging, some slow mass movement commonly occurs. Catastrophic landslides are the most hazardous mass movement. However, more rock material on the whole is moved by the greater number of slow mass movements than by catastrophic landslides.

One form of slow mass movement is called solifluction. **Solifluction** is the process by which water-saturated soil slips over hard or frozen layers. Solifluction occurs in arctic and mountainous climates where the subsoil is permanently frozen. In spring and summer, only the top layer of soil thaws. The moisture from this layer cannot penetrate the frozen layers beneath. So, the surface layer becomes muddy and slowly flows downslope, or downhill. Solifluction can also occur in warmer regions, where the subsoil consists of hard clay. The clay layer acts like the frozen subsoil in arctic climates by forming a waterproof barrier.

Creep

The extremely slow downhill movement of weathered rock material is known as **creep**. Soil creep moves the most soil of all types of mass movements. But creep may go unnoticed unless buildings, fences, or other surface objects move along with soil.

Many factors contribute to soil creep. Water separates rock particles, which allows them to move freely. Growing plants produce a wedgelike pressure that separates particles and loosens the soil. The burrowing of animals and repeated freezing and thawing loosen rock particles and allow gravity to slowly pull the particles downhill.

As rock fragments accumulate at the base of a slope, they form piles called *talus* (TAY luhs), as shown in **Figure 6.** Talus weathers into smaller fragments, which move farther down the slope. The fragments wash into gullies, are carried into successively larger waterways, and eventually flow into rivers.

solifluction the slow, downslope flow of soil saturated with water in areas surrounding glaciers at high elevations

creep the slow downhill movement of weathered rock material

Figure 6 ▶ The movement of rock fragments downslope formed these talus cones at the base of the Canadian Rockies.

Erosion and Landforms

Through weathering and erosion, Earth's surface is shaped into different physical features, or **landforms.** There are three major landforms that are shaped by weathering and erosion—*mountains*, *plains*, and *plateaus*. Minor landforms include hills, valleys, and dunes. The shape of landforms is also influenced by rock composition.

All landforms are subject to two opposing processes. One process bends, breaks, and lifts Earth's crust and thus creates elevated, or uplifted, landforms. The other process is weathering and erosion, which wears down land surfaces.

Erosion of Mountains

During the early stages in the history of a mountain, the mountain undergoes uplift. Generally, while tectonic forces are uplifting the mountain, it rises faster than it is eroded. Mountains that are being uplifted tend to be rugged and have sharp peaks and deep, narrow valleys. When forces stop uplifting the mountain, weathering and erosion wear down the rugged peaks to rounded peaks and gentle slopes. The formations in **Figure 7** show how the shapes of mountains are influenced by uplift and erosion.

Over millions of years, mountains that are not being uplifted become low, featureless surfaces. These areas are called *peneplains* (PEE nuh PLAYNZ), which means "almost flat." A peneplain commonly has low, rolling hills, as seen in New England.

Reading Check Describe how a mountain changes after it is no longer uplifted. (See the Appendix for answers to Reading Checks.)

Figure 7 ▶ The mountains in the Patagonian Andes, shown on the left, are still being uplifted and are more rugged than the more eroded Appalachian mountains on the right.

landform a physical feature of Earth's surface

Figure 8 ▶ Ancient rivers carved plateaus into mesas, which eventually eroded into the buttes of Monument Valley in Arizona.

Erosion of Plains and Plateaus

A *plain* is a relatively flat landform near sea level. A *plateau* is a broad, flat landform that has a high elevation. A plateau is subject to much more erosion than a plain. Young plateaus, such as the Colorado Plateau in the southwestern United States, commonly have deep stream valleys that separate broad, flat regions. Older plateaus, such as those in the Catskill region in New York State, have been eroded into rugged hills and valleys.

The effect of weathering and erosion on a plateau depends on the climate and the composition and structure of the rock. In dry climates, resistant rock produces plateaus that have flat tops. As a plateau ages, erosion may dissect the plateau into smaller, tablelike areas called *mesas* (MAY suhz). Mesas ultimately erode to small, narrow-topped formations called *buttes* (BYOOTS). In dry regions, such as in the area shown in **Figure 8,** mesas and buttes have steep walls and flat tops. In areas that have wet climates, humidity and precipitation weather landforms into round shapes.

Section 4 **Review**

1. **Define** erosion. 7c

2. **List** four agents of erosion. 7c

3. **Summarize** two processes of soil erosion. 7c

4. **Identify** four farming methods that result in soil conservation. 7c, IE.1l

5. **Discuss** two ways gravity contributes to erosion. 7c

6. **Compare** rapid mass movements and slow mass movements. 7c

7. **Describe** the erosion of the three major landforms. 7c

CRITICAL THINKING

8. **Analyzing Relationships** Describe an experiment that could help you determine whether a nearby hill is undergoing creep. IE.1a

9. **Applying Ideas** Suppose you wanted to grow grapevines on a hillside in Italy. What farming methods would you use? Explain your answer. 7c, IE.1d, IE.1l

10. **Predicting Consequences** Describe two ways a small butte would change if it was in a wet climate, rather than a dry climate. IE.1d

11. **Drawing Conclusions** A hillside community has asked you to help brainstorm ways to prevent future mudflows. Describe three of your ideas. IE.1d

CONCEPT MAPPING

12. Use the following terms to create a concept map: *erosion, gullying, sheet erosion, landslide, mudflow, slump, solifluction, creep, talus, landform, mountain, plain, plateau, mesa,* and *butte.* 7c

Sections

1 Weathering Processes

Key Terms

weathering, 343
mechanical weathering, 343
abrasion, 344
chemical weathering, 346
oxidation, 346
hydrolysis, 347
carbonation, 347
acid precipitation, 348

Key Concepts

▶ Agents of mechanical weathering break rock into smaller pieces but do not change its chemical composition.

▶ Chemical weathering changes the mineral composition of rock.

▶ Types of chemical weathering include hydrolysis, carbonation, oxidation, and acid precipitation.

2 Rates of Weathering

Key Terms

differential weathering, 349

Key Concepts

▶ Rock weathers at different rates, which depend partly on its mineral composition.

▶ The greater the amount of exposure a rock has, the faster a rock weathers.

▶ Rock weathers more rapidly in regions where rainfall is abundant and where alternating freezes and thaws occur.

3 Soil

Key Terms

soil, 353
soil profile, 354
horizon, 354
humus, 354

Key Concepts

▶ The parent rock from which soil forms is the major factor that determines the composition of the soil.

▶ Thick soils form in tropical climates and temperate climates. Thin soils form in arctic climates and desert climates, where rainfall is minimal.

4 Erosion

Key Terms

erosion, 357
sheet erosion, 358
mass movement, 361
solifluction, 362
creep, 362
landform, 363

Key Concepts

▶ Natural agents often move weathered rock away from where the weathering occurred. This movement leads to erosion.

▶ Planting crops helps to conserve soil.

▶ Slow and rapid mass movements of rock, soil, and mud cause massive amounts of soil erosion.

▶ Erosion wears away landforms as it levels Earth's surface.

Using Key Terms

Use each of the following terms in a separate sentence.

1. *abrasion*
2. *humus* 🐾7c
3. *landform*

For each pair of terms, explain how the meanings of the terms differ.

4. *weathering* and *erosion* 🐾7c
5. *mechanical weathering* and *chemical weathering* 🐾7c
6. *oxidation* and *carbonation* 🐾7c
7. *soil profile* and *horizon* 🐾7c
8. *solifluction* and *creep* 🐾7c

Understanding Key Concepts

9. A common kind of mechanical weathering is called 🐾7c
   a. oxidation.
   c. carbonation.
   b. ice wedging.
   d. leaching.

10. Oxides of sulfur and nitrogen that combine with water vapor cause
    a. hydrolysis.
    b. acid rain.
    c. mechanical weathering.
    d. carbonation.

11. The surface area of rocks exposed to weathering is increased by 🐾7c
    a. burial.
    c. leaching.
    b. accumulation.
    d. jointing.

12. Chemical weathering is most rapid in 🐾7c
    a. hot, dry climates.
    b. cold, dry climates.
    c. cold, wet climates.
    d. hot, wet climates.

13. The chemical composition of soil depends to a large extent on
    a. topography.
    b. the soil's A horizon.
    c. the parent material.
    d. soil's B horizon.

14. The soil in tropical climates is often 🐾7c
    a. thick.   c. dry.
    b. thin.   d. fertile.

15. All of the following farming methods prevent gullying, *except* 🐾7c
    a. terracing.   c. contour plowing.
    b. strip-cropping.   d. irrigation.

16. The type of mass movement that moves the most soil is 🐾7c
    a. a landslide.   c. a rockfall.
    b. a mudflow.   d. creep.

17. The grinding away of rock surfaces through the mechanical action of rock or sand particles is called 🐾7c
    a. carbonation.   c. abrasion.
    b. hydrolysis.   d. erosion.

18. The process by which softer rocks wear away and leave harder rocks behind is
    a. chemical weathering.
    b. mechanical weathering.
    c. differential weathering.
    d. erosion.

Short Answer

19. What is the difference between natural rain and acid precipitation?

20. Explain two reasons why soil conservation is important. 🐾7c, IE.1l

21. Describe how a mountain changes from a rugged mountain to a peneplain.

22. Describe three landforms that are shaped by weathering and erosion.

Soil Conservationist

One hundred and fifty years ago, Boone County, Illinois, consisted mainly of rolling prairies. Today, farms and homes have replaced much of the prairies. As a soil conservationist, Lewis Nichols helps farmers and homeowners to more effectively manage their land.

Down-to-Earth Solutions

"Erosion is our number one issue here," says Nichols. "Gully erosion, the kind of erosion that forms large trenches, is the most visible kind. Farmers also have problems with sheet erosion, which can remove topsoil from entire fields." Nichols helps farmers implement conservation practices to keep valuable soil in the fields and to keep the soil out of streams and rivers. As more rural areas give way to housing developments, Nichols also visits new neighborhoods. Though most of his work is done in the field, Nichols returns to his office to develop specific conservation practices for the problems he is studying.

For Nichols, the career path to soil conservation began in a high school greenhouse. Nichols turned his interests into a profession. He earned a bachelor's degree in agronomy, which is the study of crop production and soil management.

"Everything ties back to the soil."

—Lewis Nichols

Hamburger and the Farmer

Like other soil conservationists, Nichols reaches out to communities and schools to teach the value of natural resources and to encourage conservation efforts. "We go to schools to talk to kids about conservation. We want kids to know the connection between a hamburger and the farmer that produced it," says Nichols. "I find it very rewarding to know I'm able to help society by looking out for the future and providing a better world for our children—a world where the words *natural resources* still have meaning."

◀ Irrigation in this peanut field in Oklahoma has caused erosion. Soil conservationists work with farmers to reduce erosion when possible.

SCILINKS®

NSTA
Developed and maintained by the National Science Teachers Association

For a variety of links related to this subject, go to www.scilinks.org

Topic: Careers in Earth Science
SciLinksCode: HQ60222

Chapter 15

River Systems

Sections

1 The Water Cycle

2 Stream Erosion

3 Stream Deposition

What You'll Learn

- How water moves between Earth's land, oceans, and atmosphere
- How rivers shape the land by erosion
- How rivers shape the land by deposition

Why It's Relevant

The continuous movement of water is necessary for the survival of humans and other life-forms on Earth. Water movement also shapes the land by erosion and deposition.

PRE-READING ACTIVITY

Layered Book
Before you read this chapter, create the FoldNote entitled "Layered Book" described in the Skills Handbook section of the Appendix. Label the tabs of the layered book with "Evapotranspiration," "Condensation," "Precipitation," and "Conservation." As you read the chapter, write information you learn about each category under the appropriate tab.

▶ Rivers, such as the Copper River in Alaska shown here, are major forces in eroding sediment from one place and depositing sediment in another.

California Content Standards

7c Students know the movement of matter among reservoirs is driven by Earth's internal and external sources of energy.

9c Students know the importance of water to society, the origins of California's fresh water, and the relationship between supply and need.

IE.1d Students will formulate explanations using logic and evidence.

IE.1g Students will recognize the usefulness and limitations of models and theories as scientific representations of reality.

IE.1i Students will analyze the locations, sequences, or time intervals that are characteristic of natural phenomena (e.g., relative ages of rocks, locations of planets over time, and succession of species in an ecosystem).

The Water Cycle

California Content Standards

7c Students know the movement of matter among reservoirs is driven by Earth's internal and external sources of energy.

9c Students know the importance of water to society, the origins of California's fresh water, and the relationship between supply and need.

IE.1g Students will recognize the usefulness and limitations of models and theories as scientific representations of reality.

The origin of Earth's water supply has puzzled people for centuries. Aristotle and other ancient Greek philosophers believed that rivers such as the Nile and the Danube could be supplied by rain and snow alone. It was not until the middle of the 17th century that scientists could accurately measure the amount of water received on Earth and the amount flowing in rivers. These measurements showed that Earth's surface receives up to 5 times as much water as rivers carry off. So, a more puzzling question than "Where does Earth's water come from?" is "Where does the water go?"

Movement of Water on Earth

Water is essential for humans and all other organisms. Its availability in different forms is critical for the continuation of life on Earth. More than two-thirds of Earth's surface is covered with water. Water flows in streams and rivers. It is held in lakes, oceans, and icecaps at Earth's poles. It even flows through the rock below Earth's surface as groundwater. Water is found not only in these familiar bodies of water but also in the tissues of all living creatures. In the atmosphere, water occurs as an invisible gas. This gas is called *water vapor*. Liquid water also exists in the atmosphere as small particles in clouds and fog, as shown in **Figure 1.**

Earth's water is constantly changing from one form to another. Water vapor falls from the sky as rain. Glaciers melt to form streams. Rivers flow into oceans, where liquid water escapes into the atmosphere as water vapor. This continuous movement of water on Earth's surface from the atmosphere to the land and oceans and back to the atmosphere is called the **water cycle.**

OBJECTIVES

▶ **Outline** the stages of the water cycle. 🐾 **7c**

▶ **Describe** factors that affect a water budget. 🐾 **9c**

▶ **List** two approaches to water conservation. 🐾 **9c**

KEY TERMS

water cycle
evapotranspiration
condensation
precipitation
desalination

For a variety of links related to this subject, go to www.scilinks.org

Topic: Water Cycle
SciLinks code: HQ61626

water cycle the continuous movement of water between the atmosphere, the land, and the oceans

Figure 1 ▶ The snow, the fog, and the river water in this photo are three of the forms that water takes on Earth. Invisible water vapor is also present in the air.

Evapotranspiration

The process by which liquid water changes into water vapor is called *evaporation*. Each year, about 500,000 km³ of water evaporates into the atmosphere. About 86% of this water evaporates from the ocean. The remaining water evaporates from lakes, streams, and the soil. Water vapor also enters the air by *transpiration*, the process by which plants release water vapor into the atmosphere. The total loss of water from an area, which equals the sum of the water lost by evaporation from the soil and other surfaces and the water lost by transpiration from organisms, is called **evapotranspiration**. Evapotranspiration is one part of the water cycle, which is shown in **Figure 2.**

Condensation

Another process of the water cycle is condensation. **Condensation** is the change of state from a gas to a liquid. When water vapor rises in the atmosphere, it expands and cools. As the vapor becomes cooler, some of it condenses, or changes into tiny liquid water droplets, and forms clouds.

Precipitation

The third major process of the water cycle is *precipitation*, the process by which water falls from the clouds. **Precipitation** is any form of water that falls to Earth's surface from the clouds and includes rain, snow, sleet, and hail. More than 75% of all precipitation falls on Earth's oceans. The rest falls on land and becomes runoff or groundwater. Eventually, all of this water returns to the atmosphere by evapotranspiration, condenses, and falls back to Earth's surface to begin the cycle again.

Reading Check List the forms of precipitation. (See the Appendix for answers to Reading Checks.)

evapotranspiration the total loss of water from an area, which equals the sum of the water lost by evaporation from the soil and other surfaces and the water lost by transpiration from organisms

condensation the change of state from a gas to a liquid

precipitation any form of water that falls to Earth's surface from the clouds; includes rain, snow, sleet, and hail

Figure 2 ▶ Evapotranspiration, condensation, and precipitation make up the continuous process called the *water cycle.*

Condensation

Precipitation

Evapotranspiration

Runoff

Water Budget

The continuous cycle of evapotranspiration, condensation, and precipitation establishes Earth's *water budget*. A financial budget is a statement of expected income—money coming in—and expenses—money going out. In Earth's water budget, precipitation is the income. Evapotranspiration and runoff are the expenses. The water budget of Earth as a whole is balanced because the amount of precipitation is equal to the amount of evapotranspiration and runoff. However, the water budget of a particular area, called the *local water budget*, usually is not balanced.

Factors That Affect the Water Budget

 Factors that affect the local water budget include temperature, vegetation, wind, and the amount and duration of rainfall. When precipitation exceeds evapotranspiration and runoff in an area, the result is moist soil and possible flooding. When evapotranspiration exceeds precipitation, the soil becomes dry and irrigation may be necessary. Vegetation reduces runoff in an area but increases evapotranspiration. Wind increases the rate of evapotranspiration.

The factors that affect the local water budget vary geographically. For example, the Mojave Desert in California receives much less precipitation than do the tropical rain forests of Queensland, Australia, as **Figure 3** shows.

The local water budget also changes with the seasons in most areas of Earth. In general, cooler temperatures slow the rate of evapotranspiration. During the warmer months, evapotranspiration increases. As a result, streams generally transport more water in cooler months than they do in warmer months.

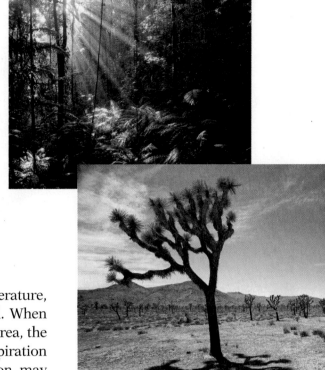

Figure 3 ▶ Tropical rain forests, such as the one in Queensland, Australia (top photo), require large amounts of rainfall annually. Deserts, such as the Mojave Desert in California (bottom photo), receive small amounts of rainfall each year.

QuickLAB 35 min

Modeling the Water Cycle

Procedure 7c, IE.1d, IE.1g

1. Place a **short glass** inside a **large plastic mixing bowl.** Add cold water to the mixing bowl until about three-fourths of the glass is covered with water. Make sure to keep the inside of the glass dry.
2. Add drops of **food coloring** (red, blue, or green) to the water in the bowl until the water has a strong color.
3. Now, add about 1 cup of dry **dirt** to the water, and stir gently until the water is muddy as well as colored.
4. Cover the bowl tightly with a **piece of plastic wrap** secured to the bowl with a **rubber band,** and place a **coin or stone** in the middle of the plastic wrap above the glass.
5. Set the bowl in the sun or under a **heat lamp** for 30 minutes to several hours. Then, observe the water that has collected in the glass.

Analysis

1. What are the processes that have taken place to allow water to collect in the glass?
2. Why is the water in the glass not muddy?
3. Is the water in the glass colored? What does this say about pollutants in water systems and the water cycle?

Water Use

On average, each person in the United States uses about 95,000 L (20,890.5 gal) of water each year. Water is used for bathing, washing clothes and dishes, watering lawns, carrying away wastes, and drinking. Agriculture and industry also use large amounts of water. As the population of the United States increases, so does the demand for water.

About 90% of the water used by cities and industry is returned to rivers or to the oceans as wastewater. Some of this wastewater contains harmful materials, such as toxic chemicals and metals, as shown in **Figure 4.** These toxic materials can pollute rivers and can harm plants and animals in the water.

Conservation of Water

While Earth holds a lot of water, only a small percentage of that water is fresh water that can be used by humans. Scientists have identified two ways to ensure that enough fresh water is available today and in the future. One way is through conservation, or the wise use of water resources. Individuals can conserve water by limiting their water use as much as possible. Governments can help conserve water by enforcing conservation laws and antipollution laws that prohibit the dumping of waste into bodies of water.

A second way to protect the water supply is to find alternative methods of obtaining fresh water. One such method is called **desalination,** which is the process of removing salt from ocean water. However, this method is expensive and is impractical for supplying water to large populations. Currently, the best way of maintaining an adequate supply of fresh water is the wise use and conservation of the fresh water that is now available.

Figure 4 ▶ Waste from this paper mill has polluted the Qingai River in China.

desalination a process of removing salt from ocean water

Section 1 Review

1. **List** two ways in which water reaches the oceans. 🐘7c

2. **Outline** the major stages of the water cycle. 🐘7c

3. **Explain** the difference between condensation and precipitation. 🐘7c

4. **Explain** why most local water budgets are not balanced. 🐘9c

5. **Describe** how vegetation and rainfall affect the local water budget. 🐘9c

6. **List** two ways to ensure the continued supply of fresh water. 🐘9c

CRITICAL THINKING

7. **Applying Concepts** Describe five ways that you can conserve water at home. 🐘9c

8. **Analyzing Processes** Why are the oceans the location of most evaporation and precipitation? 🐘7c, IE.1d

CONCEPT MAPPING

9. Use the following terms to create a concept map: *water cycle, evaporation, transpiration, evapotranspiration, condensation, precipitation,* and *water budget.* 🐘7c

7c Students know the movement of matter among reservoirs is driven by Earth's internal and external sources of energy.

IE.1d Students will formulate explanations using logic and evidence.
IE.1i Students will analyze the locations, sequences, or time intervals that are characteristic of natural phenomena (e.g., relative ages of rocks, locations of planets over time, and succession of species in an ecosystem).

A river system begins to form when precipitation exceeds evapotranspiration in a given area. After the soil in the area soaks up as much water as the soil can hold, the excess water moves downslope as runoff. As runoff moves across the land surface, it erodes rock and soil and eventually may form a narrow ditch, called a *gully*. Eventually, the processes of precipitation and erosion form a fully developed valley with a permanent stream.

Parts of a River System

A river system is made up of a main stream and **tributaries,** which are all of the feeder streams that flow into the main stream. The land from which water runs off into these streams is called a **watershed.** The ridges or elevated regions that separate watersheds are called *divides*. A river system is shown in **Figure 1.**

The relatively narrow depression that a stream follows as it flows downhill is called its *channel*. The edges of a stream channel that are above water level are called the stream's *banks*. The part of the stream channel that is below the water level is called the stream's *bed*. A stream channel gradually becomes wider and deeper as it erodes its banks and bed.

Channel Erosion

River systems change continuously because of erosion. In the process of *headward erosion*, channels lengthen and branch out at their upper ends, where runoff enters the streams. Erosion of the slopes in a watershed can also extend a river system and can add to the area of the watershed. In the process known as *stream piracy*, a stream from one watershed is "captured" by a stream from another watershed that has a higher rate of erosion. The captured stream then drains into the river system that has done the capturing.

OBJECTIVES

▶ **Summarize** how a river develops.
▶ **Describe** the parts of a river system. 🐻 7c
▶ **Explain** factors that affect the erosive ability of a river. 🐻 7c
▶ **Describe** how erosive factors affect the evolution of a river channel. 🐻 IE.1i, 7c

KEY TERMS

tributary
watershed
stream load
discharge
gradient
meander
braided stream

tributary a stream that flows into a lake or into a larger stream

watershed the area of land that is drained by a river system

Figure 1 ▶ The tributaries that run into this river are fed by runoff from surrounding land. All of the land that drains into a single river makes up the watershed of the river.

MATHPRACTICE

Water Discharge of a River River channels can carry an enormous volume of water. The water that rivers discharge can be calculated by using the following equation:

$$\text{discharge} = \begin{matrix}\text{velocity} \\ \text{of the} \\ \text{water}\end{matrix} \times \begin{matrix}\text{cross-sectional} \\ \text{area of the} \\ \text{river channel}\end{matrix}$$

In cubic meters per second (m³/s), what is the discharge of water carried by a river that moves 1.5 m/s through a cross-sectional area of 520 m²?

Stream Load

A stream transports soil, loose rock fragments, and dissolved minerals as it flows downhill. The materials carried by a stream are called the **stream load.** Stream load takes three forms: suspended load, bed load, and dissolved load. The *suspended load* consists of particles of fine sand and silt. The velocity, or rate of downstream travel, of the water keeps these particles suspended, so they do not sink to the stream bed. The *bed load* is made up of larger, coarser materials, such as coarse sand, gravel, and pebbles. This material moves by sliding and jumping along the bed. The *dissolved load* is mineral matter transported in liquid solution.

Stream Discharge

The volume of water moved by a stream in a given time period is the stream's **discharge.** The faster a stream flows, the higher its discharge and the greater the load that the stream can carry. Thus, a swift stream carries more sediment and larger particles than a slow stream does. A stream's velocity also affects how the stream cuts down and widens its channel. Swift streams erode their channels more quickly than slow-moving streams do.

Stream Gradient

The velocity of a stream depends mainly on gradient. **Gradient** is the change in elevation of a stream over a given horizontal distance. In other words, gradient is the steepness of the stream's slope. Near the *headwaters,* or the beginning of a stream, the gradient generally is steep. This area of the stream has a high velocity, which causes rapid channel erosion. As the stream nears its *mouth,* where the stream enters a larger body of water, its gradient often becomes flatter. As a result, the river's velocity and erosive power decrease. The stream channel eventually is eroded to a nearly flat gradient by the time the stream channel reaches the sea. Streams with different gradients are shown in **Figure 2.**

Figure 2 ▶ Streams that have steep gradients, such as the stream on the left, have a higher velocity than streams that have low gradients, such as the stream on the right, do.

Steep gradient

Low gradient

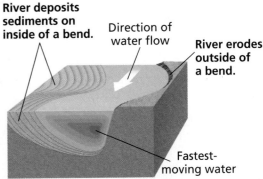

River deposits sediments on inside of a bend.

Direction of water flow

River erodes outside of a bend.

Fastest-moving water

Figure 3 ▶ Decreased velocity on the inside of a river's curve leads to the deposition of sediment, as this photo of a river in the Banff National Park in Alberta, Canada, shows.

Evolution of River Channels

As the stream's load, discharge, and gradient decrease, the erosive power of the stream decreases, which influences the evolution of the stream's channel. Over time, as the channel erodes, it becomes wider and deeper. When the stream becomes longer and wider, it is called a *river*.

Meandering Channels

As a river evolves, it may develop curves and bends. A river that has a low gradient tends to have more bends than a river that has a steep gradient does. A winding pattern of wide curves, called **meanders,** develops because as the gradient decreases, the velocity of the water decreases. When the velocity of the water decreases, the river is less able to erode down into its bed. As the water flows through the channel, more energy is directed against the banks, which causes erosion of the banks.

When a river rounds a bend, the velocity of the water on the outside of the curve increases. The fast-moving water on the outside of a river bend erodes the outer bank of that bend. However, on the inside of the curve, the velocity of the water decreases. This decrease in velocity leads to the formation of a *bar* of deposited sediment, such as sand or gravel, as shown in **Figure 3.**

As this process continues, the curve enlarges while further sediment deposition takes place on the opposite bank, where the water is moving more slowly. Meanders can become so curved that they almost form a loop, separated by only a narrow neck of land. When the river cuts across this neck, the meander can become isolated from the river, and an *oxbow lake* forms.

meander one of the bends, twists, or curves in a low-gradient stream or river

For a variety of links related to this subject, go to www.scilinks.org

Topic: River Systems
SciLinks code: HQ61314
Topic: California's Fresh Water
SciLinks code: HQ7C05

✓ Reading Check How would you describe the gradient of a river that has meanders? (See the Appendix for answers to Reading Checks.)

Figure 4 ▶ Braided streams, such as the Chisana River in Alaska, divide into multiple channels.

Graphic Organizer **Cause-and-Effect Map**

Create the **Graphic Organizer** entitled "Cause-and-Effect Map" described in the Skills Handbook section of the Appendix. Label the effects with "Meandering streams" and "Braided streams." Then, fill in the map with causes of meandering streams and braided streams and details about the causes and effects.

braided stream a stream or river that is composed of multiple channels that divide and rejoin around sediment bars

Braided Streams

Most rivers are single channels. However, under certain conditions, the presence of sediment bars between a river's banks can divide the flow of the river into multiple channels. A stream or river that is composed of multiple channels that divide and rejoin around sediment bars is called a **braided stream.** Braided streams are a direct result of a large sediment load, particularly when a high percentage of the load is composed of coarse sand and gravel. The bars form on the channel floor when the river is unable to move all of the available load.

Although braided streams, such as those in **Figure 4,** look very different from meandering channels, they can cause just as much erosion. The channel location shifts constantly such that bars between channels erode and new bars form. Sometimes, a single river can change from a braided stream to a meandering stream as the gradient and discharge change.

Section 2 Review

1. **Summarize** how a river develops. 7c

2. **Describe** the parts of a river system. 7c

3. **Explain** the processes of headward erosion and stream piracy. 7c

4. **List** the three types of stream load. 7c

5. **Explain** how stream discharge and gradient affect the erosive ability of a river. 7c

6. **Describe** the factors that control whether a river is braided or meandering. 7c, IE.1i

7. **Summarize** the process that forms an oxbow lake. IE.1i

CRITICAL THINKING

8. **Predicting Consequences** If geologic forces were to cause an uplift of the land surface, what would the effect on stream channel erosion be? 7c, IE.1d

9. **Analyzing Processes** Explain how the velocity of a stream affects the suspended load. 7c, IE.1d

CONCEPT MAPPING

10. Use the following terms to create a concept map: *braided channels, stream load, suspended load, dissolved load, bed load, meanders, stream gradient,* and *headwaters.* 7c

7c Students know the movement of matter among reservoirs is driven by Earth's internal and external sources of energy.

IE.1m Students will investigate a science-based societal issue by researching the literature, analyzing data, and communicating the find-

ings. Examples of issues include irradiation of food, cloning of animals by somatic cell nuclear transfer, choice of energy sources, and land and water use decisions in California.

The total load that a stream can carry is greatest when a large volume of water is flowing swiftly. When the velocity of the water decreases, the ability of the stream to carry its load decreases. As a result, part of the stream load is deposited as sediment.

Deltas and Alluvial Fans

A stream may deposit sediment on land or in water. For example, the load carried by a stream can be deposited when the stream reaches an ocean or a lake. As a stream empties into a large body of water, the velocity of the stream decreases sharply. The load is usually deposited at the mouth of the stream in a triangular shape. A triangular-shaped deposit that forms where the mouth of a stream enters a larger body of water is called a **delta**. The exact shape and size of a delta are determined by waves, tides, offshore depths, and the sediment load of the stream.

When a stream descends a steep slope and reaches a flat plain, the speed of the stream suddenly decreases. As a result, the stream deposits some of its load on the level plain at the base of the slope. A fan-shaped deposit called an **alluvial fan** forms on land, and its tip points upstream. In arid and semi-arid regions, temporary streams commonly form alluvial fans. Alluvial fans differ from deltas in that alluvial fans form on land instead of being deposited in water. This difference is shown in **Figure 1.**

OBJECTIVES

▶ **Explain** the two types of stream deposition. 🌞7c

▶ **Describe** one advantage and one disadvantage of living in a floodplain. 🌞7c

▶ **Identify** three methods of flood control. 🌞IE.1m

▶ **Describe** the life cycle of a lake. 🌞7c

KEY TERMS

delta
alluvial fan
floodplain

delta a fan-shaped mass of rock material deposited at the mouth of a stream; for example, deltas form where streams flow into the ocean at the edge of a continent

alluvial fan a fan-shaped mass of rock material deposited by a stream when the slope of the land decreases sharply; for example, alluvial fans form when streams flow from mountains to flat land

Figure 1 ▶ A delta, such as this one in Alaska's Prince William Sound (above), forms when a stream deposits sediment into another body of water. An alluvial fan, such as this one in California's Death Valley (right), forms when a stream deposits sediment on land.

Floodplains

The volume of water in nearly all streams varies depending on the amount of rainfall and snowmelt in the watershed. A dramatic increase in volume can cause a stream to overflow its banks and to wash over the valley floor. The part of the valley floor that may be covered with water during a flood is called a **floodplain.**

Natural Levees

When a stream overflows its banks and spreads out over the floodplain, the stream loses velocity and deposits its coarser sediment load along the banks of the channel. The accumulation of these deposits along the banks eventually produces raised banks, called *natural levees*.

Finer Flood Sediments

Not all of the load deposited by a stream in a flood will form levees. Finer sediments are carried farther out into the floodplain by the flood waters and are deposited there. A series of floods produces a thick layer of fine sediment, which becomes a source of rich floodplain soils. Swampy areas are common on floodplains because drainage is usually poor in the area between the levees and the outer walls of the valley. Despite the hazards of periodic flooding, people choose to live on floodplains, as shown in **Figure 2.** Floodplains provide convenient access to the river for shipping, fishing, and transportation. The rich soils, which are good for farming, also draw people to live on floodplains.

Figure 2 ▶ People who live in the Tonle Sap Floodplain in Cambodia have adapted to frequent flooding by building houses that are raised above the water level on stilts.

floodplain an area along a river that forms from sediments deposited when the river overflows its banks

Connection to ENVIRONMENTAL SCIENCE

The Dead Zone

Oceanographers have discovered that water in the Gulf of Mexico west of the mouth of the Mississippi River delta has a low level of oxygen during the summer. This condition, known as *hypoxia,* can suffocate crabs, shrimp, and other fish that live on the sea floor. For this reason, the area has been dubbed the Dead Zone. Hypoxia has severely affected the marine food chain in this area as well as the fishing industry.

What is the origin of the Dead Zone? Studies indicate that water flowing from the Mississippi River to the Gulf of Mexico has a high level of dissolved nitrogen and phosphorus from fertilizers that are used to grow crops in the watershed. These substances increase the growth of phytoplankton—small floating marine plants—in shallow gulf waters where the river water ends up. When these plants die and sink to the sea floor, they are broken down by bacteria that use oxygen in the process. As a result, the ocean water becomes depleted of oxygen. This process usually

Mississippi River watershed

Area of hypoxia in Gulf of Mexico

occurs in the summer when river flow is high, more sunlight is available for plant growth, and shallow gulf waters are poorly mixed with offshore water by winds.

To reduce the effects of hypoxia in the Gulf of Mexico, government officials are considering regulating the amount and type of fertilizers that can be used in the Mississippi watershed.

Soil Erosion 🔖 7c, IE.1c, IE.1d ⬥
Procedure

1. Fill a **23 cm × 33 cm pan** about half full with **moist, fine sand.**

2. Place the pan in a **sink** so that one end of the pan is resting on a **brick** and is under the water faucet.

3. Position an **additional pan or container** such that it catches any sand and water that flow out of the first pan.

4. Slowly open the faucet until a gentle trickle of water falls onto the sand in the raised end of the pan. Let the water run for 15 to 20 s.

5. Turn off the water, and draw the pattern of water flow over the sand.

6. Press the sand back into place, and carefully smooth the surface by using a **ruler.** Repeat steps 4 and 5 three more times. Each time, increase the rate of water flow slightly without splashing the sand.

Analysis

1. Describe how the rate of water flow affects erosion.

2. How does the rate of water flow affect gullies?

3. How could erosion on a real hillside be reduced without changing the rate of water flow?

4. How does the shape of a river bend change as water flows?

Human Impacts on Flooding

🔖 Human activity can contribute to the size and number of floods in many areas. Vegetation, such as trees and grass, protects the ground surface from erosion by taking in much of the water that would otherwise run off. Where this natural ground cover is removed, water can flow more freely across the surface. As a result, the likelihood of flooding increases. Logging and the clearing of land for agriculture or housing development can increase the volume and speed of runoff, which leads to more frequent flooding. Natural events, such as forest fires, can also increase the likelihood of flooding.

Flood Control

Indirect methods of flood control include forest and soil conservation measures that prevent excess runoff during periods of heavy rainfall. More-direct methods include the building of artificial structures that redirect the flow of water.

The most common method of direct flood control is the building of *dams*. The artificial lakes that form behind dams act as reservoirs for excess runoff. The stored water can be used to generate electricity, supply fresh water, and irrigate farmland. Another direct method of flood control is the building of *artificial levees*. However, artificial levees must be protected against erosion by the river. As **Figure 3** shows, when artificial levees break, flooding and property damage can result. Permanent overflow channels, or floodways, can also help prevent flooding. When the volume of water in a river increases, floodways carry away excess water and keep the river from overflowing. 🔖

✓ Reading Check Describe two ways that floods can be controlled. (See the Appendix for answers to Reading Checks.)

Figure 3 ▶ Week-long storms in Modesto, California, in 1997 broke this levee and caused flooding.

Precipitation collects in a depression and forms a lake.

A lake loses its water as the water drains away or evaporates.

As water is lost, the lake basin may eventually become dry land.

Figure 4 ▶ Compared to rivers, lakes are short lived, and some lakes may eventually dry up.

The Life Cycle of Lakes

Not all streams flow from the land to the ocean. Sometimes, water from streams collects in a depression in the land and forms a lake. Most lakes are located at high latitudes and in mountainous areas. Most of the water in lakes comes from precipitation and the melting of ice and snow. Springs, rivers, and runoff coming directly from the land are also sources of lake water.

Most lakes are relatively short lived in geologic terms. Many lakes eventually disappear because too much of their water drains away or evaporates, as shown in **Figure 4**. A common cause of excess drainage is an outflowing stream that erodes its bed below the level of a lake basin. Lakes may also lose water if the climate becomes drier and evaporation exceeds precipitation.

Lake basins may also disappear if they fill with sediments. Streams that feed a lake deposit sediments in the lake. Sediments also are carried into the lake by water that runs off the land but does not enter a stream. Most of these sediments are deposited near the shore. These sediments build up over time, which creates new shorelines and gradually fills in the lake. Organic deposits from vegetation also may accumulate in the bottom of a shallow lake. As these deposits grow denser, a bog or swamp may form. The lake basin may eventually become dry land.

Section 3 | **Review**

1. **Identify** the differences between a delta and an alluvial fan. 🐘7c

2. **Explain** the differences between the deposition of sediment in deltas and alluvial fans with the deposition of sediment on a floodplain. 🐘7c

3. **Describe** the advantages and disadvantages of living in a floodplain. 🐘7c

4. **Summarize** how human activities can affect the size and number of floods. 🐘IE.1m

5. **Identify** three methods of flood control. 🐘IE.1m

6. **Explain** why lakes are usually short lived. 🐘7c

CRITICAL THINKING

7. **Analyzing Ideas** Why are spring floods common in rivers where the headwaters are in an area of cold, snowy winters? 🐘IE.1d

8. **Making Inferences** If you were picking a material to make an artificial levee, what major characteristic would you look for? Explain your answer. 🐘IE.1d

CONCEPT MAPPING

9. Use the following terms to create a concept map: *stream deposition, delta, alluvial fan, floodplain, natural levee, dam, artificial levee,* and *lake.* 🐘7c

Chapter 15 Highlights

Sections

1 The Water Cycle

Key Terms

water cycle, 375
evapotranspiration, 376
condensation, 376
precipitation, 376
desalination, 378

Key Concepts

▶ The continuous movement of water from the atmosphere to the land and oceans and back to the atmosphere is called the *water cycle*.

▶ A region's water budget is affected by temperature, vegetation, wind, and the amount and duration of rainfall.

▶ The availability of fresh water can be enhanced through conservation efforts.

2 Stream Erosion

Key Terms

tributary, 379
watershed, 379
stream load, 380
discharge, 380
gradient, 380
meander, 381
braided stream, 382

Key Concepts

▶ A river system is made of a main stream and feeder streams, called *tributaries*.

▶ A watershed is the area of land that is drained by a river system.

▶ The erosive ability of a river is affected by stream load, stream discharge, and stream gradient.

▶ A bend in a low-gradient stream or river is called a *meander*.

▶ A river that is composed of multiple channels that divide and rejoin around sediment bars is called a *braided stream*.

3 Stream Deposition

Key Terms

delta, 383
alluvial fan, 383
floodplain, 384

Key Concepts

▶ Where a stream slows significantly, it can deposit its stream load to form deltas and alluvial fans.

▶ In floodplains, flooding commonly brings in new, rich soil for farming but can cause property damage.

▶ Floods can be controlled through forest and soil conservation and by building structures such as levees and dams.

Chapter 15 Review

Using Key Terms

Use each of the following terms in a separate sentence.

1. *water cycle* 🌋7c
2. *gradient*
3. *evapotranspiration* 🌋7c
4. *floodplain* 🌋7c

For each pair of terms, explain how the meanings of the terms differ.

5. *condensation* and *precipitation* 🌋7c
6. *watershed* and *tributary* 🌋7c
7. *stream load* and *discharge* 🌋7c
8. *delta* and *alluvial fan* 🌋7c

Understanding Key Concepts

9. The change of water vapor into liquid water is called 🌋7c
   a. runoff.
   c. evaporation.
   b. desalination.
   d. condensation.

10. In a water budget, the income is precipitation and the expense is 🌋9c
    a. evapotranspiration and runoff.
    b. condensation and saltation.
    c. erosion and conservation.
    d. conservation and sedimentation.

11. The land area from which water runs off into a stream is called a
    a. tributary.
    c. divide.
    b. watershed.
    d. gully.

12. Tributaries branch out and lengthen as a river system develops by
    a. headward erosion.
    b. condensation.
    c. saltation.
    d. runoff.

13. The stream load that includes gravel and large rocks is the 🌋7c
    a. suspended load.
    c. dissolved load.
    b. runoff load.
    d. bed load.

14. A fan-shaped formation that develops when a stream deposits its sediment at the base of a steep slope is called a(n) 🌋7c
    a. delta.
    b. meander.
    c. oxbow lake.
    d. alluvial fan.

15. The part of a valley floor that may be covered during a flood is the 🌋7c
    a. floodway.
    b. floodplain.
    c. meander.
    d. artificial levee.

16. One way to control floods indirectly is through
    a. soil conservation.
    b. dams.
    c. floodways.
    d. artificial levees.

Short Answer

17. How does a local water budget differ from the water budget of the whole Earth? 🌋9c

18. How is reducing the pollution in streams and groundwater linked to water conservation? 🌋9c

19. Describe how bank erosion can cause a river to meander. 🌋IE.1i

20. Why do most rivers that have a large sediment load also have high water velocity? 🌋7c

21. Describe how lakes fill with sediment. 🌋7c

22. What is the difference between direct and indirect methods of flood control?

7 Record the volume of water poured into the container.

8 Using container B, repeat steps 6 and 7. Record your observations.

9 Use a metric ruler to measure 1 cm above the surface of the sediment in each container. Using the grease pencil, draw a line to mark this height on the inside of each container. Pour water from the graduated cylinder into containers A and B until the water reaches the 1 cm mark.

10 Poke a nail through the very bottom of the side of container A. Place the container inside the pan. At the same time, start recording the time by using a stopwatch and pull the nail out of the container.

11 Observe the water level, and record the amount of time that the water takes to drop to the sediment surface.

12 Using container B, repeat steps 10 and 11. Record your observations.

Step 8

Step 12

ANALYZE THE RESULTS

1 **Analyzing Results** In step 8, which type of sediment held more water?

2 **Analyzing Results** Which type of sediment was the water able to flow through faster?

3 **Summarizing Results** What properties of the sediment do you think affected how the water flowed through the sediment? Explain your answer.

DRAW CONCLUSIONS

4 **Analyzing Results** On the basis of your answers to the questions above, which would water erode more quickly: an area of silt or an area of sand? Explain your answer.

5 **Drawing Conclusions** In which sediment do you think a deep stream channel is most likely to form? In which sediment is a meandering stream likely to form? Explain your answers.

Extension

1 **Applying Conclusions** Describe three ways to make slopes covered with soil more resistant to erosion.

World Watershed Sediment Yield

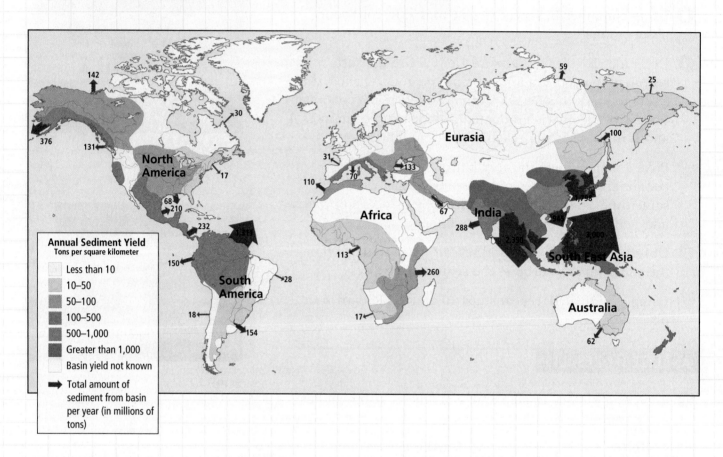

Annual Sediment Yield
Tons per square kilometer

- Less than 10
- 10–50
- 50–100
- 100–500
- 500–1,000
- Greater than 1,000
- Basin yield not known
- Total amount of sediment from basin per year (in millions of tons)

Map Skills Activity

This map shows the world's watersheds and identifies the sediment yield of each watershed basin in tons per square kilometer and the total amount of sediment that each basin dumps into the ocean in millions of tons per year. Use the map to answer the questions below.

1. **Using a Key** What area has the highest total annual sediment yield from one basin?

2. **Using a Key** What is the range of the annual sediment yield in tons per square kilometer for the United States, excluding Alaska?

3. **Analyzing Data** What is the total amount of sediment that basins in South America yield per year?

4. **Analyzing Relationships** Areas that have high relief, where the range of elevations is great, tend to have higher sediment yields than areas that have low relief, where the topography is flatter, do. Which area would you conclude has higher relief: Africa or South East Asia? Explain your answer.

5. **Making Comparisons** Both the Amazon basin, which is in northern South America, and the India basin have an annual sediment yield range of 100 to 500 tons per square kilometer. However, the total amount of sediment per year from the Amazon basin is 1,311 million tons, while the total amount of sediment per year from the India basin is 288 million tons. Explain why these two basins differ so significantly in their total sediment yield per year.

The Three Gorges Dam

China's Yangtze River is the third-longest river in the world. The Yangtze River flows through the Three Gorges region of central China, which is famous for its natural beauty and historical sites. This region is also where the Three Gorges Dam—the largest hydroelectric dam project in the world—is currently being built. When the dam is complete, the Yangtze River will rise to form a reservoir that is 595 km long— as long as Lake Superior. In other words, the reservoir will be about as long as the distance between Los Angeles and San Francisco in California!

Benefits of the Dam

The dam has several purposes, one of which is to control the water level of the Yangtze River to prevent flooding. About 1 million people died in the last century from flooding along the river. The other purpose is to provide millions of people with hydroelectric power. China now burns air-polluting coal to meet 75% of the country's energy needs. Engineers project that when the dam is completed, its turbines will provide enough electrical energy to power a city that is 10 times the size of Los Angeles. When its flow is controlled, the Yangtze River will be deep enough for ships to navigate on it, so the dam will also increase trade in a relatively poor region of China.

Disadvantages of the Dam

The project has several drawbacks, however. The reservoir behind the dam will flood an enormous area. Almost 2 million people living in the affected areas are being relocated—there are 13 cities and hundreds of villages in the area of the reservoir. As the reservoir's waters rise, fragile ecosystems and valuable archeological sites will be destroyed and scenic recreation areas will be submerged.

▲ A resident on the Yangtze River carries his belongings to higher ground after his home was destroyed when the dam caused the water level to rise.

Opponents of the project also claim that the dam will increase pollution levels in the Yangtze River. Most of the cities and factories along the river dump untreated wastes directly into the water. Some people think the reservoir will become the world's largest sewer when 1 billion tons of sewage flows into the reservoir every year.

Because the dam lies over a fault, scientists question whether the dam will be able to withstand earthquakes. If the dam were to burst, towns and cities downstream would be destroyed by the ensuing flood.

◄ An engineer on the Three Gorges Dam project celebrates the successful test of sluicing, which is the rushing of water through channels in the dam.

Extension

1. **Research** What do you think of the Three Gorges dam? Research other dam projects. After analyzing the benefits and risks of dams, write an essay describing your opinion about dam projects.

16

Groundwater

Sections

1 Water Beneath the Surface

2 Groundwater and Chemical Weathering

What You'll Learn

- How water moves under Earth's surface
- How humans use groundwater
- How groundwater shapes Earth's surface

Why It's Relevant

Groundwater is a major source of drinking water for humans and a source of fresh water for agriculture and industry. Groundwater is also a major force in shaping Earth's landforms.

PRE-READING ACTIVITY

Key-Term Fold
Before you read this chapter, create the **FoldNote** entitled "Key-Term Fold" described in the Skills Handbook section of the Appendix. Write a key term from the chapter on each tab of the key-term fold. Under each tab, write the definition of the key term.

▶ These macaque monkeys are bathing in hot springs in Jigokudani National Park in Japan. Hot springs form where molten rock in Earth's crust heats surrounding rock and the groundwater in the rock. The water then rises to the surface to form pools and springs.

 California Content Standards

7c Students know the movement of matter among reservoirs is driven by Earth's internal and external sources of energy.

9c Students know the importance of water to society, the origins of California's fresh water, and the relationship between supply and need.

IE.1a Students will select and use appropriate tools and technology (such as computer-linked probes, spreadsheets, and graphing calculators) to perform tests, collect data, analyze relationships and display data.

IE.1d Students will formulate explanations using logic and evidence.

IE.1l Students will analyze situations and solve problems that require combining and applying concepts from more than one area of science.

IE.1m Students will investigate a science-based societal issue by researching the literature, analyzing data, and communicating the findings. Examples of issues include irradiation of food, cloning of animals by somatic cell nuclear transfer, choice of energy sources, and land and water use decisions in California.

Water Beneath the Surface

California
Content
Standards

9c Students know the importance of water to society, the origins of California's fresh water, and the relationship between supply and need.

IE.1m Students will investigate a science-based societal issue by researching the literature, analyzing data, and communicating the find-ings. Examples of issues include irradiation of food, cloning of animals by somatic cell nuclear transfer, choice of energy sources, and land and water use decisions in California.

Surface water that does not run off into streams and rivers may seep down through the soil into the upper layers of Earth's crust. There, the water fills spaces, or *pores*, between rock particles. Water may also fill fractures or cavities in rock that were caused by erosion. Water that fills and moves through these spaces in rock and sediment is called **groundwater.** Groundwater is an important source of fresh water in the United States.

Properties of Aquifers

A body of rock or sediment in which large amounts of water can flow and be stored is called an **aquifer.** For water to flow freely through an aquifer, the pores or fractures in the aquifer must be connected. The ease with which water flows through an aquifer is affected by many factors, including porosity and permeability.

Porosity

In a set volume of rock or sediment, the percentage of the rock or sediment that consists of open spaces is **porosity.** One factor that affects porosity is sorting. *Sorting* is the amount of uniformity in the size of the rock or sediment particles, as **Figure 1** shows. Most particles in a well-sorted sediment are about the same size, and a few smaller particles fill the spaces between them. Poorly sorted sediment contains particles of many sizes. Small particles fill the spaces between large particles, which makes the rock less porous. Particle packing also affects porosity. Loosely packed particles leave many open spaces that can store water, so the rock has high porosity. Rock that has tightly packed particles contains few open spaces and thus has low porosity. Grain shape also affects porosity. In general, the more irregular the grain shape is, the more porous the rock or sediment is.

OBJECTIVES

▶ **Identify** properties of aquifers that affect the flow of groundwater. 🐾9c

▶ **Describe** the water table and its relationship to the land surface. 🐾9c

▶ **Compare** wells, springs, and artesian formations. 🐾9c

▶ **Describe** two land features formed by hot groundwater.

KEY TERMS

groundwater
aquifer
porosity
permeability
water table
artesian formation

groundwater the water that is beneath Earth's surface

aquifer a body of rock or sediment that stores groundwater and allows the flow of groundwater

porosity the percentage of the total volume of a rock or sediment that consists of open spaces

Figure 1 ▶ **Differences in Porosity**

Well-sorted, coarse-grained sediment has high porosity.

Well-sorted, fine-grained sediment has high porosity equal to the porosity of coarse-grained sediment.

Poorly sorted sediment that contains grains of many sizes has low porosity.

Rock is considered porous if it has many empty spaces that can fill with water.

Rock is considered permeable if its empty spaces are connected so that water may flow from one space to the next.

Figure 2 ▶ Porous rocks do not make good aquifers unless water can move freely through the rocks.

permeability the ability of a rock or sediment to let fluids pass through its open spaces, or pores

Permeability

The ease with which water passes through a porous material is called **permeability.** For a rock to be permeable, the open spaces must be connected, as shown in **Figure 2.** A rock that has high porosity is not permeable if the pores or fractures are not connected. Permeability is also affected by the size and sorting of the particles that make up a rock or sediment. The larger and better sorted the particles are, the more permeable the rock or sediment tends to be. The most permeable rocks, such as sandstone, are composed of coarse particles. Other rocks, such as limestone, may be permeable if they have interconnected cracks. Clay is a sediment composed of flat, very fine-grained particles. Because of this characteristic composition, clay is essentially *impermeable*, which means that water cannot flow through it.

QuickLAB   20 min

Permeability

Procedure 9c

1. With a **sharpened pencil**, make seven tiny holes in the bottom of each of **three paper or plastic cups.** Stretch **cheesecloth** tightly over the bottom of each cup. Secure the cloth with a **rubber band.**

2. Mark a line 2 cm from the top of one cup. Stand the cup on **three thread spools** in a **saucer or pie pan,** and fill the cup to the line with **sand.**

3. Pour **120 mL of water** into the cup. Use a **stopwatch** to time how long the water takes to drain.

4. Pour the water from the saucer into a **measuring cup.** Record the amount of water.

5. Repeat steps 2–4 with the two other cups, but fill one cup with **soil** and one with **gravel,** not sand.

6. Calculate the rates of drainage for each cup by dividing the amount of water that drained by the time the water took to drain.

7. For each cup, calculate the percentage of water retained by subtracting the amount of water drained from 120 mL. Divide this volume by 120.

Analysis

1. Which cup had the highest drainage rate?

2. A sample with a high drainage rate and a low percentage of water retained is highly permeable. Which sample was the most permeable? Which sample was the least permeable?

Zones of Aquifers

Gravity pulls water down through soil and rock layers until the water reaches impermeable rock. Water then begins to fill, or saturate, the spaces in the rock above the impermeable layer. As more water soaks into the ground, the water level rises underground and forms two distinct zones of groundwater, as shown in **Figure 3**.

Zone of Saturation

The layer of an aquifer in which the pore space is completely filled with water is the *zone of saturation*. The term *saturated* means "filled to capacity." The zone of saturation is the lower of the two zones of groundwater. The upper surface of the zone of saturation is called the **water table.**

Zone of Aeration

The zone that lies between the water table and Earth's surface is called the *zone of aeration*. The zone of aeration is composed of three regions. The uppermost region of the zone of aeration holds soil moisture—water that forms a film around grains of topsoil. The bottom region, just above the water table, is the capillary fringe. Water is drawn up from the zone of saturation into the capillary fringe by capillary action. *Capillary action* is caused by the attraction of water molecules to other materials, such as soil. For example, when a paper towel soaks up a spill, capillary action draws moisture into the towel. Between the soil moisture region and the capillary fringe is a region that is dry—except during periods of rain—and thus contains air in its pores.

Reading Check What are the two zones of groundwater? (See the Appendix for answers to Reading Checks.)

water table the upper surface of underground water; the upper boundary of the zone of saturation

Developed and maintained by the National Science Teachers Association

For a variety of links related to this chapter, go to www.scilinks.org

Topic: Groundwater
SciLinks code: HQ60699

Figure 3 ▶ Groundwater is divided into zones that are defined by the percentage of water in a given volume of rock.

Capillary fringe

Soil moisture region

Water table

Zone of aeration

Zone of saturation

Movement of Groundwater

Like water on Earth's surface, groundwater flows downward in response to gravity. Water passes quickly through highly permeable rock and slowly through rock that is less permeable. The rate at which groundwater flows horizontally depends on both the permeability of the aquifer and the gradient of the water table. *Gradient* is the steepness of a slope. The velocity of groundwater increases as the water table's gradient increases.

Topography and the Water Table

The depth of the water table below the ground surface depends on surface topography, the permeability of the aquifer, the amount of rainfall, and the rate at which humans use the water. Generally, shallow water tables match the contours of the surface, as shown in **Figure 4.** During periods of prolonged rainfall, the water table rises. During periods of drought, the water table falls and flattens because water that leaves the aquifer is not replaced.

Only one water table exists in most areas. In some areas, however, a layer of impermeable rock lies above the main water table. This rock layer prevents water from reaching the main zone of saturation. Water collects on top of this upper layer and creates a second water table, which is called a *perched water table*.

✓ **Reading Check** What four factors affect the depth of a water table? (See the Appendix for answers to Reading Checks.)

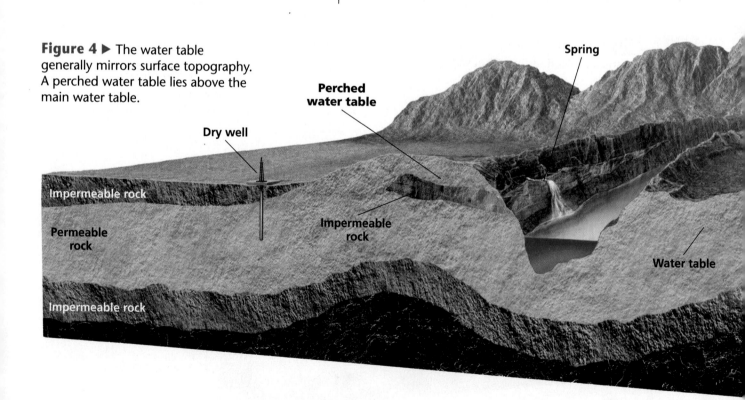

Figure 4 ▶ The water table generally mirrors surface topography. A perched water table lies above the main water table.

Spring

Perched water table

Dry well

Impermeable rock

Permeable rock

Impermeable rock

Impermeable rock

Water table

Conserving Groundwater

In many communities, groundwater is the only source of fresh water. Although groundwater is renewable, its long renewal time limits its supply. Groundwater collects and moves slowly, and the water taken from aquifers may not be replenished for hundreds or thousands of years. Communities often regulate the use of groundwater to help conserve this valuable resource. They can monitor the level of the local water table and discourage excess pumping. Some communities recycle used water. This water is purified and may be used to replenish the groundwater supply.

Surface water enters an aquifer through an area called a recharge zone. A *recharge zone* is anywhere that water from the surface can travel through permeable rock to reach an aquifer, as shown in **Figure 4.** Recharge zones are environmentally sensitive areas because pollution in the recharge zone can enter the aquifer. Therefore, recharge zones are often labeled by signs like the one shown in **Figure 5.** Pollution can enter an aquifer from waste dumps and underground storage tanks for toxic chemicals, from fertilizers and pesticides used in agriculture and on lawns, or from leaking sewage systems. If too much groundwater is pumped from an aquifer that is near the ocean, salt water from the ocean can then flow into the aquifer and contaminate the groundwater supply.

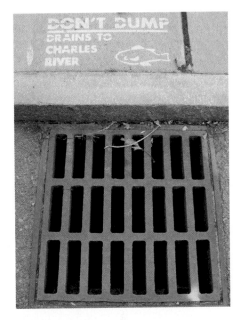

Figure 5 ▶ Water that enters this drain runs off into the Charles River and surrounding aquifers in Massachusetts.

Recharge zone

Ordinary well

Aquifer

Wells and Springs

Groundwater reaches Earth's surface through wells and springs. A *well* is a hole that is dug to below the level of the water table and through which groundwater is brought to Earth's surface. A *spring* is a natural flow of groundwater to Earth's surface in places where the ground surface dips below the water table. Wells and springs are classified into two groups—ordinary and artesian.

Ordinary Wells and Springs

Ordinary wells work only if they penetrate highly permeable sediment or rock below the water table. If the rock is not permeable enough, groundwater cannot flow into the well quickly enough to replace the water that is withdrawn.

Pumping water from a well lowers the water table around the well and forms a *cone of depression*, as shown in **Figure 6.** If too much water is taken from a well, the cone of depression may drop to the bottom of the well and the well will go dry. The lowered water table may extend several kilometers around the well and may cause surrounding wells to become dry.

Ordinary springs are usually found in rugged terrain where the ground surface drops below the water table. These springs may not flow continuously if the water table in the area has an irregular depth as a result of variable rainfall. Springs that form from perched water tables that intersect the ground surface are very sensitive to the amount of local precipitation. Thus, these springs may go dry during dry seasons or severe droughts.

Graphic
Organizer Venn Diagram
Create the Graphic Organizer entitled "Venn Diagram" described in the Skills Handbook section of the Appendix. Label the circles "Ordinary wells" and "Artesian wells." Then, fill in the diagram with characteristics that are common to both types of wells.

Figure 6 ▶ A cone of depression develops in the water table around a pumping well.

Cone of depression

Ordinary well

Flow of water

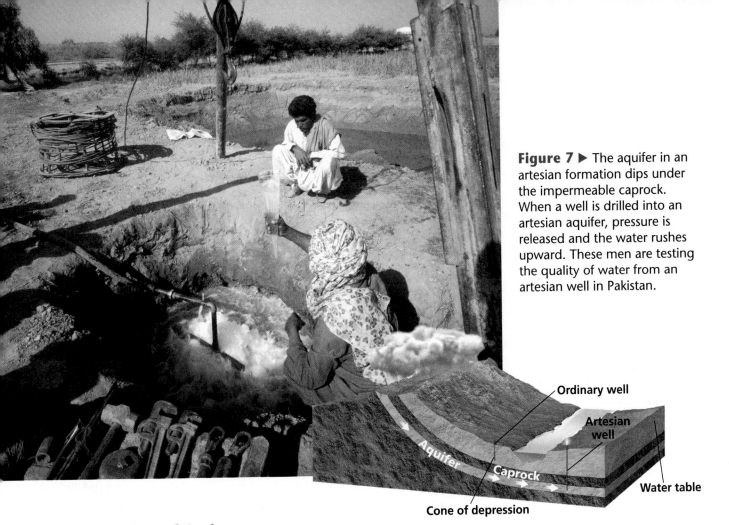

Figure 7 ▶ The aquifer in an artesian formation dips under the impermeable caprock. When a well is drilled into an artesian aquifer, pressure is released and the water rushes upward. These men are testing the quality of water from an artesian well in Pakistan.

Ordinary well

Artesian well

Aquifer

Caprock

Water table

Cone of depression

Artesian Wells and Springs

The groundwater that supplies many wells comes from local precipitation. However, the water in some wells may come from as far away as hundreds of kilometers. Water may travel through an aquifer to a distant location. Because the aquifer is so extensive, it may become part of an artesian formation, an arrangement of permeable and impermeable rock.

An **artesian formation** is a sloping layer of permeable rock that is sandwiched between two layers of impermeable rock, as shown in **Figure 7.** The permeable rock is the aquifer, and the top layer of impermeable rock is called the *caprock*. Water enters the aquifer at a recharge zone and flows downhill through the aquifer. As the water flows downward, the weight of the overlying water causes pressure in the aquifer to increase. Because the water is under pressure, when a well is drilled through the caprock, the water quickly flows up through the well and may even spout from the surface. An *artesian well* is a well through which water flows freely without being pumped.

Artesian formations are also the source of water for some springs. When cracks occur naturally in the caprock, water from the aquifer flows through the cracks. This flow forms *artesian springs*.

✔ **Reading Check** What is the difference between ordinary springs and artesian springs? (See the Appendix for answers to Reading Checks.)

artesian formation a sloping layer of permeable rock sandwiched between two layers of impermeable rock and exposed at the surface

Figure 8 ▶ The vent and underground chambers of a geyser enable water to become superheated and to eventually erupt to the surface.

Hot Springs

Groundwater is heated when it passes through rock that has been heated by magma. Hot groundwater that is at least 37°C and that rises to the surface before cooling produces a *hot spring*. When water in a hot spring cools, the water deposits minerals around the spring's edges. The deposits form steplike terraces of calcite called *travertine*. *Mud pots* form when chemically weathered rock mixes with hot water to form a sticky, liquid clay that bubbles at the surface. Mud pots are called *paint pots* when the clay is brightly colored by minerals or organic materials.

Geysers

Hot springs that periodically erupt from surface pools or through small vents are called *geysers*. A geyser consists of a narrow vent that connects one or more underground chambers with the surface. The hot rocks that make up the chamber walls superheat the groundwater. The water in the vent exerts pressure on the water in the chambers, which keeps the water in the chambers from boiling for a time. When the water in the vent finally begins to boil, the boiling water produces steam that pushes the water above it to the surface. Release of the water near the top of the vent relieves the pressure on the superheated water farther down. With the sudden release of pressure, the superheated water changes into steam and explodes toward the surface, as shown in **Figure 8**. The eruption continues until most of the water and steam are emptied from the vent and chambers. After the eruption, groundwater begins to collect again and the process is repeated, often at regular intervals.

Section 1 **Review**

1. **Identify** the difference between porosity and permeability, and explain how permeability affects the flow of groundwater. 9c

2. **Name and describe** the two zones of groundwater. 9c

3. **Describe** how the contour of a shallow water table compares with the local topography. 9c

4. **Explain** why ordinary springs often flow intermittently. 9c

5. **Define** the term *cone of depression*. 9c

6. **Compare** the rock layers in an artesian formation with those in an ordinary aquifer. 9c

7. **Compare** artesian wells and ordinary wells. 9c

CRITICAL THINKING

8. **Making Inferences** Which type of well would provide a community with a more constant source of water: an ordinary well or an artesian well? Explain your answer. 9c, IE.1d

9. **Identifying Relationships** Why is protecting the environment from pollution important for communities in recharge zones? 9c, IE.1d, IE.1m

10. **Analyzing Ideas** Why don't shallow pools of hot water erupt the way that geysers erupt?

CONCEPT MAPPING

11. Use the following terms to create a concept map: *groundwater, water table, zone of saturation,* and *zone of aeration.* 9c

7c Students know the movement of matter among reservoirs is driven by Earth's internal and external sources of energy.

9c Students know the importance of water to society, the origins of California's fresh water, and the relationship between supply and need.

IE.1l Students will analyze situations and solve problems that require combining and applying concepts from more than one area of science.

As groundwater passes through permeable rock, minerals in the rock dissolve. The warmer the rock is and the longer it is in contact with water, the greater the amount of dissolved minerals in the water. Water that contains relatively high concentrations of dissolved minerals, especially minerals rich in calcium, magnesium, and iron, is called *hard water*. Water that contains relatively low concentrations of dissolved minerals is called *soft water*.

Many people think that using hard water is unappealing. For example, more soap is needed to produce suds in hard water than in soft water. Also, many people prefer not to drink hard water because of its metallic taste. Some household appliances or fixtures may be damaged by the buildup of mineral deposits from hard water. **Figure 1** shows some results of the long-term presence of hard water.

Results of Weathering by Groundwater

One way that minerals become dissolved in groundwater is through chemical weathering. As water moves through soil and other organic materials, the water combines with carbon dioxide to form carbonic acid. This weak acid chemically weathers the rock that the acid passes through by breaking down and dissolving the minerals in the rock.

OBJECTIVES

▶ **Describe** how water chemically weathers rock. 🌅 **7c**

▶ **Explain** how caverns and sinkholes form. 🌅 **7c**

▶ **Identify** two features of karst topography. 🌅 **7c**

KEY TERMS

cavern
sinkhole
karst topography

Quick LAB 🕐 25 min

Chemical Weathering

Procedure 🌅 **7c, IE.1d**

1. Place **limestone, granite, pyrite,** and **chalk chips** into separate **small beakers**.

2. Cover the rocks in **1% HCl** solution.

3. After 20 min, observe the rocks.

Analysis

1. How have the rocks changed?

2. How is this process of change like the process of chemical weathering by groundwater?

Figure 1 ▶ Soap scum forms when soap reacts with calcium carbonate in hard water (inset). During high-water stages, hard water deposited a residue of calcium carbonate on the canyon walls that border this creek.

Figure 2 ▶ The formations in Carlsbad Caverns in New Mexico are made of calcite. *Which formations in this photo are stalagmites?*

cavern a natural cavity that forms in rock as a result of the dissolution of minerals; also a large cave that commonly contains many smaller, connecting chambers

Caverns

Rocks that are rich in the mineral calcite, such as limestone, are especially vulnerable to chemical weathering. Although limestone is not porous, vertical and horizontal cracks commonly cut through limestone layers. As groundwater flows through these cracks, carbonic acid slowly dissolves the limestone and enlarges the cracks. Eventually, a cavern may form. A **cavern** is a large cave that may consist of many smaller connecting chambers. Carlsbad Caverns in New Mexico is a good example of a large limestone cavern, as shown in **Figure 2**.

Stalactites and Stalagmites

Although a cavern that lies above the water table does not fill with water, water still passes through the rock surrounding the cavern. When water containing dissolved calcite drips from the ceiling of a limestone cavern, some of the calcite is deposited on the ceiling. As this calcite builds up, it forms a suspended, cone-shaped deposit called a *stalactite* (stuh LAK TIET). When drops of water fall on the cavern floor, calcite builds up to form an upward-pointing cone called a *stalagmite* (stuh LAG MIET). Often, a stalactite and a stalagmite will grow until they meet and form a calcite deposit called a *column*.

Connection to CHEMISTRY

How Water Dissolves Limestone

Water that falls as precipitation contains dissolved carbon dioxide, CO_2. This dissolved CO_2 causes the water to be slightly acidic. The formula for the dissolution of CO_2 is shown below.

Carbon dioxide reacts with **water** to form **carbonic acid: $H_2O + CO_2 = H_2CO_3$.**

Water that reaches the ground seeps into the soil. As the water passes through the soil, more CO_2 dissolves and the water becomes more acidic. The slightly acidic water enters fractures in limestone and dissolves the rock as the water moves through. The formula for the dissolution of limestone is shown below.

Carbonic acid dissolves **limestone** to form **calcium bicarbonate: $CaCO_3 + H_2CO_3 = Ca(HCO_3)_2$.**

Fractures widen over time, and caves develop underground. The calcium bicarbonate that forms when the limestone dissolves is deposited as the water drips and flows through the caves. This deposited calcium bicarbonate forms structures such as stalagmites and stalactites.

Carbon dioxide reacts with water to form carbonic acid.

Carbonic acid dissolves limestone to form calcium bicarbonate which is deposited in stalagmites and stalactites.

Sinkholes

A circular depression that forms at the surface when rock dissolves, when sediment is removed, or when caves or mines collapse is a **sinkhole.** Most sinkholes form by dissolution, in which the limestone or other rock dissolves where weak areas in the rock, such as fractures, previously existed. The dissolved material is carried away from the surface, and a small depression forms. *Subsidence sinkholes* form by a similar process except that as rock dissolves, overlying sediments settle into cracks in the rock and a depression forms.

Collapse sinkholes may form when sediment below the surface is removed and an empty space forms within the sediment layer. Eventually, the overlying sediments collapse into the empty space below. Collapse sinkholes may also form during dry periods, when the water table is low and caverns are not completely filled with water. Because water no longer supports the roof of the cavern, the roof may collapse. Collapse sinkholes may develop abruptly and cause extensive damage. A collapse sinkhole is shown in **Figure 3.**

Figure 3 ▶ When land overlying a cavern collapses to form a sinkhole, human-made structures, such as this highway, can be damaged.

sinkhole a circular depression that forms when rock dissolves, when overlying sediment fills an existing cavity, or when the roof of an underground cavern or mine collapses

Natural Bridges

When the roof of a cavern collapses in several places, a relatively straight line of sinkholes forms. The uncollapsed rock between each pair of sinkholes forms an arch of rock called a *natural bridge*, such as the one shown in **Figure 4.** When a natural bridge first forms, it is thick, but erosion causes the bridge to become thinner. Eventually, the natural bridge may collapse.

Reading Check How are sinkholes related to natural bridges? (See the Appendix for answers to Reading Checks.)

Figure 4 ▶ This natural bridge near San Marcos, Texas, formed when the roofs of two adjoining caverns collapsed.

Figure 5 ▶ The Stone Forest in Yunnan, China, is a dramatic example of karst topography.

karst topography a type of irregular topography that is characterized by caverns, sinkholes, and underground drainage and that forms on limestone or other soluble rock

Karst Topography

Irregular topography caused by the chemical weathering of limestone or other soluble rock by groundwater is called **karst topography.** Common features of karst topography include many closely spaced sinkholes and caverns. In karst regions, streams often disappear into cracks in the rock and then emerge in caves or through other cracks many kilometers away. In the United States, there is karst topography in Kentucky, Tennessee, southern Indiana, northern Florida, and Puerto Rico.

Generally, karst topography forms in regions where the climate is humid and where limestone formations exist at or near the surface. The plentiful precipitation in these regions commonly becomes groundwater. The groundwater flows through the limestone and reacts chemically with the calcite in the limestone. As the groundwater dissolves the limestone, cracks in the rock enlarge to form cave systems. Features of karst topography can form in relatively dry regions, too. In these areas, sinkholes may form very close together and leave dramatic arches and spires, as shown in **Figure 5.** Karst topography in these regions may indicate that the climate is becoming drier.

Section 2 Review

1. **Describe** how water chemically weathers rock. 7c

2. **Explain** how caverns form. 7c

3. **Explain** the difference between stalactites and stalagmites. 7c

4. **Identify** three common features of karst topography. 7c

5. **Describe** two ways in which a natural bridge might form.

6. **Compare** sinkholes and caverns. 7c

CRITICAL THINKING

7. **Making Inferences** If an area has a dry climate, how can the area have karst topography? 7c, IE.1d

8. **Identifying Relationships** Why might you expect to find springs in regions that have karst topography? 7c, IE.1d

CONCEPT MAPPING

9. Use the following terms to create a concept map: *groundwater, stalagmite, stalactite, natural bridge, cavern,* and *sinkhole.* 7c

Sections

1 Water Beneath the Surface

Key Terms

groundwater, 397
aquifer, 397
porosity, 397
permeability, 398
water table, 399
artesian formation, 403

Key Concepts

▶ Porosity and permeability determine how water moves through rock or sediment.

▶ Aquifers have two main zones—the zone of aeration and the zone of saturation. The upper surface of the zone of saturation is called the *water table*.

▶ The depth of the water table depends on the topography of the land, the permeability of the rock, the amount of rainfall, and the rate at which groundwater is used by humans.

▶ Groundwater can be polluted by wastes, agricultural and lawn fertilizers, agricultural and lawn pesticides, and sea water.

▶ Wells and springs may be ordinary or artesian. Artesian formations are the source of artesian wells and springs.

▶ Hot springs and geysers form when hot rock beneath Earth's surface heats groundwater.

2 Groundwater and Chemical Weathering

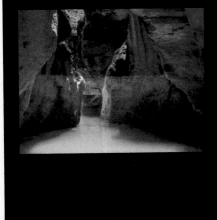

cavern, 406
sinkhole, 407
karst topography, 408

▶ Caverns form as a result of the chemical weathering of limestone.

▶ Stalagmites are calcite formations that form on the floor of a cavern. Stalactites are calcite formations that form on the roof of a cavern.

▶ Sinkholes form when rock dissolves, when sediment is removed, or when the roof of a cavern or mine collapses.

▶ Karst topography features closely spaced sinkholes, caverns, and streams that disappear into cracks in the rock and then emerge several kilometers away.

Using Key Terms

Use each of the following terms in a separate sentence.

1. *groundwater* 🔆9c
2. *water table* 🔆9c
3. *karst topography* 🔆7c

For each pair of terms, explain how the meanings of the terms differ.

4. *geyser* and *hot spring*
5. *porosity* and *permeability* 🔆9c
6. *well* and *spring* 🔆9c
7. *ordinary well* and *artesian well* 🔆9c
8. *stalactite* and *stalagmite* 🔆7c

Understanding Key Concepts

9. Any body of rock or sediment in which water can flow and be stored is called a(n) 🔆9c
   a. well.
   b. aquifer.
   c. sinkhole.
   d. artesian formation.

10. The percentage of open space in a given volume of rock is the rock's 🔆9c
    a. viscosity.
    c. permeability.
    b. capillary fringe.
    d. porosity.

11. The ease with which water can pass through a rock or sediment is called 🔆9c
    a. permeability.
    c. porosity.
    b. carbonation.
    d. velocity.

12. The slope of a water table is called the 🔆9c
    a. gradient.
    c. permeability.
    b. porosity.
    d. aquifer.

13. A natural flow of groundwater that has reached the surface is a(n) 🔆9c
    a. spring.
    c. aquifer.
    b. well.
    d. travertine.

14. Pumping water from a well causes a local lowering of the water table known as a 🔆9c
    a. cone of depression.
    b. horizontal fissure.
    c. hot spring.
    d. sinkhole.

15. Calcite formations that hang from the ceiling of a cavern are called 🔆7c
    a. stalagmites.
    c. stalactites.
    b. sinks.
    d. aquifers.

16. Regions where the results of weathering by groundwater are clearly visible have 🔆7c
    a. sink topography.
    b. karst topography.
    c. limestone topography.
    d. artesian formations.

17. When the roofs of several caverns collapse, the uncollapsed rock between sinkholes can form 🔆7c
    a. natural bridges.
    b. stalactites.
    c. limestone topography.
    d. artesian formations.

18. A layer of permeable rock that is sandwiched between layers of impermeable rock is called 🔆9c
    a. a natural bridge.
    b. karst topography.
    c. limestone topography.
    d. an artesian formation.

Short Answer

19. In regions where the water table is at the surface of the land, what type of terrain would you expect to find? 🔆9c

20. Explain the process that forms stalactites and stalagmites. Name another process in nature that produces shapes similar to the shapes of stalactites. 🔆7c

21. How does a mud pot form? 7c

22. Describe the zones of an aquifer. 9c

23. What are two ways that groundwater reaches Earth's surface? 9c

24. How are caverns and sinkholes related? 7c

25. What causes a geyser to erupt?

26. Why does it take a long time to replenish a depleted aquifer? 9c

Critical Thinking

27. Making Inferences In what type of location might pumping too much water from an aquifer lead to contamination of the groundwater supply? Explain how the water becomes contaminated. 9c, IE.1d, IE.1m

28. Analyzing Relationships Describe an artesian formation, and explain how the water in an artesian well may have entered the ground many hundreds of kilometers away. 9c, IE.1d

29. Analyzing Ideas Explain how a rock can be both porous and impermeable. 9c, IE.1d

30. Identifying Relationships Do you think that an area that has karst topography would have many surface streams or few surface streams? Explain your answer. 7c, IE.1d

Concept Mapping

31. Use the following terms to create a concept map: *porosity, sorting, permeability, ordinary well, artesian formation, highly permeable rock,* and *impermeable rock*. 9c

Math Skills

32. Evaluating Data People in Oklahoma use 11 billion gallons of water every day. The renewable water supply in Oklahoma is 68.7 billion gallons per day. What percentage of the renewable water supply do Oklahomans use every day? 9c

33. Making Conversions In an average aquifer, groundwater moves about 50 m per year. At this rate, how long would the groundwater take to flow 1 km? 9c

Writing Skills

34. Writing Persuasively Write a persuasive essay about the importance of conserving groundwater. 9c, IE.1m

35. Communicating Main Ideas Explain how overpumping at one well can affect groundwater availability in surrounding areas. 9c, IE.1m

Interpreting Graphics

The graph below shows the average annual decline in water level for the Ogallala Aquifer over 30 years. Use the graph below to answer the questions that follow.

Average Annual Rate of Decline by Decade for the Ogallala Aquifer, 1969–1999

36. Which region had the highest rate of decline from 1969 to 1999?

37. Over which decade did the aquifer have the lowest rate of decline?

38. Which years would you expect to have a higher rate of decline: the years 1999 to 2009 or the years 1989 to 1999? Explain your answer.

Understanding Concepts

Directions (1–10): **For *each* question, write on a separate sheet of paper the letter of the correct answer.**

1 Which of the following statements is FALSE?
A. Permeability affects flow through an aquifer.
B. Groundwater can be stored in an aquifer.
C. Aquifers are always a single rock layer.
D. Well-sorted sediment holds the most water.

2 The amount of surface water that seeps into the pores between rock particles is influenced by which of the following factors?
A. rock type, land slope, and climate
B. rock type, land slope, and capillary fringe
C. rock type, land slope, and sea level
D. rock type, land slope, and recharging

3 Shanghai removed 96.03 million cubic meters of groundwater in 2002 but replaced only 13.75 million cubic meters. What was the rate of groundwater depletion in Shanghai that year?
A. 109.78 million cubic meters of groundwater
B. 1,320.41 million cubic meters of groundwater
C. 6.98 million cubic meters of groundwater
D. 82.28 million cubic meters of groundwater

4 The formation of karst topography is caused by
A. the physical weathering of limestone.
B. the chemical weathering of limestone.
C. closely-spaced sinkholes.
D. irregular topography.

5 What quality distinguishes an ordinary well from an artesian well?
A. Water flows freely from an ordinary well.
B. Water is pressurized in an ordinary well.
C. Water must be pumped from an ordinary well.
D. Water comes from rainfall in an ordinary well.

6 Which of the following sediments has the highest porosity?
A. poorly sorted sediment
B. tightly packed sediments
C. coarse-grained sediment
D. fine-grained sediment

7 Many communities regulate or monitor the use of groundwater to conserve water resources. One way by which communities can conserve ground water is
A. pumping water from an aquifer and storing it elsewhere.
B. recycling used water.
C. allowing water to drain from sewage systems into an aquifer.
D. enlarging a recharge zone.

8 Which of the following statements best describes the relationship between porosity and permeability?
A. Porosity and permeability are not related.
B. Porosity describes how water flows through permeable rock.
C. Permeability is the ease with which water passes through porous rock.
D. Porous rock is always permeable.

9 Which of the following statements is NOT a way that sinkholes form?
A. Rock collapses and dissolves, leaving a sinkhole.
B. Sediments dissolve, leaving an empty space into which overlying sediments collapse.
C. Rock dissolves, and overlying sediment settles into cracks.
D. Rock dissolves and is carried away, leaving a small depression.

10 How does groundwater break down limestone?
A. by mechanical weathering
B. by forming a weak acid
C. by carrying a load
D. by absorbing minerals

Interpreting Graphics

Directions (11–12): **For *each* question below, record the correct answer on a separate sheet of paper.**

The Water Cycle

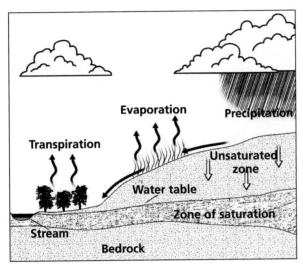

11 Which process occurs where the water table intersects with the surface?
A. stream formation
B. runoff
C. groundwater movement
D. saturation

Water Use for a Family of Four

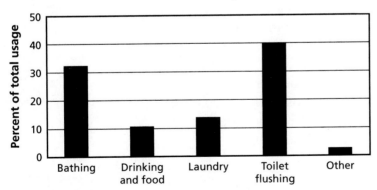

12 A family of four wants to conserve water by halving their water use in one of the five areas described in the graph above. In which area should the family halve their water use to yield the greatest conservation of water?
A. bathing
B. drinking and food
C. laundry
D. toilet flushing

Objectives

▶ **USING SCIENTIFIC METHODS**
Measure the porosity of a given volume of beads for each of three samples: large beads, small beads, and a mix of large and small beads.

▶ **Describe** how particle size and sorting of a material affect porosity.

Materials

beads, plastic, 4 mm (400)

beads, plastic, 8 mm (200)

beaker, 100 mL

graduated cylinder, 100 mL

Safety

Porosity 🖾 9c, IE.1d, IE.1a

Whether soil is composed of coarse pieces of rock or very fine particles, some pore space remains between the pieces of solid material. Porosity is calculated by dividing the volume of the pore space by the total volume of the soil sample. Thus, if 50 cm^3 of soil contains 5.0 cm^3 of pore space, the porosity of the soil sample is

$$5.0 \text{ cm}^3/50 \text{ cm}^3 = 0.10 \times 100 = 10\%.$$

The result is generally written as a percentage. In this lab, you will measure and compare the porosity of three samples that represent rock particles.

PROCEDURE

1 Fill a beaker to the top with water. Pour the water into a graduated cylinder and record the volume of water.

2 Dry the beaker, and fill it to the top with large (8 mm) plastic beads. Gently tap the beaker to settle and compact the beads. Add more beads to fill the beaker until the beads are level with the top. Record the total volume of the beads, which includes the pore space volume.

3 Fill the graduated cylinder with water to the top mark, and record the volume of water. Carefully pour the water from the cylinder into the beaker filled with the large beads until the water level just reaches the top of the beads.

Step 3

4. To determine the amount of water that you added to the beaker, subtract the volume of water in the graduated cylinder from the volume that you recorded in step 3. This difference is the volume of the pore space between the beads. Record the volume of the pore space.

5. Calculate the porosity of the beads. Record the porosity as a decimal and as a percentage.

6. Repeat steps 2–5 using small (4 mm) beads.

7. Drain and dry both sets of beads. Mix together equal volumes of the small and large beads. Using the mixed-size beads, repeat steps 2–5.

Step 4

ANALYSIS AND CONCLUSION

1. **Analyzing Methods** Do the 8 mm beads in step 2 represent well-sorted large rock particles, well-sorted small rock particles, or unsorted rock particles?

2. **Analyzing Methods** Do the 4 mm beads in step 6 represent well-sorted large rock particles, well-sorted small rock particles, or unsorted rock particles?

3. **Analyzing Methods** Do the mixed beads in step 7 represent well-sorted or unsorted rock particles?

4. **Making Graphs** Compare the porosity of the large beads with the porosity of the small beads. Make a graph that shows bead size on the x-axis and porosity on the y-axis.

5. **Drawing Conclusions** In well-sorted sediment, does porosity depend on particle size? Explain your answer.

6. **Determining Cause and Effect** How did mixing the bead sizes affect the porosity? Explain the effect.

Extension

1. **Designing Experiments** How would mixing coarse gravel with fine sand affect the porosity of the gravel? Conduct an experiment to find out if your answer is correct.

Water Level in the Southern Ogallala

KEY

WATER–LEVEL CHANGE,
IN FEET, 1980 TO 1999

Declines
- More than 60
- 40 to 60
- 20 to 40
- 10 to 20
- 5 to 10

No significant change
- –5 to 5

Rises
- 5 to 10
- 10 to 20
- 20 to 40
- More than 40

Area of little or no saturated thickness

Area with 50 to 100 feet of water–level
decline, predevelopment to 1980
(Luckey and others, 1981)

Area with 100 to 175 feet of water–level
decline, predevelopment to 1980
(Luckey and others, 1981)

Map Skills Activity

This map shows water-level change in regions of the Ogallala Aquifer, which supplies much of the drinking water in the midwestern United States. Use the map to answer the questions below.

1. **Using a Key** From predevelopment to 1980, how many areas had a decline in water level of 50 to 100 ft?

2. **Using a Key** From 1980 to 1999, how many areas had a decline in water level of more than 60 ft?

3. **Making Comparisons** Is the area in which the water level declined 50 to 100 ft before 1980 larger than or smaller than the area in which the water level declined more than 60 ft from 1980 to 1999?

4. **Identifying Trends** Has the overall amount of decline in the water-table level increased or decreased since 1980?

5. **Analyzing Relationships** What may have caused the trend that you identified in question 4? What may have changed between 1980 and 1999 that could account for the trend?

Disappearing Land

On May 8, 1981, in Winter Park, Florida, a resident saw a sycamore tree disappear. A sinkhole had swallowed the tree, and that disappearance was only the beginning.

When it first appeared, at about 8:00 P.M., the cone-shaped sinkhole was 13 m wide and 7 m deep. Overnight, the hole expanded to a diameter of 27 m. Before noon the next day, the hole expanded to a size of 300 m in diameter—the size of a football field—and 37 m deep. In the process, it consumed about 160,000 m^3 of ground.

The Winter Park Sinkhole

This destructive sinkhole resulted from a combination of natural processes and human activities. Collapse sinkholes, such as the one in Winter Park, occur when the sediment overlying a cavern collapses into a cavity formed by groundwater. However, the rapid expansion of this sinkhole may have been the result of the collapse of the cavern roof. Such a collapse may have resulted from the removal of too much water from an aquifer that was already depleted after a two-year drought.

The Money Pit

Eventually, the Winter Park sinkhole swallowed up several houses, part of a four-lane highway, a swimming pool, a parking lot, five cars, and a truck. The cost of the damage reached about $2 million. When the sinkhole finally stabilized, the city of Winter Park turned the hole into a municipal lake.

Extension

1. **Applying Ideas** What might Winter Park residents do to prevent the formation of more sinkholes?

Winter Park, Florida

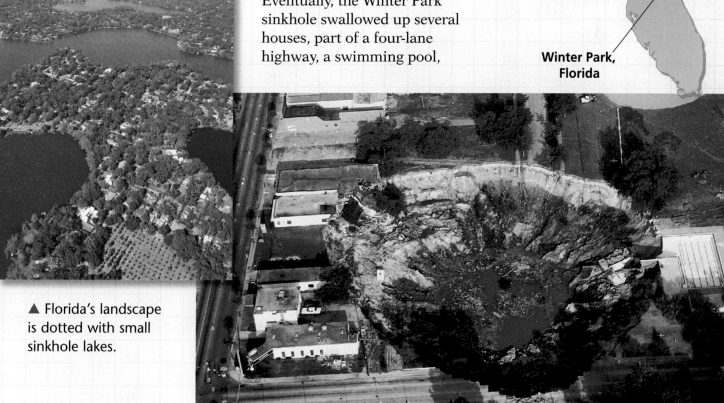

▲ Florida's landscape is dotted with small sinkhole lakes.

Sections

1 Glaciers: Moving Ice

2 Glacial Erosion and Deposition

3 Ice Ages

What You'll Learn

- How glaciers form and move
- What landforms glaciers create
- What factors drive glacial cycles

Why It's Relevant

Earth's surface was reshaped by glaciers during the last glacial period. Glaciers provide information about past and present climates and are key indicators of current climatic change.

PRE-READING ACTIVITY

Double Door
Before you read the chapter, create the FoldNote entitled "Double Door" described in the Skills Handbook section of the Appendix. Write "Alpine glaciers" on one flap of the double door and "Continental glaciers" on the other flap. As you read the chapter, write the characteristics of each type of glacier under the appropriate flap.

▶ The brilliant blue color of Alaska's Mendenhall Glacier is characteristic of glacial ice. Ice crystals in the glacier scatter more blue light than any other color, which makes the ice look blue.

 California Content Standards

6c Students know how Earth's climate has changed over time, corresponding to changes in Earth's geography, atmospheric composition, and other factors, such as solar radiation and plate movement.

7c Students know the movement of matter among reservoirs is driven by Earth's internal and external sources of energy.

IE.1a Students will select and use appropriate tools and technology (such as computer-linked probes, spreadsheets, and graphing calculators) to perform tests, collect data, analyze relationships and display data.

IE.1d Students will formulate explanations using logic and evidence.

IE.1g Students will recognize the usefulness and limitations of models and theories as scientific representations of reality.

IE.1i Students will analyze the locations, sequences, or time intervals that are characteristic of natural phenomena (e.g., relative ages of rocks, locations of planets over time, and succession of species in an ecosystem).

IE.1k Students will recognize the cumulative nature of scientific evidence.

IE.1l Students will analyze situations and solve problems that require combining and applying concepts from more than one area of science.

IE.1m Students will investigate a science-based societal issue by researching the literature, analyzing data, and communicating the findings. Examples of issues include irradiation of food, cloning of animals by somatic cell nuclear transfer, choice of energy sources, and land and water use decisions in California.

<table><tr><td>**Section** 1</td><td># Glaciers: Moving Ice</td></tr></table>

California Content Standards

IE.1d Students will formulate explanations using logic and evidence.

A single snowflake is lighter than a feather. However, if you squeeze a handful of snow, you make a firm snowball. In a process similar to making a snowball, natural forces compact snow to make a large mass of moving ice called a **glacier.**

Formation of Glaciers

At high elevations and in polar regions, snow may remain on the ground all year and form an almost motionless mass of permanent snow and ice called a *snowfield*. Snowfields form as ice and snow accumulate above the snowline. The *snowline* is the elevation above which ice and snow remain throughout the year, as shown in **Figure 1.**

Average temperatures at high elevations and in polar regions are always near or below the freezing point of water. So, snow that falls there accumulates year after year. Cycles of partial melting and refreezing change the snow into grainy ice called *firn*.

In deep layers of snow and firn, the pressure of the overlying layers flattens the ice grains and squeezes the air from between the grains. The continued buildup of snow and firn forms a glacier that moves downslope or outward under its own weight.

The size of a glacier depends on the amount of snowfall received and the amount of ice lost. When new snow is added faster than ice and snow melt, the glacier gets bigger. When the ice melts faster than snow is added, the glacier gets smaller. Small differences in average yearly temperatures and snowfall may upset the balance between snowfall and ice loss. Thus, changes in the size of a glacier may indicate climatic change.

OBJECTIVES

▶ **Describe** how glaciers form.

▶ **Compare** two main kinds of glaciers.

▶ **Explain** two processes by which glaciers move.

▶ **Describe** three features of glaciers.

KEY TERMS

glacier
alpine glacier
continental glacier
basal slip
internal plastic flow
crevasse

glacier a large mass of moving ice

Figure 1 ▶ The snowline on the Grand Teton Mountains at Grand Teton National Park, Wyoming, is more than 3000 m above sea level.

Figure 2 ▶ An alpine glacier (above) descends through Thompson Pass in Alaska. A continental glacier (right) covers much of the land surface in Greenland.

alpine glacier a narrow, wedge-shaped mass of ice that forms in a mountainous region and that is confined to a small area by surrounding topography; examples include valley glaciers, cirque glaciers, and piedmont glaciers

continental glacier a massive sheet of ice that may cover millions of square kilometers, that may be thousands of meters thick, and that is not confined by surrounding topography

Types of Glaciers

The two main categories used to classify glaciers are alpine and continental. An **alpine glacier** is a narrow, wedge-shaped mass of ice that forms in a mountainous region and that is confined to a small area by surrounding topography, as shown in **Figure 2.** Alpine glaciers are located in Alaska, the Himalaya Mountains, the Andes, the Alps, and New Zealand.

  Continental glaciers are massive sheets of ice that may cover millions of square kilometers, that may be thousands of meters thick, and that are not confined by surrounding topography, as shown in **Figure 2.** Today, continental glaciers, also called *ice sheets*, exist only in Greenland and Antarctica. The Antarctic ice sheet covers an area of more than 13 million km^2 and is more than 4,000 m thick in some places. The Greenland ice sheet covers 1.7 million km^2 of land, and its maximum thickness is more than 3,000 m. If these ice sheets melted, the water they contain would raise the worldwide sea level by more than 80 m.

✓ **Reading Check** Where can you find continental glaciers today? (See the Appendix for answers to Reading Checks.)

Movement of Glaciers

Glaciers are sometimes called "rivers of ice." Gravity causes both glaciers and rivers to flow downward. However, glaciers and rivers move in different ways. Unlike water in a river, glacial ice cannot move rapidly or flow easily around barriers. In a year, some glaciers may travel only a few centimeters, while others may move a kilometer or more. Glaciers move by two basic processes—basal slip and internal plastic flow.

Basal Slip

One way that glaciers move is by slipping over a thin layer of water and sediment that lies between the ice and the ground. The weight of the ice in a glacier exerts pressure that lowers the melting point of ice. As a result, the ice melts where the glacier touches the ground. The water mixes with sediment at the base of the glacier. This mixture acts as a lubricant between the ice and the underlying surface. The process that lubricates a glacier's base and causes the glacier to slide forward is called **basal slip.**

Basal slip also allows a glacier to work its way over small barriers in its path by melting and then refreezing. For example, if the ice pushes against a rock barrier, the pressure causes some of the ice to melt. The water from the melted ice travels around the barrier and freezes again as the pressure is removed.

Internal Plastic Flow

Glaciers also move by a process called **internal plastic flow.** In this process, pressure deforms grains of ice under a glacier. As the grains deform, they slide over each other and cause the glacier to flow slowly. However, the rate of internal plastic flow varies for different parts of a glacier, as shown in **Figure 3.** The slope of the ground and the thickness and temperature of the ice determine the rate at which ice flows at a given point. The edges of a glacier move more slowly than the center because of friction with underlying rock. For this same reason, a glacier moves more quickly near its surface than near its base.

basal slip the process that causes the ice at the base of a glacier to melt and the glacier to slide

internal plastic flow the process by which glaciers flow slowly as grains of ice deform under pressure and slide over each other

QuickLAB ⏱ 15 min

Slipping Ice
Procedure 🏷 IE.1d
1. Squeeze flat a handful of **snow** or **shaved ice** until you notice a change in the particles.
2. Place the squeezed ice on a **tray.** Place a **heavy weight** on the squeezed ice.
3. Lift one end of the tray to a 30° incline, and record your observations.

Analysis
1. What does squeezing do to the particles of snow or ice?
2. How is squeezing the snow or ice similar to the formation of a glacier?
3. What did you observe when you placed the squeezed ice on the tray? What glacial movement process is modeled here?

Fastest rate of ice flow

Figure 3 ▶ A line of blue stakes driven into a alpine glacier moves to the position of the red stakes as the glacier flows. This measurement shows that the central part of the glacier moves faster than its edges.

Figure 4 ▶ Crevasses (right) are large cracks in a glacier. The composite photograph below shows what an iceberg might look like if you could see the entire iceberg.

crevasse in a glacier, a large crack or fissure that results from ice movement

Features of Glaciers

While the interior of a glacier moves by internal plastic flow and the entire glacier moves by basal slip, the low pressure on the surface ice causes the surface ice to remain brittle. The glacier flows unevenly beneath the surface, and regions of tension and compression build under the brittle surface. As a result, large cracks, called **crevasses** (kruh VAS uhz), form on the surface, as shown in **Figure 4.** Some crevasses may be as deep as 50 m!

Continental glaciers move outward in all directions from their centers toward the edges of their landmasses. Some parts of the ice sheets may move out over the ocean and form *ice shelves*. When the tides rise and fall, large blocks of ice, called *icebergs*, may break from the ice shelves and drift into the ocean. Because most of an iceberg is below the surface of the water, as shown in **Figure 4,** icebergs pose a hazard to ships. The area above water of one of the largest icebergs ever observed in the Antarctic was twice the size of Connecticut!

Section 1 Review

1. **Identify** two regions in which snow accumulates year after year.

2. **Describe** the process by which glaciers form.

3. **Compare** an alpine glacier and a continental glacier.

4. **Explain** how internal plastic flow and basal slip move glaciers.

5. **Describe** two features of glaciers.

6. **Compare** a glacier and a snowfield.

7. **Explain** how a crevasse forms.

CRITICAL THINKING

8. **Making Inferences** If glaciers could move only by internal plastic flow, what might happen to the rate at which glaciers move? Explain your answer. IE.1d

9. **Identifying Relationships** How can changes in the size of a glacier indicate climate change? IE.1d

10. **Analyzing Ideas** If icebergs are visible at sea level, why do they pose a hazard to ships? IE.1d

CONCEPT MAPPING

11. Use the following terms to create a concept map: *glacier, firn, snowline, snowfield, alpine glacier, continental glacier, basal slip, internal plastic flow, ice shelf, iceberg,* and *crevasse.*

7c Students know the movement of matter among reservoirs is driven by Earth's internal and external sources of energy.

IE.1d Students will formulate explanations using logic and evidence.
IE.1l Students will analyze situations and solve

problems that require combining and applying concepts from more than one area of science.

Many of the landforms in Canada and in the northern United States were created by glaciers. Large lakes, solitary boulders on flat plains, and jagged ridges are just a few examples of landforms created by glaciers. Glaciers created these landforms through the processes of erosion and deposition.

Glacial Erosion

Like rivers, glaciers are agents of erosion. Both a river and a glacier can pick up and carry rock and sediment. However, because of the size and density of glaciers, landforms that result from glacial action are very different from those that rivers form. For example, deep depressions in rock form when a moving glacier loosens and dislodges, or plucks, a rock from the bedrock at the base or side of the glacier. The rock plucked by the glacier is then dragged across the bedrock and causes abrasions. As shown in **Figure 1**, long parallel grooves in the bedrock are left behind and show the direction of the glacier's movement.

OBJECTIVES

▶ **Describe** the landscape features that are produced by glacial erosion. 🐻 7c

▶ **Name** and describe five features formed by glacial deposition. 🐻 7c

▶ **Explain** how glacial lakes form. 🐻 7c

KEY TERMS

cirque
arête
horn
erratic
glacial drift
till
moraine
kettle
esker

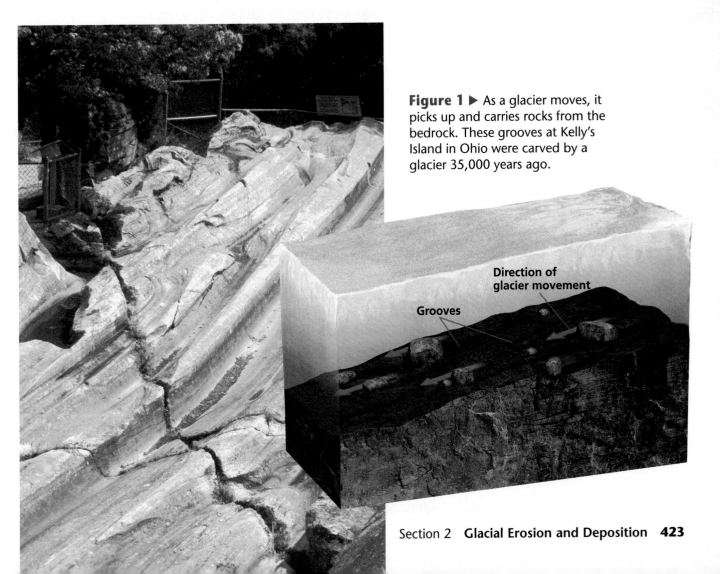

Figure 1 ▶ As a glacier moves, it picks up and carries rocks from the bedrock. These grooves at Kelly's Island in Ohio were carved by a glacier 35,000 years ago.

Direction of glacier movement

Grooves

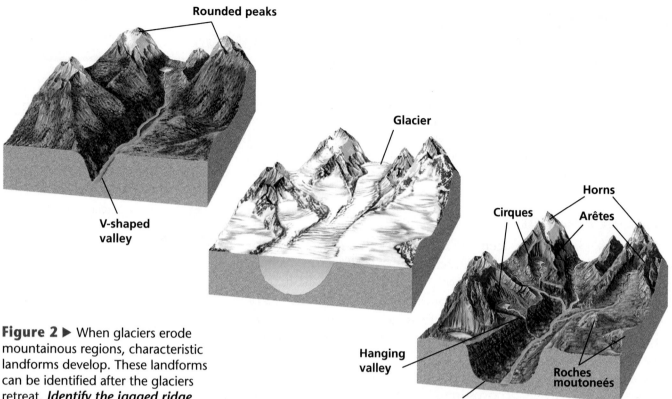

Rounded peaks

V-shaped valley

Glacier

Cirques

Horns

Arêtes

Hanging valley

Roches moutoneés

U-shaped valley

Figure 2 ▶ When glaciers erode mountainous regions, characteristic landforms develop. These landforms can be identified after the glaciers retreat. *Identify the jagged ridge that separates bowl-shaped depressions.*

cirque a deep and steep bowl-like depression produced by glacial erosion

arête a sharp, jagged ridge that forms between cirques

horn a sharp, pyramid-like peak that forms because of the erosion of cirques

Landforms Created by Glacial Erosion

Glaciers have shaped many mountain ranges and have created unique landforms by erosive processes. The glacial processes that change the shape of mountains begin in the upper end of the valley where an alpine glacier forms. As a glacier moves through a narrow, V-shaped river valley, rock from the valley walls breaks off and the walls become steeper. The moving glacier also pulls blocks of rock from the floor of the valley. These actions create a bowl-shaped depression called a **cirque** (SUHRK). A sharp, jagged ridge called an **arête** (uh RAYT) forms between cirques. When several arêtes join, they form a sharp, pyramid-like peak called a **horn**, as shown in **Figure 2**.

As the glacier flows down through an existing valley, the glacier picks up large amounts of rock. These rock fragments, which range in size from microscopic particles to large boulders, become embedded in the ice.

Rock particles embedded in the ice may polish solid rock as the ice moves over the rock. Large rocks carried by the ice may gouge deep grooves in the bedrock. Glaciers may also round large rock projections. These rounded projections usually have a smooth, gently sloping side facing the direction from which the glacier came. The other side is steep and jagged because rock is pulled away as the ice passes. The resulting rounded knobs of rock are called *roches moutonnées* (ROHSH moo tuh NAY), which means "sheep rocks" in French.

✓ Reading Check How does a glacier form a cirque? (See the Appendix for answers to Reading Checks.)

U-Shaped Valleys

A stream forms the V shape of a valley. As a glacier scrapes away a valley's walls and floor, this original V shape becomes a U shape, as shown in **Figure 3**. Because glacial erosion is the only way by which U-shaped valleys form, scientists can use this feature to determine whether a valley has been glaciated in the past.

Small tributary glaciers in adjacent valleys may flow into a main alpine glacier. Because a small tributary glacier has less ice and less cutting power than the main alpine glacier does, the small glacier's U-shaped valley is not cut as deeply into the mountains. When the ice melts, the tributary valley is suspended high above the main valley floor and is called a *hanging valley*. When a stream flows from a hanging valley, a waterfall forms.

Figure 3 ▶ Jollie Valley, a U-shaped glaciated valley, is located in the Southern Alps of New Zealand.

Erosion by Continental Glaciers

The landscape eroded by continental glaciers differs from the sharp, rugged features eroded by alpine glaciers. Continental glaciers erode by leveling landforms to produce a smooth, rounded landscape. Continental glaciers smooth and round exposed rock surfaces in a way similar to the way that bulldozers flatten landscapes. Rock surfaces are also scratched and grooved by rocks carried at the base of the ice sheet. These scratches and grooves are parallel to the direction of glacial movement.

Quick**LAB**   25 min

Glacial Erosion

Procedure 7c, IE.1d, IE.1g

1. Put a mixture of sand, gravel, and rock in the bottom of a 15 cm × 10 cm × 5 cm plastic container. Fill the container with water to a depth of about 4 cm. Freeze the container until the water is solid. Remove the ice block from the container.

2. Use a rolling pin or large dowel to flatten some modeling clay into a rectangle about 20 cm × 10 cm × 1 cm.

3. Grasp the ice block firmly with a hand towel. Place the block with the gravel-and-rock side down at one end of the clay. Press down on the ice block, and push it along the length of the flat clay surface.

4. Sketch the pattern made in the clay by the ice block.

5. Next, press a 2 cm layer of damp sand into the bottom of a shallow, rectangular box. As in step 3, push the ice block along the surface of the sand, but press down lightly.

6. Repeat steps 3 and 4, but use a soft, wooden board in place of the clay.

Analysis

1. Describe the effects of the ice block on the clay, on the sand, and on the wood.

2. Did any clay, sand, or wood become mixed with material from the ice block? Did the ice deposit material on any surface?

3. What glacial land features are represented by the features of the clay model? the sand model? the wood model?

Glacial Deposition

Glaciers are also agents of deposition. Deposition occurs when a glacier melts. A glacier will melt if it reaches low, warm elevations or if the climate becomes warmer. As the glacier melts, it deposits all of the material that it has accumulated, which may range in size from fine sediment to large rocks.

Large rocks that a glacier transports from a distant source are called **erratics.** Because a glacier carries an erratic a long distance, the composition of an erratic usually differs from that of the bedrock over which the erratic lies.

Various other landforms develop as glaciers melt and deposit sediment, as shown in **Figure 4.** The general term for all sediments deposited by a glacier is **glacial drift.** Unsorted glacial drift that is deposited directly from a melting glacier is called the **till.** Till is composed of sediments from the base of the glacier and is commonly left behind when glacial ice melts. Another type of glacial drift is stratified drift. *Stratified drift* is material that has been sorted and deposited in layers by streams flowing from the melted ice, or *meltwater.*

erratic a large rock transported from a distant source by a glacier

glacial drift rock material carried and deposited by glaciers

till unsorted rock material that is deposited directly by a melting glacier

Figure 4 ▶ Moraines, glacial lakes, drumlins, meltwater streams, and outwash plains are some examples of landforms created by glacial deposition.

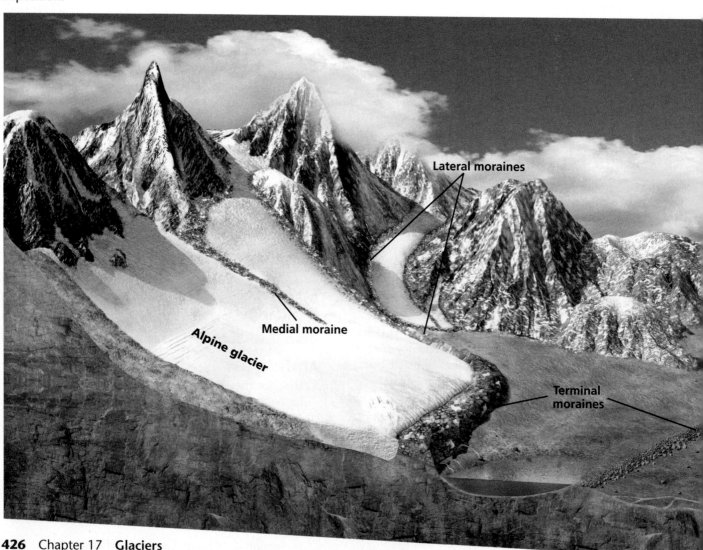

Lateral moraines

Medial moraine

Alpine glacier

Terminal moraines

Till Deposits

Landforms that result when a glacier deposits till are called *moraines*. **Moraines** are ridges of unsorted sediment on the ground or on the glacier itself. There are several types of moraines, as shown in **Figure 4**. A *lateral moraine* is a moraine that is deposited along the sides of an alpine glacier, usually as a long ridge. When two or more alpine glaciers join, their adjacent lateral moraines combine to form a *medial moraine*.

The unsorted material left beneath the glacier when the ice melts is the *ground moraine*. The soil of a ground moraine is commonly very rocky. An ice sheet may mold ground moraine into clusters of drumlins. *Drumlins* are long, low, tear-shaped mounds of till. The long axes of the drumlins are parallel to the direction of glacial movement.

Terminal moraines are small ridges of till that are deposited at the leading edge of a melting glacier. These moraines have many depressions that may contain lakes or ponds. Large terminal moraines, some of which are more than 100 km long, can be seen across the Midwest, especially south of the Great Lakes.

✓ Reading Check Which glacial deposit is a tear-shaped mound of sediment? (See the Appendix for answers to Reading Checks.)

moraine a landform that is made from unsorted sediments deposited by a glacier

Graphic Organizer Spider Map

Create the **Graphic Organizer** entitled "Spider Map" described in the Skills Handbook section of the Appendix. Label the circle "Moraines." Create a leg for each type of moraine. Then, fill in the map with details about each type of moraine.

Erratics

Outwash plain

Drumlins

Kettle

Meltwater streams

Continental glacier

427

Figure 5 ▶ This kettle lake in Saskatchewan, Canada, formed as a result of glacial deposition.

kettle a bowl-like depression in a glacial drift deposit

esker a long, winding ridge of gravel and coarse sand deposited by glacial meltwater streams

Outwash Plains

When a glacier melts, streams of meltwater flow from the edges, the surface, and beneath the glacier. Glacial meltwater may have beautiful colors, such as milky white, emerald green, or turquoise blue, because it carries very fine sediment. The meltwater carries drift as well as rock particles and deposits them in front of the glacier as a large outwash plain. An *outwash plain* is a deposit of stratified drift that lies in front of a terminal moraine and is crossed by many meltwater streams.

Kettles

Most outwash plains are pitted with depressions called **kettles.** A kettle forms when a chunk of glacial ice is buried in drift. As the ice melts, a cavity forms in the drift. The drift collapses into the cavity and produces a depression. Kettles commonly fill with water to form kettle lakes, such as the one shown in **Figure 5.**

Eskers

When continental glaciers recede, **eskers** (ES kuhrz)—long, winding ridges of gravel and sand—may be left behind. These ridges consist of stratified drift deposited by streams of meltwater that flow through ice tunnels within the glaciers. Eskers may extend for tens of kilometers, like raised, winding roadways.

✓ **Reading Check** How do eskers form? (See the Appendix for answers to Reading Checks.)

The Flooding of Venice

The city of Venice, Italy, is famous for its canals and priceless art treasures. Venice is built on about 120 islands in the Adriatic Sea.

A City Underwater

The waters of the Adriatic Sea constantly threaten Venice. Every year, winter storms cause sea water to flood the city's public squares, walkways, and buildings. Venice's famous St. Mark's Square may flood more than 100 times per year. Overexposure to floodwaters is slowly eroding the foundations of the city's Byzantine and Renaissance architecture. The city's sidewalks are buckled because the water has eroded the ground underneath them.

These floods are the result of three factors: erosion, rising sea level, and sinking land. Erosion of barrier beaches and sandbars allows high tides to reach farther into Venice. Also, the Adriatic Sea is rising. Its average sea level has risen 11 cm over the last 100 years, and Venice has sunk 13 cm.

The weight of added sediments is causing the city to sink about 1 mm per year. Removal of too much groundwater and the weight of the buildings within the city have caused additional sinkage.

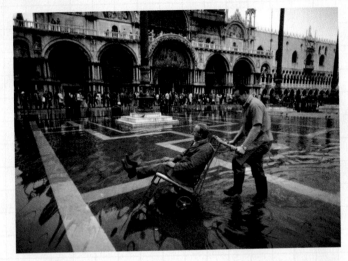

◄ Flooding in St. Mark's square invites residents to be creative about their transportation.

An Uncertain Future

To prevent future and permanent damage to Venice, the city restricts the pumping of groundwater. Pavement is often raised to help keep the city above water and to minimize erosion caused by floodwaters. Massive floodgates have been built to block high tides that threaten the city. In addition, city planners are constructing a system to pump fluids into the aquifer below the lagoon to raise the level of water in the aquifer.

◄ Flooding causes erosion in wood, brick, and stone. Many building foundations are slowly dissolving into the waters of the Adriatic Sea.

Extension

1. **Researching Trends**
   Research another area of the world that is grappling with regular flooding. How is that city or town dealing with the erosion that is caused by flooding?

▶ Oceans affect coastlines, climates, and aquatic life around the world. As shown in this satellite image of the Bahamas in the Caribbean Sea, ocean currents and tides have shaped the sand and seaweed beds so that from space the beds appear to be blue flames of a fire.

Sections

1 The Water Planet

2 Features of the Ocean Floor

3 Ocean-Floor Sediments

What You'll Learn

- Why scientists study the ocean
- What the features of the ocean basins are
- How ocean-floor sediments are classified

Why It's Relevant

The oceans interact with the atmosphere and the land to affect weather, climate, and the shape of continents. Exploration of the oceans explains how these interactions shape Earth's surface.

PRE-READING ACTIVITY

Booklet
Before you read the chapter, create the **FoldNote** entitled "Booklet" described in the Skills Handbook section of the Appendix. Label each page of the booklet with a main idea from the chapter. As you read the chapter, write what you learn about each main idea on the appropriate page of the booklet.

▶ The ocean floors contain evidence of changes in Earth over time and of human endeavors. This is the wreckage of the *Ora Verde,* a ship that was lost near the Grand Cayman Islands.

California Content Standards

3a Students know features of the ocean floor (magnetic patterns, age, and sea-floor topography) provide evidence of plate tectonics.

7c Students know the movement of matter among reservoirs is driven by Earth's internal and external sources of energy.

IE.1a Students will select and use appropriate tools and technology (such as computer-linked probes, spreadsheets, and graphing calculators) to perform tests, collect data, analyze relationships and display data.

IE.1d Students will formulate explanations using logic and evidence.

IE.1g Students will recognize the usefulness and limitations of models and theories as scientific representations of reality.

The Water Planet

IE.1a Students will select and use appropriate tools and technology (such as computer-linked probes, spreadsheets, and graphing calcula-tors) to perform tests, collect data, analyze relationships, and display data.
IE.1d Students will formulate explanations using logic and evidence.
IE.1g Students will recognize the usefulness and limitations of models and theories as scientific representations of reality.

Nearly three-quarters of Earth's surface lies beneath a body of salt water called the **global ocean.** No other known planet has a similar covering of liquid water. Only Earth can be called the *water planet*.

The global ocean contains more than 97% of all of the water on Earth. Although the ocean is the most prominent feature of Earth's surface, the ocean is only about 1/4,000 of Earth's total mass and only 1/800 of Earth's total volume.

Divisions of the Global Ocean

As shown in **Figure 1,** the global ocean is divided into five major oceans. These major oceans are the Atlantic, Pacific, Indian, Arctic, and Southern Oceans. Each ocean has special character-istics. The Pacific Ocean is the largest ocean on Earth's surface. It contains more than one-half of the ocean water on Earth. With an average depth of 4.3 km, the Pacific Ocean is also the deepest ocean. The next largest ocean is the Atlantic Ocean. The Atlantic Ocean has an average depth of 3.9 km. The Indian Ocean is the third-largest ocean and has an average depth of 3.9 km. The Southern Ocean extends from the coast of Antarctica to 60°S latitude. The Arctic Ocean is the smallest ocean, and it surrounds the North Pole.

A **sea** is a body of water that is smaller than an ocean and that may be partially surrounded by land. Examples of major seas include the Mediterranean, Caribbean, and South China Seas.

OBJECTIVES

▶ **Name** the major divisions of the global ocean.

▶ **Describe** how oceanographers study the ocean. IE.1a

▶ **Explain** how sonar works. IE.1a

KEY TERMS

global ocean
sea
oceanography
sonar

global ocean the body of salt water that covers nearly three-fourths of Earth's surface

sea a large, commonly saline body of water that is smaller than an ocean and that may be partially or completely surrounded by land

Figure 1 ▶ The global ocean is divided into oceans and seas. *How many oceans are on Earth?*

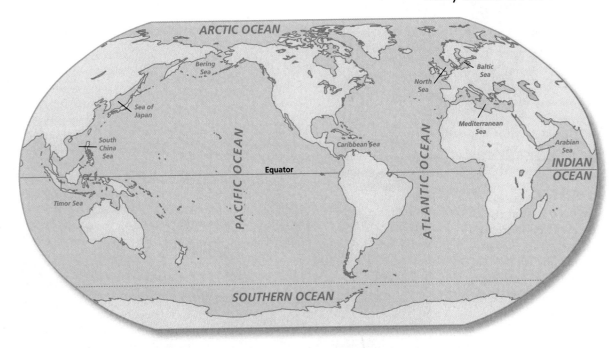

Exploration of the Ocean

The study of the physical characteristics, chemical composition, and life-forms of the ocean is called **oceanography**. Although some ancient civilizations studied the ocean, modern oceanography did not begin until the 1850s.

oceanography the scientific study of the ocean, including the properties and movement of ocean water, the characteristics of the ocean floor, and the organisms that live in the ocean

The Birth of Oceanography

An American naval officer named Matthew F. Maury used records from navy ships to learn about ocean currents, winds, depths, and weather conditions. In 1855, he published these observations as one of the first textbooks about the oceans. Then, from 1872 to 1876, a team of scientists aboard the British Navy ship HMS *Challenger* crossed the Atlantic, Indian, and Pacific Oceans. The scientists measured water temperatures at great depths and collected samples of ocean water, sediments, and thousands of marine organisms. The voyages of the HMS *Challenger* laid the foundation for the modern science of oceanography.

Today, many ships perform oceanographic research. In the 1990s and in the beginning of the 21st century, the research ship *JOIDES Resolution* was the world's largest and most sophisticated scientific drilling ship. Samples drilled by *JOIDES Resolution,* shown in **Figure 2,** provide scientists with valuable information about plate tectonics and the ocean floor. The Japanese ship *CHIKYU*, which is operated by the Integrated Ocean Drilling Program, is one of the most advanced drilling ship now in use.

✔ Reading Check List three characteristics of the ocean that oceanographers study. (See the Appendix for answers to Reading Checks.)

Figure 2 ▶ Reentry cones (above) are used so that core samples can later be taken from the same place on the ocean floor. Scientists aboard the research ship *JOIDES Resolution* (right) perform scientific studies of the ocean floor.

Figure 3 ▶ Active sonar sends out a pulse of sound. The pulse, called a *ping* because of the way it sounds, reflects when it strikes a solid object.

Reflected sound waves

Sound waves from ship

Sonar

Oceanographic research ships are often equipped with sonar. **Sonar** is a system that uses acoustic signals and returned echoes to determine the location of objects or to communicate. Sonar is an acronym for ***sound navigation and ranging***. A sonar transmitter sends out a continuous series of sound waves from a ship to the ocean floor, as shown in **Figure 3**. The sound waves travel about 1,500 m/s through sea water and bounce off the solid ocean floor. The waves reflect back to a receiver. Scientists measure the time that the sound waves take to travel from the transmitter, to the ocean floor, and to the receiver in order to calculate the depth of the ocean floor. Scientists then use this information to make maps and profiles of the ocean floor.

sonar *sound navigation and ranging,* a system that uses acoustic signals and returned echoes to determine the location of objects or to communicate

Quick**LAB**
 30 min

Sonar
Procedure

IE.1a, IE.1d, IE.1g

1. Use **heavy string** to tie one end of a **spring** securely to a **doorknob.** Pull the spring taut and parallel to the floor. You will need to keep the tension of the spring constant throughout the lab.

2. Use **masking tape** to mark the floor directly beneath the hand that is holding the spring taut. Use a **meterstick** to measure and record the distance from that hand to the doorknob.

3. Note the time on a **stopwatch or clock with a second hand.** Hold the spring taut, and hit the spring horizontally to create a compression wave.

4. Check the time again to see how long the pulse takes to travel to the doorknob and back to your hand. Record the time.

5. Repeat steps 2–4 three times. Each time, hold the spring 60 cm closer to the doorknob. Keep tension constant by gathering coils as necessary.

6. Calculate the rate of travel for each trial by multiplying the distance between your hand and the doorknob by 2. Then, divide by the number of seconds the pulse took to travel to the doorknob and back.

Analysis

1. Did the rate the pulse traveled change during the course of the investigation?

2. If a pulse took 3 s to travel to the doorknob and back to your hand, what is the distance from the doorknob to your hand?

3. How is the apparatus you used similar to sonar? How is the apparatus different than sonar? Explain.

Submersibles

Underwater research vessels, called *submersibles*, also enable oceanographers to study the ocean depths. Some submersibles are piloted by people. One such submersible is the *bathysphere*, a spherical diving vessel that remains connected to the research ship for communications and life support. Another type of piloted submersible, called a *bathyscaph*, is a self-propelled, free-moving submarine. One of the most well-known bathyscaphs is the *Alvin*. Another modern submersible, called *Nautile* (NOH teel), is shown in **Figure 4.**

Other modern submersibles are submarine robots. They can take photographs, collect mineral samples from the ocean floor, and perform many other tasks. These robot submersibles are remotely piloted and allow oceanographers to study the ocean depths for long periods of time.

Underwater Research

Submersibles have helped scientists make exciting discoveries about the deep ocean. During one dive in a submersible, startled oceanographers saw communities of unusual marine life living at depths and temperatures where scientists thought that almost no life could exist. Giant clams, blind white crabs, and giant tube worms were some of the strange life-forms that were discovered. Many of these life-forms have unusual adaptations that allow them to live in hostile environments. The angler fish, shown in **Figure 4,** can produce its own light, which attracts prey.

Figure 4 ▶The submersible *Nautile* (top) carries enough oxygen to keep a three-person crew underwater for more than five hours. Deep-sea submersibles have discovered many strange organisms in the deep ocean, such as this angler fish (bottom).

Section 1 Review

1. **Name** the five major divisions of the global ocean.

2. **Explain** the difference between an ocean and a sea.

3. **Define** *oceanography*.

4. **Describe** two ways that oceanographers study the ocean. IE.1a

5. **Explain** how sonar works. IE.1a

6. **Describe** two aspects of the ocean that submersibles are used to study. IE.1a

7. **List** three types of submersibles. IE.1a

CRITICAL THINKING

8. **Evaluating Ideas** Most submarines use sonar as a navigation aid. How would sonar enable an underwater vessel to move through the ocean depths? IE.1a, IE.1d

9. **Analyzing Methods** Why are submarine robots more practical for deep-ocean research than submersibles designed to carry people are? IE.1a, IE.1d

CONCEPT MAPPING

10. Use the following terms to create a concept map: *oceanography, submersible, bathysphere, bathyscaph, robot submersible,* and *sonar.* IE.1a

Features of the Ocean Floor

3a Students know features of the ocean floor (magnetic patterns, age, and sea floor topography) provide evidence of plate tectonics.

IE.1d Students will formulate explanations using logic and evidence.

The ocean floor can be divided into two major areas, as shown in **Figure 1**. The **continental margins** are shallow parts of the ocean floor that are made of continental crust and a thick wedge of sediment. The other major area is the **deep-ocean basin,** which is made of oceanic crust and a thin sediment layer, is the deep part of the ocean beyond the continental margin.

Continental Margins

The line that divides the continental crust from the oceanic crust is not abrupt or distinct. Shorelines are not the true boundaries between the oceanic crust and the continental crust. The boundaries are actually some distance offshore and beneath the ocean and the thick sediments of the continental margin.

Continental Shelf

Continents are outlined in most places by a zone of shallow water where the ocean covers the edge of the continent. The part of the continent that is covered by water is called a *continental shelf*. The shelf usually slopes gently from the shoreline and drops about 0.12 m every 100 m. The average depth of the water covering a continental shelf is about 60 m. Although it is underwater, a continental shelf is part of the continental margin, not the deep-ocean basin.

Changes in sea level affect the continental shelves. During glacial periods, continental ice sheets hold large amounts of water. So, sea level falls and exposes more of the continental shelf to weathering and erosion. But if ice sheets melt adding water to the oceans, sea level rises and covers the continental shelf.

OBJECTIVES

▶ **Describe** the main features of the continental margins. **3a**

▶ **Describe** the main features of the deep-ocean basin. **3a**

KEY TERMS

continental margin
deep-ocean basin
trench
abyssal plain

continental margin the shallow sea floor that is located between the shoreline and the deep-ocean bottom

deep-ocean basin the part of the ocean floor that is under deep water beyond the continent margin and that is composed of oceanic crust and a thin layer of sediment

For a variety of links related to this subject, go to www.scilinks.org

Topic: Ocean-Floor Features
SciLinks code: HQ61067

Deep-ocean basin — Continental margin — Trench — Mid-ocean ridge — Abyssal plain

Figure 1 ▶ The ocean floor includes the continental margins and the deep-ocean basin. *What are three other major features of the ocean floor?*

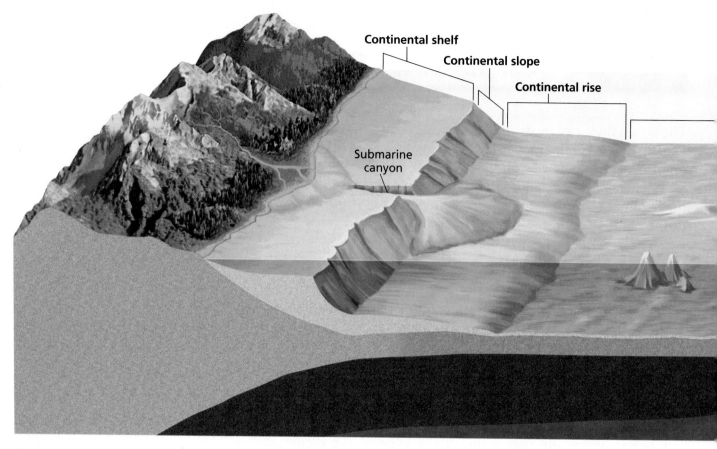

Continental shelf

Continental slope

Continental rise

Submarine canyon

Figure 2 ▶ The ocean floor is made of distinct areas and features.

Continental Slope and Continental Rise

At the seaward edge of a continental shelf is a steep slope called a *continental slope*. The boundary between the continental crust and the oceanic crust is located at the base of the continental slope. Along the continental slope, the ocean depth increases by several thousand meters within a distance of a few kilometers, as shown in **Figure 2.** The continental shelf and continental slope may be cut by deep V-shaped valleys. These deep valleys are called *submarine canyons*. These deep canyons are often found near the mouths of major rivers. Other canyons may form over time as very dense currents called *turbidity currents* carry large amounts of sediment down the continental slopes. Turbidity currents form when earthquakes cause underwater landslides or when large sediment loads run down a slope. These sediments form a raised wedge at the base of the continental slope called a *continental rise*.

Deep-Ocean Basins

Deep-ocean basins also have distinct features, as shown in **Figure 2.** These features include broad, flat plains; submerged volcanoes; gigantic mountain ranges; and deep trenches. In the deep-ocean basins, the mountains are higher and the plains are flatter than any features found on the continents are.

✓ Reading Check What features are located in the deep-ocean basins? (See the Appendix for answers to Reading Checks.)

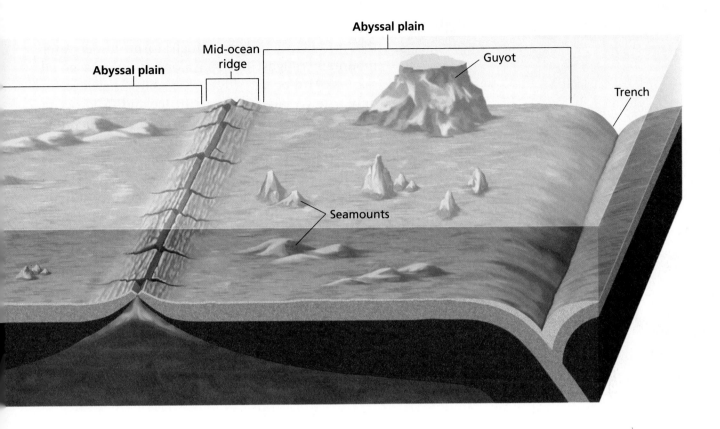

Abyssal plain · **Mid-ocean ridge** · **Abyssal plain** · Guyot · Trench · Seamounts

Trenches

Long, narrow depressions located in the deep-ocean basins are called **trenches.** At more than 11,000 m deep, the Mariana Trench, in the western Pacific Ocean, is the deepest place in Earth's crust. Trenches form where one tectonic plate subducts below another plate. Earthquakes occur near trenches. Volcanic mountain ranges and volcanic island arcs also form near trenches.

Abyssal Plains

The vast, flat areas of the deep-ocean basins where the ocean is more than 4 km deep are called **abyssal plains** (uh BIS uhl PLAYNZ). Abyssal plains cover about half of the deep-ocean basins and are the flattest regions on Earth. In some places, the ocean depth changes less than 3 m over more than 1,300 km.

Layers of fine sediment cover the abyssal plains. Ocean currents and wind carry some sediments from the continental margins. Other sediment is made by organisms that live in the ocean and settle to the ocean floor when they die.

The thickness of sediments on the abyssal plains is determined by three factors. The age of the oceanic crust is one factor. Older crust is generally covered with thicker sediments than younger crust is. The distance from the continental margin to the abyssal plain also determines how much sediment reaches the plain from the continent. Third, the sediment cover on abyssal plains that are bordered by trenches is generally thinner than the sediment cover on abyssal plains that are not bordered by trenches.

trench a long, narrow, and steep depression that forms on the ocean floor as a result of subduction of a tectonic plate, that runs parallel to the trend of a chain of volcanic islands or the coastline of a continent, and that may be as deep as 11 km below sea level; also called an *ocean trench* or a *deep-ocean trench*

abyssal plain a large, flat, almost level area of the deep-ocean basin

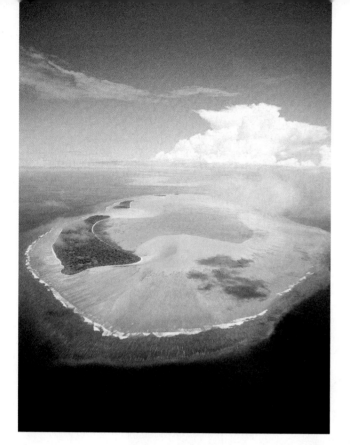

Figure 3 ▶ The white ridges in this photo are coral reefs of an atoll that formed in the shallow waters around a volcanic island. Erosion is changing the island into a guyot.

Mid-Ocean Ridges

The most prominent features of ocean basins are the *mid-ocean ridges*, which form underwater mountain ranges that run along the floors of all oceans. Mid-ocean ridges rise above sea level in only a few places, such as in Iceland. Mid-ocean ridges form where plates pull away from each other. A narrow depression, or rift, runs along the center of the ridge. Through this rift, magma reaches the sea floor and forms new lithosphere. This new lithosphere is less dense than the old lithosphere. As the new lithosphere cools, it becomes denser and begins to sink as it moves away from the rift. Fault-bounded blocks of crust that form parallel to the ridges as the lithosphere cools and contracts are called *abyssal hills*.

As ridges adjust to changes in the direction of plate motions, they break into segments that are bounded by faults. These faults create areas of rough topography called *fracture zones*, which run perpendicular across the ridge.

Seamounts

Submerged volcanic mountains that are taller than 1 km are called *seamounts*. Seamounts form in areas of increased volcanic activity called *hot spots*. Seamounts that rise above the ocean surface form oceanic islands. As tectonic plate movements carry islands away from a hot spot, the islands sink and are eroded by waves to form flat-topped, submerged seamounts called *guyots* (GEE OHZ) or *tablemounts*. An intermediate stage in this process, called an *atoll*, is shown in **Figure 3**.

Section 2 Review

1. **Describe** the three main sections of the continental margins. 3a

2. **Describe** where the boundary between the oceanic crust and the continental crust is located. 3a

3. **Explain** how turbidity currents are related to submarine canyons. 3a

4. **List** four main features of the deep-ocean basins, and describe one characteristic of each feature. 3a

5. **Compare** seamounts, guyots, and atolls. 3a

6. **Explain** the difference between the meanings of the terms *continental margin, continental shelf, continental slope,* and *continental rise.*

CRITICAL THINKING

7. **Making Inferences** The Pacific Ocean is surrounded by trenches, but the Atlantic Ocean is not. In addition, the Pacific Ocean is wider than the Atlantic Ocean, and much of the crust under the Pacific Ocean is very young. Which ocean's abyssal plain has thicker sediments? Explain your answer. 3a, IE.1d

8. **Determining Cause and Effect** If sea level were to fall significantly, what would happen to the continental shelves? IE.1d

CONCEPT MAPPING

9. Use the following terms to create a concept map: *continental margin, deep-ocean basin, continental shelf, continental slope, continental rise, trench, abyssal plain,* and *mid-ocean ridge.*

7c Students know the movement of matter among reservoirs is driven by Earth's internal and external sources of energy.

IE.1a Students will select and use appropriate tools and technology (such as computer-linked probes, spreadsheets, and graphing calculators) to perform tests, collect data, analyze relationships, and display data.

IE.1d Students will formulate explanations using logic and evidence.

Continental shelves and slopes are covered with sediments. Sediments are carried into the ocean by rivers, are washed away from the shoreline by wave erosion, or settle to the ocean bottom when the organisms that created them die. The composition of ocean sediments varies and depends on which part of the ocean floor the sediments form in. The sediments are fairly well sorted by size. Coarse gravel and sand are usually found close to shore because these heavier sediments do not move easily offshore. Lighter particles are suspended in ocean water and are usually deposited at a great distance from shore.

Sources of Deep Ocean–Basin Sediments

Sediments found in the deep-ocean basin, which is beyond the continental margin, are generally finer than those found in shallow water. Samples of the sediments in the deep-ocean basins can be gathered by scooping up sediments or by taking core samples. **Core samples** are cylinders of sediment that are collected by drilling into sediment layers on the ocean floor. **Figure 1** shows a core sample being studied aboard the research vessel *JOIDES Resolution*.

The study of sediment samples shows that most of the sediments in the deep-ocean basins are made of materials that settle slowly from the ocean water above. These materials may come from organic or inorganic sources.

OBJECTIVES

▶ **Describe** the formation of ocean-floor sediments. 7c

▶ **Explain** how ocean-floor sediments are classified by their physical composition.

KEY TERMS

core sample
nodule

core sample a cylindrical piece of sediment, rock, soil, snow, or ice that is collected by drilling

Figure 1 ▶ A scientist studies a core sample that was brought up from the drill aboard the research ship *JOIDES Resolution*.

Figure 2 ▶ This picture of sediment emptying out of the Mahakam River in Indonesia was taken by astronauts aboard the space shuttle *Columbia*.

Inorganic Sediments

Some ocean-basin sediments are rock particles that were carried from land by rivers. When a river empties into the ocean, the river deposits its sediment load, as shown in **Figure 2.** Most of these sediments are deposited along the shore and on the continental shelf. However, large quantities of these sediments occasionally slide down continental slopes to the ocean floor below. The force of the slide creates powerful turbidity currents that spread the sediments over the deep-ocean basins. Other deep ocean–basin sediments consist of fine particles of rock, including volcanic dust, that have been blown great distances out to sea by the wind. These particles land on the surface of the water, sink, and gradually settle to the bottom of the ocean.

Icebergs also provide sediments that can end up on the ocean basins. As a glacier moves across the land, the glacier picks up rock. The rock becomes embedded in the ice and moves with the glacier. When an iceberg breaks from the glacier, drifts out to sea, and melts, the rock material sinks to the ocean floor.

Even meteorites contribute to deep ocean-basin sediments. Much of a meteorite vaporizes as it enters Earth's atmosphere. The remaining cosmic dust falls to Earth's surface. Because most of Earth's surface is ocean, most meteorite fragments fall into the ocean and become part of the sediments on the ocean floor.

Connection to PHYSICS

Turbidity Currents

Underwater landslides can be caused by earthquakes or can happen when the sediment-water mixture becomes denser than the surrounding water. These landslides form currents called *turbidity currents*.

Gravity powers turbidity currents. As the dense sediment mixture moves downhill, it picks up sediment. This added sediment increases the current's density, which increases the current's speed. Turbidity currents can travel at speeds of more than 100 km/h.

The speed and composition of these currents make them powerful agents of erosion. One turbidity current may move billions of kilograms of mud, rock, and sand down a slope. Sediments are deposited as the speed of the current decreases. A turbidity current may gain enough momentum that it does not stop at the continental rise. Thus, it may spread sediment hundreds of kilometers onto the abyssal plain.

This simulated turbidity current was created in a laboratory. The density of the sediment-filled water causes it to move downhill like a landslide does.

Figure 3 ▶ Nodules, such as these mined from the East Pacific Rise, are rich in a variety of minerals.

MATHPRACTICE

Ocean-floor Sediments Ocean-floor sediments are composed of an average of 54% biogenic sediments, 45% Earth rocks and dust, less than 1% precipitation of dissolved materials (nodules and phosphorite), and less than 1% of rocks and dust from space. If you collected 10,000 kg of ocean-floor sediment, how many kilograms of each type of ocean-floor sediment would you expect to find?

Biogenic Sediments

In many places on the ocean floor, almost all of the sediments are *biogenic,* meaning that the sediments were originally produced by living organisms. Biogenic sediments are the remains of marine plants and animals. The two most common compounds that make up organic sediments are silica, SiO_2, and calcium carbonate, $CaCO_3$. Silica comes primarily from microscopic organisms called *diatoms* and *radiolarians*. Calcium carbonate comes mostly from the skeletons of tiny organisms called *foraminiferans*.

Chemical Deposits

When substances that are dissolved in ocean water crystallize, these materials can form mineral deposits on the ocean floor. Some of these mineral deposis are potato-shaped lumps called **nodules.** Nodules, such as the ones shown in **Figure 3,** are commonly located on the abyssal plains. Nodules are composed mainly of the oxides of manganese, nickel, copper, and iron. Other minerals, such as phosphorite, are also carried in the ocean water before they crystallize and form mineral deposits on the ocean floor.

✔ **Reading Check** How do nodules form? (See the Appendix for answers to Reading Checks.)

QuickLAB ⏱ 20 min

Diatoms ▨ IE.1d

Procedure

1. Observe **diatoms** under a **microscope.**
2. Sketch what you see. Make sure to note the magnification.

Analysis

1. What characteristics of the diatoms did you observe?
2. Propose one possible function for each of the structures you observed.

nodule a lump of minerals that is made of oxides of manganese, iron, copper, or nickel and that is found in scattered groups on the ocean floor

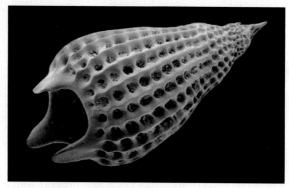

Figure 4 ▶ The remains of diatoms (left) and radiolarians (right), both magnified hundreds of times in these photos, are important components of biogenic sediments on the ocean floor.

Physical Classification of Sediments

Deep ocean-floor sediments can be classified into two basic types. *Muds* are very fine silt- and clay-sized particles of rock. One common type of mud on the abyssal plains is red clay. Red clay is made of at least 40% clay particles and is mixed with silt, sand, and biogenic material. This clay can vary in color from red to gray, blue, green, or yellow-brown. About 40% of the ocean floor is covered with soft, fine sediment called *ooze*. At least 30% of the ooze is biogenic materials, such as the remains of microscopic sea organisms. The remaining material is fine mud.

Ooze can be classified into two types. *Calcareous ooze* is ooze that is made mostly of calcium carbonate. Calcareous ooze is never found below a depth of 5 km, because at depths between 3 km and 5 km, calcium carbonate dissolves in the deep, cold ocean water. *Siliceous ooze*, which can be found at any depth, is made of mostly silicon dioxide, which comes from the shells of radiolarians and diatoms. Examples of remains of these organisms are shown in **Figure 4.** Most siliceous ooze is found in the cool, nutrient-rich ocean waters around Antarctica because of the abundance of diatoms and radiolarians in that location.

Section 3 Review

1. **Describe** the formation of two different types of ocean-floor sediments. 🐘 7c

2. **Summarize** how icebergs contribute to deep ocean-basin sediments.

3. **Explain** how substances that are dissolved in ocean water travel to the ocean floor.

4. **Explain** how ocean-floor sediments are classified by physical composition.

5. **Describe** how scientists define the word *mud*.

6. **Compare** the compositions of calcareous ooze and siliceous ooze.

CRITICAL THINKING

7. **Making Inferences** What could you infer from a core sample of a layer of sediment that contains volcanic ash and dust? 🐘 IE.1d

8. **Applying Ideas** Some businesses have tried to develop methods of extracting nodules from the ocean. Name two factors that businesses should consider when they are determining whether extracting nodules is profitable. 🐘 IE.1d

CONCEPT MAPPING

9. Use the following terms to create a concept map: *nodule, inorganic sediment, biogenic sediment, diatom, chemical deposit,* and *ocean-floor sediment.*

Sections

1 The Water Planet

Key Terms

global ocean, 471
sea, 471
oceanography, 472
sonar, 473

Key Concepts

▶ The global ocean can be divided into five major oceans—the Pacific, Atlantic, Indian, Arctic, and Southern Oceans—and many smaller seas.

▶ Oceanography is the study of the oceans and the seas. Oceanographers study the ocean using research ships, sonar, and submersibles.

▶ Sonar is a system that uses acoustic signals and echo returns to determine the location of objects or to communicate.

2 Features of the Ocean Floor

continental margin, 475
deep-ocean basin, 475
trench, 477
abyssal plain, 477

▶ The areas around continents that are shallow parts of the ocean floor are called *continental margins*.

▶ Continental margins include the continental shelf, the continental slope, and the continental rise.

▶ Features of deep-ocean basins include trenches, abyssal plains, mid-ocean ridges, and seamounts.

3 Ocean-Floor Sediments

core sample, 479
nodule, 481

▶ Core samples are taken by drilling into sediment layers. Scientists study core samples to learn about the composition and characteristics of ocean-floor sediments.

▶ Ocean-floor sediments form from inorganic and biogenic materials as well as from chemical deposits.

▶ Based on physical characteristics, deep ocean–floor sediments are classified as mud or as ooze.

Using Key Terms

Use each of the following terms in a separate sentence.

1. *oceanography*
2. *sonar* IE.1a
3. *core sample*

For each pair of terms, explain how the meanings of the terms differ.

4. *ocean* and *sea*
5. *submersible* and *nodule* IE.1a
6. *continental margin* and *deep-ocean basin* 3a
7. *global ocean* and *sea*
8. *mud* and *ooze*

Understanding Key Concepts

9. A self-propelled, free-moving submarine that is equipped for ocean research is a IE.1a
   a. turbidity.
   b. bathysphere.
   c. bathyscaph.
   d. guyot.

10. A system that is used for determining the depth of the ocean floor is IE.1a
   a. a guyot.
   b. radiolarians.
   c. a bathysphere.
   d. sonar.

11. The parts of the ocean floor that are made up of continental crust are called 3a
   a. continental margins.
   b. abyssal plains.
   c. mid-ocean ridges.
   d. trenches.

12. The accumulation of sediments at the base of the continental slope is called the 7c
   a. trench.
   b. turbidity current.
   c. continental margin.
   d. continental rise.

13. The deepest parts of the ocean are called
   a. trenches.
   b. submarine canyons.
   c. abyssal plains.
   d. continental rises.

14. Large quantities of the inorganic sediment that makes up the continental rise come from 7c
   a. turbidity currents.
   b. earthquakes.
   c. diatoms.
   d. nodules.

15. Potato-shaped lumps of minerals on the ocean floor are called
   a. guyots.   c. foraminiferans.
   b. nodules.   d. diatoms.

16. Very fine particles of silt and clay that have settled to the ocean floor are called 7c
   a. muds.   c. guyots.
   b. seamounts.   d. nodules.

Short Answer

17. What is the differences between a seamount and a guyot? 3a

18. Explain how sonar is used to study the oceans. IE.1a

19. List three ways that scientists can learn about the deep ocean. IE.1a

20. How do fine sediments reach the deep-ocean bottom? 7c

21. What effects do deep-ocean trenches have on the sediment thickness of the abyssal plain?

22. List the three main types of ocean-floor sediments, and describe how they are deposited. 7c

Oceanographer

Lynne Talley is a physical oceanographer. Physical oceanographers study waves, tides, and currents in the ocean and the interactions between the ocean and the atmosphere. Talley's research focuses on large-scale patterns of ocean circulation that govern the worldwide movement of ocean waters. Her oceanography career began with a love for physics. Scientists also enter the field of oceanography from the fields of mathematics, geology, engineering, chemistry, biology, or ecology.

Going to Sea

Unlike the many oceanographers who use remote-sensing aircraft and Earth-orbiting satellites to collect data, Talley is a seagoing oceanographer. She uses direct

▼ Lynne Talley uses this rosette sampler to take samples of ocean water at various depths.

measurement techniques to collect data. Every two years, she goes to sea on a month-long research cruise. Scientists on the cruise measure the temperature, salinity, and dissolved oxygen of ocean waters at various depths. Water samples are analyzed for chemical "fingerprints," such as the isotope helium-3. The presence of helium-3 may indicate that the sampled waters were near the surface during thermonuclear weapons testing that began in the 1950s.

After each cruise, Talley uses computer programs to analyze the data collected on the cruise. "Because oceans cover almost three-fourths of the world's surface, they have a huge impact on climate," says Talley. By studying the global movements of ocean waters, Talley can trace the global movement of heat. She uses her data as a basis for building

> "I chose oceanography because it's so environmental and large scale. You can see it and touch it."
> —Lynne Talley Ph.D.

numerical models that help scientists predict future oceanic and atmospheric conditions.

Predicting Future Climate

Discovering how heat moves around Earth gives scientists a better understanding of global warming. Nations around the world are developing regulations to control global warming. Talley says that it is critical that such regulations be based on accurate data. "You must understand the actual processes occurring right now in order to predict change. You can't make up a model unless you understand the system."

Chapter 20

Ocean Water

Sections

1 Properties of Ocean Water

2 Life in the Oceans

3 Ocean Resources

What You'll Learn

- What the properties of ocean water are
- How life survives in the ocean
- Why ocean resources are important

Why It's Relevant

Earth's oceans play a vital role in Earth's ecology. Resources from the ocean provide humans with food, fuel, and fresh water.

PRE-READING ACTIVITY

FOLDNOTES

Four-Corner Fold

Before you read the chapter, create the FoldNote entitled "Four-Corner Fold" described in the Skills Handbook section of the Appendix. Label each flap of the four-corner fold with a topic. Write what you know about each topic under the appropriate flap. As you read the chapter, add other information that you learn.

▶ To avoid predators, chevron barracuda school in a spiraling tornado near the ocean surface in Kimbe Bay, Papua New Guinea. These fish get all of the nutrients they need for life from the ocean water in which they live.

California Content Standards

5d Students know properties of ocean water, such as temperature and salinity, can be used to explain the layered structure of the oceans, the generation of horizontal and vertical ocean currents, and the geographic distribution of marine organisms.

7b Students know the global carbon cycle: the different physical and chemical forms of carbon in the atmosphere, oceans, biomass, fossil fuels, and the movement of carbon among these reservoirs.

7d* Students know the relative residence times and flow characteristics of carbon in and out of its different reservoirs.

IE.1d Students will formulate explanations using logic and evidence.

IE.1m Students will investigate a science-based societal issue by researching the literature, analyzing data, and communicating the findings. Examples of issues include irradiation of food, cloning of animals by somatic cell nuclear transfer, choice of energy sources, and land and water use decisions in California.

Properties of Ocean Water

California Content Standards

5d Students know properties of ocean water, such as temperature and salinity, can be used to explain the layered structure of the oceans, the generation of horizontal and vertical ocean currents, and the geographic distribution of marine organisms.

IE.1d Students will formulate explanations using logic and evidence.

Pure liquid water is tasteless, odorless, and colorless. However, the water in the ocean is not pure. Many solids and gases are dissolved in the ocean. In addition to dissolved substances, small particles of matter and tiny organisms are also suspended in ocean water. Ocean water is a complex mixture of chemicals that sustains a variety of plant and animal life.

Scientists describe ocean water by using a variety of properties, such as the presence of dissolved gases and the presence of dissolved solids, salinity, temperature, density, and color. Scientists study all of these properties to understand the complex interactions between the oceans, the atmosphere, and the land.

OBJECTIVES

▶ **Describe** the chemical composition of ocean water. 5d

▶ **Describe** the salinity, temperature, density, and color of ocean water. 5d

KEY TERMS

salinity
pack ice
thermocline
density

Dissolved Gases

The two principal gases in the atmosphere are nitrogen, N_2, and oxygen, O_2. These two gases are also the main gases dissolved in ocean water. While carbon dioxide, CO_2, is not a major component of the atmosphere, a large amount of this gas is dissolved in ocean water. Other atmospheric gases are also present in the ocean in small amounts.

Ocean water dissolves gases from a variety of sources, as shown in **Figure 1.** Gases may enter ocean water from water in streams and rivers. Some of the gases in ocean water come from volcanic eruptions beneath the ocean. Gases are also released directly into ocean water by organisms that live in the ocean. For example, many plants in the ocean make oxygen as a product of photosynthesis. However, most oxygen in the ocean enters at the surface of the ocean from the atmosphere.

Figure 1 ▶ Gases can enter the ocean from streams, volcanoes, organisms, and the atmosphere.

Gases enter the ocean directly from the atmosphere.

Some gases in the ocean come from underwater volcanoes and marine organisms.

Gases enter the ocean from streams and rivers.

Temperature and Dissolved Gases

The temperature of water affects the amount of gas that dissolves in water. Gases dissolve more readily in cold water than in warm water. You may have noticed this phenomenon when your glass of soda quickly goes "flat" on a warm day. The soda goes flat quickly because the CO_2 that makes the soda bubbly escapes into the air. But if the soda is kept in the refrigerator, the soda will retain its fizz longer. Because cold water dissolves gases more readily, water at the surface of the ocean in cold regions dissolves larger amounts of gases than water in warm tropical regions does.

Gases also can return to the atmosphere from the ocean. If the water temperature rises, less gas will remain dissolved, and the excess gas will be released into the atmosphere. For example, warm equatorial ocean waters tend to release CO_2 into the atmosphere, but ocean waters at cooler, higher latitudes take up large amounts of CO_2. Therefore, the ocean and the atmosphere are continuously exchanging gases as water temperatures change.

The Oceans as a Carbon Sink

Oceans contain more than 60 times as much carbon as the atmosphere does. Dissolved CO_2 may be trapped in the oceans for hundreds to thousands of years. Because of this ability to dissolve and contain a large amount of CO_2, the oceans are commonly referred to as a *carbon sink*. Because gaseous CO_2 affects the atmosphere's ability to trap thermal energy from the sun, the oceans are important in the regulation of climate.

Connection to CHEMISTRY

How Substances Dissolve

A water molecule is one oxygen atom bonded to two hydrogen atoms. The oxygen atom pulls electrons away from the hydrogen atoms, which gives the hydrogen atoms a partial positive charge and gives the oxygen atom a partial negative charge. This uneven distribution of charges allows the water molecule to attract both positive and negative ions.

The figure at right shows how a sodium chloride, NaCl, crystal dissolves in water. The partially negative oxygen atoms in water molecules attract the positively charged sodium ions of the salt. The partially positive hydrogen atoms in the water molecules attract the negatively charged chloride ions of the salt. When the force of attraction between the ions and the water molecules becomes stronger than the force of attraction between the sodium and chloride atoms, the ions are pulled away from the crystal. The ions are then surrounded by water molecules. Eventually, all of the ions in the crystal are pulled into solution, and the substance is completely dissolved.

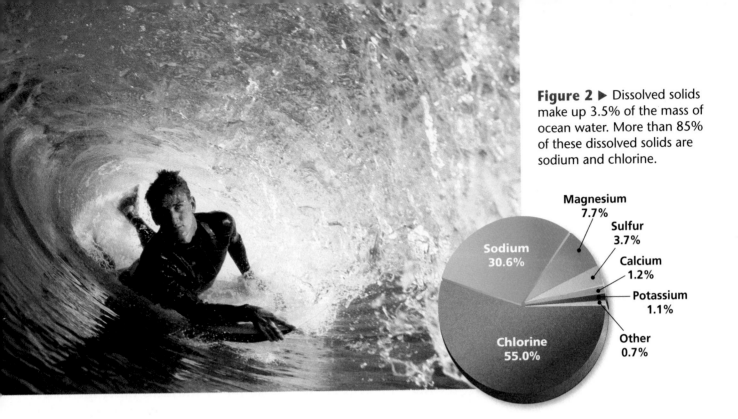

Figure 2 ▶ Dissolved solids make up 3.5% of the mass of ocean water. More than 85% of these dissolved solids are sodium and chlorine.

Magnesium 7.7%
Sulfur 3.7%
Sodium 30.6%
Calcium 1.2%
Potassium 1.1%
Chlorine 55.0%
Other 0.7%

Dissolved Solids

Ocean water is 96.5% pure water, or H_2O. Dissolved solids make up about 3.5% of the mass of ocean water. These dissolved solids, commonly called *sea salts*, give the ocean its salty taste.

Most Abundant Elements

Solids dissolved in ocean water are composed of about 75 chemical elements. The six most abundant elements in ocean water are chlorine, sodium, magnesium, sulfur, calcium, and potassium. The salt halite, which is made of sodium and chloride ions, makes up more than 85% of the ocean's dissolved solids. The remaining dissolved solids consist of various other salts and minerals, as shown in **Figure 2.** *Trace elements* are elements that exist in very small amounts. Gold, zinc, and phosphorus are some of the trace elements that are found in the ocean.

Sources of Dissolved Solids

Most of the elements that form sea salts come from three main sources—volcanic eruptions, chemical weathering of rock on land, and chemical reactions between sea water and newly formed sea-floor rocks. Each year, rivers carry about 400 billion kilograms of dissolved solids into the ocean. Most of these dissolved solids are salts. As water evaporates from the ocean, salts and other minerals remain in the ocean. Only a small fraction of these salts and minerals are returned to the land in the water that falls as rain and snow during the water cycle.

☑ **Reading Check** How do dissolved solids enter the ocean? (See the Appendix for answers to Reading Checks.)

QuickLAB ⏱ 10 min

Dissolving Solids

Procedure 🔬 5d, IE.1d

1. Heat **200 ml of water** in a **beaker** over a **hot plate** until the water is about 60°C.

2. Dissolve **table salt** in the water 1 tsp at a time until no more salt will dissolve. Record the total amount of salt that dissolves.

3. Dissolve table salt 1 tsp at a time into **200 ml of water** that has been chilled in the refrigerator to about 5°C. Record the total amount of salt that dissolves.

Analysis

1. Which water sample dissolved the most salt?

2. Describe what would happen to the dissolved salt in the hot water if the hot water was chilled to 10°C.

Salinity of Ocean Water

One of the biggest differences between ocean water and fresh water is the high concentration of salts in ocean water. **Salinity** is a measure of the amount of dissolved salts and other solids in a given liquid. Salinity is measured by the number of grams of dissolved solids in 1,000 g of ocean water. For example, if 1,000 g of ocean water contained 35 g of solids, the salinity of the sample would be about 35 parts salt per 1,000 parts ocean water. This measurement is written as *salinity* = 35 parts per thousand, or 35‰. Thus, the ocean is about 3.5% salts. However, fresh water is less than 0.1% salt or has a salinity of 1‰.

Factors That Change Salinity

Precipitation such as rain and snow is composed only of freash water. When ocean surface water evaporates or freezes, only water molecules are removed from the ocean; dissolved salts and other solids remain. Where the rate of evaporation is higher than the rate of precipitation, the salinity of surfaces water increases. Therefore, in equatorial waters, where the rate of precipitation is highest, the salinity is lower than it is in subtropical waters, where rates of evaporation are highest.

Over most of the surface of the ocean, salinity ranges from 33‰ to 36‰. The global ocean has an average salinity of 34.7‰. However, salinity at particular locations can vary greatly, as shown in **Figure 3.** The salinity of the Red Sea, for example, is more than 40‰. The high salinity is due to the hot, dry climate around the Red Sea, which causes high levels of evaporation.

Figure 3 ▶ The average surface salinity of the global ocean varies from one location to another. *What effect do river mouths tend to have on the salinity of the surrounding ocean water?*

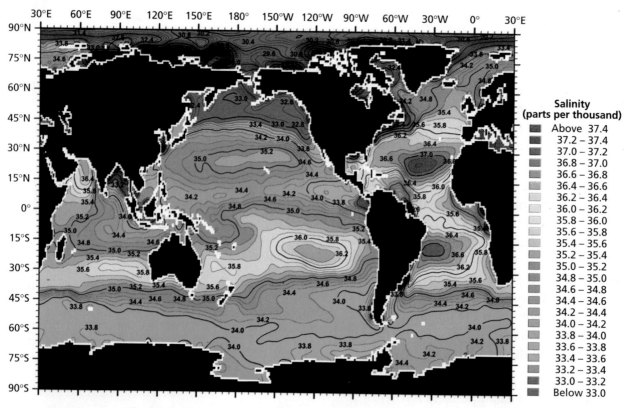

Salinity (parts per thousand)

Above 37.4
37.2 – 37.4
37.0 – 37.2
36.8 – 37.0
36.6 – 36.8
36.4 – 36.6
36.2 – 36.4
36.0 – 36.2
35.8 – 36.0
35.6 – 35.8
35.4 – 35.6
35.2 – 35.4
35.0 – 35.2
34.8 – 35.0
34.6 – 34.8
34.4 – 34.6
34.2 – 34.4
34.0 – 34.2
33.8 – 34.0
33.6 – 33.8
33.4 – 33.6
33.2 – 33.4
33.0 – 33.2
Below 33.0

Temperature of Ocean Water

Like ocean salinity, ocean temperature varies depending on depth and location on the surface of the oceans. The range of ocean temperatures is affected by the amount of solar energy an area receives and by the movement of water in the ocean.

Surface Water

The mixing of the ocean's surface water distributes heat downward to a depth of 100 to 300 m. Thus, the temperature of this zone of surface water is relatively constant and decreases only slightly as depth increases. However, the temperature of surface water does decrease as latitude increases. Therefore, polar surface waters are much cooler than the surface waters in the Tropics, as explained in **Figure 4.**

The total amount of solar energy that reaches the surface of the ocean is much greater at the equator than in areas near the North and South Poles. In tropical waters, ocean surface temperatures of about 30°C are common. Surface temperatures in polar oceans, however, often drop as low as –1.9°C. Because ocean water freezes at about –1.9°C, vast areas of sea ice exist in polar oceans. A floating layer of sea ice that completely covers an area of the ocean surface is called **pack ice.** Usually, pack ice is no more than 5 m thick because the ice insulates the water below and prevents it from freezing. In the middle latitudes, the ocean surface temperature varies depending on the seasons. In some areas, the ocean surface temperature may vary by as much as 10°C to 20°C between summer and winter.

Figure 4 ▶ The surface temperature of tropical ocean water (right) can be as high as 30°C. However, the surface temperature of polar ocean water (left) is below the freezing point of fresh water.

pack ice a floating layer of sea ice that completely covers an area of the ocean surface

Reading Check What factors affect the surface temperature of the ocean? (See the Appendix for answers to Reading Checks.)

The Thermocline

Because the sun cannot directly heat ocean water below the surface layer, the temperature of the water decreases sharply as depth increases. In most places in the ocean, this sudden decrease in temperature begins close to the surface. The layer in a body of water in which water temperature drops with increased depth faster than it does in other layers is called the **thermocline.**

The thermocline exists because the water near the surface becomes less dense as energy from the sun warms the water. This warm water cannot mix easily with the cold, dense water below. Thus, a thermocline marks the distinct separation between the warm surface water and the cold deep water. Below the thermocline, the temperature of the water continues to decrease, but it decreases very slowly, as shown in **Figure 5.** Changing temperature or shifting currents may alter the depth of the thermocline or cause the thermocline to disappear. Nevertheless, a thermocline is usually present beneath much of the ocean surface.

Deep Water

In the deep zones of the ocean, the temperature of the water is usually about 2°C. The colder the water is, the denser it is. The density of cold, deep water controls the slow movement of deep ocean currents. This movement occurs when the cold, dense water at the poles sinks and flows beneath warm water toward the equator. Cold, deep ocean water also holds more dissolved gases than warm, shallow ocean water does.

thermocline a layer in a body of water in which water temperature drops with increased depth faster than it does in other layers

Figure 5 ▶ The temperature of ocean water decreases as depth increases. Just below the surface is a thermocline, an area where the water temperature decreases sharply.

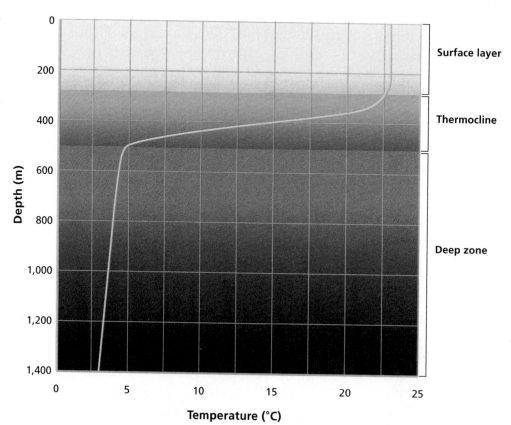

Density of Ocean Water

The mass of a substance per unit volume is that substance's **density**. For example, 1 cm³ of pure water has a mass of 1 g. So, the density of pure water is 1 g/cm³. Different liquids have different densities, as shown in **Figure 6.** Two factors affect the density of ocean water: salinity and the temperature of the water. Dissolved solids, which are mainly salts, add mass to the water. The large amount of dissolved solids in ocean water makes it denser than pure fresh water. Ocean water has a density between 1.026 g/cm³ and 1.028 g/cm³.

Ocean water becomes denser as it becomes colder and less dense as it becomes warmer. Water temperature affects the density of ocean water more than salinity does. Therefore, the densest ocean water is found in the polar regions, where the ocean surface is coldest. This cold, dense water sinks and moves through the ocean basins near the ocean floor.

Figure 6 ▶ This graduated cylinder contains six liquids that have different densities. From top to bottom they are corn oil, water, shampoo, dish detergent, anti-freeze, and maple syrup. *Which liquid has the lowest density?*

✔ **Reading Check** Explain why ocean water is denser than fresh water. (See the Appendix for answers to Reading Checks.)

density the ratio of the mass of a substance to the volume of the substance; commonly expressed as grams per cubic centimeter for solids and liquids and as grams per liter for gases

QuickLAB   20 min

Density Factors

Procedure 🌞 5d, IE.1d

1. Fill a **deep, clear plastic container** half full with **room temperature water**.
2. In a **1 L beaker,** mix **1/8 cup of table salt, a few drops of red food coloring**, and 1 L of room temperature water. Stir the mixture until the salt is dissolved.
3. Add the red saltwater mixture to the water in the clear plastic container. Record your observations.
4. In the **1 L beaker,** mix a **few drops of blue food coloring** with water that is 8°C.
5. Slowly add the cold, blue water to the clear plastic container in step 3. Record your observations.

Analysis

1. Describe what happened when you added the red salt water to the fresh water. Which is denser: fresh water or salt water?
2. What happened when you added the cold water to the room temperature water? Which is denser: cold water or room temperature water?

3. What would you expect to happen if the blue water was heated, instead of cooled?
4. Based on your observations, where would you expect the water in the ocean to be the least dense? the most dense?
5. Describe water layering where a river empties into the ocean.

Color of Ocean Water

Have you ever wondered why the ocean appears blue, as shown in **Figure 7?** The color of ocean water is determined by the way it absorbs or reflects sunlight. White light from the sun contains light from all the visible wavelengths of the electromagnetic spectrum. Much of the sunlight penetrates the surface of the ocean and is absorbed by the water. Water absorbs most of the wavelengths, or colors, of visible light. Only the blue wavelengths tend to be reflected. The reflection of this blue light makes ocean water appear blue.

Figure 7 ▶ Ocean water appears blue as far as 100 m below the surface.

Why Is Ocean Color Important?

Substances or organisms in ocean water, such as phytoplankton, can affect the color of the water. *Phytoplankton* are microscopic plants in the ocean that provide food to many of the ocean's organisms. Phytoplankton absorb red and blue light, but reflect green light. Therefore, the presence and amount of phytoplankton can affect the shade of blue of the ocean.

By studying variations in the color of the ocean, scientists can determine the presence of phytoplankton in the ocean. Because phytoplankton require nutrients, the presence or absence of phytoplankton can indicate the health of the ocean. If the color of an area of the ocean indicates that no phytoplankton is present, pollution may have prevented phytoplankton growth.

Section 1 Review

1. **Describe** how water temperature affects the ability of the ocean water to dissolve gases. 5d

2. **Summarize** how freezing and evaporation affect salinity. 5d

3. **Describe** the composition of ocean water. 5d

4. **Define** *thermocline.* 5d

5. **Describe** how temperature and salinity affect the density of ocean water. 5d

6. **Explain** how the density of ocean water drives the movement of deep ocean currents. 5d

7. **Explain** why shallow ocean water appears to be blue in color. 5d

CRITICAL THINKING

8. **Making Inferences** Why does the surface temperature of ocean water in middle latitudes vary during the year? 5d, IE.1d

9. **Understanding Relationships** Why would surface water in the North Sea be more likely to contain a high percentage of dissolved gases than the surface water in the Caribbean Sea would? 5d, IE.1d

10. **Predicting Consequences** If global temperatures increase, how would this change affect the ability of the oceans to absorb CO_2? 5d, IE.1d

11. **Identifying Relationships** If an area of the ocean has a large decrease in phytoplankton, how would this change affect other ocean organisms? Explain your answer. IE.1d

CONCEPT MAPPING

12. Use the following terms to create a concept map: *ocean water, salinity, temperature, density, dissolved solids,* and *dissolved gas.* 5d

Section 2 — Life in the Oceans

California Content Standards

5d Students know properties of ocean water, such as temperature and salinity, can be used to explain the layered structure of the oceans, the generation of horizontal and vertical ocean currents, and the geographic distribution of marine organisms.

IE.1d Students will formulate explanations using logic and evidence.

Most marine organisms depend on two major factors for their survival—the essential nutrients available in ocean water and sunlight. Variations in either of these factors affect the ability of aquatic organisms to survive and flourish.

Ocean Chemistry and Marine Life

The chemistry of the ocean is a balance of dissolved gases and solids that are essential to marine life. Marine organisms help maintain the chemical balance of ocean water. They do this by removing nutrients and gases from the ocean while returning other nutrients and gases to the ocean. For example, marine plants absorb large amounts of carbon, hydrogen, oxygen, and sulfur. They also absorb other elements such as nitrogen, phosphorus, and silicon. Marine organisms also return nutrients and gases to the ocean. For example, photosynthetic marine plants remove carbon dioxide from ocean water to produce oxygen.

Marine organisms, such as the sea horse shown in **Figure 1,** also help recycle nutrients in the ocean. During a marine organism's lifetime, the organism absorbs and stores nutrients from the ocean. These nutrients are eventually returned to the water when the organism dies. For example, bacteria in the water digest the remains of the dead organisms. The bacteria then release the essential nutrients from the dead organisms into the ocean.

OBJECTIVES

▶ **Explain** how marine organisms alter the chemistry of ocean water. 5d

▶ **Explain** why plankton can be called *the foundation of life in the ocean.* 5d

▶ **Describe** the major zones of life in the ocean. 5d

KEY TERMS

upwelling
plankton
nekton
benthos
benthic zone
pelagic zone

Figure 1 ▶ Like many marine organisms, this sea horse gets many of the nutrients it needs from the ocean water.

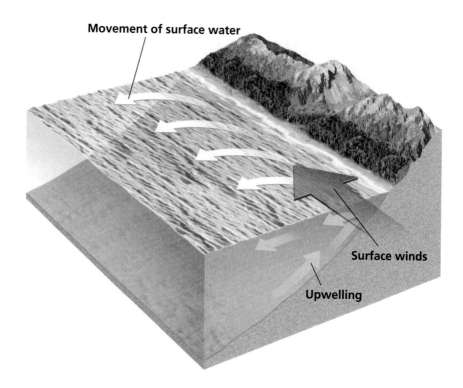

Movement of surface water

Surface winds

Upwelling

Figure 2 ▶ Upwelling is caused by offshore movement of surface water. *How might stormy weather affect the process of upwelling?*

upwelling the movement of deep, cold, and nutrient-rich water to the surface

plankton the mass of mostly microscopic organisms that float or drift freely in the waters of aquatic (freshwater and marine) environments

nekton all organisms that swim actively in open water, independent of currents

benthos organisms that live at the bottom of oceans or bodies of fresh water

Figure 3 ▶ Plankton are so tiny that you need a microscope to see them.

Upwelling

The distribution of life in the ocean depends on the way life-supporting nutrients cycle in the ocean water. In general, all of the elements necessary for life are consumed by organisms near the surface. Elements are then released back into the ocean water when organisms die, sink to lower depths, and decay. Thus, deep water is a storage area for the nutrients needed for life. These nutrients must, however, return to the surface before most organisms in the ocean can use them.

One way that nutrients return to the surface is through a process called upwelling. **Upwelling** is the movement of deep, cold, and nutrient-rich water to the surface, as shown in **Figure 2.** When wind blows steadily parallel to a coastline, surface water moves farther offshore. The deep, cold water then rises to replace the surface water that has moved away from the shore.

Marine Food Webs

Because most marine organisms need sunlight as well as nutrients, most marine organisms live in the upper 100 m of water. Free-floating, microscopic plants and animals called **plankton** live within the sunlit zone. Plankton, shown in **Figure 3,** form the base of the complex food webs in the ocean. The plankton are consumed primarily by small marine organisms, which, in turn, become food for larger marine animals. These larger animals fall into two groups. All organisms that swim actively in open water, such as fish, dolphins, and squid, are called **nekton.** The organisms that live on the ocean floor are called **benthos.** Benthos include marine plants and animals, such as oysters, sea stars, and crabs, that live in sunlit, shallow waters.

Ocean Environments

The ocean can be divided into two basic environments, as shown in **Figure 4.** These zones are the bottom region, or **benthic zone**, and the upper region, or **pelagic zone**. The amount of sunlight, the water temperature, and the water pressure determine the distribution of marine life within these zones.

Benthic Zones

The shallowest benthic zone lies between the low-tide and high-tide lines and is called the *intertidal zone*. Shifting tides and breaking waves make this zone a continually changing environment for the marine organisms that flourish there.

Most of the organisms that live in the benthic zone live in the shallow *sublittoral zone*. This continuously submerged zone is located on the continental shelves and is populated by organisms such as sea stars, brittle stars, and sea lilies.

The *bathyal zone* begins at the continental slope and extends to a depth of 4,000 m. Because little or no sunlight reaches this zone, plant life is scarce. Examples of animals that live in the bathyal zone are octopuses, sea stars, and brachiopods.

The *abyssal zone* has no sunlight because it begins at a depth of 4,000 m and extends to a depth of 6,000 m. Organisms that live in the abyssal darkness include sponges and worms.

The *hadal zone* is confined to the ocean trenches, which are deeper than 6,000 m below the surface of the water. This zone is virtually unexplored, and scientists think that life in the hadal zone is sparse.

✓ **Reading Check** Which benthic zone has the most marine life? Why? **(See the Appendix for answers to Reading Checks.)**

benthic zone the bottom region of oceans and bodies of fresh water

pelagic zone the region of an ocean or body of fresh water above the benthic zone

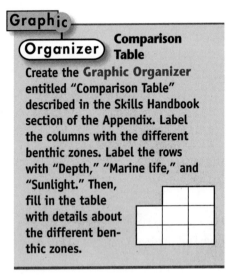

Graphic Organizer **Comparison Table**

Create the **Graphic Organizer** entitled "Comparison Table" described in the Skills Handbook section of the Appendix. Label the columns with the different benthic zones. Label the rows with "Depth," "Marine life," and "Sunlight." Then, fill in the table with details about the different benthic zones.

Figure 4 ▶ This diagram shows the classification and location of marine environments.

Figure 5 ▶ Fish and marine mammals are examples of organisms that live in the pelagic zone.

Pelagic Zones

The region of the ocean above the benthic zone is the pelagic zone. The area of the pelagic zone above the continental shelves is called the *neritic zone*. The neritic zone has abundant sunlight, moderate temperatures, and relatively low water pressure, which are ideal factors for marine life. Nekton fill the zone's waters and are the source of much of the fish and seafood that humans eat.

The *oceanic zone* extends into the deep waters beyond the continental shelf. It is divided into four zones, based on depth. The epipelagic zone is the uppermost area of the oceanic zone. It is sunlit and populated by marine life, such as the dolphins shown in **Figure 5.** The mesopelagic, bathypelagic, and abysso-pelagic zones occur at increasingly greater depths. The amount of marine life in the pelagic zone decreases as depth increases.

Section 2 Review

1. **Explain** the effects marine organisms have on the chemistry of ocean water. 5d

2. **Summarize** the process of upwelling, and describe its importance to marine organisms. 5d

3. **Explain** how plankton form the base of ocean food webs. 7b

4. **Identify** the two major zones of the ocean environment. 5d

5. **Compare** the sublittoral and neritic zones, and name some organisms found in each zone. 5d

CRITICAL THINKING

6. **Analyzing Processes** How can the movement of wind currents alter the chemistry of a given area of the ocean? 5d, IE.1d

7. **Making Predictions** How would life in the ocean change if the area of all regions of upwelling decreased? 5d, IE.1d

CONCEPT MAPPING

8. Use the following terms to create a concept map: *pelagic zone, neritic zone, benthic zone, ocean environment,* and *oceanic zone.* 5d

Section 3 Ocean Resources

 California Content Standards

IE.1d Students will formulate explanations using logic and evidence.
IE.1m Students will investigate a science-based societal issue by researching the literature, analyzing data, and communicating the findings. Examples of issues include irradiation of food, cloning of animals by somatic cell nuclear transfer, choice of energy sources, and land and water use decisions in California.

The ocean supplies humans with a number of natural resources. It is a major source of food and minerals, and it provides a means of transportation. Furthermore, the growth of Earth's population has created new interest in the sea as a source of fresh water.

Fresh Water from the Ocean

The increasing demand for fresh water for things such as drinking water, industry, and irrigation can be met by converting ocean water to fresh water. One way of increasing the freshwater supply is through desalination, as shown in **Figure 1. Desalination** is the extraction of fresh water from salt water. Although desalination may provide needed fresh water, the process is generally costly.

Methods of Desalination

One method of desalination is distillation. During *distillation*, ocean water is heated to remove salt. Heat causes liquid water to evaporate and leaves dissolved salts behind. When the water vapor condenses, the result is pure fresh water. However, the process of evaporating liquid water often requires a large amount of costly heat energy.

Another method of desalination is *freezing*. When water freezes, the first ice crystals that form do not contain salt. The ice can be removed and melted to obtain fresh water. This process requires about one-sixth the energy needed for distillation.

Reverse osmosis desalination is a popular method for desalinating ocean water. It includes the use of special membranes that allow water under high pressure to pass through and that block the dissolved salts.

OBJECTIVES

▶ **Describe** three important resources of the ocean.

▶ **Explain** the threat water pollution poses to marine organisms. IE.1m

KEY TERMS

desalination
aquaculture

desalination a process of removing salt from ocean water

Figure 1 ▶ After salt water from the Persian Gulf has undergone desalination, much of the resulting fresh water is stored in these towers in Kuwait.

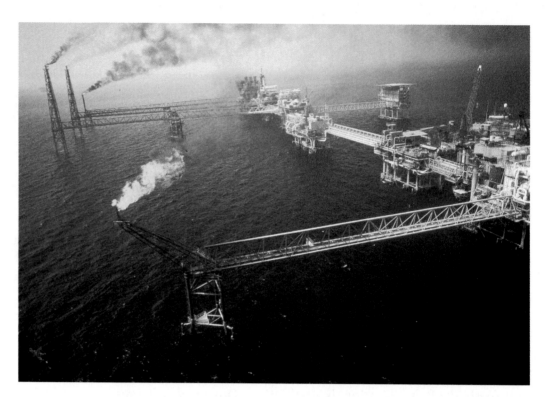

Figure 2 ▶ Offshore oil rigs, such as this one in the Gulf of Mexico, produce about one-fourth of the world's oil.

MATHPRACTICE

Ocean's Gold One cubic kilometer of ocean water contains about 6 kg of gold. If you must process 4 million liters of ocean water to get an amount of gold worth 4¢, how many liters of water would have to be processed to get gold worth $1?

Mineral and Energy Resources

Salt is one mineral resource that can be obtained from the ocean. Other minerals and energy resources can also be extracted from the oceans. While some valuable minerals are easily extracted from the oceans, others are costly or difficult to extract.

Petroleum

The most valuable resource in the ocean is the petroleum found beneath the sea floor. Offshore oil and natural gas deposits exist along continental margins around the world. About one-fourth of the world's oil is now obtained from offshore wells, such as the one shown in **Figure 2.** As a result of new drilling techniques, oil and gas can be extracted far offshore and from great depths.

Nodules

Potato-shaped lumps of minerals, called *nodules*, are found on the abyssal floor of the ocean. Nodules are a valuable source of manganese, iron, copper, nickel, cobalt, and phosphates. However, the recovery of nodules is expensive and difficult because they are located in very deep water. Because country borders are observed only close to land, the question of who has the right to mine minerals from the ocean floor has not been answered.

Trace Minerals

The ocean is also the main source of magnesium and bromine. However, the concentration of most other useful chemicals that are dissolved in the oceans is very small. The extraction of minerals found only in trace amounts is too costly to be practical.

Food from the Ocean

Of all of the resources that the ocean supplies, the one in greatest demand is food. Seafood, which is an important source of protein, can be harvested through fishing or through aquaculture.

Fishing

Because fish are a significant food source for people around the world, fishing has become an important industry. But when the ocean is overfished, or overharvested, over a long period of time, fish populations can collapse. A collapse may damage the ecosystem and threaten the fishing industry. To prevent overharvesting, many governments have passed laws to manage fishing.

Aquaculture

Another way to deal with the high demand for seafood is by farming aquatic life. **Aquaculture** is the raising of aquatic plants and animals for human use or consumption. Catfish, salmon, oysters, and shrimp are already grown on large aquatic farms. Similar methods may be used to breed fish and seaweed in ocean farms, such as the one shown in **Figure 3.** A major problem for aquaculturalists is that the ocean farms are susceptible to pollution and that the farms may be a local source of pollution.

Under the best conditions, an ocean farm could produce more food than an agricultural farm of the same size does. For example, in agriculture, only the top layers of soil can be used. In contrast, ocean farms may use a wide range of depths to produce food. Someday, the nutrient-rich bottom water may be pumped to the surface as a way of fertilizing aquatic farms.

Reading Check List the benefits and problems of aquaculture. (See the Appendix for answers to Reading Checks.)

For a variety of links related to this chapter, go to www.scilinks.org

Topic: Ocean Resources
SciLinks code: HQ61065

aquaculture the raising of aquatic plants and animals for human use or consumption

Figure 3 ▶ Aquaculture establishments, such as this seaweed farm in Madagascar, provide a reliable, economical source of food.

Ocean-Water Pollution

The oceans have been used as a dumping ground for many kinds of wastes including garbage, sewage, and nuclear waste. Until recently, most wastes were diluted or destroyed as they spread throughout the ocean. But the growth of the world population and the increased use of more-toxic substances have reduced the ocean's ability to absorb wastes and renew itself.

Productive coastal areas and beaches are in the greatest danger of being polluted because they are closest to sources of pollution, as shown in **Figure 4.** Pollution has destroyed clam and oyster beds, sea birds have become tangled in plastic products, and beaches have been closed because of sewage and oil spills.

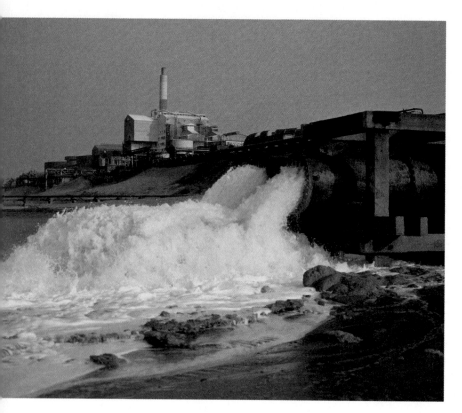

Figure 4 ▶ Pollution can damage the ocean's ecosystem and make seafood unsafe to eat.

Besides being found in coastal waters, pollutants can be found in most other areas of the oceans. Traces of mercury, of the insecticide DDT, and of lead from gasoline have been detected in the ocean. In some areas of the world, concentrations of pollutants are so high that the fish have become unsafe for humans to eat. Recognizing the affects of dumping waste in the ocean, scientists and governments have been working to reduce pollution. For example, the use of DDT has been banned in the United States and the use of leaded gasoline has been reduced. 🪶

Section 3 Review

1. **Describe** three methods of desalinating ocean water.

2. **Explain** why distillation can be an expensive method of desalination.

3. **List** two important mineral resources in the ocean.

4. **Identify** the most valuable resource that can be obtained from the ocean.

5. **Define** the term *aquaculture,* and explain why aquaculture is important.

6. **Explain** why beaches are especially vulnerable to ocean pollution. 🔲IE.1m

CRITICAL THINKING

7. **Making Inferences** Describe how the mining of nodules may create problems between countries. 🔲IE.1d

8. **Predicting Consequences** How would pollution of oceans affect the fishing industry? 🔲IE.1m

9. **Analyzing Relationships** How could humans be affected if microscopic marine organisms absorb small amounts of mercury? 🔲IE.1d, IE.1m

CONCEPT MAPPING

10. Use the following terms to create a concept map: *desalination, distillation, freezing, reverse osmosis, petroleum, aquaculture, fishing, salt, ocean resource,* and *pollution.*

Sections

1 Properties of Ocean Water

Key Terms

salinity, 496
pack ice, 497
thermocline, 498
density, 499

Key Concepts

▶ Cold ocean water dissolves gases more readily than warm ocean water does.

▶ The ocean is a carbon sink that dissolves CO_2 from the atmosphere.

▶ Dissolved solids make up 3.5% of the mass of ocean water.

▶ Salinity is a measure of the amount of dissolved salts in ocean water.

▶ Temperature of ocean water is dependent on depth and latitude.

▶ Density of ocean water is dependent on temperature and salinity.

▶ The color of ocean water is affected by the presence of phytoplankton.

2 Life in the Oceans

upwelling, 502
plankton, 502
nekton, 502
benthos, 502
benthic zone, 503
pelagic zone, 503

▶ Marine organisms help maintain the chemical balance of ocean water by using nutrients for life processes and by returning the nutrients to the water after death.

▶ Plankton form the base of complex ocean food webs by acting as food for other marine organisms.

▶ There are two major zones of life in the ocean: benthic and pelagic. Each zone supports different types of organisms.

3 Ocean Resources

desalination, 505
aquaculture, 507

▶ The ocean is valuable as a source of fresh water, minerals, and food.

▶ Fresh water can be obtained from the ocean by the methods of desalination, freezing, and reverse osmosis desalination.

▶ Ocean-water pollution threatens both marine organisms and humans by damaging food resources in the ocean.

Using Key Terms

Use each of the following terms in a separate sentence.

1. *thermocline* 🐾 5d
2. *upwelling* 🐾 5d
3. *desalination*

For each pair of terms, explain how the meanings of the terms differ.

4. *salinity* and *density* 🐾 5d
5. *plankton* and *nekton* 🐾 5d, 7b
6. *benthic zone* and *pelagic zone* 🐾 5d
7. *upwelling* and *aquaculture* 🐾 5d

Understanding Key Concepts

8. The amount of dissolved salts in ocean water is called the water's 🐾 5d
   a. salinity.
   b. nekton.
   c. plankton.
   d. density.

9. When liquid water is warmed, its density 🐾 5d
   a. increases.
   b. decreases.
   c. remains the same.
   d. doubles.

10. Although most of the various wavelengths of visible light are absorbed by ocean water, the one wavelength that is most often reflected is the color 🐾 5d
    a. violet.
    b. green.
    c. yellow.
    d. blue.

11. Drifting marine plants and animals are known as 🐾 7b
    a. plankton.
    b. benthos.
    c. nekton.
    d. sea stars.

12. Marine animals that can swim to search for food and avoid predators are called 🐾 7b
    a. phytoplankton.
    b. zooplankton.
    c. nekton.
    d. benthos.

13. Which of the following ocean environments experiences the most change? 🐾 5d
    a. intertidal zone
    b. abyssal zone
    c. bathyal zone
    d. neritic zone

14. Which of the following methods is *not* used for producing fresh water by desalinating ocean water?
    a. distillation
    b. evaporation
    c. reverse osmosis
    d. aquaculture

15. Lumps of minerals on the ocean floor are called
    a. nekton.
    b. nodules.
    c. benthos.
    d. plankton.

16. Aquaculture is another name for
    a. desalination.
    b. distillation.
    c. ocean farming.
    d. rapid temperature changes.

Short Answer

17. Describe the process of upwelling, and explain its effects on marine life. 🐾 5d

18. What are the six most abundant elements dissolved in ocean water? 🐾 5d

19. How are temperature, salinity, and density related? 🐾 5d

20. Describe how an oil spill would affect a fishing industry. 🐾 IE.1m

21. List three important resources from the ocean, and describe how they are obtained.

22. What effects does ocean pollution have on humans? 🐾 IE.1m

5a Students know how differential heating of Earth results in circulation patterns in the atmosphere and oceans that globally distrib- ute the heat. **5b** Students know the relationship between the rotation of Earth and the circular motions of ocean currents and air in pressure centers. **IE.1d** Students will formulate explanations using logic and evidence.

The water in the ocean moves in giant streams called **currents.** Many ocean currents are complex and difficult to trace. Oceanographers identify ocean currents by studying the physical and chemical characteristics of the ocean water. They also identify currents by mapping the paths of debris that is dumped or washed overboard from ships, as shown in **Figure 1.** From these data, scientists have mapped a detailed pattern of ocean currents around the world. Scientists place ocean currents into two major categories: surface currents and deep currents.

Factors That Affect Surface Currents

Currents that move on or near the surface of the ocean and are driven by winds are called **surface currents.** Surface currents are controlled by three factors: air currents, Earth's rotation, and the location of the continents.

All surface currents are affected by winds. Winds are caused by the uneven heating of the atmosphere. Variations in air temperature lead to variations in air density and pressure. Colder, denser air sinks and forms areas of high pressure. Air moves away from high-pressure areas to lower pressure areas. This movement gives rise to wind.

Because *wind* is moving air, wind has kinetic energy. The wind passes this energy to the ocean as the air moves across the ocean surface. As energy is transferred from the air to the ocean, the water at the ocean's surface begins to move.

OBJECTIVES

▶ **Describe** how wind patterns, the rotation of Earth, and continental barriers affect surface currents in the ocean. 📖 5a, 5b

▶ **Identify** the major factor that determines the direction in which a surface current circulates. 📖 5b

▶ **Explain** how differences in the density of ocean water affect the flow of deep currents. 📖 5d

KEY TERMS

current
surface current
Coriolis effect
gyre
Gulf Stream
deep current

current in geology, a horizontal movement of water in a well-defined pattern, such as a river or stream

surface current a horizontal movement of ocean water that is caused by wind and that occurs at or near the ocean's surface

Figure 1 ▶ Glass floats, which are used to hold up Japanese fishing nets, have been carried by surface currents from off the coasts of Japan to this beach in northwest Hawaii.

Global Wind Belts

Global wind belts, such as the trade winds and westerlies shown in **Figure 2,** are a major factor affecting the flow of ocean surface water. The *trade winds* are located just north and south of the equator. In the Northern Hemisphere, trade winds blow from the northeast. In the Southern Hemisphere, they blow from the southeast. In both hemispheres, trade-wind belts push currents westward across the tropical latitudes of all three major oceans.

The *westerlies* are located in the middle latitudes. In the Northern Hemisphere, westerlies blow from the southwest. In the Southern Hemisphere, they blow from the northwest. Westerlies push ocean currents eastward in the higher latitudes of the Northern and Southern Hemispheres.

Continental Barriers

The continents are another major influence on surface currents. The continents act as barriers to surface currents. When a surface current flows against a continent, the current is deflected and divided.

The Coriolis Effect

Global wind belts and ocean currents do not flow in straight lines. Wind belts and ocean currents follow a curved or circular pattern that is caused by Earth's rotation. As Earth spins on its axis, ocean currents and wind belts curve. The curving of the path of oceans and winds due to Earth's rotation is called the **Coriolis effect.** The wind belts and the Coriolis effect cause huge circles of moving water, called **gyres,** to form. In the Northern Hemisphere, water flow in gyres is to the right, or clockwise. In the Southern Hemisphere, the flow is to the left, or counterclockwise.

Coriolis effect the apparent curving of the path of a moving object from an otherwise straight path due to Earth's rotation

gyre a huge circle of moving ocean water found above and below the equator

Figure 2 ▶ Global winds and the Coriolis effect together drive the surface currents of the oceans in great circular patterns. The photo at right shows a gyre in the Pacific Ocean off the east coast of Japan.

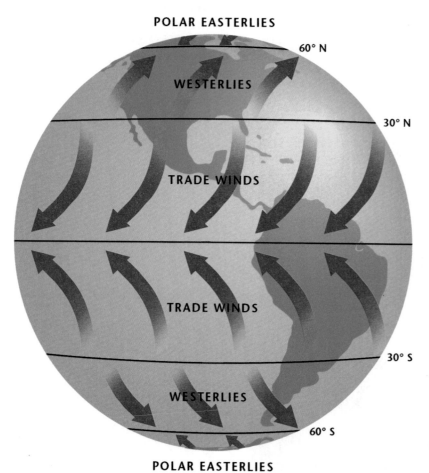

POLAR EASTERLIES

60° N

WESTERLIES

30° N

TRADE WINDS

TRADE WINDS

30° S

WESTERLIES

60° S

POLAR EASTERLIES

Major Surface Currents

The major surface currents of the world are shown in **Figure 3.** The major currents in the equatorial region and in the Northern and Southern Hemispheres are described below.

Equatorial Currents

Warm equatorial currents are located in the Atlantic, Pacific, and Indian Oceans. Each of these oceans has two warm-water equatorial currents that move in a westward direction. Between these westward-flowing currents lies a weaker, eastward-flowing current called the *Equatorial Countercurrent.*

Currents in the Southern Hemisphere

In the Southern Hemisphere, the currents in gyres move counterclockwise. In the most southerly regions of the oceans, constant westward winds produce the world's largest current, the *Antarctic Circumpolar Current,* also known as *West Wind Drift.* No continents interrupt the movement of this current that completely circles Antartica and crosses all three major oceans.

The Indian Ocean surface currents follow two patterns. Currents in the southern Indian Ocean follow a circular, counterclockwise gyre. Currents in the northern Indian Ocean are governed by *monsoons,* winds whose directions change seasonally.

✓ **Reading Check** What is the world's largest ocean current? (See the Appendix for answers to Reading Checks.)

Figure 4 ▶ Surface currents in the Atlantic Ocean form the North Atlantic Gyre. The Sargasso Sea in the center of the gyre results from this pattern of currents. The organisms below are commonly found in the Sargasso Sea.

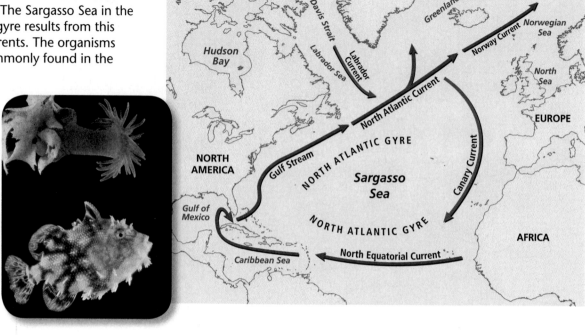

Gulf Stream the swift, deep, and warm Atlantic current that flows along the eastern coast of the United States toward the north

Ocean Currents

Procedure 🖐 5b, IE.1d, IE.1g

1. Fill a shallow pan with water.
2. Sprinkle paper confetti on the surface of the water.
3. Blow across the surface of the water through a drinking straw to produce a clockwise current.
4. Blow through the straw to make a counterclockwise current. Try to make two currents.

Analysis

1. Draw a diagram of the currents. Draw the straw's positions, and use arrows to show air and water direction.
2. How does this activity relate to what happens in ocean currents?

Currents in the North Atlantic

In the North Atlantic Ocean, warm water moves through the Caribbean Sea and Gulf of Mexico and north along the east coast of North America in a swift, warm current called the **Gulf Stream.** Farther north, the cold-water Labrador Current, which flows south, joins the Gulf Stream. South of Greenland, the Gulf Stream widens and slows until it becomes a vast, slow-moving warm current known as the *North Atlantic Current.* Near western Europe, the North Atlantic Current splits. One part becomes the Norway Current, which flows northward along the coast of Norway and keeps that coast ice-free all year. The other part is deflected southward and becomes the cool Canary Current, which eventually warms and rejoins the North Equatorial Current.

As **Figure 4** shows, the Gulf Stream, the North Atlantic Current, the Canary Current, and the North Equatorial Current form the North Atlantic Gyre. At the center of this gyre lies a vast area of calm, warm water called the *Sargasso Sea.* The Sargasso Sea is named after *sargassum,* the brown seaweed that floats on the sea's surface in this area. The pattern of winds and currents around the Sargasso Sea concentrates all kinds of floating debris, such as orange peels and plastic cups, in this area.

Currents in the North Pacific

The pattern of currents in the North Pacific is similar to that in the North Atlantic. The warm Kuroshio Current, the Pacific equivalent of the Gulf Stream, flows northward along the east coast of Asia. This current then flows toward North America as the North Pacific Drift. It eventually flows southward along the California coast as the cool California Current.

Deep Currents

In addition to having wind-driven surface currents, the ocean has **deep currents,** cold, dense currents far below the surface. Deep currents move much more slowly than surface currents do. Deep currents form as cold, dense water of the polar regions sinks and flows beneath warmer ocean water.

The movement of polar waters is a result of differences in density. When water cools, it contracts and the water molecules move closer together. This contraction makes the water denser, and the water sinks. When water warms, it expands and the water molecules move farther apart. The warm water is less dense, so it rises above the cold water. Temperature determines density.

Salinity, too, determines the density of water. The water in polar regions has high salinity because of the large amount of water frozen in icebergs and sea ice. When water freezes, the salt in the water does not freeze but stays in the unfrozen water. So, unfrozen polar water has a high salt concentration and is denser than water that has a lower salinity. This dense polar water sinks and forms a deep current that flows beneath less dense surface currents, as shown in **Figure 5.**

Antarctic Bottom Water

The temperature of the water near Antarctica is very cold, –2°C. The water's salinity is high. These two factors make the water off the coast of Antarctica the densest and coldest ocean water in the world. This dense, cold water sinks to the ocean bottom and forms a deep current called the *Antarctic Bottom Water.* The Antarctic Bottom Water moves slowly northward along the ocean bottom for thousands of kilometers to a latitude of about 40°N. It takes hundreds of years for the current to make the trip.

Reading Check Why is Antarctic Bottom Water the densest in the world? (See the Appendix for answers to Reading Checks.)

deep current a streamlike movement of ocean water far below the surface

Graphic Organizer Comparison Table

Create the **Graphic Organizer** entitled "Comparison Table" described in the Skills Handbook section of the Appendix. Label the columns with "Surface currents" and "Deep currents." Label the rows with "Salinity," "Temperature," and "Density." Then, fill in the table with details about the salinity, temperature, and density of each current.

Figure 5 ▶ The very dense and highly saline Antarctic Bottom Water travels beneath less dense North Atlantic Deep Water.

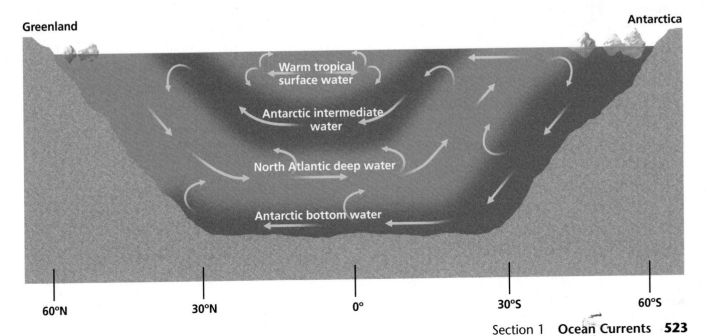

Greenland

Antarctica

Warm tropical surface water

Antarctic intermediate water

North Atlantic deep water

Antarctic bottom water

60°N   30°N   0°   30°S   60°S

North Atlantic Deep Water

In the North Atlantic, south of Greenland, the water is very cold and has a high salinity. This cold, salty water forms a deep current that moves southward under the northward-flowing Gulf Stream. Near the equator, this deep current divides. One part begins to rise, reverse direction, and flow northward again. The rest of the current continues southward toward Antarctica and flows over the colder, denser Antarctic Bottom Water.

Deep Atlantic currents exist near the Mediterranean Sea, too. Every summer in the region, evaporation increases and precipitation decreases. These changes increase the salinity, and thus the density, of the water of the Mediterranean. This denser water sinks and flows through the strait of Gibraltar into the Atlantic Ocean. In turn, surface water from the Atlantic, which is less saline and less dense than deep current water is, flows into the Mediterranean Sea, as shown in **Figure 6.**

Figure 6 ▶ The dense, highly saline water of the Mediterranean Sea forms a deep current as it flows through the strait of Gibraltar and into the less dense Atlantic Ocean.

Turbidity Currents

A turbidity current is a strong current caused by an underwater landslide. A turbidity current occurs when large masses of sediment that have accumulated along a continental shelf or continental slope suddenly break loose and slide downhill. The landslide mixes the nearby water with sediment. The sediment causes the water to become cloudy, or turbid, and denser than the surrounding water. The dense water mass of the turbidity current moves beneath the less dense, clear water.

Section 1 Review

1. **Describe** the force that drives most surface currents. 🔋 5b

2. **Identify** the winds that affect the surface currents on either side of the equator. 🔋 5b

3. **Identify** the winds that affect the surface currents in the middle latitudes. 🔋 5b

4. **Describe** how density affects the flow of deep currents. 🔋 5d

5. **List** the factors that affect the density of ocean water. 🔋 5d

6. **List** three major surface currents and two major deep currents. 🔋 5b

CRITICAL THINKING

7. **Predicting Consequences** Describe how surface currents would be affected if Earth did not rotate. 🔋 5b, IE.1d

8. **Identifying Relationships** Explain how the distribution of solar energy around Earth affects ocean surface currents. 🔋 5a, 5b, IE.1d

CONCEPT MAPPING

9. Use the following terms to create a concept map: *ocean currents, surface currents, deep currents, Gulf Stream, North Atlantic Current, Antarctic Bottom Water, gyres,* and *Coriolis effect.* 🔋 5b

5a Students know how differential heating of Earth results in circulation patterns in the atmosphere and oceans that globally distribute the heat.
IE.1d Students will formulate explanations using logic and evidence.
IE.1g Students will recognize the usefulness and limitations of models and theories as scientific representations of reality.

A **wave** is a periodic disturbance in a solid, liquid, or gas as energy is transmitted through the medium. One kind of wave is described as the periodic up-and-down movement of water. Such a wave has two basic parts—a *crest* and a *trough*, as shown in **Figure 1.** The crest is the highest point of a wave. The trough is the lowest point between two crests. The *wave height* is the vertical distance between the crest and the trough of a wave. The *wavelength* is the horizontal distance between two consecutive crests or between two consecutive troughs. The **wave period** is the time required for two consecutive wave crests to pass a given point. The speed at which a wave moves is calculated by dividing the wave's wavelength by its period.

$$wave\ speed = \frac{wavelength}{wave\ period}$$

Wave Energy

The uneven heating of Earth's atmosphere causes pressure differences that make air move. This moving air is called *wind*. Wind then transfers the energy received from the sun to the ocean and forms waves. Small waves, or ripples, form as a result of friction between the moving air and water. As a ripple receives more energy from wind, the ripple grows into a larger wave. The longer that wind blows from a given direction, the more energy is transferred from wind to water and the larger the wave becomes.

The smoothness of the ocean's surface is generally disrupted by many small waves moving in different directions. Because of their large surface area, larger waves receive more energy from the wind than smaller waves do. Thus, larger waves grow larger, and smaller waves die out.

OBJECTIVES

▶ **Describe** the formation of waves and the factors that affect wave size. 5a

▶ **Explain** how waves interact with the coastline. 5a

▶ **Identify** the cause of destructive ocean waves.

KEY TERMS

wave
wave period
fetch
refraction

wave a periodic disturbance in a solid, liquid, or gas as energy is transmitted through a medium

wave period the time required for two consecutive wave crests to pass a given point

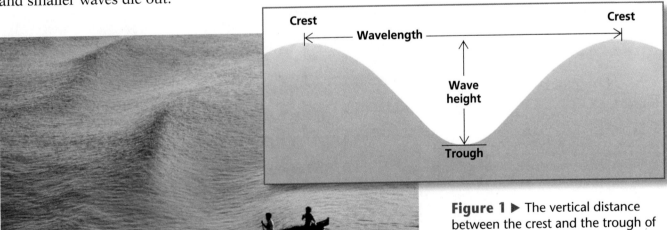

Figure 1 ▶ The vertical distance between the crest and the trough of a wave is the wave height. In a series of waves, the wave height may be similar for all of the waves, as shown in the photo at left.

Figure 2 ▶ Like the bottle in this diagram, water molecules do not travel horizontally through the water with the wave.

Water Movement in a Wave

Although the energy of a wave moves from water molecule to water molecule in the direction of the wave, the water itself moves very little. This fact can be demonstrated by observing the movement of a bottle floating on the water as a wave passes. The bottle appears to move up and down, but it moves in a circular path, as shown in **Figure 2.** As the wave passes, the bottle returns to where it started.

As a wave moves across the surface of the ocean, only the energy of the wave, not the water, moves in the direction of the wave. The water molecules within the wave move in a circular motion. During a single wave period, each water particle moves in one complete circle. At the end of the wave period, a circling water particle ends up almost exactly where it started.

As a wave passes a given point, the circle traced by a water particle on the ocean surface has a diameter that is equal to the height of the wave. Because waves receive their energy from wind pushing against the surface of the ocean, the energy received decreases as the depth of the water increases. As a result, water at various depths receives varying amounts of energy. Thus, the diameter of a water molecule's circular path decreases as water depth increases, as shown in **Figure 3.** Below a depth of about one-half the wavelength, there is almost no circular motion of water molecules.

✓ Reading Check Why does the diameter of a water molecule's circular path in a wave decrease as depth increases? (See the Appendix for answers to Reading Checks.)

Figure 3 ▶ Wave energy decreases as depth increases. As a result, the diameter of a water molecule's circular path in the wave also decreases.

Wavelength

Wave height

Direction of wave movement

Negligible water movement below a depth of one-half wavelength

Energy from the Ocean

The search for renewable energy sources has led to some ingenious ways of tapping the ocean for energy. Scientists have found ways to generate electricity from three ocean features: waves, tides, and heat.

Wave Energy

Most wave-power systems use buoys and the up-and-down motion of waves to run pumps that force water or air through turbine generators. A newer design uses piezoelectric plastic (pie EE zoh ee LEK trik PLAS tik), a material that produces electricity when stretched.

Tidal Energy

Tides can generate electricity in a way similar in principle to the way that hydroelectric plants on rivers generate electricity. At high tide, a dam built across a bay or inlet traps water. As the tide ebbs, this water is released through the dam's turbines to drive electric generators.

Thermal Energy

The process of producing electricity from the heat energy contained in ocean water is called *ocean thermal energy conversion* (OTEC). OTEC plants rely on steam to turn their turbine generators. Warm surface water is pumped through a vacuum chamber, which turns the water to steam. The steam then turns special low-pressure turbines.

Ocean power is not as cost effective as electricity from fuel-burning or nuclear power plants is. However, as ocean power technology becomes more reliable and more efficient, the ocean's renewable energy may become more affordable.

Extension

1. **Determining Cause and Effect** What do all three types of ocean power have in common?
2. **Research** Write a short report that explains how using energy from waves, tides, or heat in the ocean could help reduce pollution of the air and ocean.

▼ Tidal power plants, such as this one in France, rely on the flow of tides to turn turbines that generate electricity.

◀ This wave-power energy station in Scotland generates 500 kilowatts of electricity, enough to power 300 homes.

Unit 7 ATMOSPHERIC FORCES

▶ Wall clouds, such as this one near Adrian, Texas, are small clouds that form underneath large storm clouds. The beginning of a tornado can be seen in the circulation of dust on the ground under this wall cloud. Tornadoes tend to form under wall clouds.

Sections

1 Characteristics of the Atmosphere

2 Solar Energy and the Atmosphere

3 Atmospheric Circulation

What You'll Learn

- Which gases make up the atmosphere
- How solar energy interacts with the atmosphere
- What causes wind

Why It's Relevant

The atmosphere affects all living things on Earth. It provides the air that we breathe, protection from solar radiation, and the insulation that maintains the global temperature of Earth.

PRE-READING ACTIVITY

Booklet
Before you read this chapter, create the FoldNote entitled "Booklet" described in the Skills Handbook section of the Appendix. Label each page of the booklet with a main idea from the chapter. As you read the chapter, write what you learn about each main idea on the appropriate page of the booklet.

▶ This image was captured by a satellite that was monitoring a large storm over the Atlantic Ocean. Storms are only one small feature of Earth's dynamic atmosphere.

California Content Standards

4b Students know the fate of incoming solar radiation in terms of reflection, absorption, and photosynthesis.

4c Students know the different atmospheric gases that absorb the Earth's thermal radiation, and the mechanism and significance of the greenhouse effect.

4d* Students know the differing greenhouse conditions on Earth, Mars, and Venus; the origins of those conditions; and the climatic consequences of each.

5a Students know how differential heating of Earth results in circulation patterns in the atmosphere and oceans that globally distribute the heat.

5b Students know the relationship between the rotation of Earth and the circular motions of ocean currents and air in pressure centers.

5c Students know the origin and effects of temperature inversions.

7a Students know the carbon cycle of photosynthesis and respiration and the nitrogen cycle.

7c Students know the movement of matter among reservoirs is driven by Earth's internal and external sources of energy.

8a Students know the thermal structure and chemical composition of the atmosphere.

8b Students know how the composition of Earth's atmosphere has evolved over geologic time and know the effect of outgassing, the variations of carbon dioxide concentration and the origin of atmospheric oxygen.

8c Students know the location of the ozone layer in the upper atmosphere, its role in absorbing ultraviolet radiation, and the way in which this layer varies both naturally and in response to human activities.

IE.1a Students will select and use appropriate tools and technology (such as computer-linked probes, spreadsheets, and graphing calculators) to perform tests, collect data, analyze relationships and display data.

IE.1d Students will formulate explanations using logic and evidence.

IE.1g Students will recognize the usefulness and limitations of models and theories as scientific representations of reality.

IE.1m Students will investigate a science-based societal issue by researching the literature, analyzing data, and communicating the findings. Examples of issues include irradiation of food, cloning of animals by somatic cell nuclear transfer, choice of energy sources, and land and water use decisions in California.

Characteristics of the Atmosphere

California Content Standards

5c Students know the origin and effects of temperature inversions.
8a Students know the thermal structure and chemical composition of the atmosphere.
8c Students know the location of the ozone layer in the upper atmosphere, its role in absorbing ultraviolet radiation, and the way in which this layer varies both naturally and in response to human activities.

The layer of gases that surrounds Earth is called the **atmosphere**. The atmosphere is made up of a mixture of chemical elements and compounds that is commonly called *air*. The atmosphere protects Earth's surface from the sun's radiation and helps regulate the temperature of Earth's surface.

Composition of the Atmosphere

As the graph in **Figure 1** shows, the most abundant elements in air are the gases nitrogen, oxygen, and argon. The composition of dry air is nearly the same everywhere on Earth's surface and up to an altitude of about 80 km. The two most abundant compounds in air are the gases carbon dioxide, CO_2, and water vapor, H_2O. In addition to containing gaseous elements and compounds, the atmosphere commonly carries various kinds of tiny solid particles, such as dust and pollen.

Nitrogen in the Atmosphere

Nitrogen makes up about 78% of Earth's atmosphere. Nitrogen in the atmosphere is maintained through a process called the *nitrogen cycle*. During the nitrogen cycle, nitrogen moves from air to the soil and then to plants and animals and eventually returns to the air, as shown in **Figure 1.**

Nitrogen is removed from the air mainly by the action of nitrogen-fixing bacteria. These microscopic organisms live in the soil and on the roots of certain plants. The bacteria chemically change nitrogen from the air into nitrogen compounds that are vital to the growth of all plants. When animals eat plants, nitrogen compounds enter the animals' bodies. Nitrogen compounds are then returned to the soil through animal wastes or by the decay of dead organisms. Decay releases nitrogen back into the atmosphere. A similar nitrogen cycle takes place between marine organisms and ocean water.

OBJECTIVES

▶ **Describe** the composition of Earth's atmosphere. 🐻 4c, 8b, 8a

▶ **Explain** how two types of barometers work. 🐻 IE.1a

▶ **Identify** the layers of the atmosphere. 🐻 8a, 8c

▶ **Identify** two effects of air pollution. 🐻 5c, IE.1m

KEY TERMS

atmosphere
ozone
atmospheric pressure
troposphere
stratosphere
mesosphere
thermosphere

atmosphere a mixture of gases that surrounds a planet, such as Earth

Figure 1 ▶ The pie graph shows the composition of dry air by volume at sea level. Nitrogen in the atmosphere is kept at a relatively constant level by the nitrogen cycle.

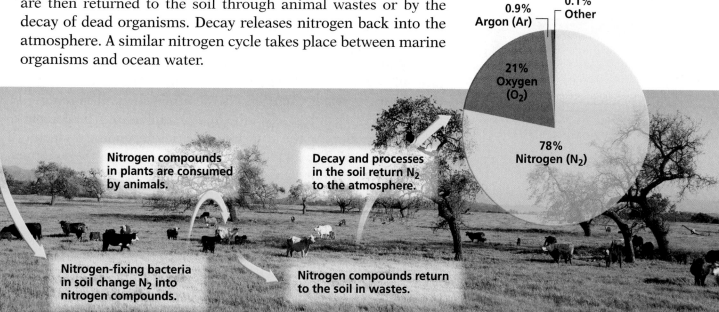

0.1% Other
0.9% Argon (Ar)
21% Oxygen (O_2)
78% Nitrogen (N_2)

Nitrogen compounds in plants are consumed by animals.

Decay and processes in the soil return N_2 to the atmosphere.

Nitrogen-fixing bacteria in soil change N_2 into nitrogen compounds.

Nitrogen compounds return to the soil in wastes.

Figure 2 ▶ Several processes interact to maintain stable amounts of oxygen, carbon dioxide, and water in the atmosphere.

Oxygen in the Atmosphere

Oxygen makes up about 21% of Earth's atmosphere. As shown in **Figure 2**, natural processes maintain the chemical balance of oxygen in the atmosphere. Animals, bacteria, and plants remove oxygen from the air as part of their life processes. Forest fires, the burning of fuels, and the weathering of some rocks also remove oxygen from air. These processes would quickly use up most atmospheric oxygen if various processes that add oxygen to air did not take place.

Land and ocean plants produce large quantities of oxygen in a process called *photosynthesis*. During photosynthesis, plants use sunlight, water, and carbon dioxide to produce their food, and they release oxygen as a byproduct. The amount of oxygen produced by plants each year equals the amount consumed by all animal life processes. Thus, the oxygen content of the air remains at about 21% of Earth's atmosphere.

Water Vapor in the Atmosphere

As water evaporates from oceans, lakes, streams, and soil, it enters air as the invisible gas *water vapor*. Plants and animals give off water vapor during transpiration, one of their life processes. But as water vapor enters the atmosphere, it is removed by the processes of condensation and precipitation. The percentage of water vapor in the atmosphere varies depending on factors such as time of day, location, and season. Because the amount of water vapor in air varies, the composition of the atmosphere is usually given as that of dry air. Dry air has less than 1% water vapor. Moist air may contain as much as 4% water vapor.

✓ Reading Check Does transpiration increase the amount of water vapor in the atmosphere or decrease the amount of water vapor in the atmosphere? (See the Appendix for answers to Reading Checks.)

Ozone in the Atmosphere

Although it is present only in small amounts, a form of oxygen called **ozone** is an important component of the atmosphere. The oxygen that we breathe, O_2, has two atoms per molecule, but ozone, O_3, has three atoms. Ozone in the upper atmosphere forms the *ozone layer*, which absorbs harmful ultraviolet radiation from the sun. Without the ozone layer, living organisms would be severely damaged by the sun's ultraviolet rays. Unfortunately, a number of human activities damage the ozone layer. Compounds known as *chlorofluorocarbons*, or CFCs, which were previously used in refrigerators and air conditioners, and exhaust compounds, such as nitrogen oxide, break down ozone and have caused parts of the ozone layer to weaken, as **Figure 3** shows.

Particulates in the Atmosphere

In addition to containing gases, the atmosphere contains various tiny solid particles, called *particulates*. Particulates can be volcanic dust, ash from fires, microscopic organisms, or mineral particles lifted from soil by winds. Pollen from plants and particles from meteors that have vaporized are also particulates. When tiny drops of ocean water are tossed into the air as sea spray, the drops evaporate. Left behind in the air are tiny crystals of salt, another type of particulate. Four common sources of particulates are shown in **Figure 4.** Large, heavy particles remain in the atmosphere only briefly, but tiny particles can remain suspended in the atmosphere for months or years.

ozone a gas molecule that is made up of three oxygen atoms

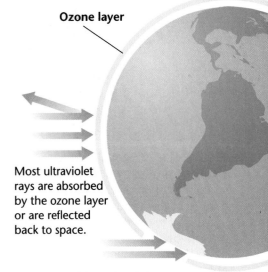

Ozone layer

Most ultraviolet rays are absorbed by the ozone layer or are reflected back to space.

More ultraviolet rays penetrate to Earth's surface through the weakened ozone layer.

Figure 3 ▶ Harmful ultraviolet radiation can reach Earth's surface through the weakened ozone layer over Antarctica.

Figure 4 ▶ Sources of Particulates

Volcanic ash and dust can remain in the atmosphere for years.

The wind carries pollen from plant to plant.

Tornadoes and windstorms carry dirt and dust high into the atmosphere.

As seaspray evaporates, salt particles are left in the atmosphere.

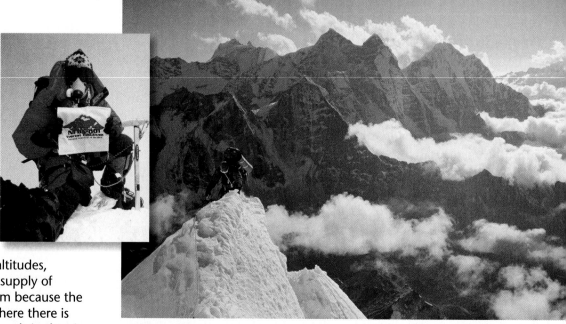

Figure 5 ▶ At high altitudes, climbers must carry a supply of oxygen to breathe from because the density of the atmosphere there is very low. So, oxygen levels in the air are too low to supply the climber. In 2001, Eric Weihenmeyer (shown above) was the first blind person to reach the summit of Mount Everest.

atmospheric pressure the force per unit area that is exerted on a surface by the weight of the atmosphere

Atmospheric Pressure

Gravity holds the gases of the atmosphere near Earth's surface. As a result, the air molecules are compressed together and exert force on Earth's surface. The pressure exerted on a surface by the atmosphere is called **atmospheric pressure.** Atmospheric pressure is exerted equally in all directions—up, down, and sideways.

Earth's gravity keeps 99% of the total mass of the atmosphere within 32 km of Earth's surface. The remaining 1% extends upward for hundreds of kilometers but gets increasingly thinner at high altitudes, as shown in **Figure 5.** Because the pull of gravity is not as strong at higher altitudes, the air molecules are farther apart and exert less pressure on each other at higher altitudes. Thus, atmospheric pressure decreases as altitude increases.

Atmospheric pressure also changes as a result of differences in temperature and in the amount of water vapor in the air. In general, as temperature increases, atmospheric pressure at sea level decreases. The reason is that molecules move farther apart when the air is heated. So, fewer particles exert pressure on a given area, and the pressure decreases. Similarly, air that contains a lot of water vapor is less dense than drier air because water vapor molecules have less mass than nitrogen or oxygen molecules do. The lighter water vapor molecules replace an equal number of heavier oxygen and nitrogen molecules, which makes the volume of air less dense.

Measuring Atmospheric Pressure

Meteorologists use three units for atmospheric pressure: atmospheres (atm), millimeters or inches of mercury, and millibars (mb). *Standard atmospheric pressure,* or 1 atmosphere, is equal to 760 mm of mercury, or 1000 millibars. The average atmospheric pressure at sea level is 1 atm. Meteorologists measure atmospheric pressure by using an instrument called a *barometer.*

Mercurial Barometers

Meteorologists use two main types of barometers. One type is the *mercurial barometer,* a model of which is shown in **Figure 6.** Atmospheric pressure presses on the liquid mercury in a well at the base of the barometer. The pressure holds the mercury up to a certain height inside a tube. The height of the mercury inside the tube varies with the atmospheric pressure. The greater the atmospheric pressure is, the higher the mercury rises.

Aneroid Barometers

The type of barometer most commonly used today is called an *aneroid barometer.* Inside an aneroid barometer is a sealed metal container from which most of the air has been removed to form a partial vacuum. Changes in atmospheric pressure cause the sides of the container to bend inward or bulge out. These changes move a pointer on a scale. Aneroid barometers can be constructed to keep a continuous record of atmospheric pressure.

An aneroid barometer can also measure altitude above sea level. When used for this purpose, an aneroid barometer is called an *altimeter.* The scale on an altimeter registers altitude instead of pressure. At high altitudes, the atmosphere is less dense and exerts less pressure than at low altitudes. So, a lowered pressure reading can be interpreted as an increased altitude reading.

Reading Check What is inside an aneroid barometer? (See the Appendix for answers to Reading Checks.)

Figure 6 ▶ The height of the mercury in this mercurial barometer indicates barometric pressure. *What is the barometric pressure shown?*

QuickLAB

25 min (over 5 days)

Barometric Pressure

Procedure IE.1a, IE.1g

1. Use a rubber band to secure plastic wrap tightly over the open end of a coffee can.
2. Use tape to secure one end of a 10 cm drinking straw onto the plastic wrap near the center of the can.
3. Use scissors and a metric ruler to cut a piece of cardboard 10 cm wide. The cardboard should also be at least 13 cm taller than the can.
4. Fold the cardboard so that it stands upright and extends at least 3 cm above the top of the straw.
5. Place the cardboard near the can so that the free end of the straw just touches the front of the cardboard. Mark an X where the straw touches.
6. Draw three horizontal lines on the cardboard: one that is level with the X, one that is 2 cm above the X, and one that is 2 cm below the X.

7. Position the cardboard so that the straw touches the X. Tape the base of the cardboard in place.
8. Observe the level of the straw at least once per day over a 5-day period. Record any changes that you see.

Analysis

1. What factors affect how your model works? Explain.
2. What does an upward movement of the straw indicate? What does a downward movement indicate?
3. Compare your results with the barometric pressures listed in your local newspaper. What may have caused your results to differ from the newspaper's?

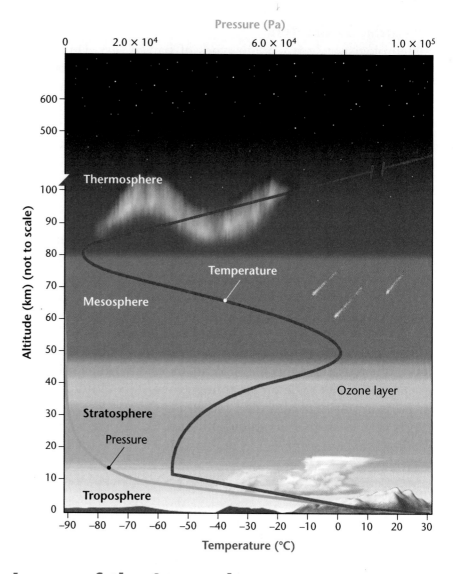

Figure 7 ▶ The red line indicates the temperature at various altitudes in the atmosphere. The green line indicates atmospheric pressure at various altitudes.

troposphere the lowest layer of the atmosphere, in which temperature drops at a constant rate as altitude increases; the part of the atmosphere where weather conditions exist

Layers of the Atmosphere

Earth's atmosphere has a distinctive pattern of temperature changes with increasing altitude, as shown in **Figure 7.** The temperature differences mainly result from how solar energy is absorbed as it moves through the atmosphere. Scientists identify four main layers of the atmosphere based on these differences.

The Troposphere

The atmospheric layer that is closest to Earth's surface and in which nearly all weather occurs is called the **troposphere.** Almost all of the water vapor and carbon dioxide in the atmosphere is found in this layer. Temperature within the troposphere decreases as altitude increases because air in this layer is heated from below by thermal energy that radiates from Earth's surface. The temperature within the troposphere decreases at the average rate of 6.5°C per kilometer as the distance from Earth's surface increases. However, at an average altitude of 12 km, the temperature stops decreasing. This zone is called the *tropopause* and represents the upper boundary of the troposphere. The altitude of this boundary varies with latitude and season.

The Stratosphere

The layer of the atmosphere called the **stratosphere** extends from the tropopause to an altitude of nearly 50 km. Almost all of the ozone in the atmosphere is concentrated in this layer. In the lower stratosphere, the temperature is almost –60°C. In the upper stratosphere, the temperature increases as altitude increases because air in the stratosphere is heated from above by absorption of solar radiation by ozone. The temperature of the air in this layer rises steadily to a temperature of about 0°C at an altitude of about 50 km above Earth's surface. This zone, called the *stratopause*, marks the upper boundary of the stratosphere.

The Mesosphere

Located above the stratopause and extending to an altitude of about 80 km is the **mesosphere.** In this layer, temperature decreases as altitude increases. The upper boundary of the mesosphere, called the *mesopause*, has an average temperature of nearly –90°C, which is the coldest temperature in the atmosphere. Above this boundary temperatures again begin to increase.

The Thermosphere

The atmospheric layer above the mesopause is called the **thermosphere.** In the thermosphere, temperature increases steadily as altitude increases because nitrogen and oxygen atoms absorb solar radiation. Because air particles in the thermosphere are very far apart, they do not strike a thermometer often enough to produce an accurate temperature reading. Therefore, special instruments are needed. These instruments have recorded temperatures of more than 1,000°C in the thermosphere.

The lower region of the thermosphere, at an altitude of 80 to 400 km, is commonly called the *ionosphere*. In the ionosphere, solar radiation that is absorbed by atmospheric gases causes the atoms of gas molecules to lose electrons and to produce ions and free electrons. Interactions between solar radiation and the ionosphere cause the phenomena known as *auroras*, which are shown in **Figure 8.**

There are not enough data about temperature changes in the thermosphere to determine its upper boundary. However, above the ionosphere is the region where Earth's atmosphere blends into the almost complete vacuum of space. This zone of indefinite altitude, called the *exosphere*, extends for thousands of kilometers above the ionosphere.

✔ **Reading Check** What is the lower region of the thermosphere called? (See the Appendix for answers to Reading Checks.)

stratosphere the layer of the atmosphere that lies between the troposphere and the mesosphere and in which temperature increases as altitude increases; contains the ozone layer

mesosphere the coldest layer of the atmosphere, between the stratosphere and the thermosphere, in which temperature decreases as altitude increases

thermosphere the uppermost layer of the atmosphere, in which temperature increases as altitude increases; includes the ionosphere

Figure 8 ▶ Auroras can be seen from space as well as from the ground.

Temperature Inversions

Any substance that is in the atmosphere and that is harmful to people, animals, plants, or property is called an *air pollutant*. Today, the main source of air pollution is the burning of fossil fuels, such as coal and petroleum. As these fuels burn, they may release harmful chemical substances, such as sulfur dioxide gas, hydrocarbons, nitrogen oxides, carbon monoxide, and lead, into the air.

Certain weather conditions can make air pollution worse. One such condition is a *temperature inversion*, the layering of warm air on top of cool air. Warm air, which is less dense than cool air is, can trap cool, polluted air beneath it. In some areas, topography may make air pollution even worse by keeping the polluted inversion layer from dispersing, as **Figure 9** shows. Under conditions in which air cannot circulate up and away from an area, trapped automobile exhaust can produce *smog*, a general term for air pollution that indicates a combination of smoke and fog.

Air pollution can be controlled only by preventing the release of pollutants into the atmosphere. International, federal, and local laws have been passed to reduce the amount of air pollutants produced by automobiles and industry.

Figure 9 ▶ During a temperature inversion, polluted cool air becomes trapped beneath a warm-air layer.

Section 1 Review

1. **Describe** the composition of dry air at sea level. 8a

2. **Identify** five main components of the atmosphere. 8a

3. **Explain** the cause of atmospheric pressure. 5b

4. **Explain** how the two types of barometers measure atmospheric pressure. IE.1a

5. **Identify** the layer of the atmosphere in which weather occurs. 8a

6. **Compare** the four main layers of the atmosphere. 8a, 8c

7. **Identify** the two atmospheric layers that contain air as warm as 25°C. 8a

CRITICAL THINKING

8. **Drawing Conclusions** Why is atmospheric pressure generally lower beneath a mass of warm air than beneath a mass of cold air? IE.1d

9. **Making Calculations** Calculate how much colder air is at the top of Mount Everest, which is almost 9 km above sea level, than air is at the Indian coastline. (Hint: On average, the temperature in the troposphere decreases by 6.5°C per kilometer of altitude.) 8a, IE.1d

10. **Applying Ideas** Which industrial city would have fewer air-pollution incidents related to temperature inversions: one on the Great Plains or one near the Rocky Mountains? Explain your answer. 5c, IE.1d, IE.1m

11. **Applying Concepts** In 1982, Larry Walters rose to an altitude of approximately 4,900 m on a lawn chair attached to 45 helium-filled weather balloons. Give two reasons why Walters' trip was dangerous. 8a, IE.1d

CONCEPT MAPPING

12. Use the following terms to create a concept map: *oxygen, atmosphere, air, nitrogen, water vapor, ozone,* and *particulates*. 4c, 8a

4b Students know the fate of incoming solar radiation in terms of reflection, absorption, and photosynthesis.

4c Students know the different atmospheric gases that absorb the Earth's thermal radiation, and the mechanism and significance of the greenhouse effect.

8a Students know the thermal structure and chemical composition of the atmosphere.

Earth's atmosphere is heated by the transfer of energy from the sun. Some of the heat in the atmosphere comes from the absorption of the sun's rays by gases in the atmosphere. Some heat enters the atmosphere indirectly as ocean and land surfaces absorb solar energy and then give off that energy as heat.

Radiation

All of the energy that Earth receives from the sun travels through space between Earth and the sun as radiation. *Radiation* includes all forms of energy that travel through space as waves. Visible light is the form of radiation that human eyes can detect. However, there are many other forms of radiation that humans cannot see, such as ultraviolet light, X rays, and radio waves.

Radiation travels through space in the form of waves at a very high speed—approximately 300,000 km/s. The distance from any point on a wave to the identical point on the next wave, for example from crest to crest, is called the *wavelength* of a wave. The various types of radiation differ in the length of their waves. Visible light, for example, consists of waves that have various wavelengths that are seen as different colors. The wavelengths of ultraviolet rays, X rays, and gamma rays are shorter than those of visible light. Infrared waves and radio waves have relatively long wavelengths. The waves that make up all forms of radiation are called *electromagnetic waves*. Almost all of the energy that reaches Earth from the sun is in the form of electromagnetic waves. The **electromagnetic spectrum**, shown at the bottom of **Figure 1**, consists of the complete range of wavelengths of electromagnetic waves.

OBJECTIVES

▶ **Explain** how radiant energy reaches Earth. 4b

▶ **Describe** how visible light and infrared energy warm Earth. 4c, 4b

▶ **Summarize** the processes of radiation, conduction, and convection. 4b, 5a

KEY TERMS

electromagnetic spectrum
albedo
greenhouse effect
conduction
convection

electromagnetic spectrum all of the frequencies or wavelengths of electromagnetic radiation

Figure 1 ▶ The sun emits radiation whose wavelengths range throughout the electromagnetic spectrum. Five images of the sun are shown above. Each image shows radiation emitted at different wavelengths.

| Radio | Infrared | Visible | Ultraviolet | X-ray |

Visible light

Radio/TV ———————→ ←Microwaves→ ←—Infrared—→ ←Ultraviolet→ ←X rays→ ←Gamma rays

10^4 10^3 10^2 10^1 10^0 10^{-1} 10^{-2} 10^{-3} 10^{-4} 10^{-5} 10^{-6} 10^{-7} 10^{-8} 10^{-9} 10^{-10} 10^{-11} 10^{-12} 10^{-13} 10^{-14}

Wavelength (m)

The Atmosphere and Solar Radiation

As solar radiation passes through Earth's atmosphere, the atmosphere affects the radiation in several ways. The upper atmosphere absorbs almost all radiation that has a wavelength shorter than the wavelengths of visible light. Molecules of nitrogen and oxygen in the thermosphere and mesosphere absorb the X rays, gamma rays, and ultraviolet rays. In the stratosphere, ultraviolet rays are absorbed and act upon oxygen molecules to form ozone.

Most of the solar rays that reach the lower atmosphere, such as visible and infrared waves, have longer wavelengths. Most incoming infrared radiation is absorbed by carbon dioxide, water vapor, and other complex molecules in the troposphere. As visible light waves pass through the atmosphere, only a small amount of this radiation is absorbed. **Figure 2** shows the percentage of solar energy that is reflected and absorbed by the atmosphere.

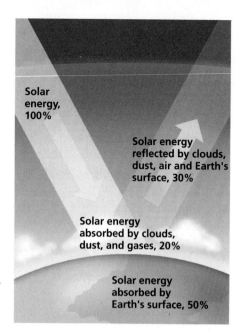

Figure 2 ▶ About 70% of the solar energy that reaches Earth is absorbed by Earth's land and ocean surfaces and by the atmosphere. The remainder is reflected back into space.

Scattering

Clouds, dust, water droplets, and gas molecules in the atmosphere disrupt the paths of radiation from the sun and cause scattering. Scattering occurs when particles and gas molecules in the atmosphere reflect and bend the solar rays. This deflection causes the rays to travel out in all directions without changing their wavelengths. Scattering sends some of the radiation back into space. The remaining radiation continues toward Earth's surface. As a result of scattering, sunlight that reaches Earth's surface comes from all directions. In addition, scattering makes the sky appear blue and makes the sun appear red at sunrise and sunset.

Connection to PHYSICS

The Ozone "Hole"

Ozone, O_3, is a naturally occurring gas that is present primarily in the stratosphere. The thin layer of ozone that surrounds Earth prevents most of the sun's ultraviolet (UV) radiation from reaching Earth's surface. Overexposure to UV radiation is dangerous to living things because it damages DNA. DNA is the genetic material that carries the information for inherited characteristics. UV radiation also makes the body more susceptible to skin cancer.

The protective ozone layer is not distributed around Earth evenly. Scientists have observed that ozone concentrations vary with latitude and with the time of year. In 1985, scientists discovered that the ozone layer was unusually thin in regions over Antarctica. This "ozone hole" allows greater amounts of UV radiation to reach Earth's surface. Scientists discovered that chemicals called chlorofluorocarbons (CFCs) were causing the ozone layer to break down. CFCs were used as coolants in refrigerators and air conditioners.

Satellite image of the ozone "hole" (purple) in 1980

Satellite image of the same ozone "hole" in 2000

CFCs were also used in spray cans such as those used for household products and paint. The discovery of a connection between CFCs and the weakening ozone layer led to an international ban on CFCs.

CFCs can act to destroy ozone continuously for 60 to 120 years. So, CFCs released 30 years ago may still be destroying ozone today. It will take many years for the ozone layer to completely recover.

Table 1 ▼

Percentage of Solar Radiation		
Surface	Reflected	Absorbed
Soils (dark colored)	5–10	90–95
Desert	20–40	60–80
Grass	5–25	75–95
Forest	5–10	90–95
Snow	50–90	10–50
Water (high sun angle)	5–10	90–95
Water (low sun angle)	50–80	20–50

Table 1 ▶ Reflection and Absorption Rates of Various Materials

Reflection

When solar energy reaches Earth's surface, the surface either absorbs or reflects the energy. The amount of energy that is absorbed or reflected depends on characteristics such as the color, texture, composition, volume, mass, transparency, state of matter, and specific heat of the material on which the solar radiation falls. The intensity and amount of time that a surface material receives radiation also affects how much energy is reflected or absorbed.

The fraction of solar radiation that is reflected by a particular surface is called the **albedo.** Because 30% of the solar energy that reaches Earth's atmosphere is either reflected or scattered, Earth is said to have an albedo of 0.3. **Table 1** shows the amount of incoming solar radiation that is absorbed and reflected by various surfaces.

albedo the fraction of solar radiation that is reflected off the surface of an object

Figure 3 ▶ Hot air near the surface of this road bends light rays. *What objects in this photo appear to be reflected?*

Absorption and Infrared Energy

The sun constantly emits radiation. Solar radiation that is not reflected is absorbed by rocks, soil, water, and other surface materials. When Earth's surface absorbs solar radiation, the radiation's short-wavelength infrared rays and visible light heat the surface materials. Then, the heated materials convert the energy into infrared rays of longer-wavelengths and reemit it as those waves. Gas molecules, such as water vapor and carbon dioxide, in the atmosphere absorb these infrared rays. The absorption of thermal energy from the ground heats the lower atmosphere and keeps Earth's surface much warmer than it would be if there were no atmosphere. Sometimes, warm air near Earth's surface bends light rays to produce an effect called a *mirage,* as **Figure 3** shows.

2 Energy from the sun is absorbed by Earth's surface and then is radiated into the atmosphere as heat, some of which escapes into space.

3 Greenhouse gases also absorb some of the energy from Earth and radiate it back toward the lower atmosphere and Earth's surface.

1 Solar radiation passes through the atmosphere and warms Earth's surface.

Figure 4 ▶ One process that helps heat Earth's atmosphere is similar to the process that heats a greenhouse.

greenhouse effect the warming of the surface and lower atmosphere of Earth that occurs when carbon dioxide, water vapor, and other gases in the air absorb and reradiate infrared radiation

For a variety of links related to this subject, go to www.scilinks.org

Topic: Greenhouse Effect
SciLinks code: HQ60694

The Greenhouse Effect

One of the ways in which the gases of the atmosphere absorb and reradiate infrared rays, shown in **Figure 4,** can be compared to the process that keeps a greenhouse warm. The glass of a greenhouse allows visible light and infrared rays from the sun to pass through and warm the surfaces inside of the greenhouse. But the glass prevents the infrared rays that are emitted by the warmed surfaces within the greenhouse from escaping. Similarly, Earth's atmosphere slows the escape of energy that radiates from Earth's surface. Because this process is similar to the process that heats a greenhouse, it is called the **greenhouse effect.**

Human Impact on the Greenhouse Effect

Generally, the amount of solar energy that enters Earth's atmosphere is about equal to the amount that escapes into space. However, human activities may change this balance and may cause the average temperature of the atmosphere to increase. For example, measurements indicate that the amount of carbon dioxide in the atmosphere has been increasing in recent years. These increases have been attributed to the burning of more fossil fuels. These increases seem likely to continue in the future. Increases in the amount of carbon dioxide may intensify the greenhouse effect and may cause Earth to become warmer in some areas and cooler in others.

Variations in Temperature

Radiation from the sun does not heat Earth equally at all places at all times. In addition, a slight delay occurs between the absorption of energy and an increase in temperature. Earth's surface must absorb energy for a time before enough heat has been absorbed and reradiated from the ground to change the temperature of the atmosphere. For a similar reason, the warmest hours of the day are usually mid- to late afternoon even though solar radiation is most intense at noon. The temperature of the atmosphere in any region on Earth's surface depends on several factors, including latitude, surface features, and the time of year and day.

Latitude and Season

Latitude is the primary factor that affects the amount of solar energy that reaches any point on Earth's surface. Because Earth is a sphere, the sun's rays do not strike all areas at the same angle, as shown in **Figure 5.** The rays of the sun strike the ground near the equator at an angle near 90°. At the poles, the sunlight strikes the ground at a much smaller angle. When sunlight hits Earth's surface at an angle smaller than 90°, the energy is spread out over a larger area and is less intense. Thus, the energy that reaches the equator is more intense than the energy that strikes the poles, so average temperatures are higher near the equator than near the poles.

Temperature varies seasonally because of the tilt of Earth's axis. As Earth revolves around the sun once each year, the portion of Earth's surface that receives the most intense sunlight changes. For part of the year, the Northern Hemisphere is tilted toward the sun and receives more direct sunlight. During this time of year, temperatures are at their highest. For the other part of the year, the Southern Hemisphere is tilted toward the sun. During this time, the Northern Hemisphere receives less direct sunlight, and the temperatures there are at their lowest.

Water in the Air and on the Surface

Because water vapor stores heat, the amount of water in the air affects the temperature of a region. The thinner air at high elevations contains less water vapor and carbon dioxide to absorb the heat. As a result, those areas become warm during the day but cool very quickly at night. Similarly, desert temperatures may vary widely between day and night because little water vapor is present to hold the heat of the day.

Land areas close to large bodies of water generally have more moderate temperatures. In other words, these areas will be cooler during the day and warmer at night than inland regions that have the same general weather conditions are. The reason for these moderate temperatures is that water heats up and cools down slower than land does, so the temperature of water changes less than the temperature of land does.

The wind patterns in an area also affect temperature. A region that receives winds off the ocean waters has more moderate temperatures than does a similar region in which the winds blow from the land.

Reading Check Why are deserts generally colder at night than other areas are? (See the Appendix for answers to Reading Checks.)

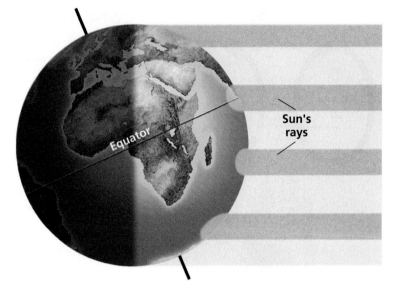

Figure 5 ▶ Temperatures are higher at the equator because solar energy is concentrated in a small area. Farther north and south, the same amount of solar energy is spread out over a larger area.

Convection cells

Cool air

Warm air

Figure 6 ▶ During convection, energy is carried away by heated air as it rises above cooler, denser air.

conduction the transfer of energy as heat through a material

convection the movement of matter due to differences in density that are caused by temperature variations; can result in the transfer of energy as heat

Conduction

The molecules in a substance move faster as they become heated. These fast-moving molecules cause other molecules to move faster. Collisions between the particles result in the transfer of energy, which warms the substance. The transfer of energy as heat from one substance to another by direct contact is called **conduction.** Solid substances, in which the molecules are close together, make relatively good conductors. Because the molecules of air are far apart, air is a poor conductor. Thus, conduction heats only the lowest few centimeters of the atmosphere, where air comes into direct contact with the warmed surface of Earth.

Convection

The heating of the lower atmosphere is primarily the result of the distribution of heat through the troposphere by convection. **Convection** is the process by which air, or other matter, rises or sinks because of differences in temperature. Convection occurs when gases or liquids are heated unevenly. As air is heated by radiation or conduction, it becomes less dense and is pushed up by nearby cooler air. In turn, this cooler air becomes warmer, and the cycle repeats, as shown in **Figure 6.**

The continuous cycle in which cold air sinks and warm air rises warms Earth's atmosphere evenly. Because warm air is less dense than cool air is, warm air exerts less pressure than the same volume of cooler air does. So, the atmospheric pressure is lower beneath a mass of warm air. As dense, cool air moves into a low-pressure region, the less dense, warmer air is pushed upward. These pressure differences, which are the result of the unequal heating that causes convection, create winds.

Section 2 Review

1. **Explain** how radiant energy reaches Earth. 🔆4b

2. **List and describe** the types of electromagnetic waves. 🔆4b

3. **Describe** how gases and particles in the atmosphere interact with light rays. 🔆4b, 4c

4. **Describe** how visible light and infrared energy warm Earth. 🔆4b, 4c

5. **Explain** how variations in the intensity of sunlight can cause temperature differences on Earth's surface. 🔆4b

6. **Summarize** the processes of conduction and convection. 🔆4b, 5a

CRITICAL THINKING

7. **Making Inferences** Why do scientists study all wavelengths of the electromagnetic spectrum? 🔆IE.1d

8. **Applying Concepts** Explain how fans in convection ovens help cook food more evenly. 🔆4b, IE.1d

9. **Applying Conclusions** You decide not to be outside during the hottest hours of a summer day. When will the hottest hours probably be? How do you know? 🔆4b, IE.1d

CONCEPT MAPPING

10. Use the following terms to create a concept map: *electromagnetic waves, infrared waves, greenhouse effect, ultraviolet waves, visible light, scattering,* and *absorption.* 🔆4b, 4c

Atmospheric Circulation

California Content Standards

5a Students know how differential heating of Earth results in circulation patterns in the atmosphere and oceans that globally distribute the heat.
5b Students know the relationship between the rotation of Earth and the circular motions of ocean currents and air in pressure centers.
IE.1d Students will formulate explanations using logic and evidence.

Pressure differences in the atmosphere cause the movement of air worldwide. The air near Earth's surface generally flows from the poles toward the equator. The reason for this flow is that air moves from high-pressure regions to low-pressure regions. High-pressure regions form where cold air sinks toward Earth's surface. Low-pressure regions form where warm air rises away from Earth's surface.

The Coriolis Effect

The circulation of the atmosphere and of the oceans is affected by the rotation of Earth on its axis. Earth's rotation causes its diameter to be greatest through the equator and smallest through the poles. Because each point on Earth makes one complete rotation every day, points near the equator travel farther and faster in a day than points closer to the poles do. When air moves toward the poles, it travels east faster than the land beneath it does. As a result, the air follows a curved path. The tendency of a moving object to follow a curved path rather than a straight path because of the rotation of Earth is called the **Coriolis effect,** which is shown in **Figure 1.**

Winds that blow from high-pressure areas to lower-pressure areas curve as a result of the Coriolis effect. The Coriolis effect deflects moving objects along a path that depends on the speed, latitude, and direction of the object. Objects are deflected to the right in the Northern Hemisphere and are deflected to the left in the Southern Hemisphere.

The faster an object travels, the greater the Coriolis effect on that object is. The Coriolis effect also noticeably changes the paths of large masses that travel long distances, such as air or ocean currents. In general, the Coriolis effect is detectable only on objects that move very fast or that travel over long distances.

Figure 1 ▶ Because of Earth's rotation, an object that travels north from the equator will curve to the east. This curving is called the *Coriolis effect.*

OBJECTIVES

▶ **Explain** the Coriolis effect. 5b
▶ **Describe** the global patterns of air circulation, and name three global wind belts. 5a
▶ **Identify** two factors that form local wind patterns. 5a

KEY TERMS

Coriolis effect
trade winds
westerlies
polar easterlies
jet stream

Coriolis effect the curving of the path of a moving object from an otherwise straight path due to Earth's rotation

Air moving south from the pole is deflected to the right because the air moves east slower than the ground beneath it does.

North Pole

Air moving north from the equator is deflected to the right because the air is moving east faster than the ground beneath it is.

Equator

Direction of Earth's rotation

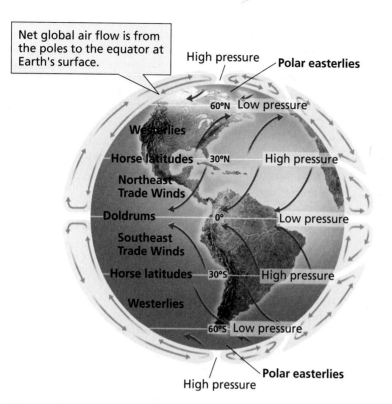

Net global air flow is from the poles to the equator at Earth's surface.

High pressure
Polar easterlies
60°N Low pressure
Westerlies
Horse latitudes 30°N High pressure
Northeast Trade Winds
Doldrums 0° Low pressure
Southeast Trade Winds
Horse latitudes 30°S High pressure
Westerlies
60°S Low pressure
High pressure
Polar easterlies

Figure 2 ▶ Each hemisphere has three wind belts. Wind belts are the result of pressure differences at the equator, the subtropics, the subpolar regions, and the poles. Winds in the belts curve because of the Coriolis effect. ***Do winds in the Northern Hemisphere curve clockwise or counterclockwise?***

trade winds prevailing winds that blow from east to west from 30° latitude to the equator in both hemispheres

westerlies prevailing winds that blow from west to east between 30° and 60° latitude in both hemispheres

polar easterlies prevailing winds that blow from east to west between 60° and 90° latitude in both hemispheres

Global Winds

The air that flows from the poles toward the equator does not flow in a single, straight line. Each hemisphere contains three looping patterns of flow called *convection cells*. Each of these convection cells correlates to an area of Earth's surface, called a *wind belt*, that is characterized by winds that flow in one main direction. These winds are called *prevailing winds*. All six wind belts are shown in **Figure 2.**

Trade Winds

In both hemispheres, the winds that flow toward the equator between 30° and 0° latitude are called **trade winds.** Like all winds, the trade winds are named according to the direction from which they flow. In the Northern Hemisphere, the trade winds flow from the northeast and are called the *northeast trade winds*. In the Southern Hemisphere, the trade winds are called the *southeast trade winds*. These wind belts are called *trade winds* because many trading ships sailed on these winds from Europe in the 18th and 19th centuries.

Westerlies

Between 30° and 60° latitude, some of the descending air moving toward the poles is deflected by the Coriolis effect. This flow creates the **westerlies,** which exist in another wind belt in each hemisphere. In the Northern Hemisphere, the westerlies are southwest winds. In the Southern Hemisphere, they are northwest winds. The westerlies blow throughout the contiguous United States.

✓ Reading Check Name two ways in which the trade winds of the Northern Hemisphere differ from the westerlies of the Northern Hemisphere. (See the Appendix for answers to Reading Checks.)

Polar Easterlies

Toward the poles, or poleward, of the westerlies—at about 60° latitude—is a zone of low pressure. This zone of low pressure separates the westerlies from a third wind belt in each hemisphere. Over the polar regions themselves, descending cold air creates areas of high pressure. Surface winds created by the polar high pressure are deflected by the Coriolis effect and become the **polar easterlies.** The polar easterlies are strongest where they flow off Antarctica. Where the polar easterlies meet warm air from the westerlies, a stormy region known as a *front* forms.

The Doldrums and Horse Latitudes

As **Figure 2** shows, the trade wind systems of the Northern Hemisphere and Southern Hemisphere meet at the equator in a narrow zone called the *doldrums*. In this warm zone, most air movement is upward and surface winds are weak and variable. As the air approaches 30° latitude, it descends and a high-pressure zone forms. These subtropical high-pressure zones are called the *horse latitudes*. Here, too, surface winds are weak and variable.

Wind and Pressure Shifts

As the sun's rays shift northward and southward during the changing seasons of the year, the positions of the pressure belts and wind belts shift. Although the area that receives direct sunlight can shift by up to 47° north and south of the equator, the average shift for the pressure belts and wind belts is only about 10° of latitude. However, even this small change causes some areas of Earth's surface to be in different wind belts during different times of the year. In southern Florida, for example, westerlies prevail in the winter, but trade winds dominate in the summer.

Jet Streams

Narrow bands of high-speed winds that blow in the upper troposphere and lower stratosphere are **jet streams.** These winds exist in the Northern Hemisphere and Southern Hemisphere.

One type of jet stream is a polar jet stream. Polar jet streams form as a result of density differences between cold polar air and the warmer air of the middle latitudes. These bands of winds, which are about 100 km wide and 2 to 3 km thick, are located at altitudes of 10 to 15 km. Polar jet streams can reach speeds of 500 km/h and can affect airline routes and the paths of storms.

Another type of jet stream is a subtropical jet stream. In the subtropical regions, very warm equatorial air meets the cooler air of the middle latitudes, and the *subtropical jet streams* form. Unlike the polar jet streams, the subtropical jet streams do not change much in speed or position. A subtropical jet stream is shown in **Figure 3.**

jet stream a narrow band of strong winds that blow in the upper troposphere

Figure 3 ▶ Clouds in this jet stream are traveling high over Egypt. This remarkable photograph was taken by *Gemini 12* astronauts.

Figure 4 ▶ Sea breezes keep these kites aloft during the afternoon. Overnight, land breezes will blow the flags toward the ocean.

Local Winds

Winds also exist on a scale that is much smaller than a global scale. Movements of air are influenced by local conditions, and local temperature variations commonly cause local winds. Local winds are not part of the global wind belts. Gentle winds that extend over distances of less than 100 km are called *breezes*.

Land and Sea Breezes

Equal areas of land and water may receive the same amount of energy from the sun. However, land surfaces heat up faster than water surfaces do. Therefore, during daylight hours, a sharp temperature difference develops between a body of water and the land along the water's edge. This temperature difference is apparent in the air above the land and water. The warm air above the land rises as the cool air from above the water moves in to replace the warm air. A cool wind moving from water to land, called a *sea breeze*, generally forms in the afternoon, as shown in **Figure 4.** Overnight, the land cools more rapidly than the water does, and the sea breeze is replaced by a *land breeze*. A land breeze flows from the cool land toward the warmer water.

Mountain and Valley Breezes

During the daylight hours in mountainous regions, a gentle valley breeze blows upslope. This *valley breeze* forms when warm air from the valleys moves upslope. At night, the mountains cool more quickly than the valleys do. At that time, cool air descends from the mountain peaks to create a *mountain breeze*. Areas near mountains may experience a warm afternoon that turns to a cold evening soon after sunset. This evening cooling happens because cold air flows down mountain slopes and settles in valleys.

Section 3 Review

1. **Describe** the pattern of air circulation between an area of low pressure and an area of high pressure. 5b

2. **Explain** how the Coriolis effect affects wind flow. 5b

3. **Name and describe** Earth's three global wind belts. 5a

4. **Summarize** the importance of the jet streams. 5a

5. **Identify** two factors that create local wind patterns. 5a

CRITICAL THINKING

6. **Applying Concepts** Determine whether wind moving south from the equator will curve eastward or westward because of the Coriolis effect. 5b, IE.1d

7. **Inferring Relationships** Which has a lower pressure: the air in your lungs as you inhale or the air outside your body? Explain. IE.1d

8. **Applying Ideas** While visiting the Oregon coast, you decide to hike toward the ocean, but you are not sure of the direction. The time is 4:00 P.M. How might the breeze help you find your way? 5a, IE.1d

CONCEPT MAPPING

9. Use the following terms to create a concept map: *wind, sea breeze, global winds, trade winds, westerlies, local winds, polar easterlies, land breeze, mountain breeze,* and *valley breeze.* 5a

Sections

1 Characteristics of the Atmosphere

2 Solar Energy and the Atmosphere

3 Atmospheric Circulation

Key Terms

atmosphere, 547
ozone, 549
atmospheric pressure, 550
troposphere, 552
stratosphere, 553
mesosphere, 553
thermosphere, 553

electromagnetic spectrum, 555
albedo, 557
greenhouse effect, 558
conduction, 560
convection, 560

Coriolis effect, 561
trade winds, 562
westerlies, 562
polar easterlies, 562
jet stream, 563

Key Concepts

► Earth's atmosphere is the mixture of gases, called *air,* that surrounds Earth. Mixed with the gases that make up air are solid particles called *particulates.*

► Atmospheric pressure is the force exerted on Earth's surface by the weight of the atmosphere. It is measured by using a barometer.

► The atmosphere is divided into four major layers whose temperature and pressure vary.

► Air pollution can be harmful to people, animals, plants, and property.

► Most of the energy that reaches Earth from the sun is in the form of electromagnetic radiation.

► Visible light and infrared rays from the sun penetrate Earth's atmosphere and heat materials on the surface.

► The upper atmosphere is heated by absorption of radiation from the sun. The lower atmosphere is heated by conduction from Earth's surface and by convection of air.

► Air-pressure differences due to the unequal heating of Earth in combination with Earth's rotation cause the global wind belts.

► A surface feature, such as a body of water, a mountain, or a valley, can influence local wind patterns.

Using Key Terms

Use each of the following terms in a separate sentence.

1. *atmosphere* 🐜8a
2. *electromagnetic spectrum*
3. *Coriolis effect* 🐜5b

For each pair of terms, explain how the meanings of the terms differ.

4. *troposphere* and *stratosphere* 🐜8a
5. *mesosphere* and *thermosphere* 🐜8a
6. *conduction* and *convection* 🐜5a
7. *trade winds* and *westerlies* 🐜5a
8. *polar easterlies* and *westerlies* 🐜5a

Understanding Key Concepts

9. During one part of the nitrogen cycle, nitrogen is removed from the air mainly by nitrogen-fixing 🐜7c
   a. bacteria.
   c. minerals.
   b. waves.
   d. crystals.

10. The atmosphere contains tiny solid particles called 🐜8a
    a. gases.
    c. meteors.
    b. particulates.
    d. nitrogen.

11. A barometer measures 🐜IE.1a
    a. atmospheric pressure.
    b. wind speed.
    c. ozone concentration.
    d. wavelengths.

12. Almost all of the water and carbon dioxide in the atmosphere is in the 🐜8a
    a. exosphere.
    c. troposphere.
    b. ionosphere.
    d. stratosphere.

13. The process by which the atmosphere slows Earth's loss of heat to space is called the 🐜4c, 8a
    a. greenhouse effect.
    c. doldrums.
    b. Coriolis effect.
    d. convection cell.

14. Energy as heat can be transferred within the atmosphere in three ways—radiation, conduction, and 🐜5a
    a. transpiration.
    b. temperature inversion.
    c. weathering.
    d. convection.

15. A vertical looping pattern of airflow is known as 🐜5a
    a. the Coriolis effect.
    c. a trade wind.
    b. a convection cell.
    d. a westerly.

16. A gentle wind that covers less than 100 km is called 🐜5a
    a. a jet stream.
    c. a breeze.
    b. the doldrums.
    d. a trade wind.

17. Which of the following layers of the atmosphere is closest to the ground? 🐜8a
    a. troposphere
    c. mesosphere
    b. thermosphere
    d. exosphere

18. Which of the following layers of the atmosphere is closest to space? 🐜8a
    a. troposphere
    c. mesosphere
    b. ionosphere
    d. exosphere

Short Answer

19. List the three main elemental gases that compose the atmosphere. 🐜8a

20. What is atmospheric pressure, and how is it measured? 🐜IE.1a

21. List and describe the four main layers of the atmosphere. 🐜8a

22. What happens to visible light that enters Earth's atmosphere? 🐜5a, 8c

23. How is heat energy transferred by Earth's atmosphere? 🐜5a

24. How does latitude affect the temperature of a region? 🐜5a

Energy from the Wind

For more than a thousand years, people have used windmills for tasks such as grinding grain or pumping water. Today, more and more people are rediscovering the benefits of wind power, and the number of wind turbines used to generate electricity continues to grow.

A New Take on an Old Idea

One result of the renewed interest in wind power is the reintroduction of the Darrieus turbine. Invented in 1920, the Darrieus turbine resembles an upside-down eggbeater. The Darrieus turbine is designed to catch winds blowing from all directions, and most of its moving parts are located on the ground. The bend in the blades can be changed to maximize efficiency, and the turbine's shape—taller than it is wide—minimizes land use.

Other, more recent technological advances in wind turbines include the use of lighter and less costly materials and the use of faster airfoil blades. Instead of being flat like earlier blades, an airfoil blade is shaped like an airplane wing. This shape allows air to flow smoothly over the blades and enables the airfoil to use the lifting force of the wind more effectively.

Energy of the Future

Using the wind to generate electricity consumes no fuels and produces no wastes. Also, wind itself costs nothing and is available in certain areas in a limitless supply. However, wind power has some disadvantages. One disadvantage is the unpredictability of wind speed and wind direction. Wind farms can also be noisy, unattractive, and deadly to migrating birds.

Thousands of wind turbines have been installed in California, Texas, and other states. Because of the steady increase in wind power use in European countries such as the Netherlands, Denmark, Germany, and England, wind power is quickly becoming the sustainable energy source of choice for utility companies worldwide.

Extension

1. **Making Predictions** What problems might arise in wind turbines placed between 20° and 40° latitude?

▼ A modern wind farm

▲ A modern Darrieus turbine

573

Chapter 23

Water in the Atmosphere

Sections

1 Atmospheric Moisture

2 Clouds and Fog

3 Precipitation

What You'll Learn

- How water enters the atmosphere
- How clouds form
- How precipitation forms

Why It's Relevant

Severe weather conditions can put lives in danger. Understanding how water moves through the atmosphere provides a basis for understanding weather.

PRE-READING ACTIVITY

Two-Panel Flip Chart
Before you read this chapter, create the FoldNote entitled "Two-Panel Flip Chart" described in the Skills Handbook section of the Appendix. Label the flaps of the two-panel flip chart with "Clouds" and "Precipitation." As you read the chapter, write information you learn about each category under the appropriate flap.

▶ Dark clouds, such as the clouds near Rosston, Oklahoma, shown here, usually signal the coming of a thunderstorm. The clouds look dark because they are so thick that little solar radiation passes through them.

 California Content Standards

7a Students know the carbon cycle of photosynthesis and respiration and the nitrogen cycle.
7c Students know the movement of matter among reservoirs is driven by Earth's internal and external sources of energy.
IE.1a Students will select and use appropriate tools and technology (such as computer-linked probes, spreadsheets, and graphing calculators) to perform tests, collect data, analyze relationships and display data.
IE.1d Students will formulate explanations using logic and evidence.
IE.1l Students will analyze situations and solve problems that require combining and applying concepts from more than one area of science.
IE.1m Students will investigate a science-based societal issue by researching the literature, analyzing data, and communicating the findings. Examples of issues include irradiation of food, cloning of animals by somatic cell nuclear transfer, choice of energy sources, and land and water use decisions in California.

Atmospheric Moisture

California Content Standards

7a Students know the carbon cycle of photosynthesis and respiration and the nitrogen cycle.
7c Students know the movement of matter among reservoirs is driven by Earth's internal and external sources of energy.
IE.1a Students will select and use appropriate tools and technology (such as computer-linked probes, spreadsheets, and graphing calculators) to perform tests, collect data, analyze relationships, and display data.

Water in the atmosphere exists in three states, or *phases*. One phase is known as a gas called *water vapor*. The other two phases of water are the solid phase known as *ice* and the liquid phase known as *water*.

Changing Forms of Water

Water changes from one phase to another when heat energy is absorbed or released, as shown in **Figure 1**. Molecules of ice are held almost stationary in a definite crystalline arrangement. However, when energy is absorbed by the ice, the molecules move more rapidly. They break from their fixed positions and slide past each other in the fluid form of a liquid.

When more energy is absorbed by liquid water, the water changes from a liquid to a gas. Because the additional energy causes the movement of molecules in liquid water to speed up, the molecules collide more frequently with each other. Such collisions can cause the molecules to move so rapidly that the fastest-moving molecules escape from the liquid to form invisible water vapor in a process called *evaporation*.

Latent Heat

The heat energy that is absorbed or released by a substance during a phase change is called **latent heat.** When liquid water evaporates, the water absorbs energy from the environment. This energy becomes potential energy between the molecules. When water vapor changes back into a liquid through the process of *condensation*, energy is released to the surrounding air and the molecules move closer together. Likewise, latent heat is absorbed when ice thaws, and latent heat is released when water freezes.

OBJECTIVES

▶ **Explain** how heat energy affects the changing phases of water. 7c

▶ **Explain** what absolute humidity and relative humidity are, and describe how they are measured. IE.1a

▶ **Describe** what happens when the temperature of air decreases to the dew point or below the dew point. 7a

KEY TERMS

latent heat
sublimation
dew point
absolute humidity
relative humidity

latent heat the heat energy that is absorbed or released by a substance during a phase change

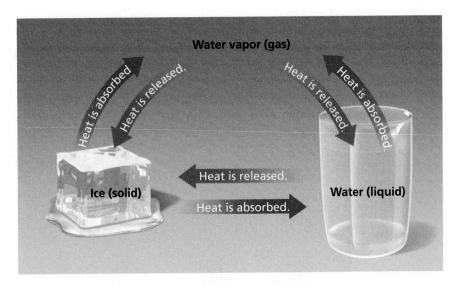

Figure 1 ▶ Water exists in three states, called *phases*. As it changes from one phase to another, water either absorbs or releases heat energy.

Evaporation

Most water enters the atmosphere through the process of evaporation. Because the largest amounts of solar energy reach Earth near the equator, most evaporation takes place over the oceans of the equatorial region. However, water vapor also enters the atmosphere by evaporation from lakes, ponds, streams, and soil. Plants release water into the atmosphere in a process called transpiration. Volcanoes and burning fuels also release small amounts of water vapor into the atmosphere.

Sublimation

Ice commonly changes into a liquid before changing into a gas. However, in some cases, ice can change directly into water vapor without becoming a liquid. The process by which a solid changes directly into a gas is called **sublimation.** When the air is dry and the temperature is below freezing, ice and snow may sublimate into water vapor. Water vapor can also turn directly into ice without becoming a liquid.

sublimation the process in which a solid changes directly into a gas (the term is sometimes also used for the reverse process)

✓ **Reading Check** Summarize the conditions under which sublimation commonly occurs. (See the Appendix for answers to Reading Checks.)

Connection to PHYSICS

Light and Water in the Atmosphere

The interaction of water and light in the atmosphere can create a number of visual effects. When visible light passes through raindrops, the raindrops *refract*, or bend the light rays, which separates the white light into the colors that make up the entire visible spectrum. You can see these colors in rainbows, glories, and coronas. *Coronas* are small, multicolored circles that surround the sun or moon. *Glories* are small, multicolored circles that surround the shadow of an object on which light is shining.

Sun dogs, sun pillars, halos, and rings are caused by the interaction of light rays and ice crystals in the atmosphere. In general, the ice crystals do not separate the light into different colors, so these phenomena involve white light. *Sun dogs* are bright spots that appear in the sky, often on either side of the sun. *Sun pillars* are bright shafts of light that extend up and down from the sun or moon. *Halos* and *rings* are fuzzy or bright rings that are commonly seen around the sun and the moon.

Crepuscular rays are slanting sunbeams that form when sunlight is intermittently interrupted by clouds or fog. The clouds cast shadows that appear to break up the sunlight to form smaller, individual rays.

A *mirage* is one of two types of optical illusions that form when light rays are refracted as they pass through a boundary between hot air and cool air. The first type, called an *inferior mirage,* occurs when light passes from a layer of cool air to a layer of hot air close to the ground. When the light rays enter the hot air, they bend upward and cause the sky to appear as a pool of water on the ground. The other type, a *superior mirage,* is an image of an object that seems to be suspended in the sky. This type occurs when light rays pass through a layer of warm air into a layer of cool air below.

Sun dogs, such as these below, are caused when ice crystals in the atmosphere interact with light rays.

Figure 2 ▶ When water comes into contact with dry air, some of the water molecules evaporate into the dry air. The addition of the water molecules to the air causes the air pressure to increase. This increase in pressure is due to vapor pressure.

Humidity

Water vapor in the atmosphere is known as *humidity*. Humidity is controlled by rates of condensation and evaporation. The rate of evaporation is determined by the temperature of the air. The higher the temperature is, the higher the rate of evaporation is. The rate of condensation is determined by vapor pressure. Vapor pressure is the part of the total atmospheric pressure that is caused by water vapor, as shown in **Figure 2.** When vapor pressure is high, the condensation rate is high.

When the rate of evaporation and the rate of condensation are in equilibrium, the air is said to be "saturated." The temperature at which the condensation rate equals the evaporation rate is called the **dew point.** At temperatures below the dew point, net condensation occurs, and liquid water droplets form.

Absolute Humidity

One way to express the amount of moisture in air is by absolute humidity. **Absolute humidity** is the mass of water vapor contained in a given volume of air. In other words, absolute humidity is a measure of the actual amount of water vapor in the air. Absolute humidity is calculated by using the following equation:

$$absolute\ humidity = \frac{mass\ of\ water\ vapor\ (grams)}{volume\ of\ air\ (cubic\ meters)}$$

However, as air moves, its volume changes as a result of temperature and pressure changes. Therefore, meteorologists prefer to describe humidity by using the mixing ratio of air. The *mixing ratio* is the mass of water vapor in a unit of air relative to the mass of the dry air. For example, the very moist air in tropical regions might have 18 g of water vapor in 1 kg of air, or a mixing ratio of 18 g/kg. On the other hand, the cold, dry air in polar regions commonly has a mixing ratio of less than 1 g/kg. Because this measurement uses only units of mass, it is not affected by changes in temperature or pressure.

dew point at constant pressure and water vapor content, the temperature at which the rate of condensation equals the rate of evaporation

absolute humidity the mass of water vapor per unit volume of air that contains the water vapor, usually expressed as grams of water vapor per cubic meter of air

Figure 3 ▶ Dew forms on surfaces such as grass and spider webs when the temperature of air reaches the dew point.

relative humidity the ratio of the amount of water vapor in the air to the amount of water vapor needed to reach saturation at a given temperature

MATHPRACTICE

Relative Humidity
Relative humidity can be calculated by using the following equation:

$$\text{relative humidity} = \left[\frac{\text{amount of water vapor in air}}{\text{amount of water vapor needed to reach saturation}} \right] \times 100$$

Air at 20°C is saturated when it contains 14 g/kg of water vapor. What is the relative humidity of a volume of air that is 20°C and that contains 10 g/kg of water vapor?

Relative Humidity

A more common way to express the amount of water vapor in the atmosphere is by *relative humidity*. **Relative humidity** is a ratio of the actual water vapor content of the air to the amount of water vapor needed to reach saturation. In other words, relative humidity is a measure of how close the air is to reaching the dew point. For example, at 25°C, air is saturated when it contains 20 g of water vapor per 1 kg of air. If air that is 25°C contains 5 g of water vapor, the relative humidity is expressed as 5/20, or 25%.

If the temperature does not change, the relative humidity will increase if moisture enters the air. Relative humidity can also increase if the moisture in the air remains constant but the temperature decreases. If the temperature increases as the moisture in the air remains constant, the relative humidity will decrease.

Reaching the Dew Point

When the air is nearly saturated with a relative humidity of almost 100%, only a small temperature drop is needed for air to reach its dew point. Air may cool to its dew point by conduction when the air is in contact with a cold surface. During the night, grass, leaves, and other objects near the ground lose heat. Their surface temperatures often drop to the dew point of the surrounding air. Air, which normally remains warmer than surfaces near the ground do, cools to the dew point when it comes into contact with cooler objects, such as grass. The resulting form of condensation, shown in **Figure 3,** is called *dew.* Dew is most likely to form on cool, clear nights when there is little wind.

If the dew point falls below the freezing temperature of water, water vapor may change directly into solid ice crystals, or *frost.* Because frost forms when water vapor turns directly into ice, frost is not frozen dew. Frozen dew is relatively uncommon. Unlike frost, frozen dew forms as clear beads of ice.

✔ **Reading Check** How does dew differ from frost? (See the Appendix for answers to Reading Checks.)

Measuring Humidity

Meteorologists are interested in measuring humidity so that they can better predict weather conditions. Relative humidity can be measured by using a variety of instruments, such as a thin polymer film, a psychrometer, a dew cell, and a hair hygrometer.

Using Thin Polymer Film to Measure Humidity

Humidity is commonly measured by a humidity sensor that uses a *thin polymer film*. The relative humidity of the surrounding air affects the ability of the thin polymer film to absorb or release water vapor. The amount of water vapor the thin polymer film contains changes the film's ability to conduct electricity. The polymer film's ability to conduct electricity is affected by the relative humidity of the surrounding air. Thus, by measuring the polymer film's ability to store electricity, relative humidity can be determined.

Using Psychrometers to Measure Humidity

A *psychrometer,* shown in **Figure 4,** is another instrument that is used to measure relative humidity. It consists of two identical thermometers. The bulb of one thermometer is covered with a damp wick, while the bulb of the other thermometer remains dry. When the psychrometer is held by a handle and whirled through the air, the air circulates around both thermometers. As a result, the water in the wick of the wet-bulb thermometer evaporates. Evaporation requires heat, so heat escapes from the thermometer. Consequently, the temperature of the wet-bulb thermometer is lower than that of the dry-bulb thermometer. The difference between the dry-bulb temperature and the wet-bulb temperature is used to calculate relative humidity. If there is no difference between the wet-bulb temperature and dry-bulb temperature, no water evaporated from the wet-bulb thermometer. Thus, the air is saturated and the relative humidity is 100%.

Figure 4 ▶ A psychrometer is commonly used with a table that lists relative humidity based on differences between wet-bulb and dry-bulb readings.

Figure 5 ▶ Scientists use weather balloons, such as this one in Antarctica, to send electric hygrometers into the high altitudes of the atmosphere.

Other Methods for Measure Humidity

Another instrument that has been used to measure relative humidity is the *dew cell*. Dew cells consist of a ceramic cylinder with electrodes attached to it and treated with lithium chloride, LiCl. When LiCl absorbs water from the air, the dew cells ability to conduct electricity increases. By detecting the electrical resistance of LiCl as it is heated and cooled, the dew cell can determine the dew point.

The *hair hygrometer* determines relative humidity based on the principle that hair becomes longer as relative humidity increases. As relative humidity decreases, hair becomes shorter.

Measuring Humidity at High Altitudes

To measure humidity at high altitudes, scientists use an electric hygrometer. The hygrometer may be carried up into the atmosphere in an instrument package known as a *radiosonde*. The radiosonde is attached to a weather balloon, such as the one shown in **Figure 5.** The electric hygrometer is triggered by passing an electric current through a moisture-attracting chemical substance. The amount of moisture changes the electrical conductivity of the chemical substance. The change can then be expressed as the relative humidity of the surrounding air.

Section 1 Review

1. **Explain** how most water vapor enters the air. 7c

2. **Identify** the principal source from which most water vapor enters the atmosphere. 7c

3. **Identify** the process by which ice changes directly into a gas. 7c

4. **Define** *humidity*.

5. **Compare** relative humidity with absolute humidity.

6. **Describe** what happens when the temperature of air decreases to the dew point or below the dew point. 7c

7. **Identify** four instruments that are used to measure relative humidity. IE.1a

CRITICAL THINKING

8. **Predicting Consequences** Explain what would happen to a sample of air whose relative humidity is 100% if the temperature decreased. 7c, IE.1d

9. **Identifying Relationships** Which region of Earth would you expect to have a higher absolute humidity: the equatorial region or the polar regions? IE.1d

CONCEPT MAPPING

10. Use the following terms to create a concept map: *humidity, water vapor, dew point, absolute humidity, dew cell, psychrometer, hygrometer, evaporation, condensation,* and *relative humidity.* 7c, IE.1a

California Content Standards

7c Students know the movement of matter among reservoirs is driven by Earth's internal and external sources of energy.

IE.1d Students will formulate explanations using logic and evidence.

Clouds are collections of small water droplets or ice crystals that fall slowly through the air. Ice crystals and water droplets form when condensation or sublimation occurs more rapidly than evaporation does. People commonly think that clouds are high in the sky and fog is close to the ground. However, clouds are not limited to high altitudes. Fog is actually a cloud that forms near or on Earth's surface.

Cloud Formation

For water vapor to condense and form a cloud, a solid surface on which condensation can take place must be available. Although the lowest layer of the atmosphere, the *troposphere,* does not contain any large solid surfaces, it contains millions of suspended particles of ice, salt, dust, and other materials. Because the particles are so small—less than 0.001 mm in diameter—they remain suspended in the atmosphere for a long time. The suspended particles that provide the surfaces necessary for water vapor to condense are called **condensation nuclei.** As water molecules collect on the nuclei, water droplets form, as **Figure 1** shows.

In addition, for clouds to form, the rate of evaporation must initially be in equilibrium with the rate of condensation. When this condition occurs, the air is said to be "saturated" with water vapor. When the temperature of the saturated air drops, condensation occurs more rapidly than evaporation does. As a result of this net condensation, clouds begin to form. Because the rate of evaporation decreases as temperature decreases, cooling of air may lead to net condensation. Four major processes can cause the cooling that is necessary for clouds to form.

OBJECTIVES

▶ **Describe** the conditions that are necessary for clouds to form. 7c

▶ **Explain** the four processes of cooling that can lead to the formation of clouds. 7c

▶ **Identify** the three types of clouds.

▶ **Describe** four ways in which fog can form. 7c

KEY TERMS

cloud
condensation nucleus
adiabatic cooling
advective cooling
stratus cloud
cumulus cloud
cirrus cloud
fog

---

cloud a collection of small water droplets or ice crystals suspended in the air, which forms when the air is cooled and condensation occurs

condensation nucleus a solid particle in the atmosphere that provides the surface on which water vapor condenses

---

Figure 1 ▶ **Formation of a Water Droplet**

Water molecules are electrically attracted to the sodium ions, Na⁺, and the chlorine ions, Cl⁻, in a salt crystal.

The water molecules and ions form a solution. Additional water molecules are attracted to the solution, and the droplet gets bigger.

Adiabatic Cooling

As a mass of air rises, the surrounding atmospheric pressure decreases. Because of the lower pressure, the molecules in the rising air move farther apart. Thus, fewer collisions between the molecules happen. The resulting decrease in the amount of energy that transfers between molecules decreases the temperature of the air. The process by which the temperature of a mass of air decreases as the air rises and expands is called **adiabatic cooling** (AD ee uh BAT ik KOOL ing).

adiabatic cooling the process by which the temperature of an air mass decreases as the air mass rises and expands

Adiabatic Lapse Rate

The rate at which the temperature of a parcel of air changes as the air rises or sinks is called the *adiabatic lapse rate*. The adiabatic lapse rate of clear air is about –1°C for every 100 m that the air rises. Air that is below the dew point—and thus is cloudy—cools more slowly, however. The average adiabatic lapse rate for cloudy air varies between –0.5°C and –0.9°C per 100 m that the air rises. The slower rate of cooling of moist air results from the release of latent heat as the water condenses.

Condensation Level

The process through which clouds form by adiabatic cooling is shown in **Figure 2**. Earth's surface absorbs energy from the sun and then reradiates that energy as heat. The air close to Earth's surface absorbs the heat. As the air warms, it rises, expands, and then cools. When the air cools to a temperature that is below the dew point, net condensation causes clouds to form. The altitude at which this net condensation begins is called the *condensation level*. The condensation level is marked by the base of the clouds. Further condensation allows clouds to rise and expand above the condensation level.

Reading Check What is the source of heat that warms the air and leads to cloud formation? (See the Appendix for answers to Reading Checks.)

Figure 2 ▶ Notice in this illustration that temperature and dew point are the same at an altitude of 1,000 m. Above that altitude, condensation begins and clouds, such as the clouds in the image on the right, form.

1,000 m — 10°C
Dewpoint = 10°C

Rising, expanding, and cooling air

500 m — 15°C
Dewpoint = 11°C

20°C
0 m — Dewpoint = 12°C

Figure 3 ▶ Clouds can form as air is pushed up along a mountain slope and is cooled to below the dew point.

Mixing

Some clouds form when one body of moist air mixes with another body of moist air that has a different temperature. The combination of the two bodies of air causes the temperature of the air to change. This temperature change may cool the combined air to below its dew point, which results in cloud formation.

Lifting

The forced upward movement of air commonly results in the cooling of air and in cloud formation. Air can be forced upward when a moving mass of air meets sloping terrain, such as a mountain range. As the rising air expands and cools, clouds form. As **Figure 3** shows, entire mountaintops can be covered with clouds that formed in this way.

The large cloud formations associated with storm systems also form by lifting. These clouds form when a mass of cold, dense air enters an area and pushes a less dense mass of warmer air upward.

Advective Cooling

Another cooling process that is associated with cloud formation is advective cooling. **Advective cooling** is the process by which the temperature of an air mass decreases as the air mass moves over a cold surface, such as a cold ocean or land surface. As air moves over a surface that is colder than the air is, the cold surface absorbs heat from the air and the air cools. If the air cools to below its dew point, clouds form.

advective cooling the process by which the temperature of an air mass decreases as the air mass moves over a cold surface

Figure 4 ▶ A variety of cloud types can be identified by their altitude and shape. *What cloud types form at or above 6,000 m?*

Classification of Clouds

Clouds are classified by their shape and their altitude. The three basic cloud forms are stratus clouds, cumulus clouds, and cirrus clouds. There are also three altitude groups: low clouds (0 to 2,000 m), middle clouds (2,000 to 6,000 m), and high clouds (above 6,000 m). This classification system is shown in **Figure 4.**

Stratus Clouds

Clouds that have a flat, uniform base and that begin to form at very low altitudes are called **stratus clouds.** *Stratus* means "sheet-like" or "layered." The base of stratus clouds is low and may almost touch Earth's surface. Stratus clouds form where a layer of warm, moist air lies above a layer of cool air. When the overlying warm air cools below its dew point, wide clouds appear. Stratus clouds cover large areas of sky and often block out the sun. Usually, very little precipitation falls from stratus clouds.

Two variations of stratus clouds are known as *nimbostratus* and *altostratus.* The prefix *nimbo-* and the suffix *-nimbus* mean "rain." Unlike other stratus clouds, the dark nimbostratus clouds can cause heavy precipitation. Altostratus clouds form at the middle altitudes. They are generally thinner than the low stratus clouds and usually produce very little precipitation.

Cumulus Clouds

Low-altitude, billowy clouds that commonly have a top that resembles cotton balls and a dark bottom are called **cumulus clouds.** *Cumulus* means "piled" or "heaped." Cumulus clouds usually look fluffy, as shown in **Figure 5.** These clouds form when warm, moist air rises and cools. As the cooling air reaches its dew point, the clouds form. The flat base that is characteristic of most cumulus clouds represents the condensation level.

The height of a cumulus cloud depends on the stability of the troposphere, which is the layer of the atmosphere that touches Earth's surface, and on the amount of moisture in the air. On hot, humid days, cumulus clouds reach their greatest heights. High, dark storm clouds known as *cumulonimbus clouds,* or thunderheads, are often accompanied by rain, lightning, and thunder. If the base of cumulus clouds begins at middle altitudes, the clouds are called *altocumulus clouds*. Low clouds that are a combination of stratus and cumulus clouds are called *stratocumulus clouds*.

cumulus cloud a low-level, billowy cloud that commonly has a top that resembles cotton balls and a dark bottom

cirrus cloud a feathery cloud that is composed of ice crystals and that has the highest altitude of any cloud in the sky

Cirrus Clouds

Feathery clouds that are composed of ice crystals and that have the highest altitude of any cloud in the sky are **cirrus clouds.** Cirrus clouds are also shown in **Figure 5.** *Cirro-* and *cirrus* mean "curly." Cirrus clouds form at altitudes above 6,000 m. These clouds are made of ice crystals because the temperatures are low at such high altitudes. Because these clouds are thin, light can easily pass through them.

Cirrocumulus clouds are rare, high-altitude, billowy clouds composed entirely of ice crystals. Cirrocumulus clouds commonly appear just before a snowfall or a rainfall. Long, thin clouds called *cirrostratus clouds* form a high, transparent veil across the sky. A halo may appear around the sun or moon when either is viewed through a cirrostratus cloud. This halo effect is caused by the bending of light rays as they pass through the ice crystals.

✓ **Reading Check** Why are cirrus clouds commonly composed of ice crystals? (See the Appendix for answers to Reading Checks.)

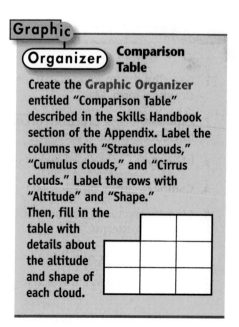

Graphic Organizer Comparison Table

Create the **Graphic Organizer** entitled "Comparison Table" described in the Skills Handbook section of the Appendix. Label the columns with "Stratus clouds," "Cumulus clouds," and "Cirrus clouds." Label the rows with "Altitude" and "Shape." Then, fill in the table with details about the altitude and shape of each cloud.

Fog

Like clouds, **fog** is the result of the condensation of water vapor in the air. The obvious difference between fog and clouds is that fog is very near the surface of Earth. However, fog also differs from clouds because of how fog forms.

Radiation Fog

One type of fog forms from the nightly cooling of Earth. The layer of air in contact with the ground becomes chilled to below the dew point, and the water vapor in that layer condenses into droplets. This type of fog is called *radiation fog* because it results from the loss of heat by radiation. Radiation fog is thickest in valleys and low places because dense, cold air sinks to low elevations. Radiation fog is often quite thick around cities, where smoke and dust particles act as condensation nuclei.

Figure 6 ▶ Steam fog covers the Yakima River in Washington.

fog water vapor that has condensed very near the surface of Earth because air close to the ground has cooled

Other Types of Fog

Another type of fog, *advection fog*, forms when warm, moist air moves across a cold surface. Advection fog is common along coasts, where warm, moist air from above the water moves in over a cooler land surface. Advection fog forms over the ocean when warm, moist air is carried over cold ocean currents.

An *upslope fog* forms by the lifting and cooling of air as air rises along land slopes. *Steam fog* is a shallow layer of fog that forms when cool air moves over an inland warm body of water, such as a river, as shown in **Figure 6.**

Section 2 Review

1. **Describe** the conditions that are necessary for clouds to form. 🖼 7c

2. **Explain** the four processes of cooling that can lead to cloud formation. 🖼 7c

3. **Identify** the cloud types that form at 8,000 m.

4. **Compare** cirrus, cumulus, and stratus clouds.

5. **Identify** the type of cloud that is known for causing thunderstorms.

6. **Compare** clouds with fog.

7. **Describe** four ways in which fog can form. 🖼 7c

CRITICAL THINKING

8. **Applying Ideas** Explain why air expands when it rises. 🖼 7c, IE.1d

9. **Making Predictions** How might an increase in pollution affect cloud formation? 🖼 7c, IE.1d

10. **Making Comparisons** Which type of cloud has the lowest condensation level? Which type has the highest condensation level? 🖼 7c, IE.1d

CONCEPT MAPPING

11. Use the following terms to create a concept map: *cloud, cirrus, condensation level, advective cooling, adiabatic cooling, stratus, cumulus,* and *fog.* 🖼 7c

---

Section 3 Precipitation

California Content Standards

7c Students know the movement of matter among reservoirs is driven by Earth's internal and external sources of energy.

IE.1a Students will select and use appropriate tools and technology (such as computer-linked probes, spreadsheets, and graphing calcula-

tors) to perform tests, collect data, analyze relationships, and display data.
IE.1d Students will formulate explanations using logic and evidence.

Any moisture that falls from the air to Earth's surface is called **precipitation.** The four major types of precipitation are rain, snow, sleet, and hail.

Forms of Precipitation

Rain is liquid precipitation. Normal raindrops are between 0.5 and 5 mm in diameter. They may vary from a fine mist to large drops in a torrential rainstorm. If the raindrops are smaller than 0.5 mm in diameter, the rain is called *drizzle*. Drizzle results in only a small amount of total precipitation.

The most common form of solid precipitation is *snow*, which consists of ice particles. These particles may fall as small pellets, as individual crystals, or as crystals that combine to form snowflakes. Snowflakes tend to be large at temperatures near 0°C and become smaller at lower temperatures.

When rain falls through a layer of freezing air near the ground, clear ice pellets, called *sleet*, can form. In some cases, the rain does not freeze until it strikes a surface near the ground. There, it forms a thick layer of ice called *glaze ice*, as shown in **Figure 1.** The condition in which glaze ice is produced is commonly referred to as an *ice storm*.

Hail is solid precipitation in the form of lumps of ice. The lumps can be either spherical or irregularly shaped. Hail usually forms in cumulonimbus clouds. Convection currents within the clouds carry raindrops to high levels, where the drops freeze before they fall. If the frozen raindrops are carried upward again, they can accumulate additional layers of ice until they are too heavy for the convection currents to carry them. They then fall to the ground. Large hailstones can damage crops and property.

OBJECTIVES

▶ **Identify** the four forms of precipitation.

▶ **Compare** the two processes that cause precipitation. **7c**

▶ **Describe** two ways that precipitation is measured. **IE.1a**

▶ **Explain** how rain can be produced artificially. **IE.1m**

KEY TERMS

precipitation
coalescence
supercooling
cloud seeding

precipitation any form of water that falls to Earth's surface from the clouds; includes rain, snow, sleet, and hail

Figure 1 ▶ Glaze ice forms as rain freezes on surfaces near the ground, such as on these flowers.

Figure 2 ▶ During coalescence, as cloud droplets fall, they collide and combine with small droplets. The resulting larger droplets fall as rain.

coalescence the formation of a large droplet by the combination of smaller droplets

supercooling a condition in which a substance is cooled below its freezing point, condensation point, or sublimation point without going through a change of state

Causes of Precipitation

Most cloud droplets have a diameter of about 20 micrometers, which is smaller than the period at the end of this sentence. Droplets of this size fall very slowly through the air. A droplet must increase in diameter by about 100 times to fall as precipitation. Two natural processes cause cloud droplets to grow large enough to fall as precipitation: coalescence and supercooling.

Coalescence

The formation of a large droplet by the combination of smaller droplets is called **coalescence** (кон uh LES uhnts) and is shown in **Figure 2.** Large droplets fall much faster through the air than small ones do. As these larger droplets drift downward, they collide and combine with smaller droplets. Each large droplet continues to coalesce until it contains a million times as much water as it did originally.

Supercooling

Precipitation also forms by the process of supercooling. **Supercooling** is a condition in which a substance is cooled to below its freezing point, condensation point, or sublimation point without changing state. Supercooled water droplets may have a temperature as low as –50°C. Yet even at this low temperature, the water droplets do not freeze. They cannot freeze because too few *freezing nuclei* on which ice can form are available. Freezing nuclei are solid particles that are suspended in the air and that have structures similar to the crystal structure of ice. Most water from the supercooled water droplets evaporates. The water vapor then condenses on the ice crystals that have formed on the freezing nuclei. The ice crystals rapidly increase in size until they gain enough mass to fall as snow, as shown in **Figure 3.** If ice crystals melt and turn into rain as they pass through air whose temperature is above freezing, they form the big raindrops that are common in summer thunderstorms.

Figure 3 ▶ Most of the rain and snow in the middle and high latitudes of Earth are the result of the formation of ice crystals in supercooled clouds.

Figure 4 ▶ Doppler radar helps meteorologists track storms, such as Tropical Storm Barry over the southeastern United States. The colors represent the intensity of rainfall. Reds and yellows indicate areas of heaviest rainfall, while blues and greens denote areas of lighter rainfall.

Measuring Precipitation

Meteorologists use a variety of instruments to measure precipitation. For example, a *rain gauge* may be used to measure rainfall.

Amount of Precipitation

In one type of rain gauge, rainwater passes through a funnel into a calibrated container, where the amount of rainfall can then be measured. In another type of rain gauge, rain caught in a funnel fills a bucket. Each time the bucket fills with a given amount of rainwater, the bucket tips and sets off an electrical device that records the amount. As the bucket tips, it activates a switch that releases the water from the bucket.

Snow depth is simply determined with a measuring stick. The water content of the snow is determined by melting a measured volume of snow and by measuring the amount of water that results. On average, 10 cm of snow will melt to produce about 1 cm of water.

Doppler Radar

The intensity of precipitation can be measured using Doppler radar. Doppler radar images, such as the one in **Figure 4,** are commonly used by meteorologists for communicating weather forecasts. Doppler radar works by bouncing radio waves off rain or snow. By timing how long the wave takes to return, meteorologists can detect the location, direction of movement, and intensity of precipitation. This information is very valuable in saving lives because people can be warned of an approaching storm.

SCILINKS®

NSTA
Developed and maintained by the
National Science Teachers Association

For a variety of links related to this subject, go to www.scilinks.org

Topic: Precipitation
SciLinks code: HQ61202

✔ **Reading Check** What aspects of precipitation can Doppler radar measure? (See the Appendix for answers to Reading Checks.)

Weather Modification

In areas suffering from drought, scientists may attempt to induce precipitation through cloud seeding, as shown in **Figure 5**. Cloud seeding is the process of introducing freezing nuclei or condensation nuclei into a cloud to cause rain to fall.

Methods of Cloud Seeding

One method of cloud seeding uses silver iodide crystals, which resemble ice crystals, as freezing nuclei. The silver iodide is released from burners on the ground or from flares dropped from aircraft. Another method of cloud seeding uses powdered dry ice, which is dropped from aircraft to cool cloud droplets and to cause ice crystals to form. As the ice crystals fall, they may melt to form raindrops.

Improving Cloud Seeding

In some cases, seeded clouds produce more precipitation than unseeded clouds do. In other experiments, cloud seeding does not cause a significant increase in precipitation. In some instances, cloud seeding appears to cause less precipitation. Thus, meteorologists have concluded that cloud seeding may increase precipitation under some conditions but decrease it under others. Research is underway to identify the conditions that cause increased precipitation. Eventually, cloud seeding may become a way to overcome many drought-related problems. Cloud seeding could also help control severe storms by releasing precipitation from clouds before a storm can become too large.

Figure 5 ▶ Special equipment attached to the wings of cloud-seeding planes releases freezing nuclei into clouds. Meteorologists hope that cloud seeding will induce rain to fall on drought-stricken areas.

cloud seeding the process of introducing freezing nuclei or condensation nuclei into a cloud in order to cause rain to fall

---

Section 3 Review

1. **Identify** four forms of precipitation.

2. **Compare** coalescence and supercooling. 7c

3. **Identify** the instrument that measures amounts of rainfall. IE.1a

4. **Describe** how the amount of snowfall can be measured. IE.1a

5. **Explain** how Doppler radar can be used to measure the intensity of precipitation. IE.1a

6. **Describe** how precipitation can be induced or increased artificially. IE.1m

CRITICAL THINKING

7. **Predicting Consequences** If water could not remain liquid during supercooling, how would the potential for precipitation in colder climates be affected? 7c, IE.1d

8. **Making Inferences** Explain how cloud seeding could be dangerous if it is not done properly. IE.1d, IE.1m

CONCEPT MAPPING

9. Use the following terms to create a concept map: *precipitation, rain, snow, glaze ice, hail, coalescence, supercooling, freezing nucleus, sleet,* and *drizzle.* 7c

Sections

1 Atmospheric Moisture

Key Terms

latent heat, 575
sublimation, 576
dew point, 577
absolute humidity, 577
relative humidity, 578

Key Concepts

▶ Latent heat is released or absorbed when water changes from one state to another.

▶ Relative humidity is a ratio of the actual amount of water vapor in the air to the amount of water vapor needed to reach saturation.

▶ When air reaches the dew point, the rate of condensation equals the rate of evaporation. Below the dew point, net condensation causes dew to form.

2 Clouds and Fog

cloud, 581
condensation nucleus, 581
adiabatic cooling, 582
advective cooling, 583
stratus cloud, 584
cumulus cloud, 585
cirrus cloud, 585
fog, 586

▶ Clouds form when water vapor cools and condenses on condensation nuclei.

▶ Water vapor can cool and condense by adiabatic cooling, by the mixing of two bodies of moist air that have different temperatures, by lifting of air, and by advective cooling.

▶ The three major forms of clouds are stratus clouds, cumulus clouds, and cirrus clouds.

▶ The four types of fog are radiation fog, advection fog, upslope fog, and steam fog.

3 Precipitation

precipitation, 587
coalescence, 588
supercooling, 588
cloud seeding, 590

▶ The major forms of precipitation are rain, snow, sleet, and hail.

▶ Coalescence and supercooling are two processes by which cloud droplets become large enough to fall as precipitation.

▶ A rain gauge is used to measure liquid precipitation. Snow is measured by its depth and water content.

▶ Cloud seeding is one way in which meteorologists try to induce precipitation.

Using Key Terms

Use each of the following terms in a separate sentence.

1. *latent heat* 🦏 7c
2. *condensation nucleus* 🦏 7c
3. *precipitation* 🦏 7c

For each pair of terms, explain how the meanings of the terms differ.

4. *coalescence* and *supercooling* 🦏 7c
5. *stratus cloud* and *cumulus cloud*
6. *adiabatic cooling* and *advective cooling* 🦏 7c
7. *relative humidity* and *absolute humidity*
8. *cloud* and *fog* 🦏 7c

Understanding Key Concepts

9. When the temperature of the air decreases, the rate of evaporation 🦏 7c
   a. increases.
   b. varies.
   c. stays the same.
   d. decreases.

10. The type of fog that results when moist air moves across a cold surface is 🦏 7c
    a. radiation fog.
    b. ground fog.
    c. advection fog.
    d. steam fog.

11. Changes in temperature that result from the cooling of rising air or the warming of sinking air are 🦏 7c
    a. adiabatic.
    b. relative.
    c. advective.
    d. latent.

12. Clouds form when the water vapor in air condenses as 🦏 7c
    a. the air is heated.
    b. the air is cooled.
    c. snow falls.
    d. the air is superheated.

13. The prefix *nimbo-* and suffix *-nimbus* mean
    a. high.
    b. billowy.
    c. rain.
    d. layered.

14. The fog that results from the nightly cooling of Earth is called 🦏 7c
    a. steam fog.
    b. upslope fog.
    c. radiation fog.
    d. advection fog.

15. Rain that freezes when it strikes a surface produces 🦏 7c
    a. sleet.
    b. glaze ice.
    c. hail.
    d. frost.

16. Clouds in which the water droplets remain liquid below 0°C are said to be 🦏 7c
    a. saturated.
    b. supersaturated.
    c. superheated.
    d. supercooled.

17. In one method of cloud seeding, silver iodide crystals are used as 🦏 IE.1m
    a. freezing nuclei.
    b. cloud droplets.
    c. dry ice.
    d. latent heat.

18. An instrument that uses the electrical conductance of the chemical lithium chloride to measure relative humidity is the 🦏 IE.1a
    a. hygrometer.
    b. rain gauge.
    c. psychrometer.
    d. dew cell.

Short Answer

19. Explain how the transfer of energy affects the changing forms of water. 🦏 7c

20. Explain how a psychrometer measures humidity. 🦏 IE.1a

21. Describe how frost forms. 🦏 7c

22. Describe how precipitation is measured. 🦏 IE.1a

23. Describe how cloud seeding may increase precipitation. 🦏 IE.1m

24. Explain how clouds are classified.

Hail

Hail is precipitation in the form of a lump of ice that starts as a raindrop falling from clouds. Updraft convection currents carry the raindrop back into freezing cloud regions, where layer after layer of supercooled water is added to the frozen drops. The added water also freezes and increases the sizes of the hailstones. Some hailstones have grown from this process to the size of grapefruits. The largest hailstone ever recorded had a circumference of more than 47 cm.

Hailstones often consist of alternating layers of clear ice and cloudy ice. The clear ice forms as a hailstone passes through a layer of very moist air. The cloudy layer forms when water droplets freeze to the surface of the hailstone and trap air bubbles between them.

Downdraft

Updraft

▲ Hailstones commonly consist of alternating layers of clear ice and cloudy ice.

Hail's Destructive Power

A hailstorm that lasts only a few minutes can cause tremendous damage. For example, hail has been responsible for some airplane crashes. It has torn holes in the roofs of houses and automobiles and in the cabins of aircraft. Hail has killed people, livestock, and wildlife, and it has stripped plants of their leaves.

In July 1984, a hailstorm in Germany caused $1 billion worth of damage to crops, trees, buildings, and vehicles. Trees were stripped of their bark. Crops were destroyed, and 400 people were injured.

The Cost of Hail

Hail destroys more than $200 million worth of wheat, corn, soybeans, and other crops in the United States each year. Hailstorms can have a devastating effect on individual farmers. Unlike drought, hail does not cause gradual damage. Instead, a family's entire crop, which may represent work over an entire year, can be wiped out within minutes.

◀ A strawberry farmer in Atwater, California, investigates damage to his crop. Seventy-five to eighty percent of his crop was destroyed by a hailstorm.

Extension

1. **Analyzing Processes** If you cut a hailstone in half, you would see layering. Explain why.

Chapter 24 Weather

Sections

1 Air Masses

2 Fronts

3 Weather Instruments

4 Forecasting the Weather

What You'll Learn

- How air masses affect weather
- How fronts lead to severe weather
- How scientists forecast weather

Why It's Relevant

Weather affects many different aspects of our lives every day. Studying the weather helps scientists make forecasts and warn people of dangerous weather.

PRE-READING ACTIVITY

Key Term Fold Before you read this chapter, create the **FoldNote** entitled "Key-Term Fold" described in the Skills Handbook section of the Appendix. Write a key term from the chapter on each tab of the key-term fold. Under each tab, write the definition of the key term.

▶ During a thunderstorm, clouds may discharge a spark of electricity called lightning. This bolt of lightning struck near Sugar Loaf Mountain in Rio De Janeiro, Brazil.

California Content Standards

5a Students know how differential heating of Earth results in circulation patterns in the atmosphere and oceans that globally distribute the heat.

6a Students know weather (in the short run) and climate (in the long run) involve the transfer of energy into and out of the atmosphere.

IE.1a Students will select and use appropriate tools and technology (such as computer-linked probes, spreadsheets, and graphing calculators) to perform tests, collect data, analyze relationships and display data.

IE.1d Students will formulate explanations using logic and evidence.

IE.1g Students will recognize the usefulness and limitations of models and theories as scientific representations of reality.

IE.1m Students will investigate a science-based societal issue by researching the literature, analyzing data, and communicating the findings. Examples of issues include irradiation of food, cloning of animals by somatic cell nuclear transfer, choice of energy sources, and land and water use decisions in California.

California Content Standards

5a Students know how differential heating of Earth results in circulation patterns in the atmosphere and oceans that globally distrib-ute the heat.
6a Students know weather (in the short run) and climate (in the long run) involve the
transfer of energy into and out of the atmosphere.
IE.1d Students will formulate explanations using logic and evidence.

Differences in air pressure are caused by unequal heating of Earth's surface. The region along the equator receives more solar energy than the regions at the poles do. The heated equatorial air rises and creates a low-pressure belt. Conversely, cold air near the poles sinks and creates high-pressure centers. Differences in air pressure at different locations on Earth create wind patterns.

How Air Moves

Air moves from areas of high pressure to areas of low pressure. Therefore, there is a general, worldwide movement of surface air from the poles toward the equator. At high altitudes, the warmed air flows from the equator toward the poles. Temperature and pressure differences on Earth's surface create three wind belts in the Northern Hemisphere and three wind belts in the Southern Hemisphere. The *Coriolis effect,* which occurs when winds are deflected by Earth's rotation, also influences wind patterns. The processes that affect air movement also influence storms, such as the one shown in **Figure 1.**

Formation of Air Masses

When air pressure differences are small, air remains relatively stationary. If the air remains stationary or moves slowly over a uniform region, the air takes on the characteristic temperature and humidity of that region. A large body of air throughout which temperature and moisture are similar is called an **air mass.** Air masses that form over frozen polar regions are very cold and dry. Air masses that form over tropical oceans are warm and moist.

OBJECTIVES

▶ **Explain** how an air mass forms. 5a
▶ **List** the four main types of air masses.
▶ **Describe** how air masses affect the weather of North America. 6a

KEY TERM

air mass

air mass a large body of air throughout which temperature and moisture content are similar

Figure 1 ▶ The motion of Earth's atmosphere can lead to the formation of powerful storms such as Hurricane Florence, which was photographed by astronauts on the shuttle *Atlantis* over the Atlantic Ocean in 1994.

Table 1 ▼

Air Masses		
Source region	Type of air	Symbol
Continental	dry	c
Maritime	moist	m
Tropical	warm	T
Polar	cold	P

Types of Air Masses

Air masses are classified according to their source regions. The source regions also determine the temperature and the humidity of the air mass. The source regions for cold air masses are polar areas. The source regions for warm air masses are tropical areas. Air masses that form over the ocean are called *maritime*. Air masses that form over land are called *continental*. Maritime air masses are moist, and continental air masses are dry. Air masses and the symbols used to designate them are listed in **Table 1.** The combination of tropical or polar air and continental or maritime air results in air masses that have distinct characteristics.

Continental Air Masses

Continental air masses form over large landmasses, such as northern Canada, northern Asia, or the southwestern United States. Because these air masses form over land, the level of humidity is very low. An air mass may remain over its source region for days or weeks. However, the air mass will eventually move into other regions because of global wind patterns. In general, continental air masses bring dry weather conditions when they move into another region. There are two types of continental air masses: *continental polar* (cP) and *continental tropical* (cT). Continental polar air masses are cold and dry. Continental tropical air masses are warm and dry.

Maritime Air Masses

Maritime air masses form over oceans or other large bodies of water. These air masses take on the characteristics of the water over which they form. The humidity in these air masses tends to be higher than that of the continental air masses. When these very moist masses of air travel to a new location, they commonly bring more precipitation and fog, as shown in **Figure 2.**

The two different maritime air masses are *maritime polar* (mP) and *maritime tropical* (mT). Maritime polar air masses are moist and cold. Maritime tropical air masses are moist and warm.

Figure 2 ▶ A maritime air mass brings fog that rolls in off the coast of California.

North American Air Masses

The four types of air masses that affect the weather of North America come from six regions. These air masses, their source locations, their movements, and the weather they bring are summarized in **Table 2.** The general directions of the air masses' movements are shown in **Figure 3.** An air mass usually brings the weather of its source region, but an air mass may change as it moves away from its source region. For example, cold, dry air may become warmer and more moist as it moves from land to the warm ocean. As the lower layers of air are warmed, the air rises. This warmed air may then create clouds and precipitation.

Table 2 ▼

Air Masses of North America			
Air mass	**Source location**	**Movement**	**Weather**
cP	polar regions in Canada	south-southeast	cold and dry
mP	polar Pacific; polar Atlantic	southeast; southwest-south	cold and moist
cT	U.S. southwest	north-northeast	warm and dry
mT	tropical Pacific; tropical Atlantic	northeast; north-northwest	warm and moist

Tropical Air Masses

Continental tropical air masses form over the deserts of the southwestern United States. These air masses bring dry, hot weather in the summer. They do not form in the winter. Maritime tropical air masses form over the warm water of the tropical Atlantic Ocean. They bring mild, often cloudy weather to the eastern United States in the winter. In the summer, they bring hot, humid weather and thunderstorms. Maritime tropical air masses also form over warm areas of the Pacific Ocean. But these air masses do not usually reach the Pacific coast. In the winter, maritime tropical air masses bring moderate precipitation to the coast and the southwestern deserts.

Reading Check Which air mass brings dry, hot weather in the summer? (See the Appendix for answers to Reading Checks.)

For a variety of links related to this subject, go to www.scilinks.org

Topic: Air Masses
SciLinks code: HQ60031

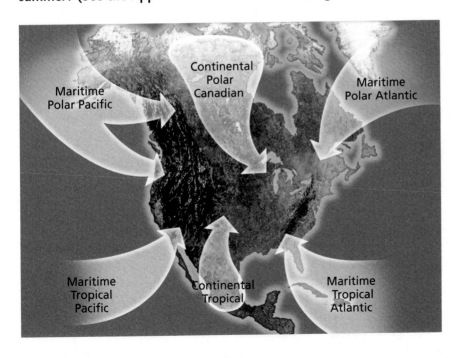

Figure 3 ▶ The four types of air masses that influence the weather in North America come from six regions and are named according to their source regions.

Figure 4 ▶ Maritime polar Atlantic air masses can bring heavy snowfall, such as in this snowstorm that hit New York City in 2003.

Polar Air Masses

Polar air masses from three regions—northern Canada and the northern Pacific and Atlantic Oceans—influence weather in North America. Continental polar air masses form over ice- and snow-covered land. These air masses move into the northern United States and can occasionally reach as far south as the Gulf Coast of the United States. In summer, the air masses usually bring cool, dry weather. In winter, they bring very cold weather to the northern United States.

Maritime polar air masses form over the North Pacific Ocean and are very moist, but they are not as cold as continental polar Canadian air masses. In winter, these maritime polar Pacific air masses bring rain and snow to the Pacific Coast. In summer, they bring cool, often foggy weather. As they move inland and eastward over the Cascades, the Sierra Nevada, and the Rocky Mountains, these cold air masses lose much of their moisture and warm slightly. Thus, they may bring cool and dry weather by the time they reach the central United States.

Maritime polar Atlantic air masses move generally eastward toward Europe. But they sometimes move westward over New England and eastern Canada. In winter, they can bring cold, cloudy weather and snow, as shown in **Figure 4.** In summer, these air masses can produce cool weather, low clouds, and fog.

Section 1 Review

1. **Define** *air mass.*

2. **Explain** how an air mass forms. 🌐 5a

3. **Identify** the location where a cold, dry air mass would form.

4. **List** the four main types of air masses.

5. **Describe** how the four main types of air masses affect the weather of North America. 🌐 6a

6. **Describe** the air mass that forms over the warm waters of the Atlantic Ocean. What letters designate the source region of this air mass?

CRITICAL THINKING

7. **Making Predictions** How would temperature and humidity at a given location change when a maritime tropical air mass is replaced by a continental polar air mass? 🌐 6a, IE.1d

8. **Recognizing Relationships** In which direction would you expect a tropical air mass near the coast of Europe to travel? Explain your answer. 🌐 IE.1d

CONCEPT MAPPING

9. Use the following terms to create a concept map: *maritime polar Pacific, maritime polar, continental polar Canadian, air mass, continental polar,* and *maritime polar Atlantic.*

IE.1d Students will formulate explanations using logic and evidence.

When two unlike air masses meet, density differences usually keep the air masses separate. A cool air mass is dense and does not mix with the less-dense air of a warm air mass. Thus, a boundary, called a *front,* forms between air masses. A typical front is several hundred kilometers long. However, some fronts may be several thousand kilometers long. Changes in middle-latitude weather usually take place along the various types of fronts. Fronts do not exist in the Tropics because no air masses that have significant temperature differences exist there.

Types of Fronts

For a front to form, one air mass must collide with another air mass. The kind of front that forms is determined by how the air masses move in relationship to each other.

Cold Fronts

When a cold air mass overtakes a warm air mass, a **cold front** forms. The moving cold air lifts the warm air. If the warm air is moist, clouds will form. Large cumulus and cumulonimbus clouds typically form along fast-moving cold fronts. Storms that form along a cold front are usually short-lived and are sometimes violent. A long line of heavy thunderstorms, called a *squall line,* shown in **Figure 1,** may occur in the warm, moist air just ahead of a fast-moving cold front. A slow-moving cold front lifts the warm air ahead of it more slowly than a fast-moving front does. A slow-moving cold front typically produces weaker storms and lighter precipitation than a fast-moving cold front does.

OBJECTIVES

▶ **Compare** the characteristic weather patterns of cold fronts with those of warm fronts.

▶ **Describe** how a midlatitude cyclone forms.

▶ **Describe** the development of hurricanes, thunderstorms, and tornadoes.

KEY TERMS

cold front
warm front
stationary front
occluded front
midlatitude cyclone
thunderstorm
hurricane
tornado

cold front the front edge of a moving mass of cold air that pushes beneath a warmer air mass like a wedge

Figure 1 ▶ As a cold air mass overtakes a warm air mass, a line of thunderstorms called a *squall line* forms. The photo shows a squall line over the North Atlantic Ocean.

Cold Front

Warm air mass

Cold air mass

Squall line

Warm Front

Occluded Front

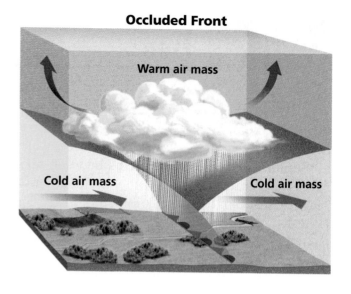

Figure 2 ▶ As a warm air mass rises over a cold air mass (left), a warm front forms at the boundary of the two air masses. An occluded front (right) forms when a cold air mass lifts a warm air mass off the ground.

warm front the front edge of advancing warm air mass that replaces colder air with warmer air

stationary front a front of air masses that moves either very slowly or not at all

occluded front a front that forms when a cold air mass overtakes a warm air mass and lifts the warm air mass off the ground and over another air mass

midlatitude cyclone an area of low pressure that is characterized by rotating wind that moves toward the rising air of the central low-pressure region

Warm Fronts

When a cold air mass retreats from an area, a **warm front** forms. The less dense warm air rises over the cooler air. The slope of a warm front is gradual, as shown in **Figure 2.** Because of this gentle slope, clouds may extend far ahead of the surface location, or *base*, of the front. A warm front generally produces precipitation over a large area and may cause violent weather.

Stationary and Occluded Fronts

Sometimes, when two air masses meet, the cold air moves parallel to the front, and neither air mass is displaced. A front at which air masses move either very slowly or not at all is called a **stationary front.** The weather around a stationary front is similar to that produced by a warm front. An **occluded front** usually forms when a fast-moving cold front overtakes a warm front and lifts the warm air off the ground completely, as shown in **Figure 2.**

Polar Fronts and Midlatitudes Cyclones

Over each of Earth's polar regions is a dome of cold air that may extend as far as 60° latitude. The boundary where this cold polar air meets the tropical air mass of the middle latitudes, especially over the ocean, is called the *polar front.* Waves commonly develop along the polar front. A *wave* is a bend that forms in a cold front or a stationary front. This wave is similar to the waves that moving air produces when it passes over a body of water. However, waves that form in a cold front or stationary front are much larger. They are the beginnings of low-pressure storm centers called midlatitude cyclones or *wave cyclones.* **Midlatitude cyclones** are areas of low pressure that are characterized by rotating wind that moves toward the rising air of the central, low-pressure region. These cyclones strongly influence weather patterns in the middle latitudes.

Stages of a Midlatitude Cyclone

A midlatitude cyclone usually lasts several days. The stages of formation and dissipation of a midlatitude cyclone are shown in **Figure 3.** In North America, midlatitude cyclones generally travel about 45 km/h in an easterly direction as they spin counterclockwise. They follow several storm tracks, or routes, as they move from the Pacific coast to the Atlantic coast. As they pass over the western mountains, they may lose their moisture and energy.

Anticyclones

Unlike the air in a midlatitude cyclone, the air of an *anticyclone* sinks and flows outward from a center of high pressure. Because of the Coriolis effect, the circulation of air around an anticyclone is clockwise in the Northern Hemisphere. Anticyclones bring dry weather, because their sinking air does not promote cloud formation. If an anticyclone stagnates over a region for a few days, the anticyclone may cause air pollution problems. After being stationary for a few weeks, anticyclones may cause droughts.

SCi LINKS **NSTA**
Developed and maintained by the National Science Teachers Association

For a variety of links related to this subject, go to www.scilinks.org

Topic: Fronts and Severe Weather
SciLinks code: HQ60624

✔ **Reading Check** How is the air of an anticyclone different from that of a midlatitude cyclone? (See the Appendix for answers to Reading Checks.)

Figure 3 ▶ Stages of a Midlatitude Cyclone

❶ Midlatitude cyclones occur along a cold or a stationary front. Winds move parallel to the front but in opposite directions on each side of the front.

❷ A wave forms when a bulge of cold air develops and advances slightly ahead of the rest of the front.

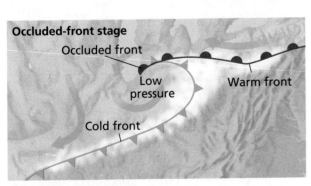

❸ As the fast-moving part of the cold front overtakes the warm front, an occluded front forms and the storm reaches its highest intensity.

❹ Eventually, the system generally loses all of its energy and the midlatitude cyclone dissipates.

Severe Weather

Severe weather is weather that may cause property damage or loss of life. Severe weather may include large quantities of rain, lightning, hail, strong winds, or tornadoes. This type of weather causes billions of dollars in damage each year.

Thunderstorms

A heavy storm that is accompanied by rain, thunder, lightning, and strong winds is called a **thunderstorm.** Thunderstorms develop in three distinct stages. In the first stage, or *cumulus stage*, warm, moist air rises, and the water vapor within the air condenses to form a cumulus cloud. In the next stage, called the *mature stage*, condensation continues as the cloud rises and becomes a dark cumulonimbus cloud. Heavy, torrential rain and hailstones may fall from the cloud. While strong updrafts continue to rise, downdrafts form as air is dragged downward by the falling precipitation. During the final stage, or *dissipating stage*, the strong downdrafts stop air currents from rising. The thunderstorm dissipates as the supply of water vapor decreases.

Lightning

During a thunderstorm, clouds discharge electricity in the form of *lightning*. The released electricity heats the air, and the air expands rapidly and produces the loud noise known as *thunder*. For lightning to occur, the clouds must have areas that carry distinct electrical charges. The upper part of the cloud usually carries a positive charge, while the lower part carries mainly a negative charge. Lightning is a huge spark that travels within the cloud or between the cloud and ground to equalize electrical charges. **Figure 4** shows an example of lightning.

---

thunderstorm a usually brief, heavy storm that consists of rain, strong winds, lightning, and thunder

---

MATHPRACTICE

Thunderstorm Distance The time between when a person sees a lightning strike and when he or she hears thunder indicates how far away the lightning bolt was from that person. Sound travels approximately 1 km in 3 s. The lapse time in seconds divided by 3 is roughly the number of kilometers between the viewer and the lightning. If 27 seconds pass between a flash of lightning and the sound of thunder, how far away was the lightning strike from the viewer?

Figure 4 ▶ The average lightning flash lasts only about a quarter of a second, but lightning causes more than $330,000,000 in damage per year in the United States.

15,000

Altitude (m)

10,000

5,000

Sea
level

Sinking dry air

Outward-flowing
high-level winds

Eye of the
hurricane

80 km/h
winds

120 km/h
winds

Evaporation

Heavy rains

400   300   200   100   0   100   200   300   400

Distance (km)

Hurricanes

Tropical storms differ from midlatitude cyclones in several ways. Tropical storms are concentrated over a small area. They lack warm and cold fronts. Also, they are usually much more violent and destructive than midlatitude cyclones. A tropical storm that has strong wind speeds of more than 120 km/h that spiral in toward its intense low pressure center is called a **hurricane.**

Hurricanes develop over warm, tropical oceans. A hurricane begins when warm, moist air over the ocean rises rapidly. When moisture in the rising warm air condenses, a large amount of energy in the form of latent heat is released. *Latent heat* is heat energy that is absorbed or released during a phase change. This heat increases the force of the rising air.

A fully developed hurricane consists of a series of thick cumulonimbus cloud bands that spiral upward around the center of the storm, as shown in **Figure 5.** Winds increase toward the center, or eye, of the storm and reach speeds of up to 275 km/h along the eyewall. The eye itself, however, is a region of calm, clear, sinking air.

At about 700 km in diameter, hurricanes are the most destructive storms that occur on Earth. The most dangerous aspect of a hurricane is a rising sea level and large waves, called a *storm surge.* A storm surge can submerge vast low-lying coastal areas. This flooding is the reason why most deaths during hurricanes are caused by drowning.

Every hurricane is categorized on the *Saffir-Simpson scale* by using several factors. These factors include central pressure, wind speed, and storm surge. The Saffir-Simpson scale has five categories. Category 1 storms cause the least damage. Category 5 storms can result in catastrophic damage.

✔ Reading Check Where do hurricanes develop? (See the Appendix for answers to Reading Checks.)

Figure 5 ▶ Although hurricanes are the most destructive storms, the eye at the center of the hurricane is relatively calm.

hurricane a severe storm that develops over tropical oceans and whose strong winds of more then 120 km/h spiral in toward the intensely low-pressure storm center

Graphic
Organizer **Venn Diagram**
Create the **Graphic Organizer** entitled "Venn Diagram" described in the Skills Handbook section of the Appendix. Label the circles with "Hurricanes," "Cyclones," and "Anticyclones." Then, fill in the diagram with characteristics that each weather event shares with the other weather events.

Figure 6 ▶ A powerful tornado in Texas embedded this bucket in a wooden door (inset).

tornado a destructive, rotating column of air that has very high wind speeds and that maybe visible as a funnel-shaped cloud

Tornadoes

The smallest, most violent, and shortest-lived severe storm is a tornado. A **tornado** is a destructive, rotating column of air that has very high wind speeds and that is visible as a funnel-shaped cloud, as shown in **Figure 6**.

A tornado forms when a thunderstorm meets high-altitude, horizontal winds. These winds cause the rising air in the thunderstorm to rotate. A storm cloud may develop a narrow, funnel-shaped, rapidly spinning extension that reaches downward and may or may not touch the ground. If the funnel does touch the ground, it generally moves in a wandering, haphazard path. Frequently, the funnel rises and touches down again a short distance away. Tornadoes generally cover paths not more than 100 m wide. Usually, everything in that path is destroyed. Tornadoes occur in many locations, but they are most common in *Tornado Alley* in the late spring or early summer. Tornado Alley stretches from Texas up through the midwestern United States.

The destructive power of a tornado is due to mainly the speed of the winds in the funnel. These winds may reach speeds of more than 400 km/h. Most injuries and deaths caused by tornadoes occur when people are trapped in collapsing buildings or are struck by objects blown by the wind.

Section 2 Review

1. **Describe** the four main types of fronts.

2. **Compare** the characteristic weather patterns of cold fronts with those of warm fronts.

3. **Identify** the type of front that may form a squall line.

4. **Summarize** how a midlatitude cyclone forms.

5. **Describe** the stages in the development of thunderstorms.

6. **Describe** the stages in the development of hurricanes.

7. **Explain** why tornadoes are destructive.

CRITICAL THINKING

8. **Evaluating Methods** What areas of Earth should meteorologists monitor to detect developing hurricanes? Explain your answer. IE.1d

9. **Making Comparisons** Compare the destructive power of midlatitude cyclones, hurricanes, and tornadoes in terms of size, wind speed, and duration. IE.1d

CONCEPT MAPPING

10. Use the following terms to create a concept map: *tornado, hurricane, warm front, squall line, cold front, severe weather, stationary front, front, midlatitude cyclone,* and *occluded front.*

Weather Instruments

California Content Standards

IE.1a Students will select and use appropriate tools and technology (such as computer-linked probes, spreadsheets, and graphing calcula-tors) to perform tests, collect data, analyze relationships, and display data.
IE.1d Students will formulate explanations using logic and evidence.

Weather observations are based on a variety of measurements, including atmospheric pressure, humidity, temperature, wind speed, and precipitation. These measurements are made with special instruments. Meteorologists then use the measurements to forecast weather patterns.

Measuring Lower-Atmospheric Conditions

During the course of a day, the lower-atmospheric conditions at a given location can change drastically. Meteorologists use the magnitude and speed of these changes to make predictions of future weather events. To obtain accurate data from the lower atmosphere, scientists use instruments such as those shown in **Figure 1**.

Air Temperature

An instrument that measures and indicates temperature is called a **thermometer.** A common type of thermometer uses a liquid—usually mercury or alcohol—sealed in a glass tube to indicate temperature. A rise in temperature causes the liquid to expand and fill more of the tube. A drop in temperature causes the liquid to contract and fill less of the tube. A scale marked on the glass tube indicates the temperature.

Another type of thermometer is an *electrical thermometer*. As the temperature rises, the electric current that flows through the material of the electrical thermometer increases and is translated into temperature readings. A *thermistor*, or thermal resistor, is a type of electrical thermometer that responds very quickly to temperature changes. For this reason, thermistors are extremely useful where temperature change occurs rapidly.

OBJECTIVES

▶ **Identify** four instruments that measure lower-atmospheric weather conditions. IE.1a

▶ **Describe** how scientists measure conditions in the upper atmosphere. IE.1a

▶ **Explain** how computers help scientists understand weather. IE.1a

KEY TERMS

thermometer
barometer
anemometer
wind vane
radiosonde
radar

thermometer an instrument that measures and indicates temperature

SCILINKS.
Developed and maintained by the National Science Teachers Association

For a variety of links related to this subject, go to www.scilinks.org

Topic: Weather Instruments
SciLinks code: HQ61646

Figure 1 ▶ Weather instruments, such as these at Elk Mountain weather research facility in Wyoming, indicate wind speed and direction.

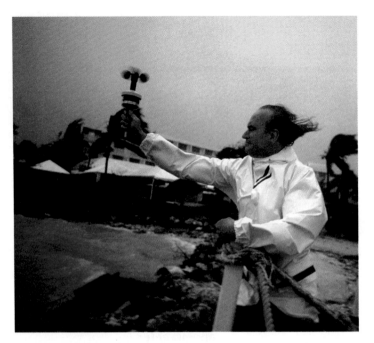

Figure 2 ▶ A meteorologist uses an anemometer during Hurricane Luis to measure wind speed.

barometer an instrument that measures atmospheric pressure

anemometer an instrument used to measure wind speed

wind vane an instrument used to determine direction of the wind

Air Pressure

Changes in air pressure affect air masses. The approach of a front is usually indicated by a drop in air pressure. Scientists use instruments called **barometers** to measure atmospheric pressure.

Wind Speed

An instrument called an **anemometer** (AN uh MAHM uht uhr) measures wind speed. A typical anemometer consists of small cups that are attached by spokes to a shaft that rotates freely. The wind pushes against the cups and causes them to rotate, as shown in **Figure 2.** This rotation triggers an electrical signal that registers the wind speed in meters per second or in miles per hour.

Wind Direction

The direction of the wind is determined by using an instrument called a **wind vane.** The wind vane is commonly an arrow-shaped device that turns freely on a pole as the tail catches the wind. Wind direction may be described by using one of 16 compass directions, such as north-northeast. Wind direction also may be recorded in degrees by moving clockwise and beginning with 0° at the north. Thus, east is 90°, south is 180°, and west is 270°.

☑ **Reading Check** Which instrument is used to measure air pressure? **(See the Appendix for answers to Reading Checks.)**

QuickLAB
15 min

Wind Chill
Procedure IE.1d

1. Place a **23 cm × 33 cm pan** on a level table. Fill the pan to a depth of 1 cm with **room temperature water.**
2. Lay a **thermometer** in the center of the pan with the bulb submerged. After 5 minutes, record the water temperature. Do not touch the thermometer.
3. Place an **electric fan** facing the pan and a few centimeters from the pan. Turn on the fan at a low speed. **CAUTION** Do not get the fan or cord wet.
4. Record the water temperature every minute until the temperature remains constant.

Analysis
1. How does the moving air affect the temperature of the water?

2. If the moving air is the same temperature as the still air in the room, what causes the water temperature to change?
3. How would you dress on a cool, windy day to stay comfortable? Explain your answer.

Doppler Radar

Conventional radar helps scientists estimate the distance to a storm and the intensity of the storm by measuring how many radio waves return. To learn more about storms, meteorologists developed a different form of radar to study weather. This form of radar, called *Doppler radar,* can measure not only the distance to a storm and the storm's overall direction and speed but also the direction that rain droplets or ice particles inside the storm are moving. This information allows scientists to identify conditions inside the storm.

Doppler radar uses the Doppler effect to read the apparent shift in wavelength of reflected radio waves as the particles that the waves reflect from move. You may have experienced the Doppler effect when an ambulance sped by you. The sound of the siren appeared to change from high-pitched as the ambulance approached to low-pitched as it moved

Lightning strikes near this Doppler radar facility in Oklahoma.

farther away. Because the wind causes the rain or ice particles to move around, the frequency of the radar signals they reflect also appear to shift. The Doppler radar measures that apparent frequency shift. Computer models then convert this information into an overall picture of the movement of the particles.

The use of Doppler radar allows meteorologists to identify dangerous conditions within a storm and to track the movement of these features. This ability allows meteorologists to warn communities of weather threats in time to save lives.

Measuring Upper-Atmospheric Conditions

Conditions of the atmosphere near Earth's surface are only a part of the complete weather picture. Scientists use several instruments to measure conditions in the upper atmosphere to obtain a better understanding of local and global weather patterns.

Radiosonde

An instrument package that is carried high into the atmosphere by a helium-filled weather balloon to measure relative humidity, air pressure, and air temperature is called a **radiosonde.** The radiosonde sends measurements as radio waves to a receiver that records the information. The path of the balloon is tracked to determine the direction and speed of high-altitude winds. When the balloon reaches a very high altitude, the balloon expands and bursts, and the radiosonde parachutes back to Earth.

Radar

Another instrument for determining weather conditions in the atmosphere is radar. **Radar,** which stands for **ra**dio **d**etection **and r**anging, is a system that uses reflected radio waves to determine the velocity and location of objects. For example, large particles of water in the atmosphere reflect radar pulses. Thus, precipitation and storms, such as thunderstorms, tornadoes, and hurricanes, are visible on a radar screen. The newest Doppler radar can indicate the precise location, movement, and extent of a storm. It can also indicate the intensity of precipitation and wind patterns within a storm.

radiosonde a package of instruments that is carried aloft by balloons to measure upper atmospheric conditions, including temperature, dew point, and wind velocity

radar **ra**dio **d**etection **and r**anging, a system that uses reflected radio waves to determine the velocity and location of objects

Figure 3 ▶ This satellite image captured Hurricane Andrew in 1992 as it approached Louisiana.

Weather Satellites

Instruments carried by weather satellites also collect important information about the atmosphere. Satellite images, such as the one shown in **Figure 3,** provide weather information for regions where observations cannot be made from the ground.

The direction and speed of the wind at the level of the clouds can also be measured by examining a continuous sequence of cloud images. For night monitoring, satellite images made by using infrared energy reveal temperatures at the tops of clouds, at the surface of the land, and at the ocean surface. Satellite instruments can also measure marine conditions. For example, the instruments can measure the temperature and flow of ocean currents and the height of ocean waves.

Computers

Meteorologists also use supercomputers to understand the weather. Before computers were available, solving the mathematical equations that describe the behavior of the atmosphere was very difficult, and sometimes impossible. In addition to solving many of these equations, computers can store weather data from around the world. These data can provide information that is useful in forecasting weather changes. Computers can also store weather records for quick retrieval. In the future, powerful computers may greatly improve weather forecasts and provide a much better understanding of the atmosphere.

Section 3 Review

1. **Identify** four instruments scientists use to measure lower-atmospheric conditions. IE.1a

2. **Explain** why scientists are interested in weather conditions in the upper atmosphere.

3. **Describe** the instruments used to measure conditions in the upper atmosphere. IE.1a

4. **Explain** how meteorologists send weather instruments into the upper atmosphere. IE.1a

5. **Summarize** how satellites help meteorologists study weather. IE.1a

6. **Summarize** how computers help scientists study weather. IE.1a

CRITICAL THINKING

7. **Recognizing Relationships** Wind is named according to the direction from which it blows. Why would a meteorologist need to know the direction wind is blowing from? IE.1d

8. **Making Inferences** If weather instruments were moved from a location in a valley to the top of a hill, what changes would you expect in the data? Explain your answer. IE.1a, IE.1d

CONCEPT MAPPING

9. Use the following terms to create a concept map: *thermometer, barometer, anemometer, radar, radiosonde, satellite, upper atmosphere, lower atmosphere,* and *weather instruments.* IE.1a

Section 4 Forecasting the Weather

IE.1a Students will select and use appropriate tools and technology (such as computer-linked probes, spreadsheets, and graphing calcula-

tors) to perform tests, collect data, analyze relationships, and display data.
IE.1d Students will formulate explanations using

logic and evidence.
IE.1g Students will recognize the usefulness and limitations of models and theories as scientific representations of reality.

Predicting the weather has challenged people for thousands of years. People in many early civilizations attributed control of weather conditions, such as wind, rain, and thunder, to gods. Some people attempted to forecast the weather by using the position of the moon and stars as the basis for their predictions.

Scientific weather forecasting began with the invention of basic weather instruments, such as the thermometer and the barometer. The invention of the telegraph in 1844 enabled meteorologists to share information about weather conditions quickly and led to the creation of national weather services. For example, the United States formed a weather-forecasting agency called the Weather Bureau. In 1970, it was renamed the *National Weather Service*. Because weather events in the United States commonly originate beyond U.S. borders, the National Weather Service exchanges weather data with other nations around the world.

OBJECTIVES

▶ **Explain** how weather stations communicate weather data. 🐾 IE.1a

▶ **Explain** how a weather map is created.

▶ **Explain** how computer models help meteorologists forecast weather. 🐾 IE.1a, IE.1g

▶ **List** three types of weather that meteorologists have attempted to control. 🐾 IE.1m

KEY TERM

station model

Global Weather Monitoring

Weather observers at stations around the world report weather conditions frequently, sometimes hourly. They record the barometric pressure and how it has changed as well as the speed and direction of surface wind. They measure precipitation, temperature, and humidity. They note the type, amount, and height of cloud cover. Observers also record visibility and general weather conditions. Similar data are gathered continuously by automated observing systems. Each station in the system sends its data to a collection center. Weather centers around the world exchange the weather information they have collected.

The World Meteorological Organization (WMO) sponsors a program called *World Weather Watch* to promote the rapid exchange of weather information. The organization helps developing countries establish or improve their meteorological services, as shown in **Figure 1.** It also offers advice on the effect of weather on natural resources and on human activities, such as farming and transportation. WMO was founded in 1873 and is now part of the United Nations.

Figure 1 ▶ One major role of the World Meteorological Organization is to train professionals to use weather instruments, such as this Bobson spectrophotometer installed at Maun, Botswana.

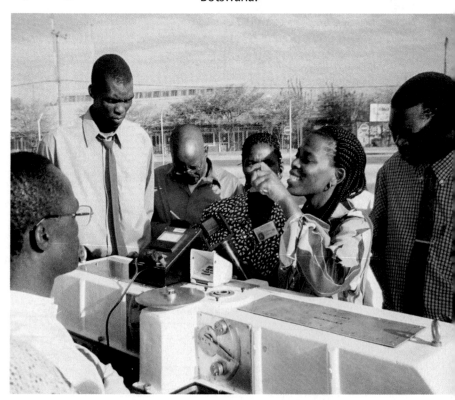

Weather Maps

The data that weather stations collect are transferred onto weather maps. Weather maps allow meteorologists to understand the current weather and to predict future weather events. To communicate weather data on a weather map, meteorologists use symbols and colors. These symbols and colors are understood and used by meteorologists around the world.

Weather Symbols

On some weather maps, clusters of meteorological symbols show weather conditions at the locations of weather stations. Such a cluster of symbols is called a **station model.** Common weather symbols describe cloud cover, wind speed, wind direction, and weather conditions, such as type of precipitation and storm activity. These symbols and a station model are shown in **Figure 2.** Notice that the symbols for cloud cover, wind speed, and wind direction are combined in one symbol in the station model.

Other information included in the station model are the air temperature and the dew point. The *dew point* is the temperature to which the air must cool in order for more water to condense than to evaporate in a given amount of time. The dew point indicates how high the humidity of the air is, or how much water is in the air.

The station model also indicates the atmospheric pressure by using a three-digit number in the upper right hand corner. If this number starts with 0, then the pressure is higher than 1,000 millibars. The position of a straight line under this figure—horizontal or angled up or down—shows whether the atmospheric pressure is steady or is rising or falling.

station model a pattern of meteorological symbols that represents the weather at a particular observing station and that is recorded on a weather map

Figure 2 ▶ Meteorologists use symbols to indicate weather conditions. The station model (lower right) shows an example of conditions around a weather station.

Highlights

Sections

1 Air Masses

Key Terms

air mass, 601

Key Concepts

▶ An air mass is a large body of air that has uniform temperature and humidity.

▶ Air masses can be described as polar, tropical, continental, and maritime. Their characteristics, which affect how they influence weather in North America, depend on their source region.

2 Fronts

cold front, 605
warm front, 606
stationary front, 606
occluded front, 606
midlatitude cyclone, 606
thunderstorm, 608
hurricane, 609
tornado, 610

▶ Cold and warm fronts are associated with characteristic weather conditions.

▶ A midlatitude cyclone is a storm that has a low-pressure center, rotating winds, and high-speed winds.

▶ Hurricanes, thunderstorms, and tornadoes are destructive storms. Thunderstorms and tornadoes are caused by the interaction of air masses with different properties.

3 Weather Instruments

thermometer, 611
barometer, 612
anemometer, 612
wind vane, 612
radiosonde, 613
radar, 613

▶ Thermometers, barometers, anemometers, and wind vanes measure lower-atmospheric weather conditions.

▶ Radiosondes, radar, satellite equipment, and computers are used to measure upper-atmospheric weather conditions.

▶ Computers are used to solve complicated mathematical equations that describe weather.

4 Forecasting the Weather

station model, 616

▶ Meteorologists prepare weather maps that are based on information from weather stations around the world.

▶ Meteorologists use different instruments to make daily and long-term forecasts of the weather.

▶ Meteorologists have attempted to control rain, hurricanes, and lightning with only limited success.

Chapter 24 Review

Using Key Terms

Use each of the following terms in a separate sentence.

1. *air mass* 🔲 5a

2. *stationary front*

3. *station model* 🔲 IE.1g

For each pair of terms, explain how the meanings of the terms differ.

4. *midlatitude cyclone* and *hurricane*

5. *wind vane* and *anemometer* 🔲 IE.1a

6. *radiosonde* and *radar* 🔲 IE.1a

7. *cold front* and *warm front*

8. *thermometer* and *barometer* 🔲 IE.1a

Understanding Key Concepts

9. Which of the following is information you would not find from a station model? 🔲 IE.1g
   a. precipitation
   b. cloud cover
   c. front
   d. wind speed

10. Continental polar Canadian air masses generally move
    a. southeasterly.
    b. northerly.
    c. northeasterly.
    d. westerly.

11. The type of front that forms when two air masses move parallel to the front between them is called
    a. stationary.
    b. occluded.
    c. polar.
    d. warm.

12. The type of front that is completely lifted off the ground by cold air is called
    a. cold.
    b. occluded.
    c. polar.
    d. warm.

13. The eye of a hurricane is a region of
    a. hailstorms.
    b. torrential rainfall.
    c. calm, clear air.
    d. strong winds.

14. The winds of a midlatitude cyclone blow in circular paths around a
    a. front.
    b. low-pressure center.
    c. high-pressure center.
    d. jet stream.

15. In the mature stage of a thunderstorm, a cumulus cloud grows until it becomes a
    a. stratocumulus cloud.
    b. altocumulus cloud.
    c. cumulonimbus cloud.
    d. cirrocumulus cloud.

16. An instrument package attached to a weather balloon is 🔲 IE.1a
    a. an anemometer.
    b. a wind vane.
    c. a thermograph
    d. a radiosonde.

17. The lines that connect points of equal atmospheric pressure on a weather map are called
    a. isobars.
    b. isotherms.
    c. highs.
    d. lows.

Short Answer

18. Describe the weather before and after an occluded front. 🔲 6a

19. What causes lightning?

20. What is the most likely location for hurricane development? Explain your answer.

21. How could a meteorologist use a station model to determine whether a cold front is approaching? 🔲 IE.1g

22. Identify the wind direction of wind given as 315°. What direction would a wind vane point in that case? 🔲 IE.1a

23. Identify the type of air mass that would most likely be responsible if the air in your region is warm and dry. What letters designate this air mass? 🔲 5a

Critical Thinking

24. Making Predictions Suppose people on Vancouver Island, off the west coast of Canada, hear reports of a midlatitude cyclone in the Gulf of Alaska. Is it likely that the midlatitude cyclone will reach their area? Explain why. IE.1d

25. Making Inferences Suppose a hurricane is passing over a Caribbean island. Suddenly, the rain and winds stop and the air becomes calm and clear. Can a person safely go outside? Explain your answer. IE.1d

26. Applying Ideas Is it safe to be in an automobile during a tornado? Explain your answer. IE.1d

27. Making Inferences An air traffic controller is monitoring nearby airplanes by radar. The controller warns an incoming pilot of a storm a few miles away. How did radar help the controller detect the storm? IE.1a, IE.1d

Concept Mapping

28. Use the following terms to create a concept map: *air mass*, *front*, *warm front*, *cold front*, *cyclones*, *thunderstorm*, *thermometer*, *hurricane*, *barometer*, and *anemometer*. 5a

Math Skills

29. Making Calculations The temperature at a station is given as 47°F . Using the equation, $°C = 5/9 \times (°F - 32)$, find the temperature in degrees Celsius.

30. Making Calculations An average of 124 tornadoes occur each year in Texas. If that is equivalent to 4.7 tornadoes per 10,000 mi^2, what is the area of Texas in square miles?

Writing Skills

31. Creative Writing Imagine that you are traveling with friends through the desert in the southwestern United States and a thunderstorm occurs. You then tell them about the type of air mass that may have brought the storm. Describe what the stages might look like by types of clouds formed, types of precipitation, and sky color.

32. Communicating Main Ideas Explain how cP and mT air masses travel across the United States, and explain why this information helps meteorologists make forecasts. 6a, IE.1d

Interpreting Graphics

The graph below shows the number of tornadoes that happened in Kansas at different times of day between January 1980 and July 2003. Use the graph to answer the questions that follow.

Number of Tornadoes by Time of Day in Kansas (1980–2003)

33. During which time of day did the least tornadoes occur?

34. Would Kansas students be more likely to experience a tornado while they are at school or while they are at home?

35. During which time of day did most tornadoes occur? Why would most tornadoes happen at this time of day?

Understanding Concepts

Directions (1–7): **For *each* question, write on a separate sheet of paper the letter of the correct answer.**

1 Making measurements in Earth's upper atmosphere can be difficult. But scientists use several tools to survey weather conditions at high altitudes. Which of the following statements describes one such tool?
A. A helium-filled balloon carries an instrument package into the atmosphere.
B. An anemometer measures wind speed.
C. A barometer measures the atmospheric pressure.
D. A thermistor measures rapid temperature changes.

2 Storms that have a lot of energy often cause a lot of damage. Of the following storms, which has the greatest amount of energy?
A. a thunderstorm
B. a tornado
C. an anticyclone
D. a Category 5 hurricane

3 Differences in air pressure result in the formation of air masses and fronts. In turn, these differences in air pressure are caused by
A. wind.
B. unequal heating of Earth's surface.
C. violent storms.
D. midlatitude cyclones.

4 Continental air masses form over large landmasses. They tend to be dry. The two types of continental land masses are continental polar and continental tropical air masses. How do they differ?
A. The continental polar air mass is smaller than the continental tropical air mass is.
B. The continental tropical air mass produces precipitation, but the continental polar air mass does not produce precipitation.
C. The continental polar air mass is colder than the continental tropical air mass is.
D. The continental tropical air mass moves into other regions, but the continental polar air mass does not move.

5 Fronts exist because of density differences between air masses. These density differences are typically due to differences in temperature—cold air is denser than warm air. In the tropics, there are few significant temperature differences. What can be concluded about fronts in the tropics?
A. Because there are no air masses, there are no fronts.
B. Fronts do not exist because there are no differences in density.
C. Air masses are less dense, so they do not form fronts.
D. Fronts do not exist because air masses are warm.

6 The amount of energy in a front can determine how strong a storm it will produce. A slow-moving cold front produces weaker storms than a fast-moving cold front does. What might this indicate about the amount of energy in each front?
A. Both fronts have the same amount of energy.
B. A slow-moving cold front does not have enough energy to produce a storm while a fast-moving cold front has enough energy to produce a storm.
C. A slow-moving cold front has less energy than a fast-moving cold front does.
D. Both fronts have enough energy to produce very violent storms.

7 Anticyclones bring dry weather, which does not promote cloud formation. If an anticyclone stays over an area for a long time, what will likely happen?
A. The anticyclone produces precipitation over a large area.
B. The anticyclone produces a squall line.
C. The anticyclone will lose its moisture and energy.
D. The anticyclone will cause a drought.

Interpreting Graphics

Directions (8–9): **For** *each* **question below, record the correct answer on a separate sheet of paper.**

Interpreting a Station Model

Weather symbols:

8 What letter indicates the current barometric reading shown in the model above?
A. letter A
B. letter B
C. letter C
D. letter D

Weather Instruments

9 Which of the weather instruments shown in the figure above uses the cooling effect of evaporation to take measurements?
A. a rain gauge
B. a psychrometer
C. a wind sock
D. an anomometer

Objectives

▶ **Construct** a pressure and temperature map.

▶ **Interpret** a weather map.

▶ **Explain** how weather patterns are related to pressure systems.

Materials

paper

pencil

pencils, colored, red, blue

Weather Map Interpretation IE.1d, IE.1g

Weather maps use various map symbols and lines to illustrate the weather conditions in an area at a given time. In this lab, you will study the symbols used on a weather map to gain an understanding of the relationships between temperature, pressure, and winds.

PROCEDURE

1. Make a copy of the weather map on the following page. This map can also be found in the Reference Tables section of the Appendix. You will use the map symbols on the same page of the Appendix to interpret the weather map. The number on the right of each station on the map represents atmospheric pressure. The number on the left represents temperature.

2. On your copy of the weather map, find stations that have a temperature of 10.0°C. Use a red pencil to draw a light line through these stations. If two adjacent stations have temperatures above and below 10°C, there is an estimated point between them that is 10.0°C. Draw a line through these estimated points to connect the stations that have temperatures of 10.0°C with a 10.0°C isotherm.

Step 2

Step 1

3 Using the same method as in step 2, draw isotherms for every two degrees of temperature. Examples are isotherms of 12.0°C, 14.0°C, and 16.0°C. Label each isotherm with the temperature it represents.

4 Find a station that has a barometric pressure of 1,004 millibars. Use a blue pencil, and follow the same method that you used in step 2 to create a 1,004 millibars isobar.

6 Using the same method as in step 3, lightly draw isobars for every 4 millibars of pressure. Examples are isobars of 1,000 mb, 1,008 mb, and 1,012 mb. Label each isobar with the pressure it represents.

ANALYSIS AND CONCLUSION

1 Identifying Trends What is the lowest temperature for which you have drawn an isotherm? What is the highest temperature for which you have drawn an isotherm? Is either isotherm a closed loop? If so, which one?

2 Making Inferences Is the air mass that is identified by the closed isotherms a cold air mass or a warm air mass? Explain your answer.

3 Analyzing Data Is there a shift in wind direction associated with either front shown on your map? Describe the shift.

4 Identifying Trends What is the value of the lowest-pressure isobar that was drawn? What is the value of the highest-pressure isobar that was drawn? Is either isobar a closed loop? If so, which one?

5 Drawing Conclusions At the time that the map represents, were there any areas of low pressure? of high pressure? Identify these areas. What weather conditions would you expect to find in those areas?

Extension

1 Making Predictions
Predict the weather conditions at Station A 24 hours after the observations for your map were made. Record your predictions in a table with columns for pressure, wind direction, wind speed, temperature, and sky condition. Also, make and record predictions for Station B and Station C.

MAPS *in Action*

Weather-Related Disasters, 1980–2003

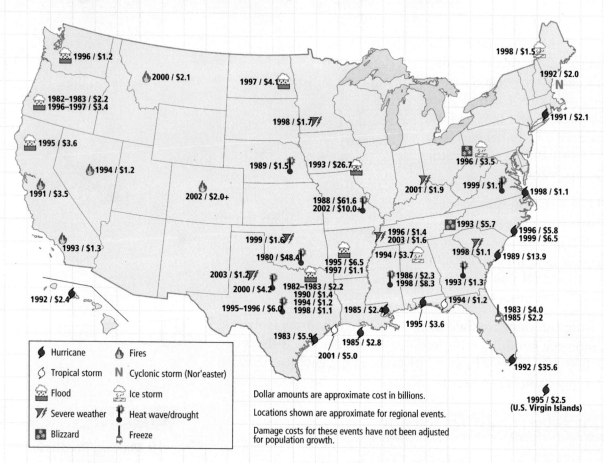

Key:

Symbol	Meaning	Symbol	Meaning
🌀	Hurricane	🔥	Fires
💧	Tropical storm	N	Cyclonic storm (Nor'easter)
🌧	Flood	❄	Ice storm
⚡	Severe weather	☀	Heat wave/drought
❄	Blizzard		Freeze

Dollar amounts are approximate cost in billions.

Locations shown are approximate for regional events.

Damage costs for these events have not been adjusted for population growth.

Map Skills Activity

This map shows the types and locations of weather disasters in the United States that caused at least $1 billion in damage. Use the map to answer the questions below.

1. **Using the Key** How many severe weather events caused more than $10 billion in damage between 1980 and 2003?

2. **Analyzing Data** Which type of weather disaster is more common—floods or fires?

3. **Making Comparisons** How do the types of disasters that happen in the western United States differ from the types of disasters that happen in the eastern United States? Explain why this difference exists.

4. **Inferring Relationships** Why might an ice storm in Alabama cause more damage than an ice storm in Maine?

5. **Identifying Trends** Almost all hurricane damage during this period happened along the coasts of the Atlantic Ocean and the Gulf of Mexico. Explain why.

6. **Analyzing Relationships** In 1996, a blizzard and floods caused $3.5 billion in damage in Ohio, Pennsylvania, and West Virginia. How might these events be related? Explain your answer.

7. **Analyzing Processes** Explain why fires are included in this map of weather-related disasters.

Meteorologist

When a hurricane threatens, most people flee, but not Shirley Murillo. Murillo boards a research aircraft and flies into the hurricane! As the plane flies through the hurricane, instruments record wind speed, wind direction, temperature, and air pressure.

Through the Eye of the Storm

Most of the flight is remarkably smooth, until the aircraft reaches the eyewall. The eyewall is a donutlike ring of turbulent thunderstorms that surround the calm eye of the storm. Once past the eyewall, the plane enters calm air. "We fly for hours going in and out of the eye, dropping instruments ... into the eye," says Murillo. Some of these instruments measure air pressure. These

data help hurricane forecasters decide if the storm is becoming weaker or stronger.

Improving Hurricane Forecasting

When she is not flying into hurricanes, Murillo is in her office at the Hurricane Research Division of the Atlantic Oceanographic and Meteorological Laboratory, an NOAA facility in Miami, Florida. Murillo studies how hurricane wind speeds change at landfall.

Murillo's research helps hurricane forecasters at the National Hurricane Center create their forecasts and advisories. Emergency managers also use it to determine areas along the coast that need to be evacuated. Scientists also use Murillo's

"Flying into a hurricane is a thrill. The data that are collected ... help save lives and property."

—Shirley Murillo

work to predict storm surge, the onshore rush of seawater caused by a hurricane's high winds and low pressure.

Rewards and Benefits

There is no doubt that Murillo's job can be exciting—and gratifying. "The most rewarding part of my job is the way in which our understanding of hurricanes and our improvement in forecasting benefit the scientific community and the public."

◀ The eye of the storm can be seen just below the plane *NOAA P-3* as it flies through Hurricane Caroline.

SciLINKS

NSTA
Developed and maintained by the
National Science Teachers Association

For a variety of links related to this subject, go to www.scilinks.org

Topic: Careers in Earth Science
SciLinks code: HQ60222

Sections

1 Factors That Affect Climate

2 Climate Zones

3 Climate Change

What You'll Learn

- What factors affect climate
- How regional climates vary
- How scientists study past climate changes and predict future climate changes

Why It's Relevant

Earth sustains life because the temperature and moisture conditions are right. By learning about climate, we can understand factors that might affect life on Earth.

PRE-READING ACTIVITY

FOLDNOTES

Tri-Fold
Before you read this chapter, create the **FoldNote** entitled "TriFold" described in the Skills Handbook section of the Appendix. Write what you know about climate in the column labeled "Know." Then, write what you want to know in the column labeled "Want." As you read the chapter, write what you learn about climate in the column labeled "Learn."

▶ Thick fur and other adaptations allow polar bears to survive and thrive in the freezing temperatures of the tundra climate.

California Content Standards

5a Students know how differential heating of Earth results in circulation patterns in the atmosphere and oceans that globally distribute the heat.

5e Students know rain forests and deserts on Earth are distributed in bands at specific latitudes.

5f* Students know the interaction of wind patterns, ocean currents, and mountain ranges results in the global pattern of latitudinal bands of rain forests and deserts.

5g* Students know features of the ENSO (El Niño southern oscillation) cycle in terms of sea-surface and air temperature variations across the Pacific and some climatic results of this cycle.

6a Students know weather (in the short run) and climate (in the long run) involve the transfer of energy into and out of the atmosphere.

6b Students know the effects on climate of latitude, elevation, topography, and proximity to large bodies of water and cold or warm ocean currents.

6c Students know how Earth's climate has changed over time, corresponding to changes in Earth's geography, atmospheric composition, and other factors, such as solar radiation and plate movement.

7b Students know the global carbon cycle: the different physical and chemical forms of carbon in the atmosphere, oceans, biomass, fossil fuels, and the movement of carbon among these reservoirs.

7d* Students know the relative residence times and flow characteristics of carbon in and out of its different reservoirs.

IE.1a Students will select and use appropriate tools and technology (such as computer-linked probes, spreadsheets, and graphing calculators) to perform tests, collect data, analyze relationships and display data.

IE.1d Students will formulate explanations using logic and evidence.

IE.1i Students will analyze the locations, sequences, or time intervals that are characteristic of natural phenomena (e.g., relative ages of rocks, locations of planets over time, and succession of species in an ecosystem).

IE.1l Students will analyze situations and solve problems that require combining and applying concepts from more than one area of science.

IE.1m Students will investigate a science-based societal issue by researching the literature, analyzing data, and communicating the findings. Examples of issues include irradiation of food, cloning of animals by somatic cell nuclear transfer, choice of energy sources, and land and water use decisions in California.

Factors That Affect Climate

California Content Standards

5g* Students know features of the ENSO (El Niño southern oscillation) cycle in terms of sea-surface and air temperature variations across the Pacific and some climatic results of this cycle. 6b Students know the effects on climate of latitude, elevation, topography, and proximity to large bodies of water and cold or warm ocean currents.

The average weather conditions for an area over a long period of time are referred to as **climate.** Climate is different from weather in that weather is the condition of the atmosphere at a particular time. Weather conditions, such as temperature, humidity, wind, and precipitation, vary from day to day. To understand climate, scientists study the features that define different climates.

Temperature and Precipitation

Climates are chiefly described by using average temperature and precipitation. To estimate the average daily temperature, add the high and low temperatures of the day and divide by two. The monthly average is the average of all of the daily averages for a given month. The yearly average temperature can be found by averaging the 12 monthly averages. However, using only average temperatures to describe climate can be misleading. As you can see in **Figure 1,** areas that have similar average temperatures may have very different temperature ranges. Another way scientists describe climate is by using the *yearly temperature range,* or the difference between the highest and lowest monthly averages.

Another major factor that affects climate is precipitation. It is also described by using monthly and yearly averages as well as ranges. As with temperature, average yearly precipitation alone cannot describe a climate. The months that have the largest amount of precipitation are important for determining climate. When describing climates, extremes of temperature and precipitation as well as averages have to be considered. The factors that have the greatest influence on both temperature and precipitation are latitude, heat absorption and release, and topography.

OBJECTIVES

▶ **Identify** two major factors used to describe climate. 6a

▶ **Explain** how latitude determines the amount of solar energy received on Earth. 6b

▶ **Describe** how the different rates at which land and water are heated affect climate. 6b, 5a, 6a

▶ **Explain** the effects of topography on climate. 6b

KEY TERMS

climate
specific heat
El Niño
monsoon

climate the average weather conditions in an area over a long period of time

Figure 1 ▶ Both St. Louis and San Francisco have the same average yearly temperature. However, St. Louis (right) has a climate of cold winters and hot summers, while San Francisco (left) has a generally mild climate all year.

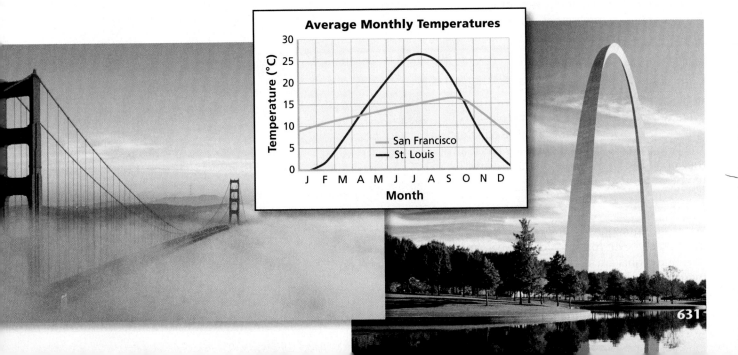

Average Monthly Temperatures

San Francisco
St. Louis

Latitude

One of the most important factors that determines a region's climate is latitude. Different latitudes on Earth's surface receive different amounts of solar energy. Solar energy determines the temperature and wind patterns of an area, which influence the average annual temperature and precipitation.

Solar Energy

The higher the latitude of an area is, the smaller the angle at which the sun's rays hit Earth is and the smaller the amount of solar energy received by the area is. At the equator, or 0° latitude, the sun's rays hit Earth at a 90° angle. So, temperatures at the equator are high. At the poles, or 90° latitudes, the sun's rays hit Earth at a smaller angle, and solar energy is spread over a large area. So, temperatures at the poles are low.

Because Earth's axis is tilted, the angle at which the sun's rays hit an area changes as Earth orbits the sun. During winter in the Northern Hemisphere, the northern half of Earth is tilted away from the sun. Thus, light that reaches the Northern Hemisphere hits Earth's surface at a smaller angle than it does in summer, when the axis is tilted toward the sun. Because of the tilt of Earth's axis during winter in the Northern Hemisphere, areas of Earth at higher northern latitudes directly face the sun for less time than during the summer. As a result, the days are shorter and the temperatures are lower during the winter months than during the summer months. **Figure 2** describes these effects.

Figure 2 ▶ Average Sea-Level Temperatures During Winter in the Northern Hemisphere

❶ In polar regions, the amount of daylight varies from 24 hours of daylight in the summer to 0 hours in the winter. Thus, the annual temperature range is very large, but the daily temperature ranges are very small.

❷ At middle latitudes, the sun's rays strike Earth at an angle of less than 90°. The energy of the rays is spread over a large area. Thus, average yearly temperatures at middle latitudes are lower than those at the equator. The lengths of days and nights vary less than they do at the poles. Therefore, the yearly temperature range is large.

Temperatures (°C)	
21 to 32	−23 to −12
10 to 21	−34 to −23
−1 to 10	−46 to −34
−12 to −1	Below −46

❸ At the equator, the sun's rays always strike Earth at a very large angle—nearly 90° for much of the year. In equatorial regions, both days and nights are about 12 hours long throughout the year. So, these regions have steady, high temperatures year-round.

Global Wind Patterns

Because Earth receives different amounts of solar energy at different latitudes, belts of cool, dense air form at latitudes near the poles, while belts of warm, less dense air form near the equator. Because cool air is dense, it forms regions of high pressure, while warm air forms regions of low pressure. Differences in air pressure create wind. Because air pressure is affected by latitude, the atmosphere is made up of global wind belts that run parallel to lines of latitude. Winds affect many weather conditions, such as precipitation, temperature, and cloud cover. Thus, regions that have different global wind belts often have different climates.

In the equatorial belt of low pressure, called the *doldrums,* the air rises and cools, and water vapor condenses. Thus, this region generally has large amounts of precipitation. The amount of precipitation generally decreases as latitude increases. In the regions between about 20° and 30° latitude in both hemispheres, or the *subtropical highs,* the air sinks, warms, and dries. Thus, little precipitation occurs in these regions. Most of the world's deserts are located in these regions. In the middle latitudes, at about 45° to 60° latitude in both hemispheres, warm tropical air meets cold polar air, which leads to belts of greater precipitation. In the high-pressure areas, above 60° latitude, the air masses are cold and dry, and average precipitation is low.

As seasons change, global wind belts shift in a north or south direction, as shown in **Figure 3.** As the wind and pressure belts shift, the belts of precipitation associated with them also shift.

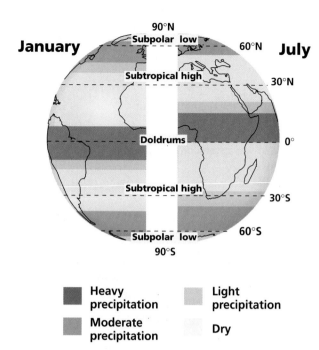

Figure 3 ▶ During winter in the Northern Hemisphere, global wind and precipitation belts shift to the south.

Heat Absorption and Release

Latitude and cloud cover affect the amount of solar energy that an area receives. However, different areas absorb and release heat differently. Land heats faster than water and thus can reach higher temperatures in the same amount of time. One reason for this difference is that the land surface is solid and unmoving. Surface ocean water, on the other hand, is liquid and moves continuously. Waves, currents, and other movements continuously replace warm surface water with cooler water from the ocean depths. This action prevents the surface temperature of the water from increasing rapidly. However, the surface temperature of the land can continue to increase as more solar energy is received. In turn, the temperature of the land or ocean influences the amount of heat that the air above the land or ocean absorbs or releases. The temperature of the air then affects the climate of the area.

✓ Reading Check How do wind and ocean currents affect the surface temperature of oceans? (See the Appendix for answers to Reading Checks.)

Specific Heat and Evaporation

Even if not in motion, water warms more slowly than land does. Water also releases heat energy more slowly than land does. This is because the specific heat of water is higher than that of land. **Specific heat** is the amount of energy needed to change the temperature of 1 g of a substance by 1°C. A given mass of water requires more energy than land of the same mass does to experience an increase in temperature of the same number of degrees.

The average temperatures of land and water at the same latitude also vary because of differences in the loss of heat through evaporation. Evaporation affects water surfaces much more than it affects land surfaces.

Ocean Currents

The temperature of ocean currents that come in contact with the air influences the amount of heat absorbed or released by the air. If winds consistently blow toward shore, ocean currents have a strong effect on air masses over land. For example, the combination of a warm Atlantic current and steady westerly winds gives northwestern Europe a high average temperature for its latitude. In contrast, the warm Gulf Stream has little effect on the eastern coast of the United States. This is because westerly winds usually blow the Gulf Stream and its warm tropical air away from the coast.

✓ **Reading Check** Why does land heat faster than water does? (See the Appendix for answers to Reading Checks.)

---

specific heat the quantity of heat required to raise a unit mass of homogeneous material 1 K or 1°C in a specified way given constant pressure and volume

MATHPRACTICE

Specific Heat

Use the following equation to calculate the amount of energy needed to heat 200 kg of water 6°C given that the specific heat of water is 4,186 J/kg•K.

energy = specific heat × mass × temperature change

QuickLAB
15 min

Evaporation

Procedure 6a, IE.1d

1. On a **piece of paper**, make a data table similar to the one shown here.
2. Assemble a **ring stand** on a **table**. Use a **meterstick** to place the support rings at heights of 20 cm and 40 cm above the base. Position a **portable clamp lamp that has an incandescent bulb** directly over the rings and at a height of 60 cm.
3. Place **three Petri dishes** or **watch glasses** as follows: one on the base of the stand and one on each of the two rings.
4. Take **three thermometers**, and lay one across each dish. Turn on the lamp. Use a **stopwatch** to record the temperature every 3 min for 9 min.
5. Remove the thermometers, and add **30 mL of water** to each of the three dishes.
6. Keep the lamp on and over the dishes for 24 h.

Dish	Temperature	Amount of water evaporated
1		
2		
3		

DO NOT WRITE IN THIS BOOK

7. Turn off the lamp. Carefully pour the water from the first dish into a **graduated cylinder**, and record any change in volume. Repeat this process for the other two dishes.

Analysis

1. At what distance from the lamp did the most water evaporate? the least water evaporate?
2. Explain the relationship between temperature and the rate of evaporation.
3. Explain why puddles of water dry out much more quickly in summer than they do in fall or winter.

El Niño–Southern Oscillation

The *El Niño–Southern Oscillation,* or *ENSO,* is a cycle of changing wind and water-current patterns in the Pacific Ocean. Every 3 to 10 years, **El Niño,** which is the warm-water phase of the ENSO, causes surface-water temperatures along the west coast of South America to rise. The event changes the interaction of the ocean and the atmosphere, which can change global weather patterns. During El Niño, typhoons, cyclones, and floods may occur in the Pacific Ocean region and southeastern United States. Droughts may strike other areas around the world, such as Indonesia and Australia. The ENSO also has a cool-water phase called *La Niña.* La Niña also affects weather patterns.

El Niño the warm-water phase of the El Niño–Southern Oscillation; a periodic occurrence in the eastern Pacific Ocean in which the surface-water temperature becomes unusually warm

monsoon a seasonal wind that blows toward the land in the summer, bringing heavy rains, and that blows away from the land in the winter, bringing dry weather

Seasonal Winds

Temperature differences between the land and the oceans sometimes cause winds to shift seasonally in some regions. During the summer, the land warms more quickly than the ocean. The warm air rises and is replaced by cool air from the ocean. Thus, the wind moves toward the land. During the winter, the land loses heat more quickly than the ocean does, and the cool air flows away from the land. Thus, the wind moves seaward. Such seasonal winds are called **monsoons.**

Monsoon climates, such as that in southern Asia, are caused by heating and cooling of the northern Indian peninsula. In the winter, continental winds bring dry weather and sometimes drought. In the summer, winds carry moisture to the land from the ocean and cause heavy rainfall and flooding, as shown in **Figure 4.** Monsoon conditions also occur in eastern Asia and affect the tropical regions of Australia and East Africa.

Figure 4 ▶ Effects of Monsoon Climates

Because monsoon rains cause regular flooding, such as this flood in eastern India, people who live in monsoon regions have adapted to living in flood conditions.

People who live in monsoon climates must adjust to periodic droughts, such as the drought that affected this cropland in southern India.

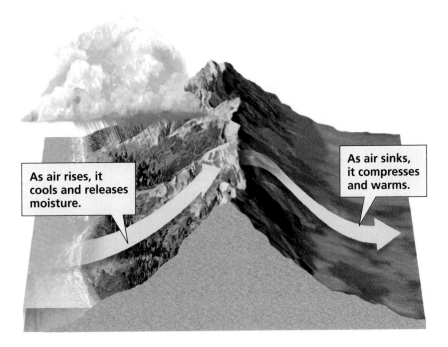

As air rises, it cools and releases moisture.

As air sinks, it compresses and warms.

Figure 5 ▶ Mountains cause air to rise, cool, and lose moisture as the air passes over the mountains. This process affects the climate on both sides of the mountain.

Topography

The surface features of the land, or *topography*, also influence climate. Topographical features, such as mountains, can control the flow of air through a region.

Elevation

The elevation, or height of landforms above sea level, produces distinct temperature changes. Temperature generally decreases as elevation increases. For example, for every 100 m increase in elevation, the average temperature decreases by 0.7°C. Even along the equator, the peaks of high mountains can be cold enough to be covered with snow.

Rain Shadows

When a moving air mass encounters a mountain range, the air mass rises, cools, and loses most of its moisture through precipitation, as shown in **Figure 5.** As a result, the air that flows down the other side of the range is usually warm and dry. This effect is called a *rain shadow*. One type of warm, dry wind that forms in this way is the *foehn* (FAYN), a dry wind that flows down the slopes of the Alps. Similar dry, warm winds that flow down the eastern slopes of the Rocky Mountains are called *chinooks*.

Section 1 **Review**

1. **Identify** two factors that are used to describe climate. 6a

2. **Explain** how latitude determines the amount of solar energy received on Earth. 6b

3. **Describe** how latitude determines wind patterns. 5a, 6b

4. **Describe** how the different rates at which land and water are heated affect climate. 5a, 6a, 6b

5. **Explain** the El Niño–Southern Oscillation cycle. 5g*

6. **Summarize** the conditions that cause monsoons. 6a

7. **Explain** how elevation affects climate. 6b

8. **Describe** a rain shadow and the resulting local winds. 6b

CRITICAL THINKING

9. **Making Inferences** If land and water had the same specific heat, how might climate be different around the world? 5a, 6a, 6b, IE.1d

10. **Analyzing Processes** On a mountain, are you likely to find more vegetation on the side facing prevailing winds or on the side facing away from them? 6b, IE.1d

11. **Recognizing Relationships** Why might you find snow-capped mountains in Hawaii even though Hawaii is closer to the equator than Florida is? 6b, IE.1d

CONCEPT MAPPING

12. Use the following terms to create a concept map: *climate, temperature range, wind, doldrums, subtropical high, monsoon, El Niño,* and *topography.* 5g*, 6a, 6b

Global Warming

Global temperatures have increased approximately 1°C over the last 100 years. Researchers are trying to determine if this increase is a natural variation or the result of human activities, such as deforestation and pollution. A gradual increase in average global temperatures is called **global warming.** This process may result from an increase in the concentration of greenhouse gases, such as CO_2, in the atmosphere.

An increase in global temperature can lead to an increase in evaporation. Increased evaporation could cause some areas to become drier than they are now. Some plants and animals would not be able to live in these drier conditions. An increase in evaporation in other areas could cause crops to suffer damage. However, an increase in temperatures due to global warming might improve conditions for crops in colder, northern regions.

An increase in global temperatures could also cause ice at the poles to melt. If a significant amount of ice melts, sea levels around the world could rise. This rise in sea levels would cause flooding around coastlines, where many cities are located.

Sea-Level Changes

Using computer models, some scientists have predicted an increase in global temperature of 2°C to 4°C during this century. An increase of only a few degrees worldwide could melt the polar icecaps and raise sea level by adding water to the oceans. On a shoreline that has a gentle slope, the shoreline could shift inland many miles, as shown in **Figure 4.** Many coastal inhabitants would be displaced, and freshwater and agricultural land resources would be diminished. Because approximately 50% of the world population lives near coastlines, this sea-level rise would have devastating effects.

global warming a gradual increase in the average global temperature that is due to a higher concentration of gases such as carbon dioxide in the atmosphere

For a variety of links related to this subject, go to www.scilinks.org

Topic: Global Warming
SciLinks code: HQ60681

Figure 4 ▶ As sea level rises, shorelines could shift inland many miles. *Which two states would lose the most area if sea level were to rise by 3 m?*

Figure 5 ▶ People from the Wangari Maathai Green Belt Movement in Kenya, Africa, prepare seedlings for planting.

What Humans Can Do

Many countries are working together to reduce the potential effects of global warming. Treaties and laws have been passed to reduce pollution. Industrial practices are being monitored and changed. Even community projects to reforest areas, such as the one shown in **Figure 5**, have been developed on a local level.

Individual Efforts

Each individual person can also help to reduce CO_2 concentrations in the atmosphere that are caused by pollution. Pollution is caused mostly by the burning of fossil fuels, such as running automobiles and using electricity. Therefore, humans can have a significant effect on pollution rates by turning lights off when they are not in use, by turning down the heat in winter, and by reducing air conditioner use in the summer. Recycling is also helpful because less energy is needed to recycle some products than to create them.

Transportation Solutions

Using public transportation and driving fuel-efficient vehicles also help release less CO_2 into the atmosphere. All vehicles burn fuel more efficiently when they are properly tuned and the tires are properly inflated. Driving at a consistent speed also allows a vehicle to burn fuel efficiently. Car manufacturers have been developing cars that are more fuel efficient. For example, *hybrid cars* use both gasoline and electricity. These cars release less CO_2 into the atmosphere from burning fuel than other cars do.

Section 3 Review

1. **Compare** four methods that climatologists use to study climate. IE.1a

2. **Identify** four factors that may cause climate change. 6c, IE.1m

3. **Describe** how orbital changes may affect climate. 6c

4. **Explain** how changes in CO_2 concentrations affect global temperatures. 6c

5. **Explain** one potential negative impact of global warming. 6c, IE.1m

6. **Identify** two ways that countries can work together to reduce the potential effects of global warming. 6c, IE.1m

7. **Identify** four ways that an individual can reduce the potential effects of global warming. IE.1m

CRITICAL THINKING

8. **Making Predictions** How would the melting of small icebergs affect sea level? Explain your answer. IE.1d, IE.1m

9. **Evaluating Models** Can short-term climate changes be explained by using the cycles described by the Milankovitch theory? Explain your answer. 6c, IE.1d

CONCEPT MAPPING

10. Use the following terms to create a concept map: *climatologist, general circulation models, global warming, ice cores, tree rings, fossils,* and *isotopes.* 6c, IE.1a, IE.1m

Sections

1 Factors That Affect Climate

Key Terms

climate, 631
specific heat, 634
El Niño, 635
monsoon, 635

Key Concepts

▶ The climate of a region is described by the region's temperature and precipitation.

▶ Latitude affects climate by determining the intensity of solar energy received by an area.

▶ The rates at which land and water are heated affect climate.

▶ Topography affects climate by causing temperature variations due to elevation and by creating rain shadows.

2 Climate Zones

tropical climate, 637
middle-latitude climate, 638
polar climate, 639
microclimate, 640

▶ Tropical subclimates are located near the equator and include tropical rain-forest, tropical desert, and savanna climates.

▶ Middle-latitude climates include marine west coast, steppe, humid continental, humid subtropical, and mediterranean climates.

▶ Polar climates include subarctic, tundra, and polar icecap climates.

▶ Microclimates are influenced by large bodies of water, by elevation, and by vegetation and urban development.

3 Climate Change

climatologist, 641
global warming, 645

▶ By using ice cores, sea-floor sediment, fossils, and tree rings, scientists have been able to study past climates.

▶ Computer-generated climate models help scientists predict possible consequences of changing certain variables in the climate system.

▶ Natural processes and human activities may be causing changes in Earth's climate, including global warming.

Using Key Terms

Use each of the following terms in a separate sentence.

1. *specific heat*

2. *microclimate* 6b

3. *climatologist*

For each pair of terms, explain how the meanings of the terms differ.

4. *climate* and *microclimate* 6b

5. *El Niño* and *monsoon* 5g*

6. *tropical climate* and *polar climate* 5e, 5f*, 6b

Understanding Key Concepts

7. At the equator, the sun's rays always strike Earth 6b
  a. at a low angle.
  b. at nearly a 90° angle.
  c. 18 hours each day.
  d. no more than 8 hours each day.

8. Which of the following is *not* used as evidence of past climates? 6c, IE.1a
  a. ice cores
  b. general circulation models
  c. tree rings
  d. fossils

9. Water cools 5a
  a. more slowly than land does.
  b. more quickly than land does.
  c. only during evaporation.
  d. during global warming.

10. Ocean currents influence temperature by 5a, 6b
  a. eroding shorelines.
  b. heating or cooling the air.
  c. washing warm, dry sediments out to sea.
  d. dispersing the rays of the sun.

11. Winds that blow in opposite directions in different seasons because of the differential heating of the land and the oceans are called 5a, 6b
  a. chinooks.   **c.** monsoons.
  b. foehn.   **d.** El Niño.

12. When a moving air mass encounters a mountain range, the air mass 6b
  a. stops moving.
  b. slows and sinks.
  c. rises and cools.
  d. reverses its direction.

13. In regions that have a mediterranean climate, almost all of the yearly precipitation falls 5e, 5f*
  a. during monsoons.
  b. in the summer.
  c. in the winter.
  d. during hurricanes.

14. The climate that has the largest annual temperature range is the 5e, 5f*
  a. subarctic climate.
  b. middle-latitude desert climate.
  c. mediterranean climate.
  d. humid continental climate.

15. The pavement and buildings in cities affect the local climate by 6b
  a. decreasing the temperature.
  b. increasing the temperature.
  c. increasing the precipitation.
  d. decreasing the precipitation.

Short Answer

16. Describe the Milankovitch theory, including how it may explain some climate changes. 6c

17. What are the possible effects of global warming? 6c, IE.1m

18. Compare marine west coast and humid continental climates. 5e, 5f*, 6b

Critical Thinking

19. Making Predictions Describe how the climate in California might be affected if all of the trees in California were cut down. 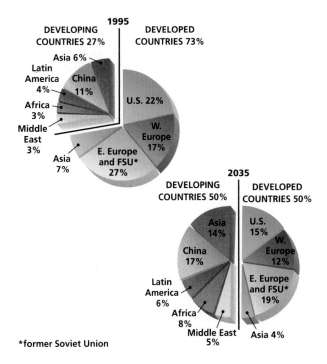 5e, 5f*, IE.1d

20. Making Inferences Explain why the vegetation in areas that have a tundra climate is sparse even though these areas receive enough precipitation to support plant life. 5e, 5f*, IE.1d

21. Analyzing Ideas Explain why climates cannot be classified only by latitude. 6b, IE.1d

22. Predicting Consequences How would global climate be affected if Earth were not tilted on its axis? Explain your reasoning. 5a, 6b

Concept Mapping

23. Use the following terms to create a concept map: *fossil, ice cores, climate, polar climate, climatologist, steppe, temperature range, tropical climate, middle-latitude climate*, and *savanna*. 6b

Math Skills

24. Using Equations Temperature generally decreases about 6.5°C for every kilometer above sea level. If T_N = temperature at new altitude, a = altitude in kilometers, and T_I = the initial temperature at sea level, what equation can be used to find the temperature at a given altitude? 6b

25. Making Calculations From 1970 to 1997, nitrogen oxides, NO_X, emissions increased from about 18.7 million to about 20.8 million tons per year. By what percentage did NO_X emissions increase from 1970 to 1997? IE.1m

Writing Skills

26. Researching Topics Research greenhouse gases to determine how they are produced. Then, write a brief essay that outlines how they can be reduced. IE.1m

27. Communicating Main Ideas Imagine that you are going to build a vacation house. Research three locations where you would like to build your house, and outline the climate features that would make each location ideal for your vacation home. 6b

Interpreting Graphics

The pie graphs below show world emissions of carbon dioxide, CO_2, in 1995 and predict emissions in 2035. Use these graphs to answer the questions that follow.

Total World Emissions of Carbon Dioxide

1995

DEVELOPING COUNTRIES 27%
DEVELOPED COUNTRIES 73%

Asia 6%
Latin America 4%
China 11%
Africa 3%
Middle East 3%
U.S. 22%
W. Europe 17%
Asia 7%
E. Europe and FSU* 27%

2035

DEVELOPING COUNTRIES 50%
DEVELOPED COUNTRIES 50%

Asia 14%
China 17%
Latin America 6%
Africa 8%
Middle East 5%
U.S. 15%
W. Europe 12%
E. Europe and FSU* 19%
Asia 4%

*former Soviet Union

28. In 1995, which country or region emitted the most CO_2? Which emitted the least CO_2? 7b

29. What percentage of the total CO_2 was emitted by developing countries in 1995? 7b

30. Why do you think researchers predict that CO_2 emissions by developing countries will equal that of developed countries by 2035? 7b

Understanding Concepts

Directions (1–9): For *each* question, write on a separate sheet of paper the letter of the correct answer.

1 Which statement best compares how land and water are heated by solar energy?
A. Water heats up faster and to a higher temperature than land does.
B. Land heats up faster and to a higher temperature than water does.
C. Water heats up more slowly but reaches a higher temperature than land does.
D. Land heats up more slowly and reaches a higher temperature than water does.

2 Which of the following statements best describes the El Niño–Southern Oscillation?
A. a change in global wind patterns that occurs in the Southern Hemisphere
B. a warming of surface waters in the eastern Pacific due to the effects of changing wind patterns on ocean currents near the equator
C. a cooling of surface waters in the eastern Pacific due to the effects of changing wind patterns on ocean currents near the equator
D. a global wind and precipitation belt between 20°N and 30°N latitude

3 The addition of carbon dioxide to Earth's atmosphere increased average global temperatures. Human activity adds more carbon dioxide to the atmosphere, which may lead to further increases in temperature. What else can increase with these increased temperatures?
A. evaporation
B. ice formation
C. human activity
D. cloud cover

4 In samples of atmospheric gases taken from ice cores, high levels of carbon dioxide indicate that the sample is from a time period that had
A. a warm climate.
B. a cool climate.
C. high amounts of precipitation.
D. low amounts of precipitation.

5 Over time, Earth's climate has changed. Which of the following was NOT a factor in that change?
A. plate tectonics
B. orbital change
C. human activity
D. winds

6 The region of Earth near the equator is called the tropics and has three types of climate. The three types of tropical climate are characterized by high temperatures and amount of precipitation, which in turn determines the vegetation that grows in the area. A tropical climate that has high rainfall results in the growth of
A. rain forests.
B. little or no vegetation.
C. open grasslands that have drought-resistant shrubs.
D. deciduous trees.

7 Climate is affected by a number of factors, including latitude, elevation, and proximity to mountains. How might mountains affect climate?
A. They increase temperature as air moves over a mountain.
B. They cause air to lose moisture as it passes over the mountains.
C. They absorb heat slower than other areas do, changing the climate.
D. They moderate area temperatures.

8 Latitude is a determining factor in the type of climate that a region has. This is due primarily to
A. the amount of solar energy a latitude receives.
B. global wind patterns.
C. the proportion of land to water.
D. ocean currents.

9 Global warming results from increased carbon dioxide in the atmosphere. This carbon dioxide is the product of many human activities. How can people reduce carbon dioxide?
A. seed clouds
B. use electricity
C. drive hybrid cars
D. eat less

Interpreting Graphics

Directions (10–12): For *each* question below, record the correct answer on a separate sheet of paper.

Two Cities Separated by Coastal Mountains

10 Which city is most likely to have the largest yearly temperature range?
A. City A would likely have the largest yearly temperature range.
B. City B would likely have the largest yearly temperature range.
C. Both cities would likely have the same temperature range.
D. There is not enough information to answer the question.

Climatograms for Two Cities

11 Based on the climatograms above, which of the two cities is in a tropical climate?
A. Nashville, TN
B. Manokwari, New Guinea
C. Both cities are in tropical climates.
D. Neither city is in a tropical climate.

12 Which month shows the most rainfall for both climates in the climatograms?
A. March
B. June
C. September
D. December

Objectives

▶ **Determine** whether land or water absorbs heat faster.

▶ **Explain** how the properties of land and water affect climate.

Materials

container (2)
heat lamp
meterstick
soil
thermometer, Celsius (2)
water

Safety

Factors That Affect Climate 5a, 6b, IE.1a, IE.1d

Many factors affect climate. One of the most significant factors that influence climate is the distribution of land and water. Because land and water absorb and release heat energy differently, they affect the atmosphere differently. In turn, the differences between land and water affect the climate. In this lab, you will explore how the properties of land and water affect climate.

ASK A QUESTION

1. How do the properties of land and water affect climate?

FORM A HYPOTHESIS

2. On a separate piece of paper, write a hypothesis that is a possible answer to the question above.

TEST THE HYPOTHESIS

3. Fill one container with soil and the other with water. Place both containers on a flat surface next to each other.

4. Place the thermometer in the soil, as shown below, and record the temperature.

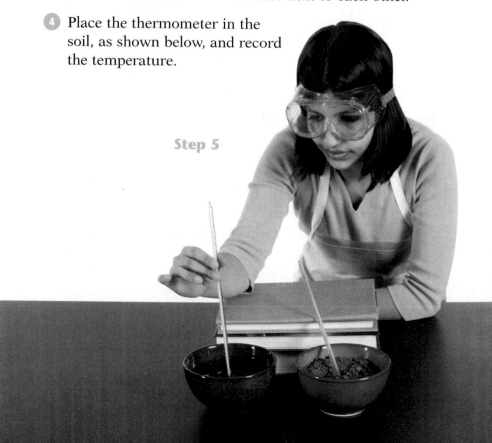

Step 5

5. Place the second thermometer in the container of water, as shown in the illustration on the previous page. The bulbs of both thermometers should be placed so that they are covered by no more than 0.5 cm of water or soil.

6. Place the heat lamp 25 cm above both containers. Turn on the heat lamp.

7. Create a data table like the one shown to the right. In the table, record the temperature of each sample at 1, 3, 5, and 10 min intervals.

8. Disconnect the lamp, and record the temperature of the soil and water after 5 min. **CAUTION** Be sure to let the heat lamp cool before storing it.

Data Table

Time (min)	Temperature of soil (°C)	Temperature of water (°C)
1		
3		
5		
10		
5 (after light off)		

DO NOT WRITE IN THIS BOOK

ANALYZE THE RESULTS

1. **Analyzing Data** Which substance absorbed more heat energy: water or soil?

2. **Analyzing Results** Which substance lost heat energy faster when the heat source was turned off: water or soil?

DRAW CONCLUSIONS

3. **Evaluating Conclusions** What conclusion can you draw about how land and water on Earth are heated by the sun?

4. **Analyzing Methods** Does this experiment describe how proximity to a body of water affects the temperature of a region? If so, explain your answer. If not, how could you test that variable?

Extension

1. **Applying Ideas** Repeat this experiment, but modify the angle at which the light strikes the surface of the soil and the water. How do your results differ from the results of the original experiment? How does the angle of the light affect temperature change in water and soil?

MAPS *in Action*

Climates of the World

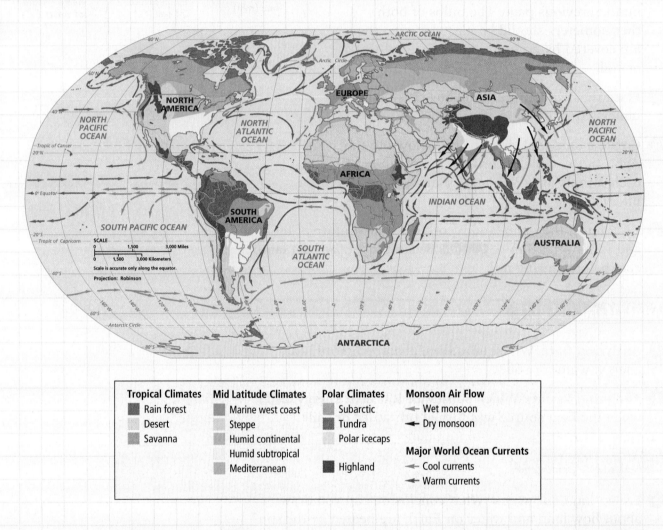

Tropical Climates
- Rain forest
- Desert
- Savanna

Mid Latitude Climates
- Marine west coast
- Steppe
- Humid continental
- Humid subtropical
- Mediterranean

Polar Climates
- Subarctic
- Tundra
- Polar icecaps
- Highland

Monsoon Air Flow
- Wet monsoon
- Dry monsoon

Major World Ocean Currents
- Cool currents
- Warm currents

Map Skills Activity

This map shows the climate regions of Earth and the locations of warm and cold ocean currents. Use the map to answer the questions below.

1. **Analyzing Data** Estimate the latitude range for the desert climate of northern Africa.

2. **Making Comparisons** Why does the eastern coast of the United States have a different climate than the western coast does even though the coasts are at similar latitudes?

3. **Analyzing Ideas** If the ocean current that flows off the western coast of Australia were a warm current, how would this type of current affect the climate of western Australia?

4. **Using a Key** Identify the latitudes where monsoons are located.

5. **Evaluating Data** Explain why the western coast of South America is desert while the inland part of the continent at the same latitude is humid.

Keeping Cool with Algae

Earth is constantly receiving energy from the sun. At the same time, Earth emits energy into space. By balancing these processes, Earth maintains its temperature. What keeps Earth from getting too hot or too cold? In seeking to answer this question, scientists look to microorganisms called *coccolithophores*.

Disappearing Carbon Dioxide

Each year, humans release more than 6 billion tons of carbon dioxide, CO_2, but only about half of that amount can be detected in the atmosphere. Where does the rest of the CO_2 go? Much of it is absorbed by coccolithophores in the oceans. These tiny algae are the primary users of CO_2. They use CO_2 to build chalky disks made of calcium carbonate. By absorbing the CO_2, these algae have a significant impact on the greenhouse effect.

DMS and Sulfur Cycles

Coccolithophores also may affect the number of clouds that form. These algae absorb sulfur compounds from ocean water to produce dimethyl sulfide, or DMS, which is then released into the air. DMS causes water vapor to condense and form clouds. As more clouds form, sunlight is blocked and photosynthesis is reduced. The number of algae begins to decline. Less DMS is produced, and fewer clouds form. When more sunlight hits the ocean, more coccolithophores can grow, and the cycle continues.

Scientists think that this process may help serve as a natural thermostat for the entire planet.

Tough Puzzles to Solve

Scientists now have a better understanding of how coccolithophores affect the atmosphere. However, scientists do not know if this knowledge can be used to help regulate climates. If scientists could promote coccolithophore growth in the ocean, atmospheric CO_2 could be reduced and more clouds could be created. As a result, the planet would cool down. However, because scientists do not know how marine ecosystems would be affected, this plan would be risky. As research continues, scientists will probably learn more about how to apply this research.

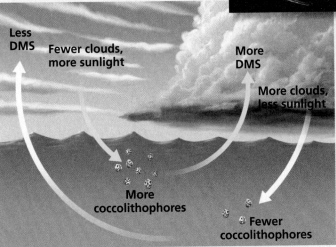

▲ This tiny microorganism may help regulate the temperature of our planet.

Extension

1. **Making Inferences** Why would predicting the effects of artificially promoting coccolithophore growth be difficult?
2. **Understanding Relationships** Find out about other marine microorganisms. How are they important to other organisms in marine ecosystems?

▶ The Starfire telescope in New Mexico provides clear images by using a laser to compensate for atmospheric turbulence.

Sections

1 Viewing the Universe

2 Movements of Earth

What You'll Learn

- How astronomers study the universe
- How different kinds of telescopes and spacecraft work
- How Earth moves and the consequences of that movement

Why It's Relevant

Understanding how scientists study space helps to explain the physical nature of the universe. Learning how Earth moves in space can help explain phenomena such as Earth's seasons.

PRE-READING ACTIVITY

Two-Panel Flip Chart

Before you read this chapter, create the FoldNote entitled "Two-Panel Flip Chart" described in the Skills Handbook section of the Appendix. Label the flaps of the two-panel flip chart with "Tools of astronomy" and "Movements of Earth." As you read the chapter, write information you learn about each category under the appropriate flap.

▶ Astronaut Bruce McCandless II tests a backpack jet propelled by nitrogen that takes him 320 ft from the space shuttle. Equipment such as the backpack helps scientists explore space.

California Content Standards

2b Students know galaxies are made of billions of stars and comprise most of the visible mass of the universe.

2d Students know that stars differ in their life cycles, and that visual, radio, and X-ray telescopes may be used to collect data that reveal those differences.

IE.1a Students will select and use appropriate tools and technology (such as computer-linked probes, spreadsheets, and graphing calculators) to perform tests, collect data, analyze relationships and display data.

IE.1d Students will formulate explanations using logic and evidence.

IE.1g Students will recognize the usefulness and limitations of models and theories as scientific representations of reality.

IE.1k Students will recognize the cumulative nature of scientific evidence.

IE.1l Students will analyze situations and solve problems that require combining and applying concepts from more than one area of science.

IE.1m Students will investigate a science-based societal issue by researching the literature, analyzing data, and communicating the findings. Examples of issues include irradiation of food, cloning of animals by somatic cell nuclear transfer, choice of energy sources, and land and water use decisions in California.

Viewing the Universe

California Content Standards

2b Students know galaxies are made of billions of stars and comprise most of the visible mass of the universe.

2d Students know that stars differ in their life cycles and that visual, radio, and X-ray telescopes may be used to collect data that reveal those differences.

IE.1d Students will formulate explanations using logic and evidence.

People studied the sky long before the telescope was invented. For example, farmers observed changes in daylight throughout the year to track seasons and to predict floods and droughts. Sailors focused on the stars to navigate through unknown territory. Today, most interest in studying the sky comes from a curiosity to discover what lies within the universe. This scientific study of the universe is called **astronomy.** Scientists who study the universe are called *astronomers.*

The Value of Astronomy

In the process of observing the universe, astronomers have made exciting discoveries, such as new planets, stars, black holes, and nebulas, such as the one shown in **Figure 1.** By studying these objects, astronomers have been able to learn more about the origin of Earth and the processes involved in the formation of our solar system.

Studying the universe is also important for the potential benefits to humans. For example, studies of how stars shine may one day lead to improved or new energy sources on Earth. Astronomers may also learn how to protect us from potential catastrophes, such as collisions between asteroids and Earth. Because of these and other contributions, astronomical research is supported by federal agencies, such as the National Science Foundation and NASA. Private foundations and industry also fund research in astronomy.

OBJECTIVES

▶ **Describe** characteristics of the universe in terms of time, distance, and organization. 2b

▶ **Identify** the visible and nonvisible parts of the electromagnetic spectrum.

▶ **Compare** refracting telescopes and reflecting telescopes. 2d, IE.1a

▶ **Explain** how telescopes for nonvisible electromagnetic radiation differ from light telescopes. 2d, IE.1a

KEY TERMS

astronomy
galaxy
astronomical unit
electromagnetic spectrum
telescope
refracting telescope
reflecting telescope

---

astronomy the scientific study of the universe

Figure 1 ▶ A nebula is a large cloud of gas and dust in space. This nebula is called the Eskimo nebula. It formed as a result of the outer layers of the central star drifting away. By studying nebulas like this one, scientists may learn if our sun will ever reach this state.

Figure 2 ▶ The Whirlpool galaxy, M51 (above), is 31 million light-years from the Milky Way. Abell 2218 (right) is one of the most massive galaxy clusters known. The galaxies' mass has distorted the light from even farther objects into the giant arcs shown here.

galaxy a collection of stars, dust, and gas bound together by gravity

astronomical unit the average distance between the Earth and the sun; approximately 150 million kilometers (symbol, AU)

Characteristics of the Universe

The study of the origin, properties, processes, and evolution of the universe is called *cosmology*. Most astronomers agree that the universe began about 14 billion years ago in one giant explosion, called the *big bang*. Since that time, the universe has continued to expand. The universe is very large, and the objects within it are extremely far apart. Telescopes are used to study some distant objects. However, astronomers also commonly use computer and mathematical models to study the universe.

Organization of the Universe

The nearest part of the universe to Earth is our solar system. The solar system includes the sun, Earth, the other planets, and many smaller objects such as asteroids and comets. The solar system is part of a **galaxy,** which is a large collection of stars, dust, and gas bound together by gravity. The galaxy in which the solar system resides is called the *Milky Way galaxy*. Beyond the Milky Way galaxy, there are billions of other galaxies, a few of which are shown in **Figure 2.**

Measuring Distances in the Universe

Because the universe is so large, the units of measurement used on Earth are too small to represent the distance between objects in space. To measure distances in the solar system, astronomers often use astronomical units. An **astronomical unit** (symbol, AU) approximates the average distance between Earth and the sun, which is 149,597,870.691 km or about 150 million km.

Astronomers also use the speed of light to measure distance. Light travels at 300,000 km/s. In one year, light travels 9.46×10^{12} km. This distance is known as a *light-year*. Aside from the sun, the closest star to Earth is 4.22 light-years away.

Observing Space

Light enables us to see the world around us and to make observations. When people look at the night sky, they see stars and other objects in space because of the light these objects emit. This visible light is only a small amount of the energy that comes from these objects. By studying other forms of energy, astronomers are able to learn more about the universe. Recall that planets do not emit light. They reflect the light from stars.

Electromagnetic Spectrum

Visible light is a form of energy that is part of the electromagnetic spectrum. The **electromagnetic spectrum** is all of the wavelengths of electromagnetic radiation. Light, radio waves, and X rays are all examples of electromagnetic radiation. The radiation is composed of traveling waves of electric and magnetic fields that oscillate at fixed frequencies and wavelengths.

Visible Electromagnetic Radiation

The human eye can see only radiation of wavelengths in the visible light range of the spectrum. When white light passes through a prism, the light is broken into a continuous set of colors, as shown in **Figure 3.** Every rainbow formed in the sky and any color spectrum formed by a prism will always have the same colors in the same order. The different colors result because each color of light has a characteristic wavelength. Though all light travels at the same speed, different colors of light have different wavelengths. For example, the shortest wavelengths of visible light are blue and violet, while the longest wavelengths of light are orange and red.

Electromagnetic radiation that has wavelengths that are shorter than the wavelengths of violet light or longer than the wavelengths of red light cannot be seen by humans. But these wavelengths can be detected by instruments that are designed to detect electromagnetic radiation that cannot be seen by human eyes. These invisible wavelengths include infrared waves, microwaves, radio waves, ultraviolet rays, X rays, and gamma rays.

✓ **Reading Check** Which type of electromagnetic radiation can be seen by humans? (See the Appendix for answers to Reading Checks.)

For a variety of links related to this subject, go to www.scilinks.org

Topic: Space Science in California
SciLinks code: HQ7C01

electromagnetic spectrum all of the frequencies or wavelengths of electromagnetic radiation

Figure 3 ▶ Visible light is broken into different colors because each color has a different wavelength. These colors can be seen when visible light is passed through a prism.

Invisible Electromagnetic Radiation

If you place a thermometer in any wavelength of the visible spectrum, the temperature reading on the thermometer will increase. In 1800, the scientist Sir Frederick William Herschel moved a thermometer beyond the red end of the visible spectrum. Even though he could not see any light on the thermometer, the temperature reading on the thermometer increased. He had discovered *infrared*, which means "below the red." Infrared is electromagnetic radiation that has waves that are longer than waves of visible light. Later, other scientists discovered radio waves, which have even longer wavelengths than infrared waves do.

The shortest wavelengths of visible light, which are shorter than the wavelengths of violet light, are the ultraviolet wavelengths. *Ultraviolet* means "beyond the violet." The X-ray wavelengths are shorter than the ultraviolet wavelengths are. The shortest wavelengths are the gamma ray wavelengths.

Telescopes

Our eyes can see detail, but some things are too small or too far away to see. Our ability to see the detail of distant objects in the sky began with the Italian scientist Galileo. In 1609, he heard of a device that used two lenses to make distant objects appear closer. He built one of the devices and turned it toward the sky. For the first time, he could see that there are craters on the moon and that the Milky Way is made of stars. An example of one of these early devices is shown in **Figure 4.**

A **telescope** is an instrument that collects electromagnetic radiation from the sky and concentrates it for better observation. While modern telescopes are able to collect and use invisible electromagnetic radiation, the first telescopes that were developed collected only visible light. Telescopes that collect only visible light are called *optical telescopes*. The two types of optical telescopes are refracting telescopes and reflecting telescopes.

telescope an instrument that collects electromagnetic radiation from the sky and concentrates it for better observation

Figure 4 ▶ A model of one of the first reflecting telescopes, which was invented by Isaac Newton, can be seen at the Royal Society in London, England.

Figure 5 ▶ Reflecting and Refracting Telescopes

Refracting telescopes use lenses to gather and focus light from distant objects.

Reflecting telescopes use mirrors to gather and focus light from distant objects.

Refracting Telescopes

Lenses are clear objects shaped to bend light in special ways. The bending of light by lenses is called *refraction*. Telescopes that use a set of lenses to gather and focus light from distant objects are called **refracting telescopes.** Refracting telescopes have an objective lens that bends light that passes through the lens and focuses the light to be magnified by an eyepiece, as shown in **Figure 5.**

One problem with refracting telescopes is that the lens focuses different colors of light at different distances. For example, if an object is in focus in red light, the object will appear out of focus in blue light. Another problem with refracting telescopes is that it is difficult to make very large lenses of the required strength and clarity. The amount of light collected from distant objects is limited by the size of the objective lens.

Reflecting Telescopes

In the mid-1600s, Isaac Newton solved the problem of color separation that resulted from the use of lenses. He invented the **reflecting telescope,** as shown in **Figure 5,** which used a curved mirror to gather and focus light from distant objects. When light enters a reflecting telescope, the light is reflected by a large curved mirror to a second mirror. The second mirror reflects the light to the eyepiece, which is a lens that magnifies and focuses the image.

Unlike objective lenses in refracting telescopes, mirrors in reflecting telescopes can be made very large without affecting the quality of the image. Thus, reflecting telescopes can be much larger and can gather more light than refracting telescopes can. The largest reflecting telescopes are a pair called the Keck Telescopes in Hawaii. Each telescope is 10 m in diameter. Astronomers are tentatively planning to build an OWL, Overwhelmingly Large Telescope, that would be 100 m in diameter.

refracting telescope a telescope that uses a set of lenses to gather and focus light from distant objects

reflecting telescope a telescope that uses a curved mirror to gather and focus light from distant objects

For a variety of links related to this subject, go to www.scilinks.org

Topic: Telescopes
SciLinks code: HQ61500

Reading Check What are the problems with refracting telescopes? (See the Appendix for the answers to Reading Checks.)

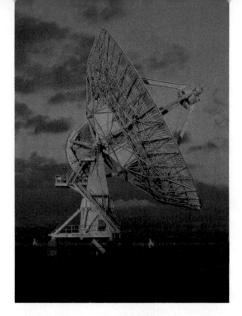

Figure 6 ▶ Radio telescopes, such as this one at the National Radio Astronomy Observatory in New Mexico, provide scientists with information about objects in space.

Telescopes for Invisible Electromagnetic Radiation

Each type of electromagnetic radiation provides scientists with information about objects in space. Scientists have developed telescopes that detect invisible radiation. For example, a radio telescope, such as the one shown in **Figure 6,** detects radio waves. There are also telescopes that detect gamma rays, X rays, and infrared rays.

One problem with using telescopes to detect invisible electromagnetic radiation is that Earth's atmosphere acts as a shield against many forms of electromagnetic radiation. Water vapor can prevent gamma rays, X rays, and most infrared and ultraviolet rays from reaching Earth's surface. So, ground-based telescopes that are used to study these forms of radiation work best at high elevations, where the air is dry. But the only way to study many forms of radiation is from space.

Space-Based Astronomy

While ground-based telescopes have been critical in helping astronomers learn about the universe, valuable information has also come from spacecraft. Spacecraft that contain telescopes and other instruments have been launched to investigate planets, stars, and other distant objects. In space, Earth's atmosphere cannot interfere with the detection of electromagnetic radiation.

☑ **Reading Check** **Why do scientists launch spacecraft beyond Earth's atmosphere? (See the Appendix for answers to Reading Checks.)**

Connection to ENVIRONMENTAL SCIENCE

Light Pollution

About 6,000 stars shine brightly enough to be seen with the unaided eye. Of those, about half are above the horizon at a time. But we can see those 3,000 stars only if the sky is very dark. Most people, however, live in or close to cities, where street lighting and other lighting casts a glow into the sky. This glow masks the fainter stars. In big cities, you may see only a handful of stars, instead of thousands!

The glow in the sky that obstructs our view of the stars is known as *light pollution*. Light pollution not only affects humans but also affects animals. Near the ocean, for example, street lighting can affect where and whether turtles come ashore to lay their eggs. On the beaches of Florida's developed coastline, bright lights may discourage female leatherback and green turtles from coming ashore to nest.

In recent years, efforts have been made to reduce light pollution. Reflectors on tops of streetlights would keep the light aimed at the ground instead of into the

sky. Reflectors would also reduce wasted electricity. Outdoor house lights and floodlights in parking lots can be directed downward to decrease light pollution. Turning off outdoor lighting when it is not needed, such as when businesses are closed, also contributes to limiting light pollution. Taking steps such as these can improve the view of the night sky without compromising safety in our neighborhoods.

Figure 7 ▶ The *Hubble Space Telescope* is in orbit around Earth, where the telescope can detect visible and nonvisible electromagnetic radiation without the obstruction of Earth's atmosphere.

Space Telescopes

The *Hubble Space Telescope,* shown in **Figure 7,** is an example of a telescope that has been launched into space to collect electromagnetic radiation from objects in space. Another example, the *Chandra X-ray Observatory* makes remarkably clear images using X rays from objects in space, such as the remnants of exploded stars. The *Compton Gamma Ray Observatory* is no longer in space, but it detected gamma rays from objects, such as black holes. The *Spitzer Space Telescope* was launched in 2003 to detect infrared radiation. The *James Webb Space Telescope* is scheduled to be launched in 2011. When deployed in space, this telescope will detect infrared radiation from objects in space.

Other Spacecraft

Since the early 1960s, spacecraft have been sent out of Earth's orbit to study other planets. Launched in 1977, the *Voyager 1* and *Voyager 2* spacecraft investigated Jupiter, Saturn, Uranus, and Neptune. These two spacecraft collected images of these planets and their moons. The *Galileo* spacecraft was in orbit around Jupiter and its moons from 1995 to 2003. This spacecraft gathered information about the composition of Jupiter's atmosphere and storm systems, which are several times larger than Earth's storm systems. The *Cassini-Huygens* spacecraft was launched in 1997, as shown in **Figure 8,** and began orbiting Saturn in 2004. In December 2004, the *Huygens* probe detached from the *Cassini* orbiter to study the atmosphere and surface of Titan, Saturn's largest moon. Like Earth, Titan has an atmosphere that is rich in nitrogen. Scientists hope to learn more about the origins of Earth by studying Titan.

Figure 8 ▶ On October 15, 1997, the *Cassini-Huygens* spacecraft was launched atop a Titan IV-Centaur rocket system. The spacecraft's journey to Saturn, which the spacecraft now orbits, took 7 years and covered 2.2 billion miles.

Figure 9 ▶ Astronaut Jerry L. Ross conducts space assembly experiments while anchored to the foot restraint on the remote manipulator system on the space shuttle.

Human Space Exploration

Spacecraft that carry only instruments and computers are described as *robotic*. These spacecraft can explore space and travel beyond the solar system. Crewed spacecraft, or those that carry humans, have never gone beyond Earth's moon.

The first humans went into space in the 1960s. Between 1969 and 1972, NASA landed 12 people on the moon. Now, crewed spaceflights only orbit Earth. Flights, such as those aboard the space shuttles, allow people to release or repair satellites and to perform scientific experiments, as shown in **Figure 9.**

Eventually, NASA would like to send people to explore Mars. However, such a voyage would be expensive, difficult, and dangerous. The loss of two space shuttles and their crews, the *Challenger* in 1986 and the *Columbia* in 2003, have focused public attention on the risks of human space exploration.

Spinoffs of the Space Program

Space programs have brought benefits to areas outside of the field of astronomy. Satellites in orbit provide information about weather all over Earth. This information helps scientists make accurate weather predictions days in advance. Other satellites broadcast television signals from around the world or allow people to navigate cars and airplanes. Inventing ways to make objects smaller and lighter so that they can go into space has also led to improved electronics. These technological developments have been applied to radios, televisions, and other equipment. Even medical equipment has benefited from space programs. For example, heart pumps have been improved based on NASA's research on the flow of fluids through rockets.

Section 1 Review

1. **Describe** characteristics of the universe in terms of time, distance, and organization. 📷 2b

2. **Identify** the parts of the electromagnetic spectrum, both visible and invisible.

3. **Explain** how astronomers use electromagnetic radiation to study space.

4. **Compare** reflecting telescopes and refracting telescopes. 📷 2d, IE.1a

5. **Explain** how a radio telescope differs from an optical telescope. 📷 2d, IE.1a

6. **Identify** two examples of space telescopes and two examples of probes. 📷 IE.1a

CRITICAL THINKING

7. **Identifying Relationships** Using the development of reflecting telescopes as an example, explain how scientific inquiry leads to advances in technology. 📷 IE.1d, IE.1k

8. **Analyzing Processes** Human space exploration is expensive and dangerous. Should NASA continue human spaceflight? 📷 IE.1d, IE.1m

CONCEPT MAPPING

9. Use the following terms to create a concept map: *electromagnetic radiation, reflecting telescope, refracting telescope, telescope, probe, astronomy, universe,* Voyager, and Cassini. 📷 IE.1a

IE.1d Students will formulate explanations using logic and evidence.
IE.1g Students will recognize the usefulness and
limitations of models and theories as scientific representations of reality.
IE.1k Students will recognize the cumulative
nature of scientific evidence.

Understanding the basic motions of Earth helps scientists understand the motions of other bodies in the solar system and the universe. These movements of Earth are also responsible for the seasons and the changes in weather.

The Rotating Earth

The spinning of Earth on its axis is called **rotation.** Each complete rotation takes about one day. The most observable effects of Earth's rotation on its axis are day and night. As Earth rotates from west to east, the sun appears to rise in the east in the morning. The sun then appears to cross the sky and set in the west. At any given moment, the hemisphere of Earth that faces the sun experiences daylight. At the same time, the hemisphere of Earth that faces away from the sun experiences nighttime.

The Foucault Pendulum

In the 19th century, the scientist Jean-Bernard-Leon Foucault, provided evidence of Earth's rotation by using a pendulum. He created a long, heavy pendulum that rocks back and forth by attaching a wire to the ceiling and then attaching a weight to the wire. Throughout the day, the bob would swing back and forth. The path of the pendulum appeared to change over time. However, it was the floor that was moving while the pendulum's path stayed constant. Because the floor was attached to Earth, one can conclude that Earth rotates. A Foucault pendulum is shown in **Figure 1.**

OBJECTIVES

▶ **Describe** two lines of evidence for Earth's rotation. IE.1k

▶ **Explain** how the change in apparent positions of constellations provides evidence of Earth's rotation and revolution around the sun.

▶ **Summarize** how Earth's rotation and revolution provide a basis for measuring time.

▶ **Explain** how the tilt of Earth's axis and Earth's movement cause seasons.

KEY TERMS

rotation
revolution
perihelion
aphelion
equinox
solstice

---

rotation the spin of a body on its axis

Figure 1 ▶ The 12 ft arc of this Foucault pendulum in Spokane, Washington, appears to change throughout the day. However, the path of the pendulum does not actually change. Instead, Earth moves the floor as Earth rotates on its axis.

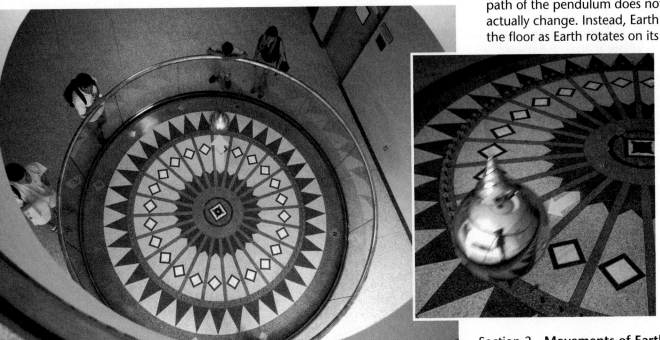

Modeling a Pendulum

Procedure 🔬 IE.1d, IE.1g, IE.1k

1. Use a yo-yo, or tie a small object at one end of a length of string for a pendulum.
2. Hold the end of the string in your fingers, and swing the pendulum.
3. Twist the string in your fingers as you allow the pendulum to continue swinging.

Analysis

1. Does the direction in which the yo-yo swings change?
2. Does the yo-yo twist around with the string?
3. How does this experiment differ from the Foucault pendulum?

revolution the motion of a body that travels around another body in space; one complete trip along an orbit

perihelion the point in the orbit of a planet at which the planet is closest to the sun

aphelion the point in the orbit of a planet at which the planet is farthest from the sun

Figure 2 ▶ As Earth revolves around its elliptical orbit, the planet is farthest from the sun in July and closest to the sun in January. The elliptical orbit in this illustration has been exaggerated for emphasis.

The Coriolis Effect

Evidence of the rotation of Earth can also be seen in the movement of ocean surface currents and wind belts. Ocean currents and wind belts do not move in a straight path. The rotation of Earth causes ocean currents and wind belts to be deflected to the right in the Northern Hemisphere. In the Southern Hemisphere, ocean currents and wind belts deflect to the left. This curving of the path of wind belts and ocean currents is caused by Earth's rotation and is called the *Coriolis effect*.

The Revolving Earth

As Earth spins on its axis, Earth also revolves around the sun. Even though you cannot feel Earth moving, it is traveling around the sun at an average speed of 29.8 km/s. The motion of a body that travels around another body in space is called **revolution.** Each complete revolution of Earth around the sun takes 365 1/4 days, or about one year.

Earth's Orbit

The path that a body follows as it travels around another body in space is called an *orbit.* Earth's orbit around the sun is not quite a circle. Earth's orbit is an ellipse. An *ellipse* is a closed curve whose shape is determined by two points, or foci, within the ellipse. In planetary orbits, one focus is located within the sun. No object may be located at the other focus.

Because its orbit is an ellipse, Earth is not always the same distance from the sun. The point in the orbit of a planet at which the planet is closest to the sun is the **perihelion.** The point in the orbit of a planet at which the planet is farthest from the sun is the **aphelion** (uh FEE lee uhn). As shown in **Figure 2,** Earth's aphelion distance is 152 million km. Its perihelion distance is 147 million km.

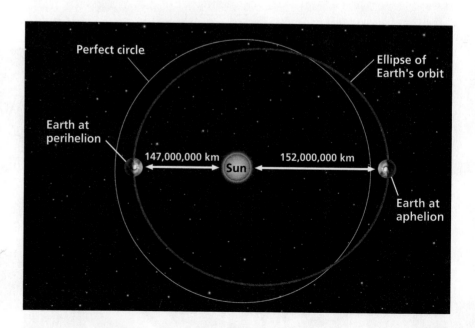

Perfect circle

Ellipse of Earth's orbit

Earth at perihelion

147,000,000 km **Sun** 152,000,000 km

Earth at aphelion

Constellations and Earth's Motion

Evidence of Earth's revolution and rotation around the sun can be seen in the motion of constellations. A *constellation* is a group of stars that are organized in a recognizable pattern. In 1930, the International Astronomical Union divided the sky into 88 constellations. Many of the names given to these constellations came from the ancient Greeks more than 2,000 years ago. Taurus, the bull, and Orion, the hunter, are some examples of names from Greek mythology that have been given to constellations.

Evidence of Earth's Rotation

If you gaze up at a constellation in the evening sky over a period of several hours, you may notice that the constellation appears to have changed its position in the sky. However, the constellation's movement has not caused the constellation's change in position. The rotation of Earth on its axis causes the change in position. Thus, Earth is moving, and the constellation is not moving.

Evidence of Earth's Revolution

A constellation's position in the evening sky will change not only because of Earth's rotation but also because of Earth's revolution around the sun. Over a period of several weeks, at the same time of the evening, a constellation's position will appear to change, as shown in **Figure 3.** But Earth's revolution around the sun causes the constellation to have different positions in the evening sky over a period of several weeks. As Earth revolves around the sun, the night side of Earth faces a different direction of the universe. Thus, different constellations will appear in the night sky as the seasons change.

Reading Check How does the movement of constellations provide evidence of Earth's rotation and revolution? (See the Appendix for answers to Reading Checks.)

Figure 3 ▶ In one month's period, the position of the constellations in the sky seen from Denver, Colorado, at 10 PM change because of the revolution of Earth.

Figure 4 ▶ This is a reconstruction of a stone calendar that the Aztecs created to help determine when to plant crops.

Graphic Organizer **Venn Diagram**
Create the **Graphic Organizer** entitled "Venn Diagram" described in the Skills Handbook section of the Appendix. Label the circles with "Day," "Month," and "Year." Then, fill in the diagram with characteristics that each period of time shares with the other periods of time.

Measuring Time

Earth's motion provides the basis for measuring time. For example, the day and year are based on periods of Earth's motion. The day is determined by Earth's rotation on its axis. Each complete rotation of Earth on its axis takes one day, which is then broken into 24 hours.

The year is determined by Earth's revolution around the sun. Each complete revolution of Earth around the sun takes 365 1/4 days, or one year.

A month is based on the moon's motion around Earth. A month was originally determined by the period between successive full moons, which is 29.5 days. The word *month* actually comes from the word *moon*. However, the number of full moons in a year is not a whole number. Therefore, a month is now determined as roughly one-twelfth of a year.

Formation of the Calendar

A *calendar* is a system created for measuring long intervals of time by dividing time into periods of days, weeks, months, and years. Many ancient civilizations created versions of calendars based on astronomical cycles. The ancient Egyptians were the first to use a calendar based on a solar year. The Babylonians used a 12 month lunar year. The Aztecs, who lived in what is now Mexico, also created a calendar, which is shown in **Figure 4.**

Because the year is 365 1/4 days long, the extra 1/4 day is usually ignored to make the number of days on a calendar a whole number. To keep the calendars on the same schedule as Earth's movements, we must account for the extra time. So, every four years, one day is added to the month of February. Any year that contains an extra day is called a *leap year.*

More than 2,000 years ago, Julius Caesar, of the Roman Empire, revised the calendar so that an extra day every four years was added. His successor, Augustus Caesar, made the extra day come at the end of the shortest month, February. He also made July and August long months with 31 days each.

The Modern Calendar

Because the year is not exactly 365 1/4 days long, over centuries, the calendar gradually became misaligned with the seasons. In the late 1500s, Pope Gregory XIII formed a committee to create a calendar that would keep the calendar aligned with the seasons. We use this calendar today. In this Gregorian calendar, century years, such as 1800 and 1900, are not leap years unless the century years are exactly divisible by 400. Thus, 2000 was a leap year even though it was a century year. However, 2100, 2200, and 2300 will not be leap years.

Time Zones

Using the sun as the basis for measuring time, we define noon as the time when the sun is highest in the sky. Because of Earth's rotation, the sun is highest above different locations on Earth at different times of day. Earth's surface has been divided into 24 standard time zones, as shown in **Figure 5**, to avoid problems created by different local times. In each zone, noon is set as the time when the sun is highest over the center of that zone. Because Earth is nearly spherical, its circumference equals 360°. If you divide 360° by the 24 hours needed for one rotation, you find that Earth rotates at a rate of 15° per hour. Therefore, each of Earth's 24 standard time zones covers about 15°. The time in each zone is one hour earlier than the time in the zone to the east of each zone.

International Date Line

There are 24 standard time zones and 24 hours in a day. But there must be some point on Earth's surface where the date changes. The *International Date Line* was established to prevent confusion. The International Date Line is a line that runs from north to south through the Pacific Ocean. When it is Friday west of the International Date Line, it is Thursday east of the line. The line is drawn so that it does not cut through islands or continents. Thus, everyone living within one country has the same date. Note where the line is drawn between Alaska and Siberia in **Figure 5**.

✔ **Reading Check** What is the purpose of the International Date Line? (See the Appendix for answers to Reading Checks.)

Figure 5 ▶ Earth has been divided into 24 standard time zones. Irregular time zones may differ between 15 to 45 minutes compared to regular time zones. *At 6 P.M. on the east coast of South America what time is it on the west coast of South America?*

Daylight Savings Time

Because of the tilt of Earth's axis, daylight time is shorter in the winter months than in the summer months. During the summer months, days are longer so that the sun rises earlier in the morning when many people are still sleeping. To take advantage of that daylight time, the United States uses *daylight savings time*. Under this system, clocks are set one hour ahead of standard time in April, which provides an additional hour of daylight during the evening. The additional hour also saves energy because the use of electricity decreases. In October, clocks are set back one hour to return to standard time. Countries in the equatorial region do not observe daylight savings time because there are not significant changes in the amount of daylight time in the equatorial region. Daylight is about 12 hours every day of the year.

The Seasons

Earth's axis is tilted at 23.5°. As Earth revolves around the sun, Earth's axis always points toward the North Star. Thus, during each revolution, the North Pole sometimes tilts toward the sun and sometimes tilts away from the sun, as shown in **Figure 6.** When the North Pole tilts toward the sun, the Northern Hemisphere has longer periods of daylight than the Southern Hemisphere does. When the North Pole tilts away from the sun, the Southern Hemisphere has longer periods of daylight.

The angle at which the sun's rays strike each part of Earth's surface changes as Earth moves through its orbit. When the North Pole tilts toward the sun, the sun's rays strike the Northern Hemisphere more directly. When the sun's rays strike Earth directly, that region receives a higher concentration of solar energy and is warmer. When the North Pole tilts away from the sun, the sun's rays strike the Northern Hemisphere less directly. When the sunlight is less direct, the concentration of solar energy is less and that region is cooler.

Reading Check What is daylight savings time? (See the Appendix for answers to Reading Checks.)

Figure 6 ▶ The direction of tilt of Earth's axis remains the same throughout Earth's orbit around the sun. Thus, the Northern Hemisphere receives more direct sunlight during summer months and less direct sunlight during winter months.

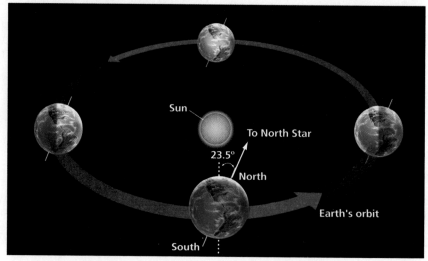

Seasonal Weather

Changes in the angle at which the sun's rays strike Earth's surface cause the seasons. When the North Pole tilts away from the sun, the angle of the sun's rays falling on the Northern Hemisphere is low. As a result, the sun's rays spread solar energy over a large area, which leads to lower temperatures. The tilt of the North Pole away from the sun also causes the Northern Hemisphere to experience fewer daylight hours. Fewer daylight hours also mean less energy and lower temperatures. Lower temperatures cause the winter seasons. At the time, the Northern Hemisphere tilts away from the sun, the Southern Hemisphere tilts toward the sun. The sun's rays strike the Southern Hemisphere at a greater angle than they do in the Northern Hemisphere, and there are more daylight hours in the Southern Hemisphere. Therefore, the Southern Hemisphere experiences the warm summer season.

Equinoxes

The seasons fall and spring begin on days called equinoxes. An **equinox** is the moment when the sun appears to cross the celestial equator. The *celestial equator* is a line drawn on the sky directly overhead from the equator on Earth. At an equinox, the sun's rays strike Earth at a 90° angle along the equator. The hours of daylight and darkness are approximately equal everywhere on Earth on that day. The *autumnal equinox* occurs on September 22 or 23 of each year and marks the beginning of fall in the Northern Hemisphere. The *vernal equinox* occurs on March 21 or 22 of each year and marks the beginning of spring in the Northern Hemisphere.

equinox the moment when the sun appears to cross the celestial equator

QuickLAB ⏱ 10 min

The Angle of the Sun's Rays IE.1d
Procedure
1. Turn the lights down low or off in the classroom.
2. Place a **piece of paper** on the floor. Hold a **flashlight** 1 m above the paper, and shine the light of the flashlight straight down on the piece of paper.
3. Have a partner outline the perimeter of the circle of light cast by the flashlight on the paper. Label the circle "90° angle." Place a clean piece of paper on the floor.
4. At a height of 1/2 m from the floor, shine the light of the flashlight on the paper at an angle. Make sure the distance between the flashlight and the paper is 1 m.
5. Have a partner outline the perimeter of the circle of light cast by the flashlight on the paper. Label the circle "low angle."

Analysis
1. Compare the two circles drawn in steps 3 and 5. Which circle concentrates the light in a smaller area?
2. Which circle would most likely model the sun's rays striking Earth during the summer season?

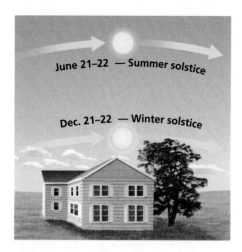

Figure 7 ▶ In the Northern Hemisphere, the sun appears to follow its highest path across the sky on the summer solstice and its lowest path across the sky on the winter solstice.

solstice the point at which the sun is as far north or as far south of the equator as possible

Summer Solstices

The seasons of summer and winter begin on days called **solstices.** Each year on June 21 or 22, the North Pole's tilt toward the sun is greatest. On this day, the sun's rays strike Earth at a 90° angle along the Tropic of Cancer, which is located at 23.5° north latitude. This day is called the *summer solstice* and marks the beginning of summer in the Northern Hemisphere. *Solstice* means "sun stop" and refers to the fact that in the Northern Hemisphere, the sun follows its highest path across the sky on that day, as shown in **Figure 7.**

The Northern Hemisphere has the most hours of daylight at the summer solstice. The farther north of the equator you are, the longer the period of daylight you have. North of the Arctic Circle, which is located at 66.5° north latitude, there are 24 hours of daylight at the summer solstice. At the other extreme, south of the Antarctic Circle, there are 24 hours of darkness at that time.

Winter Solstices

By December, the North Pole is tilted to the farthest point away from the sun. On December 21 or 22, the sun's rays strike Earth at a 90° angle along the Tropic of Capricorn, which is located at 23.5° south latitude. This day is called the *winter solstice.* It marks the beginning of winter in the Northern Hemisphere. At the winter solstice, the Northern Hemisphere has the fewest daylight hours. The sun follows its lowest path across the sky. Places that are north of the Arctic Circle then have 24 hours of darkness. However, places that are south of the Antarctic Circle have 24 hours of daylight at that time.

Section 2 Review

1. **Explain** how the apparent change of position of constellations over time provides evidence of Earth's revolution around the sun.

2. **Describe** two lines of evidence that indicate that Earth is rotating. ⬛ IE.1k

3. **Summarize** how movements of Earth provide a basis for measuring time.

4. **Explain** why today's calendars have leap years. ⬛ IE.1k

5. **Identify** two advantages in using daylight savings time.

6. **Explain** how the tilt of Earth's axis and Earth's movements cause seasons.

7. **Identify** the position of Earth in relation to the sun that causes winter in the Northern Hemisphere.

8. **Describe** the position of Earth in relation to the sun during the Northern Hemisphere's summer solstice.

CRITICAL THINKING

9. **Understanding Relationships** How can it be that Earth is at perihelion during wintertime in the Northern Hemisphere? ⬛ IE.1d

10. **Predicting Consequences** Explain how measurements of time might differ if Earth did not rotate on its axis. ⬛ IE.1d

CONCEPT MAPPING

11. Use the following terms to create a concept map: *revolution, perihelion, aphelion, rotation, ellipse, orbit, rotation, Foucault pendulum, Coriolis effect, Earth,* and *constellation.* ⬛ IE.1k

Sections

1 Viewing the Universe

Key Terms

astronomy, 659
galaxy, 660
astronomical unit, 660
electromagnetic spectrum, 661
telescope, 662
refracting telescope, 663
reflecting telescope, 663

Key Concepts

▶ The universe formed about 14 billion years ago in a giant explosion and has been expanding since that time.

▶ The electromagnetic spectrum contains all of the frequencies or wavelengths of electromagnetic radiation. Scientists use this radiation to study the universe.

▶ Refracting telescopes use lenses to gather and focus light, while reflecting telescopes use curved mirrors to gather and focus light.

▶ Space programs have led to improved technology in areas such as airplane navigation, weather forecasting, and medical equipment.

2 Movements of Earth

rotation, 667
revolution, 668
perihelion, 668
aphelion, 668
equinox, 673
solstice, 674

▶ Earth's rotation is evidenced by the change from day to night, the apparent motion of constellations, the Foucault pendulum, and the Coriolis effect.

▶ Earth's revolution around the sun is evidenced by the apparent motion of constellations.

▶ Movements of Earth provide a basis for measuring time. One revolution of Earth around the sun is equal to one year. One rotation of Earth on its axis is equal to one day.

▶ The angle of the sun's rays changes throughout the year and leads to seasonal change on Earth's surface.

Using Key Terms

Use each of the following terms in a separate sentence.

1. *electromagnetic spectrum*

2. *galaxy* 🖳 2b

3. *perihelion*

For each pair of terms, explain how the meanings of the terms differ.

4. *reflecting telescope* and *refracting telescope*

5. *solstice* and *equinox*   🖳 2d, IE.1a

6. *rotation* and *revolution*

Understanding Key Concepts

7. Stars organized into a pattern are
   a. perihelions.
   b. satellites.
   c. constellations.
   d. telescopes.

8. Days are caused by Earth's
   a. perihelion.
   b. aphelion.
   c. revolution.
   d. rotation.

9. The seasons are caused by
   a. Earth's distance from the sun.
   b. the tilt of Earth's axis.
   c. the sun's temperature.
   d. the calendar.

10. Which of the following is a tool that is used by astronomers to study radiation? 🖳 2d, IE.1a
   a. a computer model
   b. a ground-based telescope
   c. a Foucault pendulum
   d. a calendar

11. Which of the following is evidence of Earth's revolution?
   a. the Foucault pendulum
   b. the Coriolis effect
   c. night and day
   d. constellation movement

12. Which of the following forms of radiation can be shielded by Earth's atmosphere?
   a. gamma rays
   b. radio waves
   c. visible light
   d. All of the above

13. Which of the following is not a space telescope? 🖳 2d
   a. *Hubble Space Telescope*
   b. *Chandra X-ray Observatory*
   c. *Challenger*
   d. *Spitzer Space Telescope*

14. Which of the following marks the beginning of spring in the Northern Hemisphere?
   a. vernal equinox
   b. autumnal equinox
   c. summer solstice
   d. winter solstice

15. Which of the following is evidence of Earth's rotation? 🖳 IE.1k
   a. the Foucault pendulum
   b. day and night
   c. the Coriolis effect
   d. All of the above

Short Answer

16. Which two forms of electromagnetic radiation have the shortest wavelengths?

17. What is an advantage of using orbiting telescopes rather than ground-based telescopes? 🖳 2d, IE.1a

18. Why does the rotation of Earth require people to establish time zones?

19. What is a leap year, and what purpose does it serve? 🖳 IE.1k

20. What line on Earth's surface marks where the date changes?

21. How does the tilt of Earth's axis cause the seasons?

Landsat Maps of Earth

Landsat satellites have been recording images of Earth for more than three decades. In that time, these Earth-scanning satellites have logged more than a million images. As Landsat satellites periodically rescan regions, the satellites create a visual history of Earth's changing landscapes.

Say Cheese!

Landsat images resemble aerial photographs. Each image records about 30,000 km² of Earth's surface. Landsat images are not ordinary photographs, however. Each satellite uses a scanning sensor system called a *thematic mapper,* or *TM,* to create images. The TM sensors detect visible light, which is the light recorded by an ordinary camera. The TM sensors also detect other parts of the electromagnetic spectrum that humans cannot see, such as infrared light. This capability gives Landsat images much more detail than conventional photographs have.

Once a satellite sends an image back to Earth, cartographers can use computers to create a thematic map. A thematic map is a map that illustrates a particular subject or feature. Selecting different combinations of data allows cartographers to highlight features such as river deltas, geologic faults, and mineral deposits.

Earth's Changing Surface

Landsat images appeal to Earth scientists in a variety of fields. Landsat images have enabled cartographers to map remote areas of the world. The images have allowed hydrologists to find uncharted lakes. Landsat images have also helped geologists discover oil

▲ *Landsat 7* is the latest mission in the Landsat series of Earth-observation satellites.

in the Sudan, tin in Brazil, and copper in Mexico.

Recently, ecologists have begun to use Landsat images to observe changes in Earth's environment. With a series of images of the same region, taken over years, ecologists can monitor the effects of processes such as urbanization, deforestation, and soil erosion. New, useful applications of Landsat satellites may arise as the satellites continue to record Earth's changing surface.

◄ The Ganges River empties into the Bay of Bengal and forms a delta. The delta is covered by a swamp forest known as the Sunderbans.

Extension

1. **Extension** How might cartographers use Landsat images to check the accuracy of maps?

Planets of the Solar System

What You'll Learn

• How the planets of the solar system formed

• How laws of motion govern the movements of planets

• How inner planets differ from outer planets

Why It's Relevant

Understanding the formation of the planets provides a basis for understanding Earth's processes.

PRE-READING ACTIVITY

Three-Panel Flip Chart

Before you read this chapter, create the **FoldNote** entitled "Three-Panel Flip Chart" described in the Skills Handbook section of the Appendix. Label the flaps of the three-panel flip chart with "Inner planets," "Outer planets," and "Exoplanets." As you read the chapter, write information you learn about each category under the appropriate flap.

▶ This composite image shows how the Valles Marineris, a large canyon on the surface of Mars, may look from one of Mars's moons.

 California Content Standards

1a Students know how the differences and similarities among the sun, the terrestrial planets, and the gas planets may have been established during the formation of the solar system.

1b Students know the evidence from Earth and moon rocks indicates that the solar system was formed from a nebular cloud of dust and gas approximately 4.6 billion years ago.

1c Students know the evidence from geological studies of the Earth and other planets suggest that the early Earth was very different from Earth today.

1d Students know the evidence indicating that the planets are much closer to Earth than the stars are.

4d* Students know the differing greenhouse conditions on Earth, Mars, and Venus; the origins of those conditions; and the climatic consequences of each.

7b Students know the global carbon cycle: the different physical and chemical forms of carbon in the atmosphere, oceans, biomass, fossil fuels, and the movement of carbon among these reservoirs.

7d* Students know the relative residence times and flow characteristics of carbon in and out of its different reservoirs.

8b Students know how the composition of Earth's atmosphere has evolved over geologic time and know the effect of outgassing, the variations of carbon dioxide concentration, and the origin of atmospheric oxygen.

8c Students know the location of the ozone layer in the upper atmosphere, its role in absorbing ultraviolet radiation, and the way in which this layer varies both naturally and in response to human activities.

IE.1a Students will select and use appropriate tools and technology (such as computer-linked probes, spreadsheets, and graphing calculators) to perform tests, collect data, analyze relationships and display data.

IE.1d Students will formulate explanations using logic and evidence.

IE.1g Students will recognize the usefulness and limitations of models and theories as scientific representations of reality.

IE.1i Students will analyze the locations, sequences, or time intervals that are characteristic of natural phenomena (e.g., relative ages of rocks, locations of planets over time, and succession of species in an ecosystem).

IE.1k Students will recognize the cumulative nature of scientific evidence.

IE.1m Students will investigate a science-based societal issue by researching the literature, analyzing data, and communicating the findings. Examples of issues include irradiation of food, cloning of animals by somatic cell nuclear transfer, choice of energy sources, and land and water use decisions in California.

IE.1n Students will know that when an observation does not agree with an accepted scientific theory, the observation is sometimes mistaken or fraudulent (e.g., the Piltdown Man fossil or unidentified flying objects) and that the theory is sometimes wrong (e.g., the Ptolemaic model of the movement of the Sun, Moon and planets).

Formation of the Solar System

1b Students know the evidence from Earth and moon rocks indicates that the solar system was formed from a nebular cloud of dust and gas approximately 4.6 billion years ago. **1c** Students know the evidence from geological studies of Earth and other planets suggest that the early Earth was very different from Earth today.

The **solar system** consists of the sun, the planets, and all of the other bodies that revolve around the sun. **Planets** are the primary bodies that orbit the sun. Scientists have long debated the origins of the solar system. In the 1600s and 1700s, many scientists thought that the sun formed first and threw off the materials that later formed the planets. But in 1796, the French mathematician Pierre-Simon, marquis de Laplace, advanced a hypothesis that is now known as the *nebular hypothesis*.

The Nebular Hypothesis

Laplace's hypothesis states that the sun and the planets condensed at about the same time out of a rotating cloud of gas and dust called a *nebula*. Modern scientific calculations support Laplace's hypothesis and help explain how the sun and the planets formed from an original nebula of gas and dust.

Matter is spread throughout the universe. Some of this matter gathers into clouds of dust and gas, such as the one shown in **Figure 1.** Almost 5 billion years ago, the amount of gravity near one of these clouds increased as a result of a nearby supernova or other forces. The rotating cloud of dust and gas from which the sun and planets formed is called the **solar nebula.** Energy from collisions and pressure from gravity caused the center of the solar nebula to become hotter and denser. When the temperature at the center became high enough—about 10,000,000°C—hydrogen fusion began. A star, which is now called the sun, or *Sol*, formed. The sun is composed of about 99% of all of the matter that was contained in the solar nebula.

OBJECTIVES

▶ **Explain** the nebular hypothesis of the origin of the solar system. 1b

▶ **Describe** how the planets formed. 1b

▶ **Describe** the formation of the land, the atmosphere, and the oceans of Earth. 1a, 1c

KEY TERMS

solar system
planet
solar nebula
planetesimal

solar system the sun and all of the planets and other bodies that travel around it

planet a celestial body that orbits the sun, is round because of its own gravity, and has cleared the neighborhood around its orbital path

solar nebula a rotating cloud of gas and dust from which the sun and planets formed; *also* any nebula from which stars and exoplanets may form

Figure 1 ▶ The Orion nebula is about 1,500 light-years from Earth. Scientists study the nebula to learn about the processes that give birth to stars.

Formation of the Planets

While the sun was forming in the center of the solar nebula, planets were forming in the outer regions, as shown in **Figure 2.** Small bodies from which a planet originated in the early stages of formation of the solar system are called **planetesimals.** Some planetesimals joined together through collisions and through the force of gravity to form larger bodies called *protoplanets.* The protoplanets' gravity attracted other planetesimals in the solar nebula. These planetesimals collided with the protoplanets and added their masses to the protoplanets.

Eventually, the protoplanets became very large and condensed to form planets and moons. *Moons* are the smaller bodies that orbit the planets. Planets and moons are smaller and denser than the protoplanets.

Formation of the Inner Planets

The features of a newly formed planet depended on the distance between the protoplanet and the developing sun. The four protoplanets that became Mercury, Venus, Earth, and Mars were close to the sun. They contained large percentages of heavy elements, such as iron and nickel. These planets lost their less dense gases because at the temperature of the gases, gravity was not strong enough to hold the gases. Other lighter elements may have been blown or boiled away by radiation from the sun. As the denser material sank to the centers of the planets, layers formed. The less dense material was on the outer part of the planet, and the denser material was at the center. Today, the inner planets have solid surfaces that are similar to Earth's surface. The inner planets are smaller, rockier, and denser than the outer planets.

planetesimal a small body from which a planet originated in the early stages of development of the solar system

Figure 2 ▶ The Nebular Model of the Formation of the Solar System

The young solar nebula begins to collapse because of gravity.

As the solar nebula rotates, it flattens and becomes warmer near its center.

Planetesimals begin to form within the swirling disk.

Formation of the Outer Planets

Four other protoplanets became Jupiter, Saturn, Uranus, and Neptune. As a group, these outer planets are very different from the small, rocky inner planets. These outer planets formed in the colder regions of the solar nebula. They were far from the sun and therefore were cold. Thus, they did not lose their lighter elements, such as helium and hydrogen, or their ices, such as water ice, methane ice, and ammonia ice.

At first, thick layers of ice surrounded small cores of heavy elements. However, because of the intense heat and pressure in the planets' interiors, the ices melted to form layers of liquids and gases. Today, these planets are referred to as *gas giants* because they are composed mostly of gases, have low density, and are huge planets. Jupiter, for example, has a density of only 24% of Earth's density but a diameter that is 11 times Earth's diameter.

Pluto—The First Dwarf Planet

From its discovery in 1930, Pluto was known as the ninth planet. However, it is quite unlike the other outer planets, which are gas giants. In fact, Pluto is smaller than Earth's moon, and it can be best described as an ice ball that is made of frozen gases and rock. Because of its characteristics, many astronomers disagreed with Pluto's classification as a planet.

In 2006, astronomers from around the world revised the definition of *planet*. The new definition includes the first eight familiar planets, but it excludes Pluto. Pluto is part of a new category of solar system bodies called *dwarf planets*.

✓ Reading Check How is Pluto different from the outer planets? **(See the Appendix for answers to Reading Checks.)**

QuickLAB — 5 min

Water Planetesimals

Procedure 🔬 1b, IE.1g

1. Use a medicine dropper to place two drops of water about 3 cm apart on a piece of wax paper.
2. Lift one edge of the wax paper so that one drop of water moves toward the other drop until the drops collide.
3. Add a third drop of water to the wax paper. Then, repeat step 2.

Analysis

1. What happened when the water droplets collided?
2. How does this activity model the formation of protoplanets?

As planetesimals grow, their gravitational pull increases. The largest planetesimals begin to collect more of the gas and dust of the nebula.

Small planetesimals collide with larger ones, and the planets begin to grow.

The excess dust and gas is gradually removed from the solar nebula, which leaves planets around the sun and thus creates a new solar system.

Formation of Solid Earth

When Earth first formed, it was very hot. Three sources of energy contributed to the high temperature on the new planet. First, much of the energy was produced when the planetesimals that formed the planet collided with each other. Second, the increasing weight of Earth's outer layers compressed the inner layers, which generated more energy. Third, radioactive materials that emit high-energy particles were very abundant when Earth formed. When surrounding rocks absorbed these particles, the energy of the particles' motion led to higher temperatures.

Early Solid Earth

Young Earth was hot enough to melt iron, the most common of the existing heavy elements. As Earth developed, denser materials, such as molten iron, sank to its center, and less dense materials were forced to the outer layers. This process is called *differentiation.* Differentiation caused Earth to form three distinct layers, as shown in **Figure 3.** At the center is a dense *core* that is composed mostly of iron and nickel. Around the core is the very thick layer of iron- and magnesium-rich rock called the *mantle.* The outermost layer of Earth is a thin *crust* of less dense, silica-rich rock. Today, processes that shape Earth, such as plate tectonics, are driven by heat transfer and differences in density.

Present Solid Earth

Eventually, Earth's surface cooled enough for solid rock to form. The solid rock at Earth's surface formed from less dense elements that were pushed toward the surface during differentiation. Earth's surface continued to change as a result of the heat in Earth's interior as well as through impacts and through interactions with the newly forming atmosphere.

Graphic Organizer Chain-of-Events Chart

Create the **Graphic Organizer** entitled "Chain-of-Events Chart" described in the Skills Handbook section of the Appendix. Then, fill in the chart with details about each step of the formation of Earth.

Figure 3 ▶ Differentiation of Earth

During its early history, Earth cooled to form three distinct layers.

An atmosphere began to form from the water vapor and carbon dioxide released by volcanic eruptions.

Organisms produced oxygen from photosynthesis to create an oxygenated atmosphere.

Formation of Earth's Atmosphere

Like solid Earth, the atmosphere formed because of differentiation. During the original differentiation of Earth, less dense gas molecules, such as hydrogen and helium, rose to the surface. Thus, the original atmosphere of Earth consisted primarily of hydrogen and helium.

Earth's Early Atmosphere

The high concentrations of hydrogen and helium did not stay with Earth's atmosphere. Earth's gravity is too weak to hold these gases. The sun heated the gases enough so that they escaped Earth's gravity. These gases were probably blown away by the solar wind, which might have been stronger at that time than it is today. Also, Earth's magnetic field, which protects the atmosphere from the solar wind, might not have been fully developed.

Outgassing

As Earth's surface continued to form, volcanic eruptions were much more frequent than they are today. The volcanic eruptions released large amounts of gases, mainly water vapor, carbon dioxide, nitrogen, methane, sulfur dioxide, and ammonia, as shown in **Figure 4.** This process, known as *outgassing*, formed a new atmosphere.

The gases released during outgassing interacted with radiation from the sun. The solar radiation caused the ammonia and some of the water vapor in the atmosphere to break down. Most of the hydrogen that was released during this breakdown escaped into space. Some of the remaining oxygen formed *ozone*, a molecule that contains three oxygen atoms. The ozone collected in a high atmospheric layer around Earth and shielded Earth's surface from the harmful ultraviolet radiation of the sun.

Earth's Present Atmosphere

Organisms that could survive in Earth's early atmosphere developed. Some of these organisms, such as cyanobacteria and early green plants, used carbon dioxide during photosynthesis. Oxygen, a byproduct of photosynthesis, was released. So, the amount of oxygen in the atmosphere slowly increased. About 2 billion years ago, the percentage of oxygen in the atmosphere increased rapidly. Since that time, the chemical composition of the atmosphere has been similar to the present composition of the atmosphere, as shown in **Figure 5.**

Reading Check How did green plants contribute to Earth's present-day atmosphere? (See the Appendix for answers to Reading Checks.)

Figure 4 ▶ Earth's early atmosphere formed as volcanic eruptions released nitrogen, N_2; water vapor, H_2O; ammonia, NH_3; methane, CH_4; argon, Ar; sulfur dioxide, SO_2; and carbon dioxide, CO_2.

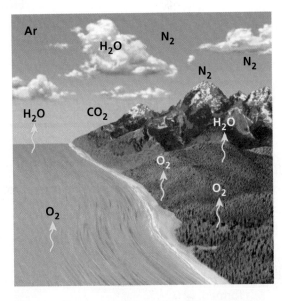

Figure 5 ▶ As Earth's surface changed, the gases in the atmosphere changed. Today, the atmosphere is 78% nitrogen, N_2; 21% oxygen, O_2; and 1% other gases.

Formation of Earth's Oceans

Some scientists think that part of Earth's water may have come from space. Icy bodies, such as comets, collided with Earth. Water from these bodies then became part of Earth's atmosphere. As Earth cooled, water vapor condensed to form rain. This liquid water collected on the surface to form the first oceans.

The first ocean was probably made of fresh water. Over millions of years, rainwater fell to Earth and ran over the land, through rivers, and into the ocean. The rainwater dissolved some of the rocks on land and carried those dissolved solids into the oceans. As more dissolved solids were carried to the oceans, the concentration of certain chemicals in the oceans increased. As the water cycled back into the atmosphere through evaporation, some of these chemicals combined to form salts. Over millions of years, water has cycled between the oceans and the atmosphere. Through this process, the oceans have become increasingly salty. Where shallow ocean water has evaporated completely, the salt precipitates and is left behind. This salt may be harvested for human use, as shown in **Figure 6.**

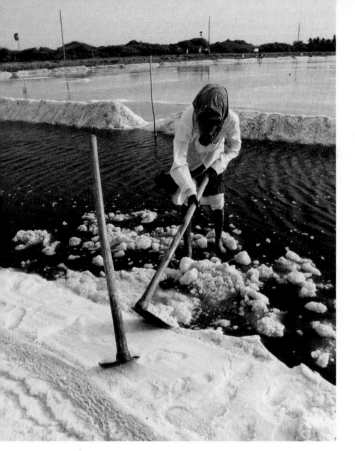

Figure 6 ▶ Salt from the ocean can be harvested from salt flats, such as this one in Habantota, Sri Lanka.

The Ocean's Effects on the Atmosphere

The oceans affect global temperatures in a variety of ways. One way the oceans affect temperature is by dissolving carbon dioxide from the atmosphere. Scientists think that early oceans also affected Earth's early climate by dissolving carbon dioxide. However, Earth's early atmosphere contained less carbon dioxide than the Earth's atmosphere does today. Thus, Earth's early climate was probably cooler than the global climate is today.

Section 1 Review

1. **Describe** the nebular hypothesis. 🐾 1b

2. **Explain** how planetesimals differ from protoplanets. 🐾 1b

3. **Describe** how planets developed. 🐾 1b

4. **Explain** why the outer planets are more gaseous than the inner planets. 🐾 1a, 1b

5. **List** three reasons that Earth was hot when it formed. 🐾 1a, 1b, 1c

6. **Summarize** the process by which the land, atmosphere, and oceans of Earth formed. 🐾 1a, 1c

CRITICAL THINKING

7. **Identifying Relationships** How does the amount of gas in an outer planet differ from the amount of gas in an inner planet? Explain your answer. 🐾 1a, IE.1d

8. **Analyzing Ideas** Explain why Earth is capable of supporting life. 🐾 1c, 8b, 8c, IE.1d

CONCEPT MAPPING

9. Use the following terms to make a concept map: *solar system, solar nebula, protoplanet, planetesimal, planet,* and *gas giant.* 🐾 1a, 1b

Models of the Solar System

California
Content
Standards

IE.1k Students will recognize the cumulative nature of scientific evidence.
IE.1n Students will know that when an obser-vation does not agree with an accepted scientific theory, the observation is sometimes mistaken or fraudulent (e.g. the Piltdown Man fossil or unidentified flying objects), and that the theory is sometimes wrong (e.g. the Ptolemaic model of the movement of the Sun, Moon, and planets).

The first astronomers who studied the sky thought that the stars, planets, and sun revolved around Earth. This idea led to the first model of the solar system. However, the model changed as scientists learned more about how the solar system works.

Early Models of the Solar System

More than 2,000 years ago, the Greek philosopher Aristotle suggested an Earth-centered, or *geocentric*, model of the solar system. In this model, the sun, the stars, and the planets revolved around Earth. However, this model did not explain why some planets sometimes appeared to move backward in the sky relative to the stars—a pattern called *retrograde motion*.

Around 130 CE, the Greek astronomer Claudius Ptolemy (TAHL uh mee) proposed changes to this model. Ptolemy thought that planets moved in small circles, called *epicycles*, as they revolved in larger circles around Earth. These epicycles seemed to explain why planets sometimes appeared to move backward.

In 1543 CE, a Polish astronomer named Nicolaus Copernicus proposed a sun-centered, or *heliocentric*, model of the solar system. In this model, the planets revolved around the sun in the same direction but at different speeds and distances from the sun. Fast-moving planets passed slow-moving planets. Therefore, planets that were slower than Earth appeared to move backward. **Figure 1** compares Ptolemy's and Copernicus's models. Later, the Italian scientist Galileo Galilei observed that four moons traveled around Jupiter. This observation showed him that objects can revolve around objects other than Earth.

OBJECTIVES

▶ **Compare** the models of the universe developed by Ptolemy and Copernicus. IE.1k, IE.1n

▶ **Summarize** Kepler's three laws of planetary motion. IE.1k

▶ **Describe** how Newton explained Kepler's laws of motion. IE.1k

KEY TERMS

eccentricity
orbital period
inertia

Figure 1 ▶ **Early Solar System Models** Ptolemy's solar system model (left) is Earth centered and has the planets moving in epicycles around Earth. Copernicus's solar model (right) is heliocentric and has the planets moving at different speeds around the sun.

Ptolemy's Model

Copernicus's Model

Kepler's Laws

Twenty years before Galileo used a telescope, a Danish astronomer named Tycho Brahe made detailed observations of the solar system. After Tycho's death, one of his assistants, Johannes Kepler, discovered patterns in Tycho's observations. These patterns led Kepler to develop three laws that explained planetary motion.

Law of Ellipses

Kepler's first law, the *law of ellipses*, states that each planet orbits the sun in a path called an ellipse, not in a circle. An *ellipse* is a closed curve whose shape is determined by two points, or *foci*, within the ellipse. In planetary orbits, one focus is located within the sun. No object is located at the other focus. The combined length of two lines, one from each focus to any one point on the ellipse, would always be the same as the length of two lines from each focus to any other one point on the same ellipse.

Elliptical orbits can vary in shape. Some orbits are elongated ellipses. Other orbit shapes are almost perfect circles. The shape of an orbit can be describe in a numerical form called eccentricity. **Eccentricity** is the degree of elongation of an elliptical orbit (symbol, e). Eccentricity is determined by dividing the distance between the foci of the ellipse by the length of the major axis. Therefore, the eccentricity of a circular orbit is $e = 0$. The eccentricity of an extreme elongated orbit, or parabolic orbit, is $e = 1$.

eccentricity the degree of elongation of an elliptical orbit (symbol, e)

✓ **Reading Check** Define and describe an ellipse. (See the Appendix for answers to Reading Checks.)

QuickLAB 🕐 15 min

Ellipses

Procedure

 IE.1d

1. Cover a **cork board** with a **piece of paper**. Put **two push pins** into the cork board 5 cm apart.
2. Tie together the ends of a **string** that is 25 cm long. Loop the string around the pins.
3. Hold the string taut with a **pencil,** and move the pencil to outline an ellipse.
4. Replace the paper with another **piece of paper**. Place the pins 10 cm apart. Outline another ellipse by using the string.
5. Use another **piece of paper**. Loop the string around one pin, and outline another ellipse.

Analysis

1. Which ellipse has an eccentricity closest to 0? Which has an eccentricity closest to 1? Describe the shape of your ellipse in terms of eccentricity.

2. Describe the ellipse as you increased the distance between the foci. Describe what would happen to the ellipse if you increased the length of the string without changing the distance between the foci.

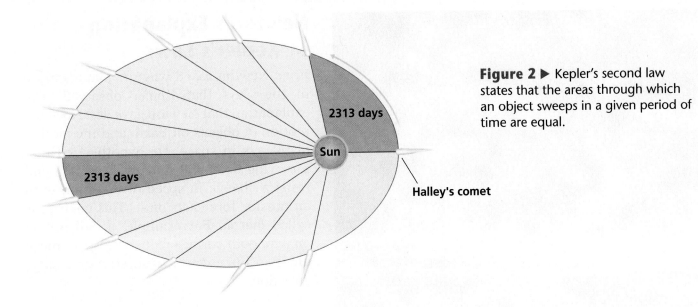

Figure 2 ▶ Kepler's second law states that the areas through which an object sweeps in a given period of time are equal.

2313 days

2313 days

Sun

Halley's comet

Law of Equal Areas

Kepler's second law, the *law of equal areas,* describes the speed at which objects travel at differnet points in their orbits. Kepler discovered Mars moves fastest in its elliptical orbit when it is closest to the sun. He calculated that a line from the center of the sun to the center of an object sweeps through equal areas in equal periods of time. This principle is illustrated in **Figure 2.**

Imagine a line that connects the center of the sun to the center of an object in orbit around the sun. When the object is near the sun, the imaginary line is short. The object moves relatively rapidly, and the line sweeps through a short, wide, pie-shaped sector. When the object is far from the sun, the line is long. However, the object moves relatively slowly when it is far from the sun, and the imaginary line sweeps through a long, thin, pie-shaped sector in the same period. Kepler's second law states that equal areas are covered in equal amounts of time as an object orbits the sun.

Laws of Periods

Kepler's third law, the *law of periods,* describes the relationship between the average distance of a planet from the sun and the orbital period of the planet. The **orbital period** is the time required for a body to complete a single orbit. According to Kepler's third law, the cube of the average distance (a) of a planet from the sun is always proportional to the square of the period (p). The mathematical formula that describes this relationship is $K \times a^3 = p^2$, where K is a constant. When distance is measured in astronomical units (AU) and the period is measured in Earth years, $K = 1$ and $a^3 = p^2$.

Scientists can find out how far away the planets are from the sun by using this law, because they can measure the orbital periods by observing the planets. Jupiter's orbital period is 11.9 Earth years. The square of 11.9 is 142. The cubed number that is equal to 142 is 5.2, so Jupiter is 5.2 AU from the sun.

MATHPRACTICE

Law of Periods
Scientists discover an asteroid that is 0.38 AU from the sun. If 1 AU = 150 million km, how long would the asteroid's orbital period be in Earth years?

orbital period the time required for a body to complete a single orbit

Newton's Explanation of Kepler's Laws

Isaac Newton asked why the planets move in the ways that Kepler observed. The explanation that Newton gave described the motion of objects on Earth and the motion of planets in space. He hypothesized that a moving body will remain in motion and resist a change in speed or direction until an outside force acts on it. This concept is called **inertia.** For example, a ball rolling on a smooth surface will continue to move unless a force causes it to stop or change direction.

Newton's Model of Orbits

Because a planet does not follow a straight path, an outside force must cause the orbit to curve. Newton gave this force the name *gravity*, and he realized that this attractive force exists between any two objects in the universe. The gravitational pull of the sun keeps objects, such as the comet shown in **Figure 3,** in orbit around the sun. While gravity pulls an object toward the sun, inertia keeps the object moving forward in a straight line. The sum of these two motions forms the ellipse of a stable orbit.

The farther from the sun a planet is, the weaker the sun's gravitational pull on the planet is. So, the outer planets are not pulled toward the sun as strongly as the inner ones are. As a result, the orbits of the outer planets are larger and are curved more gently, and the outer planets have longer periods of revolution than the inner planets do.

Figure 3 ▶ In 1997, Comet Hale-Bopp was visible in the sky above the observatory on Mauna Kea in Hawaii.

inertia the tendency of an object to resist being moved or, if the object is moving, to resist a change in speed or direction until an outside force acts on the object

Section 2 Review

1. **Compare** Ptolemy's and Copernicus's models of the universe. IE.1k, IE.1m

2. **Identify** the role that Galileo played in developing the heliocentric theory. IE.1k, IE.1m

3. **Describe** the shape of planetary orbits.

4. **Explain** the law of equal areas.

5. **Summarize** Kepler's third law of planetary orbits. IE.1k

6. **Describe** how Newton explained Kepler's laws by combining the effects of two forces. IE.1k

CRITICAL THINKING

7. **Applying Ideas** A comet's orbit is a highly elongated ellipse. So, why does a comet spend so little time in the inner solar system? IE.1d

8. **Making Comparisons** How did Kepler's explanation of the orbits of planets differ from Newton's explanation? IE.1d, IE.1k

CONCEPT MAPPING

9. Use the following terms to create a concept map: *retrograde motion, geocentric, heliocentric, ellipse, foci, gravity,* and *inertia.*

1a Students know how the differences and similarities among the sun, the terrestrial planets, and the gas planets may have been established during the formation of the solar system.
4d* Students know the differing greenhouse conditions on Earth, Mars, and Venus; the origins of those conditions; and climatic consequences of each.

The planets closest to the sun are called the *inner planets*. These planets are Mercury, Venus, Earth, and Mars. The inner planets are also called **terrestrial planets,** because they are similar to Earth. These planets consist mostly of solid rock and have metallic cores. The number of moons per planet varies from zero to two. The surfaces of inner planets have bowl-shaped depressions, called *impact craters*, that were caused by collisions of the planets with other objects in space.

Mercury

Mercury, the planet closest to the sun, circles the sun every 88 days. The ancient Romans named the planet after the messenger of the gods, who moved quickly. Mercury rotates on its axis once every 59 days.

Images of Mercury reveal a surface that is heavily cratered, as shown in **Figure 1.** The images also show a line of cliffs hundreds of kilometers long. These cliffs may be wrinkles that developed in the crust when the molten core cooled and shrank.

The absence of a significant atmosphere and the planet's slow rotation contributes to the large daily temperature range on Mercury. During the day, the temperature may reach as high as 427°C. At night, the temperature may plunge to –173°C.

OBJECTIVES

▶ **Identify** the basic characteristics of the inner planets. 1a, 4d*

▶ **Compare** the characteristics of the inner planets. 1a, 4d*

▶ **Summarize** the features that allow Earth to sustain life. 1c, 8b, 4d*

KEY TERM

terrestrial planet

---

terrestrial planet one of the highly dense planets nearest to the sun; Mercury, Venus, Mars, and Earth

Figure 1 ▶ The surface of Mercury, shown in this image captured by *Mariner 10,* probably looks much as it did shortly after the solar system formed.

Crust

Mantle

Core

Mercury	
Diameter	4,880 km, or 38% of Earth's diameter
Density	5.4 g/cm³, or 98% of Earth's density
Surface gravity	38% of Earth's surface gravity

Venus

Venus is the second planet from the sun and has an orbital period of 225 days. However, Venus rotates very slowly, only once every 243 days. In some ways, Venus is Earth's twin. The two planets are of almost the same size, mass, and density. However, Venus and Earth differ greatly in other areas.

Venus's Atmosphere

The biggest difference between Earth and Venus is Venus's atmosphere. Venus's atmospheric pressure is about 90 times the pressure on Earth. The high concentration of carbon dioxide in Venus's atmosphere and Venus's relative closeness to the sun have the strongest influences on surface temperatures. Venus's atmosphere is about 96% carbon dioxide.

Solar energy that penetrates the atmosphere heats the planet's surface. The high concentration of carbon dioxide in the atmosphere blocks most of the infrared radiation from escaping. This type of heating is called a *greenhouse effect*. On Earth, the greenhouse effect warms Earth enough to allow organisms to live on the planet. But the greenhouse effect on Venus makes the average surface temperature 464°C! This phenomenon is commonly referred to as a *runaway greenhouse effect* and makes Venus's surface temperature the highest known in the solar system.

Venus also has sulfur dioxide droplets in its upper atmosphere. These droplets form a cloud layer that reflects sunlight. The cloud layer reflects the sunlight so strongly that from Earth, Venus appears to be the brightest object in the night sky, aside from Earth's moon and the sun. Because Venus appears near the sun, Venus is usually visible from Earth only in the early morning or evening. Therefore, Venus is commonly called the *evening star* or the *morning star*.

Figure 2 ▶ Venus's surface is composed of basalt and granite rocks. However, Venus's dense atmosphere is composed primarily of carbon dioxide.

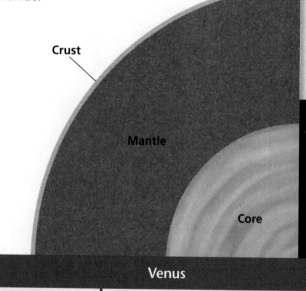

Crust

Mantle

Core

Venus	
Diameter	12,100 km, or 95% of Earth's diameter
Density	5.2 g/cm³, or 95% of Earth's density
Surface gravity	91% of Earth's surface gravity

Missions to Venus

In the 1970s, the Soviet Union sent six probes to explore the surface of Venus. The probes survived in the atmosphere long enough to transmit surface images of a rocky landscape. The images showed a smooth plain and some rocks. Other instruments carried by the probes indicated that the surface of Venus is composed of basalt and granite. These two types of rock are also common on Earth.

The United States's *Magellan* satellite orbited Venus for four years in the 1990s before the satellite was steered into the planet to collect atmospheric data. *Magellan* also bounced radio waves off Venus to produce radar images of Venus's surface.

Surface Features of Venus

From the radar mapping produced by *Magellan,* scientists discovered landforms such as mountains, volcanoes, lava plains, and sand dunes. Volcanoes and lava plains are the most common features on Venus. At an elevation of 8 km, the volcano Maat Mons, which is shown in **Figure 3,** is Venus's highest volcano.

The surface of Venus is also somewhat cratered. All of the craters are of about the same age, and they are surprisingly young. This evidence and the abundance of volcanic features on Venus's surface have led some scientists to speculate that Venus undergoes a periodic resurfacing as a result of massive volcanic activity. Heat inside the planet builds up over time, which causes the volcanoes to erupt and cover the planet's surface with lava. However, scientists think that another 100 million years may pass before volcanic activity again covers Venus's surface with lava. Venus's surface is very different from Earth's surface, which is constantly changing because of the motion of tectonic plates.

✔ **Reading Check** How is Venus different from Earth? (See the Appendix for answers to Reading Checks.)

MATHPRACTICE

Distance from the Sun Earth is about 150 million kilometers from the sun. Venus is 108.2 million kilometers from the sun. How much closer to the sun is Venus than Earth? Express your answer as a percentage.

Earth

The third planet from the sun is Earth. The orbital period of Earth is 365 1/4 days, and Earth completes one rotation on its axis every day. Earth has one large moon.

Earth has had an extremely active geologic history. Geologic records indicate that over the last 250 million years, Earth's continents separated from a single landmass and drifted to their present positions. Weathering and erosion have changed and continue to change the surface of Earth.

Water on Earth

Earth's unique atmosphere and distance from the sun allow water to exist in a liquid state. Mercury and Venus are so close to the sun that any liquid water on those planets would boil. The outer planets are so far from the sun that water freezes. Earth is the only planet known to have oceans of liquid water, as shown in **Figure 4.** However, scientists think that Jupiter's moon Europa may have an ocean under its icy crust.

Life on Earth

Scientists theorize that as oceans formed on Earth, liquid water dissolved carbon dioxide from the atmosphere. Because of this process, carbon dioxide did not build up in the atmosphere and solar heat was able to escape. Thus, Earth maintained the moderate temperatures needed to support life. Plants and cyanobacteria contributed free oxygen to the atmosphere. Earth is the only known planet that has the proper combination of water, temperature, and oxygen to support life.

Figure 4 ▶ Oceans of water and an atmosphere that can support life make Earth a unique planet.

Asthenosphere

Lithosphere

Mesosphere

Outer core

Inner core

Earth	
Diameter	12,756 km
Density	5.515 g/cm^3
Surface gravity	9.8 m/s^2

Mars	
Diameter	6,800 km, or 53% of Earth's diameter
Density	3.9 g/cm³, or 71% of Earth's density
Surface gravity	38% of Earth's surface gravity

Mars

Mars, shown in **Figure 5,** is the fourth planet from the sun. At an average distance of about 228 million kilometers from the sun, Mars is about 50% farther from the sun than Earth is. Its orbital period is 687 days, and it rotates on its axis every 24 h and 37 min. Because its axis tilts at nearly the same angle that Earth's does, Mars's seasons are much like Earth's seasons.

Mars has been geologically active in its past, which is shown in part by the presence of massive volcanoes. A system of deep canyons also covers part of the surface. Valles Marineris is a series of canyons that is as long as the United States is wide—4,000 km. The canyon is thought to be a crack that formed in the crust as the planet cooled. It was later eroded by water.

Martian Volcanoes

Tharsis Montes is one of several volcanic regions on Mars. Volcanoes in this region are 100 times as large as Earth's largest volcano. The largest volcano on Mars is Olympus Mons, which is nearly 24 km tall. It is three times as tall as Mount Everest. At 550 km across, the base of Olympus Mons is about the size of Nebraska. Scientists think that the volcano has grown so large because Mars has no moving tectonic plates. So, Olympus Mons may have had a magma source for millions of years.

Whether Martian volcanoes are still active is a question scientists have yet to answer. A *Viking* landing craft detected two geological events that produced seismic waves. These events, called *marsquakes,* may indicate that volcanoes on Mars are active.

✓ Reading Check Why are Martian volcanoes larger than Earth's volcanoes? (See the Appendix for answers to Reading Checks.)

Figure 5 ▶ Mars is called the *Red Planet* because the oxidized rocks on the planet's surface give the planet a red color.

Mars

Earth

Figure 6 ▶ The images above compare the formation of gullies by possible liquid water runoff on Mars (left) with the formation of similar gullies at Mungo National Park in Australia on Earth (right). The Mungo National Park was the site of a large lake that dried up more than 10,000 years ago.

Water on Mars

The pressure and temperature of Mars's atmosphere are too low for water to exist as a liquid on Mars's surface. However, several NASA spacecraft—such as the Mars rovers, *Spirit* and *Opportunity*, which landed on Mars in 2004—have found evidence that liquid water did exist on Mars's surface in the past. Mars has many surface features that are characteristic of erosion by water, such as branching paths that look like gullies, as shown in **Figure 6.** Scientists think that other features on Mars might be evidence of vast flood plains produced by a volume of water equal to that of all five of Earth's Great Lakes.

The surface temperature on Mars ranges from 20°C near the equator during the summer to as low as –130°C near the poles during the winter. Although most of the water on Mars is trapped in polar icecaps, data from the *Mars Global Surveyor* suggest that water may also exist as permanent frost or as a liquid just below the surface. If liquid water does exist below Mars's surface, the odds of life existing on Mars will dramatically increase. However, no solid evidence of life on Mars has been found.

Section 3 Review

1. **Explain** why Mercury has such drastically different temperatures during its day and during its night. 🐾 1a

2. **Describe** the main ways in which Venus is similar to and different from Earth. 🐾 4d*

3. **Identify** the aspects that make Earth hospitable for life. 🐾 1c, 4d*, 8b

4. **Explain** why Mars's volcanoes became so tall. 🐾 1a

5. **Explain** why Mars does not have liquid water on its surface. 🐾 1a, 4d*

6. **Compare** the characteristics of the inner planets. 🐾 1a

CRITICAL THINKING

7. **Making Comparisons** Describe the difference between the greenhouse effect on Venus and the greenhouse effect on Earth. 🐾 4d*

8. **Understanding Relationships** As rock cools, it contracts. How could this fact explain the presence of Valles Marineris on Mars? 🐾 IE.1d

CONCEPT MAPPING

9. Use the following terms to create a concept map: *Mercury, Venus, Earth, Mars, terrestrial planet, Olympus Mons, liquid water,* and *Maat Mons.* 🐾 1a

Section 4 — The Outer Planets

California Content Standards

1a Students know how the differences and similarities among the sun, the terrestrial planets, and the gas planets may have been established during the formation of the solar system.

IE.1d Students will formulate explanations using logic and evidence.

The four planets farthest from the sun are called the *outer planets*. They are separated from the inner planets by a ring of debris called the *asteroid belt*. Jupiter, Saturn, Uranus, and Neptune, which are shown in **Figure 1**, are also called **gas giants** because they are large planets that have deep, massive atmospheres made mostly of gas. Usually found past the orbit of Neptune is Pluto. Prior to 2006, Pluto was considered to be the most distant outer planet. However, in August of 2006, Pluto was reclassified as a *dwarf planet*.

Gas Giants

Although the gas giants are much larger and more massive than the terrestrial planets, the gas giants are much less dense than the terrestrial planets. Unlike the terrestrial planets, the gas giants did not lose their original gases during their formation. Their large masses give them a huge amount of gravity, which helps them retain the gases. Each of the gas giants has a thick atmosphere that is made mostly of hydrogen and helium gases. A cloud layer prevents scientists from directly observing more than the topmost part of the atmosphere of the gas giants. But each planet probably has a core made of rock and metals.

Although Saturn's rings may be the most impressive, all four gas giants have ring systems that are made of dust and icy debris that orbit the planets. Most of the debris probably came from comets or other bodies.

OBJECTIVES

▶ **Identify** the basic characteristics that make the outer planets different from terrestrial planets. **1a**

▶ **Compare** the characteristics of the outer planets. **1a**

▶ **Explain** why Pluto is now considered a dwarf planet.

KEY TERMS

gas giant
Kuiper Belt

gas giant a planet that has a deep massive atmosphere, such as Jupiter, Saturn, Uranus, or Neptune

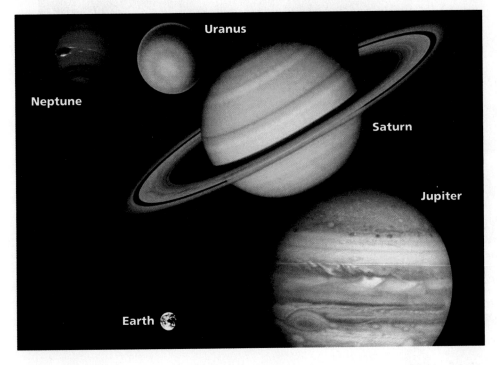

Figure 1 ▶ The four gas giants are much larger than Earth, which is the terrestrial planet shown here at the lower left.

701

Jupiter

Jupiter, shown in **Figure 2**, is the fifth planet from the sun and is by far the largest planet in the solar system. Its mass is more than 300 times that of Earth and is twice that of all the other planets combined. Jupiter's orbital period is almost 12 years. Jupiter rotates on its axis faster than any other planet rotates—once every 9 h and 50 min. Jupiter has at least 60 moons, 4 of which are the size of small planets. It also has several thin rings that are made up of millions of particles.

Jupiter's Atmosphere

Hydrogen and helium make up 92% of Jupiter, so Jupiter's composition is much like the sun's. However, when Jupiter formed about 4.6 billion years ago, it did not have enough mass to allow nuclear fusion to begin. So, Jupiter never became a star.

The alternating light and dark bands on its surface make Jupiter unique in our solar system. Orange, gray, blue, and white bands spread out parallel to the equator. The colors suggest the presence of organic molecules mixed with ammonia, methane, and water vapor. Jupiter's rapid rotation causes these gases to swirl around the planet and form the bands. The average temperature of Jupiter's outer atmospheric layers is –160°C. Jupiter also has lightning storms and thunderstorms that are much larger than those on Earth.

Reading Check **Why didn't Jupiter become a star? (See the Appendix for answers to Reading Checks.)**

Figure 2 ▶ Jupiter is easily identified by its large size and alternating light and dark bands. One of Jupiter's larger moons can be seen in front of the planet.

Transition zone

Fluid hydrogen and helium

Cloud layer

Liquid metallic hydrogen

Rocky-iron core?

Io

Jupiter	
Diameter	143,000 km, or 11 times Earth's diameter
Density	1.33 g/cm³, or 24% of Earth's density
Surface gravity	2.54 times Earth's surface gravity

Weather and Storms on Jupiter

Jupiter's most distinctive feature is its *Great Red Spot,* shown in **Figure 3.** The Great Red Spot is a giant rotating storm, similar to a hurricane on Earth, that has been raging for at least several hundred years. Several other oval spots, or storms, can be seen on Jupiter, although they are usually white. Sometimes, the smaller storms are swallowed up by the larger ones. While storms are common on Jupiter's surface, only a few of the largest storms persist for a long time.

A probe dropped by the *Galileo* spacecraft measured wind speeds on Jupiter of up to 540 km/h. Because winds are caused by temperature differences, scientists have concluded that Jupiter's internal heat affects the planet's weather more than heat from the sun does. From Earth, even by using a small telescope, you can see bands of clouds on Jupiter. These bands, which vary depending on latitude, show regions of different wind speeds.

Figure 3 ▶ Jupiter's Great Red Spot is an ongoing, massive, hurricane-like storm that is about twice the diameter of Earth.

Jupiter's Interior

Jupiter's large mass causes the temperature and pressure in Jupiter's interior to be much greater than they are inside Earth. The intense pressure and temperatures as high as 30,000°C have changed Jupiter's interior into a sea of liquid, metallic hydrogen. Electric currents in this hot liquid may be the source of Jupiter's enormous magnetic field. Scientists think that Jupiter has a solid, rocky, iron core at its center.

Connection to TECHNOLOGY

Galileo Probes Jupiter

In 1995, the spacecraft *Galileo* arrived at Jupiter and began monitoring an atmospheric probe that Galileo had launched five months earlier. The 336 kg probe transmitted data about the composition and meteorology of Jupiter's atmosphere.

The data surprised mission scientists in many ways. The wind speeds that were measured were much higher than the expected wind speeds. But the most surprising discovery was that although the levels of carbon and nitrogen that were measured were consistent with what was anticipated, only one-fifth of the expected amount of water was found.

The *Galileo* spacecraft studied Jupiter and its moons through 2003. It was then crashed into Jupiter to avoid a collision with one of Jupiter's moons, Europa. No spacecraft is now in orbit around Jupiter. NASA

is considering launching a mission to study Europa. *Galileo* discovered evidence of a possible subsurface ocean on Europa. So, scientists are excited about the possibility of life on this moon of Jupiter.

Saturn

Saturn, shown in **Figure 4,** is the sixth planet from the sun and has an orbital period of 29.5 years. Because it is so far from the sun, Saturn is very cold and has an average cloud-top temperature of –176°C. Saturn has at least 47 moons, and additional small moons continue to be discovered. Its largest moon, Titan, which has a diameter of 5,150 km, is half the size of Earth.

Saturn, like Jupiter, is made almost entirely of hydrogen and helium and has a rocky, iron core at its center. However, Saturn is much less dense than Jupiter. In fact, Saturn is the least dense planet in the solar system.

Saturn's Bands and Rings

Saturn is known for its rings, which are 2 times the planet's diameter. While the other gas giants also have rings, Saturn has the most complex and extensive system of rings. The rings are made of billions of dust and ice particles. Most of the ring debris probably came from comets or other bodies.

Like Jupiter, Saturn also has bands of colored clouds that run parallel to its equator. These bands are caused by Saturn's rapid rotation. Saturn rotates on its axis every 10 h and 30 min. This rapid rotation, paired with Saturn's low density, causes Saturn to bulge at its equator and to flatten at its poles.

Scientists are learning more about Saturn and its moons from NASA's *Cassini* spacecraft, which reached Saturn on July 1, 2004. Cassini also carried the European Space Agency's *Huygens* probe, which landed on Titan, Saturn's largest moon.

Reading Check How is Saturn similar to Jupiter? (See the Appendix for answers to Reading Checks.)

Figure 4 ▶ This composite image of Saturn taken from the *Cassini* spacecraft clearly shows the planet's rings.

Liquid hydrogen

Liquid metallic hydrogen

Icy core

Rocky-iron core?

Saturn	
Diameter	120,535 km, or 9.4 times Earth's diameter
Density	0.70 g/cm³, or 13% of Earth's density
Surface gravity	1.07 times Earth's surface gravity

Uranus	
Diameter	51,120 km, or 4 times Earth's diameter
Density	1.30 g/cm^3, or 24% of Earth's density
Surface gravity	91% of Earth's surface gravity

Uranus

Uranus, shown in **Figure 5,** is the seventh planet from the sun and the third-largest planet in the solar system. Sir William Herschel discovered Uranus in 1781. Because Uranus is nearly 3 billion kilometers from the sun, Uranus is a difficult planet to study. But the *Hubble Space Telescope* has taken images that show changes in Uranus's atmosphere. Uranus has at least 24 moons and at least 11 thin rings. Its orbital period is almost 84 years.

Uranus's Rotation

The most distinctive feature of Uranus is its unusual orientation. Most planets, including Earth, rotate with their axes perpendicular to their orbital planes as they revolve around the sun. However, Uranus's axis is almost parallel to the plane of its orbit. The rotation rate of Uranus was not discovered until 1986, when *Voyager 2* passed by Uranus. Astronomers were then able to determine that Uranus rotated once about every 17 h.

Uranus's Atmosphere

Like the other gas giants, Uranus has an atmosphere that contains mainly hydrogen and helium. The blue-green color of Uranus indicates that the atmosphere also contains significant amounts of methane. The average cloud-top temperature of Uranus is –214°C. However, astronomers believe that the planet's temperature is much higher below the clouds. There may be a mixture of liquid water and methane beneath the atmosphere. Scientists also think that the center of Uranus, which has a temperature of about 7,000°C, is a core of rock and melted elements.

Figure 5 ▶ This exaggerated-color image from the *Hubble Space Telescope* shows Uranus, two of its moons, and some of its rings.

Neptune

Neptune, shown in **Figure 6,** is the eighth planet from the sun and is similar to Uranus in size and mass. Neptune's orbital period is nearly 164 years, and the planet rotates about every 16 h. Neptune has at least 13 moons and six rings.

The Discovery of Neptune

Neptune's existence was predicted before Neptune was actually discovered. After Uranus was discovered, astronomers noted variations from its calculated orbit. They suspected that the gravity of an unknown planet was responsible for the variation. In the mid-1800s, John Couch Adams, an English mathematician, and Urbain Leverrier, a French astronomer, independently calculated the position of the unknown planet. A German astronomer, Johann Galle, discovered a bluish-green disk where Leverrier had predicted the planet would be. Astronomers named the planet Neptune after the Roman god of the sea.

Neptune's Atmosphere

Data from the *Voyager 2* spacecraft indicate that Neptune's atmosphere is made up mostly of hydrogen, helium, and methane. Neptune's upper atmosphere contains some white clouds of frozen methane. These clouds appear as continually changing bands between the equator and the poles of Neptune.

Images taken by *Voyager 2* and the *Hubble Space Telescope* indicate that Neptune has an active weather system. Neptune has the solar system's strongest winds, which exceed 1,000 km/h. A storm that is the size of Earth and that is known as the Great Dark Spot appeared and disappeared on Neptune's surface. Neptune's average cloud-top temperature is about –225°C.

Figure 6 ▶ This Great Dark Spot on Neptune was a giant storm that was similar to the Great Red Spot on Jupiter.

Fluid hydrogen

Icy-liquid mantle

Rocky-iron core?

Neptune	
Diameter	49,530 km, or 3.9 times Earth's diameter
Density	1.64 g/cm^3, or 30% of Earth's density
Surface gravity	1.2 times Earth's surface gravity

Sedna
1,300–1,800 km
in diameter

Quaoar
1,250 km

Pluto
2,302 km

Moon
3,476 km

Earth
12,756 km

Figure 7 ▶ Pluto, the prototype for dwarf planets in our solar system, is even smaller than Earth's moon. Quaoar and Sedna, as shown by these artist renditions, have a smaller diameter than Pluto.

Objects Beyond Neptune

Pluto was discovered in 1930. Until 2006, it was known as the ninth planet. Now, it is defined as a dwarf planet. Pluto orbits the sun in an unusual elongated and tilted ellipse. Pluto is usually far beyond Neptune but is closer to the sun than Neptune is for about 20 years out of its 248-year orbital period. With a diameter of 2,302 km, Pluto is smaller than Earth's moon. Astronomers think that Pluto is made up of frozen methane, rock, and ice and has an average temperature of –235°C. Infrared images show that Pluto has extensive methane icecaps and a very thin nitrogen atmosphere.

Kuiper–Belt Objects

In recent years, scientists have discovered hundreds of objects in our solar system beyond Neptune's orbit. Some of these objects are similar to Pluto in size and composition, but most are simply small chunks of ice. This region beyond Neptune's orbit is called the **Kuiper Belt** (KIE puhr BELT). Quaoar, shown in **Figure 7,** is more than half of Pluto's size. Another object, called Eris, is larger than Pluto. Like Pluto, Eris is considered to be a dwarf planet. A *dwarf planet* is any object that orbits the sun, is round because of its own gravity, but has not cleared its orbital path.

One of the most distant objects in the solar system was found beyond the Kuiper Belt in March 2004. This object, named Sedna, is about three-fourths the size of Pluto. It is currently more than twice as far from Earth as Pluto is.

Kuiper Belt a region of the solar system that starts just beyond the orbit of Neptune and that contains dwarf planets and other small bodies made mostly of ice

✔ **Reading Check** Where is the Kuiper Belt located? (See the Appendix for answers to Reading Checks.)

Exoplanets

Until the 1990s, all of the planets that astronomers had discovered were in Earth's solar system. Since then, however, more than 200 planetlike objects have been attributed to stars other than Earth's sun. Because these objects circle stars other than Earth's sun, they are called *exoplanets*. The prefix *exo-* means "outside." **Figure 8** shows an artist's rendition of an exoplanet. Most known exoplanets orbit stars that are similar to Earth's sun. Therefore, the existence of exoplanets leads some scientists to wonder if life could exist in another solar system.

Exoplanets cannot be directly observed with telescopes or satellites. Most exoplanets can be detected only because their gravity tugs on stars that they orbit. When scientists study some distant stars, they notice that the light coming from the stars shifts in wavelength. This shifting could be explained by the stars' movement slightly toward and then away from Earth. Scientists know that the gravity of an object that cannot be seen can affect a star's movement. In these cases, that object is most likely an exoplanet that orbits the star.

Most of the exoplanets that have been identified are larger than Uranus, but recently two exoplanets have been discovered that are closer to Earth in mass. Many of these exoplanets, though more massive than Jupiter, are closer to their stars than Mercury is to Earth's sun. From studying these many solar systems, scientists hope to learn more about the formation and basic arrangement of solar systems.

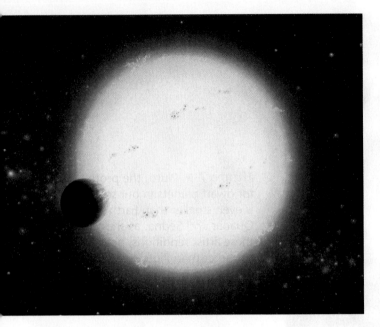

Figure 8 ▶ This illustration shows an artist's idea of a Jupiter-sized exoplanet in the foreground that was recently discovered. This exoplanet orbits a sun-like star called HD209458, which is located 150 light years from Earth.

Section 4 Review

1. **Explain** what makes Jupiter similar to the sun. 🖳 1a

2. **Compare** the characteristics of Jupiter, Saturn, Uranus, and Neptune. 🖳 1a

3. **Compare** Jupiter's Great Red Spot with weather on Earth. 🖳 1a

4. **Describe** the way in which the tilt of the axis of Uranus's rotation is unusual. 🖳 1a

5. **Explain** how Pluto differs from the outer planets of the solar system. 🖳 1a

6. **Summarize** the features of objects in the Kuiper Belt. 🖳 1a

7. **Describe** what scientists know about exoplanets, planetlike objects outside the solar system.

CRITICAL THINKING

8. **Making Comparisons** How are the compositions of the gas giants similar to the composition of the sun? 🖳 1a, IE.1d

9. **Making Inferences** Why is Pluto not considered a planet even though Neptune is sometimes farther from the sun than Pluto is? 🖳 1a, IE.1d

10. **Evaluating Conclusions** Should scientists reconsider Pluto to be a planet? Explain your answer. 🖳 1a, IE.1d

CONCEPT MAPPING

11. Use the following terms to create a concept map: *outer planet, Jupiter, Saturn, Uranus, Neptune, Pluto, gas giant, Kuiper belt,* and *Great Red Spot.* 🖳 1a

Highlights

Sections

1 Formation of the Solar System

2 Models of the Solar System

3 The Inner Planets

4 The Outer Planets

Key Terms

solar system, 685
planet, 685
solar nebula, 685
planetesimal, 686

eccentricity, 692
orbital period, 693
inertia, 694

terrestrial planet, 695

gas giant, 701
Kuiper Belt, 707

Key Concepts

▶ The solar system formed from a rotating and contracting region of gas and dust about 5 billion years ago.

▶ The planets formed from collisions of smaller bodies called *planetesimals*.

▶ As Earth cooled, differentiation caused three distinct compositional layers—the crust, the mantle, and the core—to form.

▶ Geocentric models of the solar system, such as those developed by Aristotle and Ptolemy, were replaced by the heliocentric model proposed by Copernicus.

▶ Kepler's three laws describe the motion of the planets in their orbits around the sun.

▶ The planets travel in elliptical orbits around the sun. Planets nearer to the sun travel faster than those farther from the sun do.

▶ The four inner planets share similar characteristics and are called the *terrestrial planets*. Earth, Venus, and Mars have a history of geologic activity.

▶ The terrestrial planets are denser and smaller than the gas giants.

▶ The outer planets consist of the four *gas giants*—Jupiter, Saturn, Uranus, and Neptune. Pluto is a dwarf planet usually located in the Kuiper Belt.

▶ The Kuiper Belt is a region of the solar system that is beyond Neptune's orbit and that contains small bodies made mostly of ice.

▶ Exoplanets orbit stars other than the sun.

Using Key Terms

Use each of the following terms in a separate sentence.

1. *inertia*
2. *terrestrial planet* 🔆 1a
3. *Kuiper Belt*

For each pair of terms, explain how the meanings of the terms differ.

4. *Kuiper Belt* and *orbital period*
5. *planet* and *planetesimal* 🔆 1a
6. *terrestrial planet* and *gas giant* 🔆 1a
7. *solar nebula* and *solar system* 🔆 1b

Understanding Key Concepts

8. Copernicus's model of the solar system is 🔆 IE.1k. IE.1n
   a. geocentric.
   b. lunocentric.
   c. ethnocentric.
   d. heliocentric.

9. Kepler's first law states that each planet orbits the sun in a path called a(n) 🔆 IE.1k
   a. ellipse.
   b. circle.
   c. epicycle.
   d. period.

10. The most distinctive feature of Jupiter is its
    a. Great Red Spot.
    b. Great Dark Spot.
    c. ring.
    d. elongated orbit.

11. The planet that has an axis of rotation that is almost parallel to the plane of its orbit is 🔆 1a
    a. Venus.
    b. Jupiter.
    c. Uranus.
    d. Neptune.

12. The tilt of the axis of Mars is nearly the same as that of 🔆 1a
    a. Mercury.
    b. Venus.
    c. Earth.
    d. Jupiter.

13. The planet that rotates faster than any other planet in the solar system is 🔆 1a
    a. Earth.
    b. Jupiter.
    c. Uranus.
    d. Pluto.

14. Kepler's law that describes how fast planets travel at different points in their orbits is called the law of 🔆 IE.1k
    a. ellipses.
    b. equal speeds.
    c. equal areas.
    d. periods.

15. All of the outer planets rotate with their axes perpendicular to their orbital planes *except* 🔆 1a
    a. Saturn.
    b. Jupiter.
    c. Nepture.
    d. Uranus.

16. The first atmosphere of Earth contained a large amount of 🔆 1c, 8b
    a. helium.
    b. oxygen.
    c. carbon dioxide.
    d. methane.

17. The hypothesis that states that the sun and the planets developed out of the same cloud of gas and dust is called the 🔆 1b
    a. Copernicus hypothesis.
    b. solar hypothesis.
    c. nebular hypothesis.
    d. Galileo hypothesis.

18. In the process of photosynthesis, green plants give off 🔆 8b
    a. hydrogen.
    b. oxygen.
    c. carbon dioxide.
    d. helium.

Short Answer

19. Explain how Earth's early atmosphere differs from Earth's atmosphere today. 🔆 1c, 8b

20. What is the shape of the planets' orbits?

21. What is Kepler's first law? 🔆 IE.1k

22. How did Newton's ideas about the orbits of the planets differ from Kepler's ideas? 🔆 IE.1k

23. List three features of Earth that allow it to sustain life. 🔆 4d*, 8b, 8c

24. Describe how a planet might form. 🔆 1b

25. How did differentiation help to form solid Earth? 🔆 1a, 1c

CAREER Focus

Astronomer

"As a five-year-old, I had binoculars—I'd lie on the lawn at night and use them to look at the sky," says Sandra Faber, professor of astronomy at the University of Santa Cruz, and staff member at the Lick Observatory in Santa Cruz, California.

Like a Detective Story

Faber's research focuses on the formation and evolution of galaxies and the evolution of structures in the universe. To gather data, Faber uses various kinds of telescopes, including ground-based telescopes and the *Hubble Space Telescope.* "Astronomy is like a big detective story," she says. "Information is gathered and shared among scientists, who then draw scientific conclusions about how the universe came to be." Faber is currently a core member of the Deep Extragalactic Evolutionary

Probe (DEEP) project. DEEP uses the Keck II telescope in Hawaii and the *Hubble Space Telescope* to survey faint, faraway galaxies.

A Look Back in Time

To see these galaxies, the DEEP project uses a spectrographic instrument called DEIMOS, which stands for *deep imaging multi-object spectrograph.* DEIMOS allows Faber and her colleagues to collect and analyze light that has traveled for billions of years from its original source. Astronomers call such research *look back studies.* By collecting data, Faber can look back billions of years to find answers to scientific questions about the origin of the universe.

Faber's research has given her appreciation for Earth's uniqueness. She says, "Earth is far more varied and beautiful than any other planet. It's all we've got." She also has

"Astronomy offers profound messages for our future. It provides a motivation for humans to save this planet and take advantage of its enormous possibilities."

—Sandra Faber

a special perspective on the Earth's vulnerability: "When seen from space, the Earth is small. It floats in a hostile void. Its atmosphere is thin, like the skin on an apple. Even from space, one can see visual signs of pollutants. It provides a motivation for humans to save this planet and take advantage of its enormous possibilities." In many ways, notes Faber, "Earth is like a spaceship. It's up to the crew members to maintain control."

◄ Faber studies distant galaxies from the W. M. Keck Observatory on top of the Hawaiian volcano Mauna Kea.

SCiLINKS

NSTA
Developed and maintained by the National Science Teachers Association

For a variety of links related to this subject, go to www.scilinks.org

Topic: Careers in Earth Science
SciLinks code: HQ60222

Chapter 28

Minor Bodies of the Solar System

Sections

Earth's Moon

Movements of the Moon

Satellites of
Other Planets

Asteroids, Comets,
and Meteoroids

What You'll Learn

- What Earth's moon is made of
  and how it moves
- How satellites of other planets
  differ from Earth's moon
- What comets, asteroids, and
  meteoroids are

Why It's Relevant

Small orbiting objects can
provide information about the
conditions that existed at the
beginnings of our solar system.

PRE-READING ACTIVITY

Booklet
Before you read
this chapter,
create the
FoldNote entitled "Booklet"
described in the Skills
Handbook section of the
Appendix. Label each page of
the booklet with a main idea
from the chapter. As you read
the chapter, write what you
learn about each main
idea on the appropriate
page of the booklet.

This is one idea of how an asteroid
might look as it moves toward Earth.
Asteroids are one type of small body
that travels through our solar system.

California Content Standards

1a Students know how the differences and similarities among the sun, the terrestrial planets,
and the gas planets may have been established during the formation of the solar system.
1b Students know the evidence from Earth and moon rocks indicates that the solar system was
formed from a nebular cloud of dust and gas approximately 4.6 billion years ago.
1f Students know the evidence for the dramatic effects that asteroid impacts have had in
shaping the surface of planets and their moons and in mass extinctions of life on Earth.
IE.1d Students will formulate explanations using logic and evidence.
IE.1g Students will recognize the usefulness and limitations of models and theories as scientific
representations of reality.

Earth's Moon

1b Students know the evidence from Earth and moon rocks indicates that the solar system was formed from a nebular cloud of dust and gas approximately 4.6 billion years ago. **IE.1d** Students will formulate explanations using logic and evidence. **IE.1g** Students will recognize the usefulness and limitations of models and theories as scientific representations of reality.

A body that orbits a larger body is called a **satellite.** Six of the planets in our solar system have smaller bodies that orbit around them. These natural satellites are also called **moons.** Our moon is Earth's natural satellite.

In 1957, the Soviet Union launched *Sputnik,* which was the first *artificial satellite* launched into space. In 1958, the United States launched its first artificial satellite, which was named *Explorer 1.* Thousands of artificial satellites are now in orbit around Earth, including weather satellites and space telescopes, such as the *Hubble Space Telescope.*

Exploring the Moon

Between 1969 and 1972, the United States sent six spacecraft to the moon as part of the Apollo space program. Apollo astronauts found that the moon's weak gravity affected the way they moved. They discovered that bouncing was more efficient than walking. Apollo astronauts also explored the moon's surface in a variety of specially-designed vehicles, such as the one shown in **Figure 1.**

The moon has much less mass than Earth does, so the gravity on the moon's surface is about one-sixth of the gravity on Earth. As a result, a person who has a mass of 61.2 kg and who exerts about 600 newtons (N) of force on Earth would exert only about 100 N on the moon. The gravity at the moon's surface is not strong enough to hold gases and therefore has no significant atmosphere. Because the moon has no atmosphere to absorb and transport heat, the moon's surface temperature varies greatly, from 134°C during the day to –170°C at night.

OBJECTIVES

▶ **List** four kinds of lunar surface features.

▶ **Describe** the three layers of the moon.

▶ **Summarize** the three stages by which the moon formed. 1b

KEY TERMS

satellite
moon
mare
crater

satellite a natural or artificial body that revolves around a larger celestial body

moon a celestial body that revolves around a body that is larger in mass; a natural satellite

SCiLINKS®

NSTA
Developed and maintained by the
National Science Teachers Association

For a variety of links related to this subject, go to www.scilinks.org

Topic: Earth's Moon
SciLinks code: HQ60449

Figure 1 ▶ *Apollo 17* astronaut Eugene Cernan explores the lunar surface in a Lunar Roving Vehicle.

The Lunar Surface

Because *luna* is the Latin word for "moon," any feature of the moon is referred to as *lunar*. Light and dark patches on the moon can be seen with the unaided eye. The lighter areas are rough highlands that are composed of rocks called *anorthosites*. The darker areas are smooth, reflect less light, and are called *maria* (MAHR ee uh). Each dark area is a **mare** (MAHR AY). *Mare* is Latin for "sea." Galileo named these dark areas *maria* because he thought that they looked like Earth's seas. Today, astronomers know that maria are plains of dark, solidified lava. These lava plains formed more than 3 billion years ago when lava slowly filled basins that were created by impacts of massive asteroids.

mare a large, dark area of basalt on the moon (plural, *maria*)

crater a bowl-shaped depression that forms on the surface of an object when a falling body strikes the object's surface or when an explosion occurs

Craters, Rilles, and Ridges

The surface of the moon, shown in **Figure 2**, is covered with numerous bowl-shaped depressions, called **craters.** Most of the moon's craters formed when debris left over from the formation of the solar system struck the moon about 4 billion years ago. Younger craters are characterized by bright streaks, called *rays*, that extend outward from the impact site. Even these younger craters, however, are billions of years old.

Long, deep channels called *rilles* run through the maria in some places. The moon's rilles are thought to be leftover lava channels from the formation of the maria. Some rilles are as long as 240 km. Another surface feature of the moon is ridges. Ridges are long, narrow elevations of rock that rise out of the surface and criss-cross the maria.

Reading Check Name two features of the moon. (See the Appendix for answers to Reading Checks.)

Figure 2 ▶ The largest lunar craters are named for famous scholars and scientists. The lunar surface also has millions of small, overlapping craters. *How does the shape of Mare Humboldtianum indicate that this feature once was an impact crater?*

Regolith

More meteorites have reached the surface of the moon than have reached Earth's surface because the moon has no atmosphere for protection. Over billions of years, these meteorites crushed much of the rock on the lunar surface into dust and small fragments. Today, almost all of the lunar surface is covered by a layer of dust and rock, called *regolith*. Regolith is shown in **Figure 3.** The depth of the regolith layer varies from 1 m to 6 m.

Lunar Rocks

Many lunar rocks are very similar to rocks on Earth. Lunar rocks, including the one shown in **Figure 4,** contain many of the same elements as Earth's rocks do, but lunar rocks contain different proportions of those elements. Lunar rocks are igneous, and most rocks near the surface are composed mainly of oxygen and silicon. These surface rocks are similar to the rocks in Earth's crust. Rocks from the lunar highlands are light-colored, coarse-grained anorthosites. Highland rocks are rich in calcium and aluminum. Rocks from the maria are fine-grained basalts and contain large amounts of titanium, magnesium, and iron.

Nevertheless, lunar surface rocks have only small amounts of some elements that are common on Earth. Many of these elements have low melting points and may have boiled off early in the moon's history when the moon was still molten. Also, the minerals in lunar rocks do not contain water.

One type of rock that occurs in both maria and the highlands is *breccia*. Lunar breccia contains fragments of other rocks that have been fused together. These breccias formed when meteorites struck the moon. The force of these impacts broke up rocks, and the heat from the impacts partially melted the fragments.

Figure 4 ▶ This rock is 4.3 billion to 4.5 billion years old; it is the oldest rock discovered on the moon. The rock's texture indicates that the rock has a complicated history.

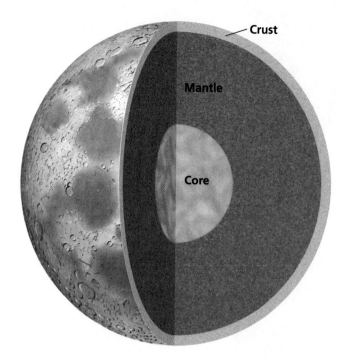

Crust

Mantle

Core

Figure 5 ▶ The moon, like Earth, has three compositional layers: the crust, the mantle, and the core.

The Interior of the Moon

Rocks of the lunar surface are about as dense as those on Earth's surface. However, the overall density of the moon is only three-fifths the density of Earth. The difference in overall density indicates that the interior of the moon is less dense than the interior of Earth.

Most of the information about the interior of the moon comes from seismographs that were placed on the moon by the Apollo astronauts. Seismographs have recorded numerous weak moonquakes, which are similar to earthquakes. More than 10,000 moonquakes have been detected. Most moonquakes occur in the mantle at a depth that is 10 times deeper than the depth at which most earthquakes occur on Earth. From these moonquakes, scientists learned that the moon's interior is layered, as shown in **Figure 5.**

The Moon's Crust

One side of the moon always faces Earth. That side is therefore called the *near side*. The other side always faces away from Earth and is called the *far side*. The pull of Earth's gravity during the moon's formation caused the crust on the far side of the moon to become thicker than the crust on the near side. On the near side, the lunar crust is about 60 km thick. On the far side, the lunar crust is up to 100 km thick. Images of the far side show that the far side's surface is mountainous and has only a few small maria. The crust of the far side appears to consist of materials that are similar to those of the rocks in the highlands on the near side.

✓ **Reading Check** Name two features of the far side of the moon. (See the Appendix for answers to Reading Checks.)

The Moon's Mantle and Core

Beneath the crust is the moon's mantle. The mantle is thought to be made of rock that is rich in silica, magnesium, and iron. Of the moon's 1,738 km radius, the mantle makes up more than half of that distance and reaches 1,000 km below the crust.

Scientists think that the moon has a small iron core that has a radius of less than 700 km. When laser beams were bounced off of small mirrors placed on the moon, scientists discovered that the moon's rotation is not uniform. This non-uniform rotation indicates that the core is neither completely solid nor completely liquid. This characteristic may explain why the moon has almost no overall magnetic field. There are, however, small areas on the moon that exhibit local magnetism.

Quick LAB ⏱ 5 min

Liquid and Solid Cores

Procedure 🖐 IE.1d, IE.1g

1. Take **one uncooked egg** and **one hardboiled egg.** With your thumb and forefinger, spin both eggs.

2. Record the amount of time each egg spins.

3. Lay **one can of solid food** and **one can of soup** on their sides, and spin both cans.

4. Record the amount of time each can spins.

Analysis

1. Which egg stopped spinning first? Which can of food stopped spinning first?

2. Which rotates more steadily: an object that has a solid core or an object that has a liquid core? Explain your answer.

The Formation of the Moon

Rocks taken from the moon by Apollo astronauts provided evidence to help astronomers understand the moon's history. Most scientists generally agree that the moon formed in three stages.

The Giant Impact Hypothesis

Most scientists think that the moon's development began when a large object collided with Earth more than 4 billion years ago. This *giant impact hypothesis* states that a Mars-sized body struck Earth early in the history of the solar system. Before the impact, Earth was molten, or heated to an almost liquid state. The collision ejected chunks of Earth's mantle into orbit around Earth. The debris eventually clumped together to form the moon, as shown in **Figure 6.**

Most of the ejected materials came from Earth's silica-rich mantle rather than from Earth's dense, metallic core. This hypothesis explains why moon rocks share many of the chemical characteristics of Earth's mantle. As the material clumped together, it continued to revolve around Earth because of Earth's gravitational pull.

Differentiation of the Lunar Interior

Early in its history, the lunar surface was covered by an ocean of molten rock. Over time, the densest materials moved toward the center of the moon and formed a small core. The least dense materials formed an outer crust. The other materials settled between the core and the outer layer to form the moon's mantle.

Meteorite Bombardment

The outer surface of the moon eventually cooled to form a thick, solid crust over the molten interior. At the same time, debris left over from the formation of the solar system struck the solid surface and produced craters and regolith.

About 3 billion years ago, the number of small objects in the solar system decreased. Less material struck the lunar surface, and few new craters formed. Craters that have rays formed during the most recent meteor impacts. During this stage of lunar development, virtually all geologic activity stopped. Because the moon cooled more than 3 billion years ago, it looks today almost exactly as it did 3 billion years ago. Therefore, the moon is a valuable source of information about the conditions that existed in the solar system long ago.

Figure 6 ▶ The First Stage of Moon Formation

Scientists think that a Mars-sized object collided with Earth and blasted part of Earth's mantle into space.

The resulting debris then began to revolve around Earth.

The material eventually joined to form Earth's moon.

Figure 7 ▶ The near side of the moon (top) has fewer visible craters than the far side (bottom) does in part because lava flows on the near side covered many of the impact sites with maria.

Lava Flows on the Moon

After impacts on the moon's surface formed deep basins, lava flowed out of cracks, or *fissures*, in the lunar crust. This lava flooded the crater basins to form maria. The presence of the maria suggests that fissure eruptions once characterized the moon, even though there is no evidence that large active volcanoes have ever been present on the moon.

Because the moon's crust is thinner on the near side than on the far side, much more lava flowed onto the surface on the near side than onto the surface of the far side of the moon. The near side of the moon has several smooth maria, but the far side has few maria and many more craters, as shown in **Figure 7.**

Scientists do not yet know how magma formed in the lunar interior or how the magma reached the surface. There is no evidence of plate tectonics or convection currents in the moon's mantle, so the magma must have formed in some other way. A large amount of energy would have been needed to produce the magma in the upper layers of the moon. Some scientists think this energy may have come from a long period of intense meteorite bombardment. Other scientists think that radioactive decay of materials may have also heated the moon's interior enough to cause magma to form. Scientists agree that the lava flows ended about 3.1 billion years ago, when the interior cooled completely.

Section 1 Review

1. **Describe** what maria on the surface of the moon look like and how they came to be known as maria.

2. **Compare** the thickness of the moon's crust on the near side with the thickness of the crust on the far side.

3. **Summarize** how and when the maria formed.

4. **Describe** how the surface of the moon would be different today if meteorites had continued to hit it at the same rate as they did 3 billion years ago.

5. **Describe** breccias and how they formed on the moon.

6. **Summarize** how scientists think the moon formed. 1b

CRITICAL THINKING

7. **Analyzing Ideas** Explain how Earth's gravity affected the moon's near side and far side differently. IE.1d

8. **Making Comparisons** Compare the features of the lunar surface created by lava flows and the features created by impacts. IE.1d

CONCEPT MAPPING

9. Use the following terms to create a concept map: *moon, meteorite, crater, rille, maria, highlands,* and *basalt*.

Movements of the Moon

IE.1d Students will formulate explanations
using logic and evidence.
IE.1g Students will recognize the usefulness and

limitations of models and theories as scientific
representations of reality.

If you looked down on the moon from above its north pole, you would see the moon rotate once on its axis every 27.3 days. However, if you stood on the moon's surface and measured the lunar day by the amount of time between sunrises, you would find that a lunar day is 29.5 Earth days long. This discrepancy is due to the fact that, while the moon is revolving around Earth, Earth and the moon are also revolving around the sun.

The Earth-Moon System

To observers on Earth, the moon appears to orbit Earth. However, if you could observe Earth and the moon from space, you would see that Earth and the moon revolve around each other. Together, they form a single system that orbits the sun.

The mass of the moon is only 1/80 that of Earth. So, the balance point of the Earth-moon system is not halfway between the centers of the two bodies. The balance point is located within Earth's interior because Earth's mass is greater than the moon's mass. This balance point is called the *barycenter*. The barycenter follows a smooth orbit around the sun, as shown in **Figure 1.**

The Moon's Elliptical Orbit

The orbit of the moon around Earth forms an ellipse that is about 5% more elongated than a circle is. Therefore, the distance between Earth and its moon varies over a month's time. When the moon is farthest from Earth, the moon is at **apogee.** When the moon is closest to Earth, the moon is at **perigee.** The average distance of the moon from Earth is 384,000 km.

OBJECTIVES

▶ **Describe** the shape of the moon's orbit around Earth.
▶ **Explain** why eclipses occur.
▶ **Describe** the appearance of four phases of the moon.
▶ **Explain** how the movements of the moon affect tides on Earth.

KEY TERMS

apogee
perigee
eclipse
solar eclipse
lunar eclipse
phase

apogee in the orbit of a satellite, the point at which the satellite is farthest from Earth

perigee in the orbit of a satellite, the point at which the satellite is closest to Earth

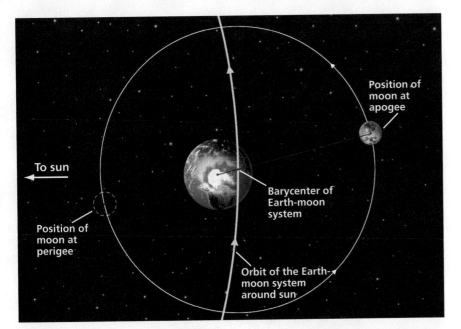

Position of moon at apogee

To sun

Barycenter of Earth-moon system

Position of moon at perigee

Orbit of the Earth-moon system around sun

Figure 1 ▶ The barycenter of the Earth-moon system orbits the sun in a smooth ellipse. The orbits of both Earth and the moon "wobble" as the bodies move around the sun. This diagram is not to scale.

Moonrise and Moonset

The moon appears to rise and set at Earth's horizon because of Earth's rotation on its axis. If you were to watch the moon rise or set on successive nights, however, you would notice that it rises or sets approximately 50 minutes later each night. This happens because of both Earth's rotation and the moon's revolution. While Earth completes one rotation each day, the moon also moves in its orbit around Earth. It takes an extra 1/29 of Earth's rotation, or 50 minutes, for the horizon to catch up to the moon.

Lunar Rotation

In addition to orbiting Earth and revolving around the sun, the moon also spins on its axis. The moon rotated rapidly when it formed, but the pull of Earth's gravity has slowed the moon's rate of rotation. The moon now spins very slowly and completes a rotation only once during each orbit around Earth. The moon revolves only once around Earth in about 27.3 days relative to the stars. Because the rotation and the revolution of the moon take the same amount of time, observers on Earth always see the same side of the moon. Therefore, images of the far side of the moon must be taken by spacecraft orbiting the moon.

As the moon orbits Earth, the part of the moon's surface that is illuminated by sunlight changes. The sun's light always illuminates half of the moon and, as shown in **Figure 2**, half the Earth. The near side of the moon is sometimes fully illuminated by the sun. At other times, depending on where the moon is in its orbit, the near side is partly or completely darkened.

☑ **Reading Check** Why are we unable to photograph the far side of the moon from Earth? (See the Appendix for answers to Reading Checks.)

Figure 2 ▶ The lunar landing module, which was also called *The Eagle,* flew to meet the command module at the end of the *Apollo 11* mission. Seen from this viewpoint, Earth is illuminated from above.

Penumbra

Umbra

Sun's rays

Eclipses

Bodies orbiting the sun, including Earth and its moon, cast long shadows into space. An **eclipse** occurs when one celestial body passes through the shadow of another. Shadows cast by Earth and the moon have two parts. In the inner, cone-shaped part of the shadow, the *umbra*, sunlight is completely blocked. In the outer part of the shadow, the *penumbra*, sunlight is only partially blocked, as shown in **Figure 3.**

Solar Eclipses

When the moon is directly between the sun and part of Earth, the shadow of the moon falls on Earth and causes a **solar eclipse.** During a *total solar eclipse*, the sun's light is completely blocked by the moon. The umbra falls on the area of Earth that lies directly in line with the moon and the sun. Outside the umbra, but within the penumbra, people see a *partial solar eclipse*. The penumbra falls on the area that immediately surrounds the umbra.

The umbra of the moon is too small to make a large shadow on Earth's surface. The part of the umbra that hits Earth during an eclipse, as shown in **Figure 4,** is never more than a few hundred kilometers across. So, a total eclipse of the sun covers only a small part of Earth and is seen only by people in particular parts of Earth along a narrow path. A total solar eclipse also never lasts more than about seven minutes at any one location. A total eclipse will not be visible in the United States until 2017, even though there is a total eclipse somewhere on Earth about every 18 months.

Figure 3 ▶ During a solar eclipse, the shadow of the moon falls on Earth. The distance between Earth and the moon in this diagram is not to scale.

eclipse an event in which the shadow of one celestial body falls on another

solar eclipse the passing of the moon between Earth and the sun; during a solar eclipse, the shadow of the moon falls on Earth

Figure 4 ▶ The dark area (right) is the shadow of the moon cast on cloudtops over Europe during a total solar eclipse in 1999. The photo was taken from the orbiting space station *Mir*. The composite (left) shows the partial and total phases of a solar eclipse over several hours.

Effects of Solar Eclipses

During a total solar eclipse, people on the ground are in the moon's umbra. In the areas on Earth's surface under the umbra, the sky becomes as dark as it does at twilight. During this period of darkness, the sunlight that is not eclipsed by the moon shows the normally invisible outer layers of the sun's atmosphere. The last bits of normal sunlight before darkness often glisten like the diamond on a ring and cause what is known as the *diamond-ring effect*. The diamond-ring effect is shown in **Figure 5.** Therefore, many people think that total solar eclipses are very beautiful.

If the moon is at or near apogee when it comes directly between Earth and the sun, the moon's umbra does not reach Earth. If the umbra fails to reach Earth, a ring-shaped eclipse occurs. This type of eclipse is called an *annular eclipse*, because *annulus* is the Latin word for "ring." During an annular eclipse, the sun is never completely blocked out. Instead, a thin ring of sunlight is visible around the outer edge of the moon. The brightness of this thin ring of ordinary sunlight prevents observers from seeing the outer layers of the sun's atmosphere that are visible during a total solar eclipse.

Reading Check What is one difference between a total solar eclipse and an annular eclipse? (See the Appendix for answers to Reading Checks.)

Figure 5 ▶ The diamond-ring effect produced by a solar eclipse can be stunning for observers on the part of Earth that falls under the moon's shadow.

QuickLAB 15 min

Eclipses

Procedure ▦ IE.1d, IE.1g

1. Make two balls from **modeling clay,** one about 4 cm in diameter and one about 1 cm in diameter.
2. Using a **metric ruler,** position the balls about 15 cm apart on a **sheet of paper,** as shown in the photo at right.
3. Turn off any nearby lights. Place a **penlight** approximately 15 cm in front of and almost level with the larger ball. Shine the light on the larger ball. Sketch your model, and note the effect of the beam of light.
4. Repeat step 3, but reverse the positions of the two balls. You may need to raise the smaller ball slightly to center its shadow on the larger ball. Sketch your model, and again note the effect of the light beam.

Analysis

1. Which planetary bodies do the larger clay ball, the smaller clay ball, and the penlight represent?

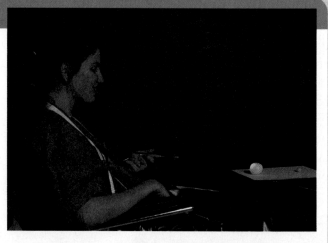

2. As viewed from Earth, what event did your model in step 3 represent? As viewed from the moon, what would your model represent?
3. As viewed from Earth, what event did your model in step 4 represent? As viewed from the moon, what would your model represent?
4. In what ways could you modify this activity to more closely model how eclipses occur?

Umbra

Penumbra

Sun's rays

Lunar Eclipses

A **lunar eclipse** occurs when Earth is positioned between the moon and the sun and when Earth's shadow crosses the lighted half of the moon. For a total lunar eclipse to occur, the entire moon must pass into Earth's umbra, as shown in **Figure 6.** When only part of the moon passes into Earth's umbra, a *partial lunar eclipse* occurs. The remainder of the moon passes through Earth's penumbra. When the entire moon passes through Earth's penumbra, a *penumbral eclipse* occurs. During a penumbral eclipse, the moon darkens so little that the eclipse is barely noticeable.

A lunar eclipse may last for more than an hour. Even during a total lunar eclipse, sunlight is bent around Earth through our atmosphere. Mainly red light reaches the moon, so the totally eclipsed moon appears to have a reddish color, as shown in the middle portion of the composite image in **Figure 7.**

Frequency of Solar and Lunar Eclipses

As many as seven eclipses may occur during a calendar year. Four may be lunar, and three may be solar or vice versa. However, total eclipses of the sun and the moon occur infrequently. Solar and lunar eclipses do not occur during every lunar orbit. This is because the orbit of the moon is not in the same plane as the orbit of Earth around the sun. The moon crosses the plane of Earth's orbit only twice in each revolution around Earth. A solar eclipse will occur only if this crossing occurs when the moon is between Earth and the sun. If this crossing occurs when Earth is between the moon and the sun, a lunar eclipse will occur.

Lunar eclipses are visible everywhere on the dark side of Earth. A total solar eclipse, however, can be seen only by observers in the small path of the moon's shadow as it moves across Earth's lighted surface. A partial solar eclipse can be seen for thousands of kilometers on either side of the path of the umbra.

Figure 6 ▶ During a lunar eclipse, the shadow of Earth falls on the moon. The distance between Earth and the moon in this diagram is not to scale.

lunar eclipse the passing of the moon through Earth's shadow at full moon

Figure 7 ▶ This composite image shows a total lunar eclipse as seen from Earth over several hours.

Phases of the Moon

On some nights, the moon shines brightly enough for you to read a book by its light. But moonlight is not produced by the moon. The moon merely reflects light from the sun. Because the moon is spherical, half of it is always lit by sunlight. As the moon revolves around Earth, however, different amounts of the near side of the moon, which faces Earth, are lighted. Therefore, the apparent shape of the visible part of the moon varies. These varying shapes, lighted by reflected sunlight, are called **phases** of the moon and are shown in **Figure 8.**

When the moon is directly between the sun and Earth, the sun's rays strike only the far side of the moon. As a result, the entire near side of the moon is dark. When the near side is dark, the moon is said to be in the *new-moon* phase. During this phase, no lighted area of the moon is visible from Earth.

phase in astronomy, the change in the illuminated area of one celestial body as seen from another celestial body; phases of the moon are caused by the changing positions of Earth, the sun, and the moon

Figure 8 ▶ Phases of the Moon

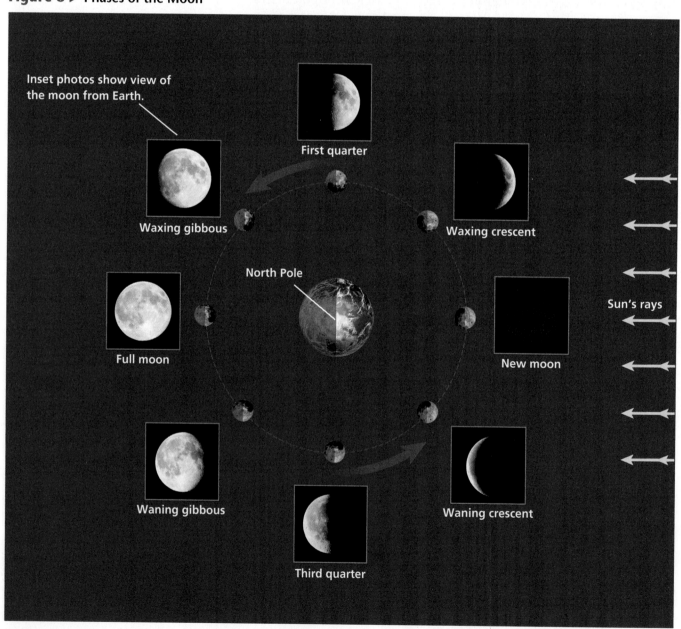

Inset photos show view of the moon from Earth.

First quarter

Waxing gibbous

Waxing crescent

North Pole

Sun's rays

Full moon

New moon

Waning gibbous

Waning crescent

Third quarter

Europa

Europa is the second closest Galilean moon to Jupiter. Europa is about the size of Earth's moon, but Europa is much less dense than Earth's moon. Astronomers think that Europa has a rock core that is covered with a crust of ice that is about 100 km thick. Images of Europa, such as the one shown in **Figure 3,** show cracks in this enormous ice sheet. Scientists have concluded from observations made from spacecraft that an ocean of liquid water may exist under this blanket of ice. If liquid water exists, simple forms of life could also exist there. Astronomers have no evidence of life on Europa, but many think Europa would be a good place to investigate the possibility of extraterrestrial life.

Figure 3 ▶ This false-color image of Europa shows immense cracks across its ice sheets.

Ganymede

Ganymede is the third Galilean moon from Jupiter. Ganymede is also the largest moon in the solar system, even larger than the planet Mercury. However, Ganymede has a relatively small mass because it is probably composed mostly of ice mixed with rock.

Images of Ganymede, such as **Figure 4,** show dark, crater-filled areas. Other light areas show marks that are thought to be long ridges and valleys. The Galileo spacecraft provided evidence to support the existence of a magnetic field around Ganymede. Ganymede and Io are the only Galilean moons that have strong magnetic fields. Both moons' magnetic fields are completely surrounded by Jupiter's much more powerful magnetic field.

Figure 4 ▶ Much of Ganymede's surface is covered with ridges and valleys.

Callisto

Of the four Galilean moons, Callisto is the farthest from Jupiter. Callisto is similar to Ganymede in size, density, and composition. However, Callisto has a much rougher surface than Ganymede does. In fact, Callisto may be one of the most densely cratered moons in our solar system.

Like craters on Earth's moon and other bodies in our solar system, craters on Callisto are the result of collisions that occurred early in the history of the solar system. **Figure 5** shows a giant impact basin that is 600 km across and a set of concentric rings that extend about 1,500 km outward in all directions from the crater.

✔ Reading Check Name one feature of each of the Galilean moons. (See the Appendix for answers to Reading Checks.)

Figure 5 ▶ "Ripples" of ice and rock radiate out from this impact crater, called *Valhalla*, on Callisto.

Figure 6 ▶ This composite image shows Saturn and many of Saturn's largest moons. The distances of the moons from Saturn and from each other are not to scale.

Moons of Saturn

Saturn has at least 47 moons. Most of them are small, icy bodies that have many craters. However, five of Saturn's moons are fairly large. These five moons and many of Saturn's other moons are shown in **Figure 6.**

Titan

Saturn's largest moon, called Titan, has a diameter of more than 5,000 km. Only Jupiter's moon Ganymede is larger. Unlike any of the other moons in our solar system, Titan has a thick atmosphere that is composed mainly of nitrogen. Titan's atmosphere is so thick that hydrocarbon smog conceals the surface.

In 2005, the *Huygens* (HIE guhnz) probe, part of the Cassini mission, gathered data about Titan's atmosphere. The information it gathered is giving scientists clues about how Titan and its atmosphere formed. When the probe got below much of the atmosphere's haze, it sent back clear images of the surface, which showed signs of flowing liquid, probably methane. *Cassini* also sent back many images of Titan, an example of which is shown in **Figure 7.**

Saturn's Other Moons

Saturn's icy moons resemble Jupiter's icy Galilean moons. Saturn's other smaller moons have irregular shapes. Scientists think that many of the smallest moons, such as Janus, were captured by Saturn's gravity.

Graphic Organizer **Comparison Table**

Create the Graphic Organizer entitled "Comparison Table" described in the Skills Handbook section of the Appendix. Label the columns with "Moons of Mars," "Moons of Jupiter," "Moons of Saturn, and "Moons of Uranus and Neptune." Fill in the table with details about each moon as you read this section.

Figure 7 ▶ This false-color image of Titan was taken by the Cassini mission. The image shows Titan in the ultraviolet and infrared wavelenghts.

Comets

Every few years, an object that looks like a star that has a tail is visible in the evening sky. This object is a comet. **Comets** are small bodies of ice, rock, and cosmic dust that follow highly elliptical orbits around the sun. The most famous is Halley's Comet, which passes by Earth every 76 years. It last passed Earth in 1986 and will return in 2061. Every 5 to 10 years, another very bright comet will be visible from Earth. Comet Hale-Bopp, shown in **Figure 3**, was particularly spectacular as it passed by Earth in 1997.

Composition of Comets

A comet has several parts. The core, or nucleus, of a comet is made of rock, metals, and ice. Cores of comets are commonly between 1 km and 100 km in diameter. A spherical cloud of gas and dust, called the *coma*, surrounds the nucleus. The coma can extend as far as 1 million kilometers from the nucleus. A comet's bright appearance largely results from sunlight reflected by the comet's coma. The nucleus and the coma form the head of the comet. In 2004, the spacecraft *Stardust* flew by a comet named Wild 2. It returned samples from the comet's coma to Earth in 2006. In 2005, the spacecraft, *Deep Impact,* slammed a probe into the nucleus of comet Temple 1. The probe released a plume of dust, giving scientists a look at what a comet's nucleus is made of.

The most spectacular parts of a comet are its tails. Tails form when sunlight causes the comet's ice to change to gas. The gas, or ion, tail of a comet streams from the comet's head. The solar wind—electrically charged particles expanding away from the sun—pushes the gas away from the comet's head. Thus, regardless of the direction the comet travels, its ion tail points away from the sun. The comet's second tail is made of dust and curves backward along the comet's orbit. Some comets have tails that are more than 80 million kilometers long.

Figure 3 ▶ A comet, such as Comet Hale-Bopp, consists of a nucleus, a coma, and two tails. The blue streak is the *ion tail,* and the white streak is the *dust tail.*

comet a small body of rock, ice, and cosmic dust that follows an elliptical orbit around the sun and that gives off gas and dust in the form of a tail as it passes close to the sun

Figure 4 ▶ Most comets come from the Oort cloud, a region in the outer solar system that is far beyond the orbit of Neptune.

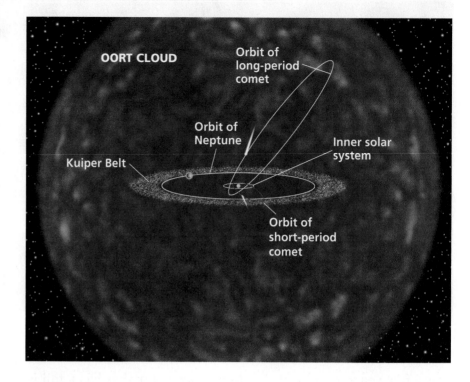

Oort cloud a spherical region that surrounds the solar system, that extends from the Kuiper Belt to almost halfway to the nearest star, and that contains billions of comets

Kuiper Belt a region of the solar system that starts just beyond the orbit of Neptune and that contains dwarf planets and other small bodies made mostly of ice

The Oort Cloud

Astronomers think that most comets originate in the Oort cloud, which is illustrated in **Figure 4.** The **Oort cloud** is a spherical cloud of dust and ice that lies far beyond Neptune's orbit and that contains the nuclei of billions of comets. The total mass of the Oort cloud is estimated to be between 10 and 40 Earth masses.

The Oort cloud surrounds the solar system and may reach as far as halfway to the nearest star. Scientists think that the matter in the Oort cloud was left over from the formation of the solar system. Studying this distant matter helps scientists understand the early history of the solar system.

Bodies within the Oort cloud circle the sun so slowly that they take a few million years to complete one orbit. But the gravity of a star that passes near the solar system may cause a comet to fall into a more elliptical orbit around the sun. The orbits of comets that pass by Jupiter may also be changed by Jupiter's gravitational force. If a comet takes more than 200 years to complete one orbit of the sun, the comet is called a *long-period comet*.

The Kuiper Belt

Recent advances in technology have allowed scientists to observe thousands of small objects beyond the orbit of Neptune. Most of these objects, including some comets, are from a flat ring called the **Kuiper Belt** (KIE puhr BELT), which is located just beyond Neptune's orbit. The Kuiper Belt is also illustrated in **Figure 4.** The dwarf planets Pluto and Eris are located in the Kuiper Belt during much of their orbits. Several other objects that are candidates for dwarf-planet status also reside in the Kuiper Belt.

Short-Period Comets

Comets called *short-period comets* take less than 200 years to complete one orbit around the sun. In recent years, astronomers have discovered that most short-period comets come from the Kuiper Belt. Some of the comets that originate in the Kuiper Belt have been forced outward into the Oort cloud by Jupiter's gravity. Many comets in the Kuiper Belt are the result of collisions between larger Kuiper-Belt objects there. Halley's comet, which has a period of 76 years, is a short-period comet.

Meteoroids

In addition to relatively large asteroids and comets, very small bits of rock or metal move throughout the solar system. These small, rocky bodies are called **meteoroids.** Most meteoroids have a diameter of less than 1 mm. Scientists think that most meteoroids are pieces of matter that become detached from passing comets. Large meteoroids—more than 1 cm in diameter—are probably the result of collisions between asteroids.

Meteors

Meteoroids that travel through space on an orbit that takes them directly into Earth's path may enter Earth's atmosphere. When a meteoroid enters Earth's atmosphere, friction between the object and the air molecules heats the meteoroid's surface. As a result of this friction and heat, most meteoroids burn up in the atmosphere. As a meteoroid burns up in Earth's atmosphere, the meteoroid produces a bright streak of light called a **meteor.** Meteors are commonly called *shooting stars.* Meteoroids sometimes also vaporize very quickly in a brilliant flash of light called a *fireball.* Observers on Earth may hear a loud noise as a fireball disintegrates.

When a large number of small meteoroids enter Earth's atmosphere in a short period of time, a *meteor shower* occurs. During the most spectacular of these showers, several meteors are visible every minute. A composite photo of a meteor shower is shown in **Figure 5.** Meteor showers occur at the same time each year. This happens because Earth intersects the orbits of comets that have left behind a trail of dust. As these particles burn up in Earth's atmosphere, they appear as meteors streaking across the sky.

Reading Check What is the difference between a meteor and a meteoroid? (See the Appendix for answers to Reading Checks.)

MATHPRACTICE

Matter From Space
Astronomers estimate that about 1 million kg of matter from meteoroids falls to Earth each day. Based on this estimate, how many kilograms of matter from meteoroids would fall on Earth in three weeks?

meteoroid a relatively small, rocky body that travels through space

meteor a bright streak of light that results when a meteoroid burns up in Earth's atmosphere

Figure 5 ▶ The straight lines in this composite photo are meteors burning up as they move through Earth's atmosphere.

Meteorites

Figure 6 ▶ Types of Meteorites

Stony

Iron

Stony-iron

Millions of meteoroids enter Earth's atmosphere each day. A few of these meteoroids do not burn up entirely in the atmosphere because they are relatively large. These meteoroids fall to Earth's surface. A meteoroid or any part of a meteoroid that is left when a meteoroid hits Earth is called a *meteorite*. Most meteorites are small and have a mass of less than 1 kg. However, large meteorites occasionally strike Earth's surface with the force of a large bomb. These impacts leave large impact craters.

Meteorites can be classified into three basic types: stony, iron, and stony-iron. These three types of meteorites are shown in **Figure 6.** *Stony meteorites* are similar in composition to rocks on Earth. Some stony meteorites contain carbon-bearing compounds that are similar to the carbon compounds in living organisms. Although most meteorites are stony, *iron meteorites* are easier to find. Iron meteorites are easier to find because they have a distinctive metallic appearance. This distinctive appearance makes iron meteorites easy to distinguish from common Earth rocks. The third type of meteorites, called *stony-iron meteorites,* contain iron and stone. Stony-iron meteorites are rare.

Astronomers think that almost all meteorites come from collisions between asteroids. The oldest meteoroids may be 100 million years older than Earth and its moon. Therefore, meteorites may provide information about how the early solar system formed.

Some rare meteorites originated on the moon or Mars. Computer simulations have shown that meteorites that hit the moon or Mars can eject rocks that then fall to Earth. Many of these rare meteorites have been found in Antarctica. Finding meteorites in Antarctica is relatively easy because they stand out against the background of snow and ice.

Section 4 Review

1. **Identify** where the asteroid belt is located in the solar system. 🔲1f

2. **Describe** the physical characteristics of asteroids. 🔲1f

3. **List** the four main parts of a comet, and identify their physical characteristics.

4. **Compare** the ion and dust tails of a comet.

5. **Explain** the relationship between the Oort cloud and comets.

6. **Describe** the location of the Kuiper Belt.

7. **Distinguish** between a meteor, a meteoroid, and a meteorite.

CRITICAL THINKING

8. **Analyzing Relationships** Explain why a comet's ion tail always points away from the sun. 🔲IE.1d

9. **Making Comparisons** Explain how both Pluto (a Kuiper-Belt object) and Ceres (an asteroid) can both be considered dwarf planets. 🔲IE.1d

10. **Making Comparisons** You find a meteorite on the ground. What kind of meteorite did you most likely find? Describe two steps of its journey from space. 🔲IE.1d

CONCEPT MAPPING

11. Use the following terms to create a concept map: *comet, asteroid, Kuiper Belt, Oort cloud, long-period comet, short-period comet,* and *meteoroid.*

Sections

1 Earth's Moon

2 Movements of the Moon

3 Satellites of Other Planets

4 Asteroids, Comets, and Meteoroids

Key Terms

satellite, 719
moon, 719
mare, 720
crater, 720

apogee, 725
perigee, 725
eclipse, 727
solar eclipse, 727
lunar eclipse, 729
phase, 730

Galilean moon, 733

asteroid, 739
comet, 741
Oort cloud, 742
Kuiper Belt, 742
meteoroid, 743
meteor, 743

Key Concepts

▶ The surface of the moon is covered by craters, rilles, and ridges.

▶ The structure of the moon's interior was determined by using seismographs.

▶ The moon may have formed when an object hit Earth more than 4 billion years ago. Lunar surface features have changed little since they formed 3 billion years ago.

▶ Eclipses occur when one planetary body passes through the shadow of another.

▶ The moon spins on its axis once during each orbit of Earth. As the moon orbits, the amount of the near side that is lighted increases and decreases, which causes phases.

▶ Tides on Earth are the result of the gravitational pull of the sun and the moon.

▶ Phobos and Deimos, the two tiny moons of Mars, are much smaller than Earth's moon.

▶ The Galilean moons are the four largest satellites of Jupiter. Jupiter, Saturn, Uranus, and Neptune have rings.

▶ Uranus and Neptune each have several moons. Pluto has at least three moons.

▶ Most asteroids are located in an asteroid belt that is located between the orbits of Mars and Jupiter.

▶ Comets come from the Oort cloud, which is far beyond Neptune's orbit, and from the Kuiper Belt, which starts just beyond Neptune's orbit.

▶ Meteoroids are small rocks in space that either burn up in Earth's atmosphere (as meteors) or stay intact to hit Earth (as meteorites).

Using Key Terms

Use each of the following terms in a separate sentence.

1. *crater*

2. *mare*

3. *Galilean moon*

For each pair of terms, explain how the meanings of the terms differ.

4. *perigee* and *apogee*

5. *Oort cloud* and *Kuiper Belt*

6. *solar eclipse* and *lunar eclipse*

7. *comet* and *asteroid* 1f

8. *meteoroid* and *meteorite*

Understanding Key Concepts

9. Dark areas on the moon that are smooth and that reflect little light are called
  a. rilles.
  b. rays.
  c. maria.
  d. breccia.

10. What happened in the most recent stage in the development of the moon? 1b
  a. The densest material sank to the core.
  b. The crust began to break.
  c. Earth's gravity captured the moon.
  d. The number of meteorites hitting the moon decreased.

11. During each orbit around Earth, the moon spins on its axis
  a. 1 time.
  b. about 29 times.
  c. about 27 times.
  d. 365 times.

12. In a lunar eclipse, the moon
  a. casts a shadow on Earth.
  b. is in Earth's shadow.
  c. is between Earth and the sun.
  d. blocks part of the sun from view.

13. When the size of the lighted part of the moon's near side is decreasing, the moon is
  a. full.
  b. waxing.
  c. annular.
  d. waning.

14. Compared with the other moons of Jupiter, the four Galilean moons are
  a. larger.
  b. farther from Jupiter.
  c. lighter.
  d. younger.

15. The main asteroid belt exists in a region between the orbits of 1f
  a. Mercury and Venus.
  b. Earth and Mars.
  c. Venus and Earth.
  d. Mars and Jupiter.

16. Meteorites can provide information about
  a. the composition of the solar system before the planets formed.
  b. the size of Earth.
  c. the destiny of the solar system.
  d. the size of the universe.

Short Answer

17. Describe how maria formed on the moon.

18. Are craters on the moon caused by volcanism or by impacts with other bodies? Explain your answer.

19. Do total eclipses of the sun occur only at full moons? Explain your answer.

20. Are any moons in the solar system bigger than planets? Explain.

21. Which planets have rings? 1a

22. Which two places in the solar system do comets come from?

23. What is the difference between natural and artificial satellites?

Critical Thinking

24. Analyzing Relationships If Earth had two moons that traveled on the same orbit and were the same distance from Earth, but formed a 90° angle with Earth, how would Earth's tides be different? **IE.1d**

25. Making Inferences How would the craters on the moon be different today if the moon had developed a dense atmosphere that moved as wind and that contained water? **IE.1d**

26. Determining Cause and Effect If meteorites had stopped hitting the moon before the outer surface of the moon cooled, how would the moon's surface be different than it is today? **IE.1d**

27. Evaluating Information Suppose that the moon spun twice on its axis during each orbit around Earth. How would the study of the moon from Earth be easier than it is currently? **IE.1d**

28. Applying Ideas The surfaces of some asteroids reflect only small amounts of light. Other asteroids reflect up to 40% of the light that falls on them. Of what kind of materials would each type of asteroid probably be composed? **1f, IE.1d**

Concept Mapping

29. Use the following terms to create a concept map: *moon, Earth, apogee, perigee, new moon, full moon, waxing, waning, solar eclipse, lunar eclipse, umbra, penumbra,* and *phase.*

Math Skills

30. Making Calculations There are 60 s in 1 min, 60 min in 1 h, 24 h in 1 day, and 365 1/4 days in a year. How many seconds are in a year?

31. Making Calculations The radius of Earth's moon is 1,738 km. The diameter of Neptune's moon Triton is 2,705 km. What percentage of Earth's moon's size is Triton?

Writing Skills

32. Creative Writing Imagine that you want to live on the moon. Describe how you would get your water and how you would acquire food and other supplies.

33. Communicating Ideas Summarize how the moon's gravity and the rotation of Earth cause tides.

Interpreting Graphics

The graph below shows the number of near-Earth asteroids discovered each year. Use the graph below to answer the questions that follow.

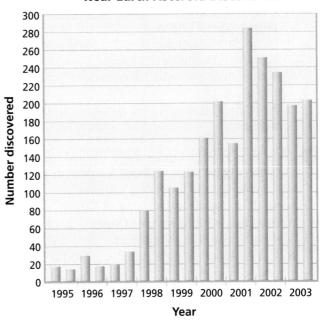

Near-Earth Asteroid Discoveries

34. Was the rate of discovery of near-Earth asteroids in 2003 higher or lower than the rate in 2000? **1f**

35. How many near-Earth asteroids were discovered in the half-year in which the most discoveries were made? **1f**

36. Which calendar year had the highest total number of near-Earth asteroid discoveries? **1f**

37. What is the total number of near-Earth asteroids discovered in the last three years shown on the graph? **1f**

Understanding Concepts

Directions (1–9): **For** *each* **question, write on a separate sheet of paper the letter of the correct answer.**

1 Because of differences in surface gravity, how much does a person who weighs 360 newtons (360 N) on Earth weigh on the moon if the moon has one-sixth the gravity of Earth?
A. 36 N
B. 60 N
C. 180 N
D. 90 N

2 Why are scientists concerned about near-Earth asteroids?
A. Near-Earth asteroids make up only a small percentage of asteroids.
B. Near-Earth asteroids might strike Earth, causing damage.
C. Near-Earth asteroids have wide, elliptical orbits.
D. Near-Earth asteroids are made of carbon materials.

3 The rings of Saturn most likely formed long after the planet formed about 5 billion years ago. Which of the following statements accurately describes each ring of Saturn?
A. It is divided into smaller ringlets, all of which orbit Saturn together.
B. It consists of a single ring composed of rock and ice pieces.
C. It is divided into smaller ringlets, each of which has an individual orbit.
D. It is part of a set of rings that are unlike those found anywhere else.

4 Which of the following statements describes why temperature variation on the moon is so large?
A. The moon has no atmosphere to provide insulation.
B. The atmosphere of the moon is made up of cold gases.
C. Gases are dense and close to the surface.
D. Dark, smooth rocks absorb the sun's heat.

5 The asteroid belt did not become a planet during the formation of the solar system because
A. the material is continually colliding with itself.
B. comets break up in the belt.
C. of Jupiter's gravity.
D. the asteroids are not massive enough.

6 Why does the moon look today almost exactly as it did 3 billion years ago?
A. The number of small objects in the solar system decreased.
B. Geologic activity on the moon increased.
C. The outer surface of the moon solidified.
D. The densest materials had moved away from the moon's surface to the core.

7 The oldest lunar rocks discovered are about 4.5 billion years old. How do these rocks compare to Earth rocks?
A. Lunar rocks contain different proportions of the elements that make up Earth rocks.
B. Lunar rocks contain water, but Earth rocks do not contain water.
C. Lunar rocks are igneous, but Earth rocks are sedimentary.
D. Lunar rocks are older than Earth rocks.

8 How do meteorites from the moon or Mars reach Earth?
A. Earth's gravity pulls meteoroids from the moon and Mars.
B. Meteorites hit the moon or Mars and eject rocks onto Earth.
C. The moon and Mars lose meteoroids into space.
D. Comets carry rocks from the moon and Mars to Earth.

9 Why have more meteorites made it to the surface of the moon than to Earth's surface?
A. The moon shields Earth from meteorites.
B. Earth is mostly covered by water.
C. The meteorites that hit the moon are larger, so they do not break up.
D. The moon has no atmosphere for protection.

Mining on the Moon

Since astronauts landed on the moon in 1969, scientists have been working toward permanent lunar bases. The biggest obstacle is the cost of transporting construction materials and life-support systems. So, scientists are developing ways to produce the materials by mining the moon's own natural resources.

Moon Mining Methods

One of the promising mining methods uses electrolysis, a process in which an electrical current is passed through a substance to change the chemical composition of the substance. Scientists hope to use electrolysis to extract iron and oxygen from lunar rocks. To test the procedure, scientists created a silicate rock like the rocks that are common on the moon. After melting the rock, they passed an electrical current through the molten rock, which caused iron and oxygen to separate from the other elements. On the moon, the extracted iron could be used to manufacture steel, and the oxygen could support human life.

Researchers also imagine using a solar-powered satellite to provide energy for everything from lunar mining to life-support systems. The satellite might use a solar concentrator and lasers to beam energy to the moon's surface. There, the laser light would be converted into electricity.

Ice Mines

Another important substance that might be mined on the moon is water in the form of ice. Many scientists think that the amount of ice that has been discovered in the craters near the poles could be of practical use. This ice was discovered where the crater rims have shielded the ice from the sun's rays and prevented it from melting.

▲ Lunar mining operations might look something like this.

Mining the moon may not be possible for many years to come. But scientists continue to develop the technology to make it possible. In addition to developing the necessary technology, many more geological studies of the moon are necessary before undertaking such a project. If mining the moon were profitable, it would help secure funding for future space exploration by opening the door to private commercial ventures.

◄ Apollo astronauts discovered valuable materials on the moon.

Extension

1. **Making Inferences** Why would solar energy be important for a lunar mining operation?

Chapter 29 — The Sun

Sections
1 Structure of the Sun
2 Solar Activity

What You'll Learn
- How the sun's interior differs from its surface layers
- How sunspots and other solar activity vary during an 11-year cycle

Why It's Relevant
The sun is the energy source that fuels most life on Earth. Understanding how the sun's energy affects Earth helps people understand how Earth interacts with the sun.

PRE-READING ACTIVITY

Table Fold
Before you read this chapter, create the FoldNote entitled "Table Fold" described in the Skills Handbook section of the Appendix. Label the columns of the table fold with "Characteristics of the sun," "Energy of the sun," "Composition of the sun," and "Layers of the sun." As you read the chapter, write examples of each topic under the appropriate column.

▶ Huge plumes of hot gas that are many times the size of Earth, called *prominences,* are occasionally visible in the sun's atmosphere. The hottest parts of the sun shown in this false-color image are white, and the coolest areas are dark red.

California Content Standards

1a Students know how the differences and similarities among the sun, the terrestrial planets, and the gas planets may have been established during the formation of the solar system.
1e Students know the Sun is a typical star and is powered by nuclear reactions, primarily the fusion of hydrogen to form helium.
IE.1a Students will select and use appropriate tools and technology (such as computer-linked probes, spreadsheets, and graphing calculators) to perform tests, collect data, analyze relationships and display data.
IE.1c Students will identify possible reasons for inconsistent results, such as sources of error or uncontrolled conditions
IE.1d Students will formulate explanations using logic and evidence.
IE.1g Students will recognize the usefulness and limitations of models and theories as scientific representations of reality.
IE.1i Students will analyze the locations, sequences, or time intervals that are characteristic of natural phenomena (e.g., relative ages of rocks, locations of planets over time, and succession of species in an ecosystem).

Structure of the Sun

California Content Standards

1e Students know the Sun is a typical star and is powered by nuclear reactions, primarily the fusion of hydrogen to form helium.

IE.1d Students will formulate explanations using logic and evidence.
IE.1g Students will recognize the usefulness and limitations of models and theories as scientific representations of reality.

Throughout much of human history, people thought that the sun's energy came from fire. People knew that burning a piece of coal or wood produced heat and light. They assumed that the sun, too, burned some type of fuel to produce its energy. But less than 100 years ago, scientists discovered that the source of the sun's energy is quite different from fire.

The Sun's Energy

The sun appears to the unaided eye as a dazzling, brilliant ball that has no distinct features. Because the sun's brightness can damage your eyes if you look directly at the sun, astronomers look at the sun only through special filters. Astronomers often use other specialized scientific instruments to study the sun.

Composition of the Sun

Scientists break up the sun's light into a spectrum (plural, *spectra*) by using a device called a *spectrograph*. Dark lines form in the spectra of stars when gases in the stars' outer layers absorb specific wavelengths of the light that passes through the layers. The temperature of these outer layers determines which gases produce visible spectral lines. By studying the spectrum of a star, scientists can determine the amounts of elements that are present in a star's atmosphere. They can also deduce the temperature, density, and pressure of the gas. Because each element produces a unique pattern of spectral lines, astronomers can match the spectral lines of starlight to those of Earth's elements, as shown in **Figure 1,** and identify the elements in the star's atmosphere.

Both hydrogen and helium occur in the sun. About 75% of the sun's mass is hydrogen, and hydrogen and helium together make up about 99% of the sun's mass. The sun's spectrum reveals that the sun contains traces of almost all other chemical elements.

OBJECTIVES

▶ **Explain** how the sun converts matter into energy in its core. 🐻 1e

▶ **Compare** the radiative and convective zones of the sun. 🐻 1e

▶ **Describe** the three layers of the sun's atmosphere. 🐻 1e

KEY TERMS

nuclear fusion
radiative zone
convective zone
photosphere
chromosphere
corona

Hydrogen

Sun's spectrum

Figure 1 ▶ When light passes through hydrogen gas and then through a slit in a prism, dark lines appear in the spectrum. Hydrogen and lines from other elements in the solar spectrum are shown in the bottom spectrograph. *How many lines are not accounted for by the presence of hydrogen in the sun's atmosphere?*

Figure 2 ▶ In the core of the sun, the nuclei of hydrogen atoms fuse to form helium. The fusion process converts mass into energy.

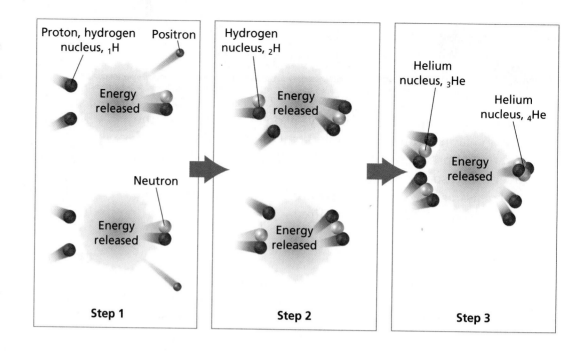

Proton, hydrogen nucleus, $_1$H   Positron

Energy released

Neutron

Energy released

Step 1

Hydrogen nucleus, $_2$H

Energy released

Energy released

Step 2

Helium nucleus, $_3$He

Helium nucleus, $_4$He

Energy released

Step 3

nuclear fusion the process by which nuclei of small atoms combine to form a new, more massive nucleus; the process releases energy

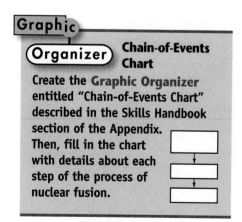

Graphic

Organizer **Chain-of-Events Chart**

Create the **Graphic Organizer** entitled "Chain-of-Events Chart" described in the Skills Handbook section of the Appendix. Then, fill in the chart with details about each step of the process of nuclear fusion.

Nuclear Fusion

A powerful atomic process known as nuclear fusion occurs inside the sun. **Nuclear fusion** is the process of combining nuclei of small atoms to form more-massive nuclei. Fusion releases huge amounts of energy. Nuclei of hydrogen atoms are the primary fuel for the sun's fusion. A hydrogen atom, the simplest of all atoms, commonly consists of only one electron and one proton. Inside the sun, however, electrons are stripped from the protons by the sun's intense heat.

Nuclear fusion produces most of the sun's energy and consists of three steps, as shown in **Figure 2.** In the first step, two hydrogen nuclei, or *protons*, collide and fuse. In this step, the positive charge of one of the protons is neutralized as that proton emits a particle called a *positron*. As a result, the proton becomes a neutron and changes the original two protons into a proton-neutron pair. In the second step, another proton combines with this proton-neutron pair to produce a nucleus made up of two protons and one neutron. In the third step, two nuclei made up of two protons and one neutron collide and fuse. As this fusion happens, two protons are released. The remaining two protons and two neutrons are fused together and form a helium nucleus. During each step of the reaction, energy is released.

The Final Product

One of the final products of the fusion of hydrogen in the sun is always a helium nucleus. The helium nucleus has about 0.7% less mass than the hydrogen nuclei that combined to form it do. The lost mass is converted into energy during the series of fusion reactions that forms helium. The energy released during the three steps of nuclear fusion causes the sun to shine and gives the sun its high temperature.

Mass Changing into Energy

The sun's energy comes from fusion, and the mass that is lost during fusion becomes energy. In 1905, the physicist Albert Einstein, then an unknown patent-office worker, proposed that a small amount of matter yields a large amount of energy. At the time, the existence of nuclear fusion was unknown. In fact, scientists had not yet discovered the nucleus of the atom. Einstein's proposal was part of his special theory of relativity. This theory included the equation $E = mc^2$. In this equation, E represents energy produced; m represents the mass, or the amount of matter, that is changed; and c represents the speed of light, which is about 300,000 km/s. Einstein's equation can be used to calculate the amount of energy produced from a given amount of matter.

By using Einstein's equation, astronomers were able to explain the huge quantities of energy produced by the sun. The sun changes more than 600 million tons of hydrogen into helium every second. Yet this amount of hydrogen is small compared with the total mass of hydrogen in the sun. During fusion, a type of subatomic particle, called a *neutrino*, is given off. Neutrinos escape the sun and reach Earth in about eight minutes. Studies of these particles indicate that the sun is fueled by the fusion of hydrogen into helium. One apparatus that collects these particles is shown in **Figure 3**. Elements other than hydrogen can fuse, too. In stars that are hotter than the sun, energy is produced by fusion reactions of the nuclei of carbon, nitrogen, and oxygen.

Reading Check How did the equation $E = mc^2$ help scientists understand the energy of the sun? (See the Appendix for answers to Reading Checks.)

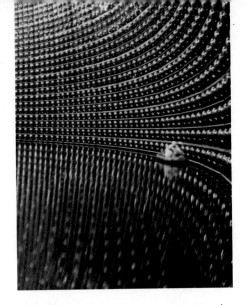

Figure 3 ▶ In Japan, this giant tank of pure water, which was only partly filled when the photo was taken, captures subatomic particles that fly out of the sun during nuclear fusion.

QuickLAB 5 min

Modeling Fusion 📖 1e, IE.1g

Procedure

1. Mark **six coins** by using a **marker** or **wax pencil**. Put a *P* for "proton" on the head side of each coin and an *N* for "neutron" on the tail side of the coins.

2. Place two coins P-side up. These two protons each represent hydrogen's simplest isotope, H. Model the fusion of these two H nuclei by placing them such that their edges touch. When they touch, flip one of them to be N-side up. This flip represents a proton becoming a neutron during fusion. The resulting nucleus, which consists of one proton and one neutron, represents the isotope hydrogen-2, ^{2}H.

3. To model the next step of nuclear fusion, place a third coin, P-side up, against the ^{2}H nucleus from step 2. This forms the isotope helium-3, or ^{3}He.

4. Repeat steps 2 and 3 to form a second ^{3}He nucleus.

5. Next, model the fusion of two ^{3}He nuclei. Move the two ^{3}He nuclei formed in step 3 so that their edges touch. When the two ^{3}He nuclei touch, move two of the protons in the two ^{3}He nuclei away from the other four particles. These four particles form a new nucleus: helium-4, or ^{4}He.

Analysis

1. Large amounts of energy are released when nuclei combine. How many energy-producing reactions did you model?

2. Create a diagram that shows the formation of ^{4}He.

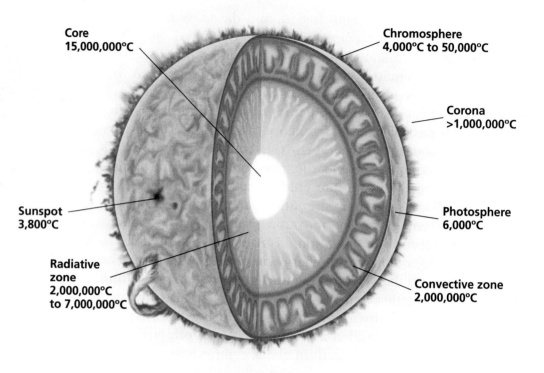

Figure 4 ▶ Energy released by fusion reactions in the core slowly works its way through the layers of the sun by the processes of radiation and convection.

Core
15,000,000°C

Chromosphere
4,000°C to 50,000°C

Corona
>1,000,000°C

Sunspot
3,800°C

Photosphere
6,000°C

Radiative
zone
2,000,000°C
to 7,000,000°C

Convective zone
2,000,000°C

The Sun's Interior

Scientists can't see inside the sun. But computer models have revealed what the invisible layers may be like. In recent years, careful studies of motions on the sun's surface have supplied more detail about what is happening inside the sun. The parts of the sun are shown in **Figure 4.**

The Core

At the center of the sun is the core. The core makes up 25% of the sun's total diameter of 1,390,000 km. The temperature of the sun's core is about 15,000,000°C. No liquid or solid can exist at such a high temperature. The core, like the rest of the sun, is made up entirely of ionized gas. The mass of the sun is 300,000 times the mass of Earth. Because of the sun's large mass, the pressure from the sun's material is so great that the center of the sun is more than 10 times as dense as iron.

The enormous pressure and high temperature of the sun's core cause the atoms to separate into nuclei and electrons. On Earth, atoms generally consist of a nucleus surrounded by one or more electrons. Within the core of the sun, however, the energy and pressure strip electrons away from the atomic nuclei. The nuclei have positive charges, so they tend to push away from each other. But the high temperature and pressure force the nuclei close enough to fuse. The most common nuclear reaction that occurs inside the sun is the fusion of hydrogen into helium.

The Radiative Zone

Before reaching the sun's atmosphere, the energy produced in the core moves through two zones of the sun's interior. The zone surrounding the core is called the **radiative zone.** The temperature in this zone ranges from about 2,000,000°C to 7,000,000°C. In the radiative zone, energy moves outward in the form of electromagnetic waves, or radiation.

The Convective Zone

Surrounding the radiative zone is the **convective zone,** where temperatures are about 2,000,000°C. Energy produced in the core moves through this zone by convection. *Convection* is the transfer of energy by moving matter. On Earth, boiling water carries energy upward by convection. In the sun's convective zone, hot gases carry energy to the sun's surface. As the hot gases move outward and expand, they lose energy. The cooling gases become denser than the other gases and sink to the bottom of the convective zone. There, the cooled gases are heated by the energy from the radiative zone and rise again. Thus, energy is transferred to the sun's surface as the gases rise and sink.

The Sun's Atmosphere

Surrounding the convective zone is the sun's atmosphere. Although the sun is made of gases, the term *atmosphere* refers to the uppermost region of solar gases. This region has three layers—the photosphere, the chromosphere, and the corona.

The Photosphere

The innermost layer of the solar atmosphere is the **photosphere.** *Photosphere* means "sphere of light." The photosphere is made of gases that have risen from the convective zone. The temperature in the photosphere is about 6,000°C. Much of the energy given off from the photosphere is in the form of visible light. The layers above the photosphere are transparent, so the visible light is the light that is seen from Earth. A photo of the sun's photosphere is shown in **Figure 5.** The dark spots are cool areas of about 3,800°C and are called *sunspots.*

✔ **Reading Check** What layers make up the sun's atmosphere? (See the Appendix for answers to Reading Checks.)

radiative zone the zone of the sun's interior that is between the core and the convective zone and in which energy moves by radiation

convective zone the region of the sun's interior that is between the radiative zone and the photosphere and in which energy is carried upward by convection

photosphere the visible surface of the sun

Figure 5 ▶ The photosphere is referred to as the sun's surface because this layer is the visible surface of the sun.

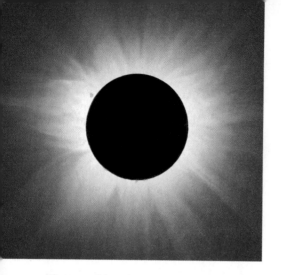

Figure 6 ▶ The corona of the sun becomes visible during a total solar eclipse.

chromosphere the thin layer of the sun that is just above the photosphere and that glows a reddish color during eclipses

corona the outermost layer of the sun's atmosphere

The Chromosphere

Above the photosphere lies the **chromosphere,** or color sphere. The chromosphere is a thin layer of gases that glows with reddish light that is typical of the color given off by hydrogen. The chromosphere's temperature ranges from 4,000°C to 50,000°C. The gases of the chromosphere move away from the photosphere. In an upward movement, gas regularly forms narrow jets of hot gas that shoot outward to form the chromosphere and then fade away within a few minutes. Some of these jets reach heights of 16,000 km.

Spacecraft study the sun from above Earth's atmosphere. These spacecraft can detect small details on the sun because they measure wavelengths of light that are blocked by Earth's atmosphere. Movies made from these spacecraft images show how features on the sun rise, change, and sometimes twist.

The Sun's Outer Parts

The outermost layer of the sun's atmosphere is the **corona** (kuh ROH nuh), or crown. The corona is a huge region of gas that has a temperature above 1,000,000°C. The corona is not very dense, but its magnetic field can stop most subatomic particles from escaping into space. However, electrons and electrically charged particles called *ions* do stream out into space as the corona expands. These particles make up the *solar wind,* which flows outward from the sun to the rest of the solar system.

The chromosphere and the corona are normally not seen from Earth because the sky during the day is too bright. Occasionally, however, the moon moves between Earth and the sun and blocks out the light of the photosphere. The sky darkens, and the corona becomes visible, as shown in **Figure 6.**

Section 1 Review

1. **Describe** how scientists use spectra to determine the composition of stars.

2. **Identify** the two elements that make up most of the sun. 🐘 1e

3. **Identify** the end products of the nuclear fusion process that occurs in the sun. 🐘 1e

4. **Explain** how the sun converts matter into energy in its core. 🐘 1e

5. **Compare** the radiative and convective zones of the sun. 🐘 1e

6. **Describe** the three layers of the sun's atmosphere. 🐘 1e

7. **Explain** why the sun's corona can be seen during an eclipse but not at other times.

CRITICAL THINKING

8. **Making Inferences** Describe whether the amount of hydrogen in the sun will increase or decrease over the next few million years. Explain your reasoning. 🐘 1e, IE.1d

9. **Analyzing Ideas** Why does fusion occur in the sun's core but not in other layers? 🐘 1e, IE.1d

10. **Predicting Consequences** What might happen to the solar wind if the sun lost its corona? 🐘 1e, IE.1d

CONCEPT MAPPING

11. Use the following terms to create a concept map: *sun, hydrogen, helium, nuclear fusion, core, radiative zone,* and *convective zone.* 🐘 1e

California Content Standards

1e Students know the Sun is a typical star and is powered by nuclear reactions, primarily the fusion of hydrogen to form helium.

IE.1i Students will analyze the locations, sequences, or time intervals that are characteristic of natural phenomena (e.g., relative

ages of rocks, locations of planets over time, and succession of species in an ecosystem).

The gases that make up the sun's interior and atmosphere are in constant motion. The energy produced in the sun's core and the force of gravity combine to cause the continuous rising and sinking of gases. The gases also move because the sun rotates on its axis. Because the sun is a ball of hot gases rather than a solid sphere, not all locations on the sun rotate at the same speed. Places close to the equator on the surface of the sun take 25.3 Earth days to rotate once. Points near the poles take 33 days to rotate once. On average, the sun rotates once every 27 days.

Sunspots

The movement of gases within the sun's convective zone and the movements caused by the sun's rotation produce magnetic fields. These magnetic fields cause convection to slow in parts of the convective zone. Slower convection causes a decrease in the amount of gas that is transferring energy from the core of the sun to these regions of the photosphere. In some places, the magnetic field is thousands of times stronger than it is in other places. Because less energy is being transferred, these regions of the photosphere are up to 3,000°C cooler than surrounding regions.

Although they still shine brightly, these cooler areas of the sun appear darker than the areas that surround them do. These cool, dark areas of gas within the photosphere are called **sunspots.** The photosphere has a grainy appearance called *granulation.* The area around the sunspots shown in **Figure 1** has visible granulation. A large sunspot can have a diameter of more than 100,000 km, which is several times the diameter of Earth.

OBJECTIVES

▶ **Explain** how sunspots are related to powerful magnetic fields on the sun. **IE.1i**

▶ **Compare** prominences, solar **1e** flares, and coronal mass ejections.

▶ **Describe** how the solar wind can cause auroras on Earth. **1e**

KEY TERMS

sunspot
prominence
solar flare
coronal mass ejection
aurora

sunspot a dark area of the photosphere of the sun that is cooler than the surrounding areas and that has a strong magnetic field

Figure 1 ▶ The diameter of this large sunspot is bigger than Earth's diameter. This image shows the granulation on the sun's surface.

Sunspots Recorded

Figure 2 ▶ The sunspot cycle lasts an average of 11 years. **When will the next high point in the cycle occur?**

The Sunspot Cycle

Astronomers have carefully observed sunspots for hundreds of years. Observations of sunspots showed astronomers that the sun rotates. Later, astronomers observed that the numbers and positions of sunspots vary in a cycle that lasts about 11 years.

A sunspot cycle begins when the number of sunspots is very low but begins to increase. Sunspots initially appear in groups about midway between the sun's equator and poles. The number of sunspots increases over the next few years until it reaches a peak of 100 or more sunspots. Then, sunspots at higher latitudes slowly disappear, and new ones appear closer to the sun's equator. **Figure 2** shows that after the peak, the number of sunspots begins to decrease until it reaches a minimum. Another 11-year cycle begins when the number of sunspots begins to increase again.

Solar Ejections

Many other solar activities are affected by the sunspot cycle. The *solar-activity cycle* is caused by the changing solar magnetic field. This cycle is characterized by increases and decreases in various types of solar activity, including solar ejections. Solar ejections are events in which the sun emits atomic particles. These events include prominences, solar flares, and coronal mass ejections.

Connection to ASTRONOMY

Total Solar Irradiance

Astronomers once thought that the sun's energy output remained steady. They called the amount of solar energy that a square centimeter of the top of Earth's atmosphere receives each second the *solar constant.* Earth's atmosphere causes an amount of energy that is less than the solar constant to reach Earth's surface.

Careful spacecraft observations made outside Earth's atmosphere have shown, however, that the solar constant isn't constant. Observations made by the Solar Maximum Mission first showed the effect. The solar constant is now being followed with special equipment on the Solar and Heliospheric Observatory (SOHO), the Active Cavity Radiometer Irradiance Monitor satellite (ACRIMSAT), and the Solar Radiation and Climate Experiment (SORCE) satellite. The ACRIMSAT and the SORCE satellite measure the entire range of solar radiation. Because this value changes, it is now officially called the *total solar irradiance* instead of the *solar constant. Irradiance* is simply the amount of energy that falls on a square centimeter of Earth each second. *Total*

means that the whole spectrum of sunlight is included, not just the visible part.

The total solar irradiance varies by about 0.2% over the 11-year sunspot cycle. It is highest when the sunspot cycle is at its maximum. Individual sunspots, however, can temporarily block a small amount of the energy that comes from the sun and thus lower the total solar irradiance.

The SORCE satellite is being used to follow total solar irradiance.

Prominences

The magnetic fields that cause sunspots also create other disturbances in the sun's atmosphere. Great clouds of glowing gases, called **prominences**, form huge arches that reach high above the sun's surface. Each solar prominence follows curved lines of magnetic force from a region of one magnetic polarity to a region of the opposite magnetic polarity. Some prominences may last for several weeks, while others may erupt and disappear in hours. The gas in prominences is very hot and is commonly associated with the chromosphere.

Solar Flares

The most violent of all solar disturbances is a **solar flare**, a sudden outward eruption of electrically charged particles, such as electrons and protons. The trigger for these eruptions is unknown. However, scientists know that solar flares release the energy stored in the strong magnetic fields of sunspots. This release of energy can lead to the formation of coronal loops, such as the ones shown in **Figure 3.**

Solar flares may travel upward thousands of kilometers within minutes, but few eruptions last more than an hour. During a peak in the sunspot cycle, 5 to 10 solar flares may occur each day. The temperature of the gas in solar flares may reach 20,000,000°C. Some of the particles from a solar flare escape into space. These particles increase the strength of the solar wind.

Coronal Mass Ejections

Particles also escape into space as **coronal mass ejections,** or parts of the corona that are thrown off the sun. As the gusts of particles strike Earth's *magnetosphere*, or the space around Earth that contains a magnetic field, the particles can generate a sudden disturbance in Earth's magnetic field. These disturbances are called *geomagnetic storms*. Although several small geomagnetic storms may occur each month, the average number of severe storms is less than one per year.

Geomagnetic storms have been known to interfere with radio communications on Earth. The high-energy particles that circulate in Earth's outer atmosphere during geomagnetic storms can also damage satellites. They can also lead to blackouts when power lines become overloaded. Not all solar activity is so dramatic, but the activity of the sun affects Earth every day.

✔ **Reading Check** How do coronal mass ejections affect communications on Earth? (See the Appendix for answers to Reading Checks.)

Figure 3 ▶ A loop of coronal gas can arch half a million kilometers or more above the sun's surface.

prominence a loop of relatively cool, incandescent gas that extends above the photosphere

solar flare an explosive release of energy that comes from the sun and that is associated with magnetic disturbances on the sun's surface

coronal mass ejection a part of coronal gas that is thrown into space from the sun

MATHPRACTICE

Magnetic Fields

Magnetic fields on the sun differ greatly from each other. Field densities at the poles are 0.001 teslas (T), while field densities near sunspots are up to 0.3 T. How many times the densities of fields at the sun's poles are densities of fields near sunspots?

Figure 4 ▶ Auroras, such as these over Canada, can fill the entire sky. When high-energy particles strike oxygen atoms in the upper atmosphere, green curtains form. When low-energy particles strike oxygen atoms, red curtains form.

aurora colored light produced by charged particles from the solar wind and from the magnetosphere that react with and excite the oxygen and nitrogen of Earth's upper atmosphere; usually seen in the sky near Earth's magnetic poles

Auroras

On Earth, a spectacular effect of the interaction between the solar wind and Earth's magnetosphere is the appearance in the sky of bands of light called **auroras** (aw RAWR uhz). **Figure 4** shows an example of an aurora. Auroras are usually seen close to Earth's magnetic poles because electrically charged particles are guided toward Earth's magnetic poles by Earth's magnetosphere. The electrically charged particles strike the atoms and gas molecules in the upper atmosphere and produce colorful sheets of light. Depending on which pole they are near, auroras are called *northern lights*—or *aurora borealis* (aw RAWR uh BAWR ee AL is)—or *southern lights*—or *aurora australis*.

Auroras normally occur between 100 and 1,000 km above Earth's surface. They are most frequent just after a peak in the sunspot cycle, especially after solar flares occur. Across the northern contiguous United States, auroras are visible about five times per year. In Alaska, however, people can see auroras almost every clear, dark night. Astronauts in orbit can also look down on Earth and see auroras. But Earth is not the only planet that has auroras. Spacecraft have recorded auroras on Jupiter and Saturn.

Section 2 Review

1. **Explain** why sunspots are cooler than surrounding areas on the sun's surface. 🐾 1e

2. **Identify** the number of sunspots that are on the sun during the peak of the sunspot cycle. 🐾 IE.1i

3. **Summarize** how the latitude of sunspots varies during the sunspot cycle. 🐾 IE.1i

4. **Explain** how prominences are different from solar flares. 🐾 1e

5. **Summarize** the cause of auroras on Earth. 🐾 1e

CRITICAL THINKING

6. **Identifying Relationships** How can a sunspot be bright but look dark? 🐾 1e, IE.1d

7. **Analyzing Ideas** Why doesn't the whole sun rotate at the same rate? 🐾 1e, IE.1d

CONCEPT MAPPING

8. Use the following terms to create a concept map: *sunspot, prominence, solar flare, solar-activity cycle,* and *coronal mass ejection.*

The Genesis Mission

What makes up the sun? Are the materials that make up Earth the same as those that make up other planets? These are only a few of the questions that NASA hoped an ambitious project called *The Genesis Mission* would answer.

Collecting Solar Wind

The Genesis mission began on August 8, 2001, when NASA launched its *Genesis* spacecraft. The spacecraft traveled 1.5 million kilometers toward the sun to an area called *Lagrange Point 1* (L1). L1 is a point in space outside Earth's magnetic field where the gravitational pulls of Earth and the sun are balanced.

Once at L1, the *Genesis* spacecraft collected electrically charged particles called *ions,* which make up solar wind. The spacecraft's solar collector contained pure materials that trapped the solar ions that collided with the collector. Another device, called the *concentrator,* consolidated the ions. The spacecraft's solar wind monitors collected data and helped coordinate the motions of the solar collectors and the concentrator. On April 1, 2004, after two years of collecting particles, the collectors were shut down in preparation for their scheduled September 8, 2004, return to Earth.

▶ The *Genesis* spacecraft collected solar wind particles.

Bringing the Sun to Earth

During the return to Earth, Genesis's parachute failed to open and the space capsule crashed into the Utah desert at nearly 200 mi/h. Scientists transported the damaged canister containing the collectors to a specially built clean room. Clean rooms are rooms in which specialized air filters and flooring reduce the number of airborne particles that may contaminate the samples.

Despite the crash, scientists remain hopeful that the samples recovered from the canister will provide enough data to help them measure the composition of the solar wind. The composition of the solar wind can be used to indirectly measure the abundance of isotopes and elements in the sun. Scientists hope to compare isotope data with data collected from comets, asteroids, and other bodies that formed at the beginning of our solar system.

Extension

1. **Evaluating Conclusions**
   Research the results of the scientists' investigation of Genesis's canister.

Chapter 30

Stars, Galaxies, and the Universe

Sections

1 Characteristics of Stars

2 Stellar Evolution

3 Star Groups

4 The Big Bang Theory

What You'll Learn

- How stars are organized by their characteristics
- How stars form and die
- How stars are grouped into clusters and galaxies
- What the universe is like and how it formed

Why It's Relevant

Our solar system is only one small part of the universe. By studying stars and galaxies, we can learn more about the formation and evolution of our universe.

PRE-READING ACTIVITY

FOLDNOTES

Layered Book Before you read this chapter, create the FoldNote entitled "Layered Book" described in the Skills Handbook section of the Appendix. Label the tabs of the layered book with "Star types," "Stellar evolution," "Star groups," and "Origin of the universe." As you read the chapter, write information you learn about each category under the appropriate tab.

▶ New stars are currently forming in the Tarantula nebula, an enormous region of dust and ionized gas.

California Content Standards

1b Students know the evidence from Earth and moon rocks indicates that the solar system was formed from a nebular cloud of dust and gas approximately 4.6 billion years ago.

1d Students know the evidence indicating that the planets are much closer to Earth than the stars are.

1e Students know the Sun is a typical star and is powered by nuclear reactions, primarily the fusion of hydrogen to form helium.

2a Students know the solar system is located in an outer edge of the disc-shaped Milky Way galaxy, which spans 100,000 light years.

2b Students know galaxies are made of billions of stars and comprise most of the visible mass of the universe.

2d Students know that stars differ in their life cycles, and that visual, radio, and X-ray telescopes may be used to collect data that reveal those differences.

2f* Students know the evidence indicating that the color, brightness, and evolution of a star are determined by a balance between gravitational collapse and nuclear fusion.

2g* Students know how the red-shift from distant galaxies and the cosmic background radiation provide evidence for the "big bang" model that suggests that the universe has been expanding for 10 to 20 billion years.

IE.1a Students will select and use appropriate tools and technology (such as computer-linked probes, spreadsheets, and graphing calculators) to perform tests, collect data, analyze relationships and display data.

IE.1d Students will formulate explanations using logic and evidence.

IE.1i Students will analyze the locations, sequences, or time intervals that are characteristic of natural phenomena (e.g., relative ages of rocks, locations of planets over time, and succession of species in an ecosystem).

IE.1k Students will recognize the cumulative nature of scientific evidence.

IE.1l Students will analyze situations and solve problems that require combining and applying concepts from more than one area of science.

Stellar Motion

Two kinds of motion are associated with stars—actual motion and apparent motion. Because stars are so far from Earth, their actual motion can be measured only with high-powered telescopes and other specialized instruments. Apparent motion, on the other hand, is much more noticeable.

Apparent Motion of Stars

The *apparent motion* of stars, or motion visible to the unaided eye, is caused by the movement of Earth. By aiming a camera at the sky and leaving the shutter open for a few hours, you can photograph the apparent motion of the stars. The curves of light in **Figure 3** record the apparent motion of stars in the northern sky. The circular trails make it seem as though the stars are moving counter-clockwise around a central star called Polaris, or the North Star. The circular pattern is caused by the rotation of Earth on its axis. Polaris is almost directly above the North Pole, and thus the star does not appear to move much.

Earth's revolution around the sun causes the stars to appear to move in a second way. Stars located on the side of the sun opposite Earth are obscured by the sun. As Earth orbits the sun, however, different stars become visible during different seasons. The visible stars appear to shift slightly to the west every night. Each night, most stars appear a small distance farther across the sky than they were the night before. After many months, they may finally disappear below the western horizon.

Reading Check Why does Polaris appear to remain stationary in the night sky? (See the Appendix for answers to Reading Checks.)

Figure 3 ▶ Stars appear as curved trails in this long-exposure photograph. These trails result from the rotation of Earth on its axis.

Circumpolar Stars

Some stars are always visible in the night sky. These stars never pass below the horizon in either their nightly or annual movements. In the Northern Hemisphere, the movement of these stars makes them appear to circle Polaris, the North Star. These circling stars are called *circumpolar stars*. The stars of the Little Dipper are circumpolar for most observers in the Northern Hemisphere. At the North Pole, all visible stars are circumpolar. The farther the observer moves from the North Pole toward the equator, the fewer circumpolar stars the observer will be able to see.

Actual Motion of Stars

Most stars have several types of *actual motion*. First, they rotate on an axis. Second, they may revolve around another star. Third, they either move away from or toward our solar system.

From a star's spectrum, astronomers can learn more about how that star is moving in space. The spectrum of a star that is moving toward or away from Earth appears to shift, as shown in **Figure 4.** The apparent shift in the wavelength of light emitted by a light source moving toward or away from an observer is called the **Doppler effect.** The colors in the spectrum of a star moving toward Earth are shifted slightly toward blue. This shift, called *blue shift,* occurs because the light waves from a star appear to have shorter wavelengths as the star moves toward Earth.

A star moving away from Earth has a spectrum that is shifted slightly toward red. This shift, called *red shift,* occurs because the wavelengths of light appear to be longer. Distant galaxies have red-shifted spectra, which indicates that these galaxies are moving away from Earth.

Doppler effect an observed change in the frequency of a wave when the source or observer is moving

Figure 4 ▶ The light from stars is shifted based on the star's movement in relationship to Earth. For example, light from stars that are moving away from Earth is shifted slightly toward the red end of the spectrum.

✓ **Reading Check** What causes starlight to shift toward the red end of the spectrum? (See the Appendix for answers to Reading Checks.)

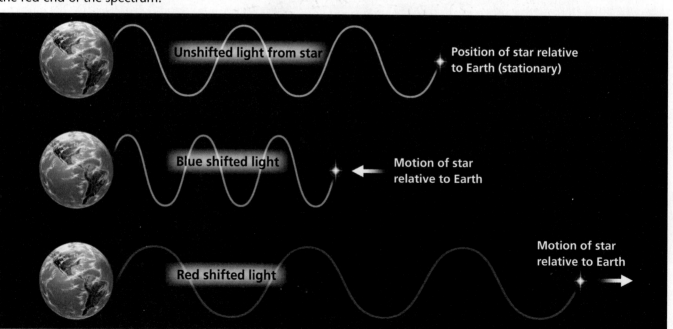

Unshifted light from star — Position of star relative to Earth (stationary)

Blue shifted light — Motion of star relative to Earth

Red shifted light — Motion of star relative to Earth

Distances to Stars

Because space is so vast, distances between the stars and Earth are measured in light-years. A **light-year** is the distance that light travels in one year. Because the speed of light is 300,000 km/s, light travels about 9.46 trillion km in one year. The light you see when you look at a star left that star sometime in the past. Light from the sun, for example, takes about 8 minutes to reach Earth. The sun is therefore 8 light-minutes from Earth. When we witness an event on the sun, such as a solar flare, the event actually took place about 8 minutes before we saw it.

Apart from the sun, the star nearest Earth is Proxima Centauri. This star is 4.2 light-years from Earth, nearly 300,000 times the distance from Earth to the sun. Polaris is about 430 light-years from Earth. When you look at Polaris, you see the star the way it was 430 years ago.

For relatively close stars, scientists can determine a star's distance by measuring **parallax,** the apparent shift in a star's position when viewed from different locations. As Earth orbits the sun, observers can study the stars from different perspectives, as shown in **Figure 5.** As Earth moves halfway around its orbit, a nearby star will appear to shift slightly relative to stars that are farther from Earth. The closer the star is to Earth, the larger the shift will be. Using this method, astronomers can calculate the distance to any star within 1,000 light-years of Earth.

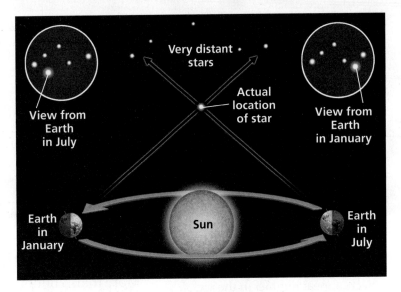

Figure 5 ▶ Observers on Earth see nearby stars against those in the distant background. The movement of Earth causes nearby stars to appear to move back and forth each year.

light-year the distance that light travels in one year

parallax an apparent shift in the position of an object when viewed from different locations

---

QuickLAB   15 min

Parallax 📖 1d, 2d, IE.1d
Procedure
1. Use a **metric ruler** and **scissors** to cut **five 1 m lengths of thread.** Use **masking tape** to tape one end of each piece of thread to the edge of a **paper plate.** Each plate should have the same diameter. One plate should be red, and four should be blue.
2. Stand on a **ladder,** and tape the free end of each piece of thread to the ceiling at various heights. Place the thread 30 cm apart in a staggered pattern. Hang the plates in a location that allows the widest field of view and movement.
3. Stand directly in front of and facing the red plate at a distance of several meters.
4. Close one eye, and sketch the position of the red plate in relation to the blue plates.

5. Take several steps back and to the right. Repeat step 4.
6. Take several more steps and make another sketch.
7. Repeat step 6.

Analysis
1. Compare your drawings. Did the red plate change position as you viewed it from different locations? Explain your answer.
2. What results would you expect if you continued to repeat step 6? Explain your answer.
3. If you noted the positions of several stars by using a powerful telescope, what would you expect to observe about their positions if you saw the same stars six months later? Explain.

Figure 6 ▶ The sun, which has an apparent magnitude of –26.8, is the brightest object in our sky. All other objects appear dimmer in the sky, so their apparent magnitudes are higher on the scale.

apparent magnitude the brightness of a star as seen from the Earth

absolute magnitude the brightness that a star would have at a distance of 32.6 light-years from Earth

Stellar Brightness

More than 3 billion stars can be seen through telescopes on Earth. Of these, only about 6,000 are visible without a telescope. Billions more stars can be observed from Earth-orbiting telescopes, such as the *Hubble Space Telescope*. The visibility of a star depends on its brightness and its distance from Earth. Astronomers use two scales to describe the brightness of a star.

The brightness of a star as it appears to us on Earth is called the star's **apparent magnitude.** The apparent magnitude of a star depends on both how much light the star emits and how far the star is from Earth. The lower the number of the star on the scale shown in **Figure 6,** the brighter the star appears to observers on Earth. The true brightness, or **absolute magnitude,** of a star is how bright the star would appear if all the stars were at a standard, uniform distance from Earth. The brighter a star actually is, the lower the number of its absolute magnitude.

Section 1 Review

1. **Describe** what astronomers analyze to determine the composition and surface temperature of a star. 2d

2. **Compare** the mass of the sun with the masses of most other stars in the universe. 2d

3. **Explain** why, as you observe the night sky over time, stars appear to move westward across the sky. 1d

4. **Describe** the units used to measure the distance to stars in terms of whether their starlight takes minutes or years to reach Earth.

5. **Describe** the method astronomers use to measure the distance to stars that are less than 1,000 light-years from Earth.

6. **Explain** the difference between apparent magnitude and absolute magnitude.

CRITICAL THINKING

7. **Identifying Relationships** How does the movement of Earth affect the apparent movement of stars in the sky? 1d, IE.1d

8. **Analyzing Ideas** Why is it better for astronomers to measure parallax by observing every six months instead of observing every year? 1d, IE.1d

9. **Understanding Relationships** If two stars have the same absolute magnitude, but one of the stars is farther from Earth than the other one, which star would appear brighter in the night sky? IE.1d

CONCEPT MAPPING

10. Use the following terms to create a concept map: *star, apparent magnitude, red shift, Doppler effect, light-year, absolute magnitude,* and *blue shift.*

California Content Standards

2d Students know that stars differ in their life cycles and that visual, radio, and X-ray telescopes may be used to collect data that reveal those differences. **2f*** Students know the evidence indicating that the color, brightness, and evolution of a star are determined by a balance between gravitational collapse and nuclear fusion. **IE.1d** Students will formulate explanations using logic and evidence.

Because a typical star exists for billions of years, astronomers will never be able to observe one star throughout its entire lifetime. Instead, they have developed theories about the evolution of stars by studying stars in different stages of development.

Classifying Stars

Plotting the surface temperatures of stars against their *luminosity,* or the total amount of energy they give off each second, reveals a consistent pattern. The graph that illustrates this pattern is the *Hertzsprung-Russell diagram,* or *H-R diagram,* a simplified version of which is shown in **Figure 1.** The graph is named for Ejnar Hertzsprung and Henry Norris Russell, the astronomers who discovered the pattern nearly 100 years ago. The temperature of a star's surface is plotted on the horizontal axis. The luminosity of a star is plotted on the vertical axis.

Astronomers use the H-R diagram to describe the life cycles of stars. Astronomers always plot the highest temperatures on the left and the highest luminosities at the top. The temperature and luminosity for most stars falls within a band that runs diagonally through the middle of the H-R diagram. This band, which extends from cool, dim, red stars at the lower right to hot, bright, blue stars at the upper left, is known as the **main sequence.** Stars within this band are called *main-sequence stars.* The sun is one example of a main-sequence star.

OBJECTIVES

▶ **Describe** how a protostar becomes a star. **2d, 2f***

▶ **Explain** how a main-sequence star generates energy. **1e**

▶ **Describe** the evolution of a star after its main-sequence stage. **2d, 2f***

KEY TERMS

main sequence
nebula
giant
white dwarf
nova
neutron star
pulsar
black hole

main sequence the location on the H-R diagram where most stars lie; it has a diagonal pattern from the lower right to the upper left

Figure 1 ▶ **The Hertzsprung-Russell Diagram**

Figure 2 ▶ The Eagle Nebula is a region in which star formation is currently taking place. This false-color image was captured by the *Hubble Space Telescope.*

nebula a large cloud of gas and dust in interstellar space; a region in space where stars are born

MATHPRACTICE

Nuclear Fusion

The sun converts nearly 545 million metric tons of hydrogen to helium every second. In the process, approximately 3.6 million metric tons of that hydrogen mass is changed into energy and radiated into space. What percentage of the converted hydrogen is changed into radiated energy? If the sun loses 3.6 million metric tons of mass per second, how many metric tons of mass will it lose in one year?

Star Formation

A star begins in a **nebula** (NEB yu luh), a cloud of gas and dust, such as the one shown in **Figure 2.** A nebula commonly consists of about 70% hydrogen, 28% helium, and 2% heavier elements. When an outside force, such as the explosion of a nearby star compresses the cloud, some of the particles move close to each other and are pulled together by gravity.

According to Newton's *law of universal gravitation,* all objects in the universe attract each other through gravitational force. This gravitational force increases as the mass of an object increases or as the distance between two objects decreases. Therefore, as gravity pulls particles closer together, the gravitational pull of the particles on each other increases. This increase in gravitational force causes more nearby particles to be pulled toward the area of increasing mass. As more particles come together, regions of dense matter begin to build up within the cloud.

Protostars

As gravity makes these dense regions more compact, any spin the region has is greatly amplified. The shrinking, spinning region begins to flatten into a disk that has a central concentration of matter called a *protostar.* Gravitational energy is converted into heat energy as more matter is pulled into the protostar. This heat energy causes the temperature of the protostar to increase.

The protostar continues to contract and increase in temperature for several million years. Eventually, the gas becomes so hot that its electrons are stripped from their parent atoms. The nuclei and free electrons move independently, and the gas is then considered a separate state of matter called plasma. *Plasma* is a hot, ionized gas that consists of an equal number of free-moving positive ions and electrons.

The Birth of a Star

Temperature continues to increase in a protostar to about 10,000,000°C. At this temperature, nuclear fusion begins. *Nuclear fusion* is a process that occurs when extremely high temperature and pressure cause less-massive atomic nuclei to combine to form more-massive nuclei and, in the process, release enormous amounts of energy. The onset of fusion marks the birth of a star. Once nuclear fusion begins in a star, the process can continue for billions of years.

A Delicate Balancing Act

As gravity increases the pressure on the matter within the star, the rate of fusion increases. In turn, the energy radiated from fusion reactions heats the gas inside the star. The outward pressures of the radiation and the hot gas resist the inward pull of gravity. The stabilizing effect of these forces is shown in **Figure 3.** This equilibrium makes the star stable in size. A main-sequence star maintains a stable size as long as the star has an ample supply of hydrogen to fuse into helium.

Reading Check How does the pressure from fusion and hot gas interact with the force of gravity to maintain a star's stability? (See the Appendix for answers to Reading Checks.)

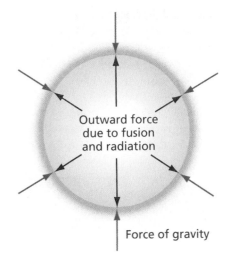

Figure 3 ▶ Stellar equilibrium is achieved when the inward force of gravity is balanced by the outward pressure from fusion and radiation inside the star.

The Main-Sequence Stage

The second and longest stage in the life of a star is the main-sequence stage. During this stage, energy continues to be generated in the core of the star as hydrogen fuses into helium. Fusion releases enormous amounts of energy. For example, when only 1 g of hydrogen is converted into helium, the energy released could keep a 100 W light bulb burning for more than 200 years.

A star that has a mass about the same as the sun's mass stays on the main sequence for about 10 billion years. More-massive stars, on the other hand, fuse hydrogen so rapidly that they may stay on the main sequence for only 10 million years. Because the universe is about 14 billion years old, massive stars that formed long ago have long since left the main sequence. Less massive stars, which are at the bottom right of the main sequence on the H-R diagram, are thought to be able to exist for hundreds of billions of years.

The stages in the life of a star cover an enormous period of time. Scientists estimate that over a period of almost 5 billion years, the sun, shown in **Figure 4**, has converted only 5% of its original hydrogen nuclei into helium nuclei. After another 5 billion years, though, with 10% of the sun's original hydrogen converted, fusion will stop in the core. When fusion stops, the sun's temperature and luminosity will change and the sun will move off the main sequence.

Figure 4 ▶ Our sun is a yellow star. It is located in the diagonal band of main-sequence stars on the H-R diagram.

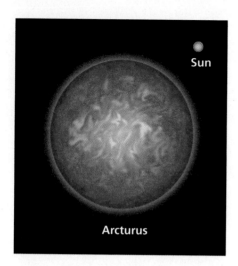

Figure 5 ▶ Arcturus is an orange giant that is about 23 times larger than the sun. Despite being about 1,000°C cooler than the sun, Arcturus gives off more than 100 times as much light as the sun does.

giant a very large and bright star whose hot core has used most of its hydrogen

Leaving the Main Sequence

A star enters its third stage when almost all of the hydrogen atoms within its core have fused into helium atoms. Without hydrogen for fuel, the core of a star contracts under the force of its own gravity. This contraction increases the temperature in the core. As the helium core becomes hotter, it transfers energy into a thin shell of hydrogen surrounding the core. This energy causes hydrogen fusion to continue in the shell of gas. The on-going fusion of hydrogen radiates energy outward, which causes the outer shell of the star to expand greatly.

Giant Stars

A star's shell of gases grows cooler as it expands. As the gases in the outer shell become cooler, they begin to glow with a reddish color. These large, red stars are known as **giants.**

Because of their large surface areas, giant stars are bright. Giants, such as the star Arcturus shown in **Figure 5,** are 10 or more times larger than the sun. Stars that contain about as much mass as the sun will become giants. As they become larger, more luminous, and cooler, they move off the main sequence. Giant stars are above the main sequence on the H-R diagram.

Supergiants

Main-sequence stars that are more massive than the sun will become larger than giants in their third stage. These highly luminous stars are called *supergiants*. These stars appear along the top of the H-R diagram. Supergiants are often at least 100 times larger than the sun. Betelgeuse, the large, orange-red star shown in **Figure 6,** is one example of a supergiant. Located in the constellation Orion, Betelgeuse is 1,000 times larger than the sun.

Though such supergiant stars make up only a small fraction of all the stars in the sky, their high luminosity makes the stars easy to find in a visual scan of the night sky. However, despite the high luminosity of supergiants, their surfaces are relatively cool.

✔ **Reading Check** Where are giants and supergiants found on the H-R diagram? (See the Appendix for answers to Reading Checks.)

Figure 6 ▶ If the sun were replaced by the red supergiant Betelgeuse, the surface of this star would be farther out than Jupiter's orbit. *How does the temperature of Betelgeuse compare with that of the sun?*

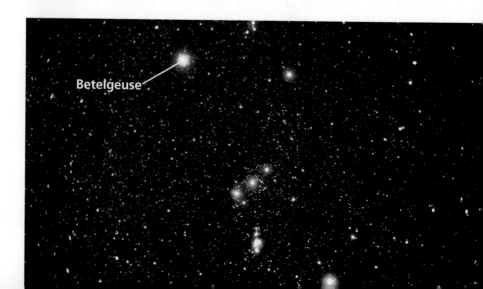

Betelgeuse

The Final Stages of a Sunlike Star

In the evolution of a medium-sized star, fusion in the core will stop after the helium atoms have fused into carbon and oxygen. With energy no longer available from fusion, the star enters its final stages.

Planetary Nebulas

As the star's outer gases drift away, the remaining core heats these expanding gases. The gases appear as a *planetary nebula*, a cloud of gas that forms around a sunlike star that is dying. Some of these clouds may form a simple sphere or ring around the star. However, many planetary nebulas form more-complex shapes. For example, the Ant nebula has a double-lobed shape, as shown in **Figure 7.**

White Dwarfs

As a planetary nebula disperses, gravity causes the remaining matter in the star to collapse inward. The matter collapses until it cannot be pressed further together. A hot, extremely dense core of matter—a **white dwarf**—is left. White dwarfs shine for billions of years before they cool completely.

White dwarfs are in the lower left of the H-R diagram. They are hot but dim. These stars are very small, about the size of Earth. As white dwarfs cool, they become fainter. This is the final stage in the life cycle of many stars.

When a white dwarf no longer gives off light, the star will become a *black dwarf.* However, this process is long, and many astronomers do not believe that any black dwarf stars yet exist.

Figure 7 ▶ The Ant nebula is a planetary nebula that is located more than 3,000 light-years from Earth in the southern constellation Norma.

white dwarf a small, hot, dim star that is the leftover center of an old star

Connection to TECHNOLOGY

Searching for Extraterrestrial Life

In 1967, scientists discovered strange, regular pulses of radio waves coming from a specific point in space. Some scientists briefly thought these pulses might be coming from an intelligent source and called them LGMs, for *Little Green Men.* Further research showed that the source of these waves was a natural phenomenon, but the idea that there might be life in the universe continued to spur scientific interest.

In 1984, the SETI Institute was founded. The name SETI stands for the Search for Extraterrestrial Intelligence. SETI is dedicated to searching for evidence of extraterrestrial life and signs of alien intelligence.

The SETI program uses telescopes all over Earth to gather data. Many of these telescopes, such as the Arecibo Observatory in Puerto Rico, gather radio data, but optical searches are also performed.

Combing through all the data that the telescopes collect is no small job. In fact, the telescopes often collect more data than SETI's computers can process. In 1998, the SETI@home project was launched by scientists at the University of California at Berkeley. This program allows anyone with a computer and an internet connection to help process the data collected.

Novas and Supernovas

Some white dwarf stars are part of a binary star system. If a white dwarf revolves around a red giant, the gravity of the very dense white dwarf may capture gases from the red giant. As these gases accumulate on the surface of the white dwarf, pressure begins to build up. This pressure may cause large explosions, which release energy and stellar material into space, to occur. Such an explosion is called a **nova.**

A nova may cause a star to become many thousands of times brighter than it normally is. However, within days, the nova begins to fade to its normal brightness. Because these explosions rarely disrupt the stability of the binary system, the process may start again and a white dwarf may become a nova several times.

A white dwarf star in a binary system may also become a *supernova,* a star that has such a tremendous explosion that it blows itself apart. Unlike an ordinary nova, a white dwarf can sometimes accumulate so much mass on its surface that gravity overwhelms the outward pressure. The star collapses and becomes so dense that the outer layers rebound and explode outward. Supernovas are thousands of times more violent than novas. The explosions of supernovas completely destroy the white dwarf star and may destroy much of the red giant.

The Final Stages of Massive Stars

Stars that have masses of more than 8 times the mass of the sun may produce supernovas without needing a secondary star to fuel them. In 1054, Chinese astronomers saw a supernova so bright that it was seen during the day for more than three weeks. At its peak, the supernova radiated an amount of energy that was equal to the output of about 400 million suns.

nova a star that suddenly becomes brighter

Life Cycle of Stars

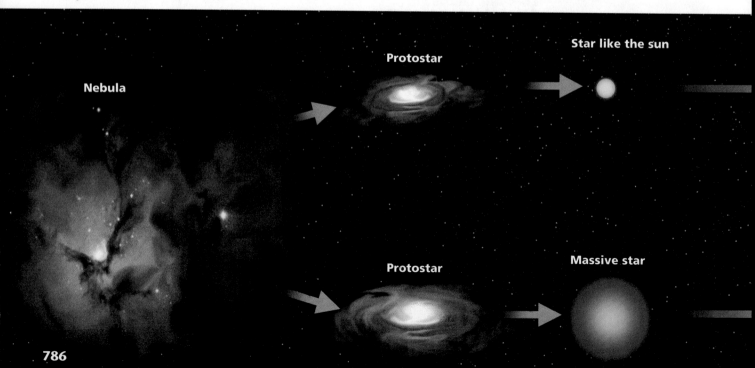

Nebula

Protostar

Star like the sun

Protostar

Massive star

Supernovas in Massive Stars

While only a small percentage of white dwarfs become supernovas, massive stars become supernovas as part of their life cycle, which is shown in **Figure 8.** After the supergiant stage, these stars contract with a gravitational force that is much greater than that of small-mass stars. The collapse produces such high pressures and temperatures that nuclear fusion begins again. This time, carbon atoms in the core of the star fuse into heavier elements such as oxygen, magnesium, or silicon.

Fusion continues until the core is almost entirely made of iron. Because iron has a very stable nuclear structure, fusion of iron into heavier elements takes energy from the star rather than giving off energy. Having used up its supply of fuel, the core begins to collapse under its own gravity. Energy released as the core collapses is transferred to the outer layers of the star, which explode outward with tremendous force. Within a few minutes, the energy released by the supernova may surpass the amount of energy radiated by a sunlike star over its entire lifetime.

✓ Reading Check What causes a supergiant star to explode as a supernova? (See the Appendix for answers to Reading Checks.)

Neutron Stars

Stars that contain about 8 or more times the mass of the sun do not become white dwarfs. After a star explodes as a supernova, the core may contract into a very small but incredibly dense ball of neutrons, called a **neutron star.** A single teaspoon of matter from a neutron star would weigh 100 million metric tons on Earth. A neutron star that has more mass than the sun may have a diameter of only about 20 km but may emit the same amount of energy as 100,000 suns. Neutron stars rotate very rapidly.

neutron star a star that has collapsed under gravity to the point that the electrons and protons have smashed together to form neutrons

Figure 8 ▶ A star the mass of the sun becomes a white dwarf near the end of its life cycle. A more massive star may become a neutron star.

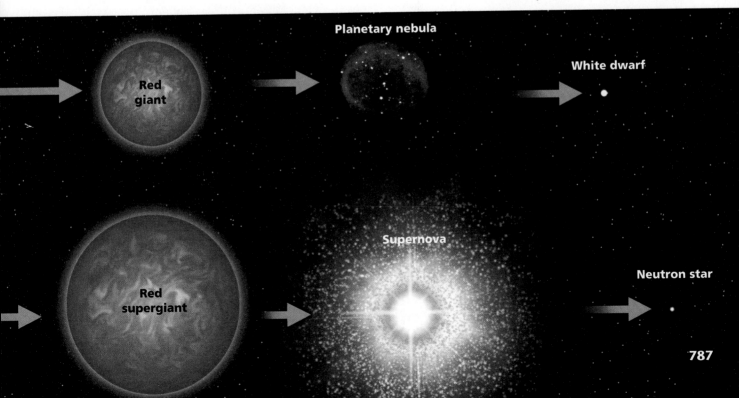

Red giant

Planetary nebula

White dwarf

Red supergiant

Supernova

Neutron star

787

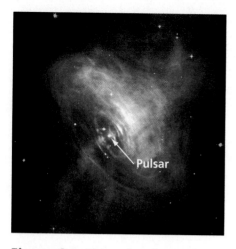

Figure 9 ▶ This pulsar, located in the heart of the Crab nebula, is still surrounded by the remains of a supernova explosion that took place less than 1,000 years ago.

pulsar a rapidly spinning neutron star that emits pulses of radio and optical energy

black hole an object so massive and dense that even light cannot escape its gravity

Pulsars

Some neutron stars emit a beam of radio waves that sweeps across space like a lighthouse light beam sweeps across water. Because we detect pulses of radio waves every time the beam sweeps by Earth, these stars are called **pulsars.** For each pulse we detect, we know that the star has rotated within that period. Newly formed pulsars, such as the one shown in **Figure 9,** are commonly surrounded by the remnants of a supernova. But most known pulsars are so old that these remnants have long since dispersed and have left behind only the spinning star.

Black Holes

Some massive stars produce leftovers too massive to become stable neutron stars. If the remaining core of a star contains more than 3 times the mass of the sun, the star may contract further under its greater gravity. The force of the contraction crushes the dense core of the star and leaves a **black hole.** The gravity of a black hole is so great that nothing, not even light, can escape it.

Because black holes do not give off light, locating them is difficult. But a black hole can be observed by its effect on a companion star. Matter from the companion star is pulled into the black hole. Just before the matter is absorbed, it swirls around the black hole. The gas becomes so hot that X rays are released. Astronomers locate black holes by detecting these X rays. Scientists then try to find the mass of the object that is affecting the companion star. Astronomers conclude that a black hole exists only if the companion star's motion shows that a massive, invisible object is present nearby.

Section 2 Review

1. **Explain** the steps that the gas in a nebula goes through as it becomes a star. 2b, 2d

2. **Describe** the process that generates energy in the core of a main-sequence star. 1e

3. **Explain** how a main-sequence star like the sun is able to maintain a stable size. 2d

4. **Describe** how nuclear fusion in a main-sequence star is different from nuclear fusion in a giant star. 1e

5. **Describe** how a star similar to the sun changes after it leaves the main-sequence stage of its life cycle. 2d

6. **Describe** what causes a nova explosion. 2d

7. **Explain** why only very massive stars can form black holes. 2d

8. **Describe** the two types of supernovas. 2d

CRITICAL THINKING

9. **Identifying Relationships** How do astronomers conclude that a supergiant star is larger than a main-sequence star of the same temperature? 2d, IE.1d

10. **Analyzing Ideas** Why would an older main-sequence star be composed of a higher percentage of helium than a young main-sequence star? 1e, IE.1d

11. **Compare and Contrast** Why does temperature increase more rapidly in a more massive protostar than in a less massive protostar? 2d, IE.1d

12. **Analyzing Ideas** How can astronomers detect a black hole if it is invisible to a normal telescope? 2d, IE.1d

CONCEPT MAPPING

13. Use the following terms to create a concept map: *main-sequence star, nebula, supergiant, white dwarf, planetary nebula, black hole, supernova, protostar, giant, pulsar,* and *neutron star.* 2d

Studying Stars in Formation

When stars are forming, they have a dim, reddish glow. As their temperature increases, they eventually become much hotter and brighter. But when they are dim and reddish, they give off most of their light in the infrared part of the spectrum. Most of this infrared light does not penetrate Earth's atmosphere, where water vapor and carbon dioxide block the light. So, astronomers have launched telescopes into space that allow them to observe stars and galaxies from above the layers of Earth's atmosphere.

The *Hubble Space Telescope*

The *Hubble Space Telescope* observes ultraviolet, visible, and infrared spectra. The telescope did not have infrared capability at first. But a camera called NICMOS, which stands for *Near Infrared Camera and Multi-Object Spectrometer,* was launched on an updating mission in which astronauts brought new equipment to the *Hubble Space Telescope.* Infrared cameras such as NICMOS have to be kept very cool, and the liquid nitrogen that originally cooled NICMOS was depleted after about two years. The next mission to the *Hubble Space Telescope* brought a new type of refrigerator to keep the camera cool.

The *Spitzer Space Telescope*

On August 25, 2003, NASA launched a new and more sensitive infrared telescope. Originally called *Space Infrared Telescope Facility,* it was renamed the *Spitzer Space Telescope.* This telescope is not orbiting Earth in the way that the *Hubble Space Telescope* does. Instead, it is far from Earth and trails Earth in its orbit around the sun. This keeps the light reflected by Earth from heating the camera.

▲ Astronauts conduct delicate repairs to the *Hubble Space Telescope* while in orbit.

The *Spitzer Space Telescope* takes images of infrared light, which has wavelengths as much as 100 times longer than the wavelengths in images taken by the *Hubble Space Telescope.* The *Spitzer Space Telescope's* high-quality images show glowing dust, cool stars, and the most distant galaxies especially well.

◀ This false-color image from the *Spitzer Space Telescope* shows the intensity of infrared emissions of the galaxy M81.

Extension

1. **Making Comparisons** What types of information can scientists determine from infrared images that they cannot determine from images taken in the visual spectrum?

California Close-Up

California's Place on Earth, page C2

Rainfall and Climate in California, page C4

California's Geologic History, page C8

California's Natural Resources, page C16

Natural Hazards in California, page C22

► California's natural beauty is evident in this photo taken at Point Lobos State Reserve. Here, the sky, the ocean, and the land all come together as if asking to be studied by Earth scientists of all types.

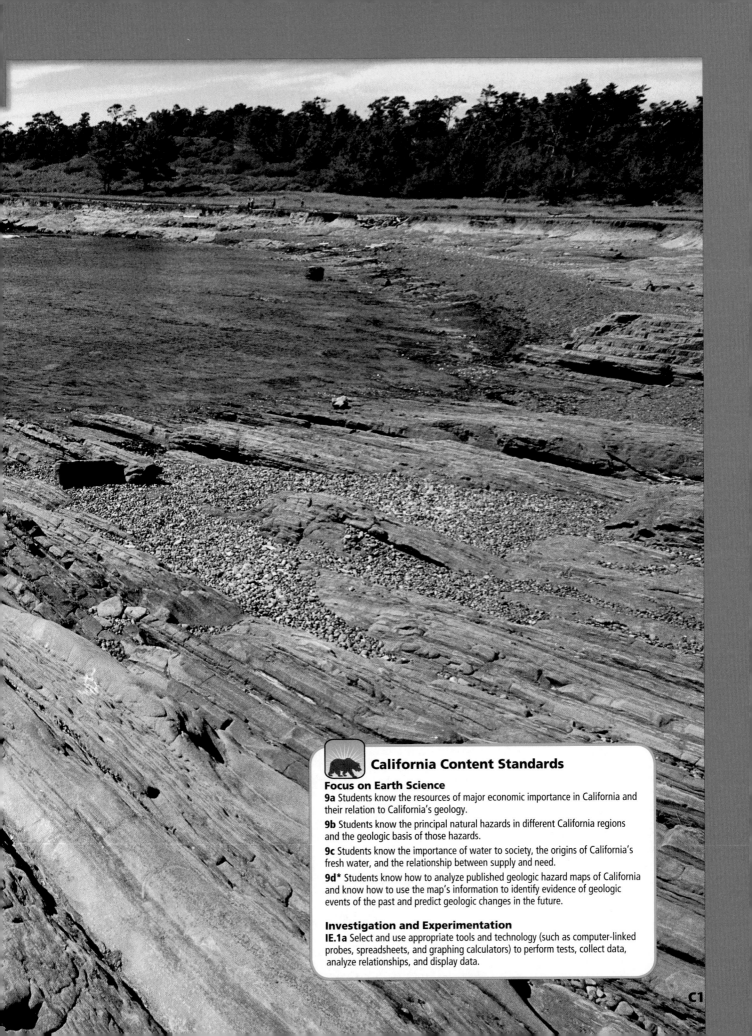

California Content Standards

Focus on Earth Science

9a Students know the resources of major economic importance in California and their relation to California's geology.

9b Students know the principal natural hazards in different California regions and the geologic basis of those hazards.

9c Students know the importance of water to society, the origins of California's fresh water, and the relationship between supply and need.

9d* Students know how to analyze published geologic hazard maps of California and know how to use the map's information to identify evidence of geologic events of the past and predict geologic changes in the future.

Investigation and Experimentation

IE.1a Select and use appropriate tools and technology (such as computer-linked probes, spreadsheets, and graphing calculators) to perform tests, collect data, analyze relationships, and display data.

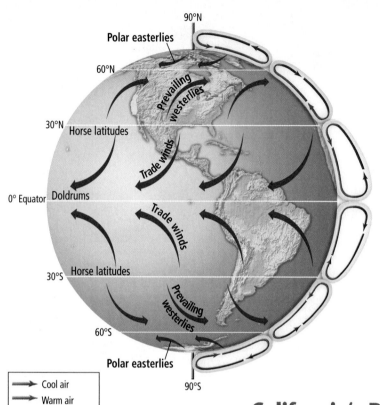

In this book, you have learned about physical processes at work in Earth's atmosphere, hydrosphere, and geosphere. In the following pages, you will learn how these physical processes affect California.

California's Place in the Atmosphere

As you can see in **Figure 1,** California is located in the Northern Hemisphere above 30°N latitude. This location puts California within the prevailing westerlies wind belt. So, the winds in California generally blow from the west, off the Pacific Ocean, to the east. However, the local patterns of wind circulation in California are determined by the state's mountains and valleys. Thus, you may encounter winds coming from different directions.

Figure 1 ▶ California (colored yellow) is located between 32°30' and 42° north latitude. Winds in these latitudes blow from west to east.

California's Place in the Hydrosphere

California's western edge meets the Pacific Ocean to form a coastline that is 1,350 km long. The ocean, therefore, is a major influence on California. An ocean current called the *California Current* flows from north to south along California's coast, as shown in **Figure 2.** This broad, slow-moving, shallow current carries cool water along the coast and moderates California's climate by cooling air that moves across the Pacific Ocean into California.

Figure 2 ▶ Cool water from the north Pacific Ocean is transported along the California coast by the California Current.

California's Place in the Geosphere

California is located near the place where three tectonic plates meet. As shown in **Figure 3,** these plates are the Pacific plate, the North American plate, and the small Juan de Fuca plate. Over time, the interaction of these three plates has made California a mountainous state.

California has two major volcanoes—Mt. Shasta (4,317 m above sea level) and Lassen Peak (3,187 m above sea level). Both volcanoes are located in the southern Cascade Mountains of northern California. California can also claim the highest and lowest points in the continental United States. Mount Whitney in the Sierra Nevada has an elevation of 4,421 m above sea level. **Figure 4** shows the eastern face of Mount Whitney.

Badwater, a salty pool in Death Valley, has an elevation of 86 m below sea level. Figure 4 shows a photo of Badwater with Telescope Peak in the Panamint Mountains shown in the distance. In fact, the elevation gain between Badwater and the summit of Telescope Peak—a horizontal distance of only 34 km—is almost 3,500 m! This difference emphasizes the great range of elevation in California.

Reading Check In what direction do winds generally blow over California? Why? (See the Appendix for answers to Reading Checks.)

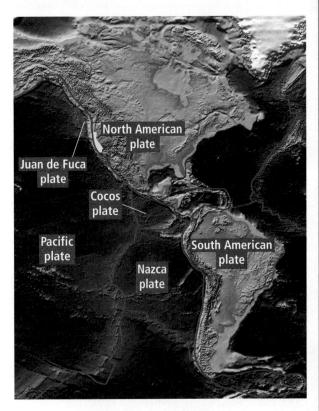

Figure 3 ▶ California is a mountainous state that is located near the point where three tectonic plates meet.

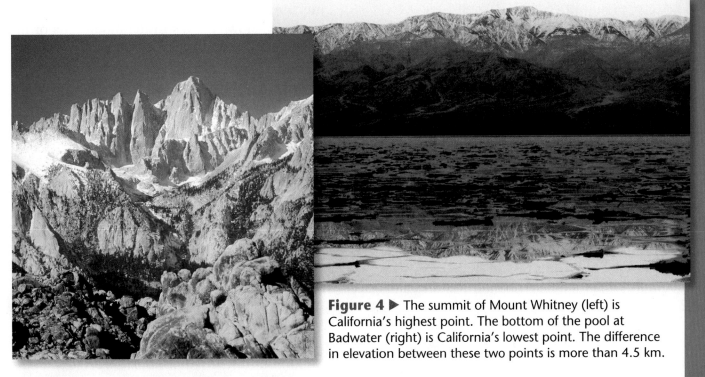

Figure 4 ▶ The summit of Mount Whitney (left) is California's highest point. The bottom of the pool at Badwater (right) is California's lowest point. The difference in elevation between these two points is more than 4.5 km.

The topography in California and California's location near the Pacific Ocean have created diverse climate patterns in the state. The climate in California ranges from cool and wet to hot and dry. Rainfall patterns have a large impact on California's climate.

Rainfall in California

The two air masses that most often cause rain in California during the winter are shown in **Figure 1.** These air masses are the Maritime Polar Pacific air mass and the Maritime Tropical Pacific air mass. As these air masses enter the mid-latitudes, they are driven across the Pacific Ocean toward California by the winds of the prevailing westerlies. As these air masses move over the Pacific Ocean, they absorb moisture from the evaporation of ocean water.

Cold Fronts

As a Maritime Polar Pacific air mass moves southeast toward California in the winter, the air mass meets warmer air from the mid-latitudes. The air mass pushes the warm air upward and forms a cold front. Rain often begins to fall over the Pacific Ocean before the cold front reaches the California coast. If rain does not begin over the ocean, then mountains will determine where rain will occur in inland California. You will learn much more about this as you continue reading. **Figure 2** shows clouds in the mountains of inland central California.

Figure 1 ▶ Two air masses directly affect the rainfall and climate of California: the Maritime Polar Pacific air mass and the Maritime Tropical Pacific air mass.

Figure 2 ▶ Low-lying clouds partially hide Cathedral Rocks in Yosemite National Park.

Rain-Shadow Zones

A map of the topography of California is shown in **Figure 3**. The map shows that mountains lie along much of the California coastline. It also shows that the highest elevations in California are in the Sierra Nevada along the eastern side of the state.

The California Coast Ranges and the Sierra Nevada create rain-shadow zones. Rainfall is heavy along the western side of the Coast Ranges and the Sierra Nevada. Much less rain, however, occurs on the eastern side of these mountains. Thus, semi-arid interior valleys and arid deserts have formed on the eastern side of the mountains. **Figure 4** contrasts the sequoia forest in the western Sierra Nevada with the arid brush of the Owens Valley on the eastern side of the Sierra Nevada.

The "Pineapple Express"

Along a cold front, conditions that cause a low-pressure, counter-clockwise circulation of the atmosphere may develop. The southern part of this circulation pattern produces southwesterly winds. As these winds move farther southward, they pull air from the Maritime Tropical Pacific air mass into southern California. The result is warm, tropical rain in southern California. The name "Pineapple Express" refers to this warm, moist air that comes from the Pacific Ocean near Hawaii.

Figure 3 ▶ The map below shows elevations within California.

Figure 4 ▶ These photos show the differences between vegetation in the Sierra Nevada and vegetation in the rain-shadow zone east of the Sierra Nevada.

Elevation in Meters

- 3,900
- 3,600
- 3,300
- 3,000
- 2,700
- 2,400
- 2,100
- 1,800
- 1,500
- 1,200
- 900
- 600
- 300
- 0
- −100

Eureka
Coast Ranges
Sacramento
San Francisco
Sierra Nevada
Owens Valley
Sequoia Forest
Coast Ranges
Los Angeles
0   100   200 Kilometers
San Diego

Annual Precipitation

Average annual precipitation in California, which includes rain, snow, and other forms, is shown in **Figure 5**. Notice that there is a relationship between California topography, which you saw in Figure 3, and average annual precipitation. That is, the mountains receive the highest annual precipitation, and the rain-shadow valleys receive very little precipitation. An example of the rain-shadow effect is shown in **Graph 1**.

You may also notice that annual precipitation decreases from north to south through the state. As cold fronts move southward through California, the cold air meets and mixes with warm air. As the air warms, rainfall stops. So, southern California receives less rainfall than does northern California. In the mountains in the northwest corner of the state, more than 305 cm (120 in.) of precipitation may fall during a year. But in the deserts in the southeastern part of the state, less than 15 cm (5 in.) of precipitation may fall during a year. In fact, differences in latitude can cause extremes in precipitation. In one year, for example, 409 cm (82.3 in.) of precipitation was recorded in the Santa Lucia Mountains along California's central coast. The town of Bagdad in the Mojave Desert of southern California, however, received no rainfall for a period of 25 months!

Figure 5 ▶ The map below shows average annual precipitation in California. Fresno, which is in the rain shadow of the coastal mountains, receives less rainfall than does San Francisco, which is located on the coast.

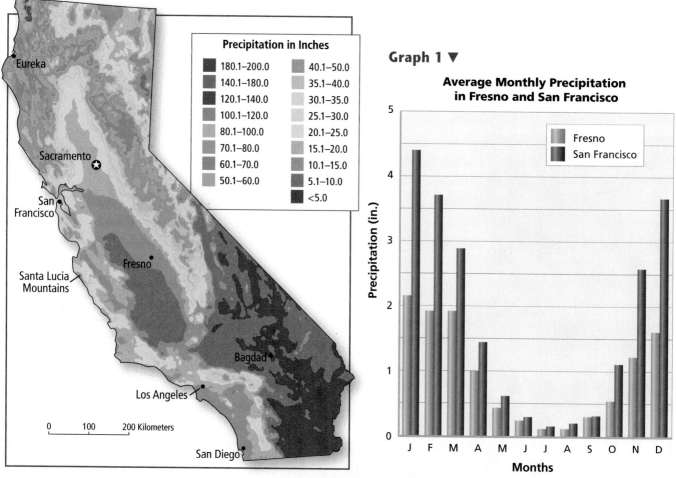

Precipitation in Inches

180.1–200.0	40.1–50.0
140.1–180.0	35.1–40.0
120.1–140.0	30.1–35.0
100.1–120.0	25.1–30.0
80.1–100.0	20.1–25.0
70.1–80.0	15.1–20.0
60.1–70.0	10.1–15.0
50.1–60.0	5.1–10.0
	<5.0

Graph 1 ▼

Average Monthly Precipitation in Fresno and San Francisco

Climate Zones in California

In California, average precipitation decreases southward. In addition, average temperatures increase southward because of a decrease in latitude. Precipitation and temperature, together with the elevation in different parts of California, produce the climate-zone patterns that are shown in **Figure 6.**

Climate Zones

There are a variety of climate zones in California. These include Mediterranean climates such as those found around the Mediterranean Sea in southern Europe and northern Africa. Areas that have a Mediterranean climate have mild winters and warm, dry summers. California also has a cold, highland/timberline climate zone. This climate zone is found at the highest elevations in the mountains. Arid mid-latitude and low-latitude deserts are located in southeastern California. These desert climate zones are dry and have hot summers and cool winters. California also has steppe climate zones. Though quite arid, these climate zones receive more precipitation than do the deserts.

In some parts of California, differences in elevation are large enough to produce several climate zones in a very small geographical area. For example, as the photos in Figure 6 show, you could play volleyball on a beach in Los Angeles and, within a two-hour drive, ski in the mountains or climb rocks in the desert.

Reading Check How does topography determine where rain falls in California? (See the Appendix for answers to Reading Checks.)

Figure 6 ▶ The map below shows the climate zones within California. The photos below show a Mediterranean climate (left), a cold winter climate (middle), and a desert climate (right).

Climate Classification System

- Steppe (hot)
- Steppe
- Steppe w/summer fog
- Arid low-latitude desert (hot)
- Arid mid-latitude desert
- Mediterranean/hot summer
- Mediterranean/cool summer
- Mediterranean/summer fog
- Cool continental/dry summer
- Cold winter/dry summer
- Highland/Timberline

Eureka

Sacramento

San Francisco

Los Angeles

0   100   200 Kilometers

San Diego

California's Geologic History

California is located on the edge of the North American continent near the point where three tectonic plates meet. Because of its location, California has a very complex geologic history. As you learn about important events in California's geologic history, you can see where they fit on the geologic time scale on p. 213.

The Ancient History of California

California began to form almost 2 billion years ago. The geologic map of California in **Figure 1** shows rocks that range in age from 1.8 billion years to the present. California's oldest rocks, however, occur in only a few scattered locations in the southernmost part of the state. The oldest of these rocks are metamorphic *gneisses* that are about 1.8 billion to 1.7 billion years old. These rocks, shown in **Figure 2**, were later intruded by magmas that formed batholiths of granite and gabbro. These batholiths range in age from 1.4 billion to 1.2 billion years. After they formed, these metamorphic and igenous rocks were uplifted and eroded.

Figure 1 ▶ The geologic map of California below shows places where rocks of different types and ages are found.

Quaternary sedimentary deposits
Tertiary and Quaternary sedimentary rocks
Tertiary sedimentary rocks
Tertiary and Quaternary volcanic rocks
Mesozoic sedimentary rocks
Metamorphosed igneous rocks
Mesozoic granitic rock
Precambrian, Paleozoic, and Mesozoic metamorphic and sedimentary rocks

Eureka
Klamath Mountains
Modoc Plateau
Basin and Range
Cascade Range
Coast Ranges
Sacramento
San Francisco
Great Valley
Sierra Nevada
Coast Ranges
Basin and Range
Mojave Desert
Transverse Ranges
Los Angeles
Peninsular Ranges
0   100   200 Kilometers
San Diego
Colorado Desert

Figure 2 ▶ This 1.7 billion–year-old gneiss is found in the San Gabriel Mountains of southern California.

Setting the Stage

About 750 million years ago, a new spreading center formed at the western edge of the North American continent, and the crust was rifted apart. The rifting that occurred is similar to the way Africa is being separated from Arabia today along the Red Sea. The new spreading center slowly moved westward away from the North American continent and created new oceanic crust as it moved.

By 650 million years ago, the spreading center was under the ocean some distance west of the continent. As the ocean opened up, rivers that flowed off the continent began to deposit sediment onto the newly created oceanic crust. This process, shown in **Figure 3**, continued for the next 500 million years until the sediment reached across the area that was to become California.

It Depends Where You Are

The rocks that formed in southeastern California consist of sandstone, shale, conglomerate, and limestone. Some of these sedimentary rocks can be seen in **Figure 4.** These rocks formed from sediment deposited in shallow water near the coastline. The oldest of these rocks formed during Precambrian time, more than 550 million years ago. Most of these rocks do not contain fossils. Younger rocks formed during the Paleozoic Era, between 550 million and 250 million years ago. Fossils of trilobites, corals, brachiopods, crinoids, clams, and snails can be found in these younger rocks.

In northwestern California, there are no rocks of Precambrian age. During the Paleozoic Era, however, sandstone, shale, conglomerate, and basalt were formed in deep ocean water. Later on, during the Mesozoic Era (250 million to 65 million years ago), these rocks in northwestern California—and many in the Sierra Nevada—were metamorphosed by contact metamorphism.

650 million years ago

250 million years ago

Figure 3 ▶ The diagrams above show the tectonic development of California from 650 million years ago (top) to 250 million years ago (bottom).

Figure 4 ▶ Sedimentary rocks are exposed in the Providence Mountains in the Mojave Desert of southern California.

C9

Pacific
Ocean

Oceanic
Trench

Future location of California

Metamorphic
rocks

Sedimentary
rocks

Volcanic
rocks

Older
sedimentary
rocks

Subducted
rocks

Intrusive
rocks

150 million years ago

Figure 5 ▶ The diagram above shows the tectonic setting of California at 150 million years ago.

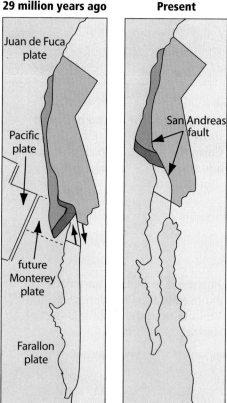

29 million years ago

Present

Juan de Fuca
plate

Pacific
plate

San Andreas
fault

future
Monterey
plate

Farallon
plate

Figure 6 ▶ The diagrams above show how crustal blocks have changed during the last 29 million years.

A Middle History of California

When the Mesozoic Era began around 250 million years ago, a major change in tectonic plate movements occurred. For the next 220 million years, the geologic development of California took place at a convergent plate boundary rather than at a spreading center. **Figure 5** shows this change. Also during this time period, various parts of the California crust had a different arrangement than they do today, as **Figure 6** shows.

Melting of the newly subducting oceanic crust produced magma that rose up through the continental crust. There, the magma solidified as igneous plutons (dikes, sills, or batholiths) or was extruded to form volcanoes and lava flows. At the same time, surface rocks were weathering and eroding, as shown in **Figure 7.** This process produced sediment that was transported west to the ocean. The batholithic rocks, most of which are made of granite, formed during the Mesozoic Era but have since been uplifted, eroded, and exposed on the surface.

Volcanic Rocks and Mountain Building

Mesozoic volcanic rocks are commonly found with Mesozoic sedimentary rocks. These volcanic rocks consist mostly of lava flows and are found on the surface along with batholithic rocks. Mesozoic sedimentary rocks are mostly sandstone, shale, and conglomerate that were deposited in the ocean off the slopes of volcanoes. In the middle of the Mesozoic Era, a mountain-building event occurred. In this event, early Mesozoic sedimentary rocks were metamorphosed, uplifted, and exposed to erosion. An angular unconformity formed between these rocks and the overlying rocks of the late Mesozoic Era.

Figure 7 ▶ The Minaret in the Sierra Nevada is an eroded portion of a caldera that existed at the top of a Mesozoic volcano.

Figure 8 ▶ The Simi Hills of Los Angeles and Ventura Counties are formed in part of sandstone created in the late Mesozoic Era.

Making Metamorphic Rocks

Late Mesozoic sedimentary rocks, shown in **Figure 8,** are also mostly sandstone, shale, and conglomerate. These rocks formed from sediment that was deposited on the continental shelf, the continental slope, in submarine canyons, and in ocean-trench environments.

Sedimentary rocks that were formed from sediment deposited far from the coastline commonly got pulled into the subduction zone. There, the rocks were thoroughly crushed and metamorphosed as the oceanic crust moved beneath the continent. Later, uplift of these subduction-zone rocks, and erosion of the overlying rocks, left the subduction-zone rocks exposed on the surface. These rocks consist of broken and jumbled blocks of sandstone, shale, and basalt of various sizes that are mixed with and bound by sand and clay particles. Some fragments of the oceanic crust rock have also been uplifted with the subduction-zone rocks.

Fossils are not common in Mesozoic rocks in California because most of the sediment from which the rocks formed was deposited in deep water where marine life was scarce. A representative Mesozoic fossil is shown in **Figure 9.**

Figure 9 ▶ This ammonite was found at La Jolla in San Diego County. Ammonites are extinct marine animals that lived during the Mesozoic Era. These relatives of the chambered nautilus lived in coiled shells that had many internal chambers.

Figure 10 ▶ West of Los Angeles at Saddle Peak in the Santa Monica Mountains, red-colored rock that formed from river sediment deposited during the Oligocene Epoch can be seen.

Up from the Deep

The pattern of deposition during the Mesozoic Era continued into the Cenozoic Era, which began 65 million years ago with an asteroid impact in Mexico. Sediment deposited during the early Cenozoic Era (Paleocene and Eocene Epochs) formed rocks that consist of sandstone, shale, and conglomerate. This sediment was also deposited on the continental shelf, on the continental slope, and in submarine canyons.

Later in the Cenozoic Era (during the Oligocene Epoch), the spreading center, which was located west of California between the Farallon and Pacific plates, moved toward the subduction zone. As the spreading center approached the subduction zone, western California was lifted out of the ocean. The shoreline moved westward from the base of the mountains, and deposition of marine sediment was replaced by deposition of non-marine river sediment. Often, rocks that formed from these river deposits are red, as shown in **Figure 10,** because of the oxidation of iron minerals in the sediment.

Late Arrivals

During the Paleocene and Eocene Epochs, marine clams and snails were common. During the Oligocene Epoch, however, the deposition of abundant nonmarine sediments brought with it fossilized mammals for the first time in California's history. These fossils include the fossils of rhinos, horses, tapirs, dogs, and rodents. They indicate that the climate in California during the early Cenozoic was humid and tropical. Several fossils from early Cenozoic rocks of California are shown in **Figure 11.**

Figure 11 ▶ Cenozoic fossils from California include (a) *Sespia californica*, a sheep-like mammal, (b) *Turritella*, a snail, and (c) *Cucullaea*, a clam.

(a)

(b)

(c)

Later in the History of California

As the spreading center neared the subduction zone, two new tectonic plate fragments—the Monterey plate and the Juan de Fuca plate—broke off of the Fallaron plate, as Figure 6 shows. The Farallon and Juan de Fuca plates continued subducting beneath the continent. But the Monterey plate became both attached to the Pacific plate and stuck under the North American plate. As a result, the Pacific plate, which was moving to the northwest, captured the part of the North American plate that is now southern California. This part broke off and ended up being dragged along with the Pacific plate. The fracture along which this separation occurred is now called the *San Andreas fault*. All of southern California southwest of the San Andreas fault is now part of the Pacific plate.

These plate movements not only pulled southern California toward the northwest, but they also stretched the whole state in an east-west direction. This stretching caused tilted fault-block mountains, with intervening graben valleys, to form across the state.

Deposition in Low Places

Because of this tectonic plate activity, deposition during the late Cenozoic Era (Miocene and Pliocene Epochs) took place in scattered valley basins between fault-block mountain ranges. In southeastern California, the valleys filled with alluvial-fan, river, and lake deposits of sandstone, shale, conglomerate, and evaporite minerals. The basins in western California were below sea level, and shallow-marine sandstone and conglomerate were deposited in the shallower basins. Deeper basins, however, were filled with deep-marine shale. **Figure 12** shows an example of deep marine shale.

SCi**LINKS**

NSTA
Developed and maintained by the
National Science Teachers Association

For a variety of links related to this subject, go to www.scilinks.org

Topic: Geology of California
SciLinks code: HK7C04

Figure 12 ▶ This outcrop of deep-marine shale (top) is located in the Santa Monica Mountains north of Malibu. Searles Lake (bottom) is an evaporite basin in the Mojave Desert of southern California.

Figure 13 ▶ The paleontologists above are uncovering a whale fossil near San Juan Capistrano. The leaf fossil was found in northern California.

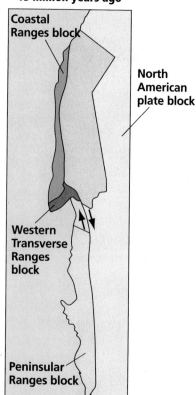

13 million years ago

Coastal Ranges block

North American plate block

Western Transverse Ranges block

Peninsular Ranges block

Figure 14 ▶ The map above shows the position of the Western Transverse Ranges block.

The End of an Era

Fossils from the late Cenozoic Era are common in California. Marine invertebrate fossils include clams, snails, and sand dollars. Marine vertebrate fossils include fish, sharks, seals, and whales. A large variety of bird and mammal fossils are preserved in the nonmarine rocks. These fossils include hawks, elephants, rhinos, camels, horses, dogs, and saber-toothed cats. Nonmarine rocks also contain abundant plant fossils, including chestnut, maple, oak, alder, hickory, and pine. These fossils indicate subtropical to more temperate and even arid climates in California. Some fossils from the late Cenozoic Era are shown in **Figure 13.**

Late Cenozoic volcanic rocks are also common in California. The volcanoes Lassen Peak and Mount Shasta are the result of the subduction that occurs as the Juan de Fuca plate continues to sink beneath the North American plate. Volcanic rocks in the central and southern parts of the state, on the other hand, are the result of the east-west stretching that occurred during the late Cenozoic Era. Also during this time, lava flows produced in Nevada flowed westward across the Sierra Nevada. This evidence suggests that the mountain range that was here during the Mesozoic and early Cenozoic Eras had eroded down to low hills by the late Cenozoic Era.

Part of California Rotates

Throughout the late Cenozoic Era, the pull of the Pacific plate on the crust southwest of the San Andreas fault caused the crust to break into numerous fragments. One of these fragments, called the *Western Transverse Ranges block*, was originally oriented in a north-south direction, parallel to and west of the Peninsular Ranges. Because of this plate movement, the Western Transverse Ranges block rotated more than 90° into its present east-west position. This rotation took about 10 million years. **Figure 14** shows the relative position of the various segments of California halfway through the rotation. Compare Figure 14 with Figure 6 for a view of the entire rotation cycle.

Making a Modern California

Beginning about 4 million years ago (during the Pliocene Epoch), the coastal basins southwest of the San Andreas fault were compressed. This compression created the mountains of the Coast Ranges and the Western Transverse Ranges. These mountain ranges are very young, and mountain building in this area is ongoing. The Sierra Nevada, which had been only low hills during the late Cenozoic Era, was uplifted to its present elevation only within the last 2 million years.

Then, less than 2 million years ago (during the Pleistocene Epoch), the climate in California became much cooler than it is today. Snow built up to great thicknesses in the high mountain valleys, and glaciers formed. Glacial ice accumulated to as much as 1,800 m thick in some of the valleys in the Sierra Nevada. The erosion of the valleys beneath the glaciers resulted in steepened side slopes and widened valley bottoms, which created broad, U-shaped valleys. Rocks that were carried down the valley by the glaciers were deposited in great piles called *glacial moraines.* When the glaciers retreated, the glaciated valleys that make the Sierra Nevada such a beautiful mountain range were revealed, as shown in **Figure 15.**

California is still active geologically, and the forces that shaped it are still operating. The San Andreas fault is still moving, and the mountains are still growing. In other words, the geologic history of California is still being written.

✓ **Reading Check** Name two features that were created by the east-west stretching of California. (See Appendix for answers to Reading checks.)

Figure 15 ▶ A lateral moraine deposit along Convict Creek in the eastern Sierra Nevada is shown at top. Yosemite Valley, a glaciated valley in the western Sierra Nevada is shown at bottom.

California's Natural Resources

California is rich in natural resources. Some of these resources are renewable. Others are nonrenewable. For those resources that are nonrenewable, wise management is necessary if Californians are to keep their present lifestyle.

Water Resources

Most of the water in California comes from rain and snowmelt. This water flows to the ocean by way of surface streams. The water also percolates into natural groundwater storage basins. Californians get most of their water from streams and underground basins.

Surface Water

Surface water is a renewable resource that meets about 60% of California's water needs. But, California is not water self-sufficient. In order to meet present water needs, some water has to be imported from outside the state. So, any future increase in population will require either better conservation methods or an increase in imported water. In addition, as **Table 1** shows, the distribution of water in California is unequal. Southern California must import much of its water.

California's surface water resources are shown in **Figure 1**. To be used in California households, surface water must be free of stream pollution at its source and must be protected from contamination during its storage in lakes and reservoirs. It must also be treated before it is sent to where it is needed. **Figure 2** shows a reservoir in which water is stored for later use.

Table 1 ▼

Distribution of Water in California		
Location	Precipitation	Water use
Northern California	75%	30%
Southern California	25%	70%

Figure 1 ▶ The map below shows streams and lakes in California.

Eureka

Sacramento

San Francisco

Los Angeles

San Diego

0   100   200 Kilometers

Figure 2 ▶ The Hollywood Reservoir, built in 1924, stores water for the Los Angeles area.

Groundwater

The remaining 40% of California's water needs are met by groundwater. Groundwater in California is contained in aquifers. In these aquifers, groundwater has collected in sediment that has filled in basins between the mountains. The location of groundwater in California is shown in **Figure 3.**

The largest aquifer in California is the Central Valley aquifer system, which is also shown in Figure 3. Groundwater in this aquifer fills a large basin between the Coast Ranges and the Sierra Nevada. The water from this system is used to irrigate farmland in the Central Valley. The availability of water has helped the Central Valley become the largest producer of agricultural products in the United States.

Most of California's population centers are located above aquifers along the coast. Groundwater in these aquifers, however, can no longer meet the demand of these growing populations. Southern California meets some of its needs by using water from northern California and the Colorado River. Some of this water is transported through the Los Angeles Aqueduct, which is shown in **Figure 4.**

Figure 3 ▶ The map above shows where water is located beneath Earth's surface in California.

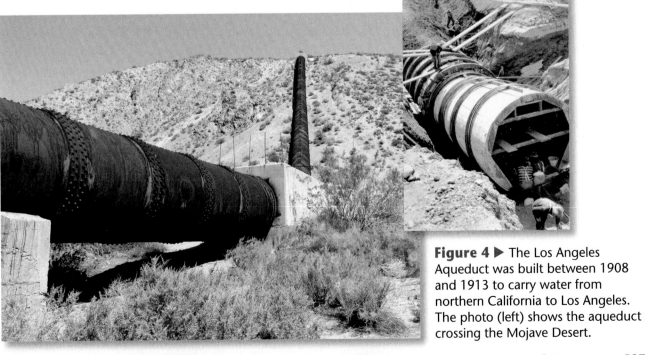

Figure 4 ▶ The Los Angeles Aqueduct was built between 1908 and 1913 to carry water from northern California to Los Angeles. The photo (left) shows the aqueduct crossing the Mojave Desert.

California's Natural Resources **C17**

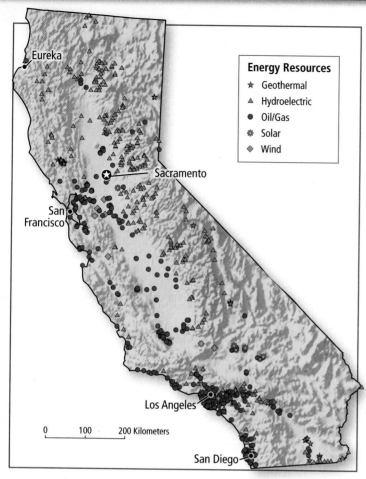

Energy Resources

Eureka

Sacramento

San Francisco

Los Angeles

San Diego

0   100   200 Kilometers

Figure 5 ▶ The map above shows the locations of important energy resources in California.

Californians need fuel, heat, and electricity to maintain their modern-day lifestyle. Oil and natural gas are largely used to provide all three of these needs. **Figure 5** shows the location of oil and gas fields in California. Other sources of energy for producing electric power in California are shown as well.

Oil and Natural Gas

Oil and natural gas are nonrenewable resources that are relatively abundant in the state. Nonrenewable resources are those that form at a rate much slower than the rate at which they are consumed. Oil and natural gas provide 78% of all of the energy used in California.

The first successful oil well in California began operating in 1865 in Humboldt County. By 1930, major oil fields had been discovered in Kern, Kings, Los Angeles, Santa Barbara, and Ventura Counties. These discoveries include the first offshore oil field to be developed in the United States, near Santa Barbara, where drilling began in 1896.

Hydroelectric Energy

Hydroelectric energy refers to electricity that has been produced using falling water. For this to happen, a river must be dammed to create a lake. The water at the base of the dam is then released through electric-generating turbines, which generate electricity. California has many operating hydroelectric dams, as shown in Figure 5. Shasta Dam shown in **Figure 6,** as well as many other dams, provide electricity as well as a constant water supply.

Figure 6 ▶ Shasta Dam provides electricity to consumers in northern California.

Geothermal Energy

Geothermal energy, a renewable resource, is generated by the heat of Earth's interior. Steam is produced in places where groundwater comes in contact with hot magma below Earth's surface. Wells can be drilled into the steam sources. The steam is used by turbines to produce electricity.

The largest geothermal field in California is The Geysers, shown in **Figure 7.** The Geysers is located in the mountains near San Francisco and supplies electricity to that city. Unfortunately, today there is little possibility of finding new geothermal energy resources in California.

Figure 7 ▶ The Geysers is one of 14 locations in California where geothermal energy is used to make electricity.

Wind Energy

Wind energy is also a renewable resource, and generating stations are being built in many of the windiest places in California. For the production of wind energy to be economical, however, the power of the wind at a given site must be more than 400 watts per square meter. Unfortunately, there are very few places in California where wind power is that high.

Solar Energy

Solar energy is a renewable resource that is growing in use in California. In fact, California has been a leader in developing solar energy for electricity generation. The largest solar electric-generating plant in the world is located in Kramer Junction in the Mojave Desert. Electricity generated by this plant is supplied to the Los Angeles area. **Figure 8** shows an early experimental solar power plant.

Figure 8 ▶ The Solar Two experimental power plant, which is located in the Mojave Desert, converted solar energy to steam to power a turbine.

Mineral Resources

California leads the United States in the production of nonfuel minerals. **Table 2** lists the nonfuel mineral products found in California. In 2004, more than 1,100 mines in the state together produced minerals valued at $3.61 billion. Some of the minerals that are mined in California are shown in **Figure 9.**

Sand and Gravel

Sand and gravel are used mostly in the construction industry and are mined from quarries in river deposits. During the winter, river flow brings new sand and gravel downstream to replace the quarried material.

Portland Cement

Portland cement is mixed with sand and gravel in the construction industry to make concrete. Portland cement is made mostly of powdered limestone mixed with clay, sand, and gypsum. All of these components are obtained from sedimentary rocks. The limestone is quarried largely from deposits in southeastern California.

Diatomite

Diatomite is a fine powder that is very porous. It is used in industry and in home swimming pools to filter water. Diatomite is made from microscopic marine plants that have died and settled to the bottom of the ocean. On the ocean bottom, these plants accumulated in thick layers. The major diatomite deposits, which are mined by open-pit methods, are found in the Coast Ranges.

Table 2 ▼

California's Nonfuel Mineral Products	
Asbestos	Pumice
Boron minerals	Pyrophyllite
Clay	Rare earth minerals
Diatomite	Saline compounds
Dolomite	Salt
Decorative rock	Sand and gravel
Dimension stone	Shale
Feldspar	Silica
Fuller's earth	Silver
Gemstones	Slate
Gypsum	Soda ash
Gold	Sodium sulfate
Iron ore	Specialty sand
Kaolin	Stone
Lignite	Talc
Lime	Titanium
Limestone	Volcanic cinder
Magnesium	Tungsten
Perlite	Zeolites

(a)

(b)

(c)

(d)

Figure 9 ▶ Some of the minerals found in California include (a) benitoite, the State gemstone, (b) gold, (c) halite, or rock salt, and (d) ulexite. Ulexite is used to make glass among other things.

Figure 10 ▶ Between 1883 and 1889, 20-mule teams carried boron minerals from Death Valley to the railroad in Mojave. The 265 km trip took 10 days to complete.

Boron Minerals

Boron minerals are used to make glass, fiberglass for insulation, water softeners, and detergents. These minerals occur as evaporite deposits in salt lakes. Ulexite, which is shown in Figure 9, is an economically valuable boron mineral.

Some boron minerals come from Cenozoic lakes. They are mined by using both open-pit and underground methods. Other deposits are found in modern dry lakes. Historic 20–mule teams, shown in **Figure 10,** pulled wagons that carried the boron mineral ore from dry-lake deposits in Death Valley. Some lake deposits are located below the water table, where the minerals are dissolved in salt solutions. To reach the minerals, miners drill holes in the lake sediment and pump the solution out.

Gold

The rush for gold in California in the 1850s brought California fame and led to early statehood. Gold is used in coins, jewelry, electronics, and dentistry. In California, gold is found in quartz veins in Paleozoic metamorphic rocks. The gold is spread unevenly throughout these quartz veins, which are mined by underground tunneling techniques.

During the Eocene Epoch, the Sierra Nevada was eroded down to the level of the gold-bearing quartz veins. The gold was transported downstream and deposited in river deposits. This type of gold is referred to as *placer gold*. These river deposits were mined by using high-pressure water hoses, which are shown in **Figure 11.** Today, recreational miners recover gold from river deposits by using small dredges to which suction hoses are attached.

Reading Check List five energy resources and five mineral resources of California. (See the Appendix for answers to Reading Checks.)

Figure 11 ▶ In the 19th century, high-pressure water hoses were used to mine placer gold (top). Today, miners use small dredges to find gold in river deposits (bottom).

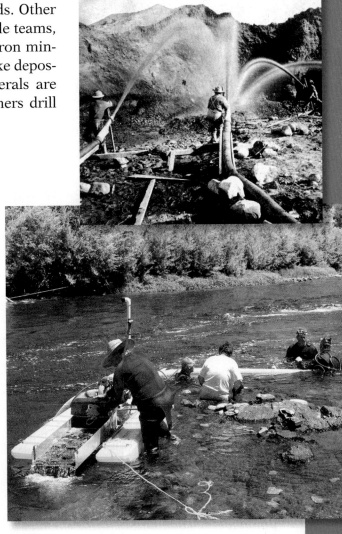

Because of its diverse geology, topography, and location, California is at risk for a variety of hazards. Earthquakes, volcanic eruptions, landslides, wave erosion, tsunamis, and flooding are natural hazards that Californians may face at some time.

Figure 1 ▶ The map below shows earthquakes of magnitude 4.5 and greater that occurred in California between 1965 and 2005.

• Earthquakes

Eureka

Sacramento

San Francisco

Los Angeles

0   100   200 Kilometers

San Diego

Earthquakes

Earthquakes occur when rocks along a fault suddenly move. California experiences more than 30 earthquakes each day. Fortunately, most of these quakes are too small to feel. However, larger earthquakes are also common, as **Figure 1** shows.

Movement along the subduction zone between the Juan de Fuca and North American plates causes some earthquakes both in the ocean and on land along the coast of northwestern California. Movement on the San Andreas fault boundary between the Pacific plate and the North American plate causes many other earthquakes along a line that runs northwest through the western part of the state. **Figure 2** shows damage caused by the Loma Prieta earthquake, which happened along the San Andreas fault. Most earthquakes happen along numerous other faults in the state.

Figure 2 ▶ The magnitude 6.9 Loma Prieta earthquake rocked San Francisco and the surrounding area for 20 s on October 17, 1989. The earthquake caused 63 deaths and the destruction of more than 1,000 homes.

Harbor Terminals SECOND RIGHT

Table 1 ▼

Most Recent Volcanic Eruptions in California	
Location	Eruption
Lassen Peak	1914 to 1917
Mono Lake	250 years ago
Clear Lake	~10,000 years ago
Amboy Crater	~10,000 years ago
Salton Buttes	~16,000 years ago
Coso Volcanic Field	Between 1 million and 40,000 years ago

MT. SHASTA, MEDICINE LAKE HIGHLAND, AND LASSEN PEAK AREA

Eureka

☐ Potential areas of volcanic hazard

0   100   200 Kilometers

CLEAR LAKE AREA

Sacramento ✪

San Francisco

MONO LAKE, LONG VALLEY AREA

OWENS RIVER, DEATH VALLEY, COSO AREA

AMBOY CRATER, LAVIC LAKE AREA

Los Angeles

SALTON BUTTES AREA

San Diego

Figure 3 ▶ The map above shows areas in California that may be subject to hazards from future volcanic eruptions.

Figure 4 ▶ This photo shows the explosive eruption of Lassen Peak on May 22, 1915. The photo was taken in Red Bluff, 65 km west of the volcano.

Volcanoes

In the past several thousand years, there have been few volcanic eruptions in California. But there are six places in the state where a volcanic eruption is possible. These places are shown in **Figure 3.** About 30% of California is located in a potential volcanic hazard area. At all of these sites, recently erupted volcanic rocks, hot springs, and geysers indicate that hot magma is still beneath Earth's surface.

The most recent volcanic eruptions that have taken place in California are shown in **Table 1.** The eruption of Lassen Peak, which is shown in **Figure 4,** lasted from 1914 to 1917. The largest single eruption during that period happened on May 22, 1915. The powerful blast shot volcanic ash more than 9,000 m into the air. The ash traveled as far as Winnemucca, Nevada, which is 320 km east of the volcano. Lava melted snow on the ground, which created a volcanic mudflow that traveled 16 km down Hat Creek. Compared with other volcanic eruptions worldwide, however, the May 1915 eruption of Lassen Peak is considered a small eruption.

Landslides

California has relatively young, steep mountains that often consist of soft, loose sedimentary rocks. These characteristics make parts of the state prone to landslides. Landslides are especially likely when rainfall rates are high. The faster a hill is saturated by rain, the more likely the hill is to suffer a landslide. Hillsides are also made less stable if they are steepened or undercut, either naturally by rivers or artificially by construction projects.

A landslide in La Conchita, a coastal town near Santa Barbara, is shown in **Figure 5.** Landslides here are not just a modern occurrence. Destructive landslides have been reported in the La Conchita area since the 1880s.

Coastal Erosion

Wherever hills or mountains border the ocean, sea cliffs will form as a result of wave erosion. As time passes, waves will continue to undercut a cliff and weaken it until it collapses into the ocean. In this way, the ocean advances and the cliff line retreats landward.

Different methods have been tried to delay the process of coastal erosion. But no method has been found to be effective in stopping the force of wave erosion. **Figure 6** shows the tremendous forces that waves can exert on a coastline. Roads and structures that are built on the beach at the base of a cliff can be threatened by wave action whenever storm waves and high tide happen at the same time.

Figure 5 ▶ On March 4, 1995, nine homes in La Conchita were buried by almost 550,000 tons of rock and soil that slid 180 m downslope.

Figure 6 ▶ Large waves that crashed against ocean-eroded cliffs caused this house in Malibu to collapse into the Pacific Ocean in February 1998.

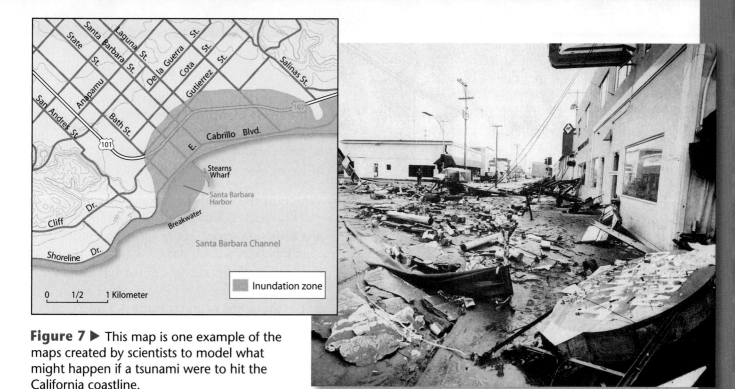

Figure 7 ▶ This map is one example of the maps created by scientists to model what might happen if a tsunami were to hit the California coastline.

Figure 8 ▶ On the night of March 27, 1964, a tsunami struck Crescent City. Flooding covered 29 city blocks and caused 11 deaths and $7.5 million in damage.

Tsunamis

Tsunamis can be generated when large earthquakes shake the ocean bottom or when large undersea landslides cause water along the ocean bottom to be displaced. Earthquakes at subduction zones and landslides in ocean trenches are common around the edges of the Pacific Ocean. Therefore, parts of the California coastline are subject to tsunamis. **Figure 7** shows the area that could be flooded if a tsunami hit Santa Barbara.

Eleven tsunamis large enough to cause damage have been recorded in California. The 1964 tsunami, which was generated by an Alaskan earthquake, produced a maximum wave height of 7 m in Crescent City. **Figure 8** shows damage caused by the tsunami.

Sea-Level Rise

Evidence indicates that global warming is increasing the rate at which glacial ice is melting around the world. As the glacial ice melts, sea level rises. As a point of reference, if all of the glacial ice in the world melted, sea level would rise about 70 m. If sea level rose this amount, some of the Los Angeles basin, major portions of the cities around San Francisco Bay, and about one-third of the Central Valley could be flooded. If such a maximum sea-level rise occurred, it would take decades to happen. Reducing global warming caused by human activity may delay this hazard.

✓ **Reading Check** Describe three natural hazards that Californians who live along the coastline may face. (See the Appendix for answers to Reading Checks.)

Understanding Key Concepts

1. The prevailing winds in California blow from which direction?
a. from the north
b. from the south
c. from the east
d. from the west

2. Which of the following mountains is the highest point in California?
a. Mt. Shasta
c. Mt. Whitney
b. Lassen Peak
d. Telescope Peak

3. Where does the warm air of a Maritime Tropical Pacific air mass originate?
a. Alaska
c. Mexico
b. Hawaii
d. Japan

4. Which of the following tectonic plates did NOT play a major role in shaping the geology of California?
a. the North American plate
b. the Cocos plate
c. the Pacific plate
d. the Juan de Fuca plate

5. Which of the following types of rock is the oldest rock found in California?
a. gneiss
c. granite
b. limestone
d. sandstone

6. The rotation of which of the following regions caused the southern California coastline to become irregular?
a. the region of the future Peninsular Ranges
b. the region of the future Coast Ranges
c. the region of the future Sierra Nevada
d. the region of the future Western Transverse Ranges

7. Which of the following energy resources provides the largest percentage of all of the energy used in California?
a. oil and natural gas
c. geothermal
b. hydroelectric
d. solar

8. Which of the following energy resources is the most plentiful renewable energy resource in California?
a. geothermal
c. solar
b. hydroelectric
d. wind

9. Which of the following statements about earthquakes in California is false?
a. California experiences more than 30 earthquakes each day.
b. Most earthquakes in California are too small to feel.
c. Earthquakes of magnitude 4.5 and greater are uncommon in California.
d. Many earthquakes in California happen at tectonic plate boundaries.

10. Movement along the San Andreas fault occurs at the boundary between which two tectonic plates?
a. the Juan de Fuca plate and the Pacific plate
b. the Juan de Fuca plate and the North American plate
c. the Pacific plate and the North American plate
d. the Pacific plate and the Cocos plate

Short Answer

11. Describe the major influence of the California Current on California.

12. Describe California's geologic location.

13. Explain why southern California receives less rainfall than northern California.

14. List two factors that determine California's climate zones.

15. Briefly describe how the San Andreas fault formed.

16. Explain how Mount Shasta and Lassen Peak are related to subduction.

17. Where are most aquifers in California located?

"Xena"—The Tenth Planet?

In January 2005, astronomers at the California Institute of Technology observed images of an unusual object in the night sky. The object, in fact, looked like it might be a good candidate for tenth planet in the solar system, after Pluto. This discovery thrilled the scientific community. But it also forced astronomers to reconsider the definition of the word *planet*.

Discovering New Planets

The object, catalogued as 2003 UB_{313}, and nicknamed "Xena," is located in the Kuiper Belt, an area located beyond the orbit of Neptune. The Kuiper Belt contains many small objects and some not so small, including Pluto and the newly discovered object.

The astronomers discovered this new object by carefully studying images made by the Samuel Oschin telescope at the Palomar Observatory, which is located on Mount Palomar in northern San Diego County, The images revealed a large object, currently three times as far from the sun as Pluto, moving through the outer solar system. The astronomers determined that this object is slightly larger than Pluto and that it orbits the sun once every 557 years

But Is It a Planet?

After making the discovery, the Caltech team submitted its data and its recommendations for an official planet name to the International Astronomical Union (IAU). The IAU is an organization that is responsible for officially naming objects in the universe.

This discovery, however, increased debate over the definition of the term *planet*. If this new object were considered a planet, then many other objects now being discovered in the solar system would also have to be considered for similar status. But if the object was not classified as a planet, then Pluto itself might not even qualify as a planet.

In August of 2006, the IAU defined the term *planet* as a celestial body that orbits the sun, is round because of its own gravity, and has cleared its orbital path of other large objects. Because Pluto is in the Kuiper Belt, it

▲ In this artist's illustration, the sun is seen from "Xena."

does not meet the last requirement in the definition. So, Pluto was reclassified as a *dwarf planet*. 2003 UB_{313} and Ceres, the largest of the asteroids, were also classified as dwarf planets. In September of 2006, the object 2003 UB_{313} was officially named Eris.

As astronomers discover more objects similar to Pluto and Eris in our solar system and beyond, those objects may also be classified as dwarf planets. Other bodies already known, may also be similarly classified. And their numbers may soon exceed that of the now eight planets of the solar system.

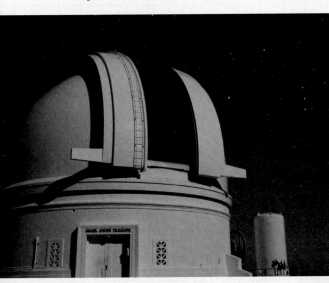

◄ The Samuel Oschin telescope at the Palomar Observatory.

Extension

1. **Applying Ideas** Find out more about the new definitions of the terms *planet* and *dwarf planet*. Prepare a five-minute presentation on how objects in the solar system are now classified.

APPENDIX CONTENTS

    Items marked with an oak leaf contain information directly related to environmental issues.

Analyzing Science Terms

You can unlock the meaning of an unfamiliar science term by analyzing its word parts. Many parts of scientific words carry a meaning that derives from Latin or Greek. The parts of words listed below provide clues to the meanings of many science terms.

Word part or root	Meaning	Application
a-	not, without	abiotic
astr-, aster-	star	astronomy
bar-, baro-	weight, pressure	barometer
batho-, bathy-	depth	batholith, bathysphere
circum-	around	circum-Pacific, circumpolar
-cline	lean, slope	anticline, syncline
-duct-	to lead, draw	conduction
eco-	environment	ecology, ecosystem
epi-	on	epicenter
ex-, exo-	out, outside of	exosphere, exfoliation, extrusion
geo-	earth	geode, geology, geomagnetic
-graph	write, writing	seismograph
hydro-	water	hydrosphere
hypo-	under	hypothesis
iso-	equal	isoscope, isostasy, isotope
-lith, -lithic	stone	Neolithic, regolith
-log-	study	ecology, geology, meteorology
magn-	great, large	magnitude
mar-	sea	marine
meta-	among, change	metamorphic, metamorphism
-meter	to measure	thermometer, spectrometer
micro-	small	microquake
-morph, -morphic	form, shape	metamorphic
nebula-	mist, cloud	nebula
neo-	new	Neolithic
paleo-	old	paleontology, Paleozoic
ped-, pedo-	ground, soil	pediment
per-	through	permeable
peri-	around	perigee, perihelion
seism-, seismo-	shake, earthquake	seismic, seismograph
sol-	sun	solar, solstice
spectro-	look at, examine	spectroscope, spectrum
-sphere	ball, globe	geosphere, lithosphere
strati-, strato-	spread, layer	stratification, stratovolcano
terra-	earth, land	terracing, terrane
thermo-	heat	thermosphere, thermometer
top-, topo-	place	topographic
trop-, tropo-	turn, respond to	tropopause, troposphere

How to Make Power Notes

Power notes help you organize the Earth science concepts you are studying by distinguishing main ideas from details. Similar to outlines, power notes are linear in form and provide you with a framework of important concepts. To make power notes, you assign a *power* of 1 to each main idea and a 2, 3, or 4 to each detail. You can use power notes to organize ideas while reading your text or to restructure your class notes for studying purposes. Practice first by using simple concepts. For example, start with a few headers or bold-faced vocabulary terms from this book. Later, you can strengthen your notes by expanding these simple words into more-detailed phrases and sentences. Use the following general format.

> **Power 1:** Main idea
> > **Power 2:** Detail or support for Power 1 idea
> > > **Power 3:** Detail or support for Power 2 concept
> > > > **Power 4:** Detail or support for Power 3 concept

1 Pick a Power 1 word or phrase from the text.

The text you choose does not have to come from your Earth science textbook. You may make power notes from your lecture notes or from another source. We'll use the term *environmental problems* as an example of a main idea.

> **Power 1:** environmental problems

2 Using the text, select some Power 2 words to support your Power 1 word.

We'll use the terms *resource depletion, pollution,* and *extinction,* which are the three main types of environmental problems.

> **Power 1:** environmental problems
> > **Power 2:** resource depletion
> > **Power 2:** pollution
> > **Power 2:** extinction

3 Select some Power 3 words to support your Power 2 words.

We'll use the terms *renewable resources* and *nonrenewable resources*. These two terms are related to *resource depletion,* which is one of the Power 2 concepts.

<u>Power 1</u>: environmental problems
    <u>Power 2</u>: resource depletion
        <u>Power 3</u>: renewable resources
        <u>Power 3</u>: nonrenewable resources
    <u>Power 2</u>: pollution
    <u>Power 2</u>: extinction

4 Continue to add powers to support and detail the main idea as necessary.

There are no restrictions on how many power numbers you can add to help you extend and organize your ideas. Words that have the same power number should have a similar relationship to the previous power but do not have to be related to each other.

<u>Power 1</u>: environmental problems
    <u>Power 2</u>: resource depletion
        <u>Power 3</u>: renewable resources
        <u>Power 3</u>: nonrenewable resources
    <u>Power 2</u>: pollution
        <u>Power 3</u>: degradable pollutants
        <u>Power 3</u>: nondegradable pollutants
    <u>Power 2</u>: extinction
        <u>Power 3</u>: pollution
        <u>Power 3</u>: habitat loss

Practice

1. Use this book's lesson on scientific methods and power notes structure to organize the following terms: *observing, hypothesizing and predicting, experimenting, organizing and analyzing data, drawing conclusions, repeating experiments, communicating results, observation, hypothesis, prediction, experiment, variable, experimental group, control group,* and *data.*

(See the last page of the Skills Handbook for the answers to practice problems.)

How to Make KWL Notes

KWL stands for *what I **K**now, what I **W**ant to know,* and *what I **L**earned.* The KWL strategy is somewhat different from other learning strategies because it prompts you to brainstorm about the subject matter before reading the assigned material. Relating new ideas and concepts with those that you have learned will help you to understand and apply the knowledge you obtain in this course. The section objectives throughout your text are ideal for using the KWL strategy. Read the objectives before reading each section, and follow the instructions in the example below.

1 | **Read the section objectives.**

You may also want to scan headings, boldfaced terms, and illustrations in the section. We'll use a few sample objectives as examples.
- List and describe the steps of the scientific method.
- Describe why a good hypothesis is not simply a guess.
- Describe the two essential parts of a good experiment.

2 | **Divide a sheet of paper into three columns. Label the columns "What I know," "What I want to know," and "What I learned."**

Here is an example table:

What I know	What I want to know	What I learned

3 | **Brainstorm about what you know about the information in the objectives, and write these ideas in the first column.**

Because this table is designed to help you blend your knowledge with new information, you do not have to write complete sentences.

4 | **Think about what you want to know about the information in the objectives. Write these ideas in the second column.**

You'll want to know the information you will be tested on, so include information from both the objectives and any other topics your teacher has given to you.

5 | **Use the third column to write down the information you learned. Do this while you read the text or just after reading the text.**

While you read, pay close attention to any information about the topics you wrote in the column entitled "What I want to know." If you do not find all of the answers you are looking for, you may need to reread the text or reference a second source. Be sure to ask your teacher for help if you cannot find the information after reading the text a second time.

When you have completed reading the text, review the ideas you brainstormed. Compare your ideas in the first column with the information you wrote down in the third column. If you find that some of the ideas are incorrect, cross them out. Before you begin studying for your test, identify and correct any misconceptions you had prior to reading.

Here is an example of what your notes might look like after using the KWL strategy:

What I know	What I want to know	What I learned
• The steps of the experimental method are predict, test, and conclude.	• What are the steps of the experimental method?	• The steps of the experimental method are observing, hypothesizing, experimenting, organizing and analyzing data, drawing conclusions, communicating results, and repeating experiments.
• A hypothesis is similar to a guess, but when you form a hypothesis, you have an idea of what might happen.	• Why is a hypothesis not a guess?	• A hypothesis is more than a guess. You have to base a hypothesis on observations and really think about what you are trying to learn. You should also design an experiment that can test if your hypothesis is wrong, but an experiment cannot prove that your hypothesis is correct.
• A good experiment includes a hypothesis and a lot of equipment.	• What are the two important parts of a good experiment?	• The two important parts of a good experiment are a single variable and a control group.

Practice

1. Use the third column from the table above to identify and correct any misconceptions in the following list of ideas.
   a. The first step of the experimental method is to predict.
   b. A hypothesis is similar to a guess.
   c. A good experiment includes a lot of equipment.

(See the last page of the Skills Handbook for the answers to practice problems.)

How to Make Two-Column Notes

Two-column notes can be used to learn and review definitions of vocabulary terms, examples of multiple-step processes, or details of specific concepts. The two-column note strategy is simple: write the term, main idea, step-by-step process, or concept in the left-hand column, and write the definition, example, or detail on the right.

One strategy for using two-column notes is to organize main ideas and their details. You will write the main ideas from your reading in the left-hand column of your paper. You can write these ideas as questions, key words, or a combination of both. Then, write details that describe these main ideas in the right-hand column of your paper.

1 Identify the main ideas.

The main ideas for a chapter are listed in the section objectives. However, you decide which ideas to include in your notes. The example below shows some main ideas from possible objectives in a section of this book.

- Define Earth science, and compare Earth science with geology.
- List the four major fields of study that contribute to Earth science.

2 Divide a blank sheet of paper into two columns, and write the main ideas in the left-hand column.

Remind yourself that your two-column notes are precisely that—notes. Do not copy whole phrases out of the book or waste your time writing ideas in complete sentences. Summarize your ideas by using short phrases that are easy for you to understand and remember. Decide how many details you need for each main idea, and write that number in parentheses under the main idea.

Main idea	Detail notes
Earth science (two definitions)	
Goals of Earth science (one main goal)	
What is studied (two main areas)	
Related fields of study (four major fields)	

3 **Write the detail notes in the right-hand column.**

List as many details as you designated in the main-idea column.

Main idea	Detail notes
Earth science (two definitions)	Earth science is the study of Earth and the universe around it. Scientific methods are the organized, logical approaches to scientific research.
Goals of Earth science (one main goal)	to understand Earth and the universe around it
What is studied (two main areas)	Earth and the universe around it • the origin, history, and structure of the solid Earth and the processes that shape it • how Earth's atmosphere, oceans, and land interact
Related fields of study (four major fields)	geology • the study of the origin, history, and structure of Earth and the processes that shape it oceanography • the study of Earth's oceans, including waves, tides, ocean currents, the ocean floor, and life in the oceans meteorology • the study of Earth's atmosphere, including weather and climate astronomy • the study of the universe beyond Earth, including planets, stars, and galaxies

You can use two-column notes to study for a short quiz or for a test on the material in an entire chapter. Cover the information in the right-hand column with a sheet of paper. Recite what you know, and then uncover the notes to check your answers. Then, ask yourself what else you know about that topic. Linking ideas in this way will help you gain a more complete picture of Earth science.

Have you ever tried to study for a test or quiz but didn't know where to start? Or have you read a chapter and found that you can remember only a few ideas? Well, FoldNotes are a fun and exciting way to help you learn and remember the ideas you encounter as you learn science!

FoldNotes are tools that you can use to organize concepts. One FoldNote focuses on a few main concepts. FoldNotes help you learn and remember how the concepts fit together. FoldNotes can help you see the "big picture." Below, you will find instructions for building 10 different FoldNotes.

Pyramid

1. Place a **sheet of paper** in front of you. Fold the lower left-hand corner of the paper diagonally to the opposite edge of the paper.

2. Cut off the tab of paper created by the fold (at the top).

3. Open the paper so that it is a square. Fold the lower right-hand corner of the paper diagonally to the opposite corner to form a triangle.

4. Open the paper. The creases of the two folds will have created an X.

5. Using **scissors,** cut along one of the creases. Start from any corner, and stop at the center point to create two flaps. Use **tape** or **glue** to attach one of the flaps on top of the other flap.

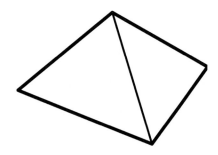

Double-Door Fold

1. Fold a **sheet of paper** in half from the top to the bottom. Then, unfold the paper.

2. Fold the top and bottom edges of the paper to the center crease.

Table Fold

1. Fold a **piece of paper** in half from the top to the bottom. Then, fold the paper in half again.

2. Fold the paper in thirds from side to side.

3. Unfold the paper completely. Carefully trace the fold lines by using a pen or pencil.

Booklet

1. Fold a **sheet of paper** in half from left to right. Then, unfold the paper.

2. Fold the sheet of paper in half again from the top to the bottom. Then, unfold the paper.

3. Refold the sheet of paper in half from left to right.

4. Fold the top and bottom edges to the center crease.

5. Completely unfold the paper.

6. Refold the paper from top to bottom.

7. Using **scissors,** cut a slit along the center crease of the sheet from the folded edge to the creases made in step 4. Do not cut the entire sheet in half.

8. Fold the sheet of paper in half from left to right. While holding the bottom and top edges of the paper, push the bottom and top edges together so that the center collapses at the center slit. Fold the four flaps to form a four-page book.

Layered Book

1. Lay **one sheet of paper** on top of **another sheet.** Slide the top sheet up so that 2 cm of the bottom sheet is showing.

2. Holding the two sheets together, fold down the top of the two sheets so that you see four 2 cm tabs along the bottom.

3. Using a **stapler,** staple the top of the FoldNote.

Two-Panel Flip Chart

1. Fold a **piece of paper** in half from the top to the bottom.

2. Fold the paper in half from side to side. Then, unfold the paper so that you can see the two sections.

3. From the top of the paper, cut along the vertical fold line to the fold in the middle of the paper. You will now have two flaps.

Key-Term Fold

1. Fold a **sheet of lined notebook paper** in half from left to right.

2. Using **scissors,** cut along every third line from the right edge of the paper to the center fold to make tabs.

Four-Corner Fold

1. Fold a **sheet of paper** in half from left to right. Then, unfold the paper.

2. Fold each side of the paper to the crease in the center of the paper.

3. Fold the paper in half from the top to the bottom. Then, unfold the paper.

4. Using **scissors,** cut the top flap creases made in step 3 to form four flaps.

Three-Panel Flip Chart

1. Fold a **piece of paper** in half from the top to the bottom.

2. Fold the paper in thirds from side to side. Then, unfold the paper so that you can see the three sections.

3. From the top of the paper, cut along each of the vertical fold lines to the fold in the middle of the paper. You will now have three flaps.

Tri-Fold

1. Fold a piece a paper in thirds from the top to the bottom.

2. Unfold the paper so that you can see the three sections. Then, turn the paper sideways so that the three sections form vertical columns.

3. Trace the fold lines by using a **pen** or **pencil.** Label the columns "Know," "Want," and "Learn."

Have you ever wished that you could draw the many concepts you learn in your science class? Sometimes, being able to see how concepts are related helps you remember what you've learned. Graphic Organizers help you see the concepts! They are a way to draw or map out concepts.

You need only a piece of paper and a pencil to make a Graphic Organizer. Below, you will find instructions for six different Graphic Organizers that are designed to help you organize the concepts you'll learn in this book.

Spider Map

1. Draw a diagram like the one shown. In the circle, write the main topic.

2. From the circle, draw legs to represent different categories of the main topic. You can have as many categories as you want.

3. From the category legs, draw horizontal lines. As you read the chapter, write details about each category on the horizontal lines.

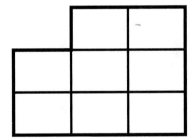

Comparison Table

1. Draw a chart like the one shown. Your chart can have as many columns and rows as you want.

2. In the top row, write the topics that you want to compare.

3. In the left column, write characteristics of the topics that you want to compare. As you read the chapter, fill in the characteristics for each topic in the appropriate boxes.

Chain-of-Events-Chart

1. Draw a box. In the box, write the first step of a process or the first event of a timeline.

2. Under the box, draw another box, and use an arrow to connect the two boxes. In the second box, write the next step of the process or the next event in the timeline.

3. Continue adding boxes until the process or timeline is finished.

Venn Diagram

1. Draw a diagram like the one shown. You may have two or three circles depending on the number of topics. Make sure the circles overlap with each other.

2. In each circle, write a topic that you want to compare with a topic in another circle.

3. In the areas of the diagram where circles overlap, fill in characteristics that the topics in the overlapping circles share.

4. In the areas of the diagram where circles do not overlap, fill in characteristics that are unique to the topic of the particular circle.

Cause-and-Effect Map

1. Draw a box, and write a cause in the box. You can have as many cause boxes as you want. The diagram shown here is one example of a cause-and-effect map.

2. Draw another box to represent an effect of the cause. You can have as many effect boxes as you want. Draw a line from each cause to the effect(s).

3. In the cause boxes, write a description, explanation, or details about the cause. In the effect boxes, explain the effects that result from the process or factor identified in the cause box.

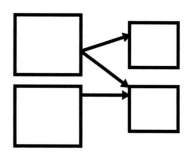

Concept Map

A concept map is a simple drawing that shows how concepts are connected to each other. Concept maps may be a good tool for visual learners to use when studying and to use to test their understanding of information in the text. Concept maps may be based on key vocabulary terms from the text. These terms are usually nouns, which make good labels for major concepts. Linking words may be used to explain relationships. A group of connected words and lines show a proposition. A proposition is another way of stating a main idea or explaining a concept.

1. Identify main ideas from the text, and write those ideas as short phrases or single words. Concepts may be vocabulary terms, important phrases, or descriptions of processes.

2. List all of the important concepts. Select a main concept for the map, and place this concept at the top or center of a piece of paper.

3. Build the map by placing the other concepts under or around the main concept, according to their importance or their relationship to the main concept.

4. Draw lines between the concepts to show relationships between ideas. Add linking words to give meaning to the arrangement of concepts. To distinguish concepts from links, place concepts in circles, ovals, or rectangles.

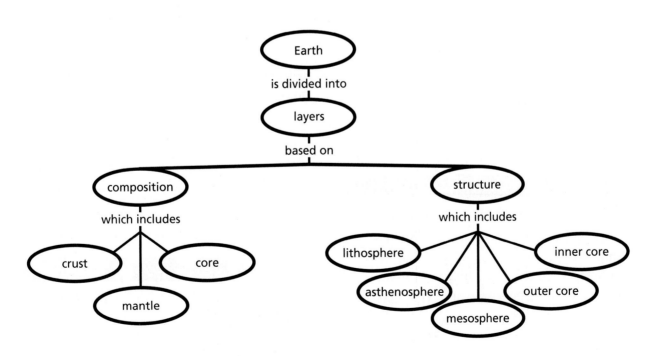

Geometry

A useful way to model the objects and substances studied in science is to consider them in terms of their shapes. For example, many of the properties of a wheel can be understood by pretending that the wheel is a perfect circle.

When you use shapes as models, the ability to calculate the area or volume of shapes is a useful skill. The table below provides equations for the area and volume of several geometric shapes.

Geometric Areas and Volumes	
Geometric shape	**Equations for shape**
Rectangle	$area = lw$
Circle	$area = \pi r^2$ $circumference = 2\pi r$
Triangle	$area = \frac{1}{2}bh$
Sphere	$surface\ area = 4\pi r^2$ $volume = \frac{4}{3}\pi r^3$
Cylinder	$surface\ area =$ $2\pi r^2 + 2\pi rh$ $volume = \pi r^2 h$
Rectangular box	$surface\ area =$ $2(lh + lw + hw)$ $volume = lwh$

Practice

1. Calculate the area of a triangle that has a base of 900.0 m and a height of 500.0 m.

2. What is the volume of a cylinder that has a diameter of 14 cm and a height of 8 cm?

3. Calculate the surface area of a cube that has sides that are 4 cm long.

(See the last page of the Skills Handbook for the answers to practice problems.)

Exponents

An exponent is a number that is written as superscript to the right of another number. The best way to explain how an exponent works is by using an example. In the value 5^4, the 4 is the exponent of the 5. The number and its exponent means that 5 is multiplied by itself 4 times as shown below:

$$5^4 = 5 \times 5 \times 5 \times 5 = 625$$

Exponents are also referred to as *powers*. Using this terminology, the above equation could be read "five to the fourth power equals 625," or "five to the power of four equals 625." Keep in mind that any number raised to the power of 0 is equal to 1: $5^0 = 1$. Also, any number raised to the power of 1 is equal to itself: $5^1 = 5$.

A scientific calculator is very helpful for solving most problems involving exponents. Many calculators have keys for squares and square roots, but scientific calculators usually have a special caret key, ^, for entering exponents. If you type in "5^4" and then press the equals sign or Enter, the calculator will determine that $5^4 = 625$ and display the answer 625.

Exponents		
	Rule	**Example**
Zero power	$x^0 = 1$	$7^0 = 1$
First power	$x^1 = x$	$6^1 = 6$
Multiplication	$(x^n)(x^m) =$ (x^{n+m})	$(x^2)(x^4) =$ $x^{(2+4)} = x^6$
Division	$\dfrac{x^n}{x^m} = x^{(n-m)}$	$\dfrac{x^8}{x^2} = x^{(8-2)} = x^6$
Exponents raised to a power	$(x^n)^m = x^{nm}$	$(5^2)^3 =$ $5^6 = 15{,}625$

Practice

1. Perform the following calculations:
   a. $9^1 =$ c. $(14^2)(14^3) =$
   b. $(3^3)^5 =$ d. $11^0 =$

(See the last page of the Skills Handbook for the answers to practice problems.)

Order of Operations

Use this phrase to remember the correct order for long mathematical problems: "Please Excuse My Dear Aunt Sally." Some people just remember the acronym "PEMDAS". This acronym stands for *parentheses, exponents, multiplication, division, addition,* and *subtraction*. This is the correct order in which to complete mathematical operations. These rules are summarized in the table below.

Order of Operations
1. Simplify groups inside parentheses. Start with the innermost group and work out.
2. Simplify all exponents.
3. Perform multiplication and division in order from left to right.
4. Perform addition and subtraction in order from left to right.

Look at the following example.

$$4^3 + 2 \times [8 - (3 - 1)] = ?$$

First, simplify the operations inside parentheses. Begin with the innermost parentheses:

$$(3 - 1) = 2$$
$$4^3 + 2 \times [8 - 2] = ?$$

Then, move on to the next-outer parentheses:

$$[8 - 2] = 6$$
$$4^3 + 2 \times 6 = ?$$

Now, simplify all exponents:

$$4^3 = 64$$
$$64 + 2 \times 6 = ?$$

Next, perform the remaining multiplication:

$$2 \times 6 = 12$$
$$64 + 12 = ?$$

Finally, perform the addition:

$$64 + 12 = 76$$

Practice
1. $2^3 \div 2 + 4 \times (9 - 2^2) =$
2. $\dfrac{2 \times (6-3) + 8}{4 \times 2 - 6} =$
(See the last page of the Skills Handbook for the answers to practice problems.)

Algebraic Rearrangements

Algebraic equations contain *constants* and *variables*. Constants are simply numbers, such as 2, 5, and 7. Variables are represented by letters such as x, y, z, a, b, and c. Variables are unspecified quantities and are also called the *unknowns*. Often, you will need to determine the value of a variable in an equation that contains algebraic expressions.

An algebraic expression contains one or more of the four basic mathematical operations: addition, subtraction, multiplication, and division. Constants, variables, or terms made up of both constants and variables can be involved in the basic operations.

The key to finding the value of a variable in an algebraic equation is that the total quantity on one side of the equals sign is equal to the quantity on the other side. If you perform the same operation on either side of the equation, the results will still be equal. To determine the value of a variable in an algebraic expression, you try to reduce the equation into a simple value that tells you exactly what x (or some other variable) equals.

Look at the simple problem below:

$$8x = 32$$

If you wish to solve for x, you can multiply or divide each side of the equation by the same factor. You can perform any operation on one side of an equation as long as you do the same thing to the other side of the equation. In this example, if you divide both sides of the equation by 8, you have the following:

$$\frac{8x}{8} = \frac{32}{8}$$

The two 8s on the left side of the equation cancel each other out, and the fraction $\frac{32}{8}$ can be reduced to give the whole number *4*. Therefore, $x = 4$.

Next, consider the following equation:

$$2x + 4 = 16$$

If you divide each side by 2, you are left with $x + 2$ on the left and 8 on the right:

$$x + 2 = 8$$

Now, you can subtract 2 from each side of the equation to find that $x = 6$. In all cases, the operation that is performed on the left side of the equals sign must also be performed on the right side.

Practice

1. Rearrange each of the following equations to give the value of the variable indicated with a letter.
   a. $8x - 32 = 128$
   b. $6 - 5(4a + 3) = 26$
   c. $-3(y - 2) + 4 = 29$
   d. $-2(3m + 5) = 14$
   e. $\left[8\frac{(8+2z)}{32} \right] + 2 = 5$
   f. $\frac{(6b + 3)}{3} - 9 = 2$

(See the last page of the Skills Handbook for the answers to practice problems.)

Scientific Notation

Many quantities that scientists deal with are very large or very small values. For example, light travels at about 300,000,000 m/s, and an electron has a mass of about
0.000 000 000 000 000 000 000 000 0009 g.
Obviously, it is difficult to read, write, and keep track of numbers such as these. We avoid this problem by using a method that deals with powers of the number 10.

Study the positive powers of 10 shown in the following table. You should be able to check these numbers by using what you know about exponents. The number of zeros in the equivalent number corresponds to the exponent of the 10, or the power to which the 10 is raised. The equivalent of 10^4 is 10,000, so the number has four zeros.

But how can we use the powers of 10 to simplify large numbers such as the speed of light? The speed of light is equal to $3 \times 100,000,000$ m/s. The factor of 10 in this number has 8 zeros, so the number can be rewritten as 10^8. So, 300,000,000 can be expressed as 3×10^8.

Powers of 10	
Power of 10	Decimal equivalent
10^4	10,000
10^3	1,000
10^2	100
10^1	10
10^0	1
10^{-1}	0.1
10^{-2}	0.01
10^{-3}	0.001

Negative exponents can be used to simplify numbers that are less than 1. Study the negative powers of 10 in the table above. In these cases, the exponent of 10 equals the number of decimal places you must move the decimal point to the right so that there is one digit just to the left of the decimal point. In the case of the mass of an electron, the decimal point has to be moved 28 decimal places to the right for the numeral 9 to be just to the left of the decimal point. The mass of the electron, about
0.000 000 000 000 000 000 000 000 0009 g, can be rewritten as about 9×10^{-28} g.

Scientific notation is a way to express numbers as a power of 10 multiplied by another number that has only one digit to the left of the decimal point. For example, 5,943,000,000 is written as 5.943×10^9 when expressed in scientific notation. The number 0.000 0832 is written as 8.32×10^{-5} when expressed in scientific notation.

Practice

1. Rewrite the following values using scientific notation.
   a. 12,300,000 m/s
   b. 0.000 000 000 0045 kg
   c. 0.000 0653 m
   d. 55,432,000,000,000 s
   e. 273.15 K
   f. 0.000 627 14 kg

(See the last page of the Skills Handbook for the answers to practice problems.)

Significant Digits

The following list can be used to review how to determine the number of *significant digits* (also called *significant figures*) in a given value or measurement. Significant digits are shown in red below.

Rules for Significant Digits:

1. All nonzero digits are significant. For example, 1,246 has four significant digits.

2. Any zeros between significant digits are also significant. For example, 1,206 has four significant digits.

3. Zeros at the end of a number but to the left of a decimal are significant if they have been measured or are the first estimated digit; otherwise, they are not significant. In this book, they will be treated as not significant. For example, 1,000 may contain from one to four significant digits, but in this book it will be assumed to have one significant digit.

4. If a value has no significant digits to the left of a decimal point, any zeros to the right of the decimal point and also to the left of a significant digit are not significant. For example, 0.0012 has only two significant digits.

5. If a value ends with zeros to the right of a decimal point, those zeros are significant. For example, 0.1200 has four significant digits.

After you have reviewed the rules, use the following table to check your understanding of the rules. Cover up the second column of the table, and try to determine how many significant digits each number in the first column has. If you get confused, refer to the rule given.

Significant Digits		
Measurement	Number of significant digits	Rule
12,345	5	1
2,400 cm	2	3
305 kg	3	2
235.0 cm	4	1 and 5
234.005 K	6	2
12.340	5	5
0.001	1	4
0.002 450	4	4 and 5

Rounding and Significant Digits

When performing mathematical operations with measurements, you must remember to keep track of significant digits. If you are adding or subtracting two measurements, your answer can have only as many decimal positions as the value that has the fewest number of decimal places. When you multiply or divide measurements, your answer can have only as many significant digits as the value that has the fewest number of significant digits.

Practice

1. Determine the number of significant digits in each of the following measurements:
   a. 65.04 mL   **c.** 0.007 504 kg
   b. 564.00 m   **d.** 1,210 K

2. Perform each of the following calculations, and report your answer with the correct number of significant digits and units:
   a. 0.004 dm + 0.12508 dm =
   b. 340 m ÷ 0.1257 s =
   c. 40.1 m × 0.2453 m =
   d. 1.03 g − 0.0456 g =

(See the last page of the Skills Handbook for the answers to practice problems.)

Line Graphs

In laboratory experiments, you will usually control one variable and see how it affects another variable. Line graphs can show these relationships clearly. For example, you might perform an experiment in which you measure the volume of a gas at different temperatures to determine how volume is related to temperature. In this experiment, you are controlling the temperature intervals at which the gas's volume is measured. Therefore, temperature is the independent variable. The volume of the gas is the dependent variable. The table below gives some sample data for an experiment that measures the volume of gas.

The independent variable is plotted on the x-axis. This axis is labeled "Temperature (K)" and has a range from 0 to 400 K. Be sure to properly label each axis, including the units.

The dependent variable is plotted on the y-axis. This axis is labeled "Volume (L)" and has a range of 0.0 to 1.4 L.

Experimental Data for Gas Volume Versus Temperature	
Temperature (K)	Gas volume (L)
0	0.0
100	0.35
200	0.70
300	1.05
400	1.4

Think of your graph as a grid that has lines running horizontally from the y-axis and vertically from the x-axis. To plot a point, find the x value on the x-axis. For the example above, plot each value for time on the x-axis. Follow the vertical line from the x-axis until it intersects the horizontal line from the y-axis at the corresponding y value. For the example, each temperature value has a corresponding volume value. Place your point at the intersection of these two lines.

The line graph below shows how the data in the table may be graphed.

Bar Graphs

Bar graphs are useful for comparing data values. If you wanted to compare the area or depth of the major oceans, you might use a bar graph. The table below gives the data for each of these quantities.

Depth of the Major Oceans	
Ocean	Depth (m)
Pacific Ocean	4,028
Atlantic Ocean	3,926
Indian Ocean	3,963
Arctic Ocean	1,205

To create a bar graph from the data in the table, begin on the x-axis by labeling four bar positions with the names of the four oceans. Label the y-axis "Depth (m)." Be sure the range on your y-axis includes 1,205 m and 4,028 m. Then, draw the bars to represent the area of each ocean.

Make sure the bar height on the y-axis matches each ocean's area value, as shown in the bar graph below.

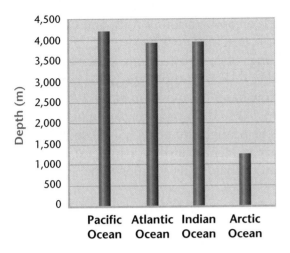

Pie Graphs

Pie graphs can help you visualize how many parts make up a whole. Frequently, pie graphs are made from percentage data. For example, you could create a pie graph that shows the percentage of different materials that make up the waste generated in cities of the United States. Study the example data in the table below.

United States Municipal Solid Waste	
Material	**Percentage of total waste**
Paper	38.1%
Yard waste	12.1%
Food waste	10.9%
Plastics	10.5%
Metals	7.8%
Rubber, leather, and textiles	6.6%
Glass	5.5%
Wood	5.3%
Other	3.2%

To create a pie graph from the data in the table, begin by drawing a circle to represent the whole, or total. Because all circles are 360°, 1% of a circle is equal to 3.6°. From this point, the pie graph can be constructed in two ways.

First, a protractor can be used to measure the number of degrees that are represented by a percentage of the circle. For example, if paper represents 38% of the municipal solid waste in the United States, that percentage would be equal to $38 \times 3.6°$, or 138.6°.

Second, the circle can be divided into 100 equal sections of 3.6° each. Then, you can shade in 38 consecutive sections and label that area "Paper." Continue to shade sections with other colors until the entire pie graph has been filled in and until each type of waste has a corresponding area in the circle, as shown in the pie graph below.

United States Municipal Solid Waste (Percentage by Weight)

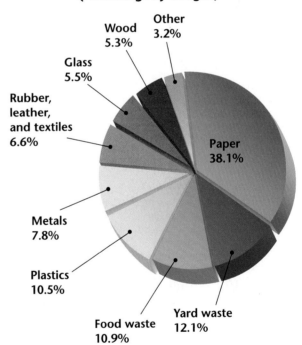

Ternary Diagrams

Ternary graphs, or ternary diagrams, show three variables on the same plot. Earth scientists use ternary diagrams to show composition of rocks and minerals and the physical states of rock material. The most common use of ternary diagrams is to represent the relative percentage of three components, such as three minerals or three elements.

The composition of any point on a ternary diagram can be described by first determining the percentage of each of the three components, as shown in the diagram below. In a ternary diagram, any point represents the relative percent-

age of three components: A, B, and C. The three components must always add up to 100%. In other words, the total composition of the mineral or rock represented by a given point on a ternary diagram is a combination of A, B, and C, so that $x\%$ A + $y\%$ B + $z\%$ C = 100%.

Readings of composition are stated as % A, % B, and % C. For example, the point in the diagram below has a composition of 40% A, 50% B, and 10% C. In most ternary diagrams, areas of the triangle are given names so that scientists can identify a rock or mineral by its name, rather than by its composition.

How to Read a Ternary Diagram

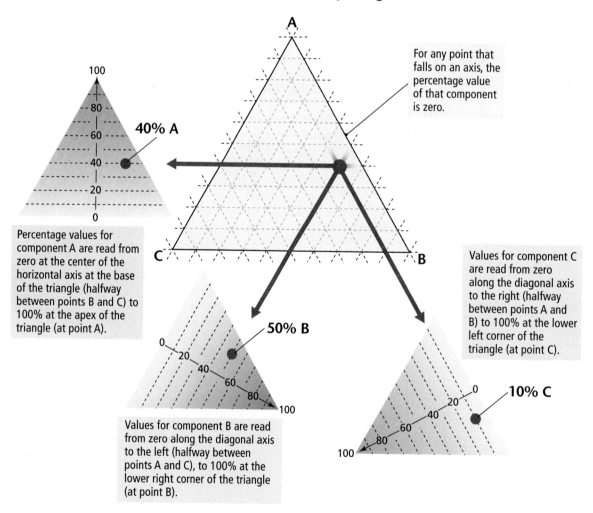

For any point that falls on an axis, the percentage value of that component is zero.

Percentage values for component A are read from zero at the center of the horizontal axis at the base of the triangle (halfway between points B and C) to 100% at the apex of the triangle (at point A).

Values for component B are read from zero along the diagonal axis to the left (halfway between points A and C), to 100% at the lower right corner of the triangle (at point B).

Values for component C are read from zero along the diagonal axis to the right (halfway between points A and B) to 100% at the lower left corner of the triangle (at point C).

Atoms and Elements

Every object in the universe is made up of particles of matter. Matter is anything that has mass and takes up space. An element is a substance that cannot be separated into simpler substances by chemical means. Elements cannot be separated in this way because each element consists of only one kind of atom. An atom is the smallest unit of an element that maintains the properties of that element.

Atomic Structure Atoms are made up of small particles called *subatomic particles*. The three major types of subatomic particles are **electrons, protons,** and **neutrons.** Electrons have a negative electrical charge, protons have a positive charge, and neutrons have no electrical charge. The protons and neutrons are packed close to one another and form the **nucleus.** The protons give the nucleus a positive charge. The electrons of an atom are located in a region around the nucleus known as an **electron cloud.** The negatively charged electrons are attracted to the positively charged nucleus.

Atomic Number To help in the identification of elements, scientists have assigned an **atomic number** to each kind of atom. The atomic number is equal to the number of protons in the atom. Atoms that have the same number of protons are all of the same element. An uncharged, or electrically neutral, atom has an equal number of protons and electrons. Therefore, the atomic number is also equal to the number of electrons in an uncharged atom. The number of neutrons, however, can vary for a given element. Atoms that have different numbers of neutrons but are of the same element are called **isotopes.**

Periodic Table of the Elements In a periodic table, the elements are arranged in order of increasing atomic number. Each element in the table is found in a separate box. In each horizontal row of the table, each element has one more electron and one more proton than

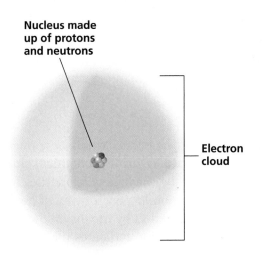

Nucleus made up of protons and neutrons

Electron cloud

▶ The nucleus of the atom contains the protons and neutrons. The protons give the nucleus a positive charge. The negatively charged electrons are in the electron cloud surrounding the nucleus.

the element to its left. Each row of the table is called a **period.** Changes in chemical properties across a period correspond to changes in the elements' electron arrangements. Each vertical column of the table, known as a **group,** contains elements that have similar properties. The elements in a group have similar chemical properties because they have the same number of electrons in their outer energy level. For example, the elements helium, neon, argon, krypton, xenon, and radon all have similar properties and are known as the *noble gases.*

Molecules and Compounds

When the atoms of two or more elements are joined chemically, the resulting substance is called a **compound.** A compound is a new substance that has properties different from those of the elements that compose it. For example, water, H_2O, is a compound formed when atoms of hydrogen, H, and oxygen, O, combine. The smallest complete unit of a compound that has all of the properties of that compound is called a **molecule.**

Chemical Formulas

A chemical formula indicates the elements that make up a compound. The chemical formula also indicates the relative number of atoms of each element present. For example, the chemical formula for water is H_2O, which indicates that each water molecule consists of two atoms of hydrogen and one atom of oxygen.

Chemical Equations

A chemical reaction occurs when a chemical change takes place. (During a chemical change, new substances that have new properties form.) A chemical equation is a useful way of describing a chemical reaction by means of chemical formulas. The equation indicates the substances that react and the products. For example, when carbon and oxygen combine, they can form carbon dioxide. The equation for this reaction is as follows:

$$C + O_2 \rightarrow CO_2$$

Acids, Bases, and pH

An ion is an atom or group of atoms that has an electrical charge because it has lost or gained one or more electrons. When an acid, such as hydrochloric acid, HCl, is mixed with water, the acid separates into ions. An acid is a compound that produces hydrogen ions, H^+, in water. The hydrogen ions then combine with a water molecule to form a hydronium ion, H_3O^+. A solution that contains hydronium ions is an acidic solution. A base, on the other hand, is a substance that produces hydroxide ions, OH^-, in water.

To determine whether a solution is acidic or basic, scientists measure pH. **pH** is a measure of how many hydronium ions are in solution. The pH scale ranges from 0 to 14. The middle point, pH = 7, is neutral, neither acidic nor basic. Acids have a pH of less than 7; bases have a pH of more than 7. The lower the number is, the stronger the acid is. The higher the number is, the stronger the base is. A pH scale is shown below.

pH Measurements of Some Common Substances

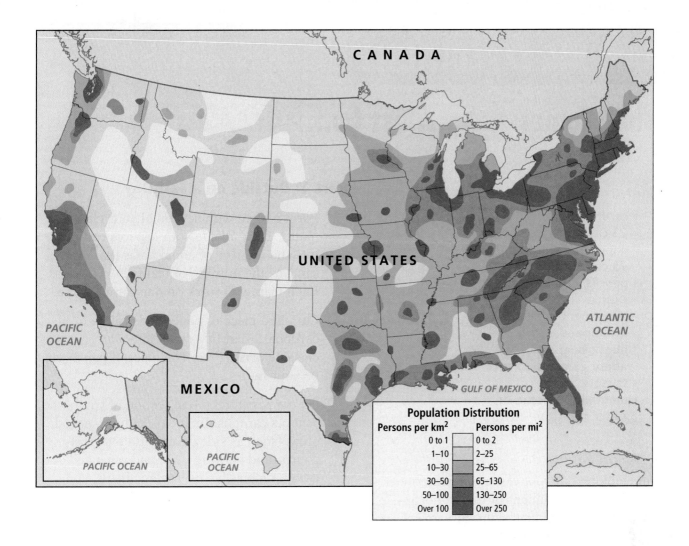

CANADA

UNITED STATES

PACIFIC OCEAN

MEXICO

ATLANTIC OCEAN

GULF OF MEXICO

PACIFIC OCEAN

PACIFIC OCEAN

Population Distribution

Persons per km²	Persons per mi²
0 to 1	0 to 2
1–10	2–25
10–30	25–65
30–50	65–130
50–100	130–250
Over 100	Over 250

1 Find your state on the map of natural resources on the previous page. What resources are produced in your state?

2 Look at the locations of the various resources. Which resources are commonly located near each other? Why do certain resources commonly occur together?

3 When tectonic plates collide, pockets of hot magma may come into contact with cooler, solid rock. Using what you know about plate tectonics and the ways in which minerals form, describe why Washington has more iron-ore deposits than Nebraska does.

4 Describe the conditions that existed in the United States millions of years ago and that resulted in the formation of the modern petroleum and natural-gas deposits.

5 Compare the map on this page with the map on the previous page. What areas have both high concentrations of people and a large reserve of natural resources? What areas have many people but few resources? How could resources be transported to areas in which they are needed?

6 Using these two maps, would you say that most cities have grown up in places in or near which there are natural resources? Why or why not? What other factors could have influenced the location of cities?

7 Imagine that you work for a company that builds electrical equipment made primarily of copper. Why might southern Arizona be a good place to locate a new plant? What might be a disadvantage of locating your plant there?

MAPPING EXPEDITIONS

What Comes Down Must Go...*WHERE?*

Materials

- cardboard, about 23 cm × 33 cm
- paper, about 23 cm × 33 cm
- pencils, red, blue, and purple
- permanent marker, fine-tipped
- plastic bag, reclosable, about 23 cm × 33 cm
- scissors
- umbrella, raincoat, or other rain gear

Imagine looking out your classroom window during a downpour. Billions of tiny raindrops splatter off of everything in sight. Streams of water fall from the roof and form dozens of puddles and streams on the ground. These miniature lakes and rivers swirl together, and tiny torrents carry away leaves, bits of trash, and other debris. A day or two later, the ground outside looks completely dry. Where did all of the water go?

In this activity, you will create a map of your school. After observing the type of ground cover and the slope of the terrain at various locations, you will predict whether rainwater will collect or run off at those locations. You will also look for possible sources of pollution and places where erosion might occur. Later, you will go outside in the rain and find out whether your predictions are correct.

Part 1: Outside on a Fair Day

1 Form a team with several of your classmates. Then, divide your school's campus into the number of equal areas that is the same as the number of teams in your class. Each team will work on one campus area.

2 Cut out a piece of paper and a piece of cardboard that fit exactly into a large reclosable plastic bag. The piece of paper will be your map.

3 On the paper, map one section of your school's campus. Include buildings, paved areas (such as sidewalks, outdoor sports courts, and parking lots), and vegetated areas (such as lawns, athletic fields, and wooded areas). The map on the next page is an example of the type of map that you will make.

4 **a.** Use a red pencil to mark the areas on your map. Draw arrows to indicate a downhill slope. Use a narrow arrow to indicate a steep slope and a wider arrow to indicate a gradual slope. Use circles to indicate flat areas.

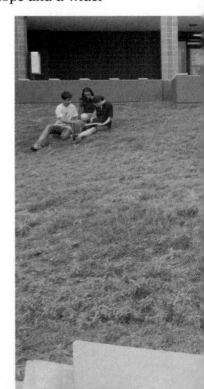

b. Use a blue pencil to draw arrows and circles that indicate where you think surface water may collect or flow during a steady rain. These areas may include low-lying areas, the roofs of buildings, gutters, and drainage ditches.

c. Use a purple pencil to mark the locations that you think might contribute pollution to the runoff. (These areas may include parking lots that contain oil stains or places where trash is usually found on the ground, such as near a dumpster.)

5 Seal your map and the piece of cardboard in the reclosable bag. When you are outside in the rain, use a permanent marker to write your observations on the outside of the bag.

Part 2: Outside During a Steady Rain

6 Dress appropriately, and go outside. Using the marker, write on your plastic-covered map the places where water collects and runs. In places where water moves along the ground, use arrows to show the water's direction. Use the letter *P* to mark the locations of pollutants that you observe in the water. Use the letter *E* to mark the locations where erosion seems to be occurring. (Look for soil or natural debris that is being washed along by moving water.)

Part 3: Back in the Classroom

7 Discuss your predictions for some of the locations. Were your predictions correct? How do you explain differences between your predictions and your observations?

8 Was the pollution that you observed suspended load, bed load, or dissolved load? Explain how there may have been pollution that you could not observe.

9 Explain how erosion on your school's campus could affect the erosion and deposition that occurs downstream from the campus.

10 Assemble the maps from your class into a single map of your school's campus. In your opinion, does most of the rainfall at your school become groundwater or runoff? Where does runoff go when it leaves your school's campus? Your school is probably part of a larger, local watershed. Find out what stream or other body of water the surface runoff in your area empties into.

Africa

MAPPING EXPEDITIONS

Where the **hippos** Roam

Materials
- pencils, assorted colors
- ruler, metric

Millions of years ago, ancestors of modern crocodiles lurked in the shallow waters of lakes and other bodies of water. Like their current descendents, they hunted fish and other animals. If you could travel back in time to visit one of those lakes, you might see the ancestors of today's hippopotamuses there, too. Antelopes might browse along the edges of the lake, and rodents of various sizes might scurry back and forth.

When paleontologists examine the fossil of a prehistoric organism, they may discover clues about the organism's life. They may also answer questions about the organism's environment: Was the area hot or cold? Was it humid or dry?

Then, by putting all of these clues together, the paleontologists may be able to learn a little more about how organisms and environments change over time.

Unfortunately, studying a fossil site is no easy task! Discoveries of complete organisms are rare. More often, a paleontologist may find a few teeth scattered over a very large area. In such cases, keeping track of where the fossils were found is very important. In this activity, you will use the data from a fossil site to create a map of fossil locations at that site. Then, you will draw some conclusions about the past environment, or *paleoenvironment*, at that location.

▶ The animals that lived near lakes millions of years ago probably had lives similar to the lives of animals that live near lakes today.

Location of Fossil Teeth				
Layer	Hippos	Rodents	Crocodiles	Bovids*
A	B11, C6, D3, I15, J10, L7, M6		C14, F7, G13, I3, L13, O2	
B	F2, J3, K1, K2	B10, B11, F13	H2, I7, K2, N5, N7	G14
C		B3, C10, D1, H8, M9, N4		A5, A6, E2, E4, E14, H7, H8, H12, K4, M1, N15

*Bovids are antelopes and other such animals.

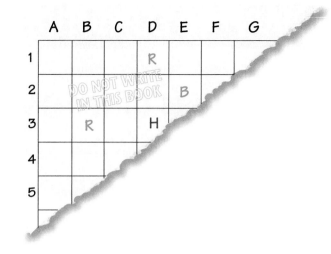

The table above shows the locations of fossils that were found spread out over 22,500 m². A team of paleontologists decided that this site, which measured 150 m × 150 m, was too large to work on all at once. So, the paleontologists decided to create a grid of 10 m squares. Starting in the northwest corner of the site, they labeled the squares from west to east with the letters A–O. Then, they numbered the squares 1–15 from north to south. Thus, each fossil could be labeled with a letter and a number that would identify where the fossil was found. For example, A1 would signify the 10 m × 10 m square in the northwest corner of the site, and O15 would signify the square in the southeast corner.

1. Create a map of the fossil site by drawing a grid similar to the one described above. The scale should be 1 cm = 10 m. Use letters to label across the top edge of the grid, and use numbers to label down the left edge of the grid. For each fossil, place a letter (*H* for a hippo fossil, *R* for a rodent fossil, *C* for a crocodile fossil, and *B* for a bovid fossil) in the square that corresponds to where the fossil was found. Use pencil color to represent the different layers of sediment, and make a key that shows which layer each color represents.

2. From the distribution of fossils in the layer of sediment just below the surface layer, what part of this site might have been underwater? Explain your answer, and devise a way to show that area on your map.

3. Describe how the environment at this site changed over time.

4. One team member wished to search this site for fossils of dry-climate plants. Which layer or layers would most likely yield fossils of such plants? Explain your answer.

5. One paleontologist suggested that tectonic uplift had raised the area's elevation over time and thus caused the climate to change. A second paleontologist thought that the area had probably lost elevation over time. With which scientist do you agree? Explain your answer.

▶ Fossils, such as these crocodile teeth, help scientists learn what an area was like millions of years ago.

MAPPING EXPEDITIONS

United States

Snapshots of the Weather

Materials
- paper, tracing
- pencil

From looking at a weather map, you might get the impression that the clouds, fronts, and other features shown are standing still. However, weather patterns change constantly, and a weather map can show only what is happening at one particular instant. For this reason, meteorologists rely on a sequence of maps to make predictions about local weather.

In this activity, you will analyze a sequence of weather maps. The maps were taken from a daily newspaper and show weather patterns that occurred in the United States during a 4-day period. You will note what information the maps show and do not show, and you will make a few predictions based on your observations.

1 Look carefully at the maps on the next page. What weather information do they show? Now, look at the weather symbols in the Reference Tables section of the Appendix. What information is not included on these maps? Why might a newspaper exclude certain types of information on daily weather maps?

2 Why would a newspaper that serves only a specific geographic region publish the weather for the entire continental United States?

3 Describe how the weather patterns in your location changed during the 4-day period shown.

4 During what season do you think this 4-day period occurred? Explain your answer.

5 Trace the outline of one weather map on a separate piece of paper, but do not include any information on the map. Predict the locations of the fronts on the day following this 4-day period. Note the locations of the fronts on your new map.

6 Predict the temperature and precipitation patterns that occur in your location on the day following this 4-day period.

▶ This tornado twisted through Manchester, South Dakota, on June 24, 2003. On the same day, South Dakota had its largest recorded outbreak of twisters ever!

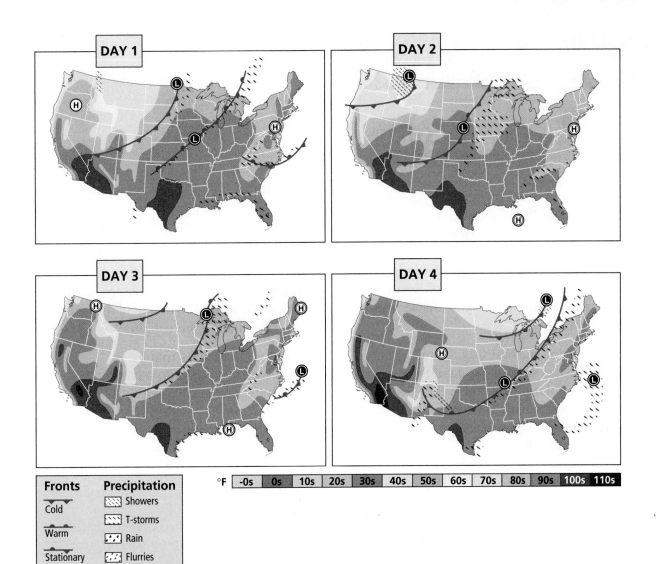

DAY 1

DAY 2

DAY 3

DAY 4

Fronts

Cold

Warm

Stationary

Precipitation

Showers

T-storms

Rain

Flurries

Snow

Ice

°F | -0s | 0s | 10s | 20s | 30s | 40s | 50s | 60s | 70s | 80s | 90s | 100s | 110s

▶ Thunderstorms, such as this one in Tucson, Arizona, bring much-needed moisture to dry regions.

MAPPING EXPEDITIONS

Stars in Your Eyes

A constellation is an arbitrary grouping of stars. The map to the right shows constellations that can be seen from the Northern Hemisphere of Earth. A Southern Hemisphere sky map, which is not provided, would show stars that can be seen from the Southern Hemisphere of Earth. Refer to the map to the right as you answer the questions below.

1 For many years, the best way to navigate at night was to use the stars as a guide. Many people used Polaris—the North Star—to orient themselves. This approach would not have worked for people all over the world, however. Why not?

2 What is the name of the constellation that contains Polaris?

3 What is the temperature of the star in the Bootes constellation, with magnitude 0?

4 The constellation Virgo can be observed from the Northern Hemisphere during the summer but not during the winter. Explain why.

5 Compare the constellation Draco on the map below with the constellation on the map to the right. What type of animal was this constellation named after?

6 Pick a group of stars that have not been connected into a constellation. Sketch the star group on a separate piece of paper. Connect the stars into a new constellation, and name your constellation.

▶ People, such as Sumerians, Greeks, Chinese, and Egyptians, have been grouping stars into constellations like these for thousands of years.

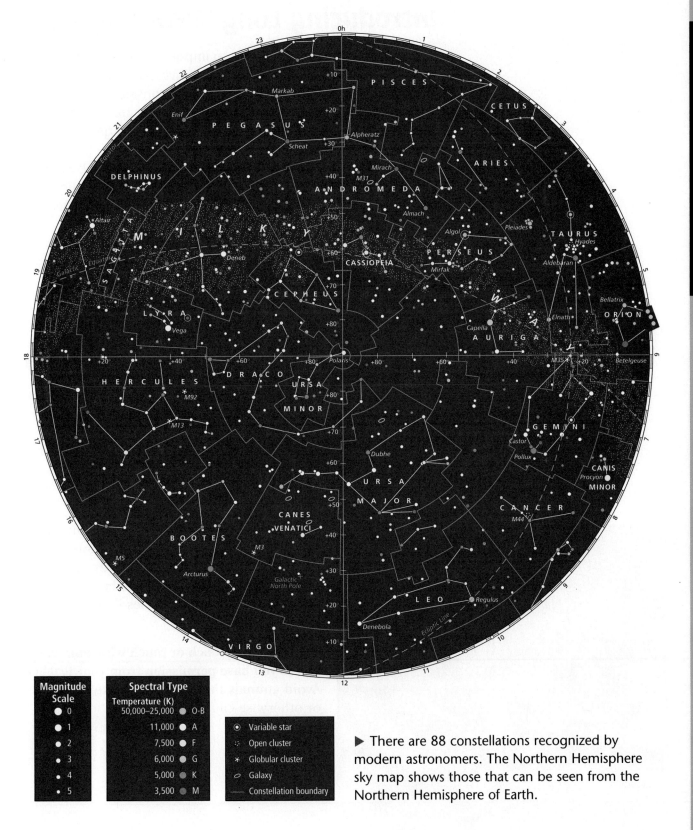

Magnitude Scale
- 0
- 1
- 2
- 3
- 4
- 5

Spectral Type
Temperature (K)
- 50,000–25,000 O-B
- 11,000 A
- 7,500 F
- 6,000 G
- 5,000 K
- 3,500 M

- ⊙ Variable star
- ⁙ Open cluster
- ✳ Globular cluster
- ⬭ Galaxy
- — Constellation boundary

▶ There are 88 constellations recognized by modern astronomers. The Northern Hemisphere sky map shows those that can be seen from the Northern Hemisphere of Earth.

Introducing Long-Term Projects

Scientific investigations that lead to important discoveries are almost never short term. Usually, these investigations last months, years, and even decades before results are considered complete and dependable. Investigations in Earth science are no exception. The long-term projects included in this section will give you practical experience in investigating Earth science the way that Earth scientists do—over extended periods of time. You will observe changes over time, keep detailed records of your observations, and draw conclusions from your data. By following these steps, you will learn firsthand what it is like to be an Earth scientist.

Safety First!

Many of the long-term projects require you to make field trips to an observation site or to conduct your activities outdoors. Advance planning is essential. You should plan carefully for these investigations and should be certain that you are aware of the safety guidelines that must be followed. The following are general guidelines for fieldwork and lab work.

Conducting Fieldwork

Find out about on-site hazards before setting out. Determine whether there are poisonous plants or dangerous animals where you are going, and know how to identify them. Also, find out about other hazards, such as steep or slippery terrain.

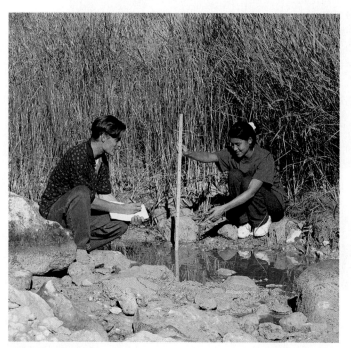

Wear protective clothing. Dress in a manner that will keep you warm, comfortable, and dry. Wear sunglasses, a hat, gloves, rain gear, or other gear to suit local weather conditions. Wear waterproof shoes if you will be near water or mud.

Do not approach or touch wild animals unless you have permission from your teacher. Avoid animals that may sting, bite, scratch, or otherwise cause injury.

Do not touch wild plants or pick wildflowers without permission from your teacher. Many wild plants can cause irritation or can be toxic, and many are protected by law. Never taste a wild plant.

Do not wander away from the group. Do not go beyond where you can be seen or heard. Travel with a partner at all times.

Report any hazards or accidents to your teacher immediately. Even if an incident seems unimportant, tell your teacher about it.

Consider the safety of the ecosystem that you will be visiting as well as your own safety. Do not remove anything from a field site without your teacher's permission. Stay on trails when possible to avoid trampling delicate vegetation. Never leave garbage behind at a field site. Strive to leave natural areas just as you find them.

Conducting Lab Work

Be aware of safety hazards. Any field or lab exercises in which there are known safety hazards will include safety cautions and icons to identify specific hazards. By being aware of safety concerns, you may avoid accidents. Know where safety equipment and emergency exits are located so that you are prepared in the event of an emergency.

Do not engage in inappropriate behavior. Most laboratory accidents are caused by carelessness, lack of attention, or inappropriate behavior. Always be aware of your surroundings, and pay attention to safety cautions.

Be neat. Keep your work area free of unnecessary clutter. Tie back loose hair and loose articles of clothing. Do not wear dangling jewelry or open-toed shoes in the lab. Never eat or drink in the laboratory.

Clean your lab station when your lab time is over. Before leaving the lab, clean up your work area. Put away all equipment and supplies, and dispose of chemicals and other materials as directed by your teacher. Turn off water, gas, and burners, and unplug electrical equipment. Wash your hands with soap and water after working on any lab.

For additional information about safety in the lab and in the field, refer to the Lab and Field Safety section in the front of this book. Don't take any chances with safety!

LONG-TERM PROJECT 1

Duration

8 or 9 months

Objectives

▶ **USING SCIENTIFIC METHODS**
Observe and record the positions of sunrise and sunset once per month.

▶ **USING SCIENTIFIC METHODS**
Graph and analyze collected data that describe the positions of sunrise and sunset.

▶ **Predict** the positions of sunrise and sunset for 3 or 4 months.

Materials

compass, magnetic

glue

paper

paper, graph

pen

pencil

poster board

scissors

twist tie (or pipe cleaner)

Safety

Positions of Sunrise and Sunset

You are probably aware that the sun rises in the east and sets in the west each day. What may not be obvious to you is that the positions of sunrise and sunset along the horizon differ from day to day in a specific pattern. As the positions of sunrise and sunset change, the amount of sunlight that an area receives also changes. In this investigation, you will observe the changes in the sun's position along the horizon at sunrise and at sunset. You will be making two observations on or near the 21st of each month for approximately 8 or 9 months (depending on the schedule of your school year).

PROCEDURE

1. Construct the bearing chart before taking any measurements. Copy the bearing chart from the next page onto a piece of paper.

2. Glue your copy of the chart to a piece of poster board. When the glue is dry, trim away the excess poster board.

3. Wrap the center of a twist tie once around the center of a pencil. Poke the ends of the twist tie through the center of the bearing chart to make a pointer for your chart.

The sun appears to rise and set at different positions relative to landmarks, such as these skyscrapers in Los Angeles, California.

④ On a cloudless morning just before sunrise, place the bearing chart on a level spot where no buildings or trees block your view of sunrise and sunset.
CAUTION Although sunlight is less intense at sunrise and sunset, you should never stare at the sun for extended periods of time.

⑤ Use the magnetic compass to determine the direction of north. Set the bearing chart so that 0° is pointing north and 180° is pointing south. (Note: Have the chart face the same direction for every observation, even months from now.) Try to align an edge of the chart with some permanent object near your observation point.

Step 1 Copy the chart below on a separate piece of paper, and use it to construct your bearing chart.

LONG-TERM PROJECTS

Step 7

Date	Position of sunrise (in degrees)	Position of sunset (in degrees)

DO NOT WRITE IN THIS BOOK

Many scientists think that ancient people used structures, such as Stonehenge in England, to predict astronomical occurrences and to determine the timing of solstices and equinoxes.

6 When the bearing chart is in place and properly aligned, measure the position of sunrise. (Note: Sunrise occurs at the instant the top of the sun appears on the horizon.) Without looking at the sun, measure its position by pointing the chart's pencil toward the sun. The shadow of the eraser end of the pencil will mark the sun's position.

7 In your lab notebook, draw a table like the one shown above. Record the position of sunrise (in degrees) in your table. That evening, measure and record the position of sunset (in degrees). (Note: Sunset occurs when the top edge of the sun drops below the horizon.)

8 Repeat steps 6 and 7 on the same date each month. (Note: On the equinoxes, the sun will rise due east and set due west. On the solstices, the sunrise and sunset will be shifted from these directions. The amount of the maximum shift will depend on the observer's latitude.)

Position of Sun at Sunrise

Step 9

9 On a sheet of graph paper, prepare a graph similar to the one shown at right. Label the graph's *y*-axis, which represents the position (in degrees) of the sun at sunrise, from 0° to 180°. The position of 90° will be in the center of the *y*-axis scale. The *x*-axis represents observation dates. Next, make a graph on which to plot the position of the sun at sunset. Label the *y*-axis of this graph from 180° to 360°.

10 On each graph, connect the points by drawing a smooth line. Estimate the positions of points between the plotted points.

ANALYSIS AND CONCLUSION

1 **Analyzing Data** On which date does the sun appear to follow the highest path across the sky? What happens to the length of daylight during this season?

2 **Analyzing Data** On which date does the sun appear to follow the lowest path across the sky? What happens to the length of daylight during this season?

3 **Analyzing Results** On which dates are the positions of the sun at sunrise and again at sunset about 180° apart? Those dates mark the beginning of which seasons?

4 **Describing Events** What general statement can you make about the pattern of sunrise and sunset according to the graphs?

5 **Forming a Hypothesis** Expand your graph to include the predicted position of the sun in June and July. Describe the pattern that you predicted.

Extension

1 **Evaluating Hypotheses** Use the process described in the investigation to chart the positions of sunrise and sunset for the months of June and July. How do your observations compare with your prediction?

2 **Making Comparisons** Use the same process to chart the positions of the moon at moonrise and moonset. Refer to an almanac when you choose the times at which you will make measurements. Do the positions of sunrise and sunset correlate to those of moonrise and moonset? What can you conclude from your observations?

LONG-TERM PROJECT 2

ENVIRONMENTAL CONNECTION

Duration

2 weeks

Objectives

▶ **USING SCIENTIFIC METHODS**
Count and record the number of particulates in the air over a 2-week period.

▶ **Analyze** how wind direction and particulate source are related.

Materials

compass, magnetic

microscope

microscope slides (8 or more)

paper, graph

pencil, grease

petroleum jelly

slide box

tape, masking or packaging, or rubber bands

Safety

Air-Pollution Watch

When certain types of pollutants are present in high concentrations, they threaten the general health and well-being of humans. Some substances that can be air pollutants include dust and smoke particles, pollen, mold spores, and waste gases. If these tiny particles remain suspended in the air for long periods of time, they are called *particulates*.

Wind direction affects the number of particulates in the air. If there is a source of particulates in an area, there will be a large number of particulates in the air when the wind blows from the direction of that source. There will be fewer particulates in the air when the wind blows from the direction opposite the source.

In this investigation, you will collect and view a few types of particulates. You will collect particulates from an outdoor site every day for 2 weeks. Then, you will examine those particulates.

PROCEDURE

1. Select a collection site in an open area, such as a large field or pasture, where the wind can blow past the site from every direction.

2. Locate a four-sided post, such as a 4 in. × 4 in. fence post, that is firmly driven into the ground. Try to choose a post whose top is at least 1 m above ground level. If there are no fences in your area, look for another four-sided structure that you could use.

Haze and smog are common in large cities, such as Los Angeles, California.

Step 3

Day	Date	Wind direction	Slide direction	Number of particulates					Total
				1	2	3	4	5	
1			N						
			S						
			E						
			W						

DO NOT WRITE IN THIS BOOK

3 Use a compass to establish north, south, east, and west directions from the post's location. Determine the direction from which the wind is blowing by watching objects, such as a flag, move in the wind. Record the wind direction and the date in a table like the one shown above.

4 Look for any phenomena that may affect air quality, such as smokestacks or heavy traffic. Record these observations and the day's weather conditions.

5 Use a grease pencil to mark on the back of each microscope slide the direction that the slide will face when placed on the post. Place each slide on the appropriate side of the post.

6 Use tape or rubber bands to attach the slides to the post, as shown on the lower-right side of this page. Use your finger to spread a thin, even film of petroleum jelly on one side of each slide.

7 Return to the site the following day. Remove the slides. Place each slide carefully in the slide box. (Note: Do not touch the greased surface.)

Step 6

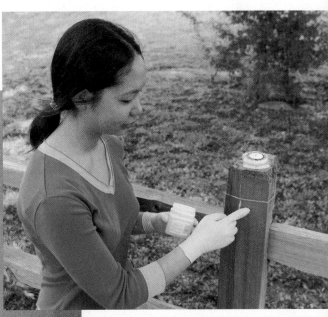

LONG-TERM PROJECT 2 *Air-Pollution Watch, continued*

8 Place new slides on the post, and record the wind direction and weather conditions.

9 Examine each slide under the microscope at 100×. Focus on one section that you have chosen at random. Count the number of particulates that you observe in the section. Record this number in column 1 of your table.

10 Move the slide, and examine another section that you have chosen at random. Count the number of particulates in this section. Record this number in column 2 of your table.

11 Repeat step 10 three more times so that you have a total of five observations per slide. Record the total number of particulates counted in the five sections.

12 Repeat steps 7 through 11 each weekday for 2 weeks.

13 When you have finished examining the slides and recording your results, total the number of particulates counted for each of the wind directions.

14 Using the data in your table, construct a bar graph. On the *y*-axis, plot the total number of particulates obtained in the past 5 days. On the *x*-axis, plot the day and wind direction. A sample graph is shown on the next page.

Step 9

A meteorologist from the National Weather Service tracks the path of a hurricane in the Gulf of Mexico.

6 On your copy of the map, put an *L* at any locations where low-pressure centers are shown on the daily weather map that you collected in step 1. Circle the *L*s with a colored pencil, and label each circle with the date.

7 Put an *H* on your map at the locations of any high-pressure centers. Circle the *H*s with a second colored pencil, and label each circle with the date.

8 Repeat steps 1–7, but use four consecutive daily weather maps that follow the first day's map, and reuse your data table and weather map. For each symbol, use the same colors that you used for the first day's map.

9 Draw arrows to connect the daily positions of each high-pressure center and of each low-pressure center.

10 Use the formula below to calculate the average velocity (in kilometers per day) of each high-pressure center and each low-pressure center. The average velocity equals the total distance traveled divided by the number of days traveled, or

$$average\ velocity = \frac{total\ distance\ traveled}{number\ of\ days}$$

Step 5

LONG-TERM PROJECTS

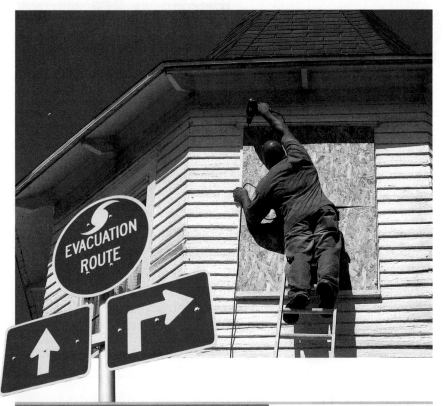

Many hurricane-prone areas have established evacuation routes to help people reach safety before a hurricane hits. This man is boarding up windows in his house to prepare for an imminent hurricane.

ANALYSIS AND CONCLUSION

1 **Analyzing Data** Generally, in which direction do the pressure centers over the United States move?

2 **Analyzing Results** From your calculations, what is the average rate of movement (in kilometers per day) of low- and high-pressure centers in winter?

3 **Making Predictions** Predict where the low- and high-pressure centers will be located on the day following the date of the last map in your series.

4 **Forming a Hypothesis** Refer to your series of daily weather maps to predict the weather for your hometown on the sixth day of the series. Write a forecast, and fill in the data table with your predictions of weather conditions.

5 **Evaluating Predictions** Was your prediction about the locations of the low- and high-pressure centers from question 3 accurate? Explain why or why not.

6 **Evaluating Hypotheses** Compare your weather prediction with the daily weather map for the appropriate day. Check the accuracy of your prediction. What factors could have caused errors in your prediction?

7 **Explaining Events** Describe the general weather conditions associated with regions of low and high atmospheric pressure.

Extension

1 **Designing Experiments** In the spring, repeat the entire investigation. What is the average rate of movement (in kilometers per day) of low- and high-pressure centers in the spring? Compare the rate of movement of pressure systems during spring and winter.

LONG-TERM PROJECT 5

Duration
6 months (October 1 to April 1)

Objectives
▶ **Record** temperature and precipitation data for eight regions.

▶ **USING SCIENTIFIC METHODS**
Graph and analyze climate features for eight regions.

▶ **Classify** regions by using two climate classification systems.

Materials
almanac

atlas

paper, graph

rain gauge (optional)

thermometer (optional)

weather reports, daily

Safety

Comparing Climate Features

A graph of the monthly temperatures and amounts of precipitation for a region is called a *climatograph*. Climatographs can be used to compare the climates of different areas or to classify an area's climate.

In this investigation, you will use climate data to compare your local climate with the climates of other regions of the United States. You will keep a daily temperature and precipitation log. You will record data every day from the first day of October until the first day of April. You will then compare your graphed data with information about the world's climates. You will use this comparison to develop a conclusion about the type of climate that your location has.

PROCEDURE

1. Listen to or watch a daily weather report for your area, or find this information in a daily newspaper or on the Internet. You may also keep your own records by using a thermometer and a rain gauge.

2. Beginning on the first day of October, keep a daily record of the high and low temperatures and of the amount of precipitation that occurs. During winter, snow should be melted before determining the amount of precipitation (in centimeters).

Rain gauges collect precipitation for scientists to measure.

3 Calculate the average temperature for each day by dividing the sum of the day's high and low temperatures by 2. Record this information.

4 At the end of each month, record the average monthly temperature given by the weather report, or calculate the average monthly temperature by dividing the sum of the daily averages by the number of days in the month. Also, record the total monthly precipitation given by the weather report.

5 Use the Internet or an almanac to look up climate data for your town or city and for seven other cities in the United States. Select one city from each of the following regions: New England, the Gulf Coast, the Midwest, the Southwest, the Pacific Northwest, the interior of Alaska, and the Hawaiian Islands.

Step 7

6 Look up the average monthly temperatures and precipitation for your town or city and for each city that you chose. Record these data in a table.

7 On your graph paper, make eight copies of the blank climatograph shown on the upper-right side of this page.

8 Label each blank climatograph with the name of one of the seven cities. Label the eighth climatograph with the name of your town or city.

9 If you recorded temperature and precipitation in English (American) units, such as degrees Fahrenheit or inches, convert your measurements to SI units, such as degrees Celsius or centimeters. Use the SI Conversions table in the Appendix of this book to convert English units to SI units.

10 For each of the eight locations, plot the average temperature for January by placing a dot in the center of the square that is located in the column representing January and in the row representing that average temperature.

11 Using the same method, plot the average precipitation for January.

12 Repeat steps 10 and 11 for each month's data for each location. Then, connect the temperature points and connect the precipitation points in order of consecutive months.

Tropical Rain Forest

Marine West Coast

Subarctic

Tropical Savanna

Humid Continental

Mediterranean

Tropical Desert

Tundra

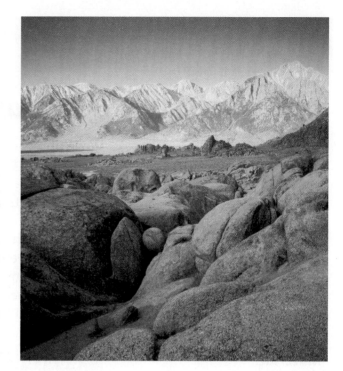

Although rain forests and deserts may have similar latitudes, the amount of precipitation that rain forests receive differs greatly from the amount that deserts receive.

ANALYSIS AND CONCLUSION

1 **Making Comparisons** Compare each of the climatographs of your seven chosen U.S. cities with the sample climatographs on the previous page. Identify the climate type or types for each location that you selected. What features of each climatograph helped you classify each region?

2 **Analyzing Results** Use the climatograph for your area to classify your regional climate. What features of your climatograph helped you identify the climate type?

3 **Examining Data** Compare the average temperatures and precipitation amounts for your location that you collected to the values that you obtained from the Internet or an almanac. Do you think that this year's climate data are typical for your region? Explain your answer.

4 **Classifying Information** How would each of the climatographs, including the one for your region, fit into the climate classification system outlined in the chapter entitled "Climate"?

5 **Evaluating Methods** In this investigation, you compared climates by looking at average precipitation and temperature. What other factors might affect the climate of an area? Give examples of each factor.

Extension

1 **Making Comparisons** Bermuda is a small island in the Atlantic Ocean. Bermuda is at about the same latitude as St. Louis, Missouri, which lies in the middle of a continent. In which of the two locations does the temperature vary least from month to month? Explain the cause of the temperature pattern in the location that has the more moderate pattern.

LONG-TERM PROJECT 6

Duration
8 months

Objectives

▶ **Observe** the position of Mars in the night sky for 8 months.

▶ **USING SCIENTIFIC METHODS** **Graph** the apparent movement of Mars through the night sky.

▶ **Identify** changes in the relative positions of Earth and Mars.

Materials

celestial sphere model (optional)

compass, magnetic

constellation charts

flashlight

metric ruler

Planetary Motions

While observing the evening sky over a period of time, you might have noticed that some objects look like stars but do not maintain a fixed position relative to the celestial sphere. These objects are the planets. As viewed from Earth at various times during the year, the patterns in the planets' motion differ from the patterns that you might expect.

In this investigation, you will observe the planet Mars in the night sky on the 1st and 15th of each month over a period of 8 months. Then, you will use your observations to draw conclusions and make predictions about planetary motion.

PROCEDURE

1 Obtain data on the positions of Mars in the night sky throughout the last year from an astronomical yearbook or from the Internet. Astronomical yearbooks can be found at most libraries.

2 Check the Internet, an almanac, or the weather section of a newspaper to find the time of night that Mars will be visible in your area.

3 Copy the star chart on the third and fourth pages of this lab onto a separate piece of paper.

4 Practice measuring angular distance by using the method shown at the bottom of this page. Always use the same hand when measuring angular distance. To have confidence in the accuracy of your measurements, you may need to practice measuring angular distance for a few days or weeks before beginning this lab.

Step 4

Estimating Angular Distance in Degrees
Hold your hand at arm's length.

1°   5°   10°   15°

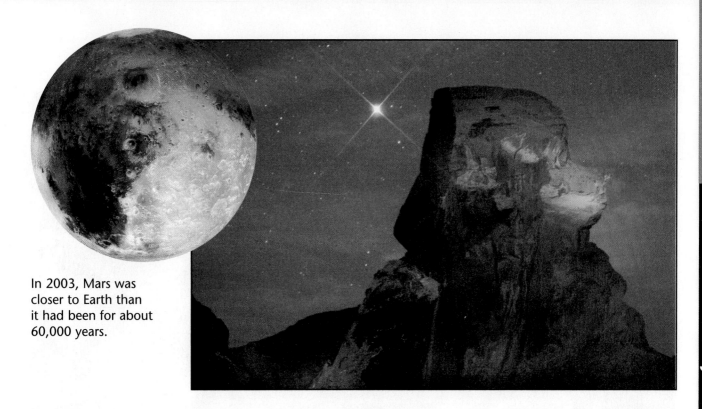

In 2003, Mars was closer to Earth than it had been for about 60,000 years.

5. On the 1st and 15th of each month, go at night to an area that gives you a clear view of the eastern, southern, and western skies. (Note: If the skies are not clear on the 1st and 15th, make observations as close to these dates as possible.)

6. At the same time each night, locate Mars in the night sky. Mars will have a dull red appearance.

7. Use your magnetic compass to position yourself facing south, and observe the position of Mars relative to the background stars.

8. Choose a constellation. Use the method illustrated at the bottom of the previous page to estimate Mars's angular distance (in degrees) from the constellation.

9. On your star chart, locate the constellation from which you measured Mars's angular distance. Draw Mars in the appropriate position relative to the constellation, and label the planet's position with the date.

10. Compare the apparent brightness of Mars with that of the background stars. Record your observation on a separate sheet of paper.

11. Repeat steps 6–10 on the 1st and 15th of each month for the next 8 months.

12. After each observation, draw an arrow from Mars's previous position to the position that you just observed. The progression of arrows will show Mars's apparent path.

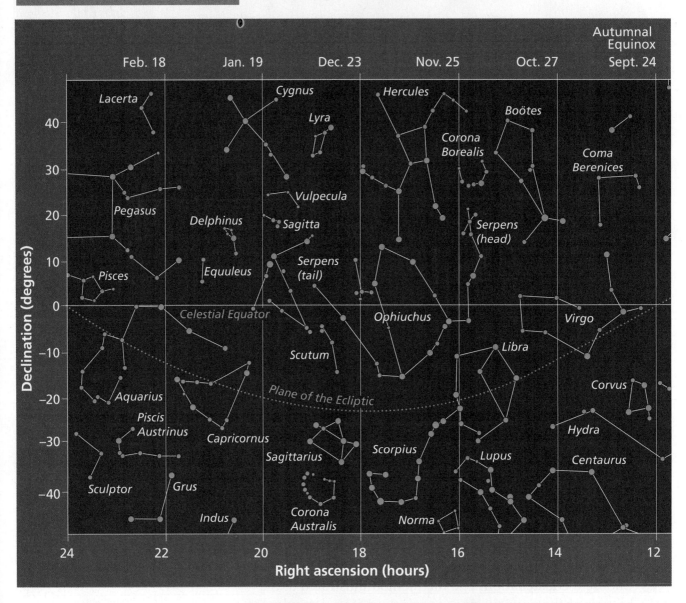

Step 3

ANALYSIS AND CONCLUSION

1 **Examining Data** In which months does Mars appear highest in the night sky? lowest in the night sky?

2 **Evaluating Results** In which direction does Mars appear to move across the sky? At any point during the year, does Mars appear to deviate from this apparent path?

3 **Making Predictions** In one year from today, will Mars be in the same position that it is in today? Explain.

4 **Drawing Conclusions** From your observations of the apparent brightness of Mars at different times of the year, what can you infer about the distance between Mars and Earth? Explain your answer.

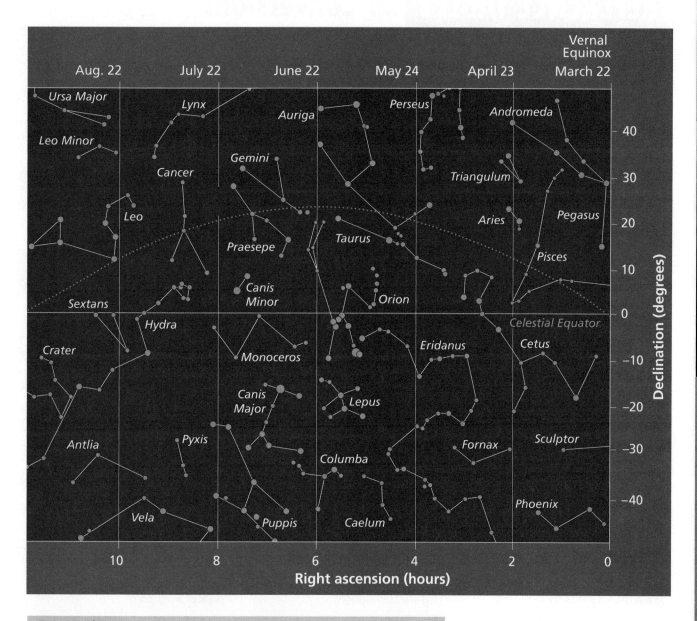

Extension

❶ **Evaluating Predictions** In the Analysis and Conclusion section of this investigation, you predicted the position of Mars in one year. Use the Internet or library to research where astronomers predict Mars will be in one year. Was your prediction accurate? Explain why or why not.

❷ **Evaluating Hypotheses** Repeat this investigation, but measure the positions of another planet, such as Venus, for the course of 8 months. Write a brief essay that explains how the paths of Mars and Venus differ.

The metric system is used for making measurements in science. The official name of this system is the Système Internationale d'Unités, or International System of Measurements (SI).

SI Units	From SI to English	From English to SI
Length		
kilometer (km) = 1,000 m	1 km = 0.62 mile	1 mile = 1.609 km
meter (m) = 100 cm	1 m = 3.28 feet	1 foot = 0.305 m
centimeter (cm) = 0.01 m	1 cm = 0.394 inch	1 inch = 2.54 cm
millimeter (mm) = 0.001 m	1 mm = 0.039 inch	
micrometer (μm) = 0.000 001 m		
nanometer (nm) = 0.000 000 001 m		
Area		
square kilometer (km^2) = 100 hectares	1 km^2 = 0.386 square mile	1 square mile = 2.590 km^2
hectare (ha) = 10,000 m^2	1 ha = 2.471 acres	1 acre = 0.405 ha
square meter (m^2) = 10,000 cm^2	1 m^2 = 10.765 square feet	1 square foot = 0.093 m^2
square centimeter (cm^2) = 100 mm^2	1 cm^2 = 0.155 square inch	1 square inch = 6.452 cm^2
Volume		
liter (L) = 1,000 mL = 1 dm^3	1 L = 1.06 fluid quarts	1 fluid quart = 0.946 L
milliliter (mL) = 0.001 L = 1 cm^3	1 mL = 0.034 fluid ounce	1 fluid ounce = 29.577 mL
microliter (μL) = 0.000 001 L		
Mass		* Equivalent weight at Earth's surface
kilogram (kg) = 1,000 g	1 kg = 2.205 pounds*	1 pound* = 0.454 kg
gram (g) = 1,000 mg	1 g = 0.035 ounce*	1 ounce* = 28.35 g
milligram (mg) = 0.001 g		
microgram (μg) = 0.000 001 g		
Energy		
British Thermal Units (BTU)	1 BTU = 1,055.056 joules	1 joule = 0.00095 BTU
Temperature		

°F 0 20 40 60 80 100 120 140 160 180 200 220

°C -20 -10 0 10 20 30 40 50 60 70 80 90 100

Freezing point of water   **Normal human body temperature**

Room temperature

Conversion of Fahrenheit to Celsius:

$$°C = \frac{5}{9}(°F - 32)$$

Conversion of Celsius to Fahrenheit:

$$°F = \frac{9}{5}(°C) + 32$$

Mineral Uses

Metallic Minerals

Mineral and chemical formula	Location of economically important deposits	Important uses
Chalcopyrite, $CuFeS_2$	Chile, U.S., and Indonesia	electrical and electronic products, wiring, telecommunications equipment, industrial machinery and equipment
Chromite, $FeCr_2O_4$	South Africa, Kazahkstan, and India	production of stainless steel, alloys, and metal plating
Galena, PbS	Australia, China, and U.S.	batteries, ammunition, glass and ceramics, and X-ray shielding
Gold, Au	South Africa, U.S., and Australia	computers, communications equipment, spacecraft, jet engines, dentistry, jewelry, and coins
Ilmenite, $FeTiO_3$	Australia, South Africa, and Canada	jet engines; missile components; and white pigment in paints, toothpaste, and candy
Magnetite, Fe_3O_4	China, Brazil, and Australia	steelmaking
Uraninite, UO_2	Canada and Australia	fuel in nuclear reactors and manufacture of radioisotopes

Nonmetallic Minerals

Mineral and chemical formula	Location of economically important deposits	Important uses
Barite, $BaSO_4$	China, India, and U.S.	weighting agent in oil well drilling fluids, automobile paint primer, and X-ray diagnostic work
Borax, $Na_2B_4O_7 \cdot 10H_2O$	Turkey, U.S., and Russia	glass, soaps and detergents, agriculture, fire retardants, and plastics and polymer additives
Calcite, $CaCO_3$	China, U.S., and Russia	cement, lime production, crushed stone, glassmaking, chemicals, and optics
Diamond, C	Australia, Democratic Republic of the Congo, and Russia	jewelry, cutting tools, drill bits, and manufacture of computer chips
Fluorite, CaF_2	China, Mexico, and South Africa	hydrofluoric acid, steelmaking, water fluoridation, solvents, manufacture of glass, and enamels
Gypsum, $CaSO_4 \cdot 2H_2O$	U.S., Iran, and Canada	wallboard, building plasters, and manufacture of cement
Halite, $NaCl$	U.S., China, and Germany	chemical production, human and animal nutrition, highway deicer, and water softener
Sulfur, S	Canada, U.S., and Russia	sulfuric acid, fertilizers, gunpowder, and tires
Kaolinite, $Al_2Si_2O_5(OH)_4$	U.S., Uzbehkistan, and Czech Republic	glossy paper and whitener and abrasive in toothpaste
Orthoclase, $KAlSi_3O_8$	Italy, Turkey, and U.S.	glass, ceramics, and soaps
Quartz, SiO_2	U.S., Germany, and France	glass, computer chips, ceramics, abrasives, and water filtration
Talc, $Mg_3Si_4O_{10}(OH)_2$	China, U.S., and Republic of Korea	ceramics, plastics, paint, paper, rubber, and cosmetics

Guide to Common Minerals

This table is used in the chapter lab for the chapter entitled "Minerals of Earth's Crust."

	Luster		Hardness	Cleavage	Fracture	Color/opacity	
Nonmetallic; light color	glassy to pearly	Scratches glass	6	two cleavage planes at nearly right angles		various colors but often white or pink; opaque	
	glassy		6	two cleavage planes at 86° and 94°		colorless, white, pink, or various colors; translucent to opaque	
	glassy and waxy		7	no cleavage	conchoidal fracture	various colors; transparent to opaque	
	glassy		6.5–7	no cleavage	conchiodal to irregular fracture	olive green; transparent to translucent	
	glassy	Does not scratch glass	2.5–3	three cleavage planes at right angles		colorless to gray; transparent to opaque	
	glassy		3	three cleavage planes at 75° and 105°		colorless or white and may be tinted; transparent to opaque	
	glassy, pearly, or silky		1–2.5	one perfect cleavage plane	conchoidal and fibrous fracture	white, pink, or gray to colorless; transparent to opaque	
	pearly to waxy		1	one cleavage plane		white to green; opaque	
	glassy or pearly		2–2.5	one cleavage plane		colorless to light gray or brown; translucent to opaque	
	glassy		4	eight cleavage planes (octahedral)		green, yellow, purple, and other colors; transparent to translucent	
	glassy		4.5–5	no cleavage	conchiodal to irregular fracture	green, blue, violet, brown, or colorless; translucent to opaque	
	silky		3.5–4	no cleavage	irregular, splintery fracture	green; translucent to opaque	
Nonmetallic; dark color	glassy and silky	Scratches glass	5–6	two cleavage planes at 56° and 124°		dark green, brown, or black; translucent to opaque	
	resinous and glassy		6.5–7.5	no cleavage	irregular fracture	dark red or green; transparent to opaque	
	pearly and glassy	Does not scratch glass	2.5–3	one cleavage plane		black to dark brown; translucent to opaque	
	metallic to earthy		5.5–6.5	no cleavage	irregular fracture	reddish brown to black; opaque	
Metallic	metallic or earthy	Does not scratch glass	1–2	one cleavage plane		black to gray; opaque	
	metallic		2.5	three cleavage planes at right angles		lead gray; opaque	
	metallic	Scratches glass	5–6	two cleavage planes at 56° and 124°		iron black; opaque	
	metallic		6–6.5	no cleavage	conchoidal to irregular fracture	brass yellow; opaque	

Streak	Specific gravity	Other properties	Mineral name and chemical formula
white	2.6	prismatic, columnar, or tabular crystals	orthoclase, $KAlSi_3O_8$
blue-gray to white	2.6 to 2.7	striations	plagioclase, $(Na, Cl)(Al, Si)_4O_8$
white	2.65	six-sided crystals	quartz, SiO_2
white to pale green	3.2 to 3.3	stubby, prismatic crystals	olivine, $(Mg, Fe)_2SiO_4$
white	2.2	cubic crystals and salty taste	halite, $NaCl$
white	2.7	may produce double image when you look through it	calcite, $CaCO_3$
white	2.2 to 2.4	thin layers and flexible	gypsum, $CaSO_4 \bullet 2H_2O$
white	2.7 to 2.8	soapy feel and thin scales	talc, $Mg_3Si_4O_{10}(OH)_2$
white	2.7 to 3	thin sheets	muscovite, $KAl_2Si_3O_{10}(OH)_2$
white	3.2	fluorescent under UV light; cubic and six-sided crystals	fluorite, CaF_2
white or pale red-brown	3.1	six-sided crystals	apatite, $Ca_5(OH, F, Cl)(PO_4)_3$
emerald green	4	fibrous, radiating aggregates or circular, banded structure	malachite, $CuCO_3 \bullet Cu(OH)_2$
pale green or white	3.2	six-sided crystals	hornblende, $(Ca, Na)_{2-3}(Mg, Fe, Al)_5$ $Si_6(Si, Al)_2O_{22}(OH)_2$
white	4.2	12- or 24-sided crystals	garnet, $Fe_3Al_2(SiO_4)_3$
white to gray	2.7 to 3.2	thin, flexible sheets	biotite, $K(Mg, Fe)_3AlSi_3O_{10}(OH)_2$
red to red-brown	5.25	granular masses	hematite, Fe_2O_3
black to dark green	2.3	greasy feel, soft, and flaky	graphite, C
lead gray to black	7.4 to 7.6	very heavy	galena, PbS
black to dark green	5.2	8- or 12-sided crystals; may be magnetic	magnetite, Fe_3O_4
greenish black	5	cubic crystals	pyrite, FeS_2

Guide to Common Rocks

This table is used in the chapter lab for the chapter entitled "Rocks."

Rock class	Grain size	Description	Rock class	Rock name
Made of crystals	Coarse grained	mostly light in color; shades of pink, gray, and white are common	igneous	granite
		dark in color; commonly black and white; heavy heft	igneous	gabbro
		foliated; layers of different minerals give a banded appearance	metamorphic	gneiss
		foliated; contains abundant amount of quartz, and may contain garnet; flaky minerals	metamorphic	schist
		nonfoliated; reacts with acid	metamorphic	marble
	Fine grained	usually light in color; many holes and spongy appearance; may float in water	igneous	pumice
		light to dark in color; glassy luster; conchoidal fracture	igneous	obsidian
		dark in color; may ring like a bell when struck with a hammer	igneous	basalt
		fine grained; foliated; cleaves into thin, flat plates	metamorphic	slate
Made of rock particles	Coarse grained	coarse-grained particles, more than 2 mm; rounded pebbles; some sorting; clay and sand are visible	sedimentary	conglomerate
		well-preserved fossils are common; can be scratched with a knife; many colors but usually white-gray; reacts with acid	sedimentary	limestone
		cube-shaped crystals; commonly colorless; does not react with acid	sedimentary	halite
	Medium grained	1/16 to 2 mm grains; mostly quartz fragments; surface feels sandy	sedimentary	sandstone
	Fine grained	soft and porous; commonly white or buff color	sedimentary	chalk
		microscopic grains; clay composition; smooth surface; hardened mud appearance	sedimentary	shale

Radiogenic Isotopes and Half-Life

Unstable isotopes, called *radiogenic isotopes* or *radioactive isotopes,* decay to form different isotopes called *daughter isotopes.* Each radiogenic isotope breaks down at a predictable rate, called its *half-life,* into a daughter isotope. Because of this predictable decay pattern, radiogenic isotopes are used to determine numeric dates for rocks. The table below describes several common radiometric dating methods.

Radiometric dating method	How it works	Parent isotope	Daughter isotope	Half-life	Effective dating range
Argon-argon dating (^{39}Ar/^{40}Ar)	Comparison made between ^{39}Ar and ^{40}Ar in a sample specially irradiated to form ^{39}Ar; ^{39}Ar is equivalent to ^{40}K in potassium-argon dating.	potassium-40 (^{40}K) irradiated to form argon-39 (^{39}Ar)	argon-40, ^{40}Ar	1.25 billion years	10,000 to 4.6 billion years
Fission track dating	Tracks of damage created by charged particles from radioactive decay that pass through a mineral's crystal lattice are counted under an electron microscope.	uranium, U	ultimately, lead, Pb, but also several other daughter isotopes	not applicable	500 years to 1 billion years
Potassium-argon dating (^{40}K/^{40}Ar)	Comparison is made between the amount of ^{40}K and amount of ^{40}Ar; over time, ^{40}K decreases and ^{40}Ar increases.	potassium-40, ^{40}K	argon-40, ^{40}Ar	1.25 billion years	50,000 to 4.6 billion years
Radiocarbon dating (^{14}C/^{12}C)	Comparison is made between the amount of ^{14}C in organic matter and the amount of ^{12}C; ^{12}C remains constant over time, and ^{14}C breaks down.	carbon-14, ^{14}C	nitrogen-14, ^{14}N	5,730 years	<80,000 years
Rubidium-strontium dating (^{87}Rb/^{87}Sr)	Comparison made between the ratio of ^{87}Sr/^{86}Sr and the ratio of ^{87}Rb/^{86}Sr to find the amount of ^{87}Sr formed by radioactive decay.	rubidium-87, ^{87}Rb	strontium-87, ^{87}Sr	48.8 billion years	10 million to 4.6 billion years
Thorium-lead dating	Comparison made between amount of ^{232}Th and the ratio of ^{208}Pb/^{204}Pb; ^{232}Th breaks into ^{208}Pb, and ^{204}Pb remains constant.	thorium-232, ^{232}Th	lead-208, ^{208}Pb	14.0 billion years	>200 million years
Uranium-lead dating (^{235}U/^{207}Pb)	Comparison made between amount of ^{235}U and the ratio of ^{207}Pb/^{204}Pb; ^{235}U breaks into ^{207}Pb, and ^{204}Pb remains constant.	uranium-235, ^{235}U	lead-207, ^{207}Pb	704 million years	10 million to 4.6 billion years
Uranium-lead dating (^{238}U/^{206}Pb)	Comparison made between amount of ^{238}U and the ratio of ^{206}Pb/^{204}Pb; ^{238}U breaks into ^{206}Pb, and ^{204}Pb remains constant.	uranium-238, ^{238}U	lead-206, ^{206}Pb	4.5 billion years	10 million to 4.6 billion years

Topographic and Geologic Map Symbols

Topographic Map Symbols

Elevation markers

Contour lines	
Index contour lines	100
Depression contour lines	
Water elevation	9600
Spot elevation	x 9136

Boundaries

National	
State	
County, parish, municipal	
Township, precinct, town	
Incorporated city, village, or town	
National or state reservation	
Small park, cemetery, airport, etc.	
Land grant	

Buildings and Structures

Buildings	
School	
Church	
Cemetery	† cem
Barn and warehouse	
Wells (non-water)	o oil o gas
Open-pit mine, quarry, or prospect	
Tunnel	
Benchmark	⊗BM △8025
National Park	
Campsite	
Bridge	

Roads and Railroads

Divided highway	
Road	
Trail	
Railroad	

Geologic Map Symbols

Sedimentary Rocks

Breccia	
Conglomerate	
Dolomite	
Limestone	
Mudstone	
Sandstone	
Siltstone	
Shale	

Igneous and Metamorphic Rocks

Extrusive	
Intrusive	
Metamorphic	

Features

River	
Water well	o ● ● ● ⊘ water
Spring	
Lake	
Glacier	

Contour Map

This map is used in the chapter lab for the chapter entitled "Models of the Earth."

Humidity and Air Pressure

The Relative Humidity table below is used in the chapter lab for the chapter entitled "Water in the Atmosphere." The Barometric Conversion Scale is used in the Long-Term Project entitled "Correlating Weather Variables" in the Appendix.

Relative Humidity (%)

Dry-bulb temperature (°C)	Difference in temperature (°C)									
	1.0	**2.0**	**3.0**	**4.0**	**5.0**	**6.0**	**7.0**	**8.0**	**9.0**	**10.0**
10	88	77	66	55	44	34	24	15	6	—
11	89	78	67	56	46	36	27	18	9	—
12	89	78	68	58	48	39	29	21	12	—
13	89	79	69	59	50	41	32	23	15	7
14	90	79	70	60	51	42	34	26	18	10
15	90	80	71	61	53	44	36	27	20	13
16	90	81	71	63	54	46	38	30	23	15
17	90	81	72	64	55	47	40	32	25	18
18	91	82	73	65	57	49	41	34	27	20
19	91	82	74	65	58	50	43	36	29	22
20	91	83	74	66	59	51	44	37	31	24
21	91	83	75	67	60	53	46	39	32	26
22	92	83	76	68	61	54	47	40	34	28
23	92	84	76	69	62	55	48	42	36	30
24	92	84	77	69	62	56	49	43	37	31
25	92	84	77	70	63	57	50	44	39	33
26	92	85	78	71	64	58	51	46	40	34
27	92	85	78	71	65	58	52	47	41	36
28	93	85	78	72	65	59	53	48	42	37
29	93	86	79	72	66	60	54	49	43	38
30	93	86	79	73	67	61	55	50	44	39
31	93	86	80	73	67	61	56	51	45	40
32	93	86	80	74	68	62	57	51	46	41
33	93	87	80	74	68	63	57	52	47	42
34	93	87	81	75	69	63	58	53	48	43
35	94	87	81	75	69	64	59	54	49	44
36	94	87	81	75	70	64	59	54	50	45
37	94	87	82	76	70	65	60	55	51	46
38	94	88	82	76	71	66	60	56	51	47
39	94	88	82	77	71	66	61	57	52	48
40	94	88	82	77	72	67	62	57	53	48

Barometric Conversion Scale

One Atmosphere 1013.2

Weather Map of the United States

This map is used in the chapter lab for the chapter entitled "Weather."

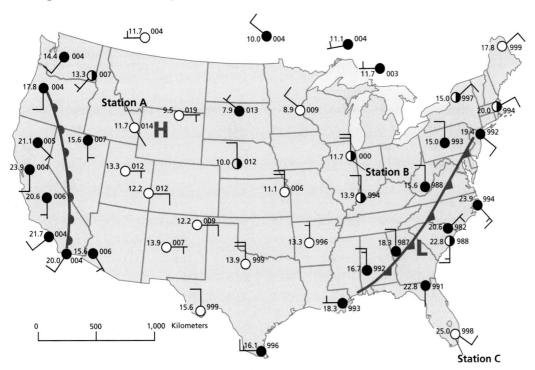

Weather Map Symbols

This chart is used in the Long-Term Project entitled "Weather Forecasting."

Cloud cover (fraction of sky covered)	○ Clear	◔ $\frac{1}{8}$	◑ Scattered	◕ $\frac{3}{8}$	◗ $\frac{4}{8}$
	◓ $\frac{5}{8}$	◕ Broken	◕ $\frac{7}{8}$	● Overcast	⊗ Obscured	No data
Wind speed (knots)	◉ Calm	│ 1 to 2	⌐ 3 to 7	⌐ 8 to 12	⌐ 13 to 17
	18 to 22	23 to 27	48 to 52	73 to 77	103 to 107
Wind direction	○— North	○ Northeast	○— East	○ Southeast
	○ South	○ Southwest	—○ West	○ Northwest
Weather conditions	❜ Drizzle	═ Fog	△ Hail	∞ Haze	● Rain	▽ Shower
	Freezing rain	Smoke	✳ Snow	Thunderstorm	Hurricane	Tropical storm

Solar System Data

Notes

The **semimajor axis** is the average distance between an object and its primary (the body the object revolves around).

Surface gravity indicated for the gas giants is calculated for the altitude at which the atmospheric pressure equals 1 bar.

Rotation period and **orbital period** are sidereal measurements (relative to the stars, not the sun).

* This value indicates distance from the sun in AU.

† This value represents the rate of rotation at the sun's equator. The sun displays differential rotation; in other words, it rotates faster at its equator than at its poles.

R This value indicates retrograde rotation or retrograde revolution.

	Sun	Mercury	Venus	Earth	Mars	Jupiter	Saturn	Uranus	Neptune
Mass (10^{24} kg)	1,989,100	0.33	4.87	5.97	0.642	1,899	568	86.8	102
Diameter (km)	1,390,000	4,880	12,100	12,756	6,800	143,000	120,535	51,120	49,530
Density (kg/m^3)	1,408	5,427	5,243	5,515	3,933	1,326	687	1,270	1,638
Surface gravity (m/s^2)	274	3.7	8.9	9.8	3.7	23.1	9	8.7	11
Escape velocity (km/s)	617.7	4.3	10.4	11.2	5	59.5	35.5	21.3	23.5
Rotation period (h)	609.12	1,407.6	5,832.5 R	23.9	24.6	9.9	10.7	17.2 R	16.1
Length of day (hours)	609.6†	4,222.6	2,802	24	24.7	9.9	10.7	17.2	16.1
Semimajor axis (10^6 km)	N/A	57.9	108.2	149.6	227.9	778.6	1,433.5	2,872.5	4,495.1
Perihelion (10^6 km)	N/A	46	107.5	147.1	206.6	740.5	1,352.6	2,741.3	4,444.5
Aphelion (10^6 km)	N/A	69.8	108.9	152.1	249.2	816.6	1,514.5	3,003.6	4,545.7
Orbital period (days)	N/A	88	224.7	365.2	687	4,331	10,747	30,589	59,800
Orbital velocity (km/s)	N/A	47.9	35	29.8	24.1	13.1	9.7	6.8	5.4
Orbital inclination (degrees)	N/A	7	3.4	0	1.9	1.3	2.5	0.8	1.8
Orbital eccentricity	N/A	0.205	0.007	0.017	0.094	0.049	0.057	0.046	0.011
Axial tilt (degrees)	7.25	0.01	2.6	23.5	25.2	3.1	26.7	82.2	28.3
Mean surface temperature (°C)	6,073	167	464	15	–65	–110	–140	–195	–200
Global magnetic field?	yes	yes	no	yes	no	yes	yes	yes	yes

	Earth's moon	Major moons of Jupiter				Major moons of Saturn			
		Io	Europa	Ganymede	Callisto	Dione	Rhea	Titan	Iapetus
Mass (10^{20} kg)	0.073	893.2	480.0	1,481.9	1,075.9	0.375	11.0	1,345.5	15.9
Diameter (km)	3,475	3,643.2	3,121.6	5,262.4	4,820.6	1,120	1,528	5,150	1,436
Density (kg/m^3)	3,340	3,530	3,010	1,940	1,830	1,500	1,240	1,881	1,020
Rotation period (days)	655.7	1.77	3.55	7.15	16.69	2.74	4.52	15.95	79.33
Semimajor axis (10^3 km)	0.384*	421.6	670.9	1,070.4	1,882.7	377.40	527.04	1,221.83	3,561.3
Orbital period (days)	27.32	1.77	3.55	7.15	16.69	2.74	4.52	15.95	79.33

	Major moons of Uranus			Major moons of Neptune		Pluto's moon	Selected asteroids		Selected comets	
	Umbriel	Titania	Oberon	Triton	Nereid	Charon	Vesta	Ceres	Chiron	Hale-Bopp
Mass (10^{20} kg)	11.7	35.2	30.1	214	0.2	19	3	8.7	—	—
Diameter (km)	1,169	1,578	1,523	2,707	340	1,186	530	960 × 932	—	—
Density (kg/m^3)	1,400	1,710	1,630	2,050	1,000	2,000	—	—	—	—
Rotation period	4.14 days	8.71 days	13.46 days	5.87 days R	unknown	6.39 days	5.342 h	9.075 h	—	—
Semimajor axis (10^3 km)	266.30	435.91	583.52	354.76	5,513.4	19,600	2.362 *	2.767 *	13.7 *	250 *
Orbital period	4.14 days	8.71 days	13.46 days	5.87 days R	360.14 days	6.39 days	3.63 y	4.60 y	50.7 y	4,000 y

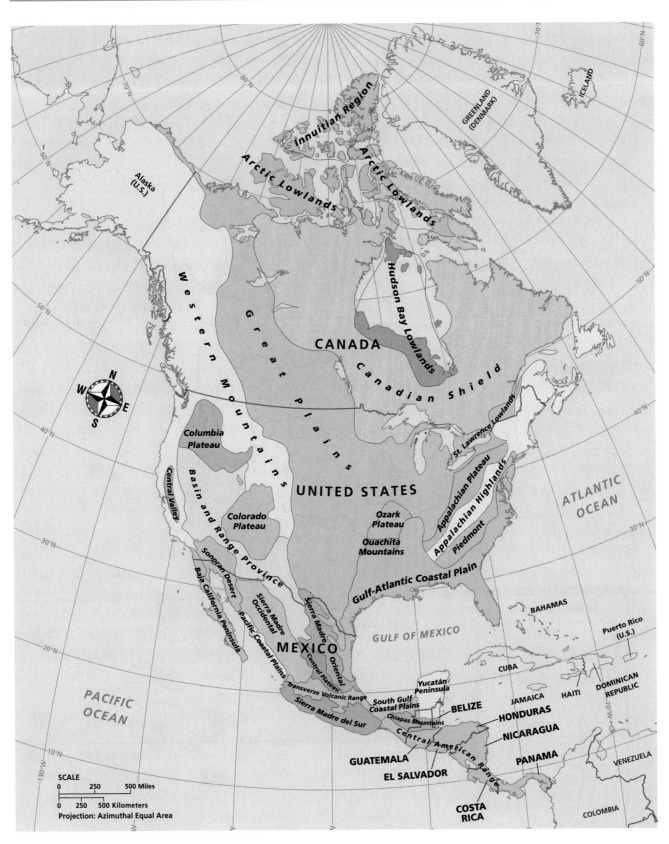

Geologic Map of North America

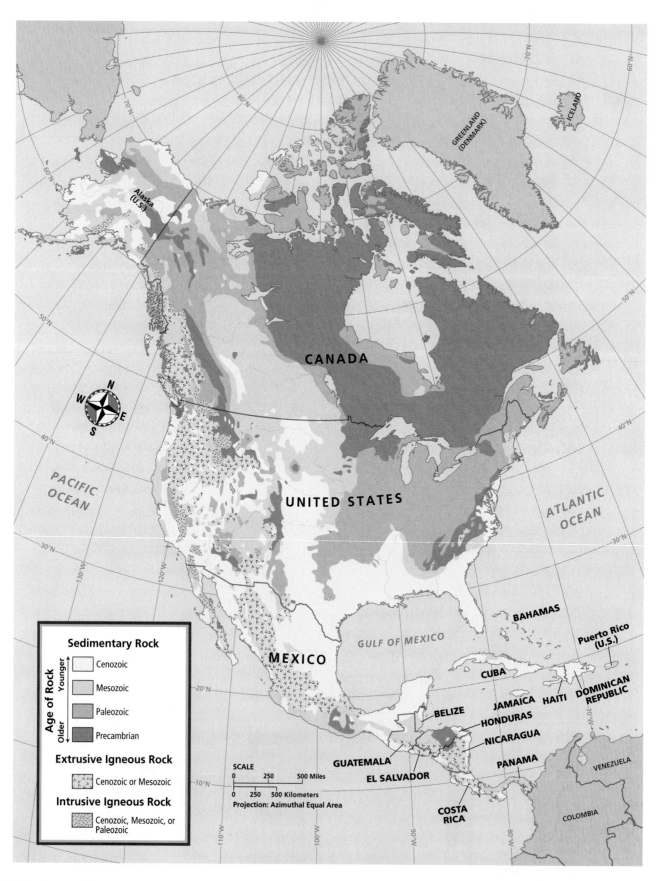

Age of Rock Younger → Older

Sedimentary Rock
- Cenozoic
- Mesozoic
- Paleozoic
- Precambrian

Extrusive Igneous Rock
- Cenozoic or Mesozoic

Intrusive Igneous Rock
- Cenozoic, Mesozoic, or Paleozoic

SCALE
0   250   500 Miles
0   250   500 Kilometers
Projection: Azimuthal Equal Area

Mineral and Energy Resources of North America

Resources

Cu	Copper	S	Sulfur
Au	Gold	U	Uranium
✎	Salt	✳	Major nuclear power plant
Ag	Silver	⬛	Hydroelectric power

Fossil Fuel Deposits of North America

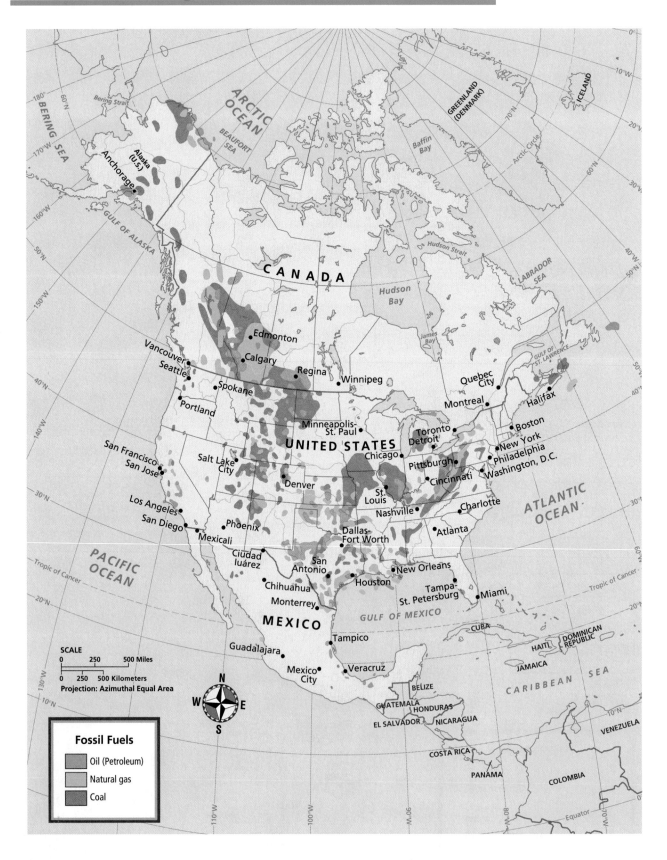

SCALE

0   250   500 Miles

0   250   500 Kilometers

Projection: Azimuthal Equal Area

Fossil Fuels

- Oil (Petroleum)
- Natural gas
- Coal

Topographic Maps of the Moon

Near Side

OCEANUS PROCELLARUM

Mare Iridum

Mare Imbrium

Apollo 15

Mare Serenitatis

Crater Copernicus

• Apollo 17

Mare Crisium

Mare Marginis

Mare Insularum

Mare Tranquillitatis

• Apollo 11

Apollo 12 •   • Apollo 14

Mare Fecunditatis

Mare Smythii

• Apollo 16

Mare Nectaris

Mare Nubium

Mare Humorum

Crater Tycho

Far Side

Mare Moscoviense

Crater Mendeleev

Crater Korolev

Crater Hertzsprung

Mare Orientale

Mare Ingenii

Crater Apollo

Mare Australe

● Apollo landing sites

-9,900 -8,000 -6,000 -4,000 -2,000 0 2,000 4,000 6,000 8,200 METERS

Color-coded topography key

Star Charts for the Northern Hemisphere

Spring

Summer

Constellations	
1	Ursa Minor
2	Draco
3	Cepheus
4	Cassiopeia
5	Auriga
6	Ursa Major
7	Boötes
8	Hercules
9	Cygnus
10	Perseus
11	Gemini
12	Cancer
13	Leo
14	Serpens
15	Sagitta
16	Pegasus
17	Pisces

Autumn

Winter

Constellations	
18	Aries
19	Taurus
20	Orion
21	Virgo
22	Libra
23	Ophiuchus
24	Aquila
25	Lepus
26	Canis Major
27	Hydra
28	Corvus
29	Scorpius
30	Sagittarius
31	Capricornus
32	Aquarius
33	Cetus
34	Columba

Maps of the Solar System

The diagram at top shows the relative sizes of the nine planets. The order of the planets from the sun is the following: Mercury, Venus, Earth, Mars, Jupiter, Saturn, Uranus, and Neptune. The diagrams at bottom show the orbits of the planets around the sun.

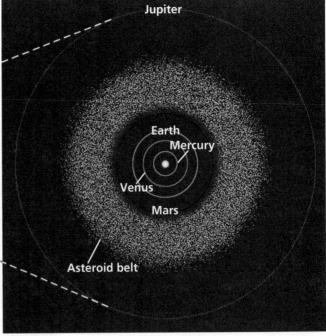

READING CHECK ANSWERS

Chapter 1 Introduction to Earth Science

Section 1
Page 7: The development of telescopes, satellites, and space probes has greatly expanded astronomers' understanding of the universe.

Section 2
Page 10: Observations may lead to interesting scientific questions and may help scientists formulate reasonable and testable hypotheses.

Page 13: Answers may vary but should include three of the following types of models: physical models, graphic models, conceptual models, computer models, and mathematical models.

Page 14: Scientists present the results of their work at professional meetings and in scientific journals.

Chapter 2 Earth as a System

Section 1
Page 28: Indirect observations are the only means available for exploring Earth's interior at depths too great to be reached by drilling.

Section 2
Page 32: Dust and rock come to Earth from space, while hydrogen atoms from the atmosphere enter space from Earth.

Page 34: An energy budget is the total distribution of energy to, from, and between Earth's various spheres.

Page 36: soil and plants

Section 3
Page 40: The amount of matter and energy in an ecosystem can supply a population of a given size, and no larger. This maximum population is the carrying capacity of the ecosystem.

Chapter 3 Models of the Earth

Section 1
Page 54: because the equator is the only parallel that divides Earth into halves

Section 2
Page 58: Because both the parallels and the meridians are equally spaced straight lines on a cylindrical projection, the parallels and meridians form a grid.

Page 61: by using a graphic scale, or a printed line divided into proportional parts that represent units of measure; a fractional scale, in which a ratio shows how distance on Earth relates to distance on a map; or a verbal scale, which expresses scale in sentence form

Section 3
Page 65: Water moves from areas of higher elevation to areas of lower elevation. Because the V shape points toward higher elevation, it points upstream.

Page 67: Scientists create soil maps to classify, map, and describe soils.

Chapter 4 Earth Chemistry

Section 1
Page 83: The atomic number is the number of protons in an atom's nucleus. The mass number is the sum of the number of protons and the number of neutrons in an atom. The atomic mass unit is used to express the mass of subatomic particles or atoms.

Section 2
Page 89: Atoms form chemical bonds by transferring electrons or by sharing electrons.

Page 91: The oxygen atom has a larger and more positively charged nucleus than the hydrogen atoms do. As a result, the oxygen nucleus pulls the electrons from the hydrogen atoms closer to it than the hydrogen nuclei pull the shared electrons from the oxygen. This unequal attraction forms a polar-covalent bond.

Chapter 5 Minerals of Earth's Crust

Section 1
Page 105: Nonsilicate minerals never contain compounds of silicon bonded to oxygen.

Page 106: The building block of the silicate crystalline structure is a four-sided structure known as the *silicon-oxygen tetrahedron*, which is one silicon atom surrounded by four oxygen atoms.

Section 2
Page 111: The strength and geometric arrangement of the bonds between the atoms that make up a mineral's internal structure determine the hardness of a mineral.

Page 113: Chatoyancy is the silky appearance of some minerals in reflected light. Asterism is the appearance of a six-sided star when a mineral reflects light.

Chapter 6 Rocks

Section 1
Page 127: As magma cools and solidifies, minerals crystallize out of the magma in a specific order that depends on their melting points.

Section 2
Page 131: Fine-grained igneous rock forms mainly from magma that cools rapidly; coarse-grained igneous rock forms mainly from magma that cools more slowly.

Page 133: A batholith is an intrusive structure that covers an area of at least 100 km^2. A stock covers an area of less than 100 km^2.

Section 3
Page 137: Three groups of clastic sedimentary rock are conglomerates and breccias, sandstones, and shales.

Page 139: Graded bedding is a type of stratification in which different sizes and types of sediments settle to different levels.

Section 4

Page 142: The high pressures and temperatures that result from the movements of tectonic plates may cause chemical changes in the minerals.

Chapter 7 Resources and Energy

Section 1

Page 156: Water creates ore deposits by eroding rock and releasing minerals and by carrying the mineral fragments and depositing them in streambeds.

Section 2

Page 161: Cap rock is a layer of impermeable rock at the top of an oil- or natural gas-bearing formation through which fluids cannot flow.

Page 162: As neutrons strike neighboring nuclei, the nuclei split and release additional neutrons that strike other nuclei and cause the chain to continue.

Section 3

Page 167: Answers may vary but should include three of the following: geothermal, solar, hydroelectric, and biomass.

Section 4

Page 170: The use of fossil fuels affects the environment when coal is mined from the surface, which destroys the land. When fossil fuels are burned, they affect the environment by creating air pollution.

Chapter 8 The Rock Record

Section 1

Page 186: Hutton reasoned that the extremely slow-working forces that changed the land on his farm had also slowly changed the rocks that make up Earth's crust. He concluded that large changes must happen over a period of millions of years.

Page 188: Because ripple marks form at the top of a rock layer, scientists can use the orientation of the ripple marks to determine which direction was "up" when the rock layers formed.

Section 2

Page 192: Varves are like tree rings in that varves are laid down each year. Thus, counting varves can reveal the age of sedimentary deposits.

Page 195: An isotope that has an extremely long half-life will not show significant or measurable changes in a young rock. In a very old rock, an isotope that has a short half-life may have decayed to the point at which too little of the isotope is left to give an accurate age measurement. So, the estimated age of the rock must be correlated to the dating method used.

Section 3

Page 199: A trace fossil is fossilized evidence of past animal movement, such as tracks, footprints, borings, or burrows, that can provide information about prehistoric life.

Chapter 9 A View of Earth's Past

Section 1

Page 211: You would find fossils of extinct animals in older layers of a geologic column.

Section 2

Page 216: Earth is approximately 4.6 billion years old.

Page 218: Answers may vary but should include three of the following: trilobites, brachiopods, jellyfish, worms, snails, and sponges.

Section 3

Page 222: Answers may vary but could include *Archaeopteryx*, pterosaurs, *Apatosaurus*, and *Stegosaurus*.

Page 225: During ice ages, water from the ocean was frozen as ice, so the amount of liquid water in the seas decreased and sea level fell.

Chapter 10 Plate Tectonics

Section 1

Page 241: Many scientists rejected Wegener's hypothesis because the mechanism that Wegener suggested was easily disproved by geologic evidence.

Page 243: New sea floor forms as magma rises to fill the rift that forms when two plates pull apart at a divergent boundary.

Page 245: The symmetrical magnetic patterns in sea-floor rocks show that rock formed at one place (at a ridge) and then broke apart and moved away from the center in opposite directions.

Section 2

Page 248: Scientists use the locations of earthquakes, volcanoes, trenches, and mid-ocean ridges to outline tectonic plates.

Page 250: Collisions at convergent boundaries can happen between two oceanic plates, between two continental plates, or between one oceanic plate and one continental plate.

Page 253: When denser lithosphere sinks into the asthenosphere, the asthenosphere must move out of the way. As the asthenosphere moves, it drags or pushes on other parts of the lithosphere, which causes movement.

Section 3

Page 256: As a plate subducts beneath another plate, islands and other land features on the subducting plate are scraped off the subducting plate and become part of the overriding plate.

Page 259: The continents Africa, South America, Antarctica, and Australia formed from Gondwanaland. The subcontinent of India was also part of Gondwanaland.

Chapter 11 Deformation of the Crust

Section 1

Page 273: Tension and shear stress can both pull rock apart.

Page 275: limbs and hinges

Page 277: A thrust fault is a type of reverse fault in which the fault plane is at a low angle relative to the surface.

Section 2

Page 281: The Himalayas are growing taller because the two plates are still colliding and causing further compression of the rock, which further uplifts the mountains.

Page 283: Answers may include three of the following: folded mountains, fault-block mountains, dome mountains, and volcanic mountains.

Chapter 12 Earthquakes

Section 1
Page 297: Rayleigh waves cause the ground to move in an elliptical, rolling motion. Love waves cause rock to move side-to-side and perpendicular to the direction the waves are traveling.

Page 298: The speed of seismic waves changes as they pass through different layers of Earth.

Section 2
Page 303: Moment magnitude is more accurate for larger earthquakes than the Richter scale is. Moment magnitude is directly related to rock properties and so is more closely related to the cause of the earthquake than the Richter scale is.

Section 3
Page 307: Scientists think that stress on a fault builds up to a critical point and is then released as an earthquake. Seismic gaps are areas in which no earthquakes have happened in a long period of time and thus are likely to be under a high amount of stress.

Chapter 13 Volcanoes

Section 1
Page 321: The denser plate of oceanic lithosphere subducts beneath the less dense plate of continental lithosphere.

Page 323: As the lithosphere moves over the mantle plume, older volcanoes move away from the mantle plume. A new hot spot forms in the lithosphere above the mantle plume as a new volcano begins to form.

Section 2
Page 326: The faster the rate of flow is and the higher the gas content is, the more broken up and rough the resulting cooled lava will be.

Page 329: A caldera may form when a magma chamber empties or when large amounts of magma are discharged, causing the ground to collapse.

Chapter 14 Weathering and Erosion

Section 1
Page 344: Two types of mechanical weathering are ice wedging and abrasion. Ice wedging is caused by water that seeps into cracks in rock and freezes. When water freezes, it expands and creates pressure on the rock, which widens and deepens cracks. Abrasion is the grinding away of rock surfaces by other rocks or sand particles. Abrasive agents may be carried by gravity, water, and wind.

Page 346: Two effects of chemical weathering are changes in the chemical composition and changes in the physical appearance of a rock.

Section 2
Page 350: Fractures and joints in a rock increase surface area and allow weathering to occur more rapidly.

Section 3
Page 355: Large amounts of rainfall and high temperatures cause thick soils to form in both tropical and temperate climates. Tropical soils have thin A horizons because of the continuous leaching of topsoil. Temperate soils have three thick layers, because leaching of the A horizon in temperate climates is much less than leaching of the A horizon in tropical climates.

Section 4
Page 358: Dust storms may form during droughts when the soil is made dry and loose by lack of moisture and wind-caused sheet erosion carries it away in clouds of dust. If all of the topsoil is removed, the remaining subsoil will not contain enough nutrients to raise crops.

Page 361: Landslides are masses of loose rock combined with soil that suddenly fall down a slope. A rockfall consists of rock falling from a steep cliff.

Page 363: When a mountain is no longer being uplifted, weathering and erosion wear down its jagged peaks to low, featureless surfaces called *peneplains*.

Chapter 15 River Systems

Section 1
Page 376: Precipitation is any form of water that falls to Earth from the clouds, including rain, snow, sleet, and hail.

Section 2
Page 381: A river that has meanders probably has a low gradient.

Section 3
Page 385: Floods can be controlled indirectly through forest and soil conservation measures that reduce or prevent runoff, or directly by building artificial structures, such as dams, levees, and floodways, to redirect water flow.

Chapter 16 Groundwater

Section 1
Page 399: The two zones of groundwater are the zone of saturation and the zone of aeration.

Page 400: The depth of a water table depends on topography, aquifer permeability, the amount of rainfall, and the rate at which humans use the groundwater.

Page 403: Ordinary springs occur where the ground surface drops below the water table. An artesian spring occurs where groundwater flows to the surface through natural cracks in the overlying cap rock.

Section 2
Page 407: A natural bridge may form when two sinkholes form close to each other. The bridge is the uncollapsed rock between the sinkholes.

Chapter 17 Glaciers

Section 1
Page 420: Continental glaciers exist only in Greenland and Antarctica.

Page 424: A moving glacier forms a cirque by pulling blocks of rock from the floor and walls of a valley and leaving a bowl-shaped depression.

Section 2
Page 427: A drumlin is a long, low, tear-shaped mound of till.

Page 428: Eskers form when meltwater from receding continental glaciers flows through ice tunnels and deposits long, winding ridges of gravel and sand.

Section 3
Page 432: The sea level was up to 140 m lower than it is now.

Chapter 18 Erosion by Wind and Waves

Section 1

Page 446: Moisture makes soil heavier, so the soil sticks and is more difficult to move. Therefore, erosion happens faster in dry climates.

Page 448: Barchan dunes are crescent shaped; transverse dunes form linear ridges.

Section 2

Page 452: Answers should include three of the following: sea cliffs, sea caves, sea arches, sea stacks, wave-cut terraces, and wave-built terraces.

Section 3

Page 457: As sea levels rise over a flat coastal plain, the shoreline moves inland and isolates dunes from the old shoreline. These dunes become barrier islands.

Chapter 19 Ocean Basins

Section 1

Page 472: Oceanographers study the physical characteristics, chemical composition, and life-forms of the ocean.

Section 2

Page 476: Trenches; broad, flat plains; mountain ranges; and submerged volcanoes are part of the deep-ocean basins.

Section 3

Page 481: When chemical reactions take place in the ocean, dissolved substances can crystallize to form nodules that settle to the ocean floor.

Chapter 20 Ocean Water

Section 1

Page 495: Dissolved solids enter the oceans from the chemical weathering of rock on land, from volcanic eruptions, and from chemical reactions between sea water and newly formed sea-floor rocks.

Page 497: Ocean surface temperatures are affected by the amount of solar energy an area receives and by the movement of water in the ocean.

Page 499: Ocean water contains dissolved solids (mostly salts) that add mass to a given volume of water. The large amount of dissolved solids in ocean water makes ocean water denser than fresh water.

Section 2

Page 503: Most marine life is found in the sublittoral zone. Life in this zone is continuously submerged, but waters are still shallow enough to allow sunlight to penetrate.

Section 3

Page 507: Aquaculture provides a reliable, economical source of food. However, aquatic farms are susceptible to pollution and they may become local sources of pollution.

Chapter 21 Movements of the Ocean

Section 1

Page 521: Because no continents interrupt the flow of the Antarctic Circumpolar Current, also called the *West Wind Drift*, it completely encircles Antarctica and crosses three major oceans. All other surface currents are deflected and divided when they meet a continental barrier.

Page 523: Antarctic Bottom Water is very cold. It also has a high salinity. The extreme cold and high salinity combine to make the water extremely dense.

Section 2

Page 526: Because waves receive energy from wind that pushes against the surface of the water, the amount of energy decreases as the depth of water increases. As a result, the diameter of the water molecules' circular path also decreases.

Page 528: Contact with the ocean floor causes friction, which slows down the bottom of the wave but not the top of the wave. Because of the difference in speed between the top and bottom of the wave, the top gets farther ahead of the bottom until the wave becomes unstable and falls over.

Section 3

Page 532: When the tidal range is small, the sun and the moon are at right angles to each other relative to Earth's orbit.

Chapter 22 The Atmosphere

Section 1

Page 548: Transpiration increases the amount of water vapor in the atmosphere.

Page 551: An aneroid barometer contains a sealed metal container that has a partial vacuum.

Page 553: The lower region of the thermosphere is called the *ionosphere.*

Section 2

Page 559: Deserts are colder at night than other areas are because the air in deserts contains little water vapor that can absorb heat during the day and release heat slowly at night.

Section 3

Page 562: They flow in opposite directions from each other, and they occur at different latitudes.

Chapter 23 Water in the Atmosphere

Section 1

Page 576: When the air is very dry and the temperature is below freezing, ice and snow change directly into water vapor by sublimation.

Page 578: Dew is liquid moisture that condenses from air on cool objects when the air is nearly saturated and the temperature drops. Frost is water vapor that condenses as ice crystals onto a cool surface directly from the air when the dew point is below freezing.

Section 2

Page 582: The source of heat that warms the air and leads to cloud formation is solar energy that is reradiated as heat by Earth's surface. As the process continues, latent heat released by the condensation may allow the clouds to expand beyond the condensation level.

Page 585: because cirrus clouds form at very high altitudes where air temperature is low

Section 3

Page 589: Doppler radar measures the location, direction of movement, and intensity of precipitation.

Chapter 24 Weather

Section 1

Page 603: a continental tropical air mass

Section 2

Page 607: The air of an anticyclone sinks and flows outward from a center of high pressure. The air of a mid-latitude cyclone rotates toward the rising air of a central, low-pressure region.

Page 609: over warm tropical seas

Section 3

Page 612: A barometer is used to measure atmospheric pressure.

Section 4

Page 617: Areas of precipitation are marked by using colors or symbols.

Page 618: Meteorologists compare computer models because different models are better at predicting different weather variables. If information from two or more models matches, scientists can be more confident of their predictions.

Chapter 25 Climate

Section 1

Page 633: Waves, currents, and other water motions continually replace warm surface waters with cooler water from the ocean depths, which keeps the surface temperature of the water from increasing rapidly.

Page 634: The temperature of land increases faster than that of water does because the specific heat of land is lower than that of water, and thus the land requires less energy to heat up than the water does.

Section 2

Page 638: marine west coast, humid continental, and humid subtropical

Section 3

Page 642: Scientists use computer models to incorporate as much data as possible to sort out the complex variables that influence climate and to make predictions about climate.

Page 644: Climate change influences humans, plants, and animals. It also affects nearby climates, sea level, and precipitation rates.

Chapter 26 Studying Space

Section 1

Page 661: The only kind of electromagnetic radiation the human eye can detect is visible light.

Page 663: Images produced by refracting telescopes are subject to distortion because of the way different colors of visible light are focused at different distances from the lens and because of weight limitations on the objective lens.

Page 664: Scientists launch spacecraft into orbit to detect radiation screened out by Earth's atmosphere and to avoid light pollution and other atmospheric distortions.

Section 2

Page 669: Constellations provide two kinds of evidence of Earth's motion. As Earth rotates, the stars appear to change position during the night. As Earth revolves around the sun, Earth's night sky faces a different part of the universe. As a result, different constellations appear in the night sky as the seasons change.

Page 671: Because time zones are based on Earth's rotation, as you travel west, you eventually come to a location where, on one side of the time zone border, the calendar moves ahead one day. The purpose of the International Dateline is to locate the border so that the transition would affect the least number of people. So that it will affect the least number of people, the International Dateline is in the middle of the Pacific Ocean, instead of on a continent.

Page 672: Daylight savings time is an adjustment that is made to standard time by setting clocks ahead one hour to take advantage of longer hours of daylight in the summer months and to save energy.

Chapter 27 Planets of the Solar System

Section 1

Page 687: Unlike the outer planets, Pluto is very small and is composed of rock and frozen gas, instead of thick layers of gases.

Page 689: Green plants release free oxygen as part of photosynthesis, which caused the concentration of oxygen gas in the atmosphere to gradually increase.

Section 2

Page 692: An ellipse is a closed curve whose shape is defined by two points inside the curve. An ellipse looks like an oval.

Section 3

Page 697: Answers may vary but should address differences in distance from the sun, density, atmospheric pressure and density, and tectonics.

Page 699: Martian volcanoes are larger than volcanoes on Earth because Mars has no moving tectonic plates. Magma sources remain in the same spot for millions of years and produce volcanic material that builds the volcanic cone higher and higher.

Section 4

Page 702: When Jupiter formed, it did not have enough mass for nuclear fusion to begin.

Page 704: Saturn and Jupiter are made almost entirely of hydrogen and helium and have rocky-iron cores, ring systems, many satellites, rapid rotational periods, and bands of colored clouds.

Page 707: The Kuiper Belt is located beyond the orbit of Neptune.

Chapter 28 Minor Bodies of the Solar System

Section 1

Page 720: Answers should include two of the following features: maria, highlands, craters, ridges, and rilles.

Page 722: The crust of the far side of the moon is thicker than the crust of the near side is. The crust of the far side also consists mainly of mountainous terrain and has only a few small maria.

Section 2

Page 726: The far side of the moon is never visible from Earth, because the moon's rotation and the moon's revolution around Earth take the same amount of time.

Page 728: During a total eclipse, the entire disk of the sun is blocked, and the outer layers of the sun become visible. During an annular eclipse, the disk of the sun is never completely blocked out, so the sun is too bright for observers on Earth to see the outer layers of the sun's atmosphere.

Page 731: When the lighted part of the moon is larger than a semicircle but the visible part of the moon is shrinking, the phase is called *waning gibbous*. When only a sliver of the near side is visible, the phase is a waning crescent.

Section 3

Page 735: Io's surface is covered with many active volcanoes. Europa's surface is covered by an enormous ice sheet. Ganymede is the largest moon in the solar system and has a strong magnetic field. Callisto's surface is heavily cratered.

Page 737: Charon is almost half the size of the body it orbits. Charon's orbital period is the same length as Pluto's day, so only one side of Pluto always faces the moon.

Section 4

Page 740: The most common type is made mostly of carbon materials. Other asteroids are made mostly of silicate minerals. The third type is composed mostly of iron and nickel.

Page 743: A meteoroid is a rocky body that travels through space. When a meteoroid enters Earth's atmosphere and begins to burn up, the meteoroid produces a meteor.

Chapter 29 The Sun

Section 1

Page 757: Einstein's equation helped scientists understand the source of the sun's energy. The equation explained how the sun could produce huge amounts of energy without burning up.

Page 759: The sun's atmosphere consists of the photosphere, the chromosphere, and the corona.

Section 2

Page 763: Coronal mass ejections generate sudden disturbances in Earth's magnetic field. The high-energy particles that circulate during these storms can damage satellites, cause power blackouts, and interfere with radio communications.

Chapter 30 Stars, Galaxies, and the Universe

Section 1

Page 777: Polaris is almost exactly above the pole of Earth's rotational axis, so Polaris moves only slightly around the pole during one rotation of Earth.

Page 778: Starlight is shifted toward the red end of the spectrum when the star is moving away from the observer.

Section 2

Page 783: The forces balance each other and keep the star in equilibrium. As gravity increases the pressure on the matter within a star, the rate of fusion increases. This increase in fusion causes a rise in gas pressure. As a result, the energy from the increased fusion and gas pressure generates outward pressure that balances the force of gravity.

Page 784: Giants and supergiants appear in the upper-right part of the H-R diagram.

Page 787: As supergiants collapse because of gravitational forces, fusion begins and continues until the supply of fuel is used up. The core begins to collapse under its own gravity and causes energy to transfer to the outer layers of the star. The transfer of energy to the outer layers causes the explosion.

Section 3

Page 790: More than 50% of all stars are in multiple-star systems.

Section 4

Page 794: All matter and energy in the early universe were compressed into a small volume at an extremely high temperature until the temperature cooled and all of the matter and energy were forced outward in all directions.

California Close-Up

Page C3: Winds in California blow from west to east because California is located in the Northern Hemisphere Westerlies wind belt.

Page C7: Increasing topography (elevation) means cooler temperatures. If a moisture-laden air mass moves up a mountain slope and cools below the dew point, clouds will form and rain might fall. As the air mass moves down the other side of the mountain, it warms to temperatures above the dew point and rain ceases. Hence, more rain falls in mountain areas than in valleys.

Page C15: The east-west stretching of California produced tilted fault-block mountains and intervening graben valleys.

Page C21: Energy sources: oil and natural gas, hydroelectric, geothermal, wind, and solar. Mineral resources: sand and gravel, Portland cement, diatomite, boron minerals, gold, or any of the other minerals listed in Table 2.

Page C25: Coastal wave erosion, tsunamis, and flooding resulting from global warming sea-level rise.

GLOSSARY/GLOSARIO

Terms and their definitions are listed in English in alphabetical order in the first column. The second column lists the equivalent term in Spanish.

A

abrasion the grinding and wearing away of rock surfaces through the mechanical action of other rock or sand particles (344)

abrasion/abrasión proceso por el cual las super-ficies de las rocas se muelen o desgastan por medio de la acción mecánica de otras rocas y partículas de arena (344)

absolute age the numeric age of an object or event, often stated in years before the present, as established by an absolute-dating process, such as radiometric dating (191)

absolute age/edad absoluta la edad numérica de un objeto o suceso, que suele expresarse en cantidad de años antes del presente, determinada por un proceso de datación absoluta, tal como la datación radiométrica (191)

absolute humidity the mass of water vapor per unit volume of air that contains the water vapor; usually expressed as grams of water vapor per cubic meter of air (577)

absolute humidity/humedad absoluta la masa de vapor de agua por unidad de volumen de aire que contiene al vapor de agua; normalmente se expresa por metro cúbico de aire (577)

absolute magnitude the brightness that a star would have at a distance of 32.6 light-years from Earth (780)

absolute magnitude/magnitud absoluta el brillo que una estrella tendría a una distancia de 32.6 años luz de la Tierra (780)

abyssal plain a large, flat, almost level area of the deep-ocean basin (477)

abyssal plain/llanura abisal un área amplia, llana y casi plana de la cuenca oceánica profunda (477)

adiabatic cooling the process by which the temperature of an air mass decreases as the air mass rises and expands (582)

adiabatic cooling/enfriamiento adiabático el proceso por medio del cual la temperatura de una masa de aire disminuye a medida que ésta se eleva y se expande (582)

advective cooling the process by which the temperature of an air mass decreases as the air mass moves over a cold surface (583)

advective cooling/enfriamiento advectivo el proceso por medio del cual la temperatura de una masa de aire disminuye a medida que ésta se mueve sobre una superficie fría (583)

air mass a large body of air throughout which temperature and moisture content are similar (601)

air mass/masa de aire un gran volumen de aire, cuya temperatura y cuyo contenido de humedad son similares en toda su extensión (601)

albedo the fraction of solar radiation that is reflected off the surface of an object (557)

albedo/albedo porcentaje de la radiación solar que la superficie de un objeto refleja (557)

alluvial fan a fan-shaped mass of rock material deposited by a stream when the slope of the land decreases sharply; for example, alluvial fans form when streams flow from mountains to flat land (383)

alluvial fan/abanico aluvial masa de materiales rocosos en forma de abanico, depositados por un arroyo cuando la pendiente del terreno disminuye bruscamente; por ejemplo, los abanicos aluviales se forman cuando los arroyos fluyen de una montaña a un terreno llano (383)

alpine glacier a narrow, wedge-shaped mass of ice that forms in a mountainous region and that is confined to a small area by surrounding topography; examples include valley glaciers, cirque glaciers, and piedmont glaciers (420)

alpine glacier/glaciar alpino una masa de hielo angosta, parecida a una cuña, que se forma en una región montañosa y que está confinada a un área pequeña por la topografía que la rodea; los glaci-ares de valle, los circos glaciares y los glaciares de pie de monte son algunos ejemplos de esto (420)

anemometer an instrument used to measure wind speed (612)

aphelion the point in the orbit of a planet at which the planet is farthest from the sun (668)

apogee in the orbit of a satellite, the point at which the satellite is farthest from Earth (725)

apparent magnitude the brightness of a star as seen from the Earth (780)

aquaculture the raising of aquatic plants and animals for human use or consumption (507)

aquifer a body of rock or sediment that stores groundwater and allows the flow of groundwater (397)

arête a sharp, jagged ridge that forms between cirques (424)

artesian formation a sloping layer of permeable rock sandwiched between two layers of impermeable rock and exposed at the surface (403)

asteroid a small, rocky object that orbits the sun; most asteroids are located in a band between the orbits of Mars and Jupiter (739)

asthenosphere the solid, plastic layer of the mantle beneath the lithosphere; made of mantle rock that flows very slowly, which allows tectonic plates to move on top of it (29, 247)

astronomical unit the average distance between the Earth and the sun; approximately 150 million kilometers (symbol, AU) (660)

astronomy the scientific study of the universe (7, 659)

atmosphere a mixture of gases that surrounds a planet or moon (33, 547)

atmospheric pressure the force per unit area that is exerted on a surface by the weight of the atmosphere (550)

atom the smallest unit of an element that maintains the chemical properties of that element (82)

anemometer/anemómetro un instrumento que se usa para medir la rapidez del viento (612)

aphelion/afelio el punto en la órbita de un planeta en que el planeta está más lejos del Sol (668)

apogee/apogeo en la órbita de un satélite, el punto en el que el satélite está más alejado de la Tierra (725)

apparent magnitude/magnitud aparente el brillo de una estrella como se percibe desde la Tierra (780)

aquaculture/acuacultura el cultivo de plantas y animales acuáticos para uso o consumo humano (507)

aquifer/acuífero un cuerpo rocoso o sedimento que almacena agua subterránea y permite que fluya (397)

arête/cresta una cumbre puntiaguda e irregular que se forma entre circos glaciares (424)

artesian formation/formación artesiana capa inclinada de rocas permeables que está en medio de dos capas de rocas impermeables y expuesta en la superficie (403)

asteroid/asteroide un objeto pequeño y rocoso que se encuentra en órbita alrededor del Sol; la mayoría de los asteroides se ubican en una banda entre las órbitas de Marte y Júpiter (739)

asthenosphere/astenosfera la capa sólida y plástica del manto, que se encuentra debajo de la litosfera; está formada por roca del manto que fluye muy lentamente, lo cual permite que las placas tectónicas se muevan en su superficie (29, 247)

astronomical unit/unidad astronómica la distancia promedio entre la Tierra y el Sol; aproximadamente 150 millones de kilómetros (símbolo: UA) (660)

astronomy/astronomía el estudio científico del universo (7, 659)

atmosphere/atmósfera una mezcla de gases que rodea un planeta o una luna (33, 547)

atmospheric pressure/presión atmosférica la fuerza por unidad de área que el peso de la atmósfera ejerce sobre una superficie (550)

atom/átomo la unidad más pequeña de un elemento que conserva las propiedades químicas de ese elemento (82)

aurora colored light produced by charged particles from the solar wind and from the magnetosphere that react with and excite the oxygen and nitrogen of Earth's upper atmosphere; usually seen in the sky near Earth's magnetic poles (764)

aurora/aurora luz de colores producida por partículas con carga del viento solar y de la magnetosfera, que reaccionan con los átomos de oxígeno y nitrógeno de la parte superior de la atmósfera de la Tierra y los excitan; normalmente se ve en el cielo cerca de los polos magnéticos de la Tierra (764)

B

barometer an instrument that measures atmospheric pressure (612)

barometer/barómetro un instrumento que mide la presión atmosférica (612)

barrier island a long ridge of sand or narrow island that lies parallel to the shore (457)

barrier island/isla barrera un largo arrecife de arena o una isla angosta ubicada paralela a la costa (457)

basal slip the process that causes the ice at the base of a glacier to melt and the glacier to slide (421)

basal slip/deslizamiento basal el proceso que hace que el hielo de la base de un glaciar se derrita y que éste se deslice (421)

beach an area of the shoreline that is made up of deposited sediment (453)

beach/playa un área de la costa que está formada por sedimento depositado (453)

benthic zone the bottom region of oceans and bodies of fresh water (503)

benthic zone/zona bentónica la región del fondo de los océanos y de las masas de agua dulce (503)

benthos organisms that live at the bottom of oceans or bodies of fresh water (502)

benthos/benthos organismos que viven en el fondo de los océanos o de las masas de agua dulce (502)

big bang theory the theory that all matter and energy in the universe was compressed into an extremely small volume that 13 billion to 15 billion years ago exploded and began expanding in all directions (794)

big bang theory/teoría del Big Bang la teoría que establece que toda la materia y la energía del universo estaban comprimidas en un volumen extremadamente pequeño que explotó hace aproximadamente 13 a 15 mil millones de años y empezó a expandirse en todas direcciones (794)

biomass plant material, manure, or any other or-ganic matter that is used as an energy source (167)

biomass/biomasa materia vegetal, estiércol o cualquier otra materia orgánica que se usa como fuente de energía (167)

biosphere the part of Earth where life exists; includes all of the living organisms on Earth (33)

biosphere/biosferavla parte de la Tierra donde existe la vida; abarca a todos los organismos vivos de la Tierra (33)

black hole an object so massive and dense that even light cannot escape its gravity (788)

black hole/hoyo negro un objeto tan masivo y denso que ni siquiera la luz puede salir de su campo gravitacional (788)

body wave in geology, a seismic wave that travels through the body of a medium (296)

body wave/onda interna en geología, una onda sísmica que se desplaza a través del cuerpo de un medio (296)

Bowen's reaction series the simplified pattern that illustrates the order in which minerals crystallize from cooling magma according to their chemical composition and melting point (127)

Bowen's reaction series/serie de reacción de Bowen el patrón simplificado que ilustra el orden en que los minerales se cristalizan a partir del magma que se enfría, de acuerdo con su composición química y punto de fusión (127)

braided stream a stream or river that is composed of multiple channels that divide and rejoin around sediment bars (382)

braided stream/corriente anastomosada una corriente o río compuesto por varios canales que se dividen y se vuelven a encontrar alrededor de barreras de sedimento (382)

C

caldera a large, circular depression that forms when the magma chamber below a volcano partially empties and causes the ground above to sink (329)

caldera/caldera una depresión grande y circular que se forma cuando se vacía parcialmente la cámara de magma que hay debajo de un volcán, lo cual hace que el suelo se hunda (329)

carbonation the conversion of a compound into a carbonate (347)

carbonation/carbonación la transformación de un compuesto a un carbonato (347)

carrying capacity the largest population that an environment can support at any given time (40)

carrying capacity/capacidad de carga la población más grande que un ambiente puede sostener en cualquier momento dado (40)

cavern a natural cavity that forms in rock as a result of the dissolution of minerals; *also* a large cave that commonly contains many smaller, connecting chambers (406)

cavern/caverna una cavidad natural que se forma en la roca como resultado de la disolución de minerales; *también,* una gran cueva que generalmente contiene muchas cámaras más pequeñas comunicadas entre sí (406)

cementation the process in which minerals precipitate into pore spaces between sediment grains and bind sediments together to form rock (135)

cementation/cementación el proceso en el cual los minerales se precipitan entre los poros de granos de sedimento y unen los sedimentos para formar rocas (135)

Cenozoic Era the current geologic era, which began 65.5 million years ago; also called the *Age of Mammals* (224)

Cenozoic Era/Era Cenozoica la era geológica actual, que comenzó hace 65.5 millones de años; también llamada *Edad de los Mamíferos* (224)

chemical sedimentary rock sedimentary rock that forms when minerals precipitate from a solution or settle from a suspension (136)

chemical sedimentary rock/roca sedimentaria química roca sedimentaria que se forma cuando los minerales precipitan a partir de una solución o se depositan a partir de una suspensión (136)

chemical weathering the process by which rocks break down as a result of chemical reactions (346)

chemical weathering/desgaste químico el proceso por medio del cual las rocas se fragmentan como resultado de reacciones químicas (346)

chromosphere the thin layer of the sun that is just above the photosphere and that glows a reddish color during eclipses (760)

chromosphere/cromosfera la delgada capa del Sol que se encuentra justo encima de la fotosfera y que resplandece con un color rojizo durante los eclipses (760)

cirque a deep and steep bowl-like depression produced by glacier erosion (424)

cirque/circo una depresión profunda y empinada, con forma de tazón, producida por erosión glaciar (424)

cirrus cloud a feathery cloud that is composed of ice crystals and that has the highest altitude of any cloud in the sky (585)

cirrus cloud/nube cirro una nube liviana formada por cristales de hielo, la cual tiene la mayor altitud de todas las nubes en el cielo (585)

clastic sedimentary rock sedimentary rock that forms when fragments of preexisting rocks are compacted and cemented together (137)

cleavage in geology, the tendency of a mineral to split along specific planes of weakness to form smooth, flat surfaces (110)

climate the average weather conditions in an area over a long period of time (631)

climatologist a scientist who gathers data to study and compare past and present climates and to predict future climate change (641)

cloud a collection of small water droplets or ice crystals suspended in the air, which forms when the air is cooled and condensation occurs (581)

cloud seeding the process of introducing freezing nuclei or condensation nuclei into a cloud in order to cause rain to fall (590)

coalescence the formation of a larger droplet by the combination of smaller droplets (588)

cold front the front edge of a moving mass of cold air that pushes beneath a warmer air mass like a wedge (605)

comet a small body of ice, rock, and cosmic dust that follows an elliptical orbit around the sun and that gives off gas and dust in the form of a tail as it passes close to the sun (741)

compaction the process in which the volume and porosity of a sediment is decreased by the weight of overlying sediments as a result of burial beneath other sediments (135)

compound a substance made up of atoms of two or more different elements joined by chemical bonds (87)

condensation the change of state from a gas to a liquid (376)

condensation nucleus a solid particle in the atmos-phere that provides the surface on which water vapor condenses (581)

clastic sedimentary rock/roca sedimentaria clástica roca sedimentaria que se forma cuando los fragmentos de rocas preexistentes se unen por compactación y cementación (137)

cleavage/exfoliación en geología, la tendencia de un mineral a agrietarse a lo largo de planos débiles específicos y formar superficies lisas y planas (110)

climate/clima las condiciones promedio del tiempo en un área durante un largo período de tiempo (631)

climatologist/climatólogo un científico que recopila datos para estudiar y comparar los climas del pasado y del presente y para predecir cambios climáticos en el futuro (641)

cloud/nube un conjunto de pequeñas gotitas de agua o cristales de hielo suspendidos en el aire, que se forma cuando el aire se enfría y ocurre condensación (581)

cloud seeding/sembrado de nubes el proceso de introducir núcleos congelados o núcleos de condensación en una nube para producir lluvia (590)

coalescence/coalescencia la formación de una gota más grande al combinarse gotas más pequeñas (588)

cold front/frente frío el borde del frente de una masa de aire frío en movimiento que empuja por debajo de una masa de aire más caliente como una cuña (605)

comet/cometa un cuerpo pequeño formado por hielo, roca y polvo cósmico que sigue una órbita elíptica alrededor del Sol y que libera gas y polvo, los cuales forman una cola al pasar cerca del Sol (741)

compaction/compactación el proceso en el que el volumen y la porosidad de un sedimento disminuyen por efecto del peso al quedar el sedimento enterrado debajo de otros sedimentos superpuestos (135)

compound/compuesto una substancia formada por átomos de dos o más elementos diferentes unidos por enlaces químicos (87)

condensation/condensación el cambio de estado de gas a líquido (376)

condensation nucleus/núcleo de condensación una partícula sólida en la atmósfera que proporciona la superficie en la que el vapor de agua se condensa (581)

conduction the transfer of energy as heat through a material (560)

conservation the preservation and wise use of natural resources (171)

constellation one of 88 regions into which the sky has been divided in order to describe the locations of celestial objects; a group of stars organized in a recognizable pattern (789)

contact metamorphism a change in the texture, structure, or chemical composition of a rock due to contact with magma (142)

continental glacier a massive sheet of ice that may cover millions of square kilometers, that may be thousands of meters thick, and that is not confined by surrounding topography (420)

continental drift the hypothesis that states that the continents once formed a single landmass, broke up, and drifted to their present locations (239)

continental margin the shallow sea floor that is located between the shoreline and the deep-ocean bottom (475)

contour line a line that connects points of equal elevation on a map (64)

convection the movement of matter due to differences in density that are caused by temperature variations; can result in the transfer of energy as heat (560)

convective zone the region of the sun's interior that is between the radiative zone and the photosphere and in which energy is carried upward by convection (759)

convergent boundary the boundary between tectonic plates that are colliding (250)

core the central part of the Earth below the mantle; *also* the center of the sun (28)

core sample a cylindrical piece of sediment, rock, soil, snow, or ice that is collected by drilling (479)

Coriolis effect the curving of the path of a moving object from an otherwise straight path due to the Earth's rotation (520, 561)

conduction/conducción transferencia de energía en forma de calor a través de un material (560)

conservation/conservación la preservación y el uso inteligente de los recursos naturales (171)

constellation/constelación una de las 88 regiones en las que se ha dividido el cielo con el fin de describir la ubicación de los objetos celestes; un grupo de estrellas organizadas en un patrón reconocible (789)

contact metamorphism/metamorfismo de contacto un cambio en la textura, estructura o composición química de una roca debido al contacto con el magma (142)

continental glacier/glaciar continental una enorme capa de hielo que puede cubrir millones de kilómetros cuadrados, tener un espesor de miles de metros y que no está confinada por la topografía que la rodea (420)

continental drift/deriva continental la hipótesis que establece que alguna vez los continentes formaron una sola masa de tierra, se dividieron y se fueron a la deriva hasta terminar en sus ubicaciones actuales (239)

continental margin/margen continental el suelo marino poco profundo que se ubica entre la costa y el fondo profundo del océano (475)

contour line/curva de nivel una línea en un mapa que une puntos que tienen la misma elevación (64)

convection/convección el movimiento de la materia debido a diferencias en la densidad que se producen por variaciones en la temperatura; puede resultar en la transferencia de energía en forma de calor (560)

convective zone/zona convectiva la región del interior del Sol que se encuentra entre la zona radiactiva y la fotosfera y en la cual la energía se desplaza hacia arriba por convección (759)

convergent boundary/límite convergente el límite entre placas tectónicas que chocan (250)

core/núcleo la parte central de la Tierra, debajo del manto; *también,* el centro del Sol (28)

core sample/muestra de sondeo un fragmento de sedimento, roca, suelo, nieve o hielo que se obtiene taladrando (479)

Coriolis effect/efecto de Coriolis la desviación de la trayectoria recta que experimentan los objetos en movimiento debido a la rotación de la Tierra (520, 561)

corona the outermost layer of the sun's atmosphere (760)

corona/corona la capa externa de la atmósfera del Sol (760)

coronal mass ejection a part of coronal gas that is thrown into space from the sun (763)

coronal mass ejection/eyección de masa coronal una parte de gas coronal que el Sol expulsa al espacio (763)

cosmic background radiation radiation uniformly detected from every direction in space; considered a remnant of the big bang (795)

cosmic background radiation/radiación cósmica de fondo radiación que se detecta de manera uniforme desde todas las direcciones en el espacio; se considera un resto del Big Bang (795)

cosmology the study of the origin, properties, processes, and evolution of the universe (793)

cosmology/cosmología el estudio del origen, propiedades, procesos y evolución del universo (793)

covalent bond a bond formed when atoms share one or more pairs of electrons (91)

covalent bond/enlace covalente un enlace formado cuando los átomos comparten uno más pares de electrones (91)

crater a bowl-shaped depression that forms on the surface of an object when a falling body strikes the object's surface or when an explosion occurs; a similar depression around the central vent of a volcano or geyser (720)

crater/cráter una depresión con forma de tazón, que se forma sobre la superficie de un objeto cuando un cuerpo en caída impacta sobre ésta o cuando se produce una explosión; una depresión similar alrededor de la chimenea de un volcán o géiser (720)

creep the slow downhill movement of weathered rock material (362)

creep/arrastre el movimiento lento y descendente de materiales rocosos desgastados (362)

crevasse in a glacier, a large crack or fissure that results from ice movement (422)

crevasse/grieta en un glaciar, una fractura o fisura grande debida al movimiento del hielo (422)

crust the thin and solid outermost layer of the Earth above the mantle (28)

crust/corteza la capa externa, delgada y sólida de la Tierra, que se encuentra sobre el manto (28)

crystal a solid whose atoms, ions, or molecules are arranged in a regular, repeating pattern (106)

crystal/cristal un sólido cuyos átomos, iones o moléculas están ordenados en un patrón regular y repetitivo (106)

cumulus cloud a low-level, billowy cloud that commonly has a top that resembles cotton balls and a dark bottom (585)

cumulus cloud/nube cúmulo una nube esponjada ubicada en un nivel bajo, cuya parte superior normalmente parece una bola de algodón y es obscura en la parte inferior (585)

current in geology, a horizontal movement of water in a well-defined pattern, such as a river or stream; the movement of air in a certain direction (519)

current/corriente en geología, un movimiento horizontal de agua en un patrón bien definido, como por ejemplo, un río o arroyo; el movimiento del aire en una cierta dirección (519)

D

deep current a streamlike movement of ocean water far below the surface (523)

deep current/corriente profunda un movimiento del agua del océano que es similar a una corriente y ocurre debajo de la superficie (523)

deep-ocean basin the part of the ocean floor that is under deep water beyond the continental margin and that is composed of oceanic crust and a thin layer of sediment (475)

deep-ocean basin/cuenca oceánica profunda la parte del fondo del océano que está bajo aguas profundas más allá del margen continental y que se compone de corteza oceánica y una delgada capa de sedimento (475)

deflation a form of wind erosion in which fine, dry soil particles are blown away (446)

deformation the bending, tilting, and breaking of Earth's crust; the change in the shape of rock in response to stress (271)

delta a fan-shaped mass of rock material deposited at the mouth of a stream; for example, deltas form where streams flow into the ocean at the edge of a continent (383)

density the ratio of the mass of a substance to the volume of the substance; commonly expressed as grams per cubic centimeter for solids and liquids and as grams per liter for gases (112, 499)

dependent variable in an experiment, the factor that changes as a result of manipulation of one or more other factors (the independent variables) (11)

desalination a process of removing salt from ocean water (378, 505)

dew point at constant pressure and water vapor content, the temperature at which the rate of condensation equals the rate of evaporation (577)

differential weathering the process by which softer, less weather resistant rocks wear away at a faster rate than harder, more weather resistant rocks do (349)

discharge the volume of water that flows within a given time (380)

divergent boundary the boundary between two tectonic plates that are moving away from each other (249)

dome mountain a circular or elliptical, almost symmetrical elevation or structure in which the stratified rock slopes downward gently from the central point of folding (283)

Doppler effect an observed change in the frequency of a wave when the source or observer is moving (778)

dune a mound of wind-deposited sand that moves as a result of the action of wind (447)

deflation/deflación una forma de erosión del viento en la que se mueven partículas de suelo finas y secas (446)

deformation/deformación el proceso de doblar, inclinar y romper la corteza de la Tierra; el cambio en la forma de una roca en respuesta a la tensión (271)

delta/delta un depósito de materiales rocosos en forma de abanico ubicado en la desembocadura de un río; por ejemplo, los deltas se forman en el lugar donde las corrientes fluyen al océano en el borde de un continente (383)

density/densidad la relación entre la masa de una substancia y su volumen; comúnmente se expresa en gramos por centímetro cúbico para los sólidos y líquidos, y como gramos por litro para los gases (112, 499)

dependent variable/variable dependiente en un experimento, el factor que cambia como resultado de la manipulación de uno o más factores (las variables independientes) (11)

desalination/desalación (o desalinización) un proceso de remoción de sal del agua del océano (378, 505)

dew point/punto de rocío a presión y contenido de vapor constantes, la temperatura a la cual la tasa de condensación iguala la tasa de evaporación (577)

differential weathering/desgaste diferencial el proceso por medio cual las rocas más blandas y menos resistentes al clima se desgastan a una tasa más rápida que las rocas más duras y resistentes al clima (349)

discharge/descarga el volumen de agua que fluye en un tiempo determinado (380)

divergent boundary/límite divergente el límite entre dos placas tectónicas que se están separando una de la otra (249)

dome mountain/domo una elevación o estructura circular o elíptica, casi simétrica, en la cual la roca estratificada se encuentra en una ligera pendiente hacia abajo a partir del punto central de plegamiento (283)

Doppler effect/efecto Doppler un cambio que se observa en la frecuencia de una onda cuando la fuente o el observador está en movimiento (778)

dune/duna un montículo de arena depositada por el viento que se mueve como resultado de la acción de éste (447)

earthquake a movement or trembling of the ground that is caused by a sudden release of energy when rocks along a fault move (295)

earthquake/terremoto un movimiento o temblor del suelo causado por una liberación súbita de energía que se produce cuando las rocas ubicadas a lo largo de una falla se mueven (295)

Earth science the scientific study of Earth and the universe around it (5)

Earth science/ciencias de la Tierra el estudio científico de la Tierra y del universo que la rodea (5)

eccentricity the degree of elongation of an elliptical orbit (symbol, *e*) (692)

eccentricity/excentricidad el grado de alargamiento de una orbita eliptica (símbolo: *e*) (692)

eclipse an event in which the shadow of one celestial body falls on another (727)

eclipse/eclipse un suceso en el que la sombra de un cuerpo celeste cubre otro cuerpo celeste (727)

ecosystem a community of organisms and their abiotic environment (39)

ecosystem/ecosistema una comunidad de organismos y su ambiente abiótico (39)

elastic rebound the sudden return of elastically deformed rock to its undeformed shape (295)

elastic rebound/rebote elástico ocurre cuando una roca deformada elásticamente vuelve súbitamente a su forma no deformada (295)

electromagnetic spectrum all of the frequencies or wavelengths of electromagnetic radiation (555, 661)

electromagnetic spectrum/espectro electromagnético todas las frecuencias o longitudes de onda de la radiación electromagnética (555, 661)

electron a subatomic particle that has a negative charge (82)

electron/electrón una partícula subatómica que tiene carga negativa (82)

element a substance that cannot be separated or broken down into simpler substances by chemical means; all atoms of an element have the same atomic number (81)

element/elemento una substancia que no se puede separar o descomponer en substancias más simples por medio de métodos químicos; todos los átomos de un elemento tienen el mismo número atómico (81)

elevation the height of an object above sea level (63)

elevation/elevación la altura de un objeto sobre el nivel del mar (63)

El Niño the warm-water phase of the El Niño–Southern Oscillation; a periodic occurrence in the eastern Pacific Ocean in which the surface-water temperature becomes unusually warm (635)

El Niño/El Niño la fase caliente de la Oscilación Sureña "El Niño"; un fenómeno periódico que ocurre en el océano Pacífico oriental en el que la temperatura del agua superficial se vuelve más caliente que de costumbre (635)

epicenter the point on Earth's surface directly above an earthquake's starting point, or focus (296)

epicenter/epicentro el punto de la superficie de la Tierra que queda justo arriba del punto de inicio, o foco, de un terremoto (296)

epoch a subdivision of geologic time that is longer than an age but shorter than a period (214)

epoch/época una subdivisión del tiempo geológico que es más larga que una edad pero más corta que un período (214)

equinox the moment when the sun appears to cross the celestial equator (673)

equinox/equinoccio el momento en que el Sol parece cruzar el ecuador celeste (673)

era a unit of geologic time that includes two or more periods (214)

era/era una unidad de tiempo geológico que incluye dos o más períodos (214)

erosion a process in which the materials of Earth's surface are loosened, dissolved, or worn away and transported from one place to another by a natural agent, such as wind, water, ice, or gravity (357)

erratic a large rock transported from a distant source by a glacier (426)

esker a long, winding ridge of gravel and coarse sand deposited by glacial meltwater streams (428)

estuary an area where fresh water from rivers mixes with salt water from the ocean; the part of a river where the tides meet the river current (456)

evapotranspiration the total loss of water from an area, which equals the sum of the water lost by evaporation from the soil and other surfaces and the water lost by transpiration from organisms (376)

evolution a heritable change in the characteristics within a population from one generation to the next; the development of new types of organisms from preexisting types of organisms over time (215)

extrusive igneous rock rock that forms from the cooling and solidification of lava at Earth's surface (131)

erosion/erosión un proceso por medio del cual los materiales de la superficie de la Tierra se aflojan, disuelven o desgastan y son transportados de un lugar a otro por un agente natural, como el viento, el agua, el hielo o la gravedad (357)

erratic/errática una piedra grande transportada de una fuente lejana por un glacial (426)

esker/esker una cumbre larga y con curvas, compuesta por grava y arena gruesa depositada por corrientes de aguas glaciares (428)

estuary/estuario un área donde el agua dulce de los ríos se mezcla con el agua salada del océano; la parte de un río donde las mareas se encuentran con la corriente del río (456)

evapotranspiration/evapotranspiración la pérdida total de agua de un área, igual a la suma del agua perdida por evaporación del suelo y otras superficies, y el agua perdida debido a la transpiración de los organismos (376)

evolution/evolución un cambio hereditario en las características de una población que se produce de una generación a la siguiente; el desarrollo de nuevos tipos de organismos a partir de organismos preexistentes a lo largo del tiempo (215)

extrusive igneous rock/roca ígnea extrusiva roca que se forma a partir del enfriamiento y la solidificación de la lava en la superficie de la Tierra (131)

F

fault a break in a body of rock along which one block slides relative to another; a form of brittle strain (277)

fault-block mountain a mountain that forms where faulting breaks Earth's crust into large blocks, which causes some blocks to drop down relative to other blocks (283)

fault zone a region of numerous, closely spaced faults (300)

felsic describes magma or igneous rock that is rich in feldspars and silica and that is generally light in color (132, 325)

fetch the distance that wind blows across an area of the sea to generate waves (527)

floodplain an area along a river that forms from sediments deposited when the river overflows its banks (384)

fault/falla una grieta en un cuerpo rocoso a lo largo de la cual un bloque se desliza respecto a otro; una forma de tensión quebradiza (277)

fault-block mountain/montaña de bloque de falla una montaña que se forma cuando una falla rompe la corteza de la Tierra en grandes bloques, lo cual hace que algunos bloques se hundan respecto a otros bloques (283)

fault zone/zona de fallas una región donde hay muchas fallas, las cuales están cerca unas de otras (300)

felsic/félsica término que describe el magma o la roca ígnea que es rica en feldespato y sílice y que en general es de color claro (132, 325)

fetch/alcance la distancia que el viento sopla en un área del mar para generar olas (527)

floodplain/llanura de inundación un área a lo largo de un río formada por sedimentos que se depositan cuando el río se desborda (384)

focus the location within Earth along a fault at which the first motion of an earthquake occurs (296)

focus/foco el lugar dentro de la Tierra a lo largo de una falla donde ocurre el primer movimiento de un terremoto (296)

fog water vapor that has condensed very near the surface of Earth because air close to the ground has cooled (586)

fog/niebla vapor de agua que se ha condensado muy cerca de la superficie de la Tierra debido al enfriamiento del aire próximo al suelo (586)

fold a form of ductile strain in which rock layers bend, usually as a result of compression (275)

fold/pliegue una forma de tensión dúctil en la cual las capas de roca se curvan, normalmente como resultado de la compresión (275)

folded mountain a mountain that forms when rock layers are squeezed together and uplifted (282)

folded mountain/montaña de plegamiento una montaña que se forma cuando las capas de roca se comprimen y se elevan (282)

foliation the metamorphic rock texture in which mineral grains are arranged in planes or bands (143)

foliation/foliación la textura de una roca metamórfica en la que los granos de mineral están ordenados en planos o bandas (143)

food web a diagram that shows the feeding relationships among organisms in an ecosystem (41)

food web/red alimenticia un diagrama que muestra las relaciones de alimentación entre los organismos de un ecosistema (41)

fossil the trace or remains of an organism that lived long ago, most commonly preserved in sedimentary rock (197)

fossil/fósil los indicios o los restos de un organismo que vivió hace mucho tiempo, comúnmente preservados en las rocas sedimentarias (197)

fossil fuel a nonrenewable energy resource formed from the remains of organisms that lived long ago; examples include oil, coal, and natural gas (159)

fossil fuel/combustible fósil un recurso energético no renovable formado a partir de los restos de organismos que vivieron hace mucho tiempo; algunos ejemplos incluyen el petróleo, el carbón y el gas natural (159)

fracture in geology, a break in a rock, which results from stress, with or without displacement, including cracks, joints, and faults; *also* the manner in which a mineral breaks along either curved or irregular surfaces (110)

fracture/fractura en geología, un rompimiento en una roca, que resulta de la tensión, con o sin desplazamiento, incluyendo grietas, fisuras y fallas; *también,* la forma en la que se rompe un mineral a lo largo de superficies curvas o irregulares (110)

G

galaxy a collection of stars, dust, and gas bound together by gravity (660, 790)

galaxy/galaxia un conjunto de estrellas, polvo y gas unidos por la gravedad (660, 790)

Galilean moon any one of the four largest satellites of Jupiter—Io, Europa, Ganymede, and Callisto—that were discovered by Galileo in 1610 (733)

Galilean moon/satélite galileano cualquiera de los cuatro satélites más grandes de Júpiter (Io, Europa, Ganímedes y Calisto) que fueron descubiertos por Galileo en 1610 (733)

gas giant a planet that has a deep, massive atmosphere, such as Jupiter, Saturn, Uranus, or Neptune (701)

gas giant/gigante gaseoso un planeta con una atmósfera masiva y profunda, como por ejemplo, Júpiter, Saturno, Urano o Neptuno (701)

gemstone a mineral, rock, or organic material that can be used as jewelry or an ornament when it is cut and polished (157)

gemstone/piedra preciosa un mineral, roca o material orgánico que se puede usar como joya u ornamento cuando se corta y se pule (157)

geologic column an ordered arrangement of rock layers that is based on the relative ages of the rocks and in which the oldest rocks are at the bottom (211)

geology the scientific study of the origin, history, and structure of Earth and the processes that shape Earth (6)

geosphere the mostly solid, rocky part of the Earth; extends from the center of the core to the surface of the crust (33)

geothermal energy the energy produced by heat within Earth (165)

giant a very large and bright star whose hot core has used most of its hydrogen (784)

glacial drift the rock material carried and deposited by glaciers (426)

glacier a large mass of moving ice (419)

global ocean the body of salt water that covers nearly three-fourths of Earth's surface (471)

global warming a gradual increase in the average global temperature that is due to a higher concentration of gases such as carbon dioxide in the atmosphere (645)

gradient the change in elevation over a given distance (380)

greenhouse effect the warming of the surface and lower atmosphere of Earth that occurs when carbon dioxide, water vapor, and other gases in the air absorb and reradiate infrared radiation (558)

groundwater the water that is beneath the Earth's surface (397)

Gulf Stream the swift, deep, and warm Atlantic current that flows along the eastern coast of the United States toward the northeast (522)

gyre a huge circle of moving ocean water found above and below the equator (520)

geologic column/columna geológica un arreglo ordenado de capas de rocas que se basa en la edad relativa de las rocas y en el cual las rocas más antiguas están al fondo (211)

geology/geología el estudio científico del origen, la historia y la estructura del planeta Tierra y los procesos que le dan forma (6)

geosphere/geosfera la parte principalmente sólida y rocosa de la Tierra; se extiende del centro del núcleo a la superficie de la corteza (33)

geothermal energy/energía geotérmica la energía producida por el calor del interior de la Tierra (165)

giant/gigante una estrella muy grande y brillante que tiene un núcleo caliente que ha usado la mayor parte de su hidrógeno (784)

glacial drift/deriva glacial el material rocoso que es transportado y depositado por los glaciares (426)

glacier/glaciar una masa grande de hielo en movimiento (419)

global ocean/océano global la masa de agua salada que cubre cerca de tres cuartas partes de la superficie de la Tierra (471)

global warming/calentamiento global un aumento gradual de la temperatura global promedio debido a una concentración más alta de gases (tales como dióxido de carbono) en la atmósfera (645)

gradient/gradiente el cambio en la elevación a lo largo de una distancia determinada (380)

greenhouse effect/efecto de invernadero el calentamiento de la superficie terrestre y de la parte más baja de la atmósfera, el cual se produce cuando el dióxido de carbono, el vapor de agua y otros gases del aire absorben radiación infrarroja y la vuelven a irradiar (558)

groundwater/agua subterránea el agua que está debajo de la superficie de la Tierra (397)

Gulf Stream/corriente del Golfo la corriente rápida, profunda y cálida del océano Atlántico que fluye por la costa este de los Estados Unidos hacia el noreste (522)

gyre/giro un círculo enorme de agua oceánica en movimiento que se encuentra debajo del ecuador (520)

half-life the time required for half of a sample of a radioactive isotope to break down by radioactive decay to form a daughter isotope (194)

half-life/vida media el tiempo que se requiere para que la mitad de una muestra de un isótopo radiactivo se descomponga por desintegración radiactiva y forme un isótopo hijo (194)

headland a high and steep formation of rock that extends out from shore into the water (452)

headland/promontorio una formación rocosa alta y empinada que se extiende de la costa hacia el agua (452)

horizon the line where the sky and the Earth appear to meet; *also* a horizontal layer of soil that can be distinguished from the layers above and below it; *also* a boundary between two rock layers that have different physical properties (354)

horizon/horizonte la línea donde parece que el cielo y la Tierra se unen; *también,* una capa horizontal de suelo que puede distinguirse de las capas que están por encima y por debajo de ella; *también,* un límite entre dos capas de roca que tienen propiedades físicas distintas (354)

horn a sharp, pyramid-like peak that forms because of the erosion of cirques (424)

horn/cuerno un pico puntiagudo en forma de pirámide que se forma debido a la erosión de los circos (424)

hot spot a volcanically active area of Earth's surface, commonly far from a tectonic plate boundary (323)

hot spot/mancha caliente un área volcánicamente activa de la superficie de la Tierra que comúnmente se encuentra lejos de un límite entre placas tectónicas (323)

humus dark, organic material formed in soil from the decayed remains of plants and animals (354)

humus/humus material orgánico obscuro que se forma en la tierra a partir de restos de plantas y animales en descomposición (354)

hurricane a severe storm that develops over tropical oceans and whose strong winds of more than 120 km/h spiral in toward the intensely low-pressure storm center (609)

hurricane/huracán tormenta severa que se desarrolla sobre océanos tropicales, con vientos fuertes que soplan a más de 120 km/h y que se mueven en espiral hacia el centro de presión extremadamente baja de la tormenta (609)

hydroelectric energy electrical energy produced by the flow of water (167)

hydroelectric energy/energía hidroeléctrica energía eléctrica producida por el flujo del agua (167)

hydrolysis a chemical reaction between water and another substance to form two or more new substances; a reaction between water and a salt to create an acid or a base (347)

hydrolysis/hidrólisis una reacción química entre el agua y otras substancias para formar dos o más substancias nuevas; una reacción entre el agua y una sal para crear un ácido o una base (347)

hydrosphere the portion of the Earth that is water (33)

hydrosphere/hidrosfera la porción de la Tierra que es agua (33)

hypothesis an idea or explanation that is based on observations and that can be tested (10)

hypothesis/hipótesis una idea o explicación que se basa en observaciones y que se puede probar (10)

ice age a long period of climatic cooling during which the continents are glaciated repeatedly (431)

ice age/edad de hielo un largo período de enfriamiento del clima, durante el cual los continentes se ven repetidamente sometidos a la glaciación (431)

igneous rock rock that forms when magma cools and solidifies (129)

igneous rock/roca ígnea una roca que se forma cuando el magma se enfría y se solidifica (129)

independent variable in an experiment, the factor that is deliberately manipulated (11)

index fossil a fossil that is used to establish the age of a rock layer because the fossil is distinct, abundant, and widespread and existed for only a short span of geologic time (200)

inertia the tendency of an object to resist being moved or, if the object is moving, to resist a change in speed or direction until an outside force acts on the object (694)

intensity in Earth science, the amount of damage caused by an earthquake (304)

internal plastic flow the process by which glaciers flow slowly as grains of ice deform under pressure and slide over each other (421)

intrusive igneous rock rock formed from the cooling and solidification of magma beneath the Earth's surface (131)

ion an atom, radical, or molecule that has gained or lost one or more electrons and has a negative or positive charge (90)

ionic bond the attractive force between oppositely charged ions, which form when electrons are transferred from one atom to another (90)

isogram a line on a map that represents a constant or equal value of a given quantity (62)

isostasy a condition of gravitational and buoyant equilibrium between Earth's lithosphere and asthenosphere (271)

isotope an atom that has the same number of protons (or the same atomic number) as other atoms of the same element do but that has a different number of neutrons (and thus a different atomic mass) (83)

independent variable/variable independiente en un experimento, el factor que se manipula deliberadamente (11)

index fossil/fósil guía un fósil que se usa para establecer la edad de una capa de roca debido a que puede diferenciarse bien de otros y es abundante; está extendido y existió sólo por un corto período de tiempo geológico (200)

inertia/inercia la tendencia de un objeto a no moverse o, si el objeto se está moviendo, la tendencia a resistir un cambio en su rapidez o dirección hasta que una fuerza externa actúe en el objeto (694)

intensity/intensidad en las ciencias de la Tierra, la cantidad de daño causado por un terremoto (304)

internal plastic flow/flujo plástico interno el proceso por medio del cual los glaciares fluyen lentamente a medida que los granos de hielo se deforman por efecto de la presión y se deslizan unos sobre otros (421)

intrusive igneous rock/roca ígnea intrusiva una roca formada a partir del enfriamiento y solidificación del magma debajo de la superficie terrestre (131)

ion/ion un átomo, radical o molécula que ha ganado o perdido uno o más electrones y que tiene una carga negativa o positiva (90)

ionic bond/enlace iónico la fuerza de atracción entre iones con cargas opuestas, que se forman cuando se transfieren electrones de un átomo a otro (90)

isogram/isograma una línea en un mapa que representa un valor constante o igual de una cantidad dada (62)

isostasy/isostasia una condición de equilibrio gravitacional y flotante entre la litosfera y la astenosfera de la Tierra (271)

isotope/isótopo un átomo que tiene el mismo número de protones (o el mismo número atómico) que otros átomos del mismo elemento, pero que tiene un número diferente de neutrones (y, por lo tanto, otra masa atómica) (83)

J

jet stream a narrow band of strong winds that blow in the upper troposphere (563)

jet stream/corriente en chorro un cinturón delgado de vientos fuertes que soplan en la parte superior de la troposfera (563)

karst topography a type of irregular topography that is characterized by caverns, sinkholes, and underground drainage and that forms on limestone or other soluble rock (408)

kettle a bowl-shaped depression in a glacial drift deposit (428)

Kuiper Belt a region of the solar system that starts just beyond the orbit of Neptune and that contains dwarf planets and other small bodies made mostly of ice (707, 742)

karst topography/topografía de karst una tipo de topografía irregular que se caracteriza por cavernas, depresiones y drenaje subterráneo y que se forma en piedra caliza o algún otro tipo de roca soluble (408)

kettle/marmita una depresión con forma de tazón en un depósito de deriva glaciar (428)

Kuiper Belt/cinturón de Kuiper una región del Sistema Solar que comienza justo después de la órbita de Neptuno y que contiene planetas enanos y otros cuerpos pequeños formados principalmente de hielo (707, 742)

lagoon a small body of water separated from the sea by a low, narrow strip of land (457)

landform a physical feature of Earth's surface (363)

latent heat the heat energy that is absorbed or released by a substance during a phase change (575)

latitude the distance north or south from the equator; expressed in degrees (53)

lava magma that flows onto Earth's surface; the rock that forms when lava cools and solidifies (320)

law of crosscutting relationships the principle that a fault or body of rock is younger than any other body of rock that it cuts through (190)

law of superposition the principle that a sedimentary rock layer is older than the layers above it and younger than the layers below it if the layers are not disturbed (187)

legend a list of map symbols and their meanings (61)

light-year the distance that light travels in one year; about 9.46 trillion kilometers (779)

lithosphere the solid, outer layer of Earth that consists of the crust and the rigid upper part of the mantle (29, 247)

lagoon/laguna una masa pequeña de agua separada del mar por una tira de tierra baja y angosta (457)

landform/accidente geográfico una característica física de la superficie terrestre (363)

latent heat/calor latente la energía calorífica que es absorbida o liberada por una substancia durante un cambio de fase (575)

latitude/latitud la distancia hacia el norte o hacia el sur del ecuador; se expresa en grados (53)

lava/lava magma que fluye a la superficie terrestre; la roca que se forma cuando la lava se enfría y se solidifica (320)

law of crosscutting relationships/ley de las relaciones entrecortadas el principio de que una falla o un cuerpo rocoso siempre es más joven que cualquier otro cuerpo rocoso que atraviese (190)

law of superposition/ley de la sobreposición el principio de que una capa de roca sedimentaria es más vieja que las capas que se encuentran arriba de ella y más joven que las capas que se encuentran debajo de ella si las capas no han sido alteradas (187)

legend/leyenda una lista de símbolos de un mapas y sus significados (61)

light-year/año luz la distancia que viaja la luz en un año; aproximadamente 9.46 trillones de kilómetros (779)

lithosphere/litosfera la capa externa y sólida de la Tierra que está formada por la corteza y la parte superior y rígida del manto (29, 247)

lode a mineral deposit within a rock formation (156)

loess fine-grained sediments of quartz, feldspar, hornblende, mica, and clay deposited by the wind (450)

longitude the angular distance east or west from the prime meridian; expressed in degrees (54)

longshore current a water current that travels near and parallel to the shoreline (454)

lunar eclipse the passing of the moon through the Earth's shadow at full moon (729)

luster the way in which a mineral reflects light (110)

lode/veta un depósito mineral que se encuentra dentro de una formación rocosa (156)

loess/loess sedimentos de grano fino de cuarzo, feldespato, horneblenda, mica y arcilla depositados por el viento (450)

longitude/longitud la distancia angular hacia el este o hacia el oeste del primer meridiano; se expresa en grados (54)

longshore current/corriente de ribera una corriente de agua que se desplaza cerca de la costa y paralela a ella (454)

lunar eclipse/eclipse lunar el paso de la Luna frente a la sombra de la Tierra cuando hay luna llena (729)

luster/brillo la forma en que un mineral refleja la luz (110)

M

mafic describes magma or igneous rock that is rich in magnesium and iron and that is generally dark in color (132, 325)

magma liquid rock produced under the Earth's surface; igneous rocks are made of magma (319)

magnitude a measure of the strength of an earthquake (303)

main sequence the location on the H-R diagram where most stars lie; it has a diagonal pattern from the lower right (low temperature and luminosity) to the upper left (high temperature and luminosity) (781)

mantle in Earth science, the layer of rock between Earth's crust and core (28)

map projection a flat map that represents a spherical surface (58)

mare a large, dark area of basalt on the moon (plural, *maria*) (720)

mass extinction an episode during which large numbers of species become extinct (221)

mass movement the movement of a large mass of sediment or a section of land down a slope (361)

mafic/máfica término que describe el magma o la roca ígnea que es rica en magnesio y hierro y que en general es de color obscuro (132, 325)

magma/magma roca líquida producida debajo de la superficie terrestre; las rocas ígneas están hechas de magma (319)

magnitude/magnitud una medida de la fuerza de un terremoto (303)

main sequence/secuencia principal la ubicación en el diagrama H-R donde se encuentran la mayoría de las estrellas; tiene un patrón diagonal de la parte inferior derecha (baja temperatura y luminosidad) a la parte superior izquierda (alta temperatura y luminosidad) (781)

mantle/manto en las ciencias de la Tierra, la capa de roca que se encuentra entre la corteza terrestre y el núcleo (28)

map projection/proyección cartográfica un mapa plano que representa una superficie esférica (58)

mare/mar lunar una gran área oscura de basalto en la Luna (720)

mass extinction/extinción masiva un episodio durante el cual grandes cantidades de especies se extinguen (221)

mass movement/movimiento masivo el movimiento hacia abajo por una pendiente de una gran masa de sedimento o una sección de terreno (361)

matter anything that has mass and takes up space (81)

meander one of the bends, twists, or curves in a low-gradient stream or river (381)

mechanical weathering the process by which rocks break down into smaller pieces by physical means (343)

meridian any semicircle that runs north and south around Earth from the geographic North Pole to the geographic South Pole; a line of longitude (54)

mesosphere literally, the "middle sphere"; the strong, lower part of the mantle between the asthenosphere and the outer core; *also* the coldest layer of the atmosphere, between the stratosphere and the thermosphere, in which temperature decreases as altitude increases (29, 553)

Mesozoic Era the geologic era that lasted from 251 million to 65.5 million years ago; also called the *Age of Reptiles* (221)

metamorphism the process in which one type of rock changes into metamorphic rock because of chemical processes or changes in temperature and pressure (141)

meteor a bright streak of light that results when a meteoroid burns up in Earth's atmosphere (743)

meteoroid a relatively small, rocky body that travels through space (743)

meteorology the scientific study of Earth's atmosphere, especially in relation to weather and climate (7)

microclimate the climate of a small area (640)

middle-latitude climate a climate that has a maximum average temperature of 8°C in the coldest month and a minimum average temperature of 10°C in the warmest month (638)

mid-latitude cyclone an area of low pressure that is characterized by rotating wind that moves toward the rising air of the central low-pressure region; the motion is counterclockwise in the Northern Hemisphere (606)

matter/materia cualquier cosa que tiene masa y ocupa un lugar en el espacio (81)

meander/meandro una de las vueltas, giros o curvas de un arroyo o río de bajo gradiente (381)

mechanical weathering/desgaste mecánico el proceso por medio del cual las rocas se rompen en pedazos más pequeños mediante medios físicos (343)

meridian/meridiano cualquier semicírculo que va de norte a sur alrededor de la Tierra, del Polo Norte geográfico al Polo Sur geográfico; una línea de longitud (54)

mesosphere/mesosfera literalmente, la "esfera media"; la parte fuerte e inferior del manto que se encuentra entre la astenosfera y el núcleo externo; *también,* la capa más fría de la atmósfera que se encuentra entre la estratosfera y la termosfera, en la cual la temperatura disminuye al aumentar la altitud (29, 553)

Mesozoic Era/Era Mesozoica la era geológica que comenzó hace 251 millones de años y terminó hace 65.5 millones de años; también llamada *Edad de los Reptiles* (221)

metamorphism/metamorfismo el proceso en el que un tipo de roca cambia a roca metamórfica debido a procesos químicos o cambios en la temperatura y la presión (141)

meteor/meteoro un rayo de luz brillante que se produce cuando un meteoroide se quema en la atmósfera de la Tierra (743)

meteoroid/meteoroide un cuerpo rocoso relativamente pequeño que viaja en el espacio (743)

meteorology/meteorología el estudio científico de la atmósfera de la Tierra, sobre todo en lo que se relaciona al tiempo y al clima (7)

microclimate/microclima el clima de un área pequeña (640)

middle-latitude climate/clima de latitud media un clima que tiene una temperatura máxima promedio de 8°C en el mes más frío y una temperatura mínima promedio de 10°C en el mes más caliente (638)

mid-latitude cyclone/ciclón de latitud media un área de baja presión caracterizada por la presencia de viento en rotación que se desplaza hacia el aire ascendente de la región central de baja presión; en el hemisferio norte, el movimiento se produce en sentido contrario al de las manecillas del reloj (606)

mid-ocean ridge a long, undersea mountain chain that has a steep, narrow valley at its center, that forms as magma rises from the asthenosphere, and that creates new oceanic lithosphere (sea floor) as tectonic plates move apart (242)

Milankovitch theory the theory that cyclical changes in Earth's orbit and in the tilt of Earth's axis occur over thousands of years and cause climatic changes (433)

mineral a natural, usually inorganic solid that has a characteristic chemical composition, an orderly internal structure, and a characteristic set of physical properties (103)

mineralogist a person who examines, analyzes, and classifies minerals (109)

mixture a combination of two or more substances that are not chemically combined (92)

Mohs hardness scale the standard scale against which the hardness of minerals is rated (111)

molecule a group of atoms that are held together by chemical forces; a molecule is the smallest unit of matter that can exist by itself and retain all of a substance's chemical properties (87)

monsoon a seasonal wind that blows toward the land in the summer, bringing heavy rains, and that blows away from the land in the winter, bringing dry weather (635)

moon a celestial body that revolves around a body that is larger in mass; a natural satellite (719)

moraine a landform that is made from unsorted sediments deposited by a glacier (427)

mountain range a series of mountains that are closely related in orientation, age, and mode of formation (279)

mid-ocean ridge/dorsal oceánica una larga cadena submarina de montañas que tiene un valle empinado y angosto en el centro, se forma a medida que el magma se eleva a partir de la astenosfera y produce una nueva litosfera oceánica (suelo marino) a medida que las placas tectónicas se separan (242)

Milankovitch theory/teoría de Milankovitch la teoría que establece que los cambios cíclicos en la órbita de la Tierra y en la inclinación de su eje se producen a lo largo de miles de años y provocan cambios climáticos (433)

mineral/mineral un sólido natural, normalmente inorgánico, que tiene una composición química característica, una estructura interna ordenada y propiedades físicas y químicas características (103)

mineralogist/minerólogo una persona que examina, analiza y clasifica los minerales (109)

mixture/mezcla una combinación de dos o más substancias que no están combinadas químicamente (92)

Mohs hardness scale/escala de dureza de Mohs la escala estándar que se usa para clasificar la dureza de un mineral (111)

molecule/molécula un conjunto de átomos que se mantienen unidos por acción de las fuerzas químicas; una molécula es la unidad más pequeña de la materia capaz de existir en forma independiente y conservar todas las propiedades químicas de una substancia (87)

monsoon/monzón viento estacional que sopla hacia la tierra en el verano, ocasionando fuertes lluvias, y que se aleja de la tierra en el invierno, ocasionando tiempo seco (635)

moon/luna un cuerpo celeste que gira alrededor de un cuerpo que tiene mayor masa; un satélite natural (719)

moraine/morrena un accidente geográfico que se forma a partir de varios tipos de sedimentos depositados por un glaciar (427)

mountain range/cinturón de montañas una serie de montañas que están íntimamente relacionadas en orientación, edad y modo de formación (279)

nebula a large cloud of gas and dust in interstellar space; a region in space where stars are born (782)

nebula/nebulosa una nube grande de gas y polvo en el espacio interestelar; una región en el espacio donde las estrellas nacen (782)

nekton all organisms that swim actively in open water, independent of currents (502)

nekton/necton todos los organismos que nadan activamente en las aguas abiertas, de manera independiente de las corrientes (502)

neutron a subatomic particle that has no charge and that is located in the nucleus of an atom (82)

neutron/neutrón una partícula subatómica que no tiene carga y que está ubicada en el núcleo de un átomo (82)

neutron star a star that has collapsed under gravity to the point that the electrons and protons have smashed together to form neutrons (787)

neutron star/estrella de neutrones una estrella que se ha colapsado debido a la gravedad hasta el punto en que los electrones y protones han chocado unos contra otros para formar neutrones (787)

nodule a lump of minerals whose composition differs from the composition of the surrounding sediment or rock; *also* a lump of minerals that is made of oxides of manganese, iron, copper, or nickel and that is found in scattered groups on the ocean floor (481)

nodule/nódulo un bulto de minerales que tienen una composición diferente a la de los sedimentos o rocas de los alrededores; *también,* un bulto de minerales compuesto por óxidos de manganeso, hierro, cobre o níquel y que se encuentra en grupos esparcidos en el fondo del océano (481)

nonfoliated the metamorphic rock texture in which mineral grains are not arranged in planes or bands (144)

nonfoliated/no foliada la textura de una roca metamórfica en la que los granos de mineral no están ordenados en planos ni bandas (144)

nonrenewable resource a resource that forms at a rate that is much slower than the rate at which it is consumed (159)

nonrenewable resource/recurso no renovable un recurso que se forma a una tasa que es mucho más lenta que la tasa a la que se consume (159)

nonsilicate mineral a mineral that does not contain compounds of silicon and oxygen (105)

nonsilicate mineral/mineral no-silicato un mineral que no contiene compuestos de sílice y oxígeno (105)

nova a star that suddenly becomes brighter (786)

nova/nova una estrella que súbitamente se vuelve más brillante (786)

nuclear fission the process by which the nucleus of a heavy atom splits into two or more fragments; the process releases neutrons and energy (162)

nuclear fission/fisión nuclear el proceso por medio del cual el núcleo de un átomo pesado se divide en dos o más fragmentos; el proceso libera neutrones y energía (162)

nuclear fusion the process by which nuclei of small atoms combine to form new, more massive nuclei; the process releases energy (164, 756)

nuclear fusion/fusión nuclear el proceso por medio del cual los núcleos de átomos pequeños se combinan y forman núcleos nuevos con mayor masa; el proceso libera energía (164, 756)

O

observation the process of obtaining information by using the senses; the information obtained by using the senses (10)

observation/observación el proceso de obtener información por medio de los sentidos; la información que se obtiene al usar los sentidos (10)

occluded front a front that forms when a cold air mass overtakes a warm air mass and lifts the warm air mass off the ground and over another air mass (606)

oceanography the scientific study of the ocean, including the properties and movements of ocean water, the characteristics of the ocean floor, and the organisms that live in the ocean (6, 472)

Oort cloud a spherical region that surrounds the solar system, that extends from the Kuiper Belt to almost halfway to the nearest star, and that contains billions of comets (742)

orbital period the time required for a body to complete a single orbit (693)

ore a natural material whose concentration of economically valuable minerals is high enough for the material to be mined profitably (155)

organic sedimentary rock sedimentary rock that forms from the remains of plants or animals (136)

oxidation a reaction that removes one or more electrons from a substance such that the substance's valence or oxidation state increases; in geology, the process by which a metallic element combines with oxygen (346)

ozone a gas molecule that is made up of three oxygen atoms (549)

occluded front/frente ocluido un frente que se forma cuando una masa de aire frío supera a una masa de aire caliente y la levanta del suelo por encima de otra masa de aire (606)

oceanography/oceanografía el estudio científico del océano, incluyendo las propiedades y los movimientos del agua, las características del fondo y los organismos que viven en él (6, 472)

Oort cloud/nube de Oort una región esférica que rodea al Sistema Solar, que se extiende desde el cinturón de Kuiper hasta la mitad del camino hacia la estrella más cercana y contiene miles de millones de cometas (742)

orbital period/período de órbita el tiempo que se requiere para que un cuerpo complete una órbita (693)

ore/mena un material natural cuya concentración de minerales con valor económico es suficientemente alta como para que el material pueda ser explotado de manera rentable (155)

organic sedimentary rock/roca sedimentaria orgánica roca sedimentaria que se forma a partir de los restos de plantas o animales (136)

oxidation/oxidación una reacción en la que uno o más electrones son removidos de una substancia, aumentado su valencia o estado de oxidación; en geología, el proceso por medio del cual un elemento metálico se combina con oxígeno (346)

ozone/ozono una molécula de gas que está formada por tres átomos de oxígeno (549)

P

pack ice a floating layer of sea ice that completely covers an area of the ocean surface (497)

paleomagnetism the study of the alignment of magnetic minerals in rock, specifically as it relates to the reversal of Earth's magnetic poles; *also* the magnetic properties that rock acquires during formation (243)

paleontology the scientific study of fossils (197)

Paleozoic Era the geologic era that followed Precambrian time and that lasted from 542 million to 251 million years ago (218)

pack ice/manto de hielo marino una capa flotante de hielo marino que cubre completamente un área de la superficie del océano (497)

paleomagnetism/paleomagnetismo el estudio de la alineación de los minerales magnéticos en la roca, específicamente en lo que se relaciona con la inversión de los polos magnéticos de la Tierra; *también,* las propiedades magnéticas que la roca adquiere durante su formación (243)

paleontology/paleontología el estudio científico de los fósiles (197)

Paleozoic Era/Era Paleozoica la era geológica que vino después del período Precámbrico; comenzó hace 542 millones de años y terminó hace 251 millones de años (218)

Pangaea the supercontinent that formed 300 million years ago and that began to break up 250 million years ago (258)

Panthalassa the single, large ocean that covered Earth's surface during the time the supercontinent Pangaea existed (258)

parallax an apparent shift in the position of an object when viewed from different locations (779)

parallel any circle that runs east and west around Earth and that is parallel to the equator; a line of latitude (53)

peer review the process in which experts in a given field examine the results and conclusions of a scientist's study before that study is accepted for publication (14)

pelagic zone the region of an ocean or body of fresh water above the benthic zone (503)

perigee in the orbit of a satellite, the point at which the satellite is closest to Earth (725)

perihelion the point in the orbit of a planet at which the planet is closest to the sun (668)

period a unit of geologic time that is longer than an epoch but shorter than an era (214)

permeability the ability of a rock or sediment to let fluids pass through its open spaces, or pores (398)

phase in astronomy, the change in the illuminated area of one celestial body as seen from another celestial body; phases of the moon are caused by the changing positions of the Earth, the sun, and the moon (730)

photosphere the visible surface of the sun (759)

placer deposit a deposit that contains a valuable mineral that has been concentrated by mechanical action (156)

planet a celestial body that orbits the sun, is round because of its own gravity, and has cleared the neighborhood around its orbital path (685)

planetesimal a small body from which a planet originated in the early stages of development of the solar system (686)

Pangaea/Pangea el supercontinente que se formó hace 300 millones de años y que comenzó a separarse hace 250 millones de años (258)

Panthalassa/Panthalassa el único gran océano que cubría la superficie de la Tierra cuando existía el supercontinente Pangea (258)

parallax/paralaje un cambio aparente en la posición de un objeto cuando se ve desde lugares distintos (779)

parallel/paralelo cualquier círculo que va hacia el Este o hacia el Oeste alrededor de la Tierra y que es paralelo al ecuador; una línea de latitud (53)

peer review/evaluación de pares el proceso en el cual los expertos en un campo dado examinan los resultados y las conclusiones de un estudio científico antes de aceptar su publicación (14)

pelagic zone/zona pelágica la región de un océano o una masa de agua dulce sobre la zona bentónica (503)

perigee/perigeo en la órbita de un satélite, el punto en el que el satélite está más cerca de la Tierra (725)

perihelion/perihelio el punto en la órbita de un planeta en el que el planeta está más cerca del Sol (668)

period/período una unidad de tiempo geológico que es más larga que una época pero más corta que una era (214)

permeability/permeabilidad la capacidad de una roca o sedimento de permitir que los fluidos pasen a través de sus espacios abiertos o poros (398)

phase/fase en astronomía, el cambio en el área iluminada de un cuerpo celeste según se ve desde otro cuerpo celeste; las fases de la Luna se producen como resultado de los cambios en la posición de la Tierra, el Sol y la Luna (730)

photosphere/fotosfera la superficie visible del Sol (759)

placer deposit/yacimiento de aluvión un yacimiento que contiene un mineral valioso que se ha concentrado debido a la acción mecánica (156)

planet/planeta un cuerpo celeste que orbita alrededor del Sol, es redondo debido a su propia fuerza de gravedad y ha despejado los alrededores de su trayectoria orbital (685)

planetesimal/planetesimal un cuerpo pequeño a partir del cual se originó un planeta en las primeras etapas de desarrollo del Sistema Solar (686)

plankton the mass of mostly microscopic organisms that float or drift freely in the waters of aquatic (freshwater and marine) environments (502)

plate tectonics the theory that explains how large pieces of the lithosphere, called plates, move and change shape (247)

polar climate a climate that is characterized by average temperatures that are near or below freezing; typical of polar regions (639)

polar easterlies prevailing winds that blow from east to west between 60° and 90° latitude in both hemispheres (562)

porosity the percentage of the total volume of a rock or sediment that consists of open spaces (397)

Precambrian time the interval of time in the geologic time scale from Earth's formation to the beginning of the Paleozoic Era, from 4.6 billion to 542 million years ago (216)

precipitation any form of water that falls to Earth's surface from the clouds; includes rain, snow, sleet, and hail (376, 587)

prominence a loop of relatively cool, incandescent gas that extends above the photosphere and above the sun's edge as seen from Earth (763)

proton a subatomic particle that has a positive charge and that is located in the nucleus of an atom; the number of protons of the nucleus is the atomic number, which determines the identity of an element (82)

pulsar a rapidly spinning neutron star that emits pulses of radio and optical energy (788)

P wave a primary wave, or compression wave; a seismic wave that causes particles of rock to move in a back-and-forth direction parallel to the direction in which the wave is traveling; P waves are the fastest seismic waves and can travel through solids, liquids, and gases (297)

pyroclastic material fragments of rock that form during a volcanic eruption (326)

plankton/plancton la masa de organismos casi microscópicos que flotan o se encuentran a la deriva en aguas (dulces y marinas) de ambientes acuáticos (502)

plate tectonics/tectónica de placas la teoría que explica cómo las grandes partes de litosfera, denominadas placas, se mueven y cambian de forma (247)

polar climate/clima polar un clima caracterizado por temperaturas cercanas o inferiores al punto de congelación; típico de las regiones polares (639)

polar easterlies/vientos polares del este vientos preponderantes que soplan de este a oeste entre los 60° y los 90° de latitud en ambos hemisferios (562)

porosity/porosidad el porcentaje del volumen total de una roca o sedimento que está formado por espacios abiertos (397)

Precambrian time/período Precámbrico el intervalo en la escala de tiempo geológico que abarca desde la formación de la Tierra hasta el comienzo de la Era Paleozoica; comenzó hace 4,600 millones de años y terminó hace 542 millones de años (216)

precipitation/precipitación cualquier forma de agua que cae de las nubes a la superficie de la Tierra; incluye a la lluvia, nieve, aguanieve y granizo (376, 587)

prominence/protuberancia una espiral de gas incandescente y relativamente frío que, vista desde la Tierra, se extiende por encima de la fotosfera y la superficie del Sol (763)

proton/protón una partícula subatómica que tiene una carga positiva y que está ubicada en el núcleo de un átomo; el número de protones que hay en el núcleo es el número atómico, y éste determina la identidad del elemento (82)

pulsar/pulsar una estrella de neutrones que gira rápidamente y emite pulsaciones de energía radioeléctrica y óptica (788)

P wave/onda P una onda primaria u onda de compresión; una onda sísmica que hace que las partículas de roca se muevan en una dirección de atrás hacia delante en forma paralela a la dirección en que viaja la onda; las ondas P son las ondas sísmicas más rápidas y pueden viajar a través de sólidos, líquidos y gases (297)

pyroclastic material/material piroclástico fragmentos de roca que se forman durante una erupción volcánica (326)

quasar quasi-stellar radio source; a very luminous object that produces energy at a high rate; quasars are thought to be the most distant objects in the universe (792)

quasar/cuasar fuente de radio cuasi-estelar; un objeto muy luminoso que produce energía a una gran velocidad; se piensa que los cuasares son los objetos más distantes del universo (792)

radar radio detection and ranging, a system that uses reflected radio waves to determine the velocity and location of objects (613)

radar/radar detección y exploración a gran distancia por medio de ondas de radio; un sistema que usa ondas de radio reflejadas para determinar la velocidad y ubicación de los objetos (613)

radiative zone the zone of the sun's interior that is between the core and the convection zone and in which energy moves by radiation (759)

radiative zone/zona radiactiva la zona del interior del Sol que se encuentra entre el núcleo y la zona de convección y en la cual la energía se mueve por radiación (759)

radiometric dating a method of determining the absolute age of an object by comparing the relative percentages of a radioactive (parent) isotope and a stable (daughter) isotope (193)

radiometric dating/datación radiométrica un método para determinar la edad absoluta de un objeto comparando los porcentajes relativos de un isótopo radiactivo (precursor) y un isótopo estable (hijo) (193)

radiosonde a package of instruments that is carried aloft by balloons to measure upper atmosphere conditions, including temperature, dew point, and wind velocity (613)

radiosonde/radiosonda un conjunto de instrumentos que llevan los globos para medir condiciones de la atmósfera superior, como la temperatura, el punto de rocío y la velocidad del viento (613)

recycling the process of recovering valuable or useful materials from waste or scrap; the process of reusing some items (171)

recycling/reciclar el proceso de recuperar materiales valiosos o útiles de los desechos o de la basura; el proceso de reutilizar algunas cosas (171)

reflecting telescope a telescope that uses a curved mirror to gather and focus light from distant objects (663)

reflecting telescope/telescopio reflector un telescopio que utiliza un espejo curvo para captar y enfocar la luz de objetos lejanos (663)

refracting telescope a telescope that uses a set of lenses to gather and focus light from distant objects (663)

refracting telescope/telescopio refractante un telescopio que utiliza un conjunto de lentes para captar y enfocar la luz de objetos lejanos (663)

refraction the bending of a wavefront as the wavefront passes between two substances in which the speed of the wave differs; *also* the process by which ocean waves bend directly toward the coastline as they approach shallow water (529)

refraction/refracción el curvamiento de un frente de ondas a medida que el frente pasa entre dos substancias en las que la velocidad de las ondas difiere; *también,* el proceso por medio del cual las olas oceánicas se curvan directamente hacia la costa a medida que se acercan a agua poco profunda (529)

regional metamorphism a change in the texture, structure, or chemical composition of a rock due to changes in temperature and pressure over a large area, generally as a result of tectonic forces (142)

regional metamorphism/metamorfismo regional un cambio en la textura, estructura o composición química de una roca debido a cambios en la temperatura y presión en un área extensa, generalmente como resultado de la acción de fuerzas tectónicas (142)

relative age the age of an object in relation to the ages of other objects (186)

relative humidity the ratio of the amount of water vapor in the air to the amount of water vapor needed to reach saturation at a given temperature (578)

relief the difference between the highest and lowest elevations in a given area; the variations in elevation of a land surface (64)

remote sensing the process of gathering and analyzing information about an object without physically being in touch with the object (57)

renewable resource a natural resource that can be replaced at the same rate at which the resource is consumed (165)

revolution the motion of a body that travels around another body in space; one complete trip along an orbit (668)

rifting the process by which Earth's crust breaks apart; can occur within continental crust or oceanic crust (255)

rock cycle the series of processes in which rock forms, changes from one type to another, is destroyed, and forms again by geologic processes (126)

rotation the spin of a body on its axis (667)

relative age/edad relativa la edad de un objeto en relación con la edad de otros objetos (186)

relative humidity/humedad relativa la proporción de la cantidad de vapor de agua que hay en el aire respecto a la cantidad de vapor de agua necesaria para alcanzar la saturación a una temperatura dada (578)

relief/relieve la diferencia entre las elevaciones más altas y las más bajas en un área dada; las variaciones en elevación de una superficie de terreno (64)

remote sensing/teledetección el proceso de recopilar y analizar información acerca de un objeto sin estar en contacto físico con el objeto (57)

renewable resource/recurso renovable un recurso natural que puede reemplazarse a la misma tasa a la que se consume (165)

revolution/revolución el movimiento de un cuerpo que viaja alrededor de otro cuerpo en el espacio; un viaje completo a lo largo de una órbita (668)

rifting/fracturación el proceso por medio del cual la corteza de la Tierra se fractura; puede producirse dentro de la corteza continental u oceánica (255)

rock cycle/ciclo de las rocas la serie de procesos por medio de los cuales una roca se forma, cambia de un tipo a otro, se destruye y se forma nuevamente por procesos geológicos (126)

rotation/rotación el giro de un cuerpo alrededor de su eje (667)

S

salinity a measure of the amount of dissolved salts in a given amount of liquid (496)

saltation the movement of sand or other sediments by short jumps and bounces that is caused by wind or water (445)

satellite a natural or artificial body that revolves around a larger celestial body (719)

scale the relationship between the distance shown on a map and the actual distance (61)

sea a large, commonly saline body of water that is smaller than an ocean and that may be partially or completely surrounded by land; *also* a subdivision of an ocean (471)

salinity/salinidad una medida de la cantidad de sales disueltas en una cantidad determinada de líquido (496)

saltation/saltación el movimiento de la arena u otros sedimentos por medio de saltos pequeños y rebotes debido al viento o al agua (445)

satellite/satélite un cuerpo natural o artificial que gira alrededor de un cuerpo celeste más grande (719)

scale/escala la relación entre la distancia que se muestra en un mapa y la distancia real (61)

sea/mar una gran masa de agua, generalmente salada, que es más pequeña que un océano y que puede estar parcial o totalmente rodeada de tierra; *también,* una subdivisión de un océano (471)

sea-floor spreading the process by which new oceanic lithosphere (sea floor) forms as magma rises to Earth's surface and solidifies at a mid-ocean ridge (243)

seismic gap an area along a fault where relatively few earthquakes have occurred recently but where strong earthquakes are known to have occurred in the past (307)

seismogram a tracing of earthquake motion that is recorded by a seismograph (301)

seismograph an instrument that records vibrations in the ground (301)

shadow zone an area on Earth's surface where no direct seismic waves from a particular earthquake can be detected (298)

sheet erosion the process by which water flows over a layer of soil and removes the topsoil (358)

silicate mineral a mineral that contains a combination of silicon and oxygen and that may also contain one or more metals (104)

silicon-oxygen tetrahedron the basic unit of the structure of silicate minerals; a silicon ion chemically bonded to and surrounded by four oxygen ions (106)

sinkhole a circular depression that forms when rock dissolves, when overlying sediment fills an existing cavity, or when the roof of an underground cavern or mine collapses (407)

soil a loose mixture of rock fragments and organic material that can support the growth of vegetation (353)

soil profile a vertical section of soil that shows the layers of horizons (354)

solar eclipse the passing of the moon between Earth and the sun; during a solar eclipse, the shadow of the moon falls on Earth (727)

solar energy the energy received by Earth from the sun in the form of radiation (166)

solar flare an explosive release of energy that comes from the sun and that is associated with magnetic disturbances on the sun's surface (763)

sea-floor spreading/expansión del suelo marino el proceso por medio del cual se forma nueva litosfera oceánica (suelo marino) a medida que el magma se eleva a la superficie de la Tierra y se solidifica en una dorsal oceánica (243)

seismic gap/brecha sísmica un área a lo largo de una falla donde han ocurrido relativamente pocos terremotos recientemente, pero donde se sabe que han ocurrido terremotos fuertes en el pasado (307)

seismogram/sismograma una traza del movimiento de un terremoto registrada por un sismógrafo (301)

seismograph/sismógrafo un instrumento que registra las vibraciones en el suelo (301)

shadow zone/zona de sombra un área de la superficie de la Tierra donde no se detectan ondas sísmicas directas de un determinado terremoto (298)

sheet erosion/erosión laminar el proceso por medio del cual el agua fluye sobre el suelo y remueve la capa superior de éste (358)

silicate mineral/mineral silicato un mineral que contiene una combinación de silicio y oxígeno y que también puede contener uno o más metales (104)

silicon-oxygen tetrahedron/tetraedro de sílice-oxígeno la unidad fundamental de la estructura de los minerales silicatos: un ion de silicio unido químicamente a cuatro iones de oxígeno, los cuales lo rodean (106)

sinkhole/depresión una depresión circular que se forma cuando la roca se funde, cuando el sedimento suprayacente llena una cavidad existente, o al colapsarse el techo de una caverna o mina subterránea (407)

soil/suelo una mezcla suelta de fragmentos de roca y material orgánico en la que puede crecer vegetación (353)

soil profile/perfil del suelo una sección vertical de suelo que muestra las capas u horizontes (354)

solar eclipse/eclipse solar el paso de la Luna entre la Tierra y el Sol; durante un eclipse solar, la sombra de la Luna cae sobre la Tierra (727)

solar energy/energía solar la energía que la Tierra recibe del Sol en forma de radiación (166)

solar flare/erupción solar una liberación explosiva de energía que proviene del Sol y que se asocia con disturbios magnéticos en la superficie solar (763)

solar nebula a rotating cloud of gas and dust from which the sun and planets formed; *also* any nebula from which stars and exoplanets may form (685)

solar system the sun and all of the planets and other bodies that travel around it (685)

solifluction the slow, downslope flow of soil saturated with water in areas surrounding glaciers at high elevations (362)

solstice the point at which the sun is as far north or as far south of the equator as possible (674)

solution a homogeneous mixture throughout which two or more substances are uniformly dispersed (92)

sonar sound navigation and ranging, a system that uses acoustic signals and returned echoes to determine the location of objects or to communicate (473)

specific heat the quantity of heat required to raise a unit mass of homogeneous material 1 K or 1ºC in a specified way given constant pressure and volume (634)

star a large celestial body that is composed of gas and that emits light; the sun is a typical star (775)

stationary front a front of air masses that moves either very slowly or not at all (606)

station model a pattern of meteorological symbols that represents the weather at a particular observing station and that is recorded on a weather map (616)

strain any change in a rock's shape or volume caused by stress; deformation (274)

stratosphere the layer of the atmosphere that lies between the troposphere and the mesosphere and in which temperature increases as altitude increases; contains the ozone layer (553)

stratus cloud a gray cloud that has a flat, uniform base and that commonly forms at very low altitudes (584)

streak the color of a mineral in powdered form (110)

solar nebula/nebulosa solar una nube de gas y polvo en rotación a partir de la cual se formaron el Sol y los planetas; *también,* cualquier nebulosa a partir de la cual se pueden formar estrellas y exoplanetas (685)

solar system/Sistema Solar el Sol y todos los planetas y otros cuerpos que se desplazan alrededor de él (685)

solifluction/soliflución el flujo lento y descendente de suelo saturado con agua en áreas que rodean glaciares a altas elevaciones (362)

solstice/solsticio el punto en el que el Sol está tan lejos del ecuador como es posible, ya sea hacia el norte o hacia el sur (674)

solution/solución una mezcla homogénea en la cual dos o más sustancias se dispersan de manera uniforme (92)

sonar/sonar navegación y exploración por medio del sonido; un sistema que usa señales acústicas y ondas de eco que regresan para determinar la ubicación de los objetos o para comunicarse (473)

specific heat/calor específico la cantidad de calor que se requiere para aumentar una unidad de masa de un material homogéneo 1 K ó 1ºC de una manera especificada, dados un volumen y una presión constantes (634)

star/estrella un cuerpo celeste grande que está compuesto de gas y emite luz; el Sol es una estrella típica (775)

stationary front/frente estacionario un frente de masas de aire que se mueve muy lentamente o que no se mueve (606)

station model/estación modelo el modelo de símbolos meteorológicos que representan el tiempo en una estación de observación determinada y que se registra en un mapa meteorológico (616)

strain/tensión cualquier cambio en la forma o volumen de una roca causado por el estrés; deformación (274)

stratosphere/estratosfera la capa de la atmósfera que se encuentra entre la troposfera y la mesosfera y en la cual la temperatura aumenta al aumentar la altitud; contiene la capa de ozono (553)

stratus cloud/nube estrato una nube gris que tiene una base plana y uniforme y que comúnmente se forma a altitudes muy bajas (584)

streak/veta el color de un mineral en forma de polvo (110)

stream load the materials other than the water that are carried by a stream (380)

stress the amount of force per unit area that acts on a rock (273)

sublimation the process in which a solid changes directly into a gas (the term is sometimes also used for the reverse process) (576)

sunspot a dark area of the photosphere of the sun that is cooler than the surrounding areas and that has a strong magnetic field (761)

supercontinent cycle the process by which supercontinents form and break apart over millions of years (258)

supercooling a condition in which a substance is cooled below its freezing point, condensation point, or sublimation point without going through a change of state (588)

surface current a horizontal movement of ocean water that is caused by wind and that occurs at or near the ocean's surface (519)

surface wave in geology, a seismic wave that travels along the surface of a medium and that has a stronger effect near the surface of the medium than it has in the interior (296)

S wave a secondary wave, or shear wave; a seismic wave that causes particles of rock to move in a side-to-side direction perpendicular to the direction in which the wave is traveling; S waves are the second-fastest seismic waves and can travel only through solids (297)

system a set of particles or interacting components considered to be a distinct physical entity for the purpose of study (31)

stream load/carga de un arroyo los materiales que lleva un arroyo, además del agua (380)

stress/estrés la cantidad de fuerza por unidad de área que se ejerce sobre una roca (273)

sublimation/sublimación el proceso por medio del cual un sólido se transforma directamente en un gas (en ocasiones, este término también se usa para describir el proceso inverso) (576)

sunspot/mancha solar un área oscura en la fotosfera del Sol que es más fría que las áreas que la rodean y que tiene un campo magnético fuerte (761)

supercontinent cycle/ciclo de los supercontinentes el proceso por medio del cual los supercontinentes se forman y se separan a lo largo de millones de años (258)

supercooling/superfrío una condición en la que una sustancia se enfría por debajo de su punto de congelación, punto de condensación o punto de sublimación sin pasar por un cambio de estado (588)

surface current/corriente superficial un movimiento horizontal del agua del océano que es producido por el viento y que ocurre en la superficie del océano o cerca de ella (519)

surface wave/onda superficial en geología, una onda sísmica que se desplaza a lo largo de la superficie de un medio, cuyo efecto es más fuerte cerca de la superficie del medio que en el interior de éste (296)

S wave/onda S una onda secundaria u onda rotacional; una onda sísmica que hace que las partículas de roca se muevan en una dirección de lado a lado, en forma perpendicular a la dirección en la que viaja la onda; las ondas S son las segundas ondas sísmicas en cuanto a velocidad y únicamente pueden viajar a través de sólidos (297)

system/sistema un conjunto de partículas o componentes que interactúan unos con otros, el cual se considera una entidad física independiente para fines de estudio (31)

T

telescope an instrument that collects electromagnetic radiation from the sky and concentrates it for better observation (662)

terrane a piece of lithosphere that has a unique geologic history and that may be part of a larger piece of lithosphere, such as a continent (256)

telescope/telescopio un instrumento que capta la radiación electromagnética del cielo y la concentra para mejorar la observación (662)

terrane/macizo autóctono un fragmento de litosfera que tiene una historia geológica única y que puede formar parte de un fragmento de litosfera mayor, como por ejemplo, un continente (256)

terrestrial planet one of the highly dense planets nearest to the sun; Mercury, Venus, Mars, and Earth (695)

theory an explanation for some phenomenon that is based on observation, experimentation, and reasoning; that is supported by a large quantity of evidence; and that does not conflict with any existing experimental results or observations (15)

thermocline a layer in a body of water in which water temperature drops with increased depth faster than it does in other layers (498)

thermometer an instrument that measures and indicates temperature (611)

thermosphere the uppermost layer of the atmosphere, in which temperature increases as altitude increases; includes the ionosphere (553)

thunderstorm a usually brief, heavy storm that consists of rain, strong winds, lightning, and thunder (608)

tidal current the movement of water toward and away from the coast as a result of the rise and fall of the tides (534)

tidal oscillation the slow, rocking motion of ocean water that occurs as the tidal bulges move around the ocean basins (533)

tidal range the difference in levels of ocean water at high tide and low tide (532)

tide the periodic rise and fall of the water level in the oceans and other large bodies of water (531)

till unsorted rock material that is deposited directly by a melting glacier (426)

topography the size and shape of the land surface features of a region, including its relief (63)

tornado a destructive, rotating column of air that has very high wind speeds and that may be visible as a funnel-shaped cloud (610)

terrestrial planet/planeta terrestre uno de los planetas muy densos que se encuentran más cerca del Sol; Mercurio, Venus, Marte y la Tierra (695)

theory/teoría una explicación sobre algún fenómeno que está basada en la observación, experimentación y razonamiento; que está respaldada por una gran cantidad de pruebas; y que no contradice ningún resultado experimental ni observación existente (15)

thermocline/termoclinal una capa en una masa de agua en la que, al aumentar la profundidad, la temperatura del agua disminuye más rápido de lo que lo hace en otras capas (498)

thermometer/termómetro un instrumento que mide e indica la temperatura (611)

thermosphere/termosfera la capa más alta de la atmósfera, en la cual la temperatura aumenta a medida que la altitud aumenta; incluye la ionosfera (553)

thunderstorm/tormenta eléctrica una tormenta fuerte y normalmente breve que consiste en lluvia, vientos fuertes, relámpagos y truenos (608)

tidal current/corriente de marea el movimiento del agua hacia la costa y de la costa hacia el mar, como resultado del ascenso y descenso de las mareas (534)

tidal oscillation/oscilación de las mareas el movimiento lento y mecedor del agua del océano que se produce cuando los abultamientos de marea se mueven alrededor de las cuencas oceánicas (533)

tidal range/rango de marea la diferencia en los niveles del agua del océano entre la marea alta y la marea baja (532)

tide/marea el ascenso y descenso periódico del nivel del agua en los océanos y otras masas grandes de agua (531)

till/arcilla glaciárica material rocoso desordenado que deposita directamente un glaciar que se está derritiendo (426)

topography/topografía el tamaño y la forma de las características de una superficie de terreno, incluyendo su relieve (63)

tornado/tornado una columna destructiva de aire en rotación cuyos vientos se mueven a velocidades muy altas y que puede verse como una nube con forma de embudo (610)

trace fossil a fossilized mark that formed in sedimentary rock by the movement of an animal on or within soft sediment (199)

trade winds prevailing winds that blow from east to west from 30° latitude to the equator in both hemispheres (562)

transform boundary the boundary between tectonic plates that are sliding past each other horizontally (251)

trench a long, narrow, and steep depression that forms on the ocean floor as a result of subduction of a tectonic plate, that runs parallel to the trend of a chain of volcanic islands or the coastline of a continent, and that may be as deep as 11 km below sea level; also called an *ocean trench* or a *deep-ocean trench* (477)

tributary a stream that flows into a lake or into a larger stream (379)

tropical climate a climate characterized by high temperatures and heavy precipitation during at least part of the year; typical of equatorial regions (637)

troposphere the lowest layer of the atmosphere, in which temperature drops at a constant rate as altitude increases; the part of the atmosphere where weather conditions exist (552)

tsunami a giant ocean wave that forms after a volcanic eruption, submarine earthquake, or landslide (305)

trace fossil/fósil traza una marca fosilizada que se formó en una roca sedimentaria por el movimiento de un animal sobre sedimento blando o dentro de éste (199)

trade winds/vientos alisios vientos prevalecientes que soplan de este a oeste desde los 30° de latitud hacia el ecuador en ambos hemisferios (562)

transform boundary/límite de transformación el límite entre placas tectónicas que se están deslizando horizontalmente una sobre otra (251)

trench/fosa submarina una depresión larga, angosta y empinada que se forma en el fondo del océano debido a la subducción de una placa tectónica; corre paralela al curso de una cadena de islas montañosas o a la costa de un continente; y puede tener una profundidad de hasta 11 km bajo el nivel del mar; también denominada *fosa oceánica* o *fosa oceánica profunda* (477)

tributary/afluente un arroyo que fluye a un lago o a otro arroyo más grande (379)

tropical climate/clima tropical un clima caracterizado por temperaturas altas y precipitación fuerte durante al menos una parte del año; típico de las regiones ecuatoriales (637)

troposphere/troposfera la capa inferior de la atmósfera, en la que la temperatura disminuye a una tasa constante a medida que la altitud aumenta; la parte de la atmósfera donde se dan las condiciones del tiempo (552)

tsunami/tsunami una ola gigante del océano que se forma después de una erupción volcánica, terremoto submarino o desprendimiento de tierras (305)

U

unconformity a break in the geologic record created when rock layers are eroded or when sediment is not deposited for a long period of time (189)

uniformitarianism a principle that geologic processes that occurred in the past can be explained by current geologic processes (185)

upwelling the movement of deep, cold, and nutrient-rich water to the surface (502)

unconformity/disconformidad una ruptura en el registro geológico, creada cuando las capas de roca se erosionan o cuando el sedimento no se deposita durante un largo período de tiempo (189)

uniformitarianism/uniformitarianismo un principio que establece que es posible explicar los procesos geológicos que ocurrieron en el pasado en función de los procesos geológicos actuales (185)

upwelling/surgencia el movimiento de las aguas profundas, frías y ricas en nutrientes hacia la superficie (502)

V

varve a banded layer of sand and silt that is de-posited annually in a lake, especially near ice sheets or glaciers, and that can be used to determine absolute age (192)

ventifact any rock that is pitted, grooved, or polished by wind abrasion (447)

volcanism any activity that includes the movement of magma toward or onto the Earth's surface (320)

volcano a vent or fissure in the Earth's surface through which magma and gases are expelled (320)

varve/sedimentos cíclicos estacionales una capa de arena y limo dispuestos en bandas, que se deposita en un lago durante un año, especialmente cerca de las capas de hielo o los glaciares, y que puede usarse para determinar la edad absoluta (192)

ventifact/ventifacto cualquier roca que es marcada, estriada o pulida por la abrasión del viento (447)

volcanism/volcanismo cualquier actividad que incluye el movimiento de magma hacia la superficie de la Tierra o sobre ella (320)

volcano/volcán una chimenea o fisura en la superficie de la Tierra a través de la cual se expulsan magma y gases (320)

W

warm front the front edge of an advancing warm air mass that replaces colder air with warmer air (606)

water cycle the continuous movement of water between the atmosphere, the land, and the oceans (375)

watershed the area of land that is drained by a river system (379)

water table the upper surface of underground water; the upper boundary of the zone of saturation (399)

wave a periodic disturbance in a solid, liquid, or gas as energy is transmitted through a medium (525)

wave period the time required for identical points on consecutive waves to pass a given point (525)

weathering the natural process by which atmospheric and environmental agents, such as wind, rain, and temperature changes, disintegrate and decompose rocks (343)

westerlies prevailing winds that blow from west to east between 30° and 60° latitude in both hemispheres (562)

white dwarf a small, hot, dim star that is the left-over center of an old star (785)

wind vane an instrument used to determine the direction of the wind (612)

warm front/frente cálido el borde del frente de una masa de aire caliente en movimiento que reemplaza al aire más frío (606)

water cycle/ciclo del agua el movimiento continuo del agua entre la atmósfera, la tierra y los océanos (375)

watershed/cuenca hidrográfica el área del terreno que es drenada por un sistema de ríos (379)

water table/capa freática el nivel más alto del agua subterránea; el límite superior de la zona de saturación (399)

wave/onda una perturbación periódica en un sólido, líquido o gas que se transmite a través de un medio en forma de energía (525)

wave period/período de onda el tiempo que se requiere para que puntos idénticos de ondas consecutivas pasen por un punto dado (525)

weathering/meteorización el proceso natural por medio del cual los agentes atmosféricos o ambientales, como el viento, la lluvia y los cambios de temperatura, desintegran y descomponen las rocas (343)

westerlies/vientos del oeste vientos preponderantes que soplan de oeste a este entre 30° y 60° de latitud en ambos hemisferios (562)

white dwarf/enana blanca una estrella pequeña, caliente y tenue que es el centro sobrante de una estrella vieja (785)

wind vane/veleta un instrumento que se usa para determinar la dirección del viento (612)

INDEX

INDEX

INDEX

INDEX

Acknowledgments, continued

Staff Credits

Editorial
Robert V. Tucek, *Executive Editor*
Clay Walton, *Senior Editor*
Debbie Starr, *Managing Editor*

Editorial Development Team
Wesley M. Bain
Angela Hemmeter
Shari Husain
Kristen McCardel
Bill Rader
Marjorie Roueché

Copyeditors
Dawn Marie Spinozza, *Copyediting Manager*
Simon Key
Jane A. Kirschman
Kira J. Watkins

Editorial Support Staff
Mary Anderson
Suzanne Krejci
Shannon Oehler

Online Products
Robert V. Tucek, *Executive Editor*
Wesley M. Bain

Design

Book Design
Kay Selke, *Director of Book Design*
Tim Hovde
Chris Stanford
Holly Whittaker

Media Design
Richard Metzger, *Design Director*
Chris Smith

Image Acquisitions
Curtis Riker, *Director*
Jeannie Taylor, *Photo Research Manager*
Elaine Tate, *Art Buyer Supervisor*
Andy Christiansen
Diana Goetting
Nadyne Wood

Cover Design
Kay Selke, *Director of Book Design*

Publishing Services
Carol Martin, *Director*

Graphic Services
Bruce Bond, *Director*
Katrina Gnader
Cathy Murphy
Nanda Patel
JoAnn Stringer

Technology Services
Laura Likon, *Director*
Juan Baquera, *Technology Services Manager*
Jeff Robinson, *Ancillary Design Manager*
Sara Buller
Lana Kaupp
Janice Noske
Margaret Sanchez
Patty Zepeda

Special Projects
John Koonz
Jennifer Schwan

eMedia
Kate Bennett, *Director*
Armin Gutzmer, *Director of Development*
Ed Blake, *Design Director*
Kimberly Cammerata, *Design Manager*
Marsh Flournoy, *Technology Project Manager*
Tara F. Ross, *Senior Project Manager*
Melanie Baccus
Lydia Doty
Cathy Kuhles
Michael Rinella

Production
Eddie Dawson, *Senior Production Manager*
Adriana Bardin-Prestwood
Kevin Dodds

Manufacturing and Inventory
Ivania Quant Lee, *Inventory Supervisor*
Wilonda leans
Jevara Jackson
Kristen Quiring

Acknowledgments, continued

Photo Credits

COVER PHOTO: John & Eliza Forder/Getty Images.

FRONTMATTER: vi (t), Terry Donnelly/Getty Images/The Image Bank; vi (c), Steve Bloom Images; vi (b), National Geophysical Data Center/National Oceanic and Atmospheric Administration/Department of Commerce; vii (Ch. 4), Steve Allen/PictureQuest; vii (Ch. 5), Richard Price/Getty Images; vii (Ch. 6), John Cleare/Worldwide Picture Library/Alamy Photos; vii (b), Richard Sisk/Panoramic Images/NGSimages.com; viii (Ch. 7), Lester Lefkowitz/CORBIS; viii (Ch. 8), Mark E. Gibson/CORBIS; viii (Ch. 9), John Gurche; viii (br), Andrew Leitch/(c)1992 the Walt Disney Co. Reprinted with permission of Discover Magazine; viii (bc), Bill Steele/A+C Anthology; ix (Ch. 10), Mats Wibe Lund; ix (Ch. 11), Roger Ressmeyer/CORBIS; ix (Ch. 12), Tom Wagner/CORBIS SABA; ix (Ch. 13), Gavriel Jecan/CORBIS; x (Ch. 14), Mark Laricchia/CORBIS ; x (Ch. 15), Jim Wark; x (Ch. 16), Joseph Van Os/Getty Images/The Image Bank; x (br), Harald Sund/Getty Images; xi (t), Liz Hymans/CORBIS; xi (Ch. 17), Andrew Wenzel/Masterfile; xi (Ch. 18), Nicole Duplaix/National Geographic Image Collection; xi (Ch. 19), Jeffrey L. Rotman/CORBIS; xii (tr), Sean Davey/AllSport/Getty Images; xii (Ch. 20), David Hall; xii (Ch. 21), eStock Photo/PictureQuest; xii (Ch. 22), Kevin Kelly/Getty Images/The Image Bank; xiii (Ch. 23), Charles Doswell III/Getty Images; xiii (Ch. 24), Getty Images/Taxi; xiii (Ch. 25), Theo Allofs/CORBIS; xiii (br), Rick Doyle/CORBIS; xiv (Ch. 26), NASA; xiv (Ch. 27), Denis Scott/CORBIS; xiv (Ch. 28), Denis Scott/CORBIS; xiv (br), Dr. Fred Espenak/Photo Researchers, Inc.; xv (t), Grant Faint/Getty Images; xv (Ch. 29), SOHO/ESA/NASA; xv (Ch. 30), Stocktrek/CORBIS; xv (inset), Barry Runk/Stan/Grant Heilman Photography

UNIT ONE: 3 (tr), Terry Donnelly/Getty Images/The Image Bank; 3 (cr), Steve Bloom Images; 3 (br), National Geophysical Data Center/National Oceanic and Atmospheric Administration/Department of Commerce; 4, Terry Donnelly/Getty Images/The Image Bank; 5, Danny Lehman/CORBIS; 6 (bl), Roger Ressmeyer/CORBIS; 6 (c), Roger Ressmeyer/CORBIS; 6 (r), Bryan and Cherry Alexander Photography; 7, Bettmann/CORBIS; 8, Dr. Howard B. Bluestein; 9 (bl), (c)Michael Sewell/Peter Arnold, Inc.; 9 (br), CSIRO/Simon Fraser/SPL/Photo Researchers, Inc.; 11, NASA; 11, NASA; 12 (tl), Sam Dudgeon/HRW; 12 (tc), Sam Dudgeon/HRW; 12 (tr), Sam Dudgeon/HRW; 12 (b), Andy Christiansen/HRW; 13 (l), Kuni/AP/Wide World Photos; 13 (r), NASA/JPL/NIMA; 14, Ric Francis/AP/Wide World Photos; 15 (bl), Aventurier Patrick/Gamma; 15 (cl), V. L. Sharpton/LPI; 15 (cr), Dr. David A. Kring; 15 (br), Courtesy of Los Alamos National Laboratories; 16, Patrick J. Endres/Alaskaphotographics.com; 17 (t), Roger Ressmeyer/CORBIS; 22, HRW; 2-3, Tom Bean/CORBIS ; 25 (t), Courtesy Ken Pierce; 25 (b), Corbis Images; 26, Steve Bloom Images; 27 (bl), Getty Images/PhotoDisc; 31 (bkgd), Douglas Faulkner/CORBIS; 31 (inset), Stuart Westmorland/CORBIS; 31 (inset), Stuart Westmorland/CORBIS; 32 (l), Andy Christiansen/HRW; 32 (r), Andy Christiansen/HRW; 33, Darrell Gulin/CORBIS; 35, Bernhard Lang/The Image Bank/Getty Images; 38, Pam Ostrow/Index Stock Imagery, Inc.; 39, Martin Harvey/Gallo Images/CORBIS; 40 (t), Raymond Gehman/CORBIS ; 40 (b), Roine Magnusson/The Image Bank/Getty Images; 42, Bob Krist; 43 (t), Getty Images/PhotoDisc; 43 (c), Bernhard Lang/The Image Bank/Getty Images; 43 (b), Bob Krist; 49, Andy Christiansen/HRW; 49, Peter Van Steen/HRW; 50, Provided by the SeaWiFS Project, NASA/Goddard Space Flight Center and ORBIMAGE/NASA/Seawifs; 51 (b), Carlos Barria/REUTERS/NewsCom; 51 (t), Martin Harvey/CORBIS; 52 (all), National Geophysical Data Center/National Oceanic and Atmospheric Administration/Department of Commerce; 55 (tl), Layne Kennedy/CORBIS; 55 (br), National Maritime Museum, London; 57 (bl), Christopher Cormack/CORBIS; 60 (bl), Courtesy U.S. Geological Survey; 60 (inset), ; 61 (tl), Simon & Schuster, Inc.; 62 (tl), Bill Frymire/Masterfile; 64 (tl), Nathan Wier/Getty Images; 64 (br), Victoria Smith/HRW; 66 (t), Courtesy U.S. Geological Survey; 67 (bl), National Conservation Resource Service; 67 (br), National Conservation Resource Service; 68 (tl), Image courtesy NSSTC Lightning Team; 69 (tl), Layne Kennedy/CORBIS; 69 (cl), Christopher Cormack/CORBIS; 69 (bl), Nathan Wier/Getty Images; 74 (b), Victoria Smith/HRW; 74 (cr), Victoria Smith/HRW; 75 (tr), Victoria Smith/HRW; 76 (t), Courtesy U.S. Geological Survey; 77 (tr), Robert Goldstrom/The Newborn Group; 77 (bl), Image Makers /Getty Images; 79 (Ch. 4), Steve Allen/PictureQuest; 79 (Ch. 5), Richard Price/Getty Images; 79 (Ch. 6), John Cleare/Worldwide Picture Library/Alamy Photos.

UNIT TWO: 78-79, Jack Dykinga/Stone/Getty Images; 79 (Ch. 7), Lester Lefkowitz/CORBIS; 80, Steve Allen/PictureQuest; 87 (bl), Andrew Lambert Photography/Photo Researchers, Inc.; 87 (bc), Andrew Lambert Photography/Photo Researchers, Inc.; 87 (br), Tony Freeman/PhotoEdit; 89 (tr), Steve Chen/CORBIS; 90 (inset), Bruce Dale/National Geographic Image Collection; 91 (tr), Charlie Winters/HRW; 92 (tl), Craig Aurness/CORBIS; 93 (bl), Steve Chen/CORBIS; 99 (cr), Victoria Smith/HRW; 101 (b), Fermilab; 101 (cr), FERMILAB/SPL/Photo

Researchers, Inc.; 102 (all), Richard Price/Getty Images; 103 (inset), Barry Runk/Grant Heilman Photography, Inc.; 103 (inset), Richard Cummins/CORBIS; 103 (inset), Doug Sokell/Visuals Unlimited; 103 (inset), Dr. E. R. Degginger/Color-Pic, Inc.; 103 (inset), Barry Runk/Stan/Grant Heilman Photography; 104 (tl), Martin Miller/Visuals Unlimited; 104 (tr), Dr. E. R. Degginger/Color-Pic, Inc.; 104 (cl), Charles D. Winters/Photo Researchers, Inc.; 105 (inset), Cabisco/Visuals Unlimited; 105 (inset), Mark Schneider/Visuals Unlimited; 105 (inset), Stonetrust, Inc.; 105 (inset), Paul Silverman/Fundamental Photographs; 105 (inset), Dr. E. R. Degginger/Color-Pic, Inc.; 105 (inset), Dr. E. R. Degginger/Color-Pic, Inc.; 105 (inset), Barry Runk/Stan/Grant Heilman Photography, Inc.; 105 (inset), Science VU/Visuals Unlimited; 105 (inset), Grace Davies Photography; 105 (inset), Geoff Tompkinson/SPL/Photo Researchers, Inc.; 105 (inset), Ken Lucas/Visuals Unlimited; 105 (inset), Ken Lucas/Visuals Unlimited; 108 (tl), Ken Lucas/Visuals Unlimited; 108 (tc), Jose Manuel Sanchez Calvate/CORBIS; 108 (tr), Breck P. Kent; 109 (bl), G. Tompkinson/Photo Researchers, Inc.; 109 (br), Mark Schneider/Visuals Unlimited; 110 (tl), E. R. Degginger/Dembinsky Photo Associates; 110 (cl), Mark A. Schneider/Visuals Unlimited; 110 (bc), Barry Runk/Stan/Grant Heilman Photography; 110 (bl), Tom Pantages Photography; 113 (tr), Dr. E. R. Degginger/Color-Pic, Inc.; 113 (cr), Dr. E. R. Degginger/Color-Pic, Inc.; 113 (inset), Victoria Smith/HRW; 114 (tl), Larry Stepanowicz / Visuals Unlimited; 115 (tl), Mark Schneider/Visuals Unlimited; 115 (bl), Mark Schneider/Visuals Unlimited; 120 (b), Victoria Smith/HRW; 123 (bl), Craig Aurness/CORBIS; 123 (tr), Courtesy of Jami Gerard-Dwyer; 124, John Cleare/Worldwide Picture Library/Alamy Photos; 125 (l), Breck P. Kent; 125 (c), Astrid & Hans-Frieder Michler/SPL/Photo Researchers, Inc.; 125 (r), Wally Eberhart/Visuals Unlimited ; 126 (br), Breck P. Kent; 126 (t), Joyce Photographics/Photo Researchers, Inc.; 126 (bl), Breck P. Kent; 128, Brand X Photos/Alamy Photos; 130 (b), Andy Christiansen/HRW; 131 (coarse), Image Copyright (c) Jerome Wyckoff; Image courtesy Earth Science World ImageBank; 131 (rhyolite), Breck P. Kent; 131 (porphyritic), Breck P. Kent; 131 (obsidian), G. R. Roberts/Natural Sciences Image Library (NSIL) of New Zealand; 131 (pumice), Wally Eberhart/Visuals Unlimited; 132 (tl), Martin Miller/Visuals Unlimited; 132 (tl, inset), Breck P. Kent; 132 (tr), Paul Harris/Getty Images/Stone; 132 (tr, inset), Victoria Smith/HRW; 134, Richard Sisk/Panoramic Images/NGSimages.com; 137 (tr, bl), Breck P. Kent; 137 (tr), Copyright Dorling Kindersley; 137 (br), Dr. E. R. Degginger/Color-Pic, Inc.; 139 (l), Russell Wood; 139 (r), Bernhard Edmaier/Photo Researchers, Inc.; 140, Tom Wagner/CORBIS SABA; 141 (br), Joyce Photographics/Photo Researchers, Inc.; 141 (cr), Wally Eberhart/Visuals Unlimited; 142, Martin Miller, University of Oregon; 143 (bl), Breck P. Kent; 143 (br), Galen Rowell/CORBIS; 144 (t), Adam Crowley/Photodisc Green/gettyimages; 144 (inset), Andy Christiansen/HRW; 145 (Sec. 1), Brand X Photos/Alamy Photos; 145 (Sec. 2), Image Copyright (c) Jerome Wyckoff; Image courtesy Earth Science World ImageBank; 145 (Sec. 2, b), Breck P. Kent; 145 (Sec. 3), Russell Wood; 145 (b), Adam Crowley/Photodisc Green/gettyimages; 150, Victoria Smith/HRW; 152, Ohio Department of Natural Resources, Division of Geological Survey; 153 (tr), NASA; 153 (c), NASA; 153 (bl), Roger Ressmeyer/CORBIS ; 154, Lester Lefkowitz/CORBIS; 156 (br), Neal Mishler/Getty Images/Photographer's Choice; 158, H. David Seawell/CORBIS; 159, Macduff Everton/CORBIS; 160 (all), Barry Runk/Stan/Grant Heilman Photography, Inc.; 164, Roger Ressmeyer/CORBIS; 165, Bob Krist; 166, Andy Christiansen/HRW; 168, Stefan Schott/Panoramic Images; 169, Peter Essick/Aurora; 170, John Lovretta, The Hawk Eye/AP/Wide World Photos; 171 (t), Jose Fuste Raga/CORBIS; 171 (b), Gary Klinkhammer/College of Oceanic and Atmospheric Sciences, Oregon State University; 172 (t), Photodisc/gettyimages; 173 (1), H. David Seawell/CORBIS; 173 (2), Macduff Everton/CORBIS; 173 (3), Bob Krist; 173 (4), Jose Fuste Raga/CORBIS; 181 (t), Applied Ecological Services; 181 (inset), Barry/Runk/Stan/Grant Heilman Photography, Inc.; 181 (b), Applied Ecological Services.

UNIT THREE: 182-183, Discovery Images/PictureQuest; 183 (Ch. 8), Mark E. Gibson/CORBIS; 183 (Ch. 7), John Gurche; 184, Mark E. Gibson/CORBIS; 185 (l), CORBIS; 185 (r), Tom Bean/CORBIS; 186, Deborah Long/Visuals Unlimited; 188 (tr), Tom Bean/CORBIS; 188 (tl), Christian Hass; 188 (tc), Gerald and Buff Corsi/Visuals Unlimited ; 191, Alan Smith/Getty Images/Stone; 192 (r), Pat O'Hara/CORBIS; 192 (l), Bruce Molnia/Terra Photo Graphics; 194 (t), Sam Dudgeon/HRW; 194 (t), Sam Dudgeon/HRW; 194 (t), Sam Dudgeon/HRW; 194 (t), Sam Dudgeon/HRW; 194 (t), Sam Dudgeon/HRW; 194, Victoria Smith/HRW; 196, James King-Holmes/SPL/Photo Researchers, Inc.; 197, Annie Griffiths Belt/CORBIS; 198 (mummy), Landmann Patrick/CORBIS SYGMA; 198 (amber), Layne Kennedy/CORBIS; 198 (tar), Nick Ut/AP/Wide World Photos; 198 (mammoth), Bettmann/CORBIS; 198 (log), Bernhard Edmaier/Photo Researchers, Inc.; 199 (leaf), Layne Kennedy/CORBIS ; 199 (mold), G. R. Roberts/Natural Sciences Image Library (NSIL) of New Zealand; 199 (coprolite), Sinclair Stammers/SPL/Photo Researchers, Inc.; 199 (gastrolith), Francios Gohier/Photo Researchers, Inc.; 200, James L. Amos/Photo Researchers, Inc.; 201 (b), James L. Amos/Photo Researchers, Inc.; 201

(c), Pat O'Hara/CORBIS; 201 (t), Tom Bean/CORBIS; 206, Victoria Smith/HRW; 207 (all), Victoria Smith/HRW; 208, Courtesy, Ohio Department of Natural Resources, Division of Geological Survey; 209 (t), Steve Bloom Images; 209 (b), Pablo Corral Vega/CORBIS; 210, John Gurche; 212, Jonathan Blair/CORBIS; 214, Reuters New Media Inc./CORBIS; 216 (l), Jim Brandenburg/Minden Pictures; 216 (r), Manfred Danegger/Peter Arnold; 217, John Reader/SPL/Photo Researchers, Inc.; 218, James L. Amos/CORBIS; 219, Kaj R. Svensson/SPL/Photo Researchers, Inc.; 220, Ken Lucas/Visuals Unlimited; 221 (bl), Chris Butler/SPL/Photo Researchers, Inc.; 221 (bc), Joe Tucciarone/SPL/Photo Researchers, Inc.; 222 (t), Doug Henderson/Reuters/NewsCom; 222 (b), James L. Amos/CORBIS; 223, Sue Ogrocki/Reuters/NewsCom; 224, Stuart Westmorland/CORBIS; 225 (bl), Wardene Weiser/Bruce Coleman, Inc.; 225, Jeff Gage/Florida Museum of Natural History; 226, Bettmann/CORBIS; 227 (t), Jonathan Blair/CORBIS; 227 (c), John Reader/SPL/Photo Researchers, Inc.; 227, Stuart Westmorland/CORBIS; 233, Jonathan Blair/CORBIS; 235 (tr), Andrew Leitch/(c)1992 the Walt Disney Co. Reprinted with permission of Discover Magazine; 235 (tc), Bill Steele/A+C Anthology; 235 (bl), Ira Block.

UNIT FOUR: 236-237, NASA; 237 (Ch. 10), Mats Wibe Lund; 237 (Ch. 11), Roger Ressmeyer/CORBIS; 237 (Ch. 12), Tom Wagner/CORBIS SABA; 237 (Ch. 13), Gavriel Jecan/CORBIS; 238 (all), Mats Wibe Lund; 239 (bl), The Granger Collection, New York.; 240 (inset), Paleontological Museum/University of Oslo, Norway; 241 (b), Galen Rowell/CORBIS; 241 (inset), British Antarctic Survey/SPL/Photo Researchers, Inc.; 242 (tl), P. Hickey/Woods Hole Oceanographic Institute; 246 (t), Courtesy of Dr. Donald Prothero; 249 (tl), NASA; 250 (br), Jacques Descloitres. MODIS Land Rapid Response Team, NASA/GSFC; 251 (t), Tom Bean/CORBIS; 253 (tr), Victoria Smith/HRW; 255 (b), Y. Arthus-B./Peter Arnold, Inc.; 255 (b), Y. Arthus-B./Peter Arnold, Inc.; 257 (cr), Michael Dick/Animals Animals/Earth Scenes; 261 (tl), British Antarctic Survey/SPL/Photo Researchers, Inc.; 261 (cr), Jacques Descloitres. MODIS Land Rapid Response Team, NASA/GSFC; 266 (b), Victoria Smith/HRW; 267 (tr), Victoria Smith/HRW; 269 (bl), Bettmann/CORBIS; 269 (inset), Walter H. F. Smith and David T. Sandwell; 270, Roger Ressmeyer/CORBIS; 272, Jeremy Woodhouse/Getty Images; 272, Jeremy Woodhouse/Getty Images; 274 (t), Tom Bean; 274 (b), Andy Christiansen/HRW; 275, Bill Bachman; 276, Photodisc Blue/Getty Images; 278, Lloyd Cluff/CORBIS; 280, Jeremy Woodhouse/Pixelchrome; 281 (t), Kim Westerskov/Getty Images/Stone; 281 (b), Alexander Stewart/Getty Images/The Image Bank; 282-283, Photodisc Green/gettyimages; 282 (sierra), Russ Bishop; 282 (colorado), George H. H. Huey/CORBIS; 282 (valley), Bob Krist/CORBIS; 283 (dome), Alan Schein Photography/CORBIS ; 283 (appalachian), James P. Blair/National Geographic Image Collection; 283 (arkansas), Zephyr Picture/Index Stock Imagery, Inc.; 284, Harvey Lloyd/Getty Images/Taxi; 285 (t), Kim Westerskov/Getty Images/Stone; 290, Victoria Smith/HRW; 292, Institute of Geological and Nuclear Sciences; 292, Institute of Geological and Nuclear Sciences; 293 (bl), Bill Bachmann/Rainbow; 293 (cr), Gavin Hellier/Nature Picture Library; 294 (all), Tom Wagner/CORBIS SABA; 300 (tl), Yann Arthus Bertrand/CORBIS; 301 (bl), Reuters/CORBIS; 302 (br), Michael S. Yamashita/CORBIS; 302 (br), Sam Dudgeon/HRW; 305 (br), Reuters/CORBIS; 306 (tr), Samuel Zuder/laif/Aurora; 309 (tl), Yann Arthus Bertrand/CORBIS; 309 (cl), Michael S. Yamashita/CORBIS; 309 (bl), Reuters/CORBIS; 316, Global Seismic Hazard Assessment Program; 317 (bl), Courtesy of Wayne Thatcher; 317 (bl), Massonet, CNES/Photo Researchers, Inc.; 317 (bkgd), Dewitt Jones/CORBIS; 318 (all), Gavriel Jecan/CORBIS; 321 (br), Barry Tessman/National Geographic Image Collection; 322 (tl), James Wall/Animals Animals/Earth Scenes; 323 (cl), Jacques Descloitres, MODIS Rapid Response Team, NASA/GSFC; 324 (t), Bill Ross/CORBIS; 325 (bl), Stuart Westmoreland/Getty Images; 326 (tl), Gary Braasch/CORBIS; 326 (tc), J. D. Griggs/CORBIS; 326 (tr), David Muench/CORBIS; 327 (b), Gary Braasch/CORBIS; 327 (cr), Robert Patrick/Corbis Sygma; 327 (cr), Juerg Alean, Switzerland/www.stromboli.net; 328 (tl), Michael Yamashita/CORBIS; 328 (cr), Mike Zens/CORBIS; 328 (cl), Yann Arthrus-Bertrand/CORBIS; 328 (br), Japack Company/CORBIS; 330 (tl), Roger Ressmeyer/CORBIS; 331 (tl), Jacques Descloitres, MODIS Rapid Response Team, NASA/GSFC; 331 (bl), Gary Braasch/CORBIS; 337 (tr), Koji Sasahara/AP/Wide World Photos; 339 (bl), InterNetwork Media/Getty Images; 339 (inset).

UNIT FIVE: 340-341, Frans Lemmens/Image Bank/Getty Images; Roger Ressmeyer/CORBIS; 341 (Ch. 14), Mark Laricchia/CORBIS ; 341 (Ch. 15), Jim Wark; 341 (Ch. 16), Joseph Van Os/Getty Images/The Image Bank; 341 (Ch. 17), Andrew Wenzel/Masterfile; 341 (Ch. 18), Nicole Duplaix/National Geographic Image Collection; 342 (all), Mark Laricchia/CORBIS ; 344 (bl), Dr. E. R. Degginger/Color-Pic, Inc.; 344 (tr), SuperStock; 345 (tl), Layne Kennedy/CORBIS; 345 (tr), W. Perry Conway/CORBIS; 345 (br), Victoria Smith/HRW; 346 (tr), Kevin Fleming/CORBIS; 348 (tr), Adam Hart-Davis/SPL/Photo Researchers, Inc.; 349 (tr), Tom Till/Getty Images; 351 (tl), Bettmann/CORBIS; 351 (tc), Joen Iaconetti/Bruce Coleman, Inc.; 352 (tl), Richard Hamilton Smith/CORBIS; 353 (bl), Jeff Vanuga/USDA/NRCS; 358 (tr), Yann Arthus-Bertrand/CORBIS; 359 (tr), Jason Hawkes/CORBIS; 359 (cr), Daniel Dancer/Peter Arnold, Inc.; 360 (tl), Jim Richardson/CORBIS; 360 (tr), Keren Su/CORBIS; 360 (tc), Grant Heilman Photography, Inc.; 361 (br), AFP/CORBIS; 361 (bl), Handout/Malacanang/Reuters/CORBIS; 362 (br), CORBIS; 363 (tl), Galen Rowell/CORBIS; 363 (tr), Steve Terrill/CORBIS; 364 (t), (c) Robert Frerck/Odyssey/Chicago; 365 (tl), Adam Hart-Davis/SPL/Photo Researchers, Inc.; 365 (cl), Richard Hamilton Smith/CORBIS; 365 (cl), Jeff Vanuga/USDA/NRCS; 365 (bl), Galen

Rowell/CORBIS; 370 (b), Victoria Smith/HRW; 371 (tr), Victoria Smith/HRW; 373 (tr), Courtesy of Lewis Nichols; 373 (bl), Grant Heilman/Grant Heilman Photography, Inc.; 374 (all), Jim Wark; 375 (bl), Annie Reynolds/PhotoLink/gettyimages; 377 (tr), Mark Taylor/Warren Photographic/Bruce Coleman, Inc.; 377 (cr), Brad Wrobleski/Masterfile; 378 (tl), Peter Turnley/CORBIS; 380 (bl), Nancy Simmerman/Getty Images; 380 (br), Rich Reid/National Geographic Image Collection; 381 (tl), Harald Sund/Getty Images; 382 (tr), Jim Wark/Airphoto; 383 (bl), Jim Wark/Airphoto; 383 (br), Martin Miller/Visuals Unlimited; 384 (tl), Kevin R. Morris/CORBIS; 385 (br), Modesto Bee/AP/Wide World Photos; 387 (tl), Annie Reynolds/PhotoLink/gettyimages; 387 (cl), Harald Sund/Getty Images; 387 (bl), Martin Miller/Visuals Unlimited; 392 (bl), Victoria Smith/HRW; 393 (tr), Victoria Smith/HRW; 393 (cr), Victoria Smith/HRW; 395 (bl), EPA/AP Wide World Photos; 395 (tr), Reuters New Media, Inc./CORBIS; 396, Joseph Van Os/Getty Images/The Image Bank; 398, Victoria Smith/HRW; 401, Charles River Watershed Association; 402, Tom Bean/CORBIS; 403, Pagasus/Visuals Unlimited; 405 (inset), Martyn F. Chillmaid/SPL/Photo Researchers, Inc.; 405 (bl), Peter Essick/Aurora; 406, Adam Woolfitt/CORBIS; 407 (t), Bettmann/CORBIS; 407, Natural Bridge Caverns; 408, Keren Su/CORBIS; 409 (t), Pagasus/Visuals Unlimited; 409, Peter Essick/Aurora; 414, Victoria Smith/HRW; 415, Victoria Smith/HRW; 416, McGuire, V.L., 2001, Water-level changes in the High Plains Aquifer, 1980 to 1999: U.S. Geological Survey Fact Sheet, FS-029-01, 2 p.; 417 (br), Leif Skoogfers/Woodfin Camp & Associates; 417 (bl), Joseph Melanson/Aero Photo-Aerials Only Gallery; 418, Andrew Wenzel/Masterfile; 419 (b), Kevin R. Morris/CORBIS; 420 (tl), Jim Wark/Airphoto; 420 (tr), Hanne & Jens Eriksen/Nature Picture Library; 422 (l), Ralph A. Clevenger/CORBIS; 422 (tr), Jim Brandenburg/Minden Pictures; 423 (bl), Ronald Gorbutt/Visuals Unlimited; 425 (tr), G. R. Roberts/Natural Sciences Image Library (NSIL) of New Zealand; 425 (br), Victoria Smith/HRW; 428 (t), Galen Rowell/CORBIS; 429 (tr), Scott T. Smith/CORBIS; 431 (bkgd), George D. Lepp/CORBIS; 434 (tl), SPL/Photo Researchers, Inc.; 435 (tl), Jim Brandenburg/Minden Pictures; 435 (cl), Scott T. Smith/CORBIS; 435 (bl), SPL/Photo Researchers, Inc.; 440 (br), Victoria Smith/HRW; 441 (tr), Victoria Smith/HRW; 443 (b), Craig Tuttle/CORBIS; 444, Nicole Duplaix/National Geographic Image Collection; 445, Mark J. Terrill/AP/Wide World Photos; 446, Jonathan Blair/CORBIS; 449 (t), John Warden/Getty Images/Stone; 449, Andy Christiansen/HRW; 450, Walter H. Hodge/Peter Arnold, Inc.; 451, David Welling; 452 (bc), Jeff Foott/DRK Photo; 452 (tl), Jeff Foott/Tom Stack & Associates; 453 (bl), G. R. Roberts/Natural Sciences Image Library (NSIL) of New Zealand; 453 (tc), Breck P. Kent; 453 (br), John S. Shelton ; 457 (t), Aerial by Caudell; 457 (bl), Frans Lanting/Minden Pictures; 457 (br), Jean-Pierre Pieuchot/Getty Images/The Image Bank; 458, Tami Chappell/Rueters/NewsCom; 459, Mark J. Terrill/AP/Wide World Photos; 459, David Welling; 459, Tami Chappell/Rueters/NewsCom; 464, HRW; 465 (t), Sam Dudgeon/HRW; 465 (c), Sam Dudgeon/HRW; 465 (b), Sam Dudgeon/HRW; 466, Joost Van der Sanden, Canada Centre for Remote Sensing/Natural Resources Canada, RADARSAT image: (c)1999 Canadian Space Agency; 467 (t), Jonathan Blair/CORBIS; 467 (b), Adam Woolfitt/CORBIS.

UNIT SIX: 468-469, USGS/NASA; 469 (Ch. 19), Jeffrey L. Rotman/CORBIS; 469 (Ch. 20), David Hall; 469 (Ch. 21), eStock Photo/PictureQuest; 470, Jeffrey L. Rotman/CORBIS; 472 (br), Ocean Drilling Program - Texas A&M University; 472 (l), Ocean Drilling Program - Texas A&M University; 473 (ship), National Oceanic and Atmospheric Administration/Department of Commerce; 473 (b), Victoria Smith/HRW; 474 (tl), Alexis Rosenfeld/SPL/Photo Researchers, Inc.; 474 (inset), David Shale/naturepl.com; 478, B. Tanaka/Getty Images/Taxi; 479, Ocean Drilling Program - Texas A&M University; 480 (t), Digital image (c) 1996 CORBIS; Original image courtesy of NASA/CORBIS; 480 (b), Courtesy Stephen Morris, Experimental Nonlinear Physics Group, University of Toronto; 481 (nodules), Tom McHugh/Photo Researchers, Inc.; 481 (bkgd), Darryl Torckler/Getty Images/Stone; 481 (nodules), Tom McHugh/Photo Researchers, Inc.; 482 (l), Jim Zuckerman/CORBIS; 482 (r), Andrew Syred/SPL/Photo Researchers, Inc.; 483 (t), Ocean Drilling Program - Texas A&M University; 483 (c), B. Tanaka/Getty Images/Taxi; 489, Victoria Smith/HRW; 490, NGDC/NOAA; 491 (t), Scripps Institution of Oceanography; 491 (b), Scripps Institution of Oceanography; 491 (bkgd), Royalty-Free/Corbis; 492 (all), David Hall; 495 (br), Sean Davey/AllSport/Getty Images; 497 (tl), Tom Stewart/CORBIS; 497 (tr), CORBIS; 499 (tc), Sam Dudgeon/HRW; 499 (br), Victoria Smith/HRW; 500 (tl), Lawson Wood/CORBIS; 501 (bl), David Hall; 502 (bl), IQ3d/Bruce Coleman, Inc.; 504 (tr), Craig Tuttle/CORBIS; 505 (bl), Steve Raymer/National Geographic Image Collection; 506 (tr), Bohemian Nomad Picturemakers/CORBIS; 507 (b), Chris Hellier/CORBIS; 508 (tl), Simon Fraser/SPL/Photo Researchers, Inc.; 509 (cl), David Hall; 509 (bl), Chris Hellier/CORBIS; 509 (tl), Sean Davey/AllSport/Getty Images; 514 (bl), Victoria Smith/HRW; 516, Courtesy of N.R. Nalli, NOAA/NESDIS, Washington, D.C.; 517 (bl), Karen J. Dodge/MWRA/RVA; 517 (tr), Digital Vision; 518 (all), eStock Photo/PictureQuest; 519 (bl), Jonathan Blair/CORBIS; 520 (br), Provided by the SeaWiFS Project, NASA/Goddard Space Flight Center, and ORBIMAGE; 522 (inset), Peter David/Nature Picture Library; 524 (inset), CORBIS; 525 (bl), Jack Fields/CORBIS; 527 (tr), Darrell Wong/Getty Images; 527 (br), Victoria Smith/HRW; 529 (tr), G. R. Roberts/Natural Sciences Image Library (NSIL) of New Zealand; 530 (tl), CORBIS; 530 (inset), CORBIS; 533 (tl), CORBIS; 533 (cl), CORBIS; 533 (br), NASA; 534 (tl), Photo Researchers, Inc.; 535 (tl), CORBIS; 535 (cl), Darrell Wong/Getty Images; 535 (bl), NASA; 540 (b), Victoria Smith/HRW; 543 (bl), SPL/Photo Researchers, Inc.; 543 (br), R. Toms/OSF/Animals Animals/Earth Scenes.

UNIT SEVEN: 544-545, (c) Warren Faidley/Weatherstock; 545 (Ch. 22), Kevin Kelly/Getty Images/The Image Bank; 545 (Ch. 23), Charles Doswell III/Getty Images; 545 (Ch. 24), Taxi/Getty; 545 (Ch. 25), Theo Allofs/CORBIS; 546, Kevin Kelly/Getty Images/The Image Bank; 547 (b), Joseph Sohm; Visions of America/CORBIS; 549 (bl), Carol Hughes; Gallo Images/CORBIS; 549 (tr), Wolfgang Kaehler/CORBIS; 549 (tl), Roger Ressmeyer/CORBIS ; 549 (tr), Royalty Free/CORBIS; 550 (tr), Chris Noble/Stone/Getty Images; 550 (tl), Didrik Johnck/CORBIS; 551, Andy Christiansen/HRW; 553, NASA/CORBIS; 554, Martin Thomas/Reuters NewMediInc./CORBIS; 555 (radio), NRAO/AUI/NSF; 555 (x-ray), NASA/JIAS/SPL/Photo Researchers, Inc.; 555 (visible), NASA/JIAS/SPL/Photo Researchers, Inc.; 555 (ultraviolet), SOHO/ESA/NASA; 555 (infrared), NOAO/SPL/Photo Researchers, Inc.; 556 (br), NASA; 556 (bl), NASA; 557, Jeremy Woodhouse/Photodisc/Getty; 563, NASA/Photo Researchers, Inc.; 564, Charles Benes/Index Stock Imagery, Inc.; 565 (t), Wolfgang Kaehler/CORBIS; 565 (c), Jeremy Woodhouse/Photodisc/Getty; 565 (b), NASA/Photo Researchers, Inc.; 572, NASA; 573 (bl), ML Sinibaldi/CORBIS; 573 (br), Roger Ressmeyer/CORBIS; 574, Charles Doswell III/Getty Images; 576 (br), Robert Wright/Ecoscence/CORBIS; 578 (tr), (c)National Geographic Image Collection; 579 (bl), Barry Runk/Stan/Grant Heilman Photography, Inc.; 580 (tl), Graham Neden/Ecoscene/CORBIS; 582 (br), Michael S. Yamashita/CORBIS; 583 (t), Chris Anderson/Aurora; 585 (tl), Royalty Free/CORBIS; 585 (tr), Gary Braasch/CORBIS; 586 (tl), Charles O'Rear/CORBIS; 587 (t), Darrell Gulin/CORBIS; 587 (bc), Gary W. Carter/CORBIS; 588 (br), Barry Runk/Stan/Grant Heilman Photography, Inc.; 589 (tl), AFP/CORBIS; 590 (tl), Jim Brandenburg/Minden Pictures; 591 (tl), Robert Wright/Ecoscence/CORBIS; 591 (cl), Michael S. Yamashita/CORBIS; 591 (bl), Gary W. Carter/CORBIS; 596 (br), Victoria Smith/HRW; 597 (tr), Victoria Smith/HRW; 599 (tr), National Center for Atmospheric Research/University Corporation for Atmospheric Research; 599 (bl), Marci Stenberg/Merced Sun-Star/AP/Wide World Photos; 600, Getty Images/Taxi; 601, NASA/CORBIS; 602, Rick Doyle/CORBIS; 604, Benjamin Lowy/Corbis; 605, CORBIS; 608, A & J Verkaik/CORBIS; 610 (inset), Jim Reed/CORBIS; 610 (tl), Howard B. Bluestein/Photo Researchers, Inc.; 611, Jonathan Blair/CORBIS; 612 (t), Philippe Giraud/CORBIS SYGMA; 612 (b), Victoria Smith/HRW; 613, Gene Rhoden/Visuals Unlimited; 614, NASA; 615, Courtesy World Meteorological Organization; 617 (t), Courtesy, The Weather Channel; 618, Jim Reed/CORBIS; 620, H. David Seawell/CORBIS; 621 (1), Benjamin Lowy/CORBIS; 621 (2), A & J Verkaik/CORBIS; 621 (3), NASA; 621 (4), Jim Reed/CORBIS; 626, HRW; 628, Data courtesy NOAA; 629 (t), Courtesy Shirley Murillo; 629 (b), NOAA; 629 (bkgd), Don Farrall/Getty Images/PhotoDisc; 630 (all), Theo Allofs/CORBIS; 631 (bl), Wolfgang Kaehler/CORBIS; 631 (br), Andrea Pistolesi/Getty Images; 635 (br), Indranil Mukherjee/AFP/Getty Images/Getty Images; 635 (bl), Reuters NewMedia, Inc./CORBIS; 639 (tl), (c) Bryan and Cherry Alexander Photography; 642 (tl), Bojan Brecelj/CORBIS; 644 (tr), Yann Arthus-Bertrand/CORBIS; 646 (tl), Wendy Stone/CORBIS; 646 (bl), Wendy Stone/CORBIS; 647 (tl), Wolfgang Kaehler/CORBIS; 647 (cl), (c) Bryan and Cherry Alexander Photography; 652 (b), Victoria Smith/HRW; 655 (c), Dee Breger/Lamont-Doherty Earth Observatory.

UNIT EIGHT: 656-657, Roger Ressmeyer/CORBIS; 657 (Ch. 28), Denis Scott/CORBIS; 657 (Ch. 26), NASA; 657 (Ch. 26), Denis Scott/CORBIS; 657 (Ch. 29), SOHO/ESA/NASA; 657 (Ch. 30), Stocktrek/CORBIS; 658 (all), NASA; 659 (bl), NASA; 660 (tr), NASA; 660 (tl), Jean-Charles Cuillandre/Canada-france-Hawaii Telescope/SPL/Photo Researchers, Inc.; 661 (br), Alfred Pasieka/SPL/Photo Researchers, Inc.; 662 (br), Michael Freeman/CORBIS; 664 (br), Bohemia Nomad Picturemakers/CORBIS; 664 (br), Glen Alison/PhotoDisc Green/gettyimages; 665 (tl), NASA; 665 (br), NASA-JPL; 666 (tl), NASA; 667 (bl), Inga Spence/Visuals Unlimited; 667 (br), Inga Spence/Visuals Unlimited; 670 (tl), Gianni Dagli Orti/CORBIS; 673 (br), Andy Christiansen/HRW; 675 (bl), Inga Spence/Visuals Unlimited; 675 (tl), Jean-Charles Cuillandre/Canada-france-Hawaii Telescope/SPL/Photo Researchers, Inc.; 680 (br), Peter van Steen/HRW; 682 (t), C. Mayhew & R. Simmon/NASA/GSFO; 683 (tr), Lockheed Martin Corporation; 683 (bl), Image courtesy of NASA Landsat Project Science Office and USGS EROS Data Center; 684 (all), Denis Scott/CORBIS; 685 (bl), Royal Observatory, Edinburgh/SPL/Photo Researchers, Inc.; 690 (tl), Lindsay Hebberd/CORBIS; 692 (br), Victoria Smith/HRW; 694 (tl), David Nunuk/SPL/Photo Researchers, Inc.; 695 (b), JPL/NASA; 696 (br), NASA/SPL/Photo Researchers, Inc.; 697 (tl), NASA/SPL/Photo Researchers, Inc.; 698 (br), ESA/PLI/CORBIS; 699 (tl), World Perspectives/Getty Images; 700 (tl), AFP/CORBIS; 700 (tr), Gordon Garradd/Photo Researchers, Inc.; 701 (bl), Kevin Kelley/Getty Images; 702 (br), NASA; 703 (tr), CORBIS; 703 (br), NASA; 704 (br), NASA/JPL/Space Science Institute; 705 (tl), NASA; 706 (br), JPL/NASA; 707 (tl), NASA/JPL-Caltech; 708 (tl), Lynette R. Cook; 709 (t), Royal Observatory, Edinburgh/SPL/Photo Researchers, Inc.; 709 (cl), David Nunuk/SPL/Photo Researchers, Inc.; 709 (bl), NASA/SPL/Photo Researchers, Inc.; 709 (b), CORBIS; 714 (b), Victoria Smith/HRW; 715 (tr), Victoria Smith/HRW; 716 (tc), Photo Researchers, Inc.; 717 (tl), George Sakkestad; 717 (br), Roger Ressmeyer/CORBIS; 717 (bkgd), NASA; 719, NASA; 720, Galileo Project/JPL/NASA; 721 (t), NASA; 721 (b), NASA; 724 (t), USGS; 724 (b), USGS; 726, NASA; 727 (bl), George Post/SPL/Photo Researchers; 727 (br), CNES/GAMMA; 728 (b), Victoria Smith/HRW; 728 (t), Royalty Free/CORBIS; 729 (b), Dr. Fred Espenak/Photo Researchers, Inc.; 730, John Bova/Photo Researchers, Inc.; 730, John Bova/Photo Researchers, Inc.; 730, John Bova/Photo Researchers, Inc.; 730, John Bova/Photo Researchers, Inc.; 730, John Bova/Photo Researchers, Inc.; 730, John Bova/Photo Researchers, Inc.; 730, John Bova/Photo Researchers, Inc.; 730, NASA; 731, John Sanford/Photo Researchers, Inc.; 733, NASA/JPL/University of Arizona; 734 (t), Galileo Project/JPL/NASA; 734 (b), Galileo Project/JPL/NASA; 735 (t), Galileo Project/JPL/NASA; 735 (c), NASA; 735 (b), NASA; 736 (t), NASA; 736 (b), NASA/JPL/Space Science Institute; 737 (t), NASA; 737 (b), Dr. R. Albrecht, ESA/ESO Space Telescope European Coordinating Facility; NASA ; 738, NASA; 739, NASA; 740, Getty Images/PhotoDisc; 741, Wally Pacholka/AstroPics.com; 743, Juan Carlos Casado; 744 (t), E.R. Degginger/Bruce Coleman, Inc.; 744 (c), Breck P. Kent/Animals Animals/Earth Scenes; 744 (b), Ken Nichols/Institute of Meteorites; 745 (1), NASA; 745 (2), CNES/GAMMA; 745 (3), Galileo Project/JPL/NASA; 745 (4), Wally Pacholka/AstroPics.com; 752, NASA; 753 (b), NASA; 753 (t), NASA; 754, SOHO/ESA/NASA; 757 (t), Kamioka Observatory, ICRR (Institute for Cosmic Ray Research), The University of Tokyo; 757 (b), Andy Christiansen/HRW; 759, NOAO/AURA/NSF; 760, Fred Espenek; 761 (bl), The Institute for Solar Physics, The Royal Swedish Academy of Sciences; 761(inset), Getty Images/Photodisc; 762, Laboratory for Atmospheric and Space Physics, University of Colorado-Boulder; 763, M. Aschwanden et al. (LMSAL), TRACE, NASA ; 764, Michael DeYoung/AlaskaStock Images; 765 (t), Fred Espenek; 765 (b), Michael DeYoung/AlaskaStock Images; 767, NASA; 770, HRW; 771, HRW; 772, Yohkoh Solar Observatory; 773 (tr), JPL/NASA; 774 (all), Stocktrek/CORBIS; 775 (b), N.A.Sharp, NOAO/NSO/Kitt Peak FTS/AURA/NSF; 776 (t), NASA/Hubble Heritage Team; 777 (b), Grant Faint/Getty Images; 779 (inset), Victoria Smith/HRW; 780 (bkgd), Roger Ressmeyer/CORBIS; 782 (tr), NASA; 783 (br), Tony Craddock/SPL/Photo Researchers, Inc.; 784 (br), Matthew Spinelli; 785 (tr), NASA The Heritage Hubble Team; 785 (inset), Photo courtesy of the NAIC/Ariecebo Observatory/NSF; 788 (tl), NASA; 790 (bl), Celestial Image Co./SPL/Photo Researchers, Inc.; 791 (tl), NASA/Gemini Observatory, GMOS Team; 791 (tr), Royal Observatory, Edinburgh/AATB/SPL/Photo Researchers, Inc.; 791 (tc), NOAO/Photo Researchers, Inc.; 792 (tr), NASA/CXC/A.Siemiginowska et al.; Illustration: CXC/M.Weiss ; 793 (br), NASA; 795 (tr), Victoria Smith/HRW; 795 (br), NASA/WMAP Science Team; 796 (tl), NASA and Hubble Heritage Team; 797 (tl), Grant Faint/Getty Images; 797 (cl), NASA The Heritage Hubble Team; 797 (cl), Celestial Image Co./SPL/Photo Researchers, Inc.; 797 (bl), NASA; 803 (tr), Victoria Smith/HRW; 805 (bl), NASA/JPL-Caltech/S. Willner (Harvard-Smithsonian Center for Astrophysics); 805 (tr), Roger Ressmeyer/CORBIS.

EARTH SCIENCE CLOSE-UP: CALIFORNIA c1 (c), Garry Black/Masterfile; c3 (br), © Thomas Hallstein/Alamy; c3 (bl), © Mark Lewis/Alamy; c4 (br), © W. Perry Conway/CORBIS; c5 (br), USGS/Modified from the National Atlas; c5 (bl), QT Luong/Terra Galleria Photography; c5 (bc), © Jon Arnold Images/Alamy; c6 (bl), USGS/Modified from the National Atlas; c7 (r), Courtesy California Department of Fish and Game/Atlas of the Biodiversity of California; c7 (bl), © Joao Canziani/Getty Images; c7 (bc), Mark Rightmire/NewsCom; c7 (br), © David Brooks/CORBIS; c8 (br), Courtesy Gene Fritsche ; c8 (cr), Courtesy Gene Fritsche; c9 (b), © Jonathan Blair/CORBIS; c10 (br), © Kirkendall-Spring Photographers; c11 (t), © Dave Welling; c11 (br), © San Diego Natural History Museum Visual Resources Collection; c12 (tl), William Rader/HRW; c12 (bc), William Rader/HRW; c12 (bl), © Marv Sloben; c12 (br), William Rader/HRW; c13 (b), QT Luong/Terra Galleria Photography; c13 (cr), William Rader/HRW; c14 (tl), Ruaridh Stewart/AP/Wide World Photos; c14 (tr), © 2006 University of California Museum of Paleontology; c15 (cr), © Noella Ballenger/Alamy; c15 (bl), Jose Fuste Raga/Corbis; c16 (bl), USGS/Modified from the National Atlas; c16 (br), © Craig Aurness/CORBIS; c17 (tr), Department of Water Resources, State of California; c17 (br), Joseph Barlow Lippincott Collection, Water Resources Center Archives - University of California, Berkeley; c17 (bl), CLUI photo by Steve Rowell; c18 (tr), Courtesy California Energy Commission; c18 (br), Mark Gibson Photography; c19 (bl), © George Steinmetz/CORBIS; c19 (tr), © Charles O'Rear/CORBIS; c20 (cl), Sam Dudgeon/HRW; c20 (bl), © Wendell E. Wilson; c20 (br), © Searles Lake Gem & Mineral Society; c20 (cr), © Wendell E. Wilson; c21 (tl), Frasher Photo Collection/Courtesy Pomona Public Library, Pomona, CA & Frashers Fotos; c21 (cr), The Granger Collection, New York; c21 (b), © Pro-Mack Mining; c22 (br), © Jim Sugar/CORBIS; c23 (cr), U. S. Geological Survey/Photo by R.E. Stinson; Courtesy National Park Service; c24 (tl), U. S. Geological Survey/Photo by Robert L. Schuster; c24 (br), Ken Lubas/LA Times; c25 (tr), © Bettmann/CORBIS; c28 (bl), Victoria Smith/HRW; c30 (t), Used with permission, California Department of Conservation, California Geological Survey; c31 (tr), NASA/JPL-Caltech ; c31 (bl), Palomar Observatory Caltech

APPENDIX: 806 (bl), R. L. Christiansen/CORBIS; 806 (bc), Stuart Westmorland/CORBIS /CORBIS; 806 (br), Jean Miele/CORBIS ; 832 (bkgd), David Muench/CORBIS; 832 (b), Victoria Smith/HRW; 833, USGS; 835, Karl Mueller/University of Colorado/AP/Wide World Photos; 836, David McNew/Getty Images/NewsCom; 838-839, Victoria Smith/HRW; 840, Chris Johns/Getty Images/National Geographic; 841, Greg Dimijian/Photo Researchers, Inc.; 842, A.T. Willett/Alamy Photos; 843, A.T. Willett/Alamy Photos; 844, Courtesy Earth and Sky; 846, HRW; 847 (tr), David Young-Wolff/PhotoEdit; 847 (c), Photodisc Green/Getty Images; 848, Digital Image copyright (c) 2006 Larry Brownstein/PhotoDisc; 850, David Gallant/CORBIS; 852-853, Robert Landau/CORBIS ; 853, Victoria Smith/HRW; 854 (r), Daniel Schaefer/HRW; 854 (l), Michael Abbey/Visuals Unlimited; 856, A & J Verkaik/CORBIS; 859, Hillery Smith/AP/Wide World Photos; 861, Michael Wirtz/Philadelphia Inquirer/NewsCom; 862, Tony Freeman/PhotoEdit; 865 (l), Galen Rowell/CORBIS; 865 (r), Paul Wakefield/Getty Images/Stone; 866 (all), HRW; 867 (r), WallyPacholka/AstroPics.com; 867 (l), Stocktrek/CORBIS.

The Periodic Table of Elements

Key:

Atomic number — 6
Symbol — **C**
Name — Carbon
Average atomic mass — 12.0107

Period

	Group 1	Group 2										

1
1
H
Hydrogen
1.007 94

2
3
Li
Lithium
6.941
| 4
Be
Beryllium
9.012 182

3
11
Na
Sodium
22.989 770
| 12
Mg
Magnesium
24.3050

Group 3 | Group 4 | Group 5 | Group 6 | Group 7 | Group 8 | Group 9

4
19 **K** Potassium 39.0983 | 20 **Ca** Calcium 40.078 | 21 **Sc** Scandium 44.955 910 | 22 **Ti** Titanium 47.867 | 23 **V** Vanadium 50.9415 | 24 **Cr** Chromium 51.9961 | 25 **Mn** Manganese 54.938 049 | 26 **Fe** Iron 55.845 | 27 **Co** Cobalt 58.933 200

5
37 **Rb** Rubidium 85.4678 | 38 **Sr** Strontium 87.62 | 39 **Y** Yttrium 88.905 85 | 40 **Zr** Zirconium 91.224 | 41 **Nb** Niobium 92.906 38 | 42 **Mo** Molybdenum 95.94 | 43 **Tc** Technetium (98) | 44 **Ru** Ruthenium 101.07 | 45 **Rh** Rhodium 102.905 50

6
55 **Cs** Cesium 132.905 43 | 56 **Ba** Barium 137.327 | 57 **La** Lanthanum 138.9055 | 72 **Hf** Hafnium 178.49 | 73 **Ta** Tantalum 180.9479 | 74 **W** Tungsten 183.84 | 75 **Re** Rhenium 186.207 | 76 **Os** Osmium 190.23 | 77 **Ir** Iridium 192.217

7
87 **Fr** Francium (223) | 88 **Ra** Radium (226) | 89 **Ac** Actinium (227) | 104 **Rf** Rutherfordium (261) | 105 **Db** Dubnium (262) | 106 **Sg** Seaborgium (266) | 107 **Bh** Bohrium (264) | 108 **Hs** Hassium (277) | 109 **Mt** Meitnerium (268)

* The systematic names and symbols for elements greater than 110 will be used until the approval of trivial names by IUPAC.

58 **Ce** Cerium 140.116 | 59 **Pr** Praseodymium 140.907 65 | 60 **Nd** Neodymium 144.24 | 61 **Pm** Promethium (145) | 62 **Sm** Samarium 150.36

90 **Th** Thorium 232.0381 | 91 **Pa** Protactinium 231.035 88 | 92 **U** Uranium 238.028 91 | 93 **Np** Neptunium (237) | 94 **Pu** Plutonium (244)

internet connect

go.hrw.com

Topic: Periodic Table
Go To: go.hrw.com
Keyword: Holt Periodic

Visit the HRW Web site for updates on the periodic table.